Burnley

A Complete Record 1882-1991

Burnley

A Complete Record
1882-1991

EDWARD LEE & RAY SIMPSON

BREEDON
BOOKS
SPORT

First published in Great Britain by
The Breedon Books Publishing Company Limited
44 Friar Gate, Derby DE1 1DA
1991

ISBN 0 907969 90 9

Printed and bound in Great Britain by Bath Press, Bath and London.
Jacket printed by The Nuffield Press, Cowley, Oxford.

Contents

Notes on the Statistics

Most of the statistical information in this book has been compiled from the archives of the *Burnley Express* and that has been the main reference point; where evidence appeared inconclusive, the *Burnley Express* version is the one reflected here. Where facts were unclear in the *Express*, two former local newspapers, the *Burnley News* and the *Burnley Gazette* were used to settle disputes. The *Lancashire Evening Telegraph* and its predecessor, the *Northern Daily Telegraph*, have also been used on a number of occasions.

Further information has been drawn from a number of sources including the club's own *Centenary Handbook* and the following: *Up the Clarets* by David Wiseman; *Burnley FC* by Tony Durkin; *The Lancashire FA Jubilee Handbook*; *The Football Grounds of England and Wales* by Simon Inglis; *Football League Players' Records 1946-1988* by Barry Hugman.

The Football League's own archives were used for attendances and players' details, as were many of the other books published in Breedon's *Complete Record* series.

Authors' Acknowledgements

Acknowledgements and grateful thanks are due to a number of people who have contributed to the cause in ensuring that this work eventually saw the light of day.

First, there is Wallace Chadwick, whose efforts in conjunction with Ray Simpson in compiling the original match-by-match details helped form the backbone to the book. Wallace is a Burnley fan of over 30 years' standing and a regular contributor to the club's match-day programme.

The authors were also fortunate to be able to call upon the assistance of Jim Creasey and Mike Davage, who tapped into their vast library of information on players. Thanks are also due to Douglas Lamming, whose contribution was received via Mike and Jim.

There are also thanks to Alan Rycroft for his collection of Burnley memorabilia; John Connolly for photographs and reminiscences; and Betty and Mike Davies for material on Betty's late father, Cecil Smith. Also, Barry Marlow telephoned 'out of the blue' from Norwich, offering to lend photographs.

Lorna Parnell and the staff at the Football League always made us welcome, as did the local library staff in Burnley, Blackburn, Darwen and Accrington.

Richard Catlow, editor of the *Burnley Express*, and his staff tolerated our incessant searching into the archives. And Steve Bott and Alan Simpson at the *Lancashire Evening Telegraph* were also tremendously helpful.

It was a pleasure to talk to former players Jack Butterfield and Jimmy McIlroy, who were able to provide first-hand knowledge and experience of a number of post-war players.

We must also thank Anton Rippon and the staff at Breedon Books for inviting us, via Joyce Pickles at Burnley FC, to contribute to their excellent series.

Finally, sincere thanks are due to our ladies, Glenys and Sandra, first of all for their patience and understanding but also for their practical help at various stages.

No doubt there are others who have contributed to the cause, perhaps without knowing it, notably the landlords of various hostelries in the Burnley area, scene of numerous 'progress meetings'.

To everyone mentioned and anyone unwittingly overlooked, thank you, one and all.

Photographic acknowledgements

Other than the sources mentioned in the acknowledgements, photographs in this book are the copyright of the *Lancashire Evening Telegraph* and Colorsport Ltd.

Introduction

IT CAN be argued that the title of this book, 'A Complete Record', is inaccurate since there will never be a totally complete account of Burnley FC, for it would be an impossible task to undertake. That is why we have not called the book '*The* Complete Record'.

From a statistical point of view there are certainly gaps. Dates and places of players' births, particularly those in the last century, are extremely difficult to locate; and other details, such as some early attendances, have had to be omitted.

Yet details of matches played are tantalizingly close to being 100 per cent complete. The glaring omission is the game against Darwen Old Wanderers at Darwen in the FA Cup in 1885. No amount of newspaper research would reveal the line-up, probably because the Burnley side consisted entirely of reserves, the first-teamers being banned as professionals.

Goalscorers, too, are a statistician's nightmare. Early newspaper references to 'scrimmages', whilst initially raising a smile with the researcher, became painful reminders of the difficulties in collating such information, especially when another source reports that particular goal as 'then Burnley scored again'.

Nevertheless, the authors believe that this book is as near to the definitive work on Burnley FC as it is possible to get. We would not claim that all the statistics are guaranteed 100 per cent correct; indeed, we would encourage readers who spot suspected inaccuracies to contact us. We will then investigate thoroughly.

Research of this kind, on a subject so dear to one's heart, is a continuing process and questionable goalscorers, scrimmages, unknowns, the rare occasion when a team line-up is debatable, all will continue to be checked and rechecked. Again, we would be grateful for any observations readers may have on details included or omitted from the book.

The *Burnley Stars A-Z* section is built up mainly of Clarets who have made a lot of appearances, scored a lot of goals (or both) for the club, players who are the very fabric of Burnley FC. Not all of them are 'names' but they have all contributed significantly in some way.

Finally, can we say that the production of this book has dominated our lives for nine months. We hope you think it has been worth it.

Edward Lee
Ray Simpson
June 1991

Burnley skipper Ray Deakin leads his side out for the 'Orient Game' in May 1987. Only victory could save the Clarets from relegation to the Vauxhall Conference. They beat the Londoners 2-1 – and the story lives on.

THE BURNLEY STORY

ON 28 April 1962, Burnley stood only three games away from a League and Cup double. Three wins and the double was theirs. But Burnley did not win any of those games and the chance of joining football's immortal sides was gone.

Few who stood on the Wembley terraces on 5 May 1962 could have imagined what the fates held in store for their beloved Clarets as 25 years later, almost to the day, they were fighting for their Football League survival.

Burnley had performed one of the most remarkable 'dives' in Football League history, from top to bottom — literally from first to 92nd — in only 25 years.

And the fickle finger of fate had added an extra twist. The Clarets became favourites to become the first team to automatically drop out of the Football League to make way for the Vauxhall Conference champions.

On that Wembley day in 1962, Burnley fans knew that their club and their team were part of a great triumvirate, one of the 'big three', a team to be feared.

The Football League Championship of 1959-60 was still fresh in their minds. They still had the magical Jimmy McIlroy as the greatest crowd-pleaser ever to don the famous Claret and Blue shirt. It all made what happened in 1987 even harder to swallow.

The date, 9 May 1987, will always be remembered as one thing in Burnley footballing folklore. It was, still is and always will be 'The Orient Game'.

It was a 'do or die' situation and real Boy's Own stuff. Even a win was not enough to ensure that Turf Moor remained the scene of Football League action — a combination of other results, notably that of Lincoln City, were also vital to the Burnley cause on a day when emotion ran in torrents.

The prospect of a Burnley win seemed to be reduced by the fact that Orient also needed to win — three points would have put them in the Fourth Division promotion play-offs — and the match was without doubt the most important in the Clarets' long and eventful history.

Had the combination of sheer endeavour and good luck not kept Burnley in the League by the skin of their teeth — they somehow managed to cling on to a 2-1 lead until the final whistle — this great club could have died on that fateful day.

Instead, things went right for the club for just about the only time in that never-to-be-forgotten season and within seconds of the final whistle, the Turf Moor pitch was a sea of claret and blue as the fans, many of them weeping, joined the players and club officials on the pitch for one of the biggest celebrations in the club's history.

They are, it is hoped, scenes which will never return to Turf Moor as Burnley strive to return to a standard of football which the club's history, ground and support deserve.

Since the 'Orient Game', the Turf Moor club has figured in the Fourth Division promotion race each season without ever managing to sustain a serious challenge until the very end.

They have also been to Wembley and, in defeat, graced the game's most famous stage in the fine Sherpa Van Trophy Final against Wolves, another great club fallen on hard times, in May 1988.

But even that great day was a far cry from the previous Wembley visit in the 1962 season, when Burnley performed the double nobody really wants — runners-up in both the First Division and the FA Cup.

It was a Final to be remembered as it included the 100th goal scored in a Wembley FA Cup Final — and it was netted by a Burnley player, Jimmy Robson. There is another reason why the 1962 Cup Final remains in the memory of most people connected with football. A scene from it is captured in a famous painting which adorns every club in the League and is also in view in other notable places.

As Football League founder members and twice winners of the First Division title, few could deny that Burnley's name is among the best known in the game.

Known far and wide as a club with the tradition of producing fine young players and always striving to play attractive football, Burnley have become one of the victims of £1 million transfers and wages which read like telephone numbers.

In the days of the maximum wage, great players were attracted to Burnley because of the club's success — and they stayed at Turf Moor because they fell in love with the club, the town and its people (it is remarkable how many players of the 1950s and 1960s still live within ten miles of the famous stadium). But as wage packets started to swell, the need to sell top-quality players to simply balance the books starved Burnley of success.

International stars like Martin Dobson, Ralph Coates, Leighton James and Brian Flynn were all sold. Dave Thomas and Steve Kindon were others to continue successful careers away from the East Lancashire mill-town club.

The sale of potential stars continued right into the 1980s when players like Michael Phelan, Trevor Steven, Brian Laws and Lee Dixon all left Turf Moor for differing reasons and made great names for themselves at great clubs and even on the international stage.

It all contributed to Burnley's plunge into the basement division and whilst the club's financial situation appeared to be getting healthier in the early 1990s, there was still a long way to go before the name of the famous claret and blue club was being mentioned in the same breath as that of clubs once privileged to be able to rub shoulders with Burnley players in the occasional Cup tie.

Football has changed beyond all recognition in the 110 or so years since the Burnley club was founded. Like many of the early clubs and Football League founder members, Burnley did not actually start life as a football club. But in the time since football became part of life as far as many Burnleyites are concerned, the club had been a forerunner in many ways — often causing controversy, always (until the loss of full membership of the Football League) an integral part of the game's decision-making process and seldom away from football's headlines.

It was in May 1882 that the Burnley Rovers Football Club held a special meeting at which it was decided that there should be a change of codes. Association Football took over from Rugby as the game played by the club then based at Calder Vale, to this day a thriving Rugby Union club in the town.

In the early part of the new club's history, the people and players connected with Burnley FC — the Rovers tag was soon dropped — were largely the same and the only major change was the shape of the ball. Public practice matches and friendlies with other local sides were the standard fare for the new club for the first few months and, whilst they attracted some local support, there could have been no cries of 'Up the Clarets' — at the time the team played in amber and black shirts and were christened 'The Hornets' by followers of the new game in the locality.

The 1882-3 season was largely made up of friendlies against clubs from elsewhere in Lancashire — by then a hotbed of enthusiasm for the new game — but in October 1882 came the club's first-ever competitive match, a Lancashire Challenge Cup clash with Astley Bridge. There was a feeling of adventure about the game with a prize at stake at the end of the day, but the Bolton outfit spoiled things for Burnley by winning 8-0.

It was not long after that game, four months later in fact, that Burnley accepted an invitation extended to them by the town's cricket club and moved across town to play at Turf Moor. Despite a 6-3 defeat at the hands of neighbours Rawtenstall, Burnley obviously liked their new surroundings and have made Turf Moor their 'home' ever since.

Before that move took place the name of Burnley Football Club had attracted its first controversy, publicly castigated by the officials from the nearby village club in Read for not fielding a 'Burnley' team. The outrage was caused by the fact that Burnley included players from Darwen, Blackburn, Accrington and Great Harwood — some of them travelling almost 20 miles to play for the Burnley club.

The following season, Burnley were casting their net even further afield in the search for good players. Scotland, Ireland and Wales were all losing some of their best footballing sons as they travelled to England in search of work and Burnley often featured as many as eight 'foreigners' for their matches.

In that second season Burnley again caused a mild sensation by refusing to join the English Football Association. The FA was banning professionalism and also barring member clubs from playing matches against non-members. Burnley were honest and stood by their professional players. Others continued their membership of the FA whilst still paying their players.

The following season Burnley were among 28 clubs threatening to form a breakaway governing body, the British Football Association. The English FA took the threat seriously and ruled that professionals would be allowed to play in all Cup competitions — County and otherwise — and inter-Association matches, provided they comply with certain conditions.

But that ruling did not help the Turf Moor side in the 1885-6 season when Burnley competed in the FA Cup for the first time. They were barred from fielding any of the large Scottish contingent in the squad for the tie against Darwen Old Wanderers

Burnley FC, winners of the Lancashire Cup in 1889-90. Back row (left to right): W.McFettridge, W.Bury, J.Kearsley (umpire), D.Spiers, E.T.White (secretary). Front row: R.Haresnape, A.McLardie, A.Lang, C.Lambie, A.Stewart, J.Hill. On ground: A.Kaye, J.Keenan.

and fielded their entire reserve team. The game resulted in an 11-0 reverse, still Burnley's heaviest defeat, and they subsequently withdrew from the Lancashire Cup when finding the same restrictions would apply.

By this stage, the club was no longer 'The Hornets', blue and white stripes were the favoured colours and Burnley earned the nickname 'Royalites' following the visit of Prince Albert to Turf Moor (see *The Turf Moor Story*).

Burnley continued to carve their own place in the ranks of the better football teams throughout the mid-1880s and when a meeting was convened in Fleet Street on the eve of the 1888 FA Cup Final to discuss the proposal that a League should be formed, Burnley were among the seven clubs represented that day. Eventually six teams from the Midlands and six from Lancashire competed in the first-ever Football League season. Professional football, incidentally, was still frowned upon south of Birmingham.

While the first-ever season created a renewed interest in the game, it did not provide the Burnley faithful with the start they wanted to organized football as the 'Turfites', 'Moorites' or 'Royalites' (they were still anything but 'Clarets') lost their opening fixture to Preston North End — the 'Invincibles' who won the League by going unbeaten and also lifted the FA Cup — and went on to finish ninth in the Football League.

The following season was a depressing affair. It was 1 March and Burnley's 18th game of the campaign before a win was registered — 7-0 against Bolton Wanderers. That victory started a mini-revival, Burnley went on to win three of their remaining games in the League and leave Stoke trailing at the foot of the table.

The League form might have made 1889-90 a bad season for Burnley, but the Lancashire Cup provided many highlights. Rossendale were beaten by the odd goal in seven, 15 were scored against Haydock, Higher Walton were swept aside 7-0. Before this remarkable run, Burnley had never won a first-round tie in the competition.

Burnley in 1896-7, the season they finished bottom of the First Division and were relegated for the first time in their history. Back row (left to right): J.Stuttard, J.Nicol, W.Place (senior), W.Tatham, T.McLintock, H.Bradshaw. Front row: J.Davidson, W.Bowes, J.Espie, A.Livingstone, W.Place (junior). On ground: J.Reynolds, H.Robertson.

Three good wins later and they were to meet their greatest East Lancashire rivals, Blackburn Rovers, in the Final at Accrington.

While the Turf Moor outfit had been floundering at the foot of the table all season, the Ewood men had fared much better to finish third. Everyone expected a Blackburn win but, led by Sandy Lang, the Burnley team pulled out all the stops to emerge 2-0 winners with Stewart and McLardie scoring the goals. It was not until the 1897-8 season that Burnley followed up that Lancashire Cup success by claiming their first national honour — and to do so they had to be relegated to the newly-formed Second Division.

For most of the 1890s Burnley had shown improved form — they even contended for the League Championship for a while in 1892-3 — but in 1896-7 they were relegated for the first time in their history. The drop inspired them into great things as they won 20 and drew eight of their 30 Second Division matches to win the title by three points from Newcastle United.

Before then, in 1895 to be exact, Burnley had again created history by being involved in the first transfer fee when selling the renowned James Crabtree to Aston Villa. The Lancashire side refused to meet terms they thought were 'exhorbitant' and thus released a player who had started his career as a full-back and had progressed to play for Burnley in every position from goal to centre-forward.

When Burnley had finished bottom of the First Division they had not been automatically relegated, but had gone down after a series of Test Matches involving the bottom two of the First Division and the top two from the Second.

And the Test Matches were to provide Burnley with the next controversial chapter in their history. Having won the Second Division championship in 1897-8, they were involved in Test Matches with Stoke, Newcastle and the 'old enemy' from Ewood Park, Blackburn Rovers.

After each team had played three games, Burnley and Stoke both had four points while Rovers and Newcastle had two each. With one game to play, both the Turf Moor side and the Potteries club needed a point to be sure of First Division status the following season — and they were due to meet each other. Apparently a gentlemen's agreement was reached, the game finished in a goalless draw and became known as the infamous 'match without a shot at goal'. The Football League immediately scrapped the Test Match system and introduced automatic promotion and relegation in its place — and the controversial outcome of the Burnley-Stoke game did neither side any real favours as the size of the League was extended for the following season and Newcastle and Blackburn both found berths in the First Division.

Burnley enjoyed their best-ever season in the First Division on their return to the top flight and finished third. But it was a flash in the pan and they were relegated the season afterwards (to make matters worse, they lost the Lancashire Cup Final against Preston North End in the same season).

If the humiliation of relegation was not bad enough, Burnley again found themselves at the centre of controversy. They had needed to win their last game of the season to have any chance of staying in the top flight. When Nottingham Forest won the game 4-0, officials from the Midlands club revealed that goalkeeper Jack Hillman had offered a bribe of £2 a player to the Forest team if they would let Burnley win. And he compounded the scandal at half-time by increasing the inducement to £5 a head as Forest were 2-0 up at that stage.

The Football League, of course, could not allow Hillman to escape unpunished. Although he later claimed he had only been joking — he was, by all accounts, a man of great humour — the Forest team had been anything but amused by his antics and the popular goalkeeper was suspended for the whole of the following season.

Burnley in 1907-08. Back row (left to right): Holden (trainer), Barron, Green, Parker. Middle row: Mr Windle, Mr Rudd, Beddows, Wolstenholme, Moffat, McFarlane, Mr Parkhouse. Front row: Bradshaw, Whittaker, R.Smith, Donaghey, A.Smith, Cretney.

The first full season of the new century saw Burnley almost complete a remarkable repeat performance of the last time they had been relegated — but this time they could only finish third and the season ended with further disappointment, this time when they lost the Lancashire Cup to Blackburn Rovers. The Edwardian decade of the 20th century continued to be a disappointment to the Turfites.

The very next season, having parted company with international players like Hillman (sold to Manchester City), Tom Morrison (transferred to Manchester United) and Billy Bannister (sold to Bolton Wanderers), saw the club again failing to escape from the Second Division and again losing the Lancashire Cup Final when coming out on the wrong end of a 1-0 scoreline when meeting Blackburn Rovers in the Final.

If that was a bad season, things got even worse for the Burnley outfit as they finished bottom of the Second Division for the first time in their history and they had to run the gauntlet of re-election.

Some notable cup runs apart, there was little for Burnley's loyal fans to cheer about until the 1911-12 season when their favourite team missed out on promotion by only two points after they lost the last game of the season. Of the FA Cup successes of that era, none was more famous than the one in 1908-09 when Bristol Rovers, Crystal Palace and Tottenham Hotspur all fell by the Burnley wayside before the Second Division side finally went out of the competition to reigning League Champions Manchester United — but again controversy surrounded that tie.

Heavy snow had limited the chances of starting the game, but the referee made the decision to get things underway and just before half-time Arthur Ogden gave

Burnley the lead. United started the second half with the increasing storm in their favour and battered away at the Burnley defence. But the back division held firm and a major Cup upset looked very much on the cards until 15 minutes before time when the referee abandoned proceedings because of the weather. When the match was replayed, Ogden scored twice but United ran out 3-2 winners and Burnley's fine Cup run was over.

While the club and its followers were starved of success for a dozen or so years, better things were to follow as the most famous combination ever to play for the Clarets led them to runners-up spot in the Second Division — and back to the First Division.

Sometime during the early 1900s Burnley had moved on from their blue and white shirts and transferred their colours to green shirts. If popular tales of the time can be believed, the club decided at the start of the 1910-11 season to try and shake off their dismal times by switching to the colours of a successful First Division side — they chose the claret and blue of Aston Villa and won promotion the very next season. The claret and blue colours have been in favour almost ever since. There have been instances of Burnley donning white or blue for home games in the years since then — but they are, and now always will be, the Clarets.

The famous combination which led them towards the First Division in 1912-13 did not come together until George Halley was signed from Bradford in March 1913 to complete the legendary half-back line of Halley, Boyle and Watson.

Although this tremendous half-back line did not play together as often as many supporters think (115 games, in fact, largely interrupted by World War One), it was without doubt the catalyst for much of Burnley's success — both in winning the FA Cup in 1914 and maintaining First Division football at such a standard that a first-ever senior title arrived at the beginning of the 1920s.

Although Burnley had to wait until the very eve of World War One to claim their first FA Cup triumph, they had come close to a first visit to the Crystal Palace for the Final the season before. That promotion season had seen them lead

Burnley's Tommy Boyle heads the winning goal against Blackburn Rovers in the fourth round of the FA Cup in 1913.

Burnley fans on their way to the 1914 FA Cup Final.

Burnley skipper Tommy Boyle receives the FA Cup from King George V, the first reigning monarch to present the trophy.

the way for much of the winter and also overcome Leeds City, Gainsborough Trinity, Middlesbrough and Blackburn Rovers on the way to the semi-final. There they met Sunderland, the First Division leaders, and lost 3-2 after a replay. The next season, while most teams would have set about trying to consolidate new-found status in the First Division, the Clarets tasted true football glory for the first time.

The First Division consolidation did take place, but Burnley went one round further in the FA Cup, made the trip to the Crystal Palace (the Wembley of its day) and won 1-0 in the Final against Liverpool.

Both teams were appearing in the Final for the first time — and King George V became the first reigning monarch to honour the competition by agreeing to present the English Cup (as it was then inscribed). Burnley's victory in the 'Royal Cup Final' remains their only success in the competition, although they have reached the Final on two other occasions. All three games feature in the *Matches to Remember* section later in this book.

The following season kicked-off after World War One was already raging. The heady triumph at the Crystal Palace and the memorable scenes in Burnley itself when the team returned were still fresh in everybody's minds when the new season got underway. But players soon started to volunteer for conflict of a far more serious nature and the last season before League football was abandoned due to hostilities saw Burnley's great side starting to break up.

But a great run towards the end of the season saw the Clarets hoist themselves into fifth position and round things off nicely by claiming their second success in the Lancashire Cup, this time by accounting for Rochdale by a 4-1 scoreline. Wartime football — both in World War One and Two — holds a special fascination for many football followers and statisticians and, therefore, warrants a special section later in this book. Suffice to say for now that many great players 'wasted' their talents at a time when victory in a football match was of little major significance when compared with what was going on elsewhere in Europe.

World War One and the later conflict both took a heavy toll on the Turf Moor club, but because players tended to play for the teams nearest to which they were stationed they also brought some great names to Burnley for a brief time.

The first full season after World War One, 1919-20, saw the Clarets picking up pretty much where they had left off and they finished the season in second place.

This is the 1919-20 Burnley team that launched Burnley towards their first ever First Division title. Back row (left to right, players only): George Halley, Tommy Boyle, Jerry Dawson, Cliff Jones, Willie Watson. Front row: Billy Nesbitt, Bob Kelly, Joe Anderson, Jimmy Lindsay, Eddie Mosscrop, Len Smelt.

But that solid start to the new era of League football seemed to have counted for nothing when the new season got underway and Burnley lost their first three games. Who could have guessed what lay in store for Burnley and their fans? Early in September the Clarets were stranded at the foot of the table but then they turned the tables on Huddersfield to beat them 3-0 and avenge a 1-0 defeat in the second match.

It was to be 26 March before they lost again — a 30-match unbeaten run which remains a First Division record to this day. The great Leeds United of the early 1970s started a season with 29 matches without defeat and in the late 1980s the mighty Liverpool team equalled that record but, just when it seemed they were going to take the run to 30 games and equal the Clarets, they lost to Everton.

The Clarets were involved in some fascinating games during the 1920-21 season which brought them their first First Division title — Oldham Athletic and Aston Villa, for instance, were both beaten 7-1 — and it looked as if Burnley, after a disastrous start, were going to go all the way through to the end of the season without losing again.

Then, on Easter Saturday, they travelled to play Manchester City at Hyde Road, the scene of their Lancashire Cup triumph against Rochdale six years earlier. The Manchester side had the best of the game from start to finish and were worthy 3-0 winners — but the Clarets did not let the defeat deter them from their steady march towards their inaugural League Championship. In the end they fairly romped home, although the end of the club's most successful season was tinged with sadness for the team and their followers as Bert Freeman — their Crystal Palace goalscoring hero of the 1914 Cup Final — announced his retirement.

The following season started in promising fashion and it looked for a while as though Burnley might be able to repeat their Championship success. They led the table on several occasions but, mainly through injuries, drifted away as the season

Burnley's 1920-21 line-up which lifted the Clarets' first Football League Championship title. Back row (left to right): Alf Bassnett, Len Smelt, David Taylor, John Haworth (secretary-manager), Jerry Dawson, Cliff Jones, Walt Weaver. Middle row: Billy Nesbitt, Bob Kelly, Joe Anderson, Benny Cross, Eddie Mosscrop. Front row: George Halley, Tommy Boyle, Willie Watson.

The Burnley side on their German tour in the close season of 1929.

drew to a close and finished third — a trio of top-three finishes since the end of the war.

If the previous season had been tinged with regret following the departure of Freeman, the end of the 1921-2 campaign was even worse — it brought about the demise of the great Halley, Boyle and Watson half-back line when Tommy Boyle, the victim of a bad leg injury, announced he would be changing roles at Turf Moor and becoming a coach.

After such a great return to League action, Burnley were hoping for great things but it was not to be and they started a steady slide down the First Division which led to relegation at the end of the 1920s. In the 1928-9 season they avoided the drop into the Second Division by seven points (they had escaped by only one point the previous season) — but in the 1929-30 season there was to be no saving them as they finished next to bottom and went down on goal-average.

Between the First Division title and relegation, much had happened at Burnley Football Club. The legendary Bob Kelly departed, sold to Sunderland for a then record transfer fee of £6,550; George Beel emerged on to the Turf Moor scene to start a career in which he would establish a number of individual goalscoring records and Jerry Dawson, the man who has appeared many more times in a Burnley shirt than any other player, finally hung up his goalkeeper's gloves. The period also saw the largest crowd ever to cram into Turf Moor — 54,755 saw Burnley beat Huddersfield 1-0 in an FA Cup tie.

Just as the 1900s had done, the 1930s started with Burnley in the Second Division — and like their predecessors of three decades before, the Burnley team could not

Action from Burnley's fourth-round FA Cup tie against First Division Sheffield United at Turf Moor in January 1933. The Clarets won 3-1 with the help of two goals from Cecil Smith.

find a quick way back to the top flight. Indeed, things nearly went the other way and in 1931-2 the Clarets avoided the plunge into the Third Division North by only two points.

Dismal League form was countered in the 1934-5 season by a rare sortie to the FA Cup semi-finals. Wins over Mansfield, Luton Town, Nottingham Forest and Birmingham gave them a semi-final date with Sheffield Wednesday at Villa Park. But the Wednesday were the favourites to win the competiton and went on to beat the Clarets 3-0.

That same season had seen the arrival of a young centre-forward named Tommy Lawton on the scene at Turf Moor. The following season saw the claret shirts disappear for a time as white shirts with black shorts with white stripes took over and Lawton made his debut at the tender age of 16 — he remains to this day the youngest player to ever pull on a first-team shirt for Burnley. The headline writers had a field day — as they did with the teenage scoring sensation right up until his departure for Everton in January 1937 when the Goodison Park club paid £7,000, then a League record, for the 17-year-old.

As the prospects of war again loomed large on the horizon, Burnley finished sixth in the 1937-8 season and 28 games into the next season they were well and truly among the promotion hopefuls before fading badly during the run-in to the end of the season and finishing 14th. When the following season got underway, World War Two was only days away and after two games play was suspended in the Football League until the end of hostilities.

There was a League of sorts and a League War Cup during the years between

Burnley skipper Alex Robinson greets Birmingham's Joe Bradford before the sixth-round FA Cup tie at Turf Moor in March 1935. Burnley won 3-2 before a crowd of 47,670.

Burnley in 1935. Back row (left to right): A.Boland (secretary), W.Dougall (trainer), T.Bromilow (manager). Middle row: J.Brown, Richmond, Scott, Wallace, Waterfield, Robinson. Front row: Hancock, G.Brown, C.Smith, Hornby, Downes.

1939 and 1946, and the 'old favourite' in the shape of the Lancashire Cup to play for as well. Burnley combined their usual blend of success and disappointment until the Football League got underway again for the 1946-7 season.

The new era of football at the end of World War One had brought golden days to Turf Moor and the fans obviously hoped for a repeat performance when the game got back into full swing after World War Two. But how many of them could have imagined just what the next 20 years would mean to the history of the Clarets?

In May 1945 there was an important new face at Turf Moor. Cliff Britton, a former Everton and England half-back, was appointed manager and a year later announced that the Clarets had a programme for promotion which would see them back in the First Division within three years. How wrong he was. They were back in the top flight at the end of the first full season of post-war soccer — and unlucky to have missed out on a Cup and promotion double when they lost at Wembley to Charlton.

Promotion after 17 years in the Second Division was obviously a great relief to Burnley and all their fans. Not only had they bounced back into action in great style following a war — they done so by returning to the claret and blue shirts which had brought so much success just before and in the three or four seasons immediately after World War One. On this occasion the strips were provided by fans who gave up their clothing coupons so that Burnley could once again become the Clarets.

Names to become famous with Burnley like Harry Potts, George Bray, Reg Attwell

Billy Morris scores the goal that put Burnley into the 1947 FA Cup semi-final after they beat Middlesbrough in a replay at Turf Moor.

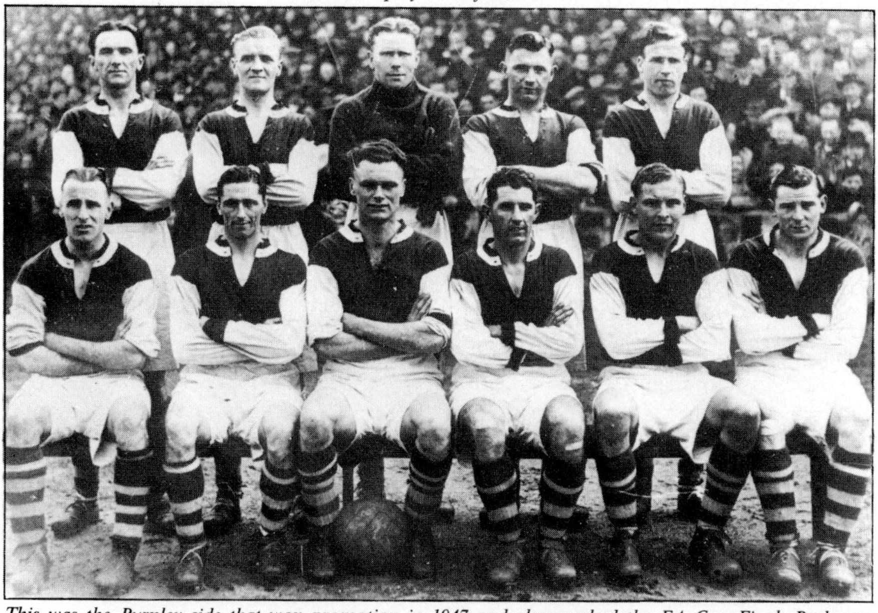

This was the Burnley side that won promotion in 1947 and also reached the FA Cup Final. Back row (left to right): Reg Attwell, Arthur Woodruff, Jimmy Strong, Harold Mather, George Bray. Front row: Jackie Chew, Billy Morris, Allan Brown, Ray Harrison, Harry Potts, Peter Kippax.

and the amateur international Peter Kippax were now established or establishing themselves on the Turf Moor scene and whilst there was much optimism about the chance of a good season in the Second Division, few even dreamt that promotion and a Cup Final appearance would be coming Burnley's way by the end of the season.

In the League, Burnley helped to set the early pace and were on top after one-third of the fixtures had been completed. As the New Year started they had dropped to third place but were only a point off the top. Even that high position seemed to count for nothing when the draw for the third round of the Cup was made and six-times winners Aston Villa were to be the guests at Turf Moor. Nobody anywhere could have predicted that Burnley would beat the First Division outfit 5-1.

The search for League honours continued and at the same time Burnley accounted for Coventry City in the fourth round of the Cup. By the time the Turf Moor team had bypassed Luton Town in a fifth-round replay there was already growing optimism about a League and Cup double — and this did not even diminish when the Clarets were drawn to play Middlesbrough away in the quarter-finals.

League points were still being collected handsomely as the 'Boro also became replay casualties and then Burnley, still second in Division Two, were drawn to meet Liverpool at Ewood Park in the semi-finals. The original tie ended goalless and when the clubs replayed at Maine Road, Ray Harrison got the only goal of the game and Burnley were on their way to Wembley for the first time.

By the time they played in an epic Final (see *Matches to Remember*), during which the ball burst for the second consecutive season, extra-time was needed for only the fourth time in Cup Final history and Charlton won by making the most of just about their only chance of the game. Burnley still had six League games to go, were still very well placed and looking set to join Manchester City in an end-of-season promotion party.

The defeat in the Final was followed by a minor hiccup and only three points came from the next four games. Those results meant that Burnley needed a point from either of their two remaining fixtures to deprive Birmingham of promotion. The Midlanders had already completed their programme and had the same number of points as the Clarets, but enjoyed a better goal-average. But Burnley were not going to wait until the last game before giving their supporters the prize they cherished most — they won promotion in their very next match by beating West Ham United on their own soil. After a 17-year absence, First Division football returned to Turf Moor.

The first season back in the top flight saw the Clarets achieve a very creditable third position — goal-average gave Manchester United the runners-up spot behind Arsenal — but they suffered a bad Cup defeat when losing 2-0 to Third Division Swindon Town, managed by Louis Page, a prodigious goalscorer in the 1920s when he played for the Clarets and became the only Burnley player to ever score six goals in the same League game (see *Matches to Remember*).

During those first few post-war seasons, great players like Tommy Cummings were making names for themselves with the Turf Moor club — but greater names were to follow and, ultimately, take the team right back to the top. And none could be more famous or more influential than a softly-spoken Irish inside-forward who joined Burnley from Glentoran in the 1949-50 season.

No player in modern times has ever commanded so much respect as Jimmy McIlroy. None has left so many fans completely awe-struck or so many opponents wondering what had hit them. 'The Magic of McIlroy' became a stock headline at local newspapers over the next dozen or so years.

He made his reserve-team debut within a week of signing in March 1950 and progressed through to the first team by October of the same year, following the sale of Harry Potts to Everton. But it was to be two more seasons before the Clarets really started their climb back to the top and became the 'Cotton Town Kings of Football'. McIlroy burst on to the Burnley scene at about the same time as another famous Jimmy — Jimmy Adamson, widely regarded as the best player anywhere never to win an international cap.

Burnley skipper Allan Brown meets Charlton's Don Welsh at Wembley before the 1947 FA Cup Final.

Jimmy Strong punches clear from Arsenal's Peter Goring at Turf Moor on the first day of the 1950-51 season.

The game was immensely popular in East Lancashire at the time and after the first handful or so games of the 1952-3 season, the Turf Moor team led the way in the First Division, having dropped only two points. Two-thirds of the way through the season they were still in with a great shout as they again topped the table, but in the end they lost touch with the leaders and finally finished sixth, three wins behind eventual Champions, Arsenal.

Next time around, following the shock sale of international winger Billy Elliot, the highest the Clarets climbed in the table was fourth and again they dropped away with a poor run in to the end of the season. The 1953-4 season is best remembered for one of the most thunderously entertaining Cup ties ever to feature the Clarets — a 5-3 home success over the mighty Manchester United, during which four goals were scored in the first six minutes (see *Matches to Remember*).

Burnley were to finish tenth the next season, having been fourth with seven games

Bill Holden heads a goal for Burnley against Wolves at Molineux in April 1953. It was a consolation for the Clarets, who lost 5-1

to play but managing to scrape together only a handful of points and the 1955-6 season saw the Burnley team make another promising start.

Again they fell away, but this time their poor finish to the season must have had something to do with a fourth-round FA Cup tie against Chelsea. Originally played at Turf Moor, the match had replays at Chelsea, St Andrew's, Highbury and White Hart Lane before Chelsea emerged 2-0 winners — the five matches still represent a club record Cup tie for the Clarets.

Notable debuts were certainly the order of the day during the 1956-7 season. John Connelly, arguably the best winger ever to play for Burnley, broke through into the first-team ranks; full-back John Angus started a career which would end on the eve of glory and earn him a testimonial; Jimmy Robson, a prolific goalscorer, and goalkeeper Adam Blacklaw both broke through for the first time; Ian Lawson scored hat-tricks in consecutive Cup ties.

One of those Cup games saw Burnley beat New Brighton 9-0 to equal their highest-ever score in the competition — they had previously won by the same score against Crystal Palace shortly after the turn of the century — but they should have hit double figures for the first time in a senior match, for Doug Winton missed a penalty! With so many new faces featuring in the team and others playing in unaccustomed positions, the team did well to finish in seventh place and the signs were good for the next couple of seasons at least.

The following season nothing much changed, although Allan Brown left the manager's chair to go to Sunderland and was eventually replaced by Harry Potts — the former player was to prove a major success in his new role. But by the time he arrived, Burnley were too far into the season for them to win any silverware and the Clarets were pleased to finish sixth, their best end to a season for a number of years. The next season they were to drop a place but history was created when

Brian Pilkington (centre) grabs Burnley's eighth goal in the 9-0 hammering of New Brighton in the 1956-7 FA Cup fourth round.

Ray Pointer notched 27 League goals — a post-war scoring record, and perhaps there were already indicatons of the glory to come in 1959-60.

Two wins got the season off to a great start, but then the Clarets lost to West Ham United. The roller-coaster start to the season continued, but after ten games they were in joint second place with Arsenal and Wolves, a point behind the Spurs (during this opening run Jimmy Adamson completed his 300th game for the club).

Eight games further into the campaign it had been all-change at the top with West Ham and Preston sharing the lead, a point ahead of Spurs with Burnley a further point in arrears. Spurs marched on, West Ham faded, and all the time it was Wolves and Burnley who formed the biggest threat to whoever held the lead. When the Clarets had ten games to play they were four points behind Spurs and a point behind Wolves and had two games in hand on them both. Burnley seemed to have blown it when they were thrashed by Wolves at Molineux and the Midlanders stayed on course for the double.

But they bounced back and when Wolves and Spurs both had only one game to play, the Turf Moor team had three to go and the title was well and truly in their sights. A win against Birmingham City and a disappointing draw in their final home game against Fulham meant that, when Burnley travelled to Maine Road for the very last game of the season, they had to win to claim the title.

The Maine Road crowd was augmented by large numbers of Wolves fans and although Burnley got off to a flying start and grabbed an early lead, City pegged them back before Trevor Meredith restored the Clarets' advantage and sent the First Division Championship trophy back to Turf Moor for the first time in 39 years (see *Matches to Remember*).

Burnley had announced their intentions and had become a force to be reckoned with for several seasons before actually getting their name inscribed again on the famous trophy but, perhaps, the most remarkable thing about the season in which they won the Championship was that they never actually topped the table until they beat Manchester City in the very last game.

The Burnley Reserve team which won the Central League and the Lancashire Senior Cup in 1961-62.

Proud Burnley parade the Football League Championship trophy through the streets of the town in 1960.

That Championship win gave Burnley the chance to take part in a tournament in America during the close season — the organizers must have known something because they invited the Clarets to cross the Atlantic and agreement was reached well before the emotional scenes at Maine Road.

It remains a shame that things did not go better in America. The competition was organized to try and increase North American interest and awareness of the finer points of soccer and Burnley joined other European clubs like Bayern Munich, Sporting Club of Portugal, Sampdoria and Brazilians, Bangu, for the event.

But the pitches were not suited to the English game, the climate was too humid, there were some angry scenes both on and off the field and in the end all those involved from Turf Moor must have been glad to get home and face the prospect of another English winter.

The new season got underway with a new competition at stake — the Football League Cup. Burnley had high hopes of attacking honours on three fronts as the old fashioned 'double' turned into a 'treble', but to this day the League Cup is the only senior honour to evade the Clarets. Of course, in those early days the competition was hardly a money-spinner and several leading clubs did not even bother to enter.

The traditional curtain-raiser to the season — the FA Charity Shield — was staged at Turf Moor and the Clarets did battle with Wolves, the side they had deprived of the double three months earlier. At the end of the day, a 2-2 draw — Burnley scored through Brian Miller and John Connelly — must have suited both clubs while leaving both sets of fans wondering just who was the best. The famous shield itself spent six months at Molineux and six at Turf Moor.

After beating Arsenal in their first game of the new season, the reigning Champions lost three times and their defence of the title looked to be in tatters. But they managed to get their act together again after that and one-third of the way into the season lay third behind Spurs and Sheffield Wednesday. In November, Burnley experienced European soccer for the first time. Given a first-round bye, they met French Champions, Stade de Reims, in the second round and won over two legs — and four days after the second leg were involved in a real epic of a match at White Hart Lane.

The scene was set for a thrilling match as Spurs, the runaway leaders, took on Burnley, the current Champions. Spurs stunned everyone by shooting into a 4-0 lead but the game finished level as Burnley proved to everyone that they were still a great team (see *Matches to Remember*).

The European dream was to die in Hamburg, where the Germans won 4-1 to take the tie 5-4 on aggregate; the FA Cup slipped from Burnley's grasp in the semi-final when they lost a Villa Park clash against Spurs; they lost in the semi-finals of the new League Cup to Aston Villa after a replay. Add to this a fourth-place finish in the League and it was quite an eventful season for the Clarets.

After the summer break, Burnley opened the new season in fine style and after 12 games led the way. By the turn of the year they were still in front, with four games to go they still topped the First Division and the Reserves clinched the Central League title.

At one stage in the season, five titles — the First Division, the FA Cup, the Central League, the Lancashire Senior Cup and the Lancashire League — were all well and truly in Burnley's sights.

A horrible run in March and April saw a second Championship title in three seasons slip from the Clarets and end up at Portman Road. The Clarets lost the FA Cup Final in a memorable game with the mighty Spurs (see *Matches to Remember*) but the season, a golden spell in a golden era for Burnley football, saw memorable highlights.

Gordon Harris (extreme left) scores Burnley's goal in Hamburg in the 1960-61 European Cup.

The dying moments in Hamburg. Jimmy McIlroy's effort hits a post and the Clarets go out 5-4 on aggregate.

The Duke of Edinburgh greets the Burnley team before the 1962 FA Cup Final against Tottenham Hotspur.

Skipper Jimmy Adamson was not only chosen as the Footballer of the Year, he was also named as England's assistant manager for that summer's World Cup in Chile.

To many followers of the game, the fact that Adamson was never chosen for the England team is a complete mystery. But something that happened the following season remains an even greater enigma.

When the news broke in the last week in February 1963, no one could believe it. Jimmy McIlroy, for 12 or so years the greatest crowd-pleaser of all time at Turf Moor, had been put on the transfer list and, later, sold to Second Division Stoke City.

The town was stunned. Man setting foot on the Moon would have been easier to believe — and that great event did not happen for another six years. Such was their disgust that many fans resolved never to pass through the Turf Moor turnstiles again — and to this day many have kept their word. And also to this day continues the mystery surrounding the transfer to the Second Division of one of the biggest names the game has ever seen.

The club simply said that McIlroy's recent performances had not consistently reached the level so dazzlingly attained by the magical Irishman since his signing from Glentoran 13 years before. But as the winter of 1962-3 was one of the worst on record and as Burnley did not actually play a League game for something like nine weeks, it is difficult to see which games he failed himself in.

It was without doubt the beginning of the end of a great era. Attendances fell, performances were undoubtedly affected and, despite stringent efforts, the good times never really came back. Although England won the World Cup three years later, the game was no longer the great institution, the great crowd-puller, the heart of a good weekend.

The abolition of the maximum wage, freedom of contract for players and spiralling transfer fees would all have their effect on the decline.

Burnley clung on to their proud First Division status for another eight seasons. Again they played in Europe and knocked on Wembley's door more than once. The stadium was virtually rebuilt as Bob Lord, the forceful chairman who made a big impression on the Football League as well as on Burnley, equipped the club which he obviously loved for life in the First Division for many years to come.

Bob Lord was, to all intents and purposes, 'Mr Burnley Football Club' from 1955 to 1981. He was a chairman with a great foresight and it is difficult to believe that anyone who had ever been connected with Burnley FC could have left such a lasting impression.

All those who encountered him have a story to tell. All relate tales of a man who knew what he wanted and went out to get it. Here was a man who was quite capable of selling Brian Clough two players when he only really wanted one. He was a man easily capable of banning football writers by the handful for simply doing their job and a man who was never far from controversy.

But he was also a man who gave Burnley their Gawthorpe training ground — still the envy of many of the top clubs — and their restyled ground, better by far than nearly every ground outside the First Division and, indeed, better than some still in the top flight. He made sure that the scouting system and youth policy were second-to-none and showed his knowledge of the game extended beyond the Burnley boundaries by rising to the rank of vice president of the Football League (he was even acting president just before his death) and chairman of the FA's Challenge Cup Committee — a face often seen on television and a voice heard often on radio as FA Cup draws were made.

Bob Lord was often the butt of the fans' anger and they called for his head on numerous occasions. But he made, and kept until just a few short months before his death, two promises throughout his time in the chairman's hot seat. The first was that Burnley would never slip below the Second Division and the second was that shares in the club would always pay a dividend — if only that was the case now.

Bob Lord finally deciding to ease his vice-like grip on the club in October 1981 and he sold the bulk of his shares. Local barrister John Jackson took over as chairman and 'Lord of Burnley' died just a couple of months later. The battle against cancer was one that Bob Lord could not win. His death left a big gap in football as a whole and at Burnley Football Club in particular. While many did not like him and some would even have claimed to have hated him, the club has never been quite the same without Bob Lord — the barrow-boy turned butcher turned influential soccer stalwart.

Whilst the 'McIlroy Mystery' obviously had a great deal to do with Bob Lord — many wanted him to go and Jimmy Mac to return — life at Burnley Football Club had to continue.

The very next season, Mac was back to haunt the Clarets for the first time since his departure from Turf Moor. Burnley travelled to the Victoria Ground and did well to fight back and draw 4-4.

A couple of months later, Burnley were up against another player with prominent claret and blue connections. At the time only the true *aficionado* of the game would have heard of Rotherham United's teenage inside-forward Frank Casper. Three and a half years later, the Turf Moor club were to break with tradition and buy Casper and by the end of his career — cut cruelly short by a never-to-be-forgotten tackle by Norman Hunter (see *Matches to Remember*) — he had joined the band of players who can boast 100 Football League goals.

Before all that was to happen, Burnley were to part company with John Connelly as falling attendances forced the club to sell him to Manchester United — another decision that left Burnley fans wondering if every player who ever showed any promise would be sold as the club tried to balance the books and stay in the First Division.

Although attendances continued to dwindle and other players were forced to leave the club — notably Jimmy Robson and Ray Pointer — Burnley managed to finish third in the League in 1965-6 and return to European action, this time in the European Fairs Cup.

Despite the undisputed glamour of playing against some of the Continent's finest players, Burnley still kept a very close eye on the League and after the first seven or eight games were again sitting on top of the First Division.

It was as divisional leaders that they went to Stuttgart for the first leg of their first European tie for seven seasons and a draw in Germany was followed by victory in Burnley and the Clarets were into the hat for the second-round draw.

At that stage they met Lausanne Sports and won 8-1 on aggregate to earn a match against Napoli for a place in the quarter-finals. But the strain of Continental travel and extra games was beginning to take its toll and Burnley slid down to mid-table obscurity.

Unfashionable, unheard of to many outside this country and unfancied, Burnley caused another major shock by putting the Italian millionaires in their place by beating them 3-0 at Turf Moor. The Italians set their stall out to gain sweet revenge

Burnley skipper Alex Elder exchanges pennants before the Fairs Cup game in Lausanne.

in Naples, but they could not find the back of the net no matter what they did (see *Matches to Remember*) and Burnley were in the last eight. It was at the quarter-final stage that Burnley's European dream was dashed. Drawn to play Eintracht, they made themselves favourites for a semi-final place by drawing 1-1 in Germany, but then contrived to lose the home leg on a night when the team really did not do itself justice and Eintracht won 2-1.

In the last match of the season, 17-year-old Dave Thomas created club history by becoming the youngest-ever player to don a claret and blue shirt for Burnley in the First Division. But Burnley finished 14th for the first of four successive seasons, parted company with Alex Elder (transferred to Stoke), Adam Blacklaw (Blackburn Rovers), Gordon Harris (Sunderland) and Brian Miller (injured and forced to retire).

Before the new season got underway, Frank Casper was on his way across the Pennines to Burnley. Shortly afterwards 19-year-old Colin Waldron was on his way north from Chelsea and by December, Steve Kindon — an apprentice signed on the same day as Casper — turned professional.

Although in general terms the 1967-8 season was something of a disappointment — relegation had been a threat until Easter yielded five invaluable points — there were two main reasons to look back at it with some satisfaction.

Firstly, Manchester United, Manchester City, Sheffield United and Everton were beaten as Burnley claimed a place in the FA Youth Cup Final. The first leg against

Skipper Mick Docherty holds aloft the FA Youth Cup as David Hartley, scorer of two goals in the 1968 Final, plants a kiss on the trophy.

Coventry saw the young Clarets — led by Mick Docherty — lose 2-1 at Highfield Road, but a 2-0 win in the return brought the prestigious trophy to Turf Moor for the first time.

The second was of a more personal nature as it saw Andy Lochhead join the élite group of Clarets to have scored 100 League goals for the club, the others being 1914 Cup Final hero, Bert Freeman; George Beel, the man with almost every goalscoring record at the club; Louis Page, the only player to have ever scored a double hat-trick for the Clarets; the legendary Jimmy McIlroy; and 'blond bombshell' Ray Pointer, who has the distinction of reaching his 100 in only 169 games — second only to the phenomenal Freeman who managed it in 152.

Attendances continued to drop as transfer fees continued to rise and at the start of the next season, Willie Morgan left the club to continue a flourishing career at Manchester United, the Old Trafford outfit writing a cheque for almost £120,000 to secure his services. It was during this season that Burnley pulled off one of their more audacious stunts. Virtually the entire first team was dropped to make way for the team with an average age of 22. There would be nothing exceptional about that these days, but in the late 1960s it still took good players anything up to five years or more to force their way into first-team soccer.

For six weeks those 'Burnley Babes' ran English soccer. They humbled the mighty Leeds United by 5-1 (see *Matches to Remember*) and won eight consecutive games — six in the League and two in the League Cup.

That run hauled them up to the fringes of the scrap for European places and took them to the semi-finals of the League Cup.

But then it was 'all-change' and back to the more usual line-up and the Clarets slumped back to mid-table obscurity and limped out of the League Cup after losing the semi-final to Swindon Town of the Third Division. Two legs failed to settle the outcome and the replay went into extra-time. Burnley grabbed an early lead in that extra-time, but then an own-goal and a late strike by Peter Noble — later to play with great distinction for the Clarets — sealed Burnley's fate.

The almost inevitable decline continued in the 1969-70 season when Burnley finished 14th for the fourth year in succession — but worse was to come in the first full season of the new decade when they were relegated with three games to go. Manager Jimmy Adamson, appointed the year before as Harry Potts became general manager, accepted most of the blame, but those of us who lived through much of that season can only remember the fact that Eric Probert was leading scorer with only five goals — so where was the real problem?

Twenty-four years in the First Division ended in unceremonious fashion. Burnley fans drew great consolation from the fact that, in the depths of their despair, one of their favourite players, Ralph Coates, had been selected for England's 22-man squad for the World Cup. But by the time Coates and the rest of the England party left for Mexico, he was a Spurs player, having signed for his new club on a motorway service station car park for around £190,000.

A swift return to the First Division looked on the cards early in the next season when Burnley lay second. But then things started to go horribly wrong and the fans began to call for Adamson's head as, for a while, it looked like Burnley were going to escape from the Second Division — but in the wrong direction! Six wins in the final 24 days of the season removed the relegation threat and Burnley climbed to a creditable but not-good-enough seventh place. Were those six wins a sign of things to come?

Well, it would certainly seem so. The next season started with a 16-match unbeaten run and by the end of the 1972-3 season Burnley had lost only four times and won the Second Division championship.

Just about every manager in football would tell you that one of the keys to

Martin Dobson leads promoted Burnley on to the pitch at Deepdale in April 1973. The Clarets now needed one point to clinch the Second Division title.

success is a settled side and Jimmy Adamson could not have asked for a much more settled campaign than the one he masterminded.

Six players — Alan Stevenson, Keith Newton, Colin Waldron, Jim Thomson, Frank Casper and Leighton James — played in each of the 42 games. Martin Dobson missed only one, Paul Fletcher was out for two, Doug Collins figured in all but five and Mick Docherty missed only seven.

The celebrations which surrounded the return to the First Division after an absence of two seasons were helped on by a testimonial match in honour of John Angus. At the start of the season the 33-year-old full-back had announced his retirement and an 18-year career with the Clarets came to a close. And, almost with the taste of celebratory champagne still with them, the Second Division's all-conquering heroes were greeted with rapturous applause when they took to the Turf Moor pitch for the testimonial. Three other teams featured in the match and all had a story to tell. One was built-up of the 'old-timers', many of whom had featured in the First Division championship 13 years before, and almost all of whom came out of retirement to honour Angus. Another was a selection of former players who had been transferred elsewhere during Angus' career and the third was built-up of youngsters and apprentices from the club — many of whom claimed their own places in Burnley's footballing history later in their careers.

Three seasons in the First Division followed. During the first of them the Clarets missed out on a place in Europe by only one place — how different things would have been if they had managed a couple more points — and were bundled out of the FA Cup in an epic semi-final by Newcastle United.

The game at Hillsborough came only a week after Burnley crushed an all-conquering Leeds side 4-1 at Elland Road (see *Matches to Remember*) but an injury sustained in that match hampered Frank Casper and subsequently the rest of the front line, while at the other end of the park, Malcolm Macdonald was making life very difficult indeed for the Burnley defence and emerged from the game with both goals.

After that came a season in which Burnley finished tenth but suffered one of their most embarrassing Cup exits, crashing out of the FA Cup at home to Wimbledon — then in the Southern League. Although Burnley were no longer a great force in the game and players were still being sold to finance the operation (Martin Dobson went to Everton for around £300,000 after three games of the 1974-5 season), few could have predicted that they were going to slip out of the First Division at the end of the next season.

They made a slow start and never really recovered from it, although Peter Noble seemed to be setting himself to become the first Burnley player to pass 20 League goals in a season since Willie Irvine had notched 29 a decade earlier. The first 16 games yielded 11 goals for the man captured from Swindon Town. But the 11th was a penalty (he never missed one for Burnley) and in taking it he picked up a niggling injury which kept him out for weeks. He came back and notched a goal in January, but then missed a further seven games and ended up collecting 13 goals from 25 starts — a strike rate which would have taken him past the 20 barrier if he had maintained it through a full season.

Manchester United came to Burnley on Easter Monday and won 1-0 to send Burnley down with a game still to play — only 11,675 fans turning up to see the performing of the 'last rites' the following Saturday when Coventry were Burnley's last First Division opponents to date.

Four seasons in the Second Division followed and then, almost inevitably, Burnley slipped into the Third Division for the first time in their 98-year history — the first full season of the new decade was their first in that division. Burnley fans everywhere knew it was only going to be a brief visit to the League's lower reaches.

And they were right as after just two seasons they were crowned as champions of the Third Division and bounced back. They started that championship in fairly dismal style by losing six of their first eight games, but then between 10 October and the end of the season they lost only twice in 38 outings to take the title on goal-difference. Winning the championship after starting the season in such a poor way was remarkable in itself — collecting the trophy when they had never topped the table until after completing their full programme of matches was quite another — although the precedent for that had been set by the 1959-60 First Division Championship side.

Life back in the Second Division was a curious mixture. Nothing would go right for the Clarets in the League, but they hardly seemed able to put a foot wrong in the Cup competitions. Bury, Middlesbrough, Coventry City and Birmingham City were all humbled by Burnley as they fought through to the quarter-finals of the League Cup. But the draw could hardly have been worse as Burnley were paired with Spurs, a team almost exclusively built-up of internationals, and the match was to take place at White Hart Lane.

Burnley made things even harder for themselves by sacking manager Brian Miller just a few hours before the match and appointing Frank Casper in his place as 'caretaker'. Everything pointed to Spurs having a bit of shooting-in practice and setting their stall out for Wembley, but Burnley won a remarkable game 4-1 (see *Matches to Remember*) and earned a plum semi-final against Liverpool. The first leg, at Anfield, was a disaster as the Clarets lost 3-0 — mainly because of missed

Burnley celebrate Derek Scott's goal at Turf Moor in the second leg of the 1983 League Cup semi-final.

chances — and although Burnley won the second leg, they never really made an impression on the Reds and said goodbye to that competition.

But the FA Cup was still in progress. Carlisle had been beaten after a replay and Swindon posed few problems. Four days after the League Cup exit, the Clarets travelled to play Crystal Palace in the fifth round, the tie being settled in a replay at Turf Moor. Despite their obvious problems, Burnley had qualified for the quarter-finals of both major domestic knock-outs, but the tiredness was to show when they lost 5-0 in a quarter-final replay at Sheffield Wednesday.

Despite a brief resurgence towards the end of that season, relegation was once more almost inevitable. Burnley said farewell to the Second Division — and parted company with Frank Casper to install John Bond in his place.

At the time there was great excitement about the appointment of one of football's best-known bosses to the Burnley hot seat, although many felt that Casper had never really been given the chance to prove himself. Burnley had only ever been relegated to the Third Division once before and had been promoted back again after two seasons. Everyone knew that the same would happen again — didn't they? But the plan was to backfire on John Bond. He was headlined as the great saviour of Burnley Football Club and the man to take the Turf Moor outfit right back to the top.

But he released many of the club's most promising young players and replaced them with men who were a testament to his Manchester City past. His only season as manager of Burnley saw the club finish 12th in the Third Division. At the end of it he moved on to new pastures and John Benson, his long time assistant at various clubs, took over.

If life under Bond was bleak for Burnley, it was ten times worse under Benson and at the end of his only season the Clarets were facing the prospect of Fourth Division football for the first time in their long and often illustrious history. They won only 11 League fixtures in the John Benson season as they finished in 21st place — the worst-ever finish by a Clarets team.

John Bond (right) and his assistant John Benson pictured before the start of the 1983-4 season, their first in charge at Turf Moor.

Despite all that, the season did have its highspots. In an FA Cup first-round tie, Burnley won 9-0 at Penrith, hitting as many goals in one game for only the third time in their history with Kevin Hird and Alan Taylor both scoring hat-tricks. And in one League game they hit seven — a feat not often recorded by Burnley in more modern times. The victims of that 7-0 win were Rotherham, Hird again scoring a hat-trick.

Benson departed and there was further great excitement about the appointment of Martin Buchan, the former Manchester United and Scotland superstar. A player who commanded great respect within the game was going to use Burnley as the launching pad for a great future in management and take the club back up the League — until he resigned in October for 'family reasons'.

Buchan's departure saw another former Old Trafford man in the Burnley job, Tommy Cavanagh took the Clarets through the remainder of their first season in the Fourth Division — and a disappointing 14th place finish. The next season saw Burnley with another manager, but this time the club had returned to a familiar face as Brian Miller was given back the job he had lost when Burnley were a Second Division club.

There was a new twist to the Football League in 1986-7, but nobody believed it would mean anything to Burnley. For the first time the team finishing bottom would be automatically relegated to make way for the Vauxhall Conference champions.

While nobody really bothered talking about that aspect of life in the Fourth Division on the opening day, it was certainly the focus of their attention on the last day of that fateful season. Burnley simply had to win to have a chance of staying in the Football League — but even a win might not be enough. Sure enough the game against Orient produced victory for the Clarets (see *Matches to Remember*) and Lincoln City lost both their final game and their Football League status.

Ian Britton celebrates the goal that kept Burnley in the Football League.

Goalscorers Grewcock (right) and Britton celebrate with manager Brian Miller.

Nobody will ever know what would have happened to Burnley had they lost. Many have private theories about closure of the club and redevelopment of Turf Moor as a housing estate, others believe that Burnley would have continued as a 'full-time' club and bounced back into the League.

Lincoln City and Darlington have both proved that relegation to the Conference need not be a death sentence and both enjoy Football League status again now. Indeed, Darlington became Fourth Division champions in 1990-91. Newport County were not so fortunate and no longer exist in that guise. The latest League casualties, Colchester United, made a sterling effort at climbing straight back into the League, but just missed out finishing runners-up to new boys Barnet.

The only thing that can be said with any certainty about that season of near-disaster is that it actually brought about the rebirth of Burnley Football Club. Ever since then it has been the best-supported club in the Fourth Division, although the 1990-91 season was the only one in which they even managed to reach the play-offs — going out in the semi-finals to Torquay United, the team eventually promoted. For whatever reason, the Turf Moor men have become the 'nearly-men' of the Fourth Division, widely respected for playing good, attractive, flowing football — but unable to get enough points to take those first tentative steps on the road back to a status more suitable for such a great old club.

The Burnley playing staff at the start of 1990-91. Back row (left to right): France, Farrell, Eli, Futcher, Williams, Pearce, Howarth, Davis. Standing: Holland (physiotherapist), Bray (kit man), Jakub, Deakin, Smyth, Francis, Measham, White, Bray, Lancashire, Bellamy (reserve-team manager), Mullen (assistant manager). Seated: Hamilton, Mumby, Deary, Grewcock, Smith, Casper (manager), Withe, Hardy, Sonner, McKay, Lawrie. On ground: Murray, Pemberton, Wallace, Rahman, Hilton, Isherwood, Seals, Hill, Vaughan, Frankum, King.

Ron Futcher gets the better of a heading duel with Doncaster Rovers' Brendan Ormsby.

The Turf Moor Story

IN ITS heyday, almost 55,000 people have crammed their way through the turnstiles at Turf Moor, the home of Burnley Football Club. The other side of the coin has seen less than 1,700 spectators there for a Football League game. Emotion has been rife and the sound of cheering fans has often filled the nearby town centre. Others have passed a few less interesting moments by letting their thoughts wander over the rolling moors which are clearly visible from Turf Moor, despite the fact that the ground stands almost at the heart of the vast East Lancashire urban conurbation.

Conceived, designed, built and extended with First Division football very much in mind, Turf Moor has been the venue for football at every level, from an England international to European Cup games, League matches in every current division and a variety of other competitions.

And whilst keeping abreast of the times, in terms of stadium quality, might have cost Burnley several key players over the seasons and, in many people's minds, might have contributed to the club's slide down the Football League, that foresight has also given Burnley an ideal launching pad for the twenty-first century and a ground which is the envy of the vast majority of clubs outside the very highest echelon.

Turf Moor became the home of Burnley FC only nine months after the club came into being and the Clarets have played there since February 1883. Only two other clubs, Preston North End and Stoke City, have been in continuous residence at their homes for longer.

Before Burnley moved into their present home, they played matches at Calder Vale, switching to Turf Moor at the invitation of the neighbouring cricket club. The cricket and football clubs went their separate ways many years ago, but they still operate as close and co-operative neighbours, a fact made evident during the 1990-91 season when the Gawthorpe training ground was snowbound and the footballers trained on the outfield at the cricket club.

First used for a local match against Rawtenstall in February 1883 — a game which Burnley lost 6-3 — Turf Moor has been continually improved, having started life very much as a field at the side of the cricket club.

By September 1884, a grandstand with 800 seats had sprung up and a natural mound had been added to and modified to accommodate a further 2,000 fans. At the same time an uncovered stand running along two sides of the pitch to hold 5,000 people was being built, a development obviously spurred on by the fact that an attendance of 12,000 — three times as many as attended that year's FA Cup Final — had been attracted for a local 'derby' against Padiham in March 1884.

Amongst the many accolades afforded to Turf Moor is the fact that it is believed to have been the first Football League ground ever visited by a member of the Royal Family. That was in October 1886, when Queen Victoria's son, Prince Albert, was amongst a crowd of 9,000 for a match between Burnley and Bolton Wanderers.

The Royal trip to Burnley had not been solely to watch Burnley, for Prince Albert was in town to open a hospital named after his mother. But the 'royal seal of approval' was of double benefit for the club — many people paid an extra guinea just to sit near the Royal party, and for some time afterwards Burnley were nicknamed throughout the football world as the Royalties.

Hectic scheduling meant that the Prince and his party could watch only the first half of the game. Burnley trailed 3-1 at that stage and were finally beaten 4-3 by the Trotters.

Whilst the new century may have dawned without too many changes at Turf

Turf Moor pictured in 1905.

Burnley players line up at Turf Moor in the 1900s.

Moor, by 1908 two sides of the ground were covered and the Brunshaw Road Stand and the Star Stand had emerged.

The Brunshaw Road Stand remained for many years but the Star Stand, which eventually made way for the Longside Terrace, was the subject of many changes and was even moved back at one stage so that an enclosure could be made in front of it for the visit of Manchester United for an FA Cup tie.

Before League football was suspended due to World War One, interest in soccer had become so intense that crowds at Turf Moor were already nudging the 50,000 mark — incredibly, equivalent to the town's population at the time — and considerable improvements were made during that period.

Football fever soon gripped the land again after the war and when Huddersfield Town visited Burnley in February 1924 for an FA Cup tie, the turnstiles were at their busiest. A crowd of 54,755 watched Burnley triumph 1-0 (one man is reported to have died in the crush) and that figure stands as a record to this day.

Two years before that, on 25 March 1922, Huddersfield had met with greater success when Turf Moor was the venue for an FA Cup semi-final. They met Notts County in front of a crowd of 46,323, won 3-1 and went on to beat Preston North End in the Cup Final at Stamford Bridge.

The year 1927 saw the only international match to be played at Turf Moor. Burnley players Louis Page and Jack Hill were drafted into the England side to try to boost local support. Another in that England line-up for the Turf Moor clash with Wales was George Brown. At the time he was a Huddersfield Town player, but later in his career he became a Claret and scored 24 goals in 35 first-team games.

Despite so much 'local knowledge' in the England team, the home side were beaten 2-1. Jack Hill scored an own-goal and Turf Moor was never again chosen as the stage for a senior international.

Things did not change very much between the wars but not long after World War Two, the Star Stand had been replaced by the terrace now known as the Longside and in 1954 the club invested £20,000 on a new roof.

Three years later, floodlights followed, officially switched on for a friendly against

Spectators crammed into Turf Moor for the FA Cup fifth-round tie against Arsenal in February 1937, when a near-record attendance was present.

local rivals, Blackburn Rovers. Those floodlights lasted for 18 years and were replaced at a cost of £30,000 in the mid-1970s. The new lights were first used for a Lancashire schoolboys match in February 1975.

Just before that, a new pitch was laid at Turf Moor. Experts in the shape of Cambridge Soil Services Limited were called in to lay a new playing surface in the 1974 close season. The new surface was slightly higher than the old one and eliminated all trace of the slope which once caused problems for players. The new pitch was laid on top of a 'state-of-the-art' drainage system designed to keep water off the playing area at all times.

Heralded as a playing surface to rival even Wembley, the new soil and grass did not do the trick for Burnley. The first time they played on it they were were beaten 2-1 by Wolves, and within two seasons they were out of the First Division.

The late-1960s and early-1970s saw the most dramatic changes ever to take place at Turf Moor. At a cost of £180,000, a new Cricket Field Stand emerged. It incorporated everything needed by a small-town club in a big league — so much so that even when there were further improvements, the Cricket Field Stand remained a fine main stand.

Players and officials change under the Cricket Field Stand and Turf Moor is one of only five League grounds where the players run out from behind a goal rather than from near the half-way line. The others are at Millwall, Blackpool, Notts County and Torquay United.

Whilst Burnley Football Club and Turf Moor have been the breeding grounds for so many innovative ideas over the years, the Cricket Field Stand has, alas, provided the club with one scheme which never took off. When the stand was completed in 1969, it boasted under-floor heating to keep a maximum of 4,500 spectators warm during the winter months. But by the time Prime Minister Edward

Prime Minister Ted Heath and Burnley chairman Bob Lord at the official opening of the Cricket Field Stand.

Heath officially opened the stand in November 1973, the oil-fired system had already been turned-off for the last time as it proved massively uneconomical.

Within months of his initial visit, Ted Heath — now Leader of the Opposition after losing a General Election — was back at Burnley, this time to officially open the £450,000 Bob Lord Stand, the replacement for the old Brunshaw Road Stand. The Bob Lord Stand is now the main stand at Turf Moor and the 'nerve centre' of the club. It can seat 2,500 spectators and includes hospitality rooms, administration offices, executive rooms, development and ticket offices, and its press-box has one of the finest views on offer to journalists anywhere in the Football League.

Next to the Bob Lord Stand and opposite the Cricket Field Stand is the Bee Hole End, the only uncovered section of the stadium. Named after a colliery which used to stand behind it, the Bee Hole End is a vast terrace with a safety limit of some 7,000 people. Although popular with many, the Bee Hole End has never commanded quite the same 'audience' as the Longside Terrace which, although split

We made it! Ecstatic Burnley fans as the final whistle sounds and the Clarets have survived in the Football League by beating Orient in the most vital game ever staged at Turf Moor.

into two sections for segregation of opposing fans and including a 'no man's land', is still the first terraced section to be filled on match days.

At the start of the 1990-91 season the capacity at Turf Moor was cut dramatically to 13,500, but much work was carried out in the first four months of the season and by January 1991, when the Clarets played host to Manchester City in the FA Cup third round, they were able to attract a sell-out audience of 20,331.

Plans are in the pipeline for future improvements and if the club returns to the Second Division, then seats will have to be installed throughout the ground.

Turf Moor has been the venue of some great moments, treasured in the memories of literally thousands of fans.

In its present form the ground is a proud testament to the dedication of those who have administered the club down the decades and those who have taken over the reins more recently and declared their intention to provide Burnley Football Club with the stadium it will need when the glory days return.

Burnley Managers

Arthur F.Sutcliffe
1893-1896

WHEN secretary Arthur Sutcliffe was asked to combine his duties with that of team manager in 1893, it was a new departure at Turf Moor, the team having been previously selected by committee.

Not too much is known about Sutcliffe but in his three years in charge, the club's position deteriorated each season and, after James Crabtree failed to reach agreement on wages in 1895, the Burnley-born England international moved on to great success at Aston Villa.

Sutcliffe had great faith in Burnley's policy of bringing Scottish players to Turf Moor and signed James Davidson, Charles McEleny and Jeremy Reynolds, all from Celtic, and David Haddow, from Motherwell, in 1895.

He also believed in home-grown talent and promoted local lad Willie Tatham as first-choice goalkeeper following Jack Hillman's departure to Everton.

Arthur Sutcliffe relinquished the position as team manager and left the club in 1896.

Harry Bradshaw
1896-1899

HARRY Bradshaw was appointed club secretary in 1891 and then chairman in 1893, shortly after Arthur Sutcliffe had succeeded him as secretary.

He replaced Sutcliffe as team manager in 1896 but at the end of the club's worst-ever season he had led the team to last place, then relegation after the Test Matches. Bradshaw had tempted the inspirational Jimmy Ross to Turf Moor and he and centre-forward Wilf Toman scored the goals that took the Clarets back to the top flight after only one season.

Bradshaw had brought big Jack Hillman back to the club and introduced young Fred Barron to the defence for a season that started promisingly but faded after the much-publicized row between Jimmy Ross and Tom Morrison. Ross was transferred to Manchester City and Wilf Toman also left the club.

In the summer of 1899, Harry Bradshaw was appointed manager of Second Division Woolwich Arsenal and within five years had taken them from the verge of bankruptcy and built a team which won promotion to the First Division in 1904.

He left Plumstead for Southern League Fulham the same year and guided the Cottagers to Football League status and an FA Cup semi-final before being appointed secretary of the Southern League in 1909, a position he held until his death in 1921, aged 68.

His son, Joe Bradshaw, also played for and managed Fulham.

J.E.Mangnall
1899-1903

ERNEST Mangnall, a former Lancashire County FA goalkeeper, was a director at Bolton Wanderers before he came to Turf Moor in 1899 to take over as secretary-manager from the departed Harry Bradshaw.

Mangnall inherited a fading team and, despite the introduction of a number of new players, notably the former England forward Edgar Chadwick from Everton, Burnley were relegated at the end of his first season.

Back in the Second Division, the club were hit by the 12-month ban on goalkeeper Jack Hillman for his part in the bribery scandal at Nottingham Forest. Mangnall signed Henry Collins from Hebburn Argyle, having already bought full-backs James Lindsay and George Lockhart.

Although third place was achieved in 1901, even relative success was short-lived and at the end of the 1902-03 season, Burnley suffered the ignominy of finishing at the very bottom of the Second Division and having to apply for re-election.

Despite the team's less than spectacular record under his control, Mangnall was appointed to Second Division Manchester United in 1903 as the man to build a promotion-winning side. He surpassed expectations by gaining promotion in 1906 and bringing two League Championships to Old Trafford, in 1908 and 1911, as well as an FA Cup Final triumph in 1909.

After being instrumental in the formation of the Central League in 1911, he left Old Trafford to join arch rivals Manchester City in 1912, where he stayed until leaving League football in 1924.

He also helped found the Football Managers' Association and upon his retirement from the game he was awarded an FA long-service medal and a testimonial game, when a combined Manchester team met Liverpool. Ernest Mangnall died in 1932.

Spen Whittaker
1903-April 1910

FOLLOWING the departure of Ernest Mangnall, the Burnley directors decided that the time had come to appoint a full-time team manager, whilst a director, Mr W.R.Thornton, would take over the secretarial duties at the club.

The man chosen to look after team affairs was Spence Whittaker, known as 'Spen', who had developed something of a reputation in local football in Accrington.

Whittaker immediately introduced numerous new players to try to seek a swift improvement on the field. David Walders came from Barrow, goalkeeper Billy Green from Brentford and Dugald McFarlane also from Barrow. The most inspired early signing, however, was probably that of Hugh Moffat from Congleton, who was a versatile player and a valuable servant to the club for a number of years.

Things did start to improve over the next few seasons, then in February 1907, Whittaker signed a young apprentice blacksmith who was to be the first member of the first great Burnley side; his name was Jerry Dawson.

The next key signing at Turf Moor was probably that of Alec Leake from Aston Villa in December 1907. Not destined to stay long enough to share in glories to come, former international Leake was an inspiration to the team during his time at the club. Then Richard Lindley and Willie Watson were both signed as the club's fortunes steadily improved.

In April 1910, however, tragedy struck. Spen Whittaker was on his way to London by train to register the signing of a new player, Harry Swift from Accrington.

When the train stopped at Crewe, it was reported that a man had fallen from a carriage some distance outside the town. When the body was discovered it was that of the Burnley manager.

A benefit match was held at Turf Moor for Whittaker's wife and family, with Manchester United providing the opposition for a Burnley team boosted by numerous guests.

R.H.Wadge
April 1910-July 1910

FOLLOWING the death of Spen Whittaker, Burnley director and former chairman R.H.Wadge temporarily assumed the duties of team manager until the end of the season, in addition to his role as honorary secretary of the club.

After John Haworth's appointment, Wadge reverted to his position as club director until, after 24 years connected with Burnley FC, he had to leave Turf Moor in 1915, to pursue business interests in the south of England.

John Haworth
July 1910-December 1924

THE Turf Moor directors once more looked to the town of Accrington to build upon the foundations laid by Spen Whittaker.

John Haworth was born in Accrington in 1876 and was brought up in a sporting family, an uncle, George Haworth, winning five England caps and skippering Accrington FC when, along with Burnley, they were founder-members of the Football League in 1888.

John Haworth was a full-back in his playing days with the Meadow Bank team but soon gave up competitive football, becoming that club's secretary. He joined Accrington Stanley, then in the North-East Lancashire Combination, as a committee man early in 1897 and became club secretary later in the year.

With Haworth as secretary, Stanley won the Lancashire Combination in 1902-03 and again in 1905-06, and it was from this background that he came to Turf Moor in 1910.

One of Haworth's first signings was Charlie Bates, who was to share in the club's triumph over the next dozen years. Bates' playing career with Burnley was short but he became an important member of the team behind the team, the trainer.

Around about this time, also, John Haworth made his mark by suggesting that the club changed the colours of their shirts from green, which the new manager considered unlucky. The director agreed and it was decided to change to the colours of the current League Champions, the claret and blue of Aston Villa.

Towards the end of his first season in charge, Haworth made his first major signing, a real coup when he persuaded the great Bert Freeman to come to Turf Moor from Everton.

The following September came the *coup de grace* when Tommy Boyle was signed from Barnsley. Haworth knew that Boyle was the man that the team needed most of all, literally the pivot around which the achievements to come would revolve.

Steady progress, rather than spectacular success, followed and, after a near-miss in 1912, promotion was achieved in 1913, together with a run to the FA Cup semi-final. Then in November 1913, another major signing was engineered by John Haworth when Bob Kelly arrived from St Helens Town.

The events surrounding the FA Cup triumph of 1914 are well documented and the following season, the last before League football was suspended, was a magnificent one. Burnley, by now, truly 'The Clarets' finished in fourth position, only three points from the title.

Better was to come in 1919-20, when Burnley were runners-up to West Brom as John Haworth and Charlie Bates planned the club's assault on the League Championship that they knew was within the team's capabilities.

After a disappointing start, the 1920-21 season was a triumph for all concerned. There was the long unbeaten run, the players perhaps all reaching their peak together, superbly led by Tommy Boyle. And behind it all was the mastermind, John Haworth, who knew every player inside-out and knew how to get the best out of each one.

Third position followed in 1921-2 but the great days were coming to an end and a period of mediocrity was in store for Burnley Football Club.

In 1924, John Haworth contracted pneumonia and died on 4 December, aged only 48. He was a man who never played football above junior level and had never before experienced management of a senior club, yet he guided the Clarets to the top honours in the game. His contribution to Burnley Football Club's success is enormous and should never be forgotten.

Albert Pickles
January 1925-September 1932

FOLLOWING the death of the enormously successful John Haworth, the club looked within to appoint his successor, local man, Albert Pickles, who had been elected to the board of directors in 1918.

Pickles was an outstanding schoolboy athlete as well as a promising amateur footballer in his younger days with Burnley Belvedere. As a 17-year-old in the late 1890s he was offered a trial by Aston Villa at the instigation of the great James Crabtree. Parental consent was not forthcoming, however, and a possible professional career in the game was lost.

Pickles faced a daunting task in trying to emulate his illustrious predecessor. The Championship side had all but broken up, attendances were falling and the prospects of lasting success looked slim.

Jack Bruton was Pickles' first signing, from Horwich RMI in March 1925. The youngster had been much sought after and was soon blooded in the first team.

Relegation was safely avoided and plans

were laid for the new season. Of course, the 1925-6 campaign was the time of a change in the offside law and with new signings Joe Devine, Andy McCluggage and the lightning-fast winger, Louis Page, the team approached the new season with confidence.

That confidence, though, evaporated on the opening day of the season when Burnley suffered a 10-0 drubbing at the hands of Aston Villa. Shortly afterwards the great Bob Kelly left the club and it was mostly downhill after that, only the one-man Louis Page show at Birmingham in April saving Burnley that season.

Relegation inevitably came in 1930 and, after two undistinguished Second Division campaigns, both George Beel and Louis Page left Turf Moor in 1932.

Two games into the 1932-3 season, after a heavy defeat at Preston, Pickles offered his resignation, which was 'reluctantly' accepted by the board.

Tom Bromilow
October 1932-July 1935

TOM Bromilow was the first Burnley manager to have played football at a professional level and one of the minority not promoted from within the club.

He joined Liverpool from Army football in 1918 and went on to become a cultured wing-half, a prominent figure in the Anfield club's League Championship successes in 1922 and 1923.

He played over 300 League games for the Reds and won five England caps, the last in 1925, before leaving to coach in Amsterdam in 1930.

Neither Bromilow nor his wife could settle in Holland and he returned to England to take up his appointment with Burnley in 1932.

His success at Turf Moor was limited. He had inherited a struggling team and with crowds dwindling and interest waning he faced an uphill struggle.

New players came and went with regularity, although one of Bromilow's achievements was to sign old campaigner Alick Robinson from Bury in 1933. Robinson became club captain and provided a degree of stability to the defence right up until the war.

In October 1934, Bromilow created a stir by signing George Brown from Aston Villa. Brown, a former England player, had starred in the great Huddersfield Town side under Herbert Chapman in the 1920s and he brought a fearsome goalscoring reputation with him. He did not let the Clarets down either, his 21 goals in his first season helping the club to a respectable 12th place in 1935.

After growing speculation in the summer of 1935, linking Bromilow with numerous positions including that of manager at Tottenham, he eventually replaced former Burnley star, Jack Tresadern, as manager of Crystal Palace.

He had two spells in charge at Selhurst

Park before the war and during the early part of World War Two he managed Leicester City, guiding them the League South title and the Midland Cup. He returned to the game in 1948 as manager of Newport County but stayed for only a short time and later scouted for Leicester.

Tommy Bromilow died on a train at Nuneaton in March 1959, aged 64.

Alf Boland
August 1935-1940

FOLLOWING the departure of Tom Bromilow, Burnley once again looked to within the club for a replacement.

Alfred Boland had been appointed assistant secretary at Burnley FC in July 1932 and when he took over as secretary from the departed Albert Pickles in November of that year, he was the youngest official in that position in the Football League.

Born and educated in Burnley, he had played for the club's junior teams in 1930, whilst working in the office of a local textile mill.

It had been decided not to appoint a manager as such, as successor to Tom Bromilow. Team affairs were to be something of a joint board effort with Alf Boland acting as the link between the officials and the players.

This situation continued into the late 1930s with Boland just starting to build the foundations of the team that would taste success after the war. Arthur Woodruff arrived in 1936, George Bray in 1937. Then came the architect of later Burnley success, Harry Potts, who came to the club in November 1937, one of the very first arrivals in Burnley's famous youth policy.

Alf Boland was a first class administrator and an eloquent contributor to the club's programme. He was unable to expand upon his team building efforts, however, and left the club in 1940.

Cliff Britton
May 1945-September 1948

BURNLEY'S immediate post-war revival was spearheaded by Cliff Britton.

Without doubt a footballing genius, Britton was a former Everton and England half-back who introduced progressive ideas in the form of new training tactics and team strategy, coupled with the experience of the players he inherited.

Contracted to take over as manager in May 1945, he assumed the role five months later on leaving the armed forces and at the club's annual meeting in February 1946 he announced a three-year plan which would give the Clarets their First Division status back.

Responsible for the signings of players like Allan Brown, Reg Attwell, Jimmy

Adamson and Tommy Cummings, Britton evolved a side based around the famed 'Iron Curtain' defence which itself evolved around the undoubted abilities of Brown.

The first full season after the war, 1946-7, proved to go beyond the wildest dreams of the three-year plan as Burnley reached the FA Cup Final, where they were beaten by Charlton Athletic and earned promotion as Second Division runners-up to Manchester City.

Born in Bristol, Britton played local league football there before signing for Bristol Rovers in 1926. Four years with the Pirates followed before he was transferred to Everton and won an FA Cup winners' medal in 1933. The following year he made his England debut and went on to play in nine full and 12 wartime internationals, many of them as an integral part of a half-back line which also featured Joe Mercer and Stan Cullis. Britton's League playing career had ended when the competition was suspended in 1939, although he had appeared in only one game when Everton won the Championship in that last pre-war season.

In September 1948, shortly after taking Burnley to third place in their first season back in the First Division, he was wooed back to Goodison Park to take over as manager from Theo Kelly, who reverted to his old position as club secretary.

Britton spent eight years as manager at Everton, during which time they lost and then regained their First Division status. He resigned in 1956, after the Everton board wanted to appoint an acting manager whilst Britton was abroad with the team.

Frank Hill
September 1948-August 1954

IF for no other reason, Frank Hill will always be remembered as the man who persuaded Jimmy McIlroy to sign for Burnley.

Scouts initially went to Glentoran to watch another player. They found he was not for sale but were told to watch the young Jimmy Mac. The scouts made two or three more visits before Hill went to Ireland and promptly signed the inspirational inside-forward.

Whilst capturing McIlroy was a definite coup for the Clarets, Hill did far more for the club than just that. He transformed them for a team who had just emerged from the Second Division wilderness into a club more than capable of holding its own against virtually any opposition. Indeed, Burnley finished in the top half of the table in each of his six seasons in charge at Turf Moor.

His time in the managerial hot-seat also featured the signing of Roy Stephenson from Liverpool and Billy Gray from Chelsea, but was controversial in that it featured the sale of Billy Elliott to Sunderland.

Born in Forfar in May 1906, Hill started his career as a wing-half with his home-town club in 1924 before being transferred to Aberdeen in 1928. After gaining three Scotland caps he moved to Arsenal in May 1932, for £3,000, and won three League Championship medals with the all-conquering Gunners' team.

In June 1936, Hill was transferred to Blackpool and became their captain. In September 1937, Southampton signed him for £2,200 and he was an automatic choice as their captain, too. But in the 1938-9 season, after being injured and then falling out with a section of the crowd at The Dell, he left Southampton to become coach and assistant trainer at Preston North End.

Hill served as an RAF flight-lieutenant in India during the war and was player-manager of Crewe Alexandra from July 1944 to September 1948, when he joined Burnley as manager.

He left Turf Moor in the 1954 close season to return to Preston as manager. In 1957 he assumed a coaching position in Baghdad before becoming manager at Notts County the following year. In 1961, Hill took over as manager at Charlton Athletic, retiring in 1965 and later scouting for Manchester City. He died in Luton in June 1970.

Allan Brown
August 1954-July 1957

ALLAN Brown brought to Burnley a style of management which was reminiscent of his playing days in a claret and blue shirt. As a centre-half and captain he had been the linchpin of the 'Iron Curtain' defence which brought Burnley success shortly after the war. As a manager, a solid defence seemed to be the focal point of his philosophy.

His first season as manager saw Burnley finish in a mid-table position and in the next two they finished seventh, a very creditable position for a small-town club.

Brown was instrumental in bringing a number of new players to the club, John Angus, Dougie Newlands and Jimmy Robson being three who went on to serve the Clarets with distinction.

In July 1957 he left Burnley to take over as manager at Sunderland, his first season at Roker Park, ending in the club's first-ever relegation from the First Division.

Brown played almost 90 games for Burnley before joining Notts County. His career finished with the Midlanders and his first coaching appointment was with Sheffield Wednesday.

Corbridge-born Brown, a Football League representative during his playing days, returned to Sheffield Wednesday after his first spell at Sunderland, going back to Roker Park after a short time in Norway.

Billy Dougall
July 1957-January 1958

THE departure of Allan Brown to Sunderland saw the elevation of club coach Billy Dougall to the manager's job, a post he occupied for less than a full season.

Dougall's first connection with Turf Moor came in 1926, when he was signed from Falkirk, and he played for the first team 60 times over the next three seasons.

In 1929 he was appointed to the club's coaching staff and figured in that capacity until his move to the manager's office almost 30 years later.

In January 1958 he relinquished the key role due to ill health but maintained his interest in the club as physiotherapist.

Harry Potts
January 1958-February 1970 & June 1977-October 1979

AT the end of his second full season as Burnley manager, former player Harry Potts had given the club the one thing it had been aiming for since the end of World War Two — the First Division title.

He inherited expert backroom staff in the shape of Billy Dougall and Ray Bennion, two of the people he classed as most influential on his own playing career, and the nucleus of a team which would become the most successful Burnley side in modern times.

Jimmy Robson began to come to prominence in Potts' early days in charge; Gordon Harris made his debut; and he spotted the potential of John Connelly. Brian Miller's move through the ranks continued and the other vital ingredient which made Burnley a great side was Alex Elder, a player who made his debut in the 1959-60 Championship season.

Those players blended alongside established Turf Moor heroes like Tommy Cummings, Jimmy Adamson, Jimmy McIlroy and Ray Pointer, and Burnley clinched the title in the very last game.

From there, Potts led Burnley in their first-ever European campaign and took them to the FA Cup Final after a 15-year gap. Neither competition was to provide Burnley with any more silverware, but the glory was undisputed and Potts was the man at the helm.

In 1963 he encountered public hostility for the first time when McIlroy was sold. Graffiti, virtually an unknown quantity, then, proclaiming 'Potts Out, bring back McIlroy' was daubed all over town and some of it can still be seen, even now.

Burnley continued to be a great force to be reckoned with and having finished third in 1965-6, they were back in Europe in the Fairs Cup. Another successful campaign followed and Burnley again achieved national and even international recognition within the game.

After 12 years, probably the most successful dozen seasons in the club's history, Potts was 'kicked upstairs' and became general manager for two years. In 1973 he became manager at Blackpool and was in charge at Bloomfield Road when the Seasiders, then in the Second Division, scored a notable FA Cup triumph over First Division Burnley in January 1976, a result which hastened the departure of Jimmy Adamson from the Turf Moor manager's office.

In 1977, Potts returned to Turf Moor for two more years as Burnley boss, replacing Joe Brown, the man who had taken over from Adamson.

The most famous incident of that spell, all of which was spent in the Second Division, came with a victory over Glasgow Celtic in the Anglo-Scottish Cup, a trophy which was won following a Final success over Oldham Athletic.

In 1979, Potts parted company with Burnley for the last time. He has had involvement in non-League football, notably as the chief scout with the now-defunct Colne Dynamos, and still lives near the scene of many of his former glories.

In both his spells as manager, Potts relied heavily on the players recruited through the club's enviable youth policy. He knew the true value of that system having been one of the first-ever products of it in the mid-1930s.

Born in Hetton-le-Hole, he began his Burnley career as a pre-war junior, playing in 165 games in the first four seasons after World War Two.

He then spent four years at Everton before becoming chief coach at Wolverhampton Wanderers. From Molineux he became manager at Shrewsbury Town, the only managerial appointment he had held before taking charge at Burnley in 1958.

Jimmy Adamson
February 1970-January 1976

JIMMY Adamson will always be dogged by one quote. Shortly after his appointment, he said that Burnley would be the 'Team of the Seventies', but at the end of his first season they were relegated to the Second Division.

When he made his prediction he had obviously not seen the club's fixtures for the 1970-71 season, as Burnley started their campaign with games against Liverpool, Everton, Manchester City, Manchester United, Leeds United and Chelsea.

They gained only two points from those opening six fixtures and never recovered from such a bad start. Adamson's bid for glory was further hampered by a pre-season injury to goalkeeper Peter Mellor and he had to draft in the services of a coach, former England international Tony Waiters, to fill the green jersey.

Relegation could have spelt disaster for many managers but Adamson was allowed time to develop his playing ideals and, after a season of consolidation in the Second Division, the Clarets, captained by Martin Dobson, stormed back into the top flight as Second Division champions.

Back in the First Division, Burnley under Adamson were unlucky to miss out on a place in Europe when finishing sixth. They also reached an FA Cup semi-final before coming across a certain Malcolm Macdonald, but from then on things started to slip away from the former 'Cotton Town Kings'.

The 1975-6 season was to be Burnley's last in the First Division and half-way through it, Adamson parted company with the club. As distressed as the fans by the repeated sale of promising players, he eventually became a victim of 'player power' following an FA Cup exit at the hands of Blackpool in January 1976.

Adamson had been blessed with a host of great young players, Leighton James and Brian Flynn being two notable examples, and was capable of some of the most astute signings. He brought Keith Newton, Alan Stevenson and Peter Noble to the club, but could not halt the fall from grace.

At the start of his last campaign at Burnley he brought Willie Morgan back to Turf Moor and also secured the services of Mike Summerbee, but no one could halt the gradual decline of the club.

On leaving Burnley he spent a short time as a coach in Holland before returning to England and spending two years as manager of Sunderland. After that he was invited to take charge of Leeds United when Jock Stein was given the managership of Scotland.

Adamson took Leeds into Europe and to a League Cup semi-final but the early promise failed to blossom into something bigger and after two years he left Elland Road, breaking all active involvement with the game.

Joe Brown
January 1976-June 1977

WHEN Jimmy Adamson resigned, the job of trying to save Burnley from relegation fell to his assistant, Joe Brown.

The Clarets, having just lost an FA Cup tie to a side from a lower division, were on a real 'downer' and there seemed to be no saving them. So it proved as Burnley slipped out of the top flight, a division they have never seriously threatened to rejoin since.

Brown was fortunate to inherit a side

full of talented players, but unfortunate to take charge when things were going so badly for them. He was eventually replaced after 16 months when it became obvious that he was not going to be the man to give them their First Division status back.

Born in Cramlington, Brown started his playing career as an apprentice with Middlesbrough. He played only 11 times for the 'Boro before being transferred to Burnley, faring no better at Burnley as a wing-half and playing only six games there. He went on to play over 200 games in five years at Bournemouth before finishing his career with a handful of appearances for Aldershot.

When he ended his brief spell as manager at Turf Moor, Brown had a variety of jobs in football and was latterly youth development officer at Old Trafford. When Manchester United won the European Cup-winners' Cup in May 1991, he could be seen on the pitch afterwards, still limping as he recovered from a hit-and-run accident which happened six months previously near United's training ground.

Brian Miller
October 1979-January 1983 & July 1986-January 1989

BRIAN Miller's two spells as manager have featured just about everything.

He was the manager who took Burnley back into the Second Division as Third Division champions; and five years later he was the man who had to guide them through those frantic days building up to the 'Orient Game'.

A season and a half later, Miller relinquished control of the first team, making way for Frank Casper for the second time.

When Miller took over as manager in October 1979, he had been with the club continuously since the end of his playing days in 1967. In many ways a background figure, there was a blaze of publicity shortly after his appointment, but for all the wrong reasons as his second match at the helm was at Queen's Park Rangers and BBC TV *Match of the Day* cameras saw a young goalkeeper called Billy O'Rourke make his debut in a 7-0 defeat.

Two seasons in the Third Division followed before Miller was in charge during the first half of the 1982-3 season, a campaign which can only be described as contradictory as Burnley struggled in the League but cut a swathe through teams from the top flight in both Cups.

Sacked in January, after a humiliating defeat at Bolton Wanderers — Bolton's 'keeper Jim McDonagh was among the scorers with a wind-assisted drop kick from his own area — Miller had just seen his son, David, make his first-team debut as a substitute for his son-in-law Derek Scott.

When he was sacked, Burnley were in the Second Division; when he returned three-and-a-half years later they were in the Fourth.

His first season was a nightmare. Burnley went out of the FA Cup to non-League opponents; and they nearly went out of the League as the first casualties of automatic relegation to the Vauxhall Conference.

The next season saw them in the Sherpa Van Final and missing the promotion play-offs by a place, but halfway through his third season Miller and the manager's office were again parted, once more by Frank Casper.

Still with the club as chief scout, Brian Miller was a player of distinction with the Clarets and made almost 380 appearances for the Turf Moor outfit.

He was the man who spotted the potential of players like Michael Phelan and Trevor Steven and groomed them for future stardom, but he also let players like Paul Fletcher and Peter Noble go. He also introduced Vince Overson, Paul Dixon, Billy Hamilton and Phil Cavener to the club, but will always be remembered as the man who had to undergo the glare of publicity surrounding the 'Orient Game'.

Frank Casper
January 1983-June 1983 & January 1989-

FRANK Casper had been on the coaching staff at Turf Moor for eight years when he assumed the role of caretaker manager following the demise of Brian Miller in January 1983.

And his career in the managerial hot-seat could not have got off to a more impressive start. On his very first day in charge, Second Division Burnley travelled to play First Division giants, Tottenham Hotspur, in the League Cup and returned home with a 4-1 win.

They went on to perform with distinction against Liverpool in the semi-final as well as reach the FA Cup quarter-final, but those Cup runs took their toll, Burnley were relegated and the 'caretaker' was out of a job following the appointment of John Bond.

Six years, almost to the day, after his appointment as 'caretaker', Casper was again in charge and again it was Brian Miller who stepped aside as he returned to Turf Moor after a successful spell at Bury as assistant to Martin Dobson.

His first two seasons saw Burnley finish in the lower reaches of the table on both occasions, but he then led the Clarets to their best Fourth Division finish — sixth — and a place in the play-offs.

Having survived the duress of much animosity from the crowd at Turf Moor, Casper brought together a team which should have won promotion automatically in 1990-91 but let itself down with a poor away record.

Casper was another manager appointed after a splendid playing career. Always a favourite of the crowd during his playing days, he has never fully enjoyed the same level of acceptance as a manager.

John Bond
June 1983-August 1984

WHEN Burnley decided to break the mould and appoint a manager who was not an 'old boy' they did it in a very big way.

It is difficult to imagine that the game had many bigger names than John Bond at the time, and Turf Moor became a regular haunt for national Press and television reporters for the next 16 months.

Bond had been in charge at Maine Road as Manchester City had slipped from the First towards the Second Division, and having been sacked he was heralded as the man most likely to take the Clarets into the Second Division, but from the other direction.

The plan, though, simply didn't work. Bond pulled off a coup by signing former £1 million players like Kevin Reeves and Steve Daley, but was guilty, in the eyes of the crowd, of signing too many of his former players, as people like Tommy Hutchison, Gerry Gow and Dennis Tueart joined the Turf Moor staff. He also signed Roger Hansbury, Joe Gallagher, Wayne Biggins and Malcom Waldron, but to make room for them he sold promising players like Trevor Steven, Brian Laws and Lee Dixon, along with established favourites like Alan Stevenson, Steve Taylor, Tommy Cassidy and Phil Cavener.

Perhaps his biggest 'sin', apart from leaving the club in the Third Division, was to take the captaincy away from Martin Dobson, the Burnley club's biggest hero

since Jimmy McIlroy, and install Hutchison in his place.

Since leaving Turf Moor, Bond has been manager at Swansea City, Birmingham City and Shrewsbury Town. His playing career was spent as a full-back, mostly with West Ham, and he managed Bournemouth and Norwich before taking over at Manchester City, a club he took to an FA Cup Final before they were relegated despite the large sums of money he spent on new players.

John Benson
August 1984-May 1985

WHEN John Bond was sacked just five days before the start of the 1984-5 season, his assistant, John Benson, took over as manager.

Initially a 'caretaker' Benson was given the job after only a month and became the man at the helm as Burnley plummeted into the Fourth Division for the first time in their 100-plus year history.

Bond had signed a number of players shortly before being sacked, but under Benson the team never gelled and he was sacked at the end of the season.

Benson and Bond had first met each other at Torquay United and became one of the best-known 'double acts' in management, but neither could repeat the success they had managed at other clubs. Benson had been Bond's assistant at Manchester City and had been left in charge when Bond was sacked in February 1983. Benson, though, could not prevent City from being relegated that season.

In his only season at Turf Moor, Benson saw Burnley equal their highest-ever score in a 'first-class' game when beating Penrith 9-0 in an FA Cup tie; they also recorded a rare 7-0 League victory when thrashing Rotherham United.

Martin Buchan
June 1985-October 1985

MARTIN Buchan's appointment was greeted with great enthusiasm. The former Scottish international and Manchester United captain was going to use Burnley as the launching pad to a successful career in management, but that career lasted just 110 days as Buchan failed to make the transition from dressing-room to manager's office.

A month after John Benson was sacked, Buchan was given a two-year contract. He never signed it. His decision to quit shocked everyone because, although Burnley were having a bad time, everyone expected the young manager to be able to turn things around.

He was bitterly disappointed by his decision but said that, however hard he tried, he could not make the change.

A model professional, Buchan played over 450 first-team games for Manchester United and had a brief spell with Oldham Athletic before accepting the opportunity of a first job in management with Burnley.

Tommy Cavanagh
October 1985-May 1986

ANOTHER well-known face from Old Trafford, Tommy Cavanagh had moved to Turf Moor to assist with first-team training when Martin Buchan was made manager.

Cavanagh, a former wing-half with

Preston, Stockport, Huddersfield, Doncaster, Bristol City and Carlisle, went to work as Tommy Docherty's assistant at Old Trafford. He was appointed 'caretaker' boss at Burnley when Buchan resigned and took over the club for the rest of the season.

But he could not help Burnley climb out of the Fourth Division and parted company at the end of the season to make way for the return of Brian Miller.

In two years, Burnley had four managers, none of whom had connections with the club. For years, fans had sought a break from the 'old boys' in a bid to inject new life into the club, but despite four attempts and four 'big' names, that break never worked.

Many people believe that the job is one that has to be in the blood, a theory highlighted by the fact that post-war success has rarely come Burnley's way with anyone other than a former player at the helm.

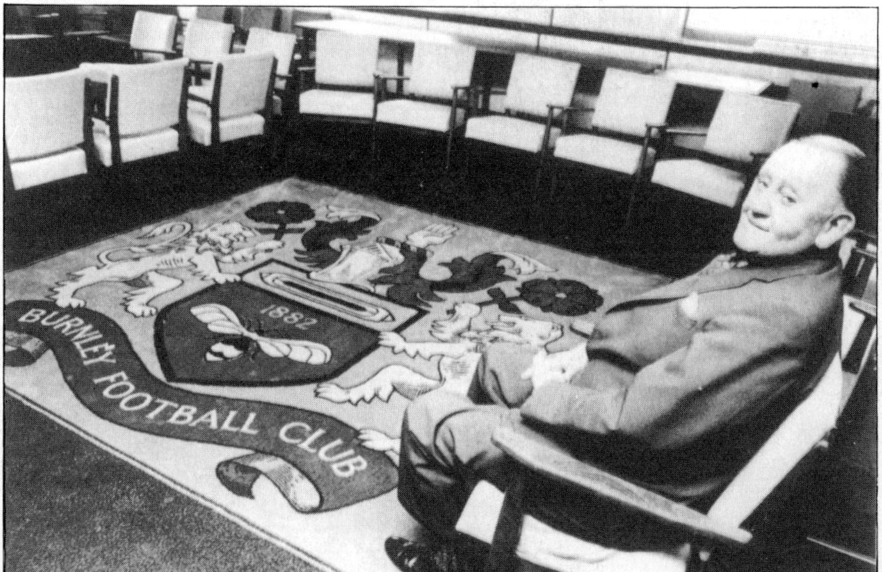

Bob Lord in the directors' room at Turf Moor, complete with a unique carpet, shortly before the opening of the Bob Lord Stand in 1974.

Burnley Stars A-Z

TED ADAMS

Edward Fairclough Adams was born in the shadow of Anfield in 1906. He came out of retirement aged 30 to keep goal for Burnley and stayed long enough to make over 100 League appearances for the club. Adams first played junior football in the local Liverpool leagues for Oakmere and Earle before joining his home-city club as a 20-year-old in May 1927. He did not break into the first team at Anfield, however, and played for numerous non-League clubs before brief spells with Barrow, Wrexham and Southport in the 1930s. He retired whilst with Southport in December 1935 but in February 1936 he was approached by Burnley manager Alf Boland and asked to come to Turf Moor. Adams went straight into the first team and vied with Tom Hetherington for the number-one spot until 1937. He missed only one League game in the last two seasons before the war, going on to play for the club until October 1940. During the hostilities he also guested for New Brighton, Chester and Wrexham before retiring. At the time of writing, Ted Adams is residing in the Burnley area and he is believed to be the oldest surviving Claret, aged 85.

	LEAGUE		*FA CUP*		*TOTAL*	
	App	*Gls*	*App*	*Gls*	*App*	*Gls*
1935-36	12	0	0	0	12	0
1936-37	16	0	3	0	19	0
1937-38	41	0	3	0	44	0
1938-39	42	0	1	0	43	0
	111	0	7	0	118	0

Many followers of the game, and not just Burnley fans, still find it difficult to believe that the inspirational Jimmy Adamson never won a full England cap. During much of his Burnley career he formed a near-legendary partnership with Jimmy McIlroy. Originally signed as an inside-right in January 1947, he made his first-team debut four years later, having moved to right-half to take Reg Attwell's number-four shirt, the former West Ham United player moving to the other wing-half position. As captain of the 1959-60 Burnley side, Adamson holds the honour of being the last Clarets player to lead a successful League Championship campaign at Turf Moor. Adamson is also the last Burnley player to lead his side out at Wembley in an FA Cup Final. Burnley may have lost that 1962 Final to Spurs, but Adamson excelled himself in the Wembley contest. He had already been named as Walter Winterbottom's assistant manager for that summer's World Cup Finals in Italy. Whilst many expected the 1962 Footballer of the Year to collect his first cap in South America, it was not to be and Adamson had only 'B' Internationals to show for a glorious career. When his playing days were over, Adamson became a successful manager with Burnley, Sunderland and Leeds United.

JIMMY ADAMSON

	LEAGUE		*FA CUP*		*FL CUP*		*OTHERS*		*TOTAL*	
	App	*Gls*	*App*	*Gls*	*App*	*Gls*	*App*	*Gls*	*App*	*Gls*
1950-51	14	0	0	0	0	0	0	0	14	0
1951-52	38	2	4	0	0	0	0	0	42	2
1952-53	41	3	4	0	0	0	0	0	45	3
1953-54	39	5	3	0	0	0	0	0	42	5
1954-55	36	0	1	0	0	0	0	0	37	0
1955-56	21	0	4	0	0	0	0	0	25	0
1956-57	36	0	4	0	0	0	0	0	40	0
1957-58	36	0	2	0	0	0	0	0	38	0
1958-59	31	1	5	1	0	0	0	0	36	2
1959-60	42	1	8	0	0	0	0	0	50	1
1960-61	30	3	5	0	3	0	5	0	43	3
1961-62	34	2	8	0	0	0	0	0	42	2
1962-63	18	0	3	0	0	0	0	0	21	0
1963-64	10	0	1	0	0	0	0	0	11	0
	426	17	52	1	3	0	5	0	486	18

Jock Aird was born in Glencraig, near Cowdenbeath, in 1926 and joined Burnley in August 1948 from the Scottish junior club Jeanfield Swifts. Competition at full-back was very fierce and it was not until April 1950 that Aird made his League debut, deputizing for Arthur Woodruff. He kept his place until the last match of the season but it was not until 1951-2, as Woodruff approached retirement, that Aird began to establish himself. He did enough to catch the eye of the international selectors and won four Scottish caps in 1954. All but a couple of his games for Burnley were at right-back but he showed his versatility by representing his country on the left flank, partnering the great Willie Cunningham of Preston North End. The potential of David Smith and a new lease of life for Harold Rudman combined to make Jock Aird seek new pastures in 1955. He joined Dundee in the summer of that year and enjoyed two more seasons before retiring from the game. Jock Aird eventually emigrated to Australia, where he made his home, but he still makes occaisional visits to Lancashire and keeps in touch with all his friends.

JOCK AIRD

	LEAGUE		*FA CUP*		*TOTAL*	
	App	*Gls*	*App*	*Gls*	*App*	*Gls*
1949-50	5	0	0	0	5	0
1950-51	2	0	0	0	2	0
1951-52	30	0	4	0	34	0
1952-53	38	0	4	0	42	0
1953-54	40	0	3	0	43	0
1954-55	17	0	0	0	17	0
	132	0	11	0	143	0

Joseph Anderson, 'Joe Andy', was signed by Burnley as one of the last pieces in the jigsaw that, when complete, would win the League Championship in 1920-21. Anderson started his Clarets career alongside Bert Freeman, but was destined to replace the great man in the formidable Burnley forward line. He was born at Bishopton, on the outskirts of Glasgow, in 1895 and played his early football with Vale of Leven, Airdrieonians, Dumbarton and Clydebank, from whom he joined Burnley in March 1920. When Benny Cross broke into the first team in September 1920, the two struck up an immediate understanding. With Bob Kelly also having his best goalscoring season, the trio hit 59 of Burnley's 79 goals between them, Anderson notching 25. He was also top scorer the following season but, as Burnley's fortunes declined and Anderson neared 30 years of age, he faded. He was transferred back to Clydebank in October 1923 and ended his playing career in 1924 with Glasgow Pollock. In his Burnley career he averaged better than a goal every other League game, no mean feat in 120 plus matches. He also scored eight goals in only four FA Cup games for the Clarets.

JOE ANDERSON

	LEAGUE		*FA CUP*		*OTHERS*		*TOTAL*	
	App	*Gls*	*App*	*Gls*	*App*	*Gls*	*App*	*Gls*
1919-20	8	6	0	0	0	0	8	6
1920-21	41	25	2	6	0	0	43	31
1921-22	36	20	1	1	1	0	38	21
1922-23	28	8	1	1	0	0	29	9
1923-24	8	5	0	0	0	0	8	5
	121	64	4	8	1	0	126	72

The archetypal one-club player, John Angus played for the Clarets in three different decades. A polished right-back, Angus signed on amateur terms from the Amble Boys' Club in 1954 and became a professional on his 17th birthday the following year. Regarded as one of the very finest right-backs of his era, Angus would have won many more than his one full England cap, had he had more ambition. Walter Winterbottom described his one England game, against Austria in 1961, as the best international debut he had ever seen and Angus was often described as a better player than England's usual right-back of the time, Jimmy Armfield. A 'cool' player, it was not unknown for Angus to trap the ball on his own goal-line and dribble it out of his own area. He won a League Championship medal and an FA Cup runners-up medal with the Clarets but scored only four goals in a career spanning over 430 games, two of them in the same game against Arsenal in October 1964. A Youth international and a Football League representative, Angus was granted a testimonial in 1972-3, a great season as Burnley returned to the top flight as Second Division champions. On retiring from Burnley, he left the game completely and returned to Amble to open a sea-front cafe. A county-standard golfer, Angus later worked as a maintenance man in his native town.

JOHN ANGUS

	LEAGUE		*FA CUP*		*FL CUP*		*OTHERS*		*TOTAL*	
	App	*Gls*	*App*	*Gls*	*App*	*Gls*	*App*	*Gls*	*App*	*Gls*
1956-57	23	0	5	0	0	0	0	0	28	0
1957-58	12	0	0	0	0	0	0	0	12	0
1958-59	23	0	3	0	0	0	0	0	26	0
1959-60	41	0	8	0	0	0	0	0	49	0
1960-61	39	0	7	0	6	0	5	0	57	0
1961-62	38	0	8	0	0	0	0	0	46	0
1962-63	42	0	3	0	0	0	0	0	45	0
1963-64	35	0	5	0	0	0	0	0	40	0
1964-65	22	2	0	0	0	0	0	0	22	2
1965-66	39	2	3	0	5	0	0	0	47	2
1966-67	26	0	0	0	1	0	6	0	33	0
1967-68	25	0	0	0	5	0	0	0	30	0
1968-69	7	0	0	0	2	0	0	0	9	0
1969-70	29	0	2	0	5	0	0	0	36	0
1970-71	35/1	0	1	0	1	0	1	0	38/1	0
1971-72	2	0	0	0	0	0	0	0	2	0
	438/1	4	45	0	25	0	12	0	520/1	4

The son of a professional footballer, Reg Attwell signed for Burnley in October 1946 after appearing as a guest for the Clarets during the war. He was fondly remembered by the fans for his cultured play at wing-half and he went on to become one of the key players in Burnley's successful, immediate post-war era. He was born at Oakengates, near Telford, in 1920 and was playing for Denaby United when West Ham United signed him in 1937. He played in only one League game for the Hammers before the war started but then appeared at Turf Moor in 1945. His performances in both wing-half positions were impressive and, after he had returned briefly to Upton Park, manager Cliff Britton secured his signature for 'a substantial fee'. He was a regular member of the promotion and Cup Final sides of 1947, forming a vital part of the 'Iron Curtain Defence' alongside Allan Brown and George Bray. Following Burnley's return to the First Division, Attwell's consistency brought him an appearance for the Football League in 1948. The level of his performances perhaps merited full England honours, but it was not to be and Attwell admitted that he did not enjoy the international scene and was content to perform at club level. He had a good attitude to training and was respected by his fellow players but he suffered from personal problems that occasionally affected his football. An incident in 1952, when he failed to appear at Turf Moor for a League match against Arsenal, was the beginning of the end of his time at Burnley. The following season he alternated with Jimmy Adamson and Bobby Seith for the number-six shirt but then, in October 1954, he moved to Bradford City. After one season at Valley Parade he retired from the game, continuing to live in Burnley, and it was in his home in the town that he died in 1986, aged 66. At his peak, Reg Attwell was one of the best wing-halves in the country in the period after the war. He will be remembered for a long time by a generation of Burnley followers for his supreme ability and sheer class.

REG ATTWELL

	LEAGUE		*FA CUP*		*TOTAL*	
	App	*Gls*	*App*	*Gls*	*App*	*Gls*
1946-47	22	0	6	0	28	0
1947-48	38	1	1	0	39	1
1948-49	35	4	3	1	38	5
1949-50	40	3	3	1	43	4
1950-51	17	1	1	0	18	1
1951-52	37	0	4	0	41	0
1952-53	34	0	4	0	38	0
1953-54	20	0	3	0	23	0
1954-55	1	0	0	0	1	0
	244	9	25	2	269	11

Horwich-born Thomas Bamford was signed by Burnley from Darwen in the close season of 1909. He replaced the veteran Fred Barron at right-back at the end of his first season, but was then himself displaced from that position by Robert Reid, signed from Cowdenbeath. Owing to Reid's consistency, Bamford played a number of games at left-back but the strength in depth at the club at that time meant keen competition for every first-team place. Bamford eventually won the vote for the right-back spot and was a model of consistency just before the war. He was an ever-present in League and Cup in the two years up to the hostilities, a run which, of course, included the FA Cup Final win at the Crystal Palace. After the war, Bamford was again up against fierce competition at right-back, Len Smelt keeping him out of the first team, and in September 1920 he signed for Rochdale, where he played for a number of years before retiring from the game.

TOM BAMFORD

	LEAGUE		*FA CUP*		*TOTAL*	
	App	*Gls*	*App*	*Gls*	*App*	*Gls*
1909-10	9	0	0	0	9	0
1910-11	15	0	3	0	18	0
1911-12	13	0	0	0	13	0
1912-13	24	0	6	0	30	0
1913-14	38	0	8	0	46	0
1914-15	38	0	3	0	41	0
	137	0	20	0	157	0

Fred Barron was the only newcomer to Burnley's ranks in the summer of 1898, following their Second Division championship success. Born in Stockton-on-Tees in 1879, he began his career at 14 years of age playing for Stockton St Mary's, where his mature approach and polished performances soon attracted the attention of some of England's leading clubs. He was 19, however, before he finally accepted Burnley's overtures. Barron immediately made the right-half position his own, but even his influence could not prevent relegation in 1900. He was elected Burnley's captain in 1902 but his first season ended with the club at rock bottom of the Second Division and having to apply for re-election. The rest of the Edwardian decade was, in the main, a mediocre period at Turf Moor. Through it all Barron remained and delivered competent performances, week in and week out, leading by example. When Jack Cretney arrived from Newcastle in 1905, Barron moved to right-back and carried on with his high level of consistency as if he had played there all his life. He missed only one game during the following two seasons but lost the captaincy when seasoned campaigner Alec Leake arrived from Aston Villa in December 1907. That year he became only the second Burnley player to make 300 League appearances for the club and later broke Joe Taylor's record of 323 games. He was still a regular in his early 30s but then lost his regular place when Bob Reid arrived from Cowdenbeath in 1910. He made his 400th and final League appearance on 1 April 1911. He retired from the game the same year and became a licensee in his adopted town, his future in the folklore of Burnley football assured.

	LEAGUE		*FA CUP*		*TOTAL*	
	App	*Gls*	*App*	*Gls*	*App*	*Gls*
1898-99	29	0	2	0	31	0
1899-1900	30	0	1	0	31	0
1900-01	34	2	3	0	37	2
1901-02	32	2	2	1	34	3
1902-03	34	3	1	0	35	3
1903-04	34	1	2	0	36	1
1904-05	33	3	2	0	35	3
1905-06	36	1	1	0	37	1
1906-07	38	1	1	0	39	1
1907-08	37	0	1	0	38	0
1908-09	31	0	5	0	36	0
1909-10	28	0	2	0	30	0
1910-11	4	0	0	0	4	0
	400	13	23	1	423	14

FRED BARRON

Alf Bassnett was born in St Helens in 1893 and, in his early years in this Rugby League stronghold, his football was with the oval ball. He converted to soccer with Star Rovers FC and played for Skelmersdale and St Helens Town, joining Eccles Borough in 1914. He fought in France in World War One, suffered in a gas attack with his regiment, the Royal Engineers, at Ypres, but made a satisfactory recovery. He joined Burnley from Eccles in June 1919 and made his League debut towards the end of his first season, scoring one of the goals in a 2-0 victory against Derby on 28 February 1920. Bassnett would have been a permanent member of most teams, but in Burnley's star-studded line-up in the 1919-22 era he had to be content with replacement status. He came in for the injured George Halley for the last third of the Championship season and deputized for all three of the first-choice half-backs during the following campaign. When Halley and Boyle both left the club, Bassnett became a regular for almost three seasons. Then, in his early 30s, he left for Lincoln City in November 1926. He spent the 1929-30 season playing for Ballymena in Northern Ireland, then returned to England to become player-manager at Hereford United in June 1930. He came back to live locally, joining Nelson in August 1931. He lived in Burnley for many years after his retirement and died in his adopted town on 24 June 1966, aged 73.

ALF BASSNETT

	LEAGUE		*FA CUP*		*OTHERS*		*TOTAL*	
	App	*Gls*	*App*	*Gls*	*App*	*Gls*	*App*	*Gls*
1919-20	6	1	0	0	0	0	6	1
1920-21	15	0	0	0	0	0	15	0
1921-22	21	1	0	0	1	0	22	1
1922-23	36	2	1	0	0	0	37	2
1923-24	36	0	7	0	0	0	43	0
1924-25	25	1	1	0	0	0	26	1
1925-26	7	0	0	0	0	0	7	0
1926-27	1	0	0	0	0	0	1	0
	147	5	9	0	1	0	157	5

George William Beel rewrote the record books in terms of goalscoring in his nine years at Burnley in the 1920s and early '30s. Some 178 League goals in all, a record seasonal total of 35 in 1927-8, 11 hat-tricks, top scorer in six of his nine seasons as a first-team regular. All this in a team that was a shadow of its illustrious predecessor and spent most of its time in the wrong half of the League table. Beel was born in Bracebridge Heath, just outside Lincoln, in 1900. After playing local football in Lincoln he had an unsuccessful trial at Manchester United in 1919 before joining Lincoln City in October that year. After spells with Merthyr Town and Chesterfield, he was transferred to Burnley from Saltergate in April 1923, with John Fisher moving in the other direction. He was seen as the successor to the once-prolific Joe Anderson and when Beel established himself as leader of the attack early the following season, Joe 'Andy' left Turf Moor to return to Clydebank. Beel played alongside Bob Kelly and Benny Cross in his first two seasons but then had to contend with the challenge of Tom Roberts, a newcomer from Preston who was, himself, no slouch at finding the net. Burnley's best season since their former glories came in 1926-7, but in the following campaign, at the end of which the Clarets were only a point from relegation, George Beel struck a vein of scoring never previously seen at Turf Moor and unequalled in more than 60 years since. Admirably supported by right winger Jack Bruton and with Louis Page on the left flank contributing over 20 goals, Beel simply could not stop scoring. In the tightest-ever First Division, only five points separated fourth from 20th and George Beel's goals undoubtedly saved Burnley from relegation, albeit delaying the drop by only two years. Another successful season for Beel followed, in a poor one for the club, then relegation came inevitably. Beel moved to inside-right, still scoring regularly but the following season he was transferred to his local club, Lincoln City, in February 1932. He moved to Rochdale in the following September and, after a season at Spotland, he was appointed player-manager at Tunbridge Wells Rangers in May 1933. George Beel, a man who will always have a special place in the history of Burnley Football Club, died at his home in Maidstone on 30 December 1980.

GEORGE BEEL

	LEAGUE		*FA CUP*		*TOTAL*	
	App	*Gls*	*App*	*Gls*	*App*	*Gls*
1922-23	1	0	0	0	1	0
1923-24	34	19	7	2	41	21
1924-25	35	10	1	0	36	10
1925-26	33	14	2	2	35	16
1926-27	36	24	3	3	39	27
1927-28	39	35	1	0	40	35
1928-29	41	30	3	2	44	32
1929-30	33	10	1	0	34	10
1930-31	41	25	2	0	43	25
1931-32	23	11	1	0	24	11
	316	178	21	9	337	187

A.A.Bell was one of the club's leading amateur players and holds the distinction of designing one of the first stands at Turf Moor. Born in Burnley in 1882, Bell was educated at Burnley Grammar School and, after completing his studies, qualified as an architect, succeeding his father, Thomas Bell in business. He played his early football with Burnley Belvedere but his real sporting love in his younger days was cricket, graduating through the junior ranks at Burnley CC and going on to represent the premier team with distinction. He captained the side which captured the Lancashire League title three years in succession in 1906-08. He was also selected to play for Lancashire 2nd XI. He had established himself in Burnley's Second Division side by this time and formed a more than useful left-wing partnership with Albert Smith. His consistency earned him amateur international recognition in 1907 and 1908 and he won three caps for his country. He retired from top class football in 1909 to concentrate on his business but in 1921 he became seriously ill and never really recovered. He died on 22 April 1923, aged only 40.

ARTHUR BELL

	LEAGUE		*FA CUP*		*TOTAL*	
	App	*Gls*	*App*	*Gls*	*App*	*Gls*
1902-03	2	1	0	0	2	1
1903-04	11	4	0	0	11	4
1904-05	5	0	0	0	5	0
1905-06	19	3	1	0	20	3
1906-07	23	12	1	1	24	12
1907-08	26	7	1	1	27	8
1908-09	15	2	0	0	15	2
	101	29	3	1	104	30

One of the veritable conveyor belt of promising youngsters from the North-East that Burnley unearthed in the 1950s and '60s, Arthur Bellamy joined the Clarets as a 17-year-old junior in June 1959. He made his mark as a constructive inside-forward in Burnley's successful youth and reserve sides but had to wait until March 1963 before being selected for the first team. It was a memorable debut as the young Bellamy, replacing the injured Jimmy Robson, scored one of the goals in a 5-2 demolition of Manchester City at Maine Road. Bellamy kept his place but then, in his first match of the following season, really arrived when he scored a glorious hat-trick against reigning League Champions, Everton, at Goodison Park. Although a dependable club man for ten seasons in the first team, Bellamy was perhaps never quite an automatic choice. Like many utility men he covered for other players and his versatility was invaluable. At the end of the 1971-2 season, Bellamy, now 30, was transferred to Chesterfield for a modest fee. In three seasons at Saltergate he made over 120 appearances, scoring a dozen goals before returning to Turf Moor. After spells as a coach to the youth and reserve teams and as assistant manager, Arthur Bellamy is still a familiar face at Turf Moor, now working as head groundsman.

ARTHUR BELLAMY

	LEAGUE		*FA CUP*		*FL CUP*		*OTHERS*		*TOTAL*	
	App	*Gls*	*App*	*Gls*	*App*	*Gls*	*App*	*Gls*	*App*	*Gls*
1962-63	13	2	0	0	0	0	0	0	13	2
1963-64	17	8	0	0	0	0	0	0	17	8
1964-65	23	3	3	0	0	0	0	0	26	3
1965-66	17/1	4	0	0	2	0	0	0	19/1	4
1966-67	11/2	0	0	0	1	0	6	0	18/2	0
1967-68	33	2	1	0	4	0	0	0	38	2
1968-69	20/2	1	2	0	4	0	0	0	26/2	1
1969-70	19/3	3	3	0	2	0	0	0	24/3	3
1970-71	24/1	0	0	0	1	0	1/1	0	26/2	0
1971-72	27/4	6	0	0	2	0	0	0	29/4	6
	204/13	29	9	0	16	0	7/1	0	236/14	29

Although an excellent goalkeeper in his own right, Adam Blacklaw undoubtedly benefited enormously from injuires to Colin McDonald. When McDonald broke an ankle at Chelsea in December 1956, Blacklaw played eight games in Burnley's first team as a 19-year-old. In March 1959, McDonald's football League career came to a tragic end and Adam Blacklaw seized his opportunity, making the position his own. His contribution to the League Championship campaign led to his first representative honours — two Scotland Under-23 caps — as the Clarets headed for the title, Blacklaw missing only one game. He was consistency itself over the following four seasons missing one game in 1960-61, then playing for three years as an ever-present, also winning the first of his three full Scottish caps, against Norway in Bergen in June 1963. Perhaps the most famous picture of Adam Blacklaw is the one of him being sent the wrong way by Danny Blanchflower from the penalty-spot in the 1962 FA Cup Final. An undoubted low point also was the last-minute incident at Anfield in February 1963, in the FA Cup fourth-round replay. With the seconds ticking away at the end of extra-time, and the score 1-1, Blacklaw unaccountably kicked the ball against Ian St John and then had to pull the Scot down to prevent him scoring. Ronnie Moran stroked in the spot-kick, Liverpool were through and Burnley were out. In 1965, Blacklaw's position between the posts came under threat from a fellow Scot, Harry Thomson, and in July 1967 he was transferred to Blackburn Rovers, where he stayed for three seasons. In 1970 he joined Blackpool but played only one game for the Seasiders, ironically deputizing for Harry Thomson, before retiring. Like so many Clarets, the big Aberdonian came back to live in the Burnley area after his playing days were over. He became a publican and these days is to be found as the steward of a popular local golf club.

ADAM BLACKLAW

	LEAGUE		*FA CUP*		*FL CUP*		*OTHERS*		*TOTAL*	
	App	*Gls*	*App*	*Gls*	*App*	*Gls*	*App*	*Gls*	*App*	*Gls*
1956-57	8	0	5	0	0	0	0	0	13	0
1957-58	3	0	0	0	0	0	0	0	3	0
1958-59	15	0	0	0	0	0	0	0	15	0
1959-60	41	0	8	0	0	0	0	0	49	0
1960-61	41	0	7	0	7	0	5	0	60	0
1961-62	42	0	8	0	0	0	0	0	50	0
1962-63	42	0	3	0	0	0	0	0	45	0
1963-64	42	0	5	0	0	0	0	0	47	0
1964-65	34	0	5	0	0	0	0	0	39	0
1965-66	27	0	3	0	3	0	0	0	33	0
1966-67	23	0	0	0	2	0	4	0	29	0
	318	0	44	0	12	0	9	0	383	0

There were few harder workers or more consistent performers for Burnley in the early days than Billy Bowes. He was the first Claret to top 200 League appearances and his 79 goals for Burnley, in completed 1901, stood as the club record until beaten by Bert Freeman some 25 years later. William Bowes was born in Armadale, Linlithgowshire, in 1870 and played his early football with Armadale Wanderers, Bathgate Rovers and Broxburn. He was secured by Burnley in February 1891, going into the League side immediately to partner Tom Nicol, also newly arrived. A skilful, speedy inside-forward, Bowes linked with a number of wingers but struck up a fine understanding with Walter Place junior, particularly in the Second Division championship season of 1897-8. The entire forward line of Morrison, Ross, Toman, Bowes and Place remained virtually unchanged all season as the club's first League honour was gained. Bowes left League football in 1901, securing employment at the local Bank Hall pit. He boosted the already very strong colliery side and helped them to win the famous Burnley Hospital Cup in 1904. His team also reached the Final in each of the following two years. A one club man, like many Clarets, Billy Bowes stayed in his adopted town until the end of his days.

BILLY BOWES

	LEAGUE		*FA CUP*		*OTHERS*		*TOTAL*	
	App	*Gls*	*App*	*Gls*	*App*	*Gls*	*App*	*Gls*
1890-91	3	1	0	0	0	0	3	1
1891-92	24	6	2	0	0	0	26	6
1892-93	28	8	2	0	0	0	30	8
1893-94	22	6	1	0	0	0	23	6
1894-95	30	8	1	1	0	0	31	9
1895-96	23	6	3	1	0	0	26	7
1896-97	28	11	1	0	4	1	33	12
1897-98	28	8	2	1	4	0	34	9
1898-99	32	10	2	1	0	0	34	11
1899-1900	29	6	1	0	0	0	30	6
1900-01	22	9	3	0	0	0	25	9
	269	79	18	4	8	1	295	84

Tommy Boyle remains to this day the only Burnley captain to lift the FA Cup. He also has the distinction, of course, of receiving the trophy on the first occasion that it was presented by the reigning monarch, King George V, after the men from Turf Moor had beaten Liverpool 1-0 at the Crystal Palace in 1914. Boyle was born in Hoyland, near Barnsley, in 1888 and played for several junior sides in the area before being signed by the Oakwell club as a 16-year-old in 1905. He soon made an impact at the club and was undoubtedly the star in a galaxy of talent that was uncovered in this dour Yorkshire mining area at the end of the Edwardian decade. In 1909-10, he was the captain and the hardest in a team of Barnsley hard men that was beaten by Newcastle United in the FA Cup Final. The nucleus of this side won the FA Cup two years later, but without Tommy Boyle. Still in the Second Division, but determined to get back to the top flight at the earliest opportunity, Burnley paid a then club record fee of £1,150 to bring Boyle to Turf Moor in September 1911. He joined Jerry Dawson, Willie Watson, Tom Bamford and Bert Freeman, who were already at the club and made his Clarets debut, ironically at Barnsley in a 1-1 draw, on the same day as Teddy Hodgson, 30 September 1911. Boyle was, without doubt, the fulcrum, around which the great Burnley sides of the next dozen years were to revolve. Within weeks he was appointed club captain, and at the end of his first season at Turf Moor, the Clarets just missed promotion by two points, finishing the campaign as the League's top scorers with 77 goals in 38 matches. The following season, 1912-13, promotion was secured, again as the League's leading scorers, together with an FA Cup run to the semi-final stage. George Halley was signed from Bradford in March that year and on 15 March Burnley's half-back line, in a 3-1 win against Bury, read 'Halley, Boyle and Watson' for the first time. The inspirational Boyle came into his own in 1913-14 as Burnley consolidated their position in the First Division and, of course, brought the FA Cup back to Turf Moor together with a unique collection of medals inscribed 'English Cup Winners'. During World War One, Bombardier Tommy Boyle fought in France and suffered serious injuries in 1917. Such was the strength of the man, however, that he made a complete recovery and when League football resumed, he led the Clarets to the runners-up spot in 1919-20. The following season went down in football history. Boyle led a truly great Burnley side to the First Division Championship and within that season the team created the record of 30 games without defeat, that still stands to this day. The best days of Boyle's career were behind him, however, and, at the age of 33 he played his last League game for Burnley's first team in February 1922. After recovering from injury he played again in the Reserves, but in April 1923 he was transferred to Wrexham as a player-coach. After coaching in Germany for a time, he returned to England to live in Blackpool, but his health began to deteriorate and financial difficulties contributed to a nervous breakdown. He was under medical treatment for the rest of his life which ended in Whittingham Hospital on 5 January 1940. He was just 50 years old. Tommy Boyle remains one of the all-time greats of Burnley Football Club. Although only 5ft 7in tall, his superb timing in the air made him one of the most powerful headers of a ball the game has seen. He was hard and strong in the tackle, and his distribution of the ball was first-class. His greatest quality, however, was his leadership. His ability to motivate the players around him was unequalled and he is arguably the club's best-ever captain. He won only one England cap and played three times for the Football League. His representative honours certainly do not reflect his contribution to the success of Burnley FC.

	LEAGUE		*FA CUP*		*OTHERS*		*TOTAL*	
	App	*Gls*	*App*	*Gls*	*App*	*Gls*	*App*	*Gls*
1911-12	29	4	1	0	0	0	30	4
1912-13	23	6	6	4	0	0	29	10
1913-14	33	7	8	1	0	0	41	8
1914-15	32	4	3	1	0	0	35	5
1919-20	29	5	2	0	0	0	31	5
1920-21	38	7	3	0	0	0	41	7
1921-22	26	3	2	1	1	0	29	4
	210	36	25	7	1	0	236	43

TOMMY BOYLE

GEORGE BRAY

Born in Oswaldtwistle in 1918, George Bray joined Burnley from Great Harwood Town in October 1937, and after impressing in the Reserves, made his Second Division debut a year later alongside Bob Johnson and Tom Gardner. He immediately made the left-half position his own and when Arthur Woodruff replaced Johnson and then Billy Morris made his first appearance the following January, a great Burnley side was beginning to take shape. The outbreak of war was to interrupt the team building plans, however, and seven years were to elapse before George Bray took up the reins of his Football League career. He missed only one game in the triumphant season 1946-7 as Burnley returned to Division One and reached the FA Cup Final. He was a virtual ever-present until 1951, when a young Jimmy Adamson broke into the side, first of all at the expense of Reg Attwell. Attwell was to move to left-half, however, and in September 1951, at the age of 32, George Bray played his last first-team game for the Clarets before retiring. Bray was a hard-tackling player who never gave less than 100 per cent. He was perhaps not quite as good a player as his brother Jack, also a wing-half and an England international before the war. George joined the Turf Moor coaching staff after he had hung up his boots and then became reserve-team trainer. Under Jimmy Adamson he became first-team trainer and he is still actively involved with the first team as kit-man. George Bray is the classic one-club man, currently in his 53rd year at Turf Moor. Long may he continue.

	LEAGUE		*FA CUP*		*TOTAL*	
	App	*Gls*	*App*	*Gls*	*App*	*Gls*
1938-39	34	0	1	0	35	0
1945-46	0	0	0	0	0	0
1946-47	41	2	9	0	50	2
1947-48	42	3	1	0	43	3
1948-49	39	1	3	1	42	2
1949-50	33	1	3	0	36	1
1950-51	42	1	1	0	43	1
1951-52	10	0	0	0	10	0
	241	8	18	1	259	9

IAN BRENNAN

Ian Brennan is a Burnley player who will always be remembered for the goal he scored at Anfield to give the Clarets a 1-0 victory against the Reds. A crowd of over 44,000 saw the men from Anfield miss the chance to go back to the top of the First Division on 28 September 1974, when Brennan picked up a loose ball eight yards in from the left touch-line. From fully 30 yards the ball never rose more than a foot off the ground after the full-back hit it with tremendous power to give England 'keeper Ray Clemence no chance. Brennan was born in Easington, Northumberland, in 1953 and came to Burnley as an apprentice in 1970. He played for the junior and reserve teams as a forward, but it was at left-back that he made his League debut in 1974. He established himself in the first team in 1974-5 but found stiff competition from Keith Newton and played only two full games the following season. Newton moved to right-back to accommodate him and Brennan made the number-three shirt his own until April 1980, when he was displaced by Steve McAdam. He was transferred to Bolton in December 1980, for £25,000, but was plagued by injury in his time at Burnden Park and was forced to retire after appearing in only 17 League games for Wanderers. He is a regular visitor to Turf Moor, like many former Clarets, still keeping an active interest in his former club's affairs.

	LEAGUE		*FA CUP*		*FL CUP*		*OTHERS*		*TOTAL*	
	App	*Gls*	*App*	*Gls*	*App*	*Gls*	*App*	*Gls*	*App*	*Gls*
1973-74	1	0	0	0	0	0	0	0	1	0
1974-75	34	1	0	0	3	0	0	0	37	1
1975-76	2/1	0	0	0	1	0	0	0	3/1	0
1976-77	31	2	2	0	0	0	0	0	33	2
1977-78	40	4	2	0	4	0	3	0	49	4
1978-79	38	4	4	0	3	1	9	1	54	6
1979-80	27/1	0	1	0	2	0	2	1	32/1	1
	173/2	11	9	0	13	1	14	2	209/2	14

Ian Britton scored ten goals for Burnley in a three-year stay. With respect to Britton, however, probably the only one that the fans remember is his header against Orient to give the Clarets a 2-0 lead and some vital breathing space in their bid to avoid the unthinkable — the loss of League status — on 9 May 1987. Britton was born in Dundee in 1954 and joined Chelsea as an apprentice in July 1971. He made his First Division debut for the Blues in December 1972 and made over 200 League appearances for the Stamford Bridge club before moving back to his home town for a short spell with Dundee United. He joined Blackpool in November 1983 and was an ever-present as the Seasiders won promotion from Division Four as runners-up in 1984-5. In three seasons at Bloomfield Road, Britton played over 100 League games. He joined Burnley, initially on loan, at the beginning of the 1986-7 campaign and scored three goals in his first season in claret and blue, the last of which was, with Neil Grewcock's opener, arguably the most important goal ever scored by a Burnley player. Britton left Turf Moor in the summer of 1989 but still lives and works in the area and is still involved in local football.

IAN BRITTON

	LEAGUE		*FA CUP*		*FL CUP*		*OTHERS*		*TOTAL*	
	App	*Gls*	*App*	*Gls*	*App*	*Gls*	*App*	*Gls*	*App*	*Gls*
1986-87	37/2	3	1	0	2	0	4	0	44/2	3
1987-88	29/3	4	0/1	0	1	0	9/1	1	39/5	5
1988-89	36/1	3	0/1	0	4	0	5/1	0	45/3	3
	102/6	10	1/2	0	7	0	18/2	1	128/10	11

Robert Edward Brocklebank was a stylish inside-forward who played for Burnley in a difficult period in their history. If he had come on the scene 15 years earlier, or later, he would certainly have made a bigger impact and possibly won international honours. He was born in Barnet in 1908, one of eight brothers, and represented Finchley District Boys before joining Finchley FC as an amateur. Aston Villa snapped him up in 1929 but in six years at Villa Park he struggled to make an impact and played only occasionally. He signed for Burnley in March 1935 and went straight into the side, playing alongside 16-year-old Tommy Lawton. Brocklebank was always immaculately turned out and earned the nickname 'The Toff'. A true gentleman, well-respected by players and fans, he was also a cricketer of note, captaining Lowerhouse in the Lancashire League. He continued to play for the Clarets during the war but in 1945 he was appointed as manager of Chesterfield. He joined Birmingham City in 1949 and after six years he moved to Hull City after a scouting spell with West Bromwich Albion. After mixed fortunes in his time at Boothferry Park, he took over at Bradford City in 1961, where he stayed for three years before leaving the game in 1964. He died in Brixham, Devon, in September 1981, aged 73.

BOB BROCKLEBANK

	LEAGUE		*FA CUP*		*TOTAL*	
	App	*Gls*	*App*	*Gls*	*App*	*Gls*
1935-36	10	2	0	0	10	2
1936-37	32	9	3	2	35	11
1937-38	42	14	3	2	45	16
1938-39	37	8	1	1	38	9
	121	33	7	5	128	38

ALLAN BROWN

Allan Brown was the iron man of Burnley Football immediately after World War Two, the centre-half and captain of a formidable team with a reputation for giving nothing away. The Burnley half-back line of Attwell, Brown and Bray was a post-war reincarnation of Halley, Boyle and Watson. Brown was born in Corbridge, on the banks of the Tyne, in 1914 and, after junior football with Spen Black & White, he signed for Huddersfield Town in 1933. He spent some time in the police force but was still with the Terriers when war broke out in 1939. He continued to play at Leeds Road throughout wartime but was transferred to Burnley in 1946. Brown was an ever-present in the 1946-7 season as he led the Clarets to promotion to the First Division and to a place at Wembley. After a season in the top flight he lost his place and in October 1948 was transferred to Notts County, where he ended his playing career. After coaching at Sheffield Wednesday, he returned to Turf Moor in 1954 as manager, a position he held for three years before leaving to manage Sunderland. In 1957, relegation befell the Wearsiders for the first time ever but Allan Brown stayed at the helm until 1964, when he rejoined Sheffield Wednesday, this time as manager. He returned to Roker Park in 1968, and, after coaching in Norway, began a well-earned retirement.

	LEAGUE		*FA CUP*		*TOTAL*	
	App	*Gls*	*App*	*Gls*	*App*	*Gls*
1946-47	42	0	9	0	51	0
1947-48	36	0	1	0	37	0
1948-49	10	0	0	0	10	0
	88	0	10	0	98	0

JIM BROWN

James Brown was born in Motherwell in 1907. One of six brothers, he was a Scottish Schoolboy international before joining the trail to the pithead, playing part-time football for Belhavenock, Maryhill and Wishaw before joining East Fife. He helped the Fifers to the Scottish Cup Final in 1927, where they were beaten by Celtic. He joined Burnley at the end of that season. Brown temporarily filled the gap at centre-half that was created by the departure of Jack Hill, but eventually he made the right-half position his own. He was a first-class club man and spent a number of years at Burnley before Manchester United saw him as the player they needed to boost their promotion campaign. Brown signed for United in June 1935 and they gained promotion at the end of his first season, with Jim Brown missing only two games and winning a championship medal. He left Old Trafford in February 1939, after over 100 League appearances, and ended his playing career with Bradford in the last season before war was declared.

	LEAGUE		*FA CUP*		*TOTAL*	
	App	*Gls*	*App*	*Gls*	*App*	*Gls*
1927-28	14	0	1	0	15	0
1928-29	11	1	0	0	11	1
1929-30	27	0	1	0	28	0
1930-31	38	2	2	0	40	2
1931-32	41	2	1	0	42	2
1932-33	19	0	0	0	19	0
1933-34	40	0	2	0	42	0
1934-35	38	0	6	0	44	0
	228	5	13	0	241	5

John Bruton was born in Westhoughton in 1903 and played his early football with Wigan Borough and Horwich RMI whilst working as a miner. He signed as a professional for Burnley in March 1925, a fee of £125 being paid to the Horwich club. He scored on his League debut at Turf Moor but it was as a goalmaker that he made his name at Burnley, providing countless opportunities for a number of forwards, notably George Beel in his record breaking season 1927-8. Bruton was a superb athlete and his game was built around sheer speed, although he was a very skilful and tricky ball-player. Bruton won three England caps in his time at Turf Moor but in December 1929, Blackburn Rovers paid £6,500 for his signature. He spent ten years at Ewood Park, making over 300 League appearances before joining the coaching staff and subsequently being appointed Rovers manager in 1947. After only two years he left Ewood Park, going on to join Bournemouth as manager in 1950, a position he held for six years. He left the game in 1956, but stayed in the south coast resort where he died on 13 March 1986, aged 82.

	LEAGUE		*FA CUP*		*TOTAL*	
	App	*Gls*	*App*	*Gls*	*App*	*Gls*
1924-25	2	1	0	0	2	1
1925-26	25	7	2	0	27	7
1926-27	42	9	3	2	45	11
1927-28	41	6	1	0	42	6
1928-29	40	11	3	0	43	11
1929-30	17	8	0	0	17	8
	167	42	9	2	176	44

JACK BRUTON

Burnley caused quite a stir when they signed Frank Casper in June 1967 because, quite simply, they did not spend money on players, everyone coming through the junior ranks. The Barnsley-born inside-forward had already scored against the Clarets for Rotherham United in an FA Cup tie and he soon started to repay his £30,000 transfer fee. Casper scored on his debut for Burnley, against Coventry City, and was the club's leading scorer in both his first two seasons. Casper's arrival and scoring prowess probably hastened the departure of Willie Irvine. An ever-present in the 1972-3 Second Division championship team, Casper maintained a strike-rate which saw him score an average of one goal in every three games, his best League tally being 18 in the 1971-2 season. A Football League representative, Casper had his career cruelly curtailed following an injury suffered during the infamous Norman Hunter 'running track' tackle at Elland Road in March 1974. He played in Burnley's last First Division season, his free-kick goal against Queen's Park Rangers being his 100th in the Football League. But the injury sustained against Leeds continued to take its toll and Casper went into coaching and then management at Burnley, Bury and then back at Burnley.

	LEAGUE		*FACUP*		*FLCUP*		*OTHERS*		*TOTAL*	
	App	*Gls*	*App*	*Gls*	*App*	*Gls*	*App*	*Gls*	*App*	*Gls*
1967-68	36/2	14	1	1	5	2	0	0	42/2	17
1968-69	41	13	2	2	8	6	0	0	51	21
1969-70	36/1	8	3	1	5	0	0	0	44/1	9
1970-71	21	4	0	0	0	0	2	1	23	5
1971-72	39/1	18	1	0	3	1	0	0	43/1	19
1972-73	42	12	2	0	1	0	2	0	47	12
1973-74	11/1	4	2	1	0	0	1	0	14/1	5
1974-75	0	0	0	0	0	0	0	0	0	0
1975-76	4/2	1	0	0	0	0	0	0	4/2	1
	230/7	74	11	5	22	9	5	1	268/7	89

FRANK CASPER

ALBERT CHEESEBROUGH

Albert Cheesebrough is one of a very small band of professional footballers who have played for Burnley, having been born in the town. He was born in the Rosegrove area in 1935 and played for the schoolboys team at town and county level before signing for Burnley on his 17th birthday. He made his League debut in April 1952, but it was not until the 1955-6 season that he became a regular in the first team and then he missed only a handful of games in the next three years, forming a quality inside-forward partnership with Jimmy McIlroy, with both players getting their quota of goals. Although only 5ft 7in tall, 'Cheesy' was powerfully built and packed a ferocious left-foot shot. His reputation grew steadily and he was rewarded with an England Under-23 cap against France in 1956. In 1958-9, Cheesebrough's place was strongly challenged by Jimmy Robson and, in June 1959, he was transferred to Leicester City for £20,000. He stayed at Filbert Street for four seasons and was in the side defeated at Wembley in 1961 by the all-conquering Spurs. He moved to Port Vale in 1963 and in 1965 joined Mansfield Town, then managed by his former Turf Moor teammate, Tommy Cummings. A broken leg at Field Mill ended his career and he left the game. He now lives and runs a business in Southport, his main sporting passion is golf and he has only a passing interest in football. His daughter, Susan, became an international gymnast.

	LEAGUE		*FA CUP*		*TOTAL*	
	App	*Gls*	*App*	*Gls*	*App*	*Gls*
1951-52	5	1	0	0	5	1
1952-53	1	0	0	0	1	0
1953-54	0	0	0	0	0	0
1954-55	7	0	1	0	8	0
1955-56	35	6	6	0	41	6
1956-57	40	8	5	4	45	12
1957-58	40	13	2	1	42	14
1959-60	14	7	2	0	16	7
	142	35	16	5	158	40

JACK CHEW

Jackie Chew was born in Blackburn in 1920 and was on Rovers' books as an amateur when war broke out in 1939. He signed for Burnley immediately hostilities ended and played an important role in the successful 1946-7 season. Known as 'Cowboy' because of his bandy legs, Chew possessed a tremendous shot and contributed a useful quota of goals from his right-wing position. He developed a fine understanding with inside-forward Billy Morris and the diminutive pair were the Clarets' regular right-wing until 1952. When Billy Gray arrived from Chelsea in the summer of 1953, he took the number-seven shirt from Jack Chew and 12 months later Chew moved to Bradford City, where he played his last season of League football. He was a talented cricketer and played for many years as a middle-order batsman for Rishton in the Lancashire League. On a famous occasion in 1964, Jackie Chew helped Rishton to a notable Worsley Cup win against Burnley, Charlie Griffiths and all, coming off the field covered in bruises after a marathon innings. Jack Chew lives locally and can be seen at Turf Moor on match days, supporting the Clarets.

	LEAGUE		*FA CUP*		*TOTAL*	
	App	*Gls*	*App*	*Gls*	*App*	*Gls*
1946-47	35	9	8	1	43	10
1947-48	34	4	0	0	34	4
1948-49	40	11	3	0	43	11
1949-50	25	5	3	0	28	5
1950-51	28	5	1	0	29	5
1951-52	24	1	4	1	28	2
1952-53	36	4	4	0	40	4
1953-54	3	0	0	0	3	0
	225	39	23	2	248	41

A midfielder who loved to get forward, Ralph Coates was capable of setting any game alight and as a Burnley player he was a great favourite with the crowd due to his whole-hearted committment. His transfer to Spurs, when the Clarets were forced to sell players in the early-1970s, was a deep-felt loss at Turf Moor. Born in Hetton-le-Hole, Coates followed a well-trodden path from the North-East when he signed for Burnley as a 16-year-old in 1962. He made his League debut in 1964 and three years later played for England Under-23s against Wales. Full honours followed and he was a member of the England party for the 1970 World Cup finals in Mexico. At the end of the 1970-71 season, after more than 200 appearances for Burnley, Coates was sold to Tottenham for just under £200,000. He helped Spurs win the UEFA Cup in 1972, scored the winning goal in the 1973 League Cup Final (after coming on as substitute) and the following year his four goals helped Tottenham to a UEFA Cup runners-up spot. In the summer of 1978, Coates was loaned to an Australian club, St George's, then joined Orient on a free transfer in October 1978 and took his overall League appearances tally past the 450 mark. He scored some grand goals for Orient, including two against Burnley on the opening day of the 1979-80 season. He retired from League football at the end of 1980-81 and is now the manager of a leisure complex in Hertfordshire, maintaining a wide variety of sporting interests.

RALPH COATES

	LEAGUE		*FA CUP*		*FL CUP*		*OTHERS*		*TOTAL*	
	App	*Gls*	*App*	*Gls*	*App*	*Gls*	*App*	*Gls*	*App*	*Gls*
1964-65	7	1	0	0	0	0	0	0	7	1
1965-66	35	5	3	0	4	1	0	0	42	6
1966-67	33	2	2	0	3	0	7	3	45	5
1967-68	25/2	6	1	0	2/2	0	0	0	28/4	6
1968-69	37	5	2	0	7	1	0	0	46	6
1969-70	39	5	3	1	5	0	0	0	47	6
1970-71	38	2	1	0	1	0	2	0	42	2
	214/2	26	12	1	22/2	2	9	3	257/4	32

When Fourth Division Grimsby Town met First Division Burnley in the League Cup in 1968-9, the Mariners' star player was midfield man Doug Collins. Although Grimsby were heavily defeated after a replay, Collins had done enough to impress the Turf Moor scouts and signed for the Clarets in September 1968 for a fee of £35,000. He was born in Newton, Lincolnshire, in 1945, first joining Rotherham United as an apprentice but beginning his League career at Grimsby in 1963. He appeared in exactly 100 League games for the Mariners, scoring 11 goals, before his move to Lancashire five years later. He went straight into Burnley's first team and held his own for the rest of the season. But then, over the next three years, he failed to establish himself as the Clarets went into decline and suffered the traumas of relegation. Collins returned to prominence in 1972-3 and missed only five games, winning a Second Division championship medal as the Clarets returned to the top flight in style. After two more good First Division seasons at Turf Moor, he was given a free transfer in relegation year 1976, joining Plymouth. He then spent a short time at Sunderland under Jimmy Adamson. He joined Rochdale as player-manager in 1979 but was sacked in 1981, then emigrated to Australia where he now combines coaching with various business interests.

DOUG COLLINS

	LEAGUE		*FA CUP*		*FL CUP*		*OTHERS*		*TOTAL*	
	App	*Gls*	*App*	*Gls*	*App*	*Gls*	*App*	*Gls*	*App*	*Gls*
1968-69	23/4	6	2	0	0	0	0	0	25/4	6
1969-70	5/1	1	0	0	2	0	0	0	7/1	1
1970-71	14/3	0	0	0	0/1	0	2	0	16/4	0
1971-72	3/5	2	0	0	0	0	0	0	3/5	2
1972-73	37	2	1	0	1	0	0	0	39	2
1973-74	37/2	4	5	0	3	0	5/1	1	50/3	5
1974-75	39	3	1	0	3	0	0	0	43	3
1975-76	14	0	0	0	3	0	0	0	17	0
	172/15	18	9	0	12/1	0	7/1	1	200/17	19

One of Turf Moor's favourite sons, John Connelly was born in St Helens, in the heart of Rugby League country, in 1938. He was serving his apprenticeship as a joiner whilst playing for St Helens Town when he joined the Clarets in November 1956. Connelly did not make an immediate impact in the first team — Billy Gray and Doug Newlands were vying for the right-wing position — and played only occasionally in his first two seasons. He made the number-seven shirt his own, however, during the 1958-9 season and finished his first campaign as a regular as second-highest scorer behind Ray Pointer. He went one better during the Championship season as Connelly, Pointer and Robson hit 57 of the team's 85 goals between them. Injury forced him to miss the run-in to the title, his replacement, Trevor Meredith, scoring the goal that clinched the trophy in the final match. Of all the goals that John Connelly scored in his Burnley career, none was more memorable than his solo effort in the away leg of the European Cup tie against Rheims. Picking up the ball in his own half, he rode a number of wild tackles and, letting fly from 25 yards, surprised the 'keeper as the ball dipped into the net. The goal effectively won the tie for Burnley and set up an epic struggle against Hamburg in the third round. He won ten England caps in his time at Turf Moor, his first was as early as 1959, and scored four goals for his country before his exciting wing play inevitably attracted the big clubs. Connelly signed for Manchester United in April 1964 and helped to bring the League title to Old Trafford in his first season, in which he missed only one game. Ten more England caps followed at United before he left Old Trafford for Blackburn Rovers, where he gave four years' sterling service. He joined Bury in 1970, where he performed with distinction for three years before retiring in 1973. John Connelly is still a familiar figure in the area, behind the counter at his fish and chip shop in Brierfield. He still watches Burnley on occasions but these days prefers to follow Burnley Belvedere, for whom his son plays. He is also a keen walker and a golfer and sees as many Lancashire League cricket matches as he can.

JOHN CONNELLY

	LEAGUE		*FA CUP*		*FL CUP*		*OTHERS*		*TOTAL*	
	App	*Gls*	*App*	*Gls*	*App*	*Gls*	*App*	*Gls*	*App*	*Gls*
1956-57	3	0	0	0	0	0	0	0	3	0
1957-58	3	0	2	1	0	0	0	0	5	1
1958-59	32	12	5	0	0	0	0	0	37	12
1959-60	34	20	8	4	0	0	0	0	42	24
1960-61	32	16	7	2	7	2	5	2	51	22
1961-62	38	17	8	3	0	0	0	0	46	20
1962-63	41	13	3	2	0	0	0	0	44	15
1963-64	32	8	5	3	0	0	0	0	37	11
	215	86	38	15	7	2	5	2	265	105

JAMES CRABTREE

One of Burnley's earliest home-grown stars, James Crabtree was a naturally gifted player who rose rapidly to international status in the 1890s. He was an important member of Aston Villa's double-winning side of 1897, yet in the space of only 11 years, he died in poverty, mentally unstable and a drunkard. He was born in Burnley in 1871 and first played for the first team as an amateur in 1889. After spells with non-League clubs he returned to Turf Moor as a professional and captained the side during much of his three-year stay. He won the first three of his 14 England caps before a supposed contractual dispute led to his transfer to Aston Villa in 1895. The move is believed to be the first time that money changed hands between Football League clubs for a player. In his first five years at Villa Park, he collected four Championship medals and an FA Cup medal as Villa dominated English football. He won 11 more England caps, a number as captain, and at his peak he was one of the best-paid players in the country. He left Villa in 1902 and after coaching in the lower leagues he retired in 1906, his drinking problems already apparent. His health deteriorated rapidly and, following a series of fits, he died on 18 June 1908, aged only 37. James Crabtree had been an all-round athlete, fit and strong. At 5ft 10in and almost 14st, he was ideally built for the powerful defender he was. His sad decline was remarkable and a tragic waste of true talent.

	LEAGUE		*FA CUP*		*TOTAL*	
	App	*Gls*	*App*	*Gls*	*App*	*Gls*
1889-90	3	1	1	0	4	1
1892-93	23	6	2	0	25	6
1893-94	18	0	1	0	19	0
1894-95	28	2	1	0	29	2
	72	9	5	0	77	9

Benjamin Cross played over 230 League games for Burnley and came to prominence in the club's halcyon days. Never a prolific scorer, he nevertheless netted over 50 League goals, his best haul being in the Championship season of 1920-21. He was born in Birkenhead in 1898 and represented Birkenhead Schoolboys, who won the English Schools' Shield in 1912. He also played twice for England Schoolboys in the same year. After the war, Cross was invited on an FA tour of Canada and subsequently joined Runcorn, who won the Cheshire County League championship in his final season with them. He was transferred to Burnley in April 1920 and made his Clarets debut in the fourth match of the following season, a 3-0 home win against Huddersfield on 6 September. Significantly, this was the first game in the run of 30 without defeat and Benny Cross missed only two more during the rest of the season. He remained a prominent first-teamer, still scoring his share of goals until 1927, when he won his only senior representative honour, playing for the Football League in a 2-2 draw against the Scottish League at Leicester. At the end of his career he played only in the very last game of the 1927-8 season, after struggling with injury. He left the game in 1929 and lived in retirement in Blackpool for many years until his death in June 1984, aged 86.

	LEAGUE		*FA CUP*		*OTHERS*		*TOTAL*	
	App	*Gls*	*App*	*Gls*	*App*	*Gls*	*App*	*Gls*
1920-21	37	14	3	1	0	0	40	15
1921-22	25	9	1	0	1	0	27	9
1922-23	42	12	1	0	0	0	43	12
1923-24	39	5	7	2	0	0	46	7
1924-25	40	6	1	0	0	0	41	6
1925-26	24	3	2	0	0	0	26	3
1926-27	29	8	2	1	0	0	31	9
1927-28	1	0	0	0	0	0	1	0
	237	57	17	4	1	0	255	61

BENNY CROSS

'The greatest goal ever scored at Turf Moor' is how Tommy Cummings' effort, on a snowy winter's day nearly 40 years ago, is still described. Billy Morris had put Burnley ahead in a League match against Newcastle United on 19 January 1952. Jackie Milburn had equalized and, with 15 minutes to go, Cummings had just robbed Milburn on the edge of the Burnley area at the Bee Hole End. The young centre-half moved quickly forward and evaded a couple of tackles as he crossed the halfway line looking to pass the ball and retreat. No one offered themselves as Cummings, still surging forward, swept past Newcastle captain and right-half Joe Harvey into the 'D'. As he reached the edge of the box, he hit the ball with tremendous power and it crashed into the net past a diving but hopelessly beaten Ronnie Simpson. The crowd went wild and it was several minutes before Newcastle kicked-off again as players from both sides congratulated the Burnley pivot. Afterwards Tommy was heard to say simply, 'I had nobody to pass to.' Tommy Cummings was born in Castledown, near Sunderland, in 1928. He was playing for Stanley United outside Consett in 1947 when he was offered a trial by Tottenham, but Spurs' loss was Burnley's gain and he signed on at Turf Moor in October 1947. Following the departure of iron man Allan Brown in 1948, the young Tommy Cummings was seen as the natural successor and he made his League debut on 18 December 1948 at Maine Road. From that moment the position was his and, apart from very occasional absences, made the centre-half berth very much his own property until 1956. Renowned as one of the fastest half-backs in the game, Cummings played for the Football League in 1951 and won three England 'B' caps, in 1953 and 1956; alas, full international honours eluded him. After a two-year spell affected by injury, he came back into contention in 1958 but competition for places in the side was fierce. During the Championship campaign he alternated with Brian Miller for the number-five shirt but ultimately both players were accommodated with Bobby Seith missing out. After a League career at Turf Moor spanning 15 seasons over three decades, Cummings moved to Mansfield Town as player-manager in March 1963 but after only 11 games retired from playing, also relinquishing his position as chairman of the PFA. After four years at Field Mill he was appointed Aston Villa manager in July 1967 but, given precious little time to make an impression at Villa Park, he was sacked in November 1968. After coaching abroad and scouting for a number of clubs, Tommy Cummings decided to put down roots in his adopted Lancashire. He has been in the licensed trade for a number of years and now runs a very pleasant hostelry on the outskirts of Burnley.

	LEAGUE		*FA CUP*		*FL CUP*		*OTHERS*		*TOTAL*	
	App	*Gls*	*App*	*Gls*	*App*	*Gls*	*App*	*Gls*	*App*	*Gls*
1948-49	18	0	2	0	0	0	0	0	20	0
1949-50	41	0	3	0	0	0	0	0	44	0
1950-51	41	0	1	0	0	0	0	0	42	0
1951-52	42	2	4	0	0	0	0	0	46	2
1952-53	42	0	4	0	0	0	0	0	46	0
1953-54	35	0	3	0	0	0	0	0	38	0
1954-55	39	0	1	0	0	0	0	0	40	0
1955-56	40	0	6	0	0	0	0	0	46	0
1956-57	2	0	0	0	0	0	0	0	2	0
1957-58	6	0	0	0	0	0	0	0	6	0
1958-59	39	0	5	0	0	0	0	0	44	0
1959-60	23	0	0	0	0	0	0	0	23	0
1960-61	25	0	2	0	6	0	1	0	34	0
1961-62	39	1	7	0	0	0	0	0	46	1
1962-63	2	0	0	0	0	0	0	0	2	0
	434	3	38	0	6	0	1	0	479	3

TOMMY CUMMINGS

Chosen by his fellow professionals as one of the Fourth Division's brightest prospects, Steve Davis leads the Burnley team with a combination of enthusiasm, determination and undoubted skill. In 1991, Davis was a recipient of a Barclays PFA Divisional Award, and as such was recognized as one of the best players in the division. As first-team skipper in the 1990-91 season, he formed a formidable partnership in central defence with new signing John Pender. Birmingham-born, Davis was an apprentice with Stoke City before signing professional terms with Crewe Alexandra. He played almost 150 games and became captain of the Gresty Road club before joining the Clarets, initially on loan. Replacing Peter Zelem in the heart of the Burnley defence, Davis formed a solid partnership with Steve Gardner early in his career. Never afraid to go forward, Davis has contributed his fair share of goals, mainly from set-pieces, but also in open play. Frequently watched by other clubs, Davis has been a virtual ever-present since moving to Turf Moor apart from a period in the 1989-90 season which he missed through injury.

STEVE DAVIS

	LEAGUE		*FA CUP*		*FL CUP*		*OTHERS**		*TOTAL*	
	App	*Gls*	*App*	*Gls*	*App*	*Gls*	App	Gls	*App*	*Gls*
1987-88	33	5	0	0	1	0	7	0	41	5
1988-89	37	0	1	0	3	0	5	1	46	1
1989-90	31	1	5	0	0	0	1	0	37	1
1990-91	46	5	3	0	3	0	9	0	61	5
	147	11	9	0	7	0	22	1	185	12

* Includes 1990-91 Play-off games.

Like many famous players, Jerry Dawson is probably best remembered for one particular match. Unlike perhaps every other player, this match was one that Dawson did not play in! In the famous FA Cup run of 1914, Jerry Dawson was probably approaching the peak of his ability. He had performed brilliantly in all the matches up to the semi-final when, in a goalless draw at Old Trafford against Sheffield United, he twisted a thigh muscle. Four days later, in the replay, reserve Ronnie Sewell took Dawson's place and a goal from Tommy Boyle sent the Clarets through to their first FA Cup Final. Sewell played in the next four League games, then, a week before the Final, Dawson reappeared for a League game at Manchester City. In a 4-1 defeat for Burnley, Dawson was again injured, this time suffering bruised ribs, and it became a race against time to get him fit for the 'Royal' Cup Final at the Crystal Palace. The town was alive with rumour. Would Dawson play or not? It was the question on everyone's lips. On the Friday before the big match, Dawson met manager John Haworth privately and said he had decided not to play. He considered that, although he felt fit, it was too much of a risk and he may not last the whole match. Sewell stepped up again and performed with distinction as the famous strike by Bert Freeman was enough to deny Liverpool and bring the FA Cup back to Turf Moor for the first and so far only time. Jerry Dawson's act of selflessness has now gone down in football history and, as a gesture of appreciation by the club and the football authorities, a special medal was struck to honour the great man. Jeremiah Dawson was born in Holme-in-Cliviger, just outside Burnley, on 18 March 1888. He first played football for nearby Portsmouth Rovers whilst serving his apprenticeship to the Cliviger village blacksmith. It was whilst playing for the village football team that he came to Burnley's attention and, after playing a few games for the Reserves, he was signed as a full-time professional in February 1907. He made his League debut two months later and, although he had little to do in a 3-0 win against Stockport at Turf Moor, his class was unmistakable. Soon after the start of the following season, stalwart Billy Green was displaced and Jerry Dawson's monumental League career had begun in earnest. Dawson was the first member of the two great teams either side of the World War One to sign for Burnley, and few would argue that his arrival at the club signalled the start of a new era at Turf Moor. Steady progress was made towards eventual promotion, the crowds came in their thousands and as the key players, Boyle, Freeman, Kelly and others began to arrive, Dawson's consistency and sheer brillance week after week was the bedrock upon which the success was built. His performances brought international recognition for the first time in February 1910, when he was chosen to represent the Football League against the Scottish League at Ewood Park. The following year his masterly display in the inter-League match at Ibrox Park led to a standing ovation by the mainly Scottish crowd. The 1913-14 season was, of course, one of club triumph but personal sadness for Jerry Dawson, but the following campaign he was as consistent as ever, Burnley finishing fourth as the clouds of war darkened over Europe. In 1919, Jerry Dawson carrried on between the posts for the Clarets, but missed eight games in mid-season with a damaged shoulder. He returned to assist the club to runners-up position at the end of the season, the highest-ever finish and a foretaste of things to come. He was injured again in the heavy defeat in the opening game of the title-winning season but after missing two games, was back in the side to play his part to the full in the memorable Championship campaign. Strangely, as he had missed the triumphant end to the 1913-14 season, he also missed the final match of the most magnificent season in the club's history. Dawson's long-awaited England debut came in Belfast on 22 October 1921, a 1-1 draw, and he won his only other full international cap the following April against Scotland in Birmingham. At 34 he was past his peak and, like many players, had lost perhaps the best years of his career to a war. On 2 December 1922 Dawson played his 400th League game for Burnley, at Middlesbrough, and the following week broke Fred Barron's appearance record which had stood since 1911. Incredibly, he played another three full seasons as first-choice 'keeper before deciding enough was enough and made his final League appearance in front of the Turf Moor faithful on Christmas Day 1928 — nine months after his 40th birthday and almost 20 years after first signing for his only League club. He joined the coaching staff at Turf Moor and continued to keep himself fit by playing cricket for Burnley Cricket Club. He was an accomplished batsman and graced the Lancashire League scene for many years. A lifelong bachelor, Jerry Dawson, lived in Cliviger all his life and died at his home on 8 August 1970, aged 82. He played well over 700 first-team games for Burnley and his record of 522 League appearances will undoubtedly stand for a very long time. Jeremiah Dawson, fresh-faced country boy, village blacksmith and dedicated professional footballer will be remembered in Burnley as long as football is played.

JERRY DAWSON

	LEAGUE		*FA CUP*		*OTHERS*		*TOTAL*	
	App	*Gls*	*App*	*Gls*	*App*	*Gls*	*App*	*Gls*
1906-07	1	0	0	0	0	0	1	0
1907-08	34	0	1	0	0	0	35	0
1908-09	36	0	6	0	0	0	42	0
1909-10	35	0	2	0	0	0	37	0
1910-11	32	0	4	0	0	0	36	0
1911-12	38	0	1	0	0	0	39	0
1912-13	30	0	6	0	0	0	36	0
1913-14	32	0	6	0	0	0	38	0
1914-15	35	0	3	0	0	0	38	0
1919-20	34	0	2	0	0	0	36	0
1920-21	39	0	3	0	0	0	42	0
1921-22	37	0	2	0	1	0	40	0
1922-23	30	0	1	0	0	0	31	0
1923-24	36	0	6	0	0	0	42	0
1924-25	36	0	1	0	0	0	37	0
1925-26	35	0	2	0	0	0	37	0
1926-27	1	0	0	0	0	0	1	0
1927-28	0	0	0	0	0	0	0	0
1928-29	1	0	0	0	0	0	1	0
	522	0	46	0	1	0	569	0

The latest player to chalk up 200 Football League appearances for the Clarets, Ray Deakin is one of only three Burnley players to have led his side out in a Wembley Final. The defeat in that 1988 Sherpa Van Final took nothing away from his captaincy and he remained a regular member of the first team, injuires apart, until the very end of the 1990-91 season when he made way for Ian Bray. More at home at left-back, Deakin carried out centre-half and sweeper duties for the Clarets and also liked to get his name on the score-sheet. Liverpool-born, Deakin was an apprentice at Everton but after four years at Goodison Park had failed to make the first-team grade. A season at Port Vale followed before Deakin returned North and played almost 150 times for Bolton Wanderers. He joined Burnley in the summer of 1985 and scored his first goal for the Clarets on New Year's Day 1986, in a 5-2 win against Wrexham. After six seasons at Turf Moor he was released at the end of 1990-91.

RAY DEAKIN

	LEAGUE		*FA CUP*		*FL CUP*		*OTHERS**		*TOTAL*	
	App	*Gls*	*App*	*Gls*	*App*	*Gls*	App	Gls	*App*	*Gls*
1985-86	46	3	2	0	2	0	6	0	56	3
1986-87	46	0	1	0	2	0	6	0	55	0
1987-88	37	3	1	0	3	0	10	0	51	3
1988-89	14	0	0	0	2	0	3	0	19	0
1989-90	32/1	0	0	0	2	0	3	0	37/1	0
1990-91	37	0	3	0	4	0	7/1	0	51/1	0
	212/1	6	7	0	15	0	35/1	0	269/2	6

* Includes 1990-91 Play-off games.

JOE DEVINE

Joseph Devine was born in Motherwell in 1905, playing junior football in the Glasgow area with Cledale and Bathgate before joining Burnley as a professional in May 1925. A slightly built but tricky inside-forward, Devine was introduced to the first team immediately, in a forward line that, on paper, was strong enough to challenge for honours. After partnering the great Bob Kelly, Devine was given the job of trying to step into his boots when Kelly moved to Sunderland in December 1925. It was an impossible task, of course, but Joe Devine made the inside-left berth was own, playing between Louis Page and George Beel. He was an ever-present in 1928-9, also having his best season for finding the net, although well behind the prolific pair, Beel and Page. As Burnley fought desperately against meagre crowds and the threat of relegation, Devine was transferred to Newcastle United for over £5,500 in January 1930. He struck up an early understanding with the legendary Hughie Gallacher, ending his first season as second-highest scorer behind the controversial Scot. He lost his place the following season and moved to Sunderland in February 1931, going on to play for Queen's Park Rangers and Birmingham before ending his Football League career with Chesterfield in 1938. In later life he became a referee in Highland League football before retiring from the game to live quietly in his native Scotland.

	LEAGUE		*FA CUP*		*TOTAL*	
	App	*Gls*	*App*	*Gls*	*App*	*Gls*
1925-26	9	2	0	0	9	2
1926-27	26	9	3	0	29	9
1927-28	17	1	0	0	17	1
1928-29	42	10	3	2	45	12
1929-30	20	5	1	0	21	5
	114	27	7	2	121	29

ARTHUR DIXON

Arthur Dixon was born in Barrowford in 1879 and played for Trawden Forest and Nelson before joining Burnley in the summer of 1900. He did not break into the first team in his first season but made his League debut alongside Joe Taylor in the 7-0 drubbing of Doncaster Rovers at Turf Moor in December 1901. He was a polished but rugged defender, strong in the tackle and, although not the biggest of men, he was good in the air. Dixon was a virtual ever-present at left-half unti 1903, when he showed his versatility by performing equally effectively at right- and left-back over the following four seasons. The year 1907 was a period of great upheaval at Turf Moor and Arthur Dixon was seen as surplus to requirements. He was transferred to Southern League Tottenham Hotspur as the White Hart Lane club prepared for Football League status, eventually achieved in 1908. Dixon returned north after one season in London, joining the other Football League newcomers, Bradford, where he stayed for a number of years. He eventually returned to live locally and died in Nelson in 1946.

	LEAGUE		*FA CUP*		*TOTAL*	
	App	*Gls*	*App*	*Gls*	*App*	*Gls*
1901-02	17	0	1	0	18	0
1902-03	32	0	1	0	33	0
1903-04	33	6	2	0	35	6
1904-05	33	1	2	0	35	1
1905-06	30	0	1	0	31	0
1906-07	30	0	1	0	31	0
	175	7	8	0	183	7

Most Burnley fans of the post-McIlroy era would cite only one player as their favourite ex-Claret. Martin Dobson was a great thinker who always seemed to have time with the ball at his feet. A player of great perception, he appeared to know where his teammates were and play accurate balls to them without even looking up. In his two spells at Burnley he played over 400 games for the Clarets and proved to be a vital cog in two championship campaigns, the Second Division in 1972-3 and the Third Division nine years later. It must all have left Bolton Wanderers kicking themselves. Rishton-born Dobson spent three years as a Burnden Park apprentice before being given a free transfer. His father persuaded Burnley boss Harry Potts to give him a trial and the former Clitheroe Grammar School pupil was immediately snapped up by Burnley. He made his debut at centre-forward in place of the injured Willie Irvine in a 3-2 defeat at Wolves and his appearances in that 1967-8 season were in a variety of positions. Over the next six seasons he played over 200 games, contributing more than 40 goals, an excellent goals-per-game ratio for a midfielder. He was captain of the Second Division title-winning team in 1972-3 and virtual ever-present the following season as Burnley narrowly missed out on a place in Europe. After three games of the 1974-5 season rumours were rife that the England international — Dobson had been capped four times by then — was about to be sold. And when the Clarets entertained Chelsea in a midweek match, the fan's worst fears were confirmed as the team emerged without Dobson. He had been sold to Everton for around £300,000 and went on to make almost 200 First Division appearances for the Toffeemen and claimed another England cap. But the Burnley fans never forgave the club for selling him in the first place, many renaming the Bob Lord stand the 'Martin Dobson Stand' in honour of their former hero. Burnley eventually bought Dobson back for £100,000 in August 1979 and having moved into central defence, he was captain and a key member of the side which won the Third Division title in 1981-2 and enjoyed two memorable Cup runs the following year. In all his time at Burnley, Dobson, a cultured, stylish player, was an automatic choice and vital component. And until John Bond arrived as manager that remained true. But Bond installed Tommy Hutchison as captain and decided, for some reason, that Dobson did not suit his style of play and made him scrap for a shirt. Many saw this as the beginning of a new career for Dobson, also a Football League representative, and expected him to move on and become a player-coach and be groomed for the managerial hot-seat. He did just that, but he did it 15 miles down the road at Bury, moving to Gigg Lane as John Bond's only season in charge at Turf Moor drew to a close. In his first season with Bury he was a player-coach, later becoming a player-manager, surrounding himself with former Clarets and steering them out of the Fourth Division. For the next four seasons he kept Bury on the fringe of the Third Division promotion race, but then towards the end of the 1988-9 season he left Gigg Lane following a contractual dispute. He is currently manager of Bristol Rovers.

MARTIN DOBSON

	LEAGUE		FA CUP		FL CUP		OTHERS		TOTAL	
	App	Gls	App	Gls	App	Gls	App	Gls	App	Gls
1967-68	11/3	3	0	0	0	0	0	0	11/3	3
1968-69	22/1	4	0	0	4	0	0	0	26/1	4
1969-70	36	6	3	3	5	2	0	0	44	11
1970-71	25	4	1	0	0	0	0	0	26	4
1971-72	42	9	1	0	3	0	0	0	46	9
1972-73	41	12	2	0	1	0	2	0	46	12
1973-74	40	4	5	2	3	0	7	1	55	7
1974-75	3	1	0	0	0	0	0	0	3	1
1979-80	29	5	2	1	2	1	3	0	36	7
1980-81	46	7	3	0	4	1	3	1	56	9
1981-82	44	3	5	0	2	0	3	0	54	3
1982-83	39	1	5	0	9	0	3	0	56	1
1983-84	28	4	4	1	1	0	3	0	36	5
	406/4	63	31	7	34	4	24	2	495/4	76

It was something of a feather in Burnley's cap when a big name in the game, Tommy Docherty, persuaded his son to accept an apprenticeship offered by the Clarets. An English Youth international, Mick Docherty signed for the Clarets in April 1967 and within 12 months had captained them to FA Youth Cup triumph. Originally a midfielder, he made his debut in the 1968-9 season and played 50 games, almost exclusively in midfield before taking over from John Angus at right-back after two games of the 1971-2 campaign. He played 68 consecutive games in the number-two shirt before injury began to plague his career. Badly injured in the opening game of the 1973-4 season, Docherty did not play again until November 1975, that game against Sheffield United being his only one of the season. Docherty played 22 games in 1975-6, leaving Burnley for Maine Road on the eve of their First Division demise towards the end of that season. He played only eight games for Manchester City before moving on again, this time to Sunderland where he became a first-team fixture. He finished his playing career at Blackpool, where a serious knee injury forced him to retire early. Since then he has been involved in a coaching and managerial capacity at a variety of clubs. He was boss at Hartlepool United before becoming assistant to his father at Wolves. After that he was assistant at Blackpool before returning to Turf Moor in January 1989 as Frank Casper's right-hand man. Just before the 1990-91 season he went to Hull City as assistant to Stan Ternent, another former Claret, but both were sacked shortly into the campaign. Docherty then transferred his allegiance to Rochdale.

	LEAGUE		FA CUP		FL CUP		OTHERS		TOTAL	
	App	Gls	App	Gls	App	Gls	App	Gls	App	Gls
1968-69	5/2	0	0	0	0/1	0	0	0	5/3	0
1969-70	16	0	0	0	0/1	0	0	0	16/1	0
1970-71	29/2	0	1	0	1	0	2	1	33/2	1
1971-72	40	0	1	0	3	0	0	0	44	0
1972-73	35	0	2	0	1	0	2	0	40	0
1973-74	1	0	0	0	0	0	1	0	2	0
1974-75	1	0	0	0	0	0	0	0	1	0
1975-76	22	0	1	0	4	0	0	0	27	0
	149/4	0	5	0	9/2	0	5	1	168/6	1

MICK DOCHERTY

Alex Elder was the only player to become established in the Championship winning side of 1959-60 who made his debut during that memorable campaign. He arrived from Glentoran in January 1959 and soon impressed in a very strong Burnley reserve side with his hard-tackling style and his mastery of the long ball out of defence. He made his first Division One appearance in September 1959 in a difficult game at Preston. The young Elder was detailed to mark the legendary Tom Finney and, although the Clarets lost the game 1-0, Elder had done enough to make the left-back position his own for the foreseeable future. Still only 18, he made his full Northern Ireland debut against Wales in April 1960, going on to win 34 caps in his time at Turf Moor; oddly, he won his only Irish Under-23 cap in 1964, four years after making his first senior international appearance. A broken ankle kept Elder out of the side for more than half of the 1963-4 season and he later asked for a transfer following a contractual dispute. He stayed at Turf Moor however and in 1965 was appointed club captain. Perhaps the most talked about own-goal in Burnley's history was scored by Alex Elder in the last home match of the 1965-6 against Leeds United. From the most acute of angles, Elder contrived to lob the ball over Adam Blacklaw to give the Yorkshiremen the points, also ensuring that Leeds clinched runners-up spot behind Liverpool — at the Clarets' expense. He was transferred to Stoke City in August 1967, spending five years in the Potteries where he played 80 League games, winning six more Irish caps, before retiring from the game in 1972.

ALEX ELDER

	LEAGUE		*FA CUP*		*FL CUP*		*OTHERS*		*TOTAL*	
	App	*Gls*	*App*	*Gls*	*App*	*Gls*	*App*	*Gls*	*App*	*Gls*
1959-60	34	0	8	0	0	0	0	0	42	0
1960-61	36	0	7	0	5	0	5	0	53	0
1961-62	41	0	8	1	0	0	0	0	49	1
1962-63	41	1	3	1	0	0	0	0	44	2
1963-64	19	1	5	0	0	0	0	0	24	1
1964-65	34	4	5	0	0	0	0	0	39	4
1965-66	39	6	3	0	4	0	0	0	46	6
1966-67	27	3	0	0	2	0	4	0	33	3
	271	15	39	2	11	0	9	0	330	17

The transfer of Jock Espie to Burnley in December 1891 was one of the earliest controversies in the club's League history. Espie arrived from Burnbank Swifts and played his first game for the Clarets at West Brom on Boxing Day 1891. Albion promptly complained to the Football League that Espie had already signed for them and that 'certain inducements' had been offered to the Scot to join Burnley. In addition, West Brom claimed that Burnley had offered them some money to keep quiet about the affair. The League decided that Espie would be suspended for a week and would not be eligible for Cup ties but Burnley FC had no action taken against them. Espie was born in Hamilton in 1868 and played for a number of clubs whilst still in his teens, including Glasgow Rangers, Motherwell and Queen's Park, before joining Burnbank Swifts. He was a solid, well-built young man at 5ft 11in and weighing over 13st and he arrived at Turf Moor having represented his country at junior level. He was equally at home at centre-forward or centre-half but it was in defence that he gave his greatest service to Burnley. Even the great James Crabtree had to make way for him in the centre of defence in 1894, Crabtree moving to right-back to enable Espie to take his place in the middle of a formidable half-back line, flanked by big Walter Place and Archie Livingstone. He was transferred to Manchester City in February 1896, but managed only one League game at Hyde Road before returning to Scotland to join Dundee the following September. He retired from football while still in his early 30s to earn his living as a face worker down the pit, but tragically, met his death in a mining accident.

JOHN ESPIE

	LEAGUE		*FA CUP*		*TOTAL*	
	App	*Gls*	*App*	*Gls*	*App*	*Gls*
1891-92	10	2	0	0	10	2
1892-93	18	1	0	0	18	1
1893-94	30	5	0	0	30	5
1894-95	26	1	1	0	27	1
1895-96	9	0	1	0	10	0
	93	9	2	0	95	9

Having joined Burnley as a midfield player. Andy Farrell has developed into being the club's most versatile player. In his early days with Turf Moor, Farrell was forced to play in defence, but the real transformation in his game came in the 1989-90 season. Long-term injuries to centre-halves Mark Monington and Steve Gardner saw the Colchester-born player move into the heart of defence alongside Steve Davis, a move which won him a place in the hearts of the fans as well as the club's Player of the Year award. The arrival of John Pender in 1990-91 deprived him of the number-five shirt, but led to another transformation as Farrell played confidently at sweeper or in midfield. Time spent in defence has armed Farrell with both excellent distribution, aerial ability and a strong tackle. His versatility was further highlighted in January 1991, when Chris Pearce was sent-off and Farrell spent eight or nine confident minutes in the green jersey. Farrell started his career with his home-town club and played over 100 games for the Layer Road outfit before joining Burnley in the summer of 1987. His first goal for the Clarets came in a 4-1 defeat against Leyton Orient. His second was a sweet strike from 25 yards which, briefly, took Burnley to the top of Division Four. Unusually, he is one of the few southern-born players to have settled with the Turf Moor club.

ANDY FARRELL

	LEAGUE		*FA CUP*		*FL CUP*		*OTHERS**		*TOTAL*	
	App	*Gls*	*App*	*Gls*	*App*	*Gls*	App	Gls	*App*	*Gls*
1987-88	45	3	1	0	4	1	11	1	61	5
1988-89	35/1	4	1	0	4	0	6	0	46/1	4
1989-90	36	2	6	0	2	0	5	1	49	3
1990-91	30/7	2	0/2	0	3/1	0	8	2	41/10	4
	146/8	11	8/2	0	13/1	1	30	4	197/11	16

* Includes 1990-91 Play-off games.

One of six ever-presents during the 1972-3 Second Division championship winning side, Paul Fletcher is perhaps best remembered for one goal. While the Bolton-born forward may have scored 71 times for the Clarets and almost 100 times in the Football League, his goal at Elland Road in 1974 remains one of the most often talked about by Burnley fans. Leeds were the all-conquering heroes of the time, but Burnley beat them 4-1 on their own pitch with Fletcher netting with an overhead bicycle-kick which was so spectacular it had to be seen to be believed. An England Under-23 international, Fletcher came to Burnley from Burnden Park. After ten seasons with the Clarets he went to Blackpool and after an injury-plagued spell with the Seasiders, drifted out of the game. Since then he has been involved in private business before rejoining football as commercial manager at the now-defunct Colne Dynamoes. He left Colne to take up a similar role at Huddersfield Town and has since become chief executive at the Leeds Road club. A very popular player and accomplished administrator, Fletcher is also highly regarded as an after-dinner speaker.

PAUL FLETCHER

	LEAGUE		*FA CUP*		*FL CUP*		*OTHERS*		*TOTAL*	
	App	*Gls*	*App*	*Gls*	*App*	*Gls*	*App*	*Gls*	*App*	*Gls*
1970-71	9	1	0	0	0	0	0	0	9	1
1971-72	42	10	1	0	3	0	0	0	46	10
1972-73	40	15	2	0	1	0	2	0	45	15
1973-74	38	13	5	2	3	0	8	6	54	21
1974-75	34	10	1	0	3	0	0	0	38	10
1975-76	17	2	0	0	1	0	0	0	18	2
1976-77	30/1	4	3	2	0	0	1	0	34/1	6
1977-78	34	7	2	2	3	1	1	0	40	10
1978-79	34/1	9	2/1	1	3	0	9	1	48/2	11
1979-80	13	0	0	0	1	0	3	0	17	0
	291/2	71	16/1	7	18	1	24	7	349/3	86

When Burnley's youth programme was at its very best, it churned out a string of international players. Brian Flynn was amongst the most capped of them. Although small in stature, Flynn was always big on committment and willing to battle it out with the burliest midfielders. Born in Port Talbot, Flynn joined the Clarets as an apprentice and made his First Division debut in February 1974 in a 1-1 draw with Arsenal. In his first spell at Burnley Flynn played most of his football in the First Division, but as the Clarets slipped out of the top flight, it was obvious that a number of star players would leave. In November 1977, after 115 games for Burnley, Flynn was sold to Leeds and became a first-team regular with the Elland Road outfit. Four and a half years and more than 150 Leeds appearances later, Flynn was back at Turf Moor, first on loan and then permanently. He played another 80 games with the Clarets before moving to Cardiff and then Doncaster. His next move was to Limerick, where former Claret Billy Hamilton was manager and Flynn became player-coach. Back 'across the water' he joined Bury before returning to Doncaster. Flynn finished his playing career with Wrexham as player-manager and then manager. In 1989-90 he successfully led Wrexham's campaign to avoid the drop into the Vauxhall Conference and the following season was forced out of retirement to play in the European Cup-winners' Cup, UEFA rules meaning he had to drop most of his regular team and field a side made up of veterans and trainees. Capped 66 times by Wales, Flynn won exactly half his international honours while with the Clarets.

BRIAN FLYNN

	LEAGUE		*FA CUP*		*FL CUP*		*OTHERS*		*TOTAL*	
	App	*Gls*	*App*	*Gls*	*App*	*Gls*	*App*	*Gls*	*App*	*Gls*
1973-74	2	0	0	0	0	0	0	0	2	0
1974-75	23/3	0	1	0	1/1	0	0	0	25/4	0
1975-76	37/2	4	1	0	5	2	0	0	43/2	6
1976-77	41	2	3	1	1	0	3	1	48	4
1977-78	12	2	0	0	4	0	3	0	19	2
1981-82	2	0	0	0	0	0	0	0	2	0
1982-83	28	1	7	1	4	0	0	0	39	2
1983-84	43	9	5	0	2	2	5	1	55	12
1984-85	5/4	1	0	0	1/1	0	3	0	9/5	1
	193/9	19	17	2	18/2	4	14	2	242/11	27

BERT FREEMAN

Bert Freeman was already an established goalscorer with a fearsome reputation when he joined Burnley from Everton in April 1911. He won two England caps whilst at Goodison and also played for the Football League against the Irish League in 1909, scoring four goals. Surprisingly, he was seen as surplus to requirements at Everton and came to Turf Moor to join the growing band of stars about to make a lasting impact on British football. He was born Bertram Clewley Freeman in Birmingham in October 1885 and, after starring in schools football, joined Aston Villa in April 1904. At 5ft 8in he was not the biggest of forwards and he failed to make an impact at Villa Park. He was transferred to Arsenal in November 1905 and, although never able to command an automatic place at Highbury, still managed 21 goals in only 44 League appearances for the Gunners before being transferred to Everton in April 1908, to join his former teammate at Highbury, Tim Coleman. His impact at Goodison was immediate and in their first full season on Merseyside, the Freeman-Coleman partnership hit 56 goals between them, with Bert Freeman netting 36 to make him the League's leading scorer as Everton finished runners-up to Newcastle United in the First Division. He won his first England cap towards the end of that season, scoring his country's second goal as they beat Wales 2-0 at Nottingham on 15 March. He played again the following month as England beat Scotland 2-0 at the Crystal Palace. He was his club's leading scorer again in 1909-10 with 22 goals, but the following season he failed to make an impact and was allowed to leave for Burnley, where he was to become one of Turf Moor's favourite sons. Seasons 1911-12 and 1912-13 were fruitful ones for Bert Freeman and Burnley as the Clarets flirted with, and then secured, promotion from Division Two. The men from Turf Moor were the League's leading scorers in both seasons and Freeman took the individual honours as the League's top marksman with 32 goals and 31 goals in only 70 appearances. He also won three more England caps in 1912, scoring twice more for his country. 1913-14 was a season of consolidation in the League as this great side wound itself up for its pending assault on both Cup and League. Teddy Hodgson was the club's leading marksman on the trail to the Crystal Palace but Bert Freeman got the one that went down in history as the Clarets lifted the FA Cup for the first time. Twelve more League goals in the last season before World War One took Freeman's total to 91 in only four years. He was now the club's leading scorer of all time, having gone way past Billy Bowes' record of 79 set in 1901. Bert Freeman had perhaps reached his peak just before the war started, and, after hostilities ceased, his best years were certainly behind him. He was still a regular in the side, however, in 1919-20 and top-scored with 12 goals as the Clarets finished as runners-up to West Brom. An important piece of history was made that season when, 32 years after League Football started, Bert Freeman became the first Burnley player to score 100 League goals, in a 2-0 win at Derby on 21 February 1920. Towards the end of the season the club felt that Freeman was not the man to lead Burnley's attack in the momentous campaign to come. They signed Joe Anderson from Clydebank and in March 1920, Freeman played alongside 'Joe Andy' for the last month of the season and scored his last two goals in claret and blue. A sad thing about the triumphant campaign in 1920-21 was that Freeman played only in the first three League games, all of which were lost, and his last appearance for the club was in the 3-0 FA Cup debacle at Hull City on 19 February 1921. He joined Wigan Borough at the end of the season and played in that club's early days in the Football League, later moving to Kettering Town before retiring in 1924. Bert Freeman, a veritable goal-scoring machine, died on 11 August 1955, aged 70.

	LEAGUE		*FA CUP*		*TOTAL*	
	App	*Gls*	*App*	*Gls*	*App*	*Gls*
1910-11	2	0	0	0	2	0
1911-12	33	32	1	1	34	33
1912-13	37	31	6	5	43	36
1913-14	31	16	8	3	39	19
1914-15	32	12	3	3	35	15
1919-20	28	12	4	0	32	12
1920-21	3	0	1	0	4	0
	166	103	23	12	189	115

There was a large clearout amongst the playing staff at Turf Moor in the summer of 1987, following the infamous Orient game. Amongst the new players brought in was promising teenage centre-half Steve Gardner. Born in Teesside, Gardner was apprenticed to Manchester United but never featured in the first team there. In his first season at Burnley he missed only five games as he formed the central defence partnership with Steve Davis which was a key feature of Burnley's run to Wembley in the Sherpa Van competition. Just prior to the 1989-90 season, Gardner broke an ankle and did not get back into first-team action until February 1990. Although he re-established himself in an injury-plagued side, Gardner was released at the end of the 1989-90 season as the way was made clear for half a dozen new faces at Turf Moor. After leaving Burnley, Gardner split his time between work in the building trade and playing in senior non-League football. He had several trials with Football League clubs but, at the time of writing, had still not forced his way back into the game.

STEVE GARDNER

	LEAGUE		*FA CUP*		*FL CUP*		*OTHERS*		*TOTAL*	
	App	*Gls*	*App*	*Gls*	*App*	*Gls*	*App*	*Gls*	*App*	*Gls*
1987-88	41/1	0	1	0	3	0	10	0	55/1	0
1988-89	44	0	1	0	4	0	6	0	55	0
1989-90	8/1	0	0	0	0	0	0	0	8/1	0
	93/2	0	2	0	7	0	16	0	118/2	0

BILLY GRAY

Outside-right Billy Gray joined Burnley from Chelsea in the summer of 1953, replacing the popular Jackie Chew. Like Chew, Gray was on the small side but he had proved very effective at Stamford Bridge, winning an England 'B' cap. Thus, it was something of a coup when the Clarets secured his signature. In a successful first season he was top scorer, forming a fine partnership with Jimmy McIlroy, the right-wing pair netting 36 goals between them. After losing his place to Doug Newlands, he moved to Nottingham Forest in June 1957. In six years at the City Ground, Gray made over 200 League appearances, also helping Forest to an FA Cup Final win over Luton Town in 1959. Durham-born Gray ended his playing career at Millwall in the 1963-4 season, at the end of which he was appointed manager at The Den. He later managed Brentford and Notts County before returning to Nottingham Forest, scene of perhaps his most successful time as a player, where he became a groundsman at the City Ground.

	LEAGUE		*FA CUP*		*TOTAL*	
	App	*Gls*	*App*	*Gls*	*App*	*Gls*
1953-54	42	19	3	1	45	20
1954-55	40	8	1	0	41	8
1955-56	31	2	6	1	37	3
1956-57	7	1	0	0	7	1
	120	30	10	2	130	32

BILLY GREEN

Goalkeeper William John Green was signed in the summer of 1903 to fill the large gap that had never been adequately filled following the departure of big Jack Hillman to Manchester City in January 1902. Green was born in Gravesend in 1882 and played as an amateur for his home-town club before joining Southern League Brentford in 1901. He stayed with the Bees for two years before moving to Burnley. At 6ft tall and well-built, Green was an immediate success at Turf Moor. His confidence and safe handling inspired his defence and he missed only three League games in his first four seasons at Burnley. Ominously, the youngster who deputized for him in the third of those games, in April 1907, was 19-year-old Jerry Dawson. After the first four games of the following season, Dawson came into the side again, this time for a rather longer stay. After a brief recall in October 1908, it was back to reserve-team football for Billy Green and in December he was transferred to Bradford to strengthen a Park Avenue side newly-elected to the Football League. Right at the end of his playing career, Green saw active service in World War One. Although he survived, he suffered serious injuries and was severely disabled but continued to maintain his links with football, visiting Turf Moor frequently in the 1920s.

	LEAGUE		*FA CUP*		*TOTAL*	
	App	*Gls*	*App*	*Gls*	*App*	*Gls*
1903-04	33	0	2	0	35	0
1904-05	34	0	2	0	36	0
1905-06	37	0	1	0	38	0
1906-07	37	0	1	0	38	0
1907-08	4	0	0	0	4	0
1908-09	2	0	0	0	2	0
	147	0	6	0	153	0

In the 1990-91 season, Neil Grewcock was the longest-serving player on the Burnley staff, having been signed in the summer of 1984 from non-League club Shepshed Charterhouse. He immediately became a crowd favourite with his scintillating right-wing runs and never scored a more vital goal than the one on 9 May 1987, which helped Burnley beat Orient and maintain their Football League status. Badly injured the following season in the Northern area semi-final of the Sherpa Van Trophy competition, Grewcock missed virtually all of the following two seasons. He played only 16 times in these two campaigns before re-establishing himself in the first-team squad in 1990-91. Grewcock started his career at his home-town club as an apprentice with Leicester City. After only a handful of appearances for Leicester, he moved to Gillingham. It was from the Priestfield Stadium that he drifted into non-League football before his career was resurrected at Turf Moor. Although usually playing a more midfield role in recent matches, Grewcock still has the ability to turn defences inside-out with runs down either flank. Although released in the summer of 1991, his goal on that famous day in May 1987 will ensure that he will always be fondly remembered by Clarets fans.

NEIL GREWCOCK

	LEAGUE		*FA CUP*		*FL CUP*		*OTHERS*		*TOTAL*	
	App	*Gls*	*App*	*Gls*	*App*	*Gls*	*App*	*Gls*	*App*	*Gls*
1984-85	44/2	6	3	1	4	2	4	0	55/2	9
1985-86	36/2	7	2	0	2	0	6	3	46/2	10
1986-87	35/1	9	1	0	1	0	5	0	42/1	9
1987-88	28/4	0	1	0	4	0	7	2	40/4	2
1988-89	12/1	1	0	0	0	0	0	0	12/1	1
1989-90	4/3	2	0	0	0/1	0	2/1	0	6/5	2
1990-91	21/9	2	3	0	1	0	5	0	30/9	2
	180/22	27	10	1	12/1	2	29/1	5	231/24	35

Scotsman George Halley was the last of the FA Cup winning side to arrive at Turf Moor when he signed from Bradford in March 1913. His debut for the Clarets, of course, on 15 March 1913, was the first time that 'Halley, Boyle and Watson' appeared on the team-sheet. He was born in Cronberry, near Ayr, in 1887 and after being spotted in local junior football he signed for nearby Kilmarnock in November 1907. He came south to England to join Bradford in May 1911, spending almost two seasons at Park Avenue before leaving to join the Clarets. Although he was a regular in the side in the Cup winning season of 1913-14, he was kept out of the team the following campaign by Levy Thorpe and played only a few games during the war. In 1919-20, he was again in competition with Thorpe and occasionally had to keep his place in the team by playing at left-back. Halley was at the top of his form, however, in the Championship season to follow and caught the eye of the Scotland selectors for the match against Ireland in Belfast in February 1921. Sadly, Halley was taken ill after Burnley's match at Villa Park early in February and, not only did he lose the chance to represent his country, he missed the rest of the Championship campaign as well. He chose not to re-sign for the club at the end of the 1921-2 season and was eventually transferred to Southend United the following November. He returned to Lancashire in 1924 to join Bacup Borough as a coach before retiring from the game.

GEORGE HALLEY

	LEAGUE		*FA CUP*		*TOTAL*	
	App	*Gls*	*App*	*Gls*	*App*	*Gls*
1912-13	8	1	0	0	8	1
1913-14	33	2	8	1	41	3
1914-15	10	0	0	0	10	0
1919-20	26	0	4	0	30	0
1920-21	26	0	2	0	28	0
1921-22	34	1	2	0	36	1
	137	4	16	1	153	5

BILLY HAMILTON

Already an Irish international by the time he signed for Burnley from Queen's Park Rangers, Billy Hamilton became an instant hit with the fans. Although not the quickest of forwards from a standing start, Hamilton was a tireless campaigner who never stopped running. Perhaps best-remembered for his exploits in the 1982 World Cup, Hamilton is the last Burnley player to have competed at the very highest level. Nobody gave Northern Ireland any hope at all, but Hamilton struck a rich partnership with Gerry Armstrong and the two goals scored by the Burnley player against Austria earned him worldwide fame. Hamilton started his career at Linfield in Northern Ireland and first played in the Football League for Queen's Park Rangers. After only nine games at Loftus Road he moved to Burnley in November 1979, scoring the first of his 58 goals in the famous Boxing Day win over Newcastle United. In his second season, Hamilton, who played 200 times for Burnley, formed a glorious partnership with Steve Taylor as the Irish striker became the most recent player to boast 50 goals for the Clarets. In his final four seasons he was a virtual ever-present, missing only nine games in those four campaigns. He joined Oxford United in time to help the club reach the First Division for the first time, but his career was curtailed by a serious injury. Hamilton teamed up with Brian Flynn for a while at Limerick where Hamilton was manager and Flynn player-coach. Hamilton is now manager of Irish League side Distillery.

	LEAGUE		*FA CUP*		*FL CUP*		*OTHERS*		*TOTAL*	
	App	*Gls*	*App*	*Gls*	*App*	*Gls*	*App*	*Gls*	*App*	*Gls*
1979-80	25	7	2	0	0	0	0	0	27	7
1980-81	46	9	3	1	4	0	3	0	56	10
1981-82	44	11	6	4	2	1	3	3	55	19
1982-83	39	13	7	2	8	4	3	1	57	20
1983-84	46	18	5	3	2	0	4	0	57	21
	200	58	23	10	16	5	13	4	252	77

PETER HAMPTON

Oldham-born Peter Hampton was brought up in the North-East and played for Durham County schoolboys as well as becoming an English Youth international. Apprenticed to Leeds United, he played more than 60 times in the Elland Road defence before being sold to Stoke City in August 1980 for £175,000. Four years later he was given a free transfer and came to Burnley where he played more than 100 games, including a vital part in the 'Orient Game'. After three seasons with Burnley, the momentous 2-1 win over Orient being the last game of his last season, he was another victim of the 1987 summer clearout. Hampton went to Rochdale but before the end of the year was on the move again, this time to Carlisle United as a player-physiotherapist. Despite calling time on his playing days, Hampton is still involved in the physiotherapy and managerial duties at Brunton Park. A family affection for the game is reflected by the fact that his father was president of Crook Town FC.

	LEAGUE		*FA CUP*		*FL CUP*		*OTHERS*		*TOTAL*	
	App	*Gls*	*App*	*Gls*	*App*	*Gls*	*App*	*Gls*	*App*	*Gls*
1984-85	44/1	1	3	0	4	0	5	0	56/1	1
1985-86	39/1	1	0	0	2	0	6	1	47/1	2
1986-87	33	0	1	0	2	0	3	0	39	0
	116/2	2	4	0	8	0	14	1	142/2	3

The penultimate game of the 1972-3 Second Division championship season saw the first-team debut, as a substitute, of Ray Hankin. Over the next three seasons the England Youth and Under-23 player was to appear over 100 times for Burnley and average one goal in every three games. The substitute appearance was as a replacement for Frank Casper and during his time with the Clarets, Hankin was involved in an almost continuous fight for shirts with Casper and Paul Fletcher. Burnley were back in the Second Division by season 1976-7 and Hankin was one of a number of players to leave the club. More than 80 games and over 30 goals for Leeds United followed and then Hankin became one of a growing number of English players to try his luck in North America. After a spell with the Vancouver Whitecaps, Hankin became a non-contract player with Arsenal but was unable to make the grade and went to Middlesbrough. After a year at Ayresome Park he was transferred to Peterborough United, his League career finishing with the Posh. Hankin has since returned to his native North-East and is involved in senior non-League football there.

RAY HANKIN

	LEAGUE		*FA CUP*		*FL CUP*		*OTHERS*		*TOTAL*	
	App	*Gls*	*App*	*Gls*	*App*	*Gls*	*App*	*Gls*	*App*	*Gls*
1972-73	0/1	0	0	0	0	0	0	0	0/1	0
1973-74	33/1	8	3	1	3	2	6	4	45/1	15
1974-75	37	14	1	0	3	1	0	0	41	15
1975-76	34	13	1	0	5	1	0	0	40	14
1976-77	6	2	0	0	1	0	3	0	10	2
	110/2	37	5	1	12	4	9	4	136/2	46

Gordon 'Bomber' Harris was a stocky, powerfully-built 'engine-room' type of player who was deceptively quick. He was renowned at Turf Moor for the cannonball shots that regularly detonated from his left foot, possessing arguably the hardest shot of any Burnley player. He was born in Worksop in 1940 and was playing for a colliery team at nearby Firbeck when Burnley spotted him and brought him to Turf Moor in January 1958. In his first two years he played only occasionally but established himself in 1961 after Brian Pilkington had left for Bolton Wanderers. His excellent ball control and his ability to take defenders on and beat them brought him England Under-23 and Football League honours before he won his only full international cap, against Poland in 1966. He was a hard man both on and off the field and occasionally there were reports of altercations with other players in training, whilst his quick temper often brought him into conflict with referees. Harris joined Sunderland for a reported £70,000 fee in 1968 going on to play over 120 League games on Wearside before retiring in 1971. He later moved back to his home area, near Worksop and worked in the coal industry as a driver.

GORDON HARRIS

	LEAGUE		*FA CUP*		*FL CUP*		*OTHERS*		*TOTAL*	
	App	*Gls*	*App*	*Gls*	*App*	*Gls*	*App*	*Gls*	*App*	*Gls*
1958-59	2	1	0	0	0	0	0	0	2	1
1959-60	2	0	0	0	0	0	0	0	2	0
1960-61	21	10	4	0	5	3	1	1	31	14
1961-62	34	14	8	3	0	0	0	0	42	17
1962-63	40	7	3	1	0	0	0	0	43	8
1963-64	32	10	5	0	0	0	0	0	37	10
1964-65	27	2	5	0	0	0	0	0	32	2
1965-66	39	7	3	1	4	1	0	0	46	9
1966-67	41	13	2	0	2	0	8	1	53	14
1967-68	20	5	0	0	5	1	0	0	25	6
	258	69	30	5	16	5	9	2	313	81

JACK HAYS

Born in Ashington in 1918, Christopher Jack Hays began his Football League career with Bradford, from whom he joined the Clarets in 1939. He never got the chance to embark upon his League career at Turf Moor because war broke out within a matter of weeks. He made his debut in the promotion season 1946-7 but with Jack Chew in the right-wing position, Hays was often in the shadow of the brilliant but unpredictable amateur Peter Kippax on the left flank. Kippax played in all the FA Cup games that season but the following campaign, Hays became the regular left winger, operating outside Harry Potts and subsequently Jimmy McIlroy. The arrival of Billy Elliott in 1951 meant the end of Jack Hays' Burnley career and in September that year he was transferred to Bury. In one season at Gigg Lane he scored twice in 27 League matches before retiring in 1952. Jack Hays was a workmanlike Football League professional who, like many others, lost his best years because of the war. He died on 2 February 1983, aged 64.

	LEAGUE		*FA CUP*		*TOTAL*	
	App	*Gls*	*App*	*Gls*	*App*	*Gls*
1945-46	0	0	2	0	2	0
1946-47	16	4	0	0	16	4
1947-48	37	3	1	0	38	3
1948-49	30	2	3	0	33	2
1949-50	36	2	1	1	37	3
1950-51	27	1	1	0	28	1
	146	12	8	1	154	13

JACK HILL

John Hendry Hill was the classic 'stopper' centre-half who enjoyed a fine reputation as a hard but fair player in the 1920s. With his red hair and standing 6ft 3in tall and at over 13st, he certainly looked the part. He was born in Hetton le Hole in 1897 and joined Plymouth Argyle in 1920 from his first club, Durham City. He captained Argyle to a mid-table position in 1921 and then twice to runners-up spot in the Third Division South as the Pilgrims went on seemingly forever destined to be bridesmaids. Burnley signed him in May 1923, for a then club record fee of £6,000. He filled the yawning gap that had been left by the departed Tommy Boyle and, like Boyle, he was a natural captain, a position he soon assumed. He won his first England cap in 1925 and gained seven more in his five years at Turf Moor, including one as captain, in a game staged at Burnley in November 1927. England were beaten 2-1 by Wales with Hill putting through his own goal. He was transferred to Newcastle United in October 1928 and was soon appointed captain as the Magpies sought to consolidate during the lean years following their Championship triumph in 1927. He won three more England caps in his three years at St James' Park. Success eluded the Geordies, however, and Hill was allowed to leave, joining Bradford City in June 1931. He left for Hull City after less than six months and, after ending his playing days at Anlaby Road, he managed the Tigers from 1934 to 1936, and continued scouting for the club for many years. Jack Hill spent his twilight years in Scotland and died in April 1972, aged 75.

	LEAGUE		*FA CUP*		*TOTAL*	
	App	*Gls*	*App*	*Gls*	*App*	*Gls*
1923-24	39	2	7	0	46	2
1924-25	25	3	1	0	26	3
1925-26	37	3	2	0	39	3
1926-27	35	1	3	0	38	1
1927-28	37	4	1	0	38	4
1928-29	11	0	0	0	11	0
	184	13	14	0	198	13

James Hill was Burnley's first consistent goalscorer over a number of seasons. Operating mainly at outside-left but equally at home in any forward position, he developed a reputation as a tricky winger with an abundance of skill and a powerful shot. Born in Paisley, Hill was transferred to Burnley from his only previous club, St Mirren, at Christmas 1889. He went straight into the League side, immediately forming an understanding with Alec Stewart and Claude Lambie as the three newcomers helped to drag the club off the bottom of the League with an unbeaten last month of the season. Jimmy Hill was the first Burnley player to reach 150 League appearances but in January 1897, he moved to Stoke where he was to give sterling service for a number of years. He ended his playing career in the early 1900s with New Brighton and Wellingborough.

JAMES HILL

	LEAGUE		*FA CUP*		*TOTAL*	
	App	*Gls*	*App*	*Gls*	*App*	*Gls*
1889-90	8	3	0	0	8	3
1890-91	16	3	2	1	18	4
1891-92	21	5	2	3	23	8
1892-93	27	6	2	1	29	7
1893-94	25	11	1	0	26	11
1894-95	20	3	1	0	21	3
1895-96	20	4	3	0	23	4
1896-97	14	1	0	0	14	1
	151	36	11	5	162	41

One of the great characters in the history of Burnley FC, Jack Hillman was also one of the most notorious. He was banned for a complete season in 1900 after attempting to bribe Nottingham Forest players to 'throw' the last match of the season to enable Burnley to avoid relegation. He was born in Tavistock, Devon, in 1870, but his family moved to Burnley when he was a child. He was spotted playing junior football and played his first game for Burnley Reserves in 1890, eventually taking over in the first team from Archibald Kaye. After four seasons at Turf Moor, Hillman was transferred to Everton, then, after a short spell with Dundee he returned to Burnley in March 1898. At over 6ft tall and 16st, 'The Burly One' drew the attention of the England selectors, winning his only international cap in the 13-2 win against Ireland at Sunderland in 1899. After the bribery scandal, Hillman moved to Manchester City in 1902, where he won a Second Division championship medal in 1903 and and FA Cup winners' medal in 1904. He ended his playing career with Millwall in 1907 before returning to Turf Moor yet again, where he became reserve-team trainer, then first-team trainer, continuing his association with the club into the mid-1920s. After his retirement from the game, big Jack continued to live in Burnley, where he ran a corner shop for a number of years. He died on 1 August 1955, aged 84.

JACK HILLMAN

	LEAGUE		*FA CUP*		*OTHERS*		*TOTAL*	
	App	*Gls*	*App*	*Gls*	*App*	*Gls*	*App*	*Gls*
1891-92	26	0	2	0	0	0	28	0
1892-93	28	0	2	0	0	0	30	0
1893-94	27	0	1	0	0	0	28	0
1894-95	19	0	0	0	0	0	19	0
1897-98	5	0	0	0	4	0	9	0
1898-99	19	0	1	0	0	0	20	0
1899-1900	31	0	1	0	0	0	32	0
1900-01	0	0	0	0	0	0	0	0
1901-02	20	0	2	0	0	0	22	0
	175	0	9	0	4	0	188	0

KEVIN HIRD

A local player who seemed to have escaped the Burnley net, Kevin Hird signed as a schoolboy for nearby Blackburn Rovers in 1973. After more than 120 appearances for the Ewood Park club, Hird became the most expensive full-back in the game when transferred to Leeds United for £357,000 in March 1979. Around 200 League appearances followed before Hird was transferred to Burnley, the club he had always supported, in August 1984. By then he was a midfielder and in each of his two seasons was second-highest scorer behind Wayne Biggins. The last Burnley player to score a Football League hat-trick, Hird netted three times (one penalty) in a 7-0 home win against Rotherham United in February 1985. Earlier the same season he had scored another hat-trick, those three coming in a 9-0 FA Cup triumph over Penrith. On leaving Turf Moor he was connected with non-League club Colne Dynamoes. A keen rock musician, Hird is now trying to put something back into the game via a soccer skills coaching school run in his home town of Colne.

	LEAGUE		*FA CUP*		*FL CUP*		*OTHERS*		*TOTAL*	
	App	*Gls*	*App*	*Gls*	*App*	*Gls*	*App*	*Gls*	*App*	*Gls*
1984-85	44	16	3	4	4	1	7	2	58	23
1985-86	39	7	2	0	2	1	3/1	0	46/1	8
	83	23	5	4	6	2	10/1	2	104/1	31

TEDDY HODGSON

Edward 'Teddy' Hodgson was a vital cog in the Burnley footballing machine that won the FA Cup in 1914. When the guns fell silent at the end of the war, however, Hodgson never played again and tragically died in 1919, aged only 33. Teddy Hodgson joined Burnley from his home-town club, Chorley, in September 1911 and made his first-team debut at Barnsley on the same day as Tommy Boyle. He soon established himself as a scheming inside-forward who was both a goalmaker and a goalscorer. In his first two seasons he averaged almost a goal every other game as well as prompting the phenomenal scoring prowess of Bert Freeman. In 1913-14 he was the top scorer during the run to the Crystal Palace with five goals including a hat-trick in the second round against Derby. In the Final he played a vital part in the winning goal, steering Billy Nesbitt's cross to Freeman, who tucked it safely away. Hodgson joined the Army in 1916 and was in Germany when hostilities ended. Having been wounded, his condition deteriorated and he was transferred to hospital back in England, where he died on 4 August 1919. Always a gentleman, Teddy Hodgson had the respect of fellow players, directors and fans alike and many people felt a personal friend had been lost. His one representative honour came for the Football League against the Scottish League in March 1914, another case of rich talent cruelly wasted by the ravages of war.

	LEAGUE		*FA CUP*		*TOTAL*	
	App	*Gls*	*App*	*Gls*	*App*	*Gls*
1911-12	20	7	0	0	20	7
1912-13	32	15	6	3	38	18
1913-14	32	12	8	5	40	17
1914-15	36	19	3	1	39	20
	120	53	17	9	137	62

'We played football as Jimmy Hogan taught us. When our soccer history is written, his name should be written in gold letters'. So said Gustave Sebez, coach of the Hungarian side that demolished England twice in six months in 1953 and 1954. Jimmy Hogan was born in Nelson in 1882, the family coming to live in Burnley when young Hogan was eight years old. He was an outstanding schoolboy footballer, a cultured inside-forward, going on to play for Burnley Belvedere before signing as a professional for Nelson. After a short spell at Rochdale he was transferred to Burnley in September 1903. After two seasons as a regular in the side he fell into dispute with the club and moved to Fulham in October 1905, going on to play for Swindon and Bolton. He went abroad in 1910 to take up a coaching appointment with the Dutch FA and then to a similar position in Austria, arriving in Vienna just a month before war was declared. He was interned for a time but in 1919 was appointed as the Hungarian national coach and spent the 1920s and early '30s in various coaching positions all over the European continent. He returned to management in England in 1934, first at Fulham, then at Aston Villa, guiding Villa to the Second Division championship in 1938. After the war he coached at Glasgow Celtic before going out to Hungary once more, advising the crack Budapest side, Honved, and of course being instrumental in England's infamous downfall in 1953. Jimmy Hogan spent 66 years in football as player, manager, coach and as a scout. It was said of him that he was better-known in the European game than in his own country, but he was proud of his Lancashire origins. 'I am a product of Burnley rec football,' he said simply, 'If you can control a ball wearing clogs, you can really play the game.' After a long illness in hospital in Burnley, Jimmy Hogan, the Grand Old Man of football, passed away on 30 January 1974, aged 94.

	LEAGUE		*FA CUP*		*TOTAL*	
	App	*Gls*	*App*	*Gls*	*App*	*Gls*
1903-04	25	5	0	0	25	5
1904-05	25	7	2	0	27	7
	50	12	2	0	52	12

JIMMY HOGAN

Born in Bolton in 1928, Bill Holden, a traditional centre-forward, was signed in November 1949 after playing for Everton as an amateur. He spent a year in the Reserves but then broke into the first team following the departure of Jack Billingham and Ray Harrison. He was a hard-working player and a consistent scorer in his five years in the League side, his abilities being acknowledged with an England 'B' cap against Scotland in 1953. Holden was never seriously challenged as leader of Burnley's attack until newcomer Peter McKay was preferred to him early in the 1955-6 season. McKay was an instant success and, after requesting a transfer, Holden moved to Sunderland in December 1955. After less than a year on Wearside, he joined Stockport County in October 1956 and in his stay at Edgeley Park scored nearly 40 goals in less than 90 games. He was transferred to Bury in March 1959 and, at the end of his first full season at Gigg Lane, won a Third Division championship medal. After a season at Halifax Town, Bill Holden retired from the game in 1963. He died some years ago.

	LEAGUE		*FA CUP*		*TOTAL*	
	App	*Gls*	*App*	*Gls*	*App*	*Gls*
1950-51	35	12	0	0	35	12
1951-52	31	12	4	1	35	13
1952-53	42	22	4	2	46	24
1953-54	39	14	3	1	42	15
1954-55	38	15	1	0	39	15
1955-56	2	0	0	0	2	0
	187	75	12	4	199	79

BILL HOLDEN

TOMMY HUTCHISON

Despite being one of the best-known players in the game and completing two ever-present seasons with the Clarets, Tommy Hutchison was never a favourite with the Burnley crowd. Hutchison had 17 Scottish caps and around 500 Football League appearances to his credit when he came to Turf Moor. But he was signed by John Bond and was given the club captaincy in place of Martin Dobson, and the crowd never forgave him for it. At Burnley he never gave less than 100 per cent to his midfield endeavours and was easily the pick of the Bond signings. Hutchison started his career at Alloa Athletic before chalking-up over 160 appearances with Blackpool and more than 300 with Coventry City. In his time with Manchester City he had the unenviable distinction of scoring at both ends during the 1981 FA Cup Final, which Spurs eventually won after a replay. He joined Burnley after a spell in Hong Kong. He followed John Bond to Swansea and in season 1989-90 was the oldest player to feature in a European tie, playing for City in a Cup-winners' Cup tie at the age of 42. The following season his contribution to the game was recognized in the form of a PFA merit award. His appearances for Swansea have taken him past the 800 Football League matches mark.

	LEAGUE		*FA CUP*		*FL CUP*		*OTHERS*		*TOTAL*	
	App	*Gls*	*App*	*Gls*	*App*	*Gls*	*App*	*Gls*	*App*	*Gls*
1983-84	46	4	5	0	2	0	6	0	59	4
1984-85	46	0	3	0	4	0	4	1	57	1
	92	4	8	0	6	0	10	1	116	5

BILLY INGHAM

As Burnley won the Second Division championship in 1972-3, several new players were already looming on the horizon. Billy Ingham started to make his mark in those Second Division days and as a utility player found himself in the number-12 shirt on numerous occasions, more, in fact, than any other Burnley player. Listed in many publications as a forward, the Stakeford-born Ingham played a great deal as both a midfielder and a full-back in his 181 League appearances for Burnley. Ingham, who came through the Turf Moor apprentice ranks, earned the nickname 'Ginger Pelé' after a goal against Chelsea in 1977 when the diminutive player won the battle on the edge of the area to half-volley the ball home. That was the most memorable of 22 goals he scored for Burnley before leaving for Bradford City. A short career at Valley Parade was followed by a spell in non-League football, but Ingham remains a familiar face in Burnley as a driver with the local 'bus company.

	LEAGUE		*FA CUP*		*FL CUP*		*OTHERS*		*TOTAL*	
	App	*Gls*	*App*	*Gls*	*App*	*Gls*	*App*	*Gls*	*App*	*Gls*
1971-72	7/2	0	0	0	0	0	0	0	7/2	0
1972-73	11/7	4	1/1	0	0	0	2	0	14/8	4
1973-74	16/8	2	2/1	0	1	0	7	0	26/9	2
1974-75	33/2	1	1	0	2	1	0	0	36/2	2
1975-76	14/6	0	1	0	0/1	0	0	0	15/7	0
1976-77	24/3	2	2	0	1	0	2	1	29/3	3
1977-78	32/1	4	2	0	3	1	3	1	40/1	6
1978-79	37	9	4	1	3	1	8	2	52	13
1979-80	7/1	0	0	0	2	0	3	1	12/1	1
1980-81	0	0	0	0	0	0	1	0	1	0
	181/30	22	13/2	1	12/1	3	26	5	232/33	31

A prolific scorer throughout his Football League career, Willie Irvine's most productive period for finding the net was at Turf Moor and his ratio of better than two goals every three games in all matches stands comparison with the best. He was born in Carrickfergus in 1943, joining Burnley as a junior in 1960. The strength and depth of attacking players at Turf Moor meant he had to wait to make his first-team debut. When he did, it was a sign of things to come as he scored at Arsenal in a 3-2 win, then, three days later, in the last match of the 1962-3 season, scored a hat-trick in a 3-1 victory over Birmingham City at Turf Moor. Although he won the first of many Irish caps in 1963, Andy Lochhead and Jimmy Robson kept Irvine out of the Burnley first team until Robson inevitably made way for him in 1964. In the three seasons from 1964-5, Irvine and Lochhead developed a marvellous partnership and hit 118 League goals between them. The total included 29 from the Irishman in 1965-6, bettered only by legends Bert Freeman and George Beel and never remotely challenged in the 25 years since. After breaking his leg in an FA Cup tie at Everton in January 1967, he was never quite the same player and moved to Preston in March 1968, going on to play for Brighton and Halifax before retiring in 1973. After building up a thriving DIY business in Burnley he now helps to run the very successful Barrowford Celtic as the manager of one of the boys' teams. He enjoys the challenge of grooming potential footballers of tomorrow. With his track record, he has a lot to offer.

	LEAGUE		*FA CUP*		*FL CUP*		*OTHERS*		*TOTAL*	
	App	*Gls*	*App*	*Gls*	*App*	*Gls*	*App*	*Gls*	*App*	*Gls*
1962-63	2	4	0	0	0	0	0	0	2	4
1963-64	7	4	0	0	0	0	0	0	7	4
1964-65	33	22	4	3	0	0	0	0	37	25
1965-66	42	29	3	5	4	3	0	0	49	37
1966-67	23	13	2	1	0	0	3	2	28	16
1967-68	17/2	6	0/1	0	4/1	5	0	0	21/4	11
	124/2	78	9/1	9	8/1	8	3	2	144/4	97

WILLIE IRVINE

Joe Jakub is the last playing link with Burnley's First Division days, having made his Clarets debut in the very last match of the 1975-6 season in his first spell with the club. Born in Falkirk in 1956, Jakub, of Polish ancestry and with a given name of 'Yanek', joined Burnley as an apprentice in December 1973. Essentially a midfield player, Jakub was versatile enough to cover at left-back for Ian Brennan before lack of opportunity led to his move to Bury in 1980. He was a virtual ever-present in his six years at Gigg Lane and made over 260 League appearances for the Shakers. At Bury he was part of a large ex-Burnley contingent which included manager Martin Dobson and assistant manager Frank Casper. He went to play in Holland midway through the 1986-7 season, spending a year and a half with the AZ67 club before returning to England, joining Chester City in the summer of 1988. His spell at Sealand Road included an impressive FA Cup performance at Turf Moor in November 1988, Chester winning 2-0. He joined the Clarets in the close season of 1989 and has played in every match — League and Cup — since his return. A busy, all-action player, he has never given less than 100 per cent effort throughout his career.

	LEAGUE		*FA CUP*		*FL CUP*		*OTHERS**		*TOTAL*	
	App	*Gls*	*App*	*Gls*	*App*	*Gls*	App	Gls	*App*	*Gls*
1975-76	1	0	0	0	0	0	0	0	1	0
1976-77	5	0	0	0	0	0	0	0	5	0
1977-78	0	0	0	0	0	0	0	0	0	0
1978-79	13	0	0	0	0	0	0	0	13	0
1979-80	23	0	0	0	2	0	1	0	26	0
1989-90	46	5	6	0	2	0	5	0	59	5
1990-91	46	3	3	0	4	0	12	1	65	4
	134	8	9	0	8	0	18	1	169	9

* Includes 1990-91 Play-off games.

JOE JAKUB

Without doubt the most exciting Burnley player of the last two decades, Leighton James was a winger of great speed and skill, and was never afraid to go for goal. The magical Welshman graced a club with a long tradition of fine wing play on three separate occasions, one of a very select band to return to the club twice. Although he spent much of his third spell as either a sweeper or a central defender, James, one of a number of international players at Turf Moor in the early 1970s, first signed for Burnley in February 1970 as a 17-year-old apprentice. He made his debut as Burnley were relegated from the First Division in season 1970-71 and from 1971 to 1974 hardly ever missed a game, playing in all the matches during the 1972-3 Second Division title winning campaign. An article in the *Sunday Express* saw James leave Turf Moor for the first time. In it the Welsh International stated that the only other club he wanted to play for was Derby County and within a fortnight Dave Mackay had paid over £300,000 for his services. In two seasons with the Rams, James never really settled and was transferred to Queen's Park Rangers. But within a year of his move to Loftus Road, James was on the move again, this time back to Turf Moor. He stayed with Burnley for almost another two seasons and played in just under another 80 games before transferring to Swansea and helping John Toshack take City into the First Division for the first time in their history. From there, James went to Sunderland, Bury and Newport County before again signing for the Clarets. In the 1986-7 season, during which Football League life was almost pronounced extinct at Turf Moor, James played 42 games and was one of the select few to be offered a contract for the following season. Having virtually dropped out of the League in 1987, Burnley fought back to narrowly miss a place in the play-offs and end up as runners-up in the Sherpa Van Trophy. James was a second-half substitute in that game and his 35-year-old legs remembered something about the Wembley turf — he had played there eight times for Wales — as for half an hour or so he threatened to turn the game upside down and give Burnley's long suffering fans something to really cheer about. A coach for a while at Turf Moor, James drifted into non-League football as player-manager with Burnley Bank Hall before his Football League career was rekindled by Bradford City, where he is in charge of the reserves and youth team. Born in Llwchyr, near Newport, South Wales, James was a glowing example of Burnley's scouting and youth policy at its very best. He played on 54 occasions with his country and scored ten international goals. Of his caps, 23 were won while he was a Burnley player. Among the exclusive band of players with more than 50 Burnley goals to their credit, James lost a lot of friends on the Turf Moor terraces following the manner of his sale to Derby County, but won many of them back through his endeavours later in his career. Burnley has been his home virtually throughout his career and James is still watched by crowds of spectators, as a batsman with the town's cricket club.

LEIGHTON JAMES

	LEAGUE		*FA CUP*		*FL CUP*		*OTHERS*		*TOTAL*	
	App	*Gls*	*App*	*Gls*	*App*	*Gls*	*App*	*Gls*	*App*	*Gls*
1970-71	3/1	0	1	0	0	0	0	0	4/1	0
1971-72	36	8	1	0	3	1	0	0	40	9
1972-73	42	10	2	0	1	0	2	1	47	11
1973-74	40	7	5	1	3	4	8	3	56	15
1974-75	42	16	1	0	3	1	0	0	46	17
1975-76	17	3	0	0	4	0	0	0	21	3
1978-79	37	3	4	1	1	0	6	1	48	5
1979-80	39	6	1	0	2	0	3	0	45	6
1986-87	42	10	1	0	2	2	5	0	50	12
1987-88	19	0	1	0	2	0	2/1	0	24/1	0
1988-89	14/4	3	0	0	1	0	1	0	16/4	3
	331/5	66	17	2	22	8	27/1	5	397/6	81

One of Burnley's hard men of the very earliest days of League football, the commanding Jack Keenan was widely regarded as one of the finest half-backs of his day. Born in Clitheroe of Irish extractions in 1864, Keenan arrived at Turf Moor from his home-town club in the mid-1880s before the advent of the Football League, quickly establishing himself in a team that consisted almost entirely of Scots. He played for his county on 12 occasions, captaining the side three times and was on the fringe of international honours. In 1888 he received a cable asking him to join the England party at Preston for the journey to Glasgow for the Scotland v England match on 17 March. He was not selected, however, and watched as England demolished the Scots 5-0. He was a virtual ever-present during the first three years of League football and was a tower of strength as Burnley defeated Blackburn Rovers 2-0 at Accrington in April 1890 to win the Lancashire Cup for the first time, the club's first honour of any description. He retired in 1893 to work in a local brewery in his adopted town and, after a year's illness, died on 16 March 1906 aged only 42.

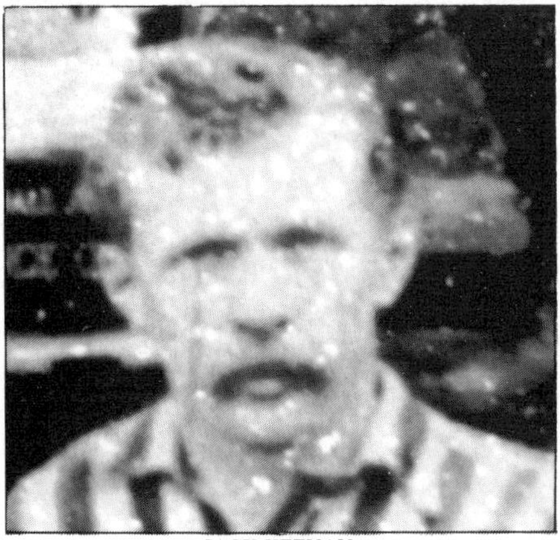

JACK KEENAN

	LEAGUE		*FA CUP*		*TOTAL*	
	App	*Gls*	*App*	*Gls*	*App*	*Gls*
1886-87	0	0	2	0	2	0
1887-88	0	0	1	0	1	0
1888-89	20	0	2	0	22	0
1889-90	18	0	1	0	19	0
1890-91	18	0	2	0	20	0
1891-92	9	0	2	0	11	0
1892-93	3	0	0	0	3	0
	68	0	10	0	78	0

One of the most naturally gifted players the game has ever seen, Bob Kelly ranks alongside Jimmy McIlroy as the greatest-ever Claret. Which of them would get the vote over the other we will never know but, imagine, what an inside-forward combination they would have made! Robert Kelly was born in Ashton-in-Makerfield near Wigan on 16 November 1894 and started his working life as a coalminer, playing part-time football first of all as a full-back with Ashton Central. He joined Earlestown in the Liverpool County Combination, then went to St Helens Town in the Lancashire Combination in September 1913. Kelly's reputation had gone before him and even at this stage people were nodding knowingly and comparing him favourably with the legendary Charlie Buchan. It was said that every game he played for St Helens Town he was watched by scouts from League clubs. It was only a matter of time before somebody stepped in, when they did it was Burnley in November 1913. A fee of £275, a record for a Lancashire Combination player, was paid to St Helens Town and Bob Kelly was on his way. He made his League debut on 15 November 1913, scoring one of the goals in a 4-0 win against Aston Villa at Turf Moor. His performance was described as exceptional but such was the strength in depth at Turf Moor that he failed to command a regular place in the League side that season, and the team went on to triumph in the FA Cup without him. The following season it was a different story and Kelly's mercurial talents were not to be denied. He established an early understanding with Bert Freeman and Teddy Hodgson and the trio scored 41 of Burnley's 61 League goals as the Clarets finished fourth, only three points from the title. After the war, Kelly carried on where he had left off and his brilliant individualism helped the Clarets to runners-up spot in the First Division in 1919-20 and also attracted the attention of the international selectors. He made his first representative appearance, in March 1920, scoring in a 4-0 victory for the Football League against the Scottish League in Glasgow. On 10 April 1920 he won his first England cap, against Scotland at Sheffield. He commanded centre stage, scoring twice as England triumphed 5-4 in a classic match. Season 1920-21, of course, saw many individual careers peak at the same time. Along with Tommy Boyle, however, Bob Kelly was the major influence on that great side and his sheer genius in ball control, his ability to avoid the fiercest of tackles and his shooting power contributed greatly to the Clarets' success. Third position in 1922 was followed by a decline in Burnley's fortunes and in December 1925, Bob Kelly was transferred to Sunderland for £6,500. Burnley were bottom of the First Division at the time and amidst an air of sporting gloom in the town, the local newspaper was moved to write categorically that his like would never be seen at Turf Moor again. He moved from Roker Park to Huddersfield Town in February 1927 as the Terriers tried to consolidate their earlier greatness. Two runners-up positions were followed by a period of mediocrity, however, and after over 200 first-team appearances Kelly was transferred to Preston in the summer of 1932. In the twilight of his career but still active, Kelly went to Carlisle United as player-manager in 1935. After only one season he joined Stockport County, where he managed the Cheshire side to the Third Division North title in 1936-7. Relegation followed immediately, however, and Bob Kelly left Stockport and football for good. He became a publican and was in business in the Blackpool area for many years until he died on 22 September 1969, aged 74. Bob Kelly won 14 caps altogether for England, 12 of them whilst at Turf Moor, and can rightfully take his place amongst the truly great players to have worn the claret and blue.

	LEAGUE		*FA CUP*		*OTHERS*		*TOTAL*	
	App	*Gls*	*App*	*Gls*	*App*	*Gls*	*App*	*Gls*
1913-14	7	1	0	0	0	0	7	1
1914-15	27	10	3	2	0	0	30	12
1919-20	38	9	4	1	0	0	42	10
1920-21	37	20	3	3	0	0	40	23
1921-22	40	16	2	1	1	0	43	17
1922-23	40	17	1	0	0	0	41	17
1923-24	37	8	7	2	0	0	44	10
1924-25	24	3	1	0	0	0	35	3
1925-26	17	4	0	0	0	0	17	4
	277	88	21	9	1	0	299	97

BOB KELLY

STEVE KINDON

Several key players came out of the FA Youth Cup run in 1967-8, when the prestigious trophy was won for the only time by Burnley. The player to perhaps, receive the highest acclaim, both at the time and in the years since, was Steve Kindon. Already a full-time professional by the time the Youth Cup was landed, Kindon was described in the local Press as 'bounding down the wing like a young kangaroo'. He was immediately nicknamed 'Skippy' by the Burnley fans, and the name has stuck ever since. Born in Warrington, Kindon attended a rugby-playing school and it was there that he developed his tremendous speed. He signed as an apprentice on the same June 1967 day that Frank Casper joined the club from Rotherham United. Within six months a full-time contract had been signed and Kindon made his debut in a 5-0 defeat at Upton Park in 1968-9. An ever-present in the following season, Kindon eventually lost his place to a combination of Leighton James and Eric Probert. Sold to Wolves in July 1972, Kindon tormented the Clarets on a couple of occasions whilst with the Molineux club. He won a Second Division championship medal with Wolves before returning to Turf Moor in November 1977. He stayed at Burnley for just over two years before being transferred to Huddersfield Town in December 1979. His move to Leeds Road came in the middle of a Fourth Division championship season, but shortly afterwards he sustained a serious leg injury and had to retire from the game. He was commercial manager at Huddersfield before becoming the general manager of a travel agency and then the sales manager of an import-export company. The former Schoolboy international was a naturally talented winger who scored over 100 League goals in his 350 games.

	LEAGUE		*FA CUP*		*FL CUP*		*OTHERS*		*TOTAL*	
	App	*Gls*	*App*	*Gls*	*App*	*Gls*	*App*	*Gls*	*App*	*Gls*
1968-69	16	4	0/1	0	5	1	0	0	21/1	5
1969-70	42	17	3	0	5	1	0	0	50	18
1970-71	29	3	0	0	1	0	1	1	31	4
1971-72	15/7	4	1	0	0/1	0	0	0	16/8	4
1977-78	27	12	2	1	0	0	0	0	29	13
1978-79	37/1	3	4	1	2	0	9	6	52/1	10
1979-80	9/2	3	0	0	1/1	0	3	1	13/3	4
	175/10	46	10/1	2	14/2	2	13	8	212/13	58

CLAUDE LAMBIE

'Lambie the leap' came to Burnley from Glasgow Thistle in January 1890 and became something of a legend at Turf Moor, even though he made only 29 League appearances over a period of four seasons. Born in a tough district of Glasgow in 1868, he soon established himself as a natural footballer and becoming a Scottish junior international in his early teens. He took the road south to pursue professionally the career he knew best and, at the end of a terrible season for Burnley, scored a hat-trick in his third game, a 7-0 victory against Bolton on 1 March 1890. He led the attack in the famous Lancashire Cup victory over Blackburn Rovers in April 1890. Lambie was skilful and very strong on the ball and, as his nickname suggests, was phenomenally good in the air, having the ability to 'hang', then time his bullet-like headers to perfection. He left Burnley to play for Clyde in the 1891-2 season and then joined the Highland Light Infantry. It was whilst he was on leave from his regiment that he played his final League games for the Clarets. In December 1892 his welcome in the town was rapturous but his stay was short-lived, only four games, none of them won, and no goals. He returned to Scotland and then left for active service in South Africa. Sadly, he next came to the public's attention when a dead body found on the railway line at King's Norton, Birmingham, in July 1921 was identified as Claude Lambie, a real footballing character who was no more.

	LEAGUE		*FA CUP*		*TOTAL*	
	App	*Gls*	*App*	*Gls*	*App*	*Gls*
1889-90	7	5	0	0	7	5
1890-91	18	16	2	1	20	17
1892-93	4	0	0	0	4	0
	29	21	2	1	31	22

Alexander Lang came to Burnley from Padiham in 1885 and was one of the club's regular full-backs, operating on the left or right side, as well as being the club captain, when League football came to Turf Moor in 1888. He was born at Bridge of Weir, near Paisley, in 1864 and came south of the border to join Padiham as a 20-year-old in 1884. He brought with him a reputation as a versatile player but it was as a hard-tackling defender that he made his name. He missed only eight League games in the first seasons of League football and was the first Burnley player to complete 100 games for the club, in March 1893. The only two goals of his League career came in the previous season and the second was the club's first-ever from a penalty-kick, in a 3-2 win against West Brom on 28 November 1891. The 'keeper Lang beat that day was Joe Reader, later to play for England. He played his last League game in March 1895 and became a publican in Burnley, although he later resumed his playing career, assisting Nelson to the Lancashire League championship. Sadly, he sustained fatal injuries in an accident at his home and died on 9 November 1901, aged only 37.

SANDY LANG

	LEAGUE		*FA CUP*		*TOTAL*	
	App	*Gls*	*App*	*Gls*	*App*	*Gls*
1886-87	0	0	0	0	0	0
1887-88	0	0	2	0	2	0
1888-89	21	0	2	1	23	1
1889-90	21	0	1	0	22	0
1890-91	18	0	2	0	20	0
1891-92	26	2	2	0	28	2
1892-93	28	0	1	0	29	0
1893-94	8	0	1	0	9	0
1894-95	1	0	0	0	1	0
	123	2	11	1	134	3

When Les Latcham joined Burnley as an apprentice shortly after his 17th birthday, he was a promising winger. When he made his first-team debut he still patrolled the flanks. But he will always be remembered as the Burnley player who put George Best 'in his pocket' on more than one occasion. Born in Stanley, Latcham joined Burnley early in 1960 and progressed through the junior ranks. He made his debut at Old Trafford in 1965, deputizing for Ralph Coates, but later in the season he was switched to full-back and, having tried both flanks, settled down at left-back. Latcham was only one game short of 150 first-team appearances when he was sold to Plymouth Argyle for £150,000 in 1971. In his time at Burnley he made most of his senior appearances as a full-back but wore just about every shirt and, indeed, settled down at centre-forward for Plymouth. He scored 13 goals in 90 League and Cup appearances for Argyle before moving back north in July 1973 to join Bradford City. By the end of that year, however, he had left League football and signed for Great Harwood. Latcham returned to the Burnley area and has worked in insurance ever since. He was manager of North-West Counties League club Nelson for a spell and has maintained his interest in the game at amateur level, where he has achieved a variety of successes.

LES LATCHAM

	LEAGUE		*FA CUP*		*FL CUP*		*OTHERS*		*TOTAL*	
	App	*Gls*	*App*	*Gls*	*App*	*Gls*	*App*	*Gls*	*App*	*Gls*
1964-65	4	1	1	0	0	0	0	0	5	1
1965-66	6	2	0	0	1	0	0	0	7	2
1966-67	20/2	3	2	0	0	0	4	1	26/2	4
1967-68	40	2	1	0	5	0	0	0	46	2
1968-69	39/1	2	2	1	7/1	0	0	0	48/2	3
1969-70	24	0	0/1	0	5	0	0	0	29/1	0
1970-71	16/1	0	0	0	0	0	1	0	17/1	0
	149/4	10	6/1	1	18/1	0	5	1	178/6	12

BRIAN LAWS

Discarded from Turf Moor by John Bond, Brian Laws progressively enhanced his career and, guided by one of the shrewdest managers in the game, he successfully held down a regular first-team place at one of England's top clubs. In addition, in his first 18 months in the First Division, Laws won two Littlewoods Cup winners' medals, a Simod Cup winners' medal and played in an FA Cup Final. Laws was born in Wallsend, Tyne and Wear, in 1961. After joining Burnley as an apprentice he progressed through the junior and reserve teams before making his League debut at right-back in the last match of the Second Division relegation season in 1980. He made the number-two shirt his own for the next three seasons, missing only a handful of games and developing a reputation as an attacking full-back who contributed his share of goals. He won a Third Division championship medal in 1981-2 and in the contradictory season to follow, played a key role in the two Cup runs. Laws left Turf Moor after the arrival of John Bond in 1983 and, after spells at Huddersfield Town and Middlesbrough, was seen by Brian Clough as a right-back of some promise. He signed for Nottingham Forest in July 1988 and, following his first-team debut in the following November has never looked back.

	LEAGUE		*FA CUP*		*FL CUP*		*OTHERS*		*TOTAL*	
	App	*Gls*	*App*	*Gls*	*App*	*Gls*	*App*	*Gls*	*App*	*Gls*
1979-80	1	0	0	0	0	0	0	0	1	0
1980-81	42	2	3	0	3	0	0	0	48	2
1981-82	44	6	6	0	2	0	3	0	55	6
1982-83	38	4	6	1	9	2	3	0	56	7
1983-84	0	0	0	0	0	0	2	0	2	0
	125	12	15	1	14	2	8	0	162	15

TOMMY LAWTON

After more than 500 goals in three years of schoolboy football in his home town of Bolton, Burnley were the first professional club off the mark to secure the signature of Tommy Lawton, one of the most prolific goalscorers and gifted centre-forwards the game has ever seen. After playing with Hayes Athletic and Rossendale United, Lawton signed for Burnley as an amateur in May 1935. He was 16 years and 163 days old when he made his League debut against Doncaster on 28 March 1936. Burnley's youngest-ever player, Lawton scored his first goals for the club, two at Swansea, a week after his debut. He signed professional forms on his 17th birthday, 6 October 1936, but it was not long before the big clubs were asking Burnley to name their price. On New Year's Day 1937, Everton paid £6,500 to take the young star to Goodison Park. Although Lawton started his Everton career alongside the immortal Dixie Dean, he was destined to replace the great man and in less than three seasons at Goodison before the outbreak of war, Lawton scored 70 goals in only 95 first-team games. He also won the first eight of his England caps in 1938-9, scoring a goal in each of the first six. He was transferred to Chelsea in November 1945, then played for Notts County and Brentford before signing for Arsenal in September 1953, the Gunners looking to him to stimulate their younger players. When he left League football in 1955, his post-war career had yielded 150 League goals in only 278 appearances. He had also won 15 more England caps and scored 16 more goals for his country. His only managerial role was at Notts County during the 1957-8 season, but he then left the game altogether to become a publican just outside Nottingham. He now lives in retirement in that city.

	LEAGUE		*FA CUP*		*TOTAL*	
	App	*Gls*	*App*	*Gls*	*App*	*Gls*
1935-36	7	5	0	0	7	5
1936-37	18	11	0	0	18	11
	25	16	0	0	25	16

The arrival of Alex Leake from Aston Villa in December 1907 was a major coup for Burnley. The 36-year-old defender had given stalwart service to both Birmingham and Villa over the previous dozen years and had won five England caps whilst at Villa Park. He was born in Small Heath, Birmingham, in 1871. A natural footballer, he played for a number of junior clubs in the Birmingham area before being signed as a professional by Small Heath in 1894, at the comparatively mature age of 23. He played over 200 games at Muntz Street before moving to Aston Villa in 1902, where he won an FA Cup winners' medal in 1905. An all-round sportsman, Alex Leake was a hard but very mild-mannered player and was soon appointed club captain after his arrival at Turf Moor. These were lean Second Division years for the Clarets and Leake was something of an elder statesman. He moved back to the Birmingham area in 1910 to end his playing career in non-League football then held coaching and training appointments at Crystal Palace and Merthyr Town. He later tried to pass on some of his vast knowledge and experience by coaching in schools all over the Midlands before his retirement. He died in Birmingham on 29 March 1938, aged 66.

ALEX LEAKE

	LEAGUE		*FA CUP*		*TOTAL*	
	App	*Gls*	*App*	*Gls*	*App*	*Gls*
1907-08	21	2	1	0	22	2
1908-09	33	0	6	0	39	0
1909-10	27	0	2	0	29	0
	81	2	9	0	90	2

A native of Bolton, Richard Lindley was spotted by a Burnley scout playing for Oswaldtwistle Rovers and was snapped up in March 1908. He made his League debut the following September and seemed to have made his mark when he scored in each of his first two games. He struggled to establish himself however and made only 16 appearances in his first three seasons at Turf Moor. His talent was not to be denied, however, and he emerged during 1911-12 as yet another star in the making as the Cup-winning team was being built. He scored 35 League goals in the three seasons which ended with the FA Cup triumph and was an ever-present in the run to the Crystal Palace in 1914. After World War One had ended, he was unable to regain his earlier form and after only six appearances during 1919-20 he was transferred to Bradford City. In May 1920, after one season at Valley Parade, he moved to Coventry City where he ended his playing career. After his retirement from football, Lindley opened a shop in Burnley and then became involved in the licensing trade, running a number of pubs in Burnley and in the Yorkshire Dales.

DICK LINDLEY

	LEAGUE		*FA CUP*		*TOTAL*	
	App	*Gls*	*App*	*Gls*	*App*	*Gls*
1908-09	10	3	0	0	10	3
1909-10	4	1	0	0	4	1
1910-11	2	0	0	0	2	0
1911-12	34	15	1	0	35	15
1912-13	33	10	6	1	39	11
1913-14	34	10	8	3	42	13
1914-15	14	2	0	0	14	2
1919-20	6	1	0	0	6	1
	137	42	15	4	152	46

ARCHIE LIVINGSTONE

Archibald Livingstone was one of the many Scots who came down to Lancashire in the 1880s. He was a loyal servant at Turf Moor, a solid dependable defender who made the left-half position his own for many years, a natural successor to Jack Keenan. He was born at Bothwell, on the Clyde, in 1877 and played his early football in Greenock, afterwards joining Glasgow Whitefield. He was transferred to Burnley from Third Lanark in March 1893, going straight into the League side where he became almost a permanent fixture. He suffered a serious injury in 1896 and missed an entire season. Such was his influence that Burnley finished bottom without him and were relegated after the Test matches. He recovered to win a Second Division championship medal in 1897-8, but after two more seasons at Turf Moor he was suddenly transferred to Nelson in the summer of 1900. He came back into League football with Burton United in 1901, but joined Southern League Brighton in 1904. Norwich City, also in the Southern League, acquired his services in 1905 and he spent six years first at Newmarket Road, then The Nest, occasionally playing first-team football but mainly coaching City's reserves and youngsters. After trying his hand at motor racing, Livingstone realized that football was what he knew best and joined Peterborough City as player-manager in 1912, where he stayed until war was declared.

	LEAGUE		*FA CUP*		*OTHERS*		*TOTAL*	
	App	*Gls*	*App*	*Gls*	*App*	*Gls*	*App*	*Gls*
1892-93	5	1	0	0	0	0	5	1
1893-94	28	0	1	0	0	0	29	0
1894-95	30	0	1	0	0	0	31	0
1895-96	23	0	0	0	0	0	23	0
1896-97	0	0	0	0	0	0	0	0
1897-98	21	1	3	0	4	0	28	1
1898-99	32	0	2	0	0	0	34	0
1899-1900	30	0	1	0	0	0	31	0
	169	2	8	0	4	0	181	2

Andy Lochhead was the sixth, and so far the last, Burnley player to complete a century of goals which he achieved in a 3-0 home win against Leeds United on the last day of the 1967-8 season. He is also one of only four Burnley players to hit five goals or more in a first-team match and is on his own as the only man to do it twice. He was born in Millgie in 1941 and signed for Burnley in December 1958 from the Renfrew club in Paisley. He was amongst the goals when he deputized for Ray Pointer in 1960-61, but it was not until 1962-3 that he made the number-nine shirt his own, Pointer moving to inside-right. Following the departure of both Pointer and Jimmy Robson, Lochhead was to form a very effective partnership with Willie Irvine. His power in the air and his skill both on and off the ball had already won him a Scottish Under-23 cap in 1962 but the Scottish selectors chose to ignore him for full honours. He went nap for the first time in the last match of the 1964-5 season, in a 6-2 drubbing of Chelsea, and repeated the feat the following January in an FA Cup replay against Bournemouth, the Clarets winning 7-0. Shortly after reaching the 100-goal mark, Lochhead left for Leicester City in October 1968. In his first season at Filbert Street he helped his new club to reach Wembley, where he picked up a runners-up medal, Leicester falling to Manchester City. He joined Aston Villa in February 1970 and, although Villa were relegated at the end of the season he won a Third Division championship medal and was top scorer as Villa bounced back two years later. After 44 goals in around 150 first-team games, he joined Oldham in 1973, going on to win his second Division Three championship medal in his first season with the Latics. He hung up his boots in 1975 and, like so many ex-Clarets, then returned to the Burnley area, where he is the steward in a popular bowling club and a frequent visitor to Turf Moor.

ANDY LOCHHEAD

	LEAGUE		*FA CUP*		*FL CUP*		*OTHERS*		*TOTAL*	
	App	*Gls*	*App*	*Gls*	*App*	*Gls*	*App*	*Gls*	*App*	*Gls*
1960-61	5	3	0	0	1	1	0	0	6	4
1961-62	2	0	0	0	0	0	0	0	2	0
1962-63	32	19	3	1	0	0	0	0	35	20
1963-64	33	11	5	3	0	0	0	0	38	14
1964-65	38	21	5	3	0	0	0	0	43	24
1965-66	34/1	15	3	5	4	3	0	0	41/1	23
1966-67	36	18	2	0	3	0	6	6	47	24
1967-68	34	13	1	0	5	2	0	0	40	15
1968-69	11	1	0	0	2	3	0	0	13	4
	225/1	101	19	12	15	9	6	6	265/1	128

Andrew McCluggage made his Burnley debut, along with Louis Page, in the infamous 10-0 débâcle at Villa Park in August 1925. In spite of this dreadful start, McCluggage made the right-back position virtually his own for the next six seasons, occasionally appearing at left-back and, more often than not, being partnered on the opposite flank by George Waterfield. McCluggage was born in Larne, Co Antrim, in 1900 and began playing football with Invervale in the Irish Junior Alliance, later joining Cliftonville. He was transferred to Bradford in 1921, where he won his first cap for Ireland in October 1923. Burnley secured his transfer in May 1925 to fill the right-back position where they had been served so well by Len Smelt since the end of war. The club and the fans were not to be disappointed as McCluggage's polished performances brought him 11 more Irish caps between 1927 and 1931. After a short unofficial spell with Dundalk, he signed for Preston in December 1931, making his North End debut at Turf Moor on Christmas Day, in a 2-2 draw. He left League football the following season and, after playing for Morecambe, hung up his boots and settled in Burnley. A typical Irishman, bright and breezy with a friendly disposition, Andy McCluggage worked as a maintenance engineer at Huncoat Pit until his death on 14 October 1954.

	LEAGUE		*FA CUP*		*TOTAL*	
	App	*Gls*	*App*	*Gls*	*App*	*Gls*
1925-26	33	5	0	0	33	5
1926-27	33	2	2	0	35	2
1927-28	29	1	1	0	30	1
1928-29	36	6	3	1	39	7
1929-30	40	6	1	0	41	6
1930-31	33	2	2	1	35	3
	204	22	9	2	213	24

ANDY McCLUGGAGE

Considered by many to be Burnley's finest goalkeeper, Colin McDonald was an England regular and just about at his peak when a broken leg, sustained representing the Football League in Dublin, ended his playing career. The son of a Football League goalkeeper, McDonald was born in Tottington, near Bury, in 1930. At school and with local side Hawkshaw St Mary's he was a left winger, only going in goal one day when the regular 'keeper failed to appear. He was a natural and was soon referred to Burnley for a trial by Jack Marshall, then on the Clarets' books. McDonald immediately impressed and signed amateur forms in the summer of of 1948 and then as a professional on his 17th birthday the following October. With Jimmy Strong at the top of his form and Joe McNulty and Des Thompson waiting in reserve, McDonald had to wait nearly six years for his first-team debut, coming in for Thompson in April 1954. He was ready for his chance and immediately became Burnley's first choice. McDonald's dedication to his craft was absolute and he worked at his game incessantly, determined to make himself the best in the business. His positional sense and his anticipation were uncanny with the result that he was rarely spectacular but always effective. He soon attracted the attention of the international selectors and, after an appearance for the Football League in 1957, made his full England debut replacing Bolton's Eddie Hopkinson in a 1-1 draw with the Soviet Union in Moscow on 18 May 1959. He played in all England's matches in the 1958 World Cup in Sweden, being voted the best goalkeeper in the tournament. The following season was to be Colin McDonald's last in the Football League. On 18 March 1959 his illustrious career came to an abrupt end. Complications set in as a result of his injury and he contracted pneumonia but thankfully recovered his health some time later. After a brief spell playing reserve-team football he retired in 1959, later coaching and scouting at various clubs including Bury, Oldham and Tranmere. Colin McDonald was indeed a Burnley great. He must rank alongside Jerry Dawson in ability if not number of games and, had injury not cut short his career so tragically he would surely have become an England great too.

	LEAGUE		*FA CUP*		*TOTAL*	
	App	*Gls*	*App*	*Gls*	*App*	*Gls*
1953-54	5	0	0	0	5	0
1954-55	39	0	1	0	40	0
1955-56	42	0	6	0	48	0
1956-57	34	0	0	0	34	0
1957-58	39	0	3	0	42	0
1958-59	27	0	5	0	32	0
	186	0	15	0	201	0

COLIN McDONALD

Bill McFettridge was yet another of the rugged Scots who dominated Burnley football in the 1880s and '90s. He partnered Jack Keenan at half-back for much of his time at Turf Moor and the pair were instrumental in the famous Lancashire Cup win against Blackburn Rovers in 1890. McFettridge was born in Govan, Glasgow, in 1862 and played his early football for the Thornliebank club in the south of the city. He came to England in 1883 to join Padiham, then a footballing power in Lancashire, before being transferred to Burnley in 1886. McFetteridge soon established himself as a versatile member of the side, playing both in attack and defence, before making the right-half position his own. He missed the first League game in 1888, but continued to perform consistently over the first four seasons of League football, his hard, robust style proving very effective in those early days. He lost his regular place in 1892 and retired from the game, aged 30, to return to his trade as a painter and decorator. In later life he also became a publican and was a popular landlord in a number of hostelries in Padiham and Burnley. McFettridge's brother, David, joined Bolton Wanderers from Cowlairs in 1891 and was the Trotters' regular left winger during the club's successful campaign in 1891-2.

BILL McFETTRIDGE

	LEAGUE		*FA CUP*		*TOTAL*	
	App	*Gls*	*App*	*Gls*	*App*	*Gls*
1886-87	0	0	2	0	2	0
1887-88	0	0	1	1	1	1
1888-89	16	0	2	0	18	0
1889-90	21	2	1	0	22	2
1890-91	21	0	2	0	23	0
1891-92	25	0	2	0	27	0
1892-93	2	0	0	0	2	0
	85	2	10	1	95	3

Of all the players that have donned the famous claret and blue of Burnley since World War Two, unquestionably the greatest of them all is the magical Irishman Jimmy McIlroy. It is difficult to compare 'modern' players to those who appeared before the war but, with the possible exception of Bob Kelly, no one would argue that 'Mac' was the finest Burnley player of all time. Even in the great Burnley side of the late 1950s and early '60s — League Champions, FA Cup Finalists, European Cup ambassadors — McIlroy was by far the most skilful individual talent in a team of all the talents. The events of early 1963 have never been totally explained but, following the departure of the great man, the club was never the same again. The fans never completely forgave, and most of them have not forgotten. Jimmy McIlroy was born in Lambeg, a small village just south of Belfast, on 25 October 1931. As a young child he never doubted that he wanted to be a footballer and he was encouraged and influenced by his father Harry, a part-time player with Distillery, and his uncle, Willie McIlroy, who was a professional with Portadown. The young McIlroy was a slightly-built boy and it was feared that his development, in life in general and in football in particular, would be affected by his physique, so he was amply fed to build him up. He practised constantly with a tennis ball and, in later life, insisted that this early concentration on ball skills was the key to his prowess. Aged ten he was picked for the school team, where he played with and against 14-year-olds. He was even more determined to make it as a professional and left school at 15 to do some manual work, to build himself up even more and to earn some money to pay his parents back for their sacrifices. After leaving school he played for the Craigavad Club near Bangor and his performances were soon being monitored by the Glentoran scouts. He later signed for that club and in 1949 played for the first team in the last match of the season. The following season he became a regular, one of his teammates being Billy Bingham, who was also a regular target for the talent scouts. Things began to move quickly and the following March, Burnley manager Frank Hill was the latest admiring Englishman to cross the water to assess McIlroy's ability. After a particularly inspired performance for Glentoran against Distillery, Hill was convinced and Jimmy Mac was on his way to Turf Moor. Early the following season, inside-left Harry Potts was transferred to Everton, McIlroy was seen as the natural replacement and on 21 October 1950, at Sunderland, he embarked upon his League career with Burnley. Within a year he won his first cap for Northern Ireland, his performance in Belfast against Scotland ensuring that he would be a permanent member of his country's line-up, as well as that of his club, well into the next decade. Following the retirement of Billy Morris in 1952, McIlroy switched to inside-right, accommodating the skilful Les Shannon at number-ten and going on to form a superb right-wing partnership with Billy Gray. In 1956, he was approaching the peak of his greatness and was acknowledged as one of the very best players in British football since the war when he was chosen in a Great Britain side to play the Rest of Europe. At Turf Moor, McIlroy's right-wing partner had changed, first to Doug Newlands, then to John Connelly, a perfect foil for Mac's trickery. Ray Pointer was by now leading the Clarets' attack and with Brian Pilkington and Jimmy Robson on the other flank, the forward line was ready to play its part in the assault on the title. In the Championship season and the two that followed, the McIlroy/Jimmy Adamson partnership was at its magnificent best and was the engine-room in a team that, but for the marvellous Tottenham side of that era, would surely have brought more silverware back to Turf Moor. In 1962, McIlroy was just edged into second place by his captain, Jimmy Adamson, as Footballer of the Year as the Clarets narrowly missed out on an FA Cup and League double. The following season, after the Cup defeat at Liverpool in February, the unbelievable news broke that Jimmy McIlroy had been placed on the transfer list. It was one of those events where everyone knows what they were doing when they heard about it. He joined Stoke City, Stanley Matthews and all, and helped the Potters win the Second Division championship in 1963, and consolidate their position in the top flight. McIlroy moved to Oldham Athletic in March 1966, where he finished his playing career, combining on-the-field appearances with managing the Latics for a short spell. He was chief coach back at the Victoria Ground for a time but then, in November 1970, spent 18 days as the manager of Bolton Wanderers after coaching at Burnden Park. He soon resigned, 'unwelcome interference in team selection' being the reason cited. These days, Jimmy McIlroy is a much-respected journalist at the *Burnley Express*, primarily a sports reporter but fast developing a reputation as a feature writer. Golf is his sporting passion, his single-figure handicap improving all the time. Jimmy Mac will always be a sporting hero in Burnley. His skill and artistry will be talked about passionately for years to come. His partnerships, at club level with Jimmy Adamson and at international level with Danny Blanchflower, were among the finest ever. Jimmy McIlroy was and is, quite simply, the greatest.

JIMMY McILROY

	LEAGUE		*FA CUP*		*FL CUP*		*OTHERS*		*TOTAL*	
	App	*Gls*	*App*	*Gls*	*App*	*Gls*	*App*	*Gls*	*App*	*Gls*
1950-51	30	5	1	0	-	-	0	0	31	5
1951-52	28	4	0	0	-	-	0	0	28	4
1952-53	38	11	3	1	-	-	0	0	41	12
1953-54	40	17	3	1	-	-	0	0	43	18
1954-55	40	3	1	0	-	-	0	0	41	3
1955-56	24	4	5	1	-	-	0	0	29	5
1956-57	40	13	5	3	-	-	0	0	45	16
1957-58	36	16	3	3	-	-	0	0	39	19
1958-59	40	6	5	1	-	-	0	0	45	7
1959-60	32	6	6	1	-	-	0	0	38	7
1960-61	33	10	7	1	3	1	5	1	48	13
1961-62	36	15	8	1	0	0	0	0	44	16
1962-63	22	6	3	0	0	0	0	0	25	6
	439	116	50	13	3	1	5	1	497	131

When Peter McKay broke into Burnley's first team in 1955, to replace centre-forward Bill Holden, he immediately impressed with his unusual style and his unlikely appearance combined with his deadly finishing. He was born in Newburgh on the Firth of Tay in 1925 and was playing for Dundee United when the Burnley scouts were recommended to have a look at him. Like numerous clubs previously, they were not immediately taken by this slightly-built player who lacked pace and was one-footed. His goals tally spoke for itself, however, and eventually Peter McKay came to Turf Moor in May 1954 at the age of 29. He played a few games in the 1954-5 season but did not sufficiently impress to become a regular. The following season he was a revelation, now aged 30, he became the first player since George Beel in 1931 to score 25 goals in a season. McKay was a goal poacher, in the team for one purpose and never straying away from the middle. He was skilled at riding the crudest of tackles as he darted between defenders. Although not good with his head, he was awkward for centre-halves to deal with, as he jumped he flicked his heels in the air and his marker kept clear or got a crack on the shins. In 1956, Allan Brown was appointed Burnley manager and the team pattern changed, every player being expected to work harder. McKay's strength was in the middle rather than foraging out on the flanks and his effectiveness suffered. He was transferred to St Mirren in 1957 and later came south again to the steel works in Corby, playing part-time for Corby Town. Shrewd judges maintained that Peter McKay was one of the best goal poachers of his day, an instinctive scorer who had the potential to go to the very top, if only he had been discovered years earlier.

PETER McKAY

	LEAGUE		*FA CUP*		*TOTAL*	
	App	*Gls*	*App*	*Gls*	*App*	*Gls*
1954-55	4	0	0	0	4	0
1955-56	34	25	6	2	40	27
1956-57	22	11	0	0	22	11
	60	36	6	2	66	38

TOM McLINTOCK

A virtual ever-present for seven years in the 1890s, Tom McLintock replaced the great Sandy Lang at left-back and continued the tradition of durable Scottish defenders at Turf Moor. He was born in Maybole, Ayrshire, and played his early football for junior clubs in the Glasgow area before joining Clyde. He then played for Kilmarnock and represented Ayrshire against Glasgow in 1892. He signed for Burnley in the summer of 1892 and, although originally a skilful right-back, made the position on the left flank his own from the first match of the following season. He won a Second Division championship medal in 1897-8, missing only one game and enjoyed two more good seasons before the club was relegated again in 1900. In his last two seasons he lost his place in defence to George Lockhart and became something of a utility player. In one match against Blackpool in 1901, playing on the left wing, he scored all the goals, including two penalties, in a 4-0 win. A shoemaker by trade, McLintock was transferred back to Kilmarnock in 1903. He ended his career in his native Scotland, where he spent the rest of his days.

	LEAGUE		*FA CUP*		*OTHERS*		*TOTAL*	
	App	*Gls*	*App*	*Gls*	*App*	*Gls*	*App*	*Gls*
1893-94	29	0	1	0	0	0	30	0
1894-95	30	0	1	0	0	0	31	0
1895-96	30	1	3	0	0	0	33	1
1896-97	27	1	1	0	4	0	32	1
1897-98	29	3	3	0	4	0	36	3
1898-99	34	2	2	0	0	0	36	2
1899-1900	34	0	1	0	0	0	35	0
1900-01	8	6	0	0	0	0	8	6
1901-02	12	1	1	0	0	0	13	1
	233	14	13	0	8	0	254	14

HAROLD MATHER

Harold Mather played all his League football for Burnley just after World War Two, he was one of the 'Iron Curtain' defence and his full-back partnership with Arthur Woodruff was one of the best around. He was born in Bolton in 1921 and, after starring in Bolton's schoolboys team, he was snapped up from under the Wanderers' noses just before the war. He played for the first team during hostilities but then, when normal League football resumed, he made the number-three shirt his own and was an ever-present in the promotion and Wembley side of 1946-7. With his ball control and his ability to beat a man, Mather was the classic overlapping full-back, except that he was discouraged from doing it by manager Cliff Britton. He was instructed to defend and this he did. With his exceptional timing he was able to dispossess the best wingers of the day. He was a virtual ever-present until 1953, but then left the club in 1955. He stayed in the game taking a number of jobs including coaching spells in South Africa and with Nelson and as player-manager of Kettering Town. He also assisted Hull City, Accrington Stanley and Limerick in Southern Ireland. Like many ex-Clarets, Harold Mather still lives in Burnley, but these days his involvement in football is restricted to watching it on television.

	LEAGUE		*FA CUP*		*TOTAL*	
	App	*Gls*	*App*	*Gls*	*App*	*Gls*
1945-46	0	0	2	0	2	0
1946-47	42	0	9	0	51	0
1947-48	38	0	1	0	39	0
1948-49	41	0	2	0	43	0
1949-50	34	0	2	0	36	0
1950-51	40	0	1	0	41	0
1951-52	40	0	4	0	44	0
1952-53	36	0	4	0	40	0
1953-54	24	0	3	0	27	0
1954-55	6	0	0	0	6	0
	301	0	28	0	329	0

In the late 1980s and early '90s, Ian Measham made the number-two shirt virtually his own property. He signed from Cambridge United in November 1988 and promptly took over from Peter Daniel. An attacking full-back at his best when Burnley adopt a sweeper system, Measham is one of the most recent players to complete 100 first-team appearances. Born in Barnsley, Measham started his career as an apprentice at Huddersfield Town. He had loan spells at Lincoln City and Rochdale before leaving Leeds Road for a new career with Cambridge United. Among the quicker full-backs in the lower divisions, Measham has been virtually an ever-present in the number-two shirt, apart from a spell in the 1989-90 season which he missed when a serious injury. Although fond of going forward, Measham has scored only one Football League goal, in a 1-1 draw against Peterborough in February 1989.

	LEAGUE		*FA CUP*		*FL CUP*		*OTHERS**		*TOTAL*	
	App	*Gls*	*App*	*Gls*	*App*	*Gls*	App	Gls	*App*	*Gls*
1988-89	30	1	1	0	0	0	3	0	34	1
1989-90	35	0	6	0	1	0	4	0	46	0
1990-91	44/1	0	3	0	2	0	9	0	58/1	0
	109/1	1	10	0	3	0	16	0	138/1	1

* Includes 1990-91 Play-off games.

IAN MEASHAM

Although Dave Merrington never really classed himself as a first-team regular at Burnley, he was made club captain in the 1979-80 season. Merrington, born in Newcastle upon Tyne, joined the Clarets as an apprentice in 1962 and made his debut at centre-half three years later, on the last day of the 1964-5 season which was memorable for the fact that Burnley beat Chelsea 6-2. On that occasion he took the number-five shirt from John Talbut but never really managed to force him out of the side. When Talbut was eventually sold to West Bromwich Albion, Merrington again had to fight for first-team recognition, this time battling it out with Sammy Todd. In the end it was a battle they both lost with the arrival of Colin Waldron from Chelsea. When Burnley were relegated at the end of the 1970-71 season, Merrington was transferred to Bristol City but a severe pre-season injury meant that he never played for them. He returned to Turf Moor as a coach and worked under manager Jimmy Adamson at Burnley, Sunderland and Leeds United. Merrington trained to be a church minister, a full-time vocation he followed for some time before returning to football as youth development officer at Southampton.

	LEAGUE		*FA CUP*		*FL CUP*		*OTHERS*		*TOTAL*	
	App	*Gls*	*App*	*Gls*	*App*	*Gls*	*App*	*Gls*	*App*	*Gls*
1964-65	1	0	0	0	0	0	0	0	1	0
1965-66	13	0	2	0	3	0	0	0	18	0
1966-67	17	0	2	0	0	0	3	0	22	0
1967-68	21/1	0	1	0	4	0	0	0	26/1	0
1968-69	19	1	1	0	4	0	0	0	24	1
1969-70	15	0	3	0	2	0	0	0	20	0
1970-71	10/1	0	0/1	0	0	0	2	1	12/2	1
	96/2	1	9/1	0	13	0	5	1	123/3	2

DAVE MERRINGTON

BRIAN MILLER

One of a small number of locally-born players to make the grade with Burnley, Brian Miller was born in Hapton in 1937 and joined the Clarets as a junior in February 1954. He made his first-team debut, deputizing for Les Shannon during the FA Cup tie marathon with Chelsea in 1956. Up against a formidable trio like Adamson, Seith and Shannon, and with the injured Tommy Cummings waiting to come back, Miller did well to force himself into the reckoning over the next few years with his solid hard-tackling style. He was an ever-present in the League Championship season and won three Under-23 caps in 1960. His sheer consistency over the following seasons was a major factor in Burnley's success and should perhaps have earned him more than his solitary full England cap in Vienna in May 1961. John Angus also made his only appearance for his country in that match, both men playing out of position, Angus at left-back and Miller at right-half, in a 3-1 defeat. Miller was an automatic choice until the end of 1966-7 when, in a match at Villa Park, so often an unlucky ground for the Clarets, a twisted knee signalled the end of a marvellous playing career for a first-class clubman. Brian Miller joined the Turf Moor coaching staff in 1967 and has been with the club in various capacities almost continuously ever since (see *Burnley Managers).*

	LEAGUE		*FA CUP*		*FL CUP*		*OTHERS*		*TOTAL*	
	App	*Gls*	*App*	*Gls*	*App*	*Gls*	*App*	*Gls*	*App*	*Gls*
1955-56	2	1	2	0	-	-	0	0	4	1
1956-57	25	0	5	0	-	-	0	0	30	0
1957-58	19	1	1	0	-	-	0	0	20	1
1958-59	17	1	2	0	-	-	0	0	19	1
1959-60	42	3	8	0	-	-	0	0	50	3
1960-61	35	5	7	2	5	1	5	1	52	9
1961-62	38	3	8	2	0	0	0	0	46	5
1962-63	42	6	3	0	0	0	0	0	45	6
1963-64	40	6	4	0	0	0	0	0	44	6
1964-65	39	1	5	0	0	0	0	0	44	1
1965-66	42	2	3	0	5	0	0	0	50	2
1966-67	38	0	2	0	3	0	8	2	51	2
	379	29	50	4	13	1	13	3	455	37

HUGH MOFFAT

Left-sided defender Hugh Moffat was born in Congleton in 1885 and played for Congleton Town and Congleton Swifts before joining Burnley as a 19-year-old amateur in January 1904. Moffat was equally at home at left-back or left-half and his career at Burnley was divided between these two positions, after he turned professional after a year at Turf Moor. Moffat was involved in a unique situation when Burnley travelled to play Chesterfield in November 1904. Moffatt missed the team's train connection in Manchester and was unable to get to the match until after it had finished. No 12th man had accompanied the team and, consequently, for the only time in the club's League history, Burnley played the whole 90 minutes with ten men. He played his last two seasons with Burnley partnering Alex Leake but then lost his place when Willie Watson arrived from Southport Central in 1909 and started to show his class. Moffatt joined Oldham in December 1910 and was a member of the Latics side promoted to Division One at the end of his first season. In 1914-15, Oldham were desperately close to winning the First Division title, a defeat at Turf Moor at the end of the season depriving Moffat of a Championship medal. After the war he spent a season at Chesterfield before returning to Congleton Town in the close season of 1920. He died in Macclesfield on 14 November 1952, aged 67.

	LEAGUE		*FA CUP*		*TOTAL*	
	App	*Gls*	*App*	*Gls*	*App*	*Gls*
1903-04	4	1	0	0	4	1
1904-05	25	1	2	0	27	1
1905-06	38	2	1	0	39	2
1906-07	31	4	1	0	32	4
1907-08	34	1	1	0	35	1
1908-09	27	1	6	0	33	1
1909-10	34	3	2	0	36	3
1910-11	8	0	0	0	8	0
	201	13	13	0	214	13

Reputed to be the first British footballer to have his own official fan club, Willie Morgan was the idol of many Burnley followers in the 1960s. A right winger of the very highest order, Morgan was snapped up by Burnley scouts from his home in Glasgow and became a 17-year-old apprentice in October 1961. On the last day of the following season he made his first-team debut as a replacement for the almost legendary figure of John Connelly. He ousted the club stalwart from the right-wing position the following campaign, when Connelly switched to the left flank for one season before his move to Manchester United. Over the next four seasons, Morgan was a virtual ever-present for Burnley before following Connelly on the path to Old Trafford in the summer of 1968. He had won a full Scotland cap whilst with Burnley and went on to win another 20 caps with United as well as gaining a Second Division championship medal. He played in Scotland's unsuccessful 1974 World Cup finals and the following year returned to Burnley to try to bolster their fight against First Division relegation. The move never worked and after only 12 appearances he was on his way again, this time to Bolton Wanderers and a five-year career with the Trotters which yielded another Second Division championship medal. In September 1980, after playing for Chicago Sting and Minnesota Kicks in the NASL, he signed for Blackpool, retiring at the end of 1981-2 to concentrate on a public relations business and improving his golf handicap. In November 1978, a libel case brought against Morgan by former Manchester United manager Tommy Docherty collapsed when Docherty admitted lying under oath.

	LEAGUE		*FA CUP*		*FL CUP*		*OTHERS*		*TOTAL*	
	App	*Gls*	*App*	*Gls*	*App*	*Gls*	*App*	*Gls*	*App*	*Gls*
1962-63	2	0	0	0	0	0	0	0	2	0
1963-64	25	4	5	1	0	0	0	0	30	5
1964-65	35	3	1	0	0	0	0	0	36	3
1965-66	39	2	3	0	5	0	0	0	47	2
1966-67	40	3	2	0	2	1	8	0	52	4
1967-68	42	7	1	0	5	0	0	0	48	7
1975-76	12/1	0	1	0	3	1	0	0	16/1	1
	195/1	19	13	1	15	2	8	0	231/1	22

WILLIE MORGAN

Born in Colwyn Bay in 1918, Billy Morris joined Burnley from Llandudno in January 1939 and went straight into the Clarets' first team. Sadly, he hardly had time to get his Turf Moor career off the ground before war intervened. Morris became an Army sergeant and served in the Far East in the conflict with Japan. When Burnley kicked-off the 1946-7 season he was one of only four players who had played for the Clarets before the war. He struck up an immediate affinity, both on and off the field, with one of the newcomers, right winger Jackie Chew. Morris was a very small, light inside-forward. He was an elusive player, difficult to mark, a man who had a knack for finishing off half-chances inside the six-yard box, simply because he was in the right place at the right time. He won his first Welsh cap against Northern Ireland in Belfast in April 1947 and, although he played four more matches for his country, he would have made far more international appearances but for some quality opposition in his position, notably Aubrey Powell, and later, Ivor Allchurch. He retired from the professional game in 1952 and played non-League football in Wales for a number of years before hanging up his boots for good. He later managed Wrexham for two short spells in the 1960s. Billy Morris still lives in Wales but is severely handicapped these days by arthritis.

	LEAGUE		*FA CUP*		*TOTAL*	
	App	*Gls*	*App*	*Gls*	*App*	*Gls*
1938-39	12	0	0	0	12	0
1945-46	0	0	2	1	2	1
1946-47	31	9	9	4	40	13
1947-48	23	4	0	0	23	4
1948-49	31	3	0	0	31	3
1949-50	34	2	3	0	37	2
1950-51	38	11	1	0	39	11
1951-52	39	18	4	1	43	19
1952-53	3	0	0	0	3	0
	211	47	19	6	230	53

BILLY MORRIS

Irishman Tom 'Ching' Morrison came to Burnley from Glentoran as a 20-year-old in February 1894 but the following September temporarily severed his connection with the club and returned home. Whilst still with Glentoran he won his first cap in a 9-0 defeat for the Irish at Derby on 9 March 1895. James Crabtree was making his second appearance in an England shirt in the same game. Morrison played twice more for his country in the Home International series of 1895 and eventually returned to England, re-signing at Turf Moor in February 1897, but too late to prevent Burnley's relegation at the end of the season. Another significant arrival at Turf Moor at the same time as Morrison was Jimmy Ross who signed from Liverpool. 'Ching' and Ross formed a marvellous right-wing partnership, with Morrison quite dazzling out on the touch-line and providing goal after goal for Ross and Wilf Toman as well as contributing half a dozen himself. The Second Division championship was secured in 1898 and promotion deservedly won after the Test matches. The team carried on in the First Division, where they had left off in the Second and for a time led the table, until a violent disagreement between Morrison and Ross affected the team's performances and they fell away. The rift between the players was so deep that Ross was transferred to Manchester City the following February. Meanwhile, Morrison continued to perform consistently with a variety of right-wing partners, over the next four years, earning four more Irish caps between 1899 and 1902. He was transferred to Manchester United in December 1902, spending a season and a half at Old Trafford before returning for a third spell at Turf Moor, this time as a trainer-coach. He managed one more appearance for the first team before he later went back to his roots in Ireland, coaching at his first club, Glentoran, where he stayed until retirement.

TOM MORRISON

	LEAGUE		*FA CUP*		*OTHERS*		*TOTAL*	
	App	*Gls*	*App*	*Gls*	*App*	*Gls*	*App*	*Gls*
1893-94	4	1	0	0	0	0	4	1
1894-95	3	0	0	0	0	0	3	0
1896-97	6	1	0	0	1	0	7	1
1897-98	29	6	3	0	4	0	36	6
1898-99	29	3	1	0	0	0	30	3
1899-1900	31	3	1	0	0	0	32	3
1900-01	30	4	3	2	0	0	33	6
1901-02	32	7	2	0	0	0	34	7
1902-03	14	1	1	0	0	0	15	1
1905-06	0	0	0	0	0	0	0	0
1906-07	1	0	0	0	0	0	1	0
	179	26	11	2	5	0	195	28

Edwin Mosscrop was born in Southport in 1892 and played for the same local junior club, Blowick, as Billy Watson. Whilst still a teenager he played for a time in the London area but then returned to his home town, joining Burnley as an amateur from Southport Central in the summer of 1912. For a time he vied with Billy Nesbitt for the right-wing spot but then claimed the left flank position as his own. He was at his brilliant best in the successful FA Cup run of 1914 and his outstanding form brought him two England caps in the Home International Championship that year. After the war, in which Mosscrop saw active service in Salonika, he was still the club's regular left winger until losing his place to Walt Weaver, newly-arrived from South Liverpool. He was not an automatic choice in the Championship side but then re-established himself at Weaver's expense the following season. He retired from the game in 1922, after a period of serious illness, and returned to Southport where he became a schoolteacher. He died on 14 March 1980, aged 87.

EDDIE MOSSCROP

	LEAGUE		*FA CUP*		*OTHERS*		*TOTAL*	
	App	*Gls*	*App*	*Gls*	*App*	*Gls*	*App*	*Gls*
1912-13	22	4	4	0	0	0	26	4
1913-14	29	2	8	0	0	0	37	2
1914-15	29	1	3	0	0	0	32	1
1919-20	31	4	2	0	0	0	33	4
1920-21	14	1	2	0	0	0	16	1
1921-22	35	7	2	1	1	0	38	8
1922-23	16	0	0	0	0	0	16	0
	176	19	21	1	1	0	198	20

Joe Neenan was the goalkeeper who made a couple of dramatic saves on a May afternoon in 1987. How important they were as they helped to preserve Burnley's Football League status. Born in Manchester, Neenan crossed the Pennines to become an apprentice with York City. He had more than 50 first-team games there before moving on to the Old Show Ground and becoming Scunthorpe United's first-choice 'keeper. He arrived at Turf Moor, initially on loan and later permanently, from Scunthorpe having made almost 200 appearances with The Iron and having formed a close friendship with Ian Botham. Neenan made his Burnley debut in a 7-0 win against Rotherham. Having made a lasting impression wtih his performance during the 'Orient Game', Neenan was one of the several close season casualties as Burnley built a new team. He went on to play for Peterborough United and also had a loan spell with League newcomers Scarborough.

JOE NEENAN

	LEAGUE		*FA CUP*		*FL CUP*		*OTHERS*		*TOTAL*	
	App	*Gls*	*App*	*Gls*	*App*	*Gls*	*App*	*Gls*	*App*	*Gls*
1984-85	9	0	0	0	0	0	2	0	11	0
1985-86	36	0	2	0	2	0	6	0	46	0
1986-87	45	0	1	0	2	0	6	0	54	0
	90	0	3	0	4	0	14	0	111	0

William Nesbitt was a member of both the FA Cup winning side of 1914 and the League Championship team of seven years later. He was a quiet man who went out of his way to avoid publicity and he was reputed to have been stone deaf from birth. He was born in Portsmouth, near Todmorden, and joined Burnley from Hebden Bridge FC in September 1911. He failed to establish himself for two years but in 1913-14 made the right-wing position his own and played his part in the Cup success, creating many goals for his colleagues. He was on the fringe of international honours, being selected to represent England in a trial match against the North just before World War One. Nesbitt missed only the first two games of the Championship season in 1920-21 and his right-wing partnership with the incomparable Bob Kelly was one of the key factors in the team's success. The Clarets flirted with honours the following season, of course, but fell away in the last third of the season, the decline coinciding with Nesbitt being injured. He missed much of the following season also and when Peter Bennie was signed from Albion Rovers in the summer of 1923, Nesbitt's days at Turf Moor were numbered. He signed for Bristol City the following October but eventually succumbed to persistent injury problems and retired.

BILLY NESBITT

	LEAGUE		*FA CUP*		*OTHERS*		*TOTAL*	
	App	*Gls*	*App*	*Gls*	*App*	*Gls*	*App*	*Gls*
1911-12	13	2	0	0	0	0	13	2
1912-13	9	1	0	0	0	0	9	1
1913-14	24	2	8	0	0	0	32	2
1914-15	19	1	2	0	0	0	21	1
1919-20	30	6	4	1	0	0	34	7
1920-21	40	5	3	0	0	0	43	5
1921-22	29	1	2	0	1	0	32	1
1922-23	8	1	0	0	0	0	8	1
	172	19	19	1	1	0	192	20

KEITH NEWTON

An inspirational signing in the summer of 1972, Keith Newton brought an element of stability to an often troublesome left-back position and in his first season with the Clarets he helped Burnley back into the First Division as an ever-present in the 1972-3 Second Division campaign. A virtual ever-present in each of his first four seasons, Newton was a cultured player who always used the ball to the greatest possible advantage. Equally at home in either full-back position, Newton used his height and athleticism to great effect. He was sound in the air and sharp in the tackle. The Manchester-born player launched a distinguished career with Blackburn Rovers in the late 1950s. He won an FA Youth Cup winners' medal with the Ewood Park club and went on to play more than 300 senior games for them before moving to Everton in 1969. He won a League Championship medal at Goodison Park but left for Burnley on a free transfer, frustrated by the role he was being expected to play. Newton won 27 full England caps before joining Burnley, the first in 1966 against Scotland and the last in the 1970 World Cup finals against West Germany. Never afraid to go forward, Newton had a fondness for firing long-range left-foot shots and was unlucky to collect only five goals in his 209 Burnley games. He dropped out of the Football League in 1978 and had a brief spell with non-League Morecambe.

	LEAGUE		*FA CUP*		*FL CUP*		*OTHERS*		*TOTAL*	
	App	*Gls*	*App*	*Gls*	*App*	*Gls*	*App*	*Gls*	*App*	*Gls*
1972-73	42	1	2	0	1	0	2	0	47	1
1973-74	39	0	5	1	2	0	8	0	54	1
1974-75	39	1	1	0	3	1	0	0	43	2
1975-76	41	2	1	0	4	0	0	0	46	2
1976-77	30	1	3	0	1	0	3	0	37	1
1977-78	18	0	1	0	3	0	3	0	25	0
	209	5	13	1	14	1	16	0	252	7

TOM NICOL

Thomas Nicol was a conscientious servant for Burnley and served the club with distinction for six years in the 1890s, being equally at home at full-back or in the forward line. He led the attack in his League debut for the Clarets and scored a hat-trick as Preston, the defending Champions, were crushed 6-2 at Turf Moor. He was born in Linlithgow in 1870 and played junior league football in the Edinburgh area before Burnley signed him from Mossend Swifts in February 1891. He went straight into the first team to replace the departed Claude Lambie and in his first full season, 1891-2, was something of a goalscoring sensation. In a modest season for the club, he hit 17 goals alternating between the right wing and centre-forward. He was certainly a utility player during the rest of his Burnley career which lasted till December 1896, when he was transferred to Blackburn Rovers. He left Ewood Park at the end of the season and ended his playing days at Southampton where he became host at one of the leading hotels in the city. Whilst with the Saints he became an expert bowls player and won many championships. He died in Southampton on 10 June 1915, aged 45.

	LEAGUE		*FA CUP*		*TOTAL*	
	App	*Gls*	*App*	*Gls*	*App*	*Gls*
1890-91	3	3	0	0	3	3
1891-92	25	17	2	1	27	18
1892-93	30	1	2	0	32	1
1893-94	22	1	1	0	23	1
1894-95	22	11	1	0	23	11
1895-96	26	8	3	1	29	9
1896-97	12	1	0	0	12	1
	140	42	9	2	149	44

As a midfielder who spent much of his time with Burnley as a full-back, Peter Noble had a goalscoring record better than many forwards. Noble, who started his career with his home-town club, Newcastle United, is one of the very few Burnley players to have scored four goals or more in the same match, and he is one of only two to do so and still not end up on the winning side. In 1975-6, Burnley's last season in the First Division, Noble was well on course to become the first player for some time to score 20 League goals in a season. It was early in that campaign that he scored all four Burnley goals in a remarkable draw against Norwich City, but he pulled a groin muscle in netting a penalty soon afterwards and missed a big chunk of the season. Noble first came to Burnley's attention in 1968-9, when he was a key member of the Swindon Town side which beat Burnley in the League Cup semi-final, accounted for the Arsenal in the Final and won promotion from the Third Division. Four years later the Clarets signed Noble to bolster their midfield after winning the Second Division championship. But in the first game, Mick Docherty was injured and Noble played at full-back for the rest the season. A very popular player with the Turf Moor crowd, Noble never missed a penalty in his professional career, but he took them only for Burnley. When he was transferred to Blackpool in the summer of 1980, many thought the move was premature, even though Noble was 35 at the time. Despite playing almost 100 times for the Seasiders, he never really settled at Bloomfield Road and his contract was cancelled in 1982. One of the many former players who still regularly visits Turf Moor, Noble runs a flourishing sports shop in the town which has been his home for almost two decades.

	LEAGUE		*FACUP*		*FLCUP*		*OTHERS*		*TOTAL*	
	App	*Gls*	*App*	*Gls*	*App*	*Gls*	*App*	*Gls*	*App*	*Gls*
1973-74	40/1	0	4	0	3	0	6	5	53/1	5
1974-75	42	12	1	0	3	2	0	0	46	14
1975-76	25/1	13	0	0	4	4	0	0	29/1	17
1976-77	42	13	3	1	1	0	3	1	49	15
1977-78	40	8	2	0	4	1	3	0	49	9
1978-79	41	14	4	0	3	1	9	1	57	16
1979-80	11	3	0	0	1	0	3	1	15	4
	241/2	63	14	1	19	8	24	8	298/2	80

PETER NOBLE

When David Thomas was transferred to Queen's Park Rangers early in Burnley's 1972-3 Second Division championship campaign, it was always going to take a special sort of player to fill his boots. The job fell to Geoff Nulty and in over 120 Burnley games he proved equal to the task. Before taking over the number-seven shirt, Nulty had played almost 50 games for Burnley in a variety of positions. Thomas last played for the Clarets against Luton in September 1972 and Nulty wore his shirt for 76 consecutive League games before being sold to Newcastle United in December 1974. Nulty became an integral part of the side which won the Second Division title in 1972-3, reached the FA Cup semi-final against Newcastle the following season and only narrowly missed out on a place in Europe. He featured prominently in that Cup semi-final and crashed a shot against United's crossbar before the Magpies had scored the first of their two goals. Born in Prescot, Nulty was an apprentice at Stoke City before joining Burnley. He signed for the Clarets in 1967 and made his Football League debut in the 1969-70 season. His career at Newcastle United lasted until July 1978, when he was transferred to Everton for £40,000. The midfielder played in only 22 games for the Blues before he was seriously injured in a Merseyside derby, Jimmy Case's tackle effectively ending his career. Nulty was retained as a coach at Everton and took up a similar role at Preston North End when Gordon Lee moved to Deepdale. Since his playing career ended, Nulty has studied for an Open University degree in social sciences.

	LEAGUE		*FACUP*		*FLCUP*		*OTHERS*		*TOTAL*	
	App	*Gls*	*App*	*Gls*	*App*	*Gls*	*App*	*Gls*	*App*	*Gls*
1969-70	5/2	1	0	0	1	1	0	0	6/2	2
1970-71	30/1	3	1	0	0	0	0/1	0	31/2	3
1971-72	11	1	0	0	0	0	0	0	11	1
1972-73	32/3	6	2	0	0/1	0	0	0	34/4	6
1973-74	42	9	5	0	3	0	8	3	58	12
1974-75	3/1	0	0	0	0	0	0	0	3/1	0
	123/7	20	8	0	4/1	1	8/1	3	143/9	24

GEOFF NULTY

PETER O'DOWD

James Peter O'Dowd was born in Halifax in 1908 and, after playing junior football in his home area, including a spell with Bradford as an amateur at Park Avenue, he was snapped up from under the noses of Yorkshire clubs by Blackburn Rovers in December 1926. He never really settled at Ewood Park, for the Rovers preferred him at left-half but O'Dowd felt he was better in the centre of defence. He signed for Burnley in March 1930 for £2,500. He was an ever-present in his time at Turf Moor, proving to have a cool head. With a commanding 6ft-plus physique, he played the game with no apparent effort but was deceptively quick on the ball. He was invited to join an FA tour of Canada in the summer of 1931 and came back amid glowing reports of his performances. O'Dowd left Turf Moor for Chelsea in November 1931, a fee of £5,000 being impossible to resist for a Burnley club struggling to make ends meet. In his first game for the Pensioners, against Everton, he had the misfortune to come up against Dixie Dean at the top of his form. Dean hit five goals in a 7-2 victory but O'Dowd was judged to have performed reasonably well. In his time at Stamford Bridge he won three England caps but in 1934 decided to try fresh pastures and signed for the Valenciennes club in Northern France for a fee of £3,000. He returned to England in March 1937 and ended his playing career with Torquay United. He died in Bournemouth in 1964, aged 56.

	LEAGUE		*FA CUP*		*TOTAL*	
	App	*Gls*	*App*	*Gls*	*App*	*Gls*
1929-30	10	3	0	0	10	3
1930-31	42	3	2	0	44	3
1931-32	13	2	0	0	13	2
	65	8	2	0	67	8

BRIAN O'NEIL

One of the Burnley crowd's favourite players in the mid- to late-1960s was a hard-tackling, no-nonsense, never-say-die midfielder called Brian O'Neil. The 'Bedlington Terrier' first arrived on the Turf Moor scene as a junior in 1960 and made his first-team debut in April 1963, taking over the number-four shirt from Jimmy Adamson. The contrast between the two players could not have been more stark: Adamson was a silky mover and a great thinker; O'Neil was a non-stop player who concentrated on moving the ball from 'A' to 'B' as quickly as possible, and covering himself with much mud in the process. For seven seasons he was a virtual ever-present and in every one of his 230-plus appearances for Burnley he gave maximum effort. During that time he won an England Under-23 cap and represented the Football League. At the end of the 1969-70 season, he was transferred to Southampton for £75,000 (their club record fee at the time) and went on to make almost 150 first-team appearances for the Saints before spending two years with Huddersfield Town. After 60 League appearances for Huddersfield he became player-manager of Bideford Town. Today, over twenty years after his move from Burnley, he is still a regular visitor to Turf Moor.

	LEAGUE		*FA CUP*		*FL CUP*		*OTHERS*		*TOTAL*	
	App	*Gls*	*App*	*Gls*	*App*	*Gls*	*App*	*Gls*	*App*	*Gls*
1962-63	2	0	0	0	0	0	0	0	2	0
1963-64	30	2	5	0	0	0	0	0	35	2
1964-65	35	3	5	0	0	0	0	0	40	3
1965-66	39	4	2	0	5	0	0	0	46	4
1966-67	39/1	4	2	0	3	0	7	1	51/1	5
1967-68	35	5	1	0	5	1	0	0	41	6
1968-69	16/1	1	0	0	4/1	0	0	0	20/2	1
1969-70	35/2	3	3	1	4	0	0	0	42/2	4
	231/4	22	18	1	21/1	1	7	1	277/5	25

When Vince Overson played his second game for Burnley on 10 November 1979, he created a special slice of Clarets history. Also in the team was his elder brother, Richard, and it was the first time two brothers had played in the same Burnley side since the Walders performed the same feat on the opening day of the 1904-05 season. Both Overson brothers were born in Kettering and joined Burnley as apprentices. Both were defenders, but only Vince went on to make the grade as a professional footballer. A tough-tackling no-nonsense central defender, Vince signed as an apprentice in 1978 and made his first-team debut in November 1979. Soon establishing himself in the place of long-serving Billy Rodaway, he won a Third Division championship medal with the Clarets in 1982-3. In the summer of 1986 he was transferred to Birmingham City for £25,000 and remained at St Andrew's until June 1991, when he said he wanted to return to a club nearer his Burnley home. Apart from a broken leg, Overson hardly missed a game while in the first-team squad at Burnley, his hard-tackling approach making him a great favourite with the crowd.

	LEAGUE		*FA CUP*		*FL CUP*		*OTHERS*		*TOTAL*	
	App	*Gls*	*App*	*Gls*	*App*	*Gls*	*App*	*Gls*	*App*	*Gls*
1979-80	22	0	2	0	0	0	0	0	24	0
1980-81	39	1	3	0	1	0	2	0	45	1
1981-82	36	4	6	0	1	0	2/1	0	45/1	4
1982-83	2/4	0	0	0	0	0	0	0	2/4	0
1983-84	38	0	5	0	1	0	4	0	48	0
1984-85	42	1	3	0	4	1	7	0	56	2
1985-86	28	0	0	0	2	0	6	0	36	0
	207/4	6	19	0	9	1	21/1	0	256/5	7

VINCE OVERSON

Louis Page holds a unique fascination for Burnley football followers as the only Claret to score a double hat-trick in a League match. The 7-1 win at Birmingham in April 1926 was towards the end of the first season under the revised offside law which had affected Burnley's defence more than any other. Ironically, had the men from Turf Moor lost that match, Burnley would have been relegated. Louis Antonio Page was born in Kirkdale, Liverpool, in 1899, one of four brothers, all of whom went on to play professional football and all of whom represented their country at baseball, a popular sport in England in the 1920s and '30s. After excelling in Liverpool schools football during World War One, Page joined the South Liverpool club from whom Stoke secured his services as a professional in the summer of 1919. He joined Northampton Town after a year and it was his prolific goalscoring record with the Cobblers which persuaded Burnley to bring him to Turf Moor for a big fee in May 1925. Part of the arrangement between the clubs was that former England international Jack Tresadern left Burnley to become player-manager at the County Ground. The flying winger was an immediate success with the Burnley fans and in his first season, outscored both the prodigious George Beel and Tom Roberts. By the time of the Birmingham match at St Andrews, the clouds of relegation were darkening and both Beel and Roberts were left out of the side. Page was not pleased to be asked to lead the attack but manager Albert Pickles' inspired team selection was more than justified as Page proceeded to make club history. He won all seven of his England caps during 1927 and scored his only goal for his country in a 9-1 destruction of Belgium in Brussels on 11 May 1927. The late-1920s and early '30s were lean times at Turf Moor and Louis Page's wing play and goals could not prevent relegation in 1930. In March 1932 he signed for Manchester United, but after only seven months at Old Trafford he moved to Port Vale, subsequently joining Yeovil & Petters United as player-manager in July 1933. After a spell as Newport County manager he moved to Swindon Town after the war and plotted Burnley's downfall in the FA Cup in 1948. His last managerial appointment was at Chester from 1953 to 1956, after which he acted as a scout for Leicester City. After a painful illness, Louis Page died in hospital in Birkenhead on 12 October 1959, aged 60. His place in the history of Burnley Football Club is forever assured.

	LEAGUE		*FA CUP*		*TOTAL*	
	App	*Gls*	*App*	*Gls*	*App*	*Gls*
1925-26	41	26	2	0	43	26
1926-27	36	13	3	2	39	15
1927-28	41	22	1	0	42	22
1928-29	39	17	3	2	42	19
1929-30	32	15	1	0	33	15
1930-31	29	13	0	0	29	13
1931-32	30	5	1	0	31	5
	248	111	11	4	259	115

LOUIS PAGE

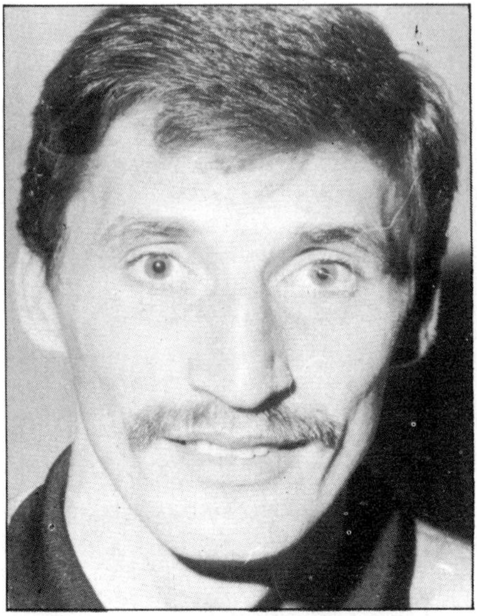

CHRIS PEARCE

One of the many players to join Burnley in the summer of 1987, Chris Pearce has been the crowd's favourite player ever since. An apprentice with Wolverhampton Wanderers, Newport-born Pearce moved to Blackburn Rovers and then Rochdale before returning to the Midlands and playing almost 50 games for Port Vale. Back in his native county, the Welsh Schoolboy international goalkeeper played 25 games for Wrexham before joining the Clarets. Burnley's most consistent 'keeper since the departure of Alan Stevenson, Pearce is capable of outstanding reflex saves, his finest hour coming at Bradford in January 1991 when he saved a penalty and made a string of exceptional saves as Burnley qualified for the Northern semi-final of the Leyland DAF Trophy. A keen golfer, Pearce is a great favourite of Burnley supporters, especially for his dancing antics which keep them entertained in quieter moments and after special victories.

	LEAGUE		*FA CUP*		*FL CUP*		*OTHERS**		*TOTAL*	
	App	*Gls*	*App*	*Gls*	*App*	*Gls*	App	Gls	*App*	*Gls*
1987-88	46	0	1	0	4	0	11	0	62	0
1988-89	39	0	1	0	4	0	4	0	48	0
1989-90	39	0	6	0	2	0	5	0	52	0
1990-91	43	0	3	0	4	0	7	0	57	0
	167	0	11	0	14	0	27	0	219	0

* Includes 1990-91 Play-off games.

MIKE PHELAN

Without doubt the best player to ever come out of the renowned Barrowford Celtic Boys' Club, Mike Phelan was destined for the top from the moment he kicked his first ball at Burnley. Unflappable, consistent, versatile and virtually injury-free (one badly broken leg apart) Phelan has performed at the very highest of levels with great distinction. He signed as an apprentice in the summer of 1980, making his first-team debut within a matter of months. Having been groomed for stardom, it was a surprise that it took him two full seasons to establish himself but when he did he became a virtual ever-present. As Burnley's slide down the League continued it was obvious that Phelan would leave Turf Moor. But it was a shock when he went to Norwich City, when both Nottingham Forest and Manchester United were displaying an interest. In his first season at Carrow Road Phelan won a Second Division championship medal and when Steve Bruce went to Old Trafford, the former Burnley player became club captain. In the summer of 1989, Phelan went to Manchester United for £750,000 and in a memorable first season won his only England cap, an FA Cup winners' medal and captained the Red Devils. His international cap came against Italy when he came on as substitute and almost scored with a shot from the edge of the area with his first touch. Equally at home in midfield, central defence or at full-back, Phelan's move to Manchester United has seen him bring his family back to his native Barrowford, and also given him the chance to watch Burnley when their matches do not conflict with Old Trafford duties. In 1990-91 he gained a European Cup-winners' Cup winners' medal and a Rumbelows League Cup runners-up medal with United.

	LEAGUE		*FA CUP*		*FL CUP*		*OTHERS*		*TOTAL*	
	App	*Gls*	*App*	*Gls*	*App*	*Gls*	*App*	*Gls*	*App*	*Gls*
1980-81	15/1	2	0	0	0	0	0	0	15/1	2
1981-82	22/1	1	2	0	1	0	3	0	28/1	1
1982-83	42	3	7	0	9	2	3	0	61	5
1983-84	44	2	4	0	2	0	7	0	57	2
1984-85	43	1	3	0	4	0	7	2	57	3
	166/2	9	16	0	16	2	20	2	218/2	13

Brian Pilkington was born in Leyland in 1933 and was playing for Leyland Motors when he signed for Burnley in April 1951. The short stocky winger made his League debut in September 1952, coming in for the injured Billy Elliott. Although he played only four more times that season, he did enough to convince manager Frank Hill of his potential. Elliott was sold to Sunderland the following summer and Pilkington became the regular left winger in the run up to the League Championship. His consistent wing play brought him England honours and he won his only full cap in a 2-0 win against Northern Ireland in Belfast in October 1954. He also won two England 'B' caps and represented the Football League. He missed only one game in the Championship campaign in 1959-60 and scored the first goal in the cliff-hanger that clinched the title at Maine Road. The following season he had to contend with the challenge of Gordon Harris and, although Pilkington scored two goals in the European Cup win against Hamburg, he was sold to Bolton Wanderers within a month. He spent three years at Burnden Park, then a season at Bury before ending his League career at Barrow, where he helped the club to gain promotion to Division Three for the first time in 1967. He returned to his first club, Leyland Motors, in 1969, taking over as manager in 1970 and later going on to manage Chorley. He still lives in Leyland, where he is an estate agent in the town as well as a local magistrate.

	LEAGUE		*FA CUP*		*FL CUP*		*OTHERS*		*TOTAL*	
	App	*Gls*	*App*	*Gls*	*App*	*Gls*	*App*	*Gls*	*App*	*Gls*
1952-53	5	0	0	0	0	0	0	0	5	0
1953-54	39	8	3	1	0	0	0	0	42	9
1954-55	35	11	0	0	0	0	0	0	35	11
1955-56	40	12	6	1	0	0	0	0	46	13
1956-57	37	5	5	2	0	0	0	0	42	7
1957-58	42	13	3	0	0	0	0	0	45	13
1958-59	39	8	5	1	0	0	0	0	44	9
1959-60	41	9	8	2	0	0	0	0	49	11
1960-61	22	1	3	0	3	1	4	2	32	4
	300	67	33	7	3	1	4	2	340	77

BRIAN PILKINGTON

Although 5ft 10in tall and over 12st, Walter Place junior, to distinguish him from his older and bigger cousin, was known as 'Little Walter'. He was born in Burnley and learned his early football playing with local sides Blue Stars and Union Stars before joining his home-town club in 1893. He soon broke into the first team, initially deputizing for the great Billy Bowes at inside-left, but played in a variety of forward positions. He was a regular member of the side for five seasons from 1894 and formed a quality left-wing partnership with Bowes, his speed and trickery down the flank coming into its own particularly in promotion year of 1897-8, when he won a Second Division championship medal. After a successful first season back in the top flight, Place could not command a regular position in 1899-1900 and played in only the last game of the season. Within days, Harry Bradshaw, who had recently left Turf Moor after three years as manager to go to Woolwich Arsenal in a similar position, signed little Walter for the Gunners. After two seasons and 42 games at Plumstead, Place returned to his home county and joined Padiham where he remained for the rest of his playing days.

	LEAGUE		*FA CUP*		*OTHERS*		*TOTAL*	
	App	*Gls*	*App*	*Gls*	*App*	*Gls*	*App*	*Gls*
1893-94	9	3	0	0	0	0	9	3
1894-95	25	5	1	0	0	0	26	5
1895-96	28	7	3	2	0	0	31	9
1896-97	29	2	1	2	2	0	32	4
1897-98	28	7	3	0	4	0	35	7
1898-99	32	6	1	0	0	0	33	6
1899-1900	1	0	0	0	0	0	1	0
	152	30	9	4	6	0	167	34

WALTER PLACE Jnr

In the years before World War One, 'Big Walter' was Burnley's most versatile player and, arguably, the most complete all-round sportsman the town had ever produced. Born in Burnley in 1870, Place first appeared for the first team as a 16-year-old in 1886 but then spent time at Colne and Bacup before returning to Turf Moor in 1890. His favourite position was right-half but he was equally at home in any forward role and, on two occasions in 1893, kept goal in the absence of Jack Hillman. As utility players often do, he suffered because of his versatility, and in his ten years with the club rarely made one position his own for any length of time. After leaving Turf Moor in 1900 he was reinstated as an amateur and captained Burnley Belvedere with distinction. He was also an accomplished athlete, being something of an expert 'backwards way' sprinter as well as the more conventional type. He was a skilful snooker player, a roller-skater of some ability and a very strong swimmer. Indeed, he is reported to have saved both human and canine life in the canal carried by aqueduct above his home town. He was a crackshot with a rifle, winning numerous prizes at local gun clubs. He played cricket to a high standard and was also a prominent bowler, occupying the presidency of the Burnley Bowlers' Association for some years. Walter Place was declared to be England's best wrestler after an international tournament at Blackburn in 1904 and his excellent performance against the Russian champion Hackenschmidt. For relaxation, Place was a breeder and flyer of homing pigeons and enjoyed some considerable success in competition. In later years he built up a reputation as a raconteur of sporting stories and won a host of friends with the sheer depth of his knowledge and experience.

WALTER PLACE Snr

	LEAGUE		*FA CUP*		*OTHERS*		*TOTAL*	
	App	*Gls*	*App*	*Gls*	*App*	*Gls*	*App*	*Gls*
1886-87	0	0	2	1	0	0	2	1
1890-91	5	2	0	0	0	0	5	2
1891-92	8	1	0	0	0	0	8	1
1892-93	2	0	0	0	0	0	2	0
1893-94	3	0	0	0	0	0	3	0
1894-95	26	0	1	0	0	0	27	0
1895-96	21	2	3	1	0	0	24	3
1896-97	30	0	1	0	4	0	35	0
1897-98	9	0	0	0	0	0	9	0
1898-99	12	1	1	0	0	0	13	1
1899-1900	20	1	1	0	0	0	21	1
	136	7	9	2	4	0	149	9

Boasting a strike ratio of better than one goal in every two games, Ray Pointer has one of the best goals-per-game ratios in Burnley history. The 'blond bombshell' failed a trial at Blackpool and returned to his native North-East. It was from Dudley Welfare that the Cramlington-born goalscorer joined the Clarets in 1957. England Under-23 honours and three full caps followed as Pointer became a vital component of the Burnley team which won the First Division title in 1959-60 and reached the FA Cup Final two years later. A Football League representative, Pointer, despite 118 goals in 222 Burnley games, lost his place to a combination of Willie Irvine and Andy Lochhead and left Burnley for Gigg Lane in 1965. He could not settle at Bury, although he did score 17 times in 19 outings. From there he went for a short spell at Coventry where he collected 13 goals in 23 games. After that Pointer, who stands second only to George Beel in the all-time goalscoring chart at Turf Moor, went to Portsmouth where he scored a further 31 goals in 149 games for Pompey, playing most of his time at Fratton Park in a midfield role. One of many former Clarets to have since involved at Bury, Pointer was a Gigg Lane coach when Bury were promoted from the Fourth Division in season 1984-5 with Martin Dobson as player-manager and Frank Casper as coach.

RAY POINTER

	LEAGUE		*FA CUP*		*FL CUP*		*OTHERS*		*TOTAL*	
	App	*Gls*	*App*	*Gls*	*App*	*Gls*	*App*	*Gls*	*App*	*Gls*
1957-58	22	8	3	2	0	0	0	0	25	10
1958-59	37	27	5	2	0	0	0	0	42	29
1959-60	42	19	8	4	0	0	0	0	50	23
1960-61	34	22	7	2	7	2	5	0	53	26
1961-62	40	25	8	1	0	0	0	0	48	26
1962-63	35	14	1	0	0	0	0	0	36	14
1963-64	10	2	3	2	0	0	0	0	13	4
1964-65	3	1	0	0	0	0	0	0	3	1
	223	118	35	13	7	2	5	0	270	133

One of the very first products of Burnley's new 'youth policy', Harry Potts was born in Hetton-le-Hole in 1920 and joined the Clarets as a professional in 1937. After making his mark in the Reserves, the young Potts had no chance to break into Second Division football before war broke out in 1939. Like more than half the team, he made his Football League debut for the Clarets on the opening day of the 1946-7 season. He was 25 years old and was one of the inspirations behind the success achieved that season. His inside-forward partner, Billy Morris, was an attack-minded player and Potts, more defensive, was the engine-room of the midfield. After four years as a virtual ever-present, during which time the club had established itself in the First Division, Potts became unsettled and asked for a transfer in the summer of 1950. With a depth of talent in the Reserves, Burnley felt able to release him and he subsequently joined Everton for a record fee the following October. Relegation befell the Goodison Park club at the end of Potts' first season and after that he was never able to command a regular first-team place, eventually joining Wolves as a coach in 1956. Harry Potts perhaps suffered more than most because of the war, hostilities breaking out just as he was about to make an impact and robbing him of seven years of his peak playing years. If the Turf Moor crowd never quite saw the best of him on the field, he was to make an even greater impact at the club in the years to come (see *Burnley Managers*).

HARRY POTTS

	LEAGUE		*FA CUP*		*TOTAL*	
	App	*Gls*	*App*	*Gls*	*App*	*Gls*
1946-47	40	15	9	2	49	17
1947-48	38	14	1	0	39	14
1948-49	36	7	3	0	39	7
1949-50	42	11	3	1	45	12
1950-51	9	0	0	0	9	0
	165	47	16	3	181	50

Scotsman Jeremy Reynolds came to Burnley from Celtic in the summer of 1895. It was a time of some upheaval at Turf Moor and Reynolds was signed to replace the departed James Crabtree at right-back, a hard act to follow indeed. He slotted in well, establishing an early understanding with left flank partner Tom McLintock. The pair were almost automatic choices over the following four years when the club experienced the contrasting fortunes of relegation and immediate promotion. Reynolds missed only one game in the Second Division championship season of 1897-8. He was a fine defender, exceptionally good in the air. It was said of him that he sometimes used his head when he should have used his feet, particularly when the ball was quite near the ground, and he suffered some facial injuries as a result. When Tom Woolfall arrived from Darwen in 1899, his place in the side was at Jeremy Reynold's expense. Reynolds decided to return home to Scotland and secured employment as a face worker down the pit.

JEREMY REYNOLDS

	LEAGUE		*FA CUP*		*OTHERS*		*TOTAL*	
	App	*Gls*	*App*	*Gls*	*App*	*Gls*	*App*	*Gls*
1895-96	27	0	3	0	0	0	30	0
1896-97	22	0	1	0	4	0	27	0
1897-98	29	0	3	0	4	0	36	0
1898-99	27	0	2	0	0	0	29	0
1899-1900	2	0	0	0	0	0	2	0
	107	0	9	0	8	0	124	0

The only Burnley player ever to score for the club at Wembley, Jimmy Robson's consolation in the 1962 Final was the 100th goal in an FA Cup Final beneath the twin towers. Robson was born in Pelton, near Chester-le-Street, in 1939 and joined Burnley on his 17th birthday in 1956. A tall, rangy player, he soon impressed in the club's junior teams and quickly got his first-team chance, donning Jimmy McIlroy's number-eight shirt for a home match against Blackpool in October 1956, and scoring a cracker in a 2-2 draw. Competition was fierce, of course, but after Robson vied with Albert Cheesebrough for the inside-left berth in 1958-9, it was Cheesebrough who was considered surplus to requirements and left the club in 1959. Although the Championship season was not Robson's best for goalscoring, he did make the football world sit up and take notice when he hit five in an 8-0 hammering of the Cup holders, Nottingham Forest, in November 1959. He had also won his only representative honour earlier that year, being chosen for the England Under-23's against West Germany and scoring in a 2-2 draw in Bochum. He was the club's top marksman in 1960-61, scoring three hat-tricks in seven games early in the season and sharing a total of 63 goals with Ray Pointer in that memorable campaign. Like the club itself, Robson was never quite the same after the departure of Jimmy McIlroy in 1963. He was transferred to Blackpool in 1965, for a bargain fee but, after the Seasiders' relegation from Division One in 1967, he joined Barnsley. After helping the Oakwell club out of the Fourth Division in 1968, he moved to Bury in 1970, giving sterling service before retiring from League football in 1973. He returned to Turf Moor briefly, assisting with the reserve team, but then joined Huddersfield Town as a coach. He now lives locally, following his trade as an electrician. Until recently he was the manager of Bacup Borough.

	LEAGUE		*FA CUP*		*FL CUP*		*OTHERS*		*TOTAL*	
	App	*Gls*	*App*	*Gls*	*App*	*Gls*	*App*	*Gls*	*App*	*Gls*
1956-57	4	1	0	0	-	-	0	0	4	1
1957-58	4	2	0	0	-	-	0	0	4	2
1958-59	33	10	3	1	-	-	0	0	36	11
1959-60	38	18	8	4	-	-	0	0	46	22
1960-61	36	25	7	5	6	4	5	3	54	37
1961-62	41	15	8	4	0	0	0	0	49	19
1962-63	16	2	2	0	0	0	0	0	18	2
1963-64	25	6	0	0	0	0	0	0	25	6
1964-65	5	0	1	0	0	0	0	0	6	0
	202	79	29	14	6	4	5	3	242	100

JIMMY ROBSON

Having made his debut in Colin Waldron's place at the end of the 1971-2 season, Liverpudlian Billy Rodaway failed to make any impression at all the following season as Burnley clinched the Second Division title to return to the top flight. A schoolboy international, Rodaway always struggled to get into the team in his natural centre-half position whilst Waldron and Jim Thomson were at the club, a fact reflected in Rodaway's occasional appearances in a number-nine shirt. When Waldron departed for Manchester United, Rodaway formed a partnership with Jim Thomson which lasted until their Burnley careers both faded in season 1980-81. He played for Peterborough United, Blackpool and Tranmere Rovers before returning to Turf Moor on a free transfer for the traumatic 1986-7 campaign. Rodaway missed only two games that season, his last match being the much fabled 'Orient Game'. Released in the summer of 1987, Rodaway went in to non-League football and played for Runcorn and Altrincham before joining Colne Dynamoes, for whom he played in the successful FA Vase Final 12 months after leaving the Clarets.

	LEAGUE		*FA CUP*		*FL CUP*		*OTHERS*		*TOTAL*	
	App	*Gls*	*App*	*Gls*	*App*	*Gls*	*App*	*Gls*	*App*	*Gls*
1971-72	2	0	0	0	0	0	0	0	2	0
1972-73	0	0	0	0	0	0	0	0	0	0
1973-74	9	0	0	0	0	0	3	0	12	0
1974-75	28/1	1	0	0	3	0	0	0	31/1	1
1975-76	15	0	0	0	0	0	0	0	15	0
1976-77	42	0	3	0	1	0	3	0	49	0
1977-78	33	0	2	0	4	0	3	0	42	0
1978-79	39	0	4	0	3	0	9	0	55	0
1979-80	28/1	0	2	0	2	0	3	0	35/1	0
1980-81	5	0	0	0	3	0	1	0	9	0
1986-87	44	2	1	0	2	0	6	0	53	2
	245/2	3	12	0	18	0	28	0	303/2	3

BILLY RODAWAY

'King James' or 'James I' was one of those Burnley players of long ago who seemed to be forever remembered long after other players of their era were forgotten. James Daniel Ross was born in Edinburgh on 28 March 1866 and played for Edinburgh St Bernard's before coming south to join Preston North End in 1884. He was joined at Deepdale by his brother, Nick, and both men were in the North End side that hammered Hyde United 26-0 in the FA Cup in 1887, Jimmy Ross helping himself to eight goals. An inside-forward of skill and artistry, Ross was one of the team of Preston 'Invincibles', who won the Cup and League double in 1889 and the League again in 1890. He also scored two goals in Preston's 5-2 win on the very first day of League football, 8 September 1888, against Burnley. After a decade at Deepdale, Ross moved to Liverpool in September 1894 and, after relegation in his first season, inspired the Reds to the Second Division championship in 1895-6. He joined Burnley in March 1897, along with Malcolm McVean, but his influence failed to prevent relegation after the Test matches. His scoring partnership with centre-forward Wilf Toman, however, was a leading factor in bringing the Second Division championship to Turf Moor the following season, Ross contributing 23 goals to break the club scoring record. The following season Ross fell out with his right-wing partner Tom Morrison and was transferred to Manchester City in February 1899. He was to play inside the legendary Billy Meredith at Hyde Road and in Ross' first game for City, he got two goals to Meredith's hat-trick in a 5-0 win against Barnsley. He netted a total of seven goals in the last nine games of the season and City went on to win the Second Division championship.

	LEAGUE		*FA CUP*		*OTHERS*		*TOTAL*	
	App	*Gls*	*App*	*Gls*	*App*	*Gls*	*App*	*Gls*
1896-97	4	1	0	0	3	0	7	1
1897-98	27	23	3	1	4	1	34	25
1898-99	20	5	2	1	0	0	22	6
	51	29	5	2	7	1	63	32

Jimmy Ross was one of British football's real characters at the end of the last century. Tragically, after only three seasons in Manchester he contracted an acute skin disease, succumbed to raging fever and died on 12 June 1902, aged only 36.

JIMMY ROSS

Gateshead-born Derek Scott made his Burnley debut as a 17-year-old in April 1975 but it was almost a year before he established himself as a regular in the number-two shirt. That season was Burnley's last in the First Division and Scott continued to dominate the right-back position until losing his place to Brian Laws. The England Schoolboy international then made a successful transition to the midfield and proved to be a more than useful asset to the team in that role. It was as a midfielder that Scott won a Third Division championship medal in 1981-2, but three years later he was transferred to Bolton Wanderers for £20,000. Scott almost moved to Burnden Park a season earlier in a deal which would have brought striker Jeff Chandler to Turf Moor. In his first season at Bolton he appeared at Wembley in the Sherpa Van Trophy Final, but a season later when the Wanderers were relegated to the Fourth Division it meant that Scott had played in all four divisions of the Football League. Given a free transfer by Bolton, Scott, the son-in-law of former Burnley manager Brian Miller, went to HFS Loans League club, Colne Dynamoes. When that club folded he became one of eight former Clarets on the books of West Lancashire League side, Burnley Bank Hall, and he is still a regular visitor to Turf Moor.

	LEAGUE		*FA CUP*		*FL CUP*		*OTHERS*		*TOTAL*	
	App	*Gls*	*App*	*Gls*	*App*	*Gls*	*App*	*Gls*	*App*	*Gls*
1974-75	2	0	0	0	0	0	0	0	2	0
1975-76	17	2	0	0	0	0	0	0	17	2
1976-77	13/1	0	1	0	1	0	3	0	18/1	0
1977-78	26	1	2	0	1	0	0	0	29	1
1978-79	35	1	4	0	3	0	7	0	49	1
1979-80	27/1	2	2	0	2	0	3	0	34/1	2
1980-81	29	9	3	0	4	1	2	1	38	11
1981-82	29/1	2	0	0	1	0	5	1	35/1	3
1982-83	34/2	2	6	0	7	2	2	0	49/2	4
1983-84	38/2	4	5	0	2	0	6	1	51/2	5
1984-85	27/1	1	0	0	3	0	4	1	34/1	2
	277/8	24	23	0	24	3	32	4	356/8	31

DEREK SCOTT

BOBBY SEITH

After a distinguished career at Turf Moor in the 1950s, the final few months of Bobby Seith's time at Burnley were tinged with sadness. He lost his place in the side in the final month of the run-in to the League title in 1960 and, after a clash with chairman Bob Lord, was placed on the transfer list and denied a fully-deserved Championship medal. He was born in Coatbridge in 1932 and, after joining Burnley as a junior, signed professional forms for the club in 1949. He was good enough to displace Jimmy Adamson at right-half when he first broke into the team in 1953, but it was ultimately at Reg Attwell's expense that he became a regular in the side. After over 200 First Division games, he signed for Dundee in the summer of 1960 and won a Scottish League Championship medal at Dens Park two years later. He finished playing in 1965 and joined the Dundee coaching staff, later moving to Rangers in a similar capacity. He left Ibrox to take up his first managerial appointment at Preston in 1968, staying at Deepdale for three years before being offered the job of Scotland's youth-team manager in 1970. He later managed Hearts for a four-year spell but now keeps in contact with the game as a knowledgable radio sports commentator in Dundee, where he lives with his wife, a Burnley girl. A qualified chiropodist, Bobby Seith will always be remembered as a cultured wing-half, strong in the tackle and an accurate passer of the ball. Certainly a loyal servant of the club who perhaps deserved a kinder send-off.

	LEAGUE		*FA CUP*		*TOTAL*	
	App	*Gls*	*App*	*Gls*	*App*	*Gls*
1953-54	23	0	0	0	23	0
1954-55	13	0	0	0	13	0
1955-56	33	0	6	0	39	0
1956-57	41	1	5	0	46	1
1957-58	32	2	3	0	35	2
1958-59	42	3	5	0	47	3
1959-60	27	0	8	0	35	0
	211	6	27	0	238	6

LES SHANNON

A member of Liverpool's successful reserve side of 1948-9, Merseysider Les Shannon was transferred to Burnley in November of that year after an outstanding display for the Reds against a Rest of the Central League team. He played a few games, replacing Jackie Chew on the right wing, but found it difficult to make his mark and it was not until the retirement of Billy Morris that Shannon came into his own. Converted to a deep-lying inside-forward, he was the perfect foil for Jimmy McIlroy and contributed 15 goals in 1952-3. He won three caps for the England 'B' side and proved to be an even better player when he moved to wing-half following the departure of crowd favourite Reg Attwell. He continued to perform with style until 1958 when, in his early 30s, the competition from younger men took its inevitable toll and he retired from playing. He had coaching spells with various clubs before joining Bury as manager in 1966 and guiding them to promotion to Division Two in 1968. He followed this by moving to Blackpool and achieving promotion there also, this time to Division One in 1970. He parted company with the Seasiders and, after many years coaching in the Middle East, now lives in his native Liverpool. Sharp-eyed television viewers may have noticed his name as an adviser in the recent Channel 4 series *The Manageress.*

	LEAGUE		*FA CUP*		*TOTAL*	
	App	*Gls*	*App*	*Gls*	*App*	*Gls*
1949-50	8	1	0	0	8	1
1950-51	0	0	0	0	0	0
1951-52	30	9	4	2	34	11
1952-53	42	15	4	1	46	16
1953-54	30	7	3	2	33	9
1954-55	42	1	1	0	43	1
1955-56	41	2	3	0	44	2
1956-57	26	2	1	0	27	2
1957-58	35	2	3	0	38	2
1958-59	8	0	0	0	8	0
	262	39	19	5	281	44

Leonard Smelt was a very popular player at Turf Moor immediately after World War One and missed only four games in his first four seasons. He was the dependable right-back in the Championship side of 1920-21. A native of Rotherham, Smelt first experienced League football with Gainsborough Trinity, then, during the war, assisted Rotherham County, Leeds City and Burnley themselves before signing professional forms for the Clarets in March 1919. He was a very consistent and reliable player and was made captain for the day on his 100th consecutive match for the first team on 17 November 1923. He won the toss and never put a foot wrong as Burnley beat West Ham 5-1. After a season coaching the 'A' team, he was given a free transfer in 1926 and joined Third Division North strugglers Barrow, where he ended his playing days. He rejoined Burnley in the summer of 1932 as a member of the coaching staff but within six months he was taken ill and died, in January 1933, aged only 47.

	LEAGUE		*FA CUP*		*OTHERS*		*TOTAL*	
	App	*Gls*	*App*	*Gls*	*App*	*Gls*	*App*	*Gls*
1919-20	42	0	4	0	0	0	46	0
1920-21	39	0	3	0	0	0	42	0
1921-22	41	0	2	0	1	0	44	0
1922-23	42	0	1	0	0	0	43	0
1923-24	31	0	7	0	0	0	38	0
1924-25	34	0	1	0	0	0	35	0
	229	0	18	0	1	0	248	0

LEN SMELT

After playing his schoolboy and junior football in the Fulledge area of Burnley, in the shadow of Turf Moor, Albert Smith was snapped up by his home-town club, signing as a professional in October 1905. A flying left winger, Smith went straight into the League side and soon made the left-flank position his own. He and Arthur Bell made a feared partnership and Albert Smith created countless goals for his namesake in the middle, Dick Smith. Albert Smith was one of a number of Burnley players who moved to Bradford around the time they entered the League. He joined the Park Avenue side in November 1908, three months into their inaugural season, and stayed until 1911. He was transferred to Rochdale where he remained throughout the wartime period before moving to Grimsby Town in 1919. He returned to Rochdale in 1923.

	LEAGUE		*FA CUP*		*TOTAL*	
	App	*Gls*	*App*	*Gls*	*App*	*Gls*
1905-06	17	4	0	0	17	4
1906-07	37	5	1	0	38	5
1907-08	37	10	1	0	38	10
1908-09	14	2	0	0	14	2
	105	21	2	0	107	21

ALBERT SMITH

CECIL SMITH

In Cecil Smith's four seasons at Turf Moor, Burnley never finished in the top half of the Second Division table. At a more successful time in the club's history, his goals-per-game ratio and his rugged, no-nonsense approach would certainly have brought him greater rewards. He was born in Wrexham in 1904 and played his early football at the end of the war with Oswestry and Welshpool before signing for his home-town club in 1925. After two seasons as leading goalscorer, he joined Wigan Borough, then in the Third Division North, before a short spell at Notts County in 1930. He left League football for a time, playing for Macclesfield, then for Cheshire League side Stalybridge Celtic, for whom he scored 77 goals in the 1931-2 season. Not surprisingly, his record haul still stands to this day. He joined Burnley in June 1932, as the Clarets sought to replace the prolific George Beel, sold to Lincoln the previous February. Cecil Smith soon established himself as a favourite with the crowd, his fearless leadership of the line bringing goals for himself and his colleagues. He became feared by goalkeepers as he thought nothing of shoulder-charging in the six-yard box at every available opportunity. His game was built around aggression, but only during matches, off the field he was a perfect gentleman. After a relatively barren spell in 1936, Smith lost his place to a youngster called Tommy Lawton. It was the beginning of the end for Cecil Smith and he was transferred to Cardiff City at the end of the season. At the end of his playing days, Smith came back to live in Burnley, working in the local hospital service, then at an engineering firm in the town before retiring. Cecil Smith, one of the real characters of Burnley football died in 1977. His spirit lives on at Turf Moor however, his daughter Betty and son-in-law, Mike are familiar figures at the ground on match days, both working hard for Burnley FC.

	LEAGUE		*FA CUP*		*TOTAL*	
	App	*Gls*	*App*	*Gls*	*App*	*Gls*
1932-33	27	14	4	2	31	16
1933-34	32	17	1	1	33	18
1934-35	18	8	6	2	24	10
1935-36	29	10	2	0	31	10
	106	49	13	5	119	54

RICHARD SMITH

Dick Smith arrived from Workington in September 1904 and went straight into the first team, scoring on his League debut. He took time to settle into his role as leader of the attack in his first two seasons, and played with numerous inside-forward partners. By 1906-07, Arthur Bell was establishing himself at inside-left and the two seemed to develop an understanding, netting 29 goals between them in a moderate season for the club. The following season brought an even better haul for the pair — 31 goals — with Smith's contribution 24, a new record for the club in League football, edging out Jimmy Ross, who netted 23 in 1897-8. It is interesting to note that Dick Smith's tally was beaten only twice more before World War One, on both occasions by the legendary Bert Freeman; and each time Burnley were the League's top scorers. He was perhaps just past his peak when he was selected as travelling reserve for the Football League against the Scottish League in Glasgow in 1909. Afterwards, his club form suffered and he lost his place to a variety of stop-gap centre-forwards who led the Clarets' attack until the advent of Bert Freeman. Dick Smith, one of Burnley's best-ever goalscoring centre-forwards, returned to Workington in 1910 to become a publican.

	LEAGUE		*FA CUP*		*TOTAL*	
	App	*Gls*	*App*	*Gls*	*App*	*Gls*
1904-05	27	8	1	0	28	8
1905-06	31	7	0	0	31	7
1906-07	36	17	1	0	37	17
1907-08	36	24	1	0	37	24
1908-09	35	13	6	5	41	18
1909-10	9	2	2	0	11	2
	174	71	11	5	185	76

Burnley's first-choice 'keeper for more than 11 years, Alan Stevenson's record with the Clarets was remarkable in that he was an ever-present in the 1972-3 Second Division championship campaign, and also in the 1981-2 Third Division title-winning season. Born in Staveley, near Chesterfield, Stevenson launched his career with the Spireites and won a Fourth Division championship medal with them in his first season, 1969-70. He moved to Burnley in January 1972 and within 18 months the Clarets were back in the First Division. Already an England Under-23 player, Stevenson was often believed to be on course for a full cap, but never made the step to the very top flight. During his 11-year spell at Burnley, only Gerry Peyton ever posed a serious threat to Stevenson's domination of the green jersey and, when Peyton was sold to Fulham, Stevenson's missed matches were almost only due to injury. The two championship seasons apart, Stevenson was also an ever-present in the 1977-8 campaign. Like many followers of the club, Stevenson was astonished to be given a free transfer in the summer of 1983, especially as he was only two games short of creating a post-war appearance record for the Clarets. He played for Rotherham United before combining playing duties with the role of commercial manager at Hartlepool United. He went on to become commercial manager with Middlesbrough before taking on the same role with West Bromwich Albion.

ALAN STEVENSON

	LEAGUE		*FA CUP*		*FL CUP*		*OTHERS*		*TOTAL*	
	App	*Gls*	*App*	*Gls*	*App*	*Gls*	*App*	*Gls*	*App*	*Gls*
1971-72	17	0	0	0	0	0	0	0	17	0
1972-73	42	0	2	0	1	0	2	0	47	0
1973-74	40	0	5	0	3	0	8	0	56	0
1974-75	39	0	1	0	3	0	0	0	43	0
1975-76	22	0	0	0	5	0	0	0	27	0
1976-77	32	0	3	0	0	0	1	0	36	0
1977-78	42	0	2	0	4	0	3	0	51	0
1978-79	42	0	4	0	3	0	9	0	58	0
1979-80	40	0	2	0	2	0	3	0	47	0
1980-81	44	0	3	0	4	0	3	0	54	0
1981-82	46	0	6	0	2	0	4	0	58	0
1982-83	32	0	5	0	9	0	3	0	49	0
	438	0	33	0	36	0	36	0	543	0

Jimmy Strong was the model 'Mr Consistency', literally the first man on the team-sheet. And, from the resumption of League football after the war in August 1946, he did not miss a single League or Cup match until March 1951. Strong played in 203 successive League matches (220 altogether), easily a club record, until injury let in Joe McNulty at Easter 1951. Strong was born in Morpeth in 1916 and signed for Hartlepool in 1934, going on to play for Chesterfield, Portsmouth and Walsall before the outbreak of war. He was a regular guest player for Burnley during the later war years and took his place as the last line of the formidable 'Iron Curtain' defence in 1946. After fending off the challenge of Joe McNulty, Strong was eventually displaced by Des Thompson in December 1952 and he decided to retire from playing. He left the game completely but continued to live locally, keeping a poultry farm before his death some years ago.

JIMMY STRONG

	LEAGUE		*FA CUP*		*TOTAL*	
	App	*Gls*	*App*	*Gls*	*App*	*Gls*
1946-47	42	0	9	0	51	0
1947-48	42	0	1	0	43	0
1948-49	42	0	3	0	45	0
1949-50	42	0	3	0	45	0
1950-51	40	0	1	0	41	0
1951-52	36	0	4	0	40	0
1952-53	20	0	0	0	20	0
	264	0	21	0	285	0

JOHN TALBUT

England Schoolboy international centre-half Oxford-born John Talbut signed for Burnley in 1957, aged 17, and made his first appearances in League football in two games against Leicester City over Christmas 1958. The competition for places in the middle of Burnley's defence was fierce, however, and with Tommy Cummings and Brian Miller around, Talbut played in only seven League games in four years. He displaced Cummings, however, as first-choice centre-half in 1962 and for three seasons made the position his own, his dependable performances winning him seven England Under-23 caps in 1964. In 1966, Talbut was no longer a regular as the central defensive combination of Miller and the newly-emerging Sam Todd was preferred. With Dave Merrington also in the wings, Talbut accepted the opportunity presented by West Brom and moved to The Hawthorns in December 1966 for £30,000. He was a virtual ever-present in his time in the Midlands and made almost 200 appearances for Albion, including their FA Cup Final win over Everton in 1968. He also gained a runners-up medal in the League Cup Final of 1970. He moved to Belgium in 1971, as player-coach to KV Mechelen, and retired three years later to open a restaurant in his adopted country.

	LEAGUE		*FA CUP*		*FL CUP*		*OTHERS*		*TOTAL*	
	App	*Gls*	*App*	*Gls*	*App*	*Gls*	*App*	*Gls*	*App*	*Gls*
1958-59	2	0	0	0	-	-	0	0	2	0
1959-60	0	0	0	0	-	-	0	0	0	0
1960-61	2	0	0	0	1	0	0	0	3	0
1961-62	3	0	0	0	0	0	0	0	3	0
1962-63	40	0	3	0	0	0	0	0	43	0
1963-64	41	0	5	0	0	0	0	0	46	0
1964-65	31	0	4	0	0	0	0	0	35	0
1965-66	13	0	2	0	2	0	0	0	17	0
1966-67	6	0	0	0	2	1	3	0	11	1
	138	0	14	0	5	1	3	0	160	1

DAVID TAYLOR

David Taylor was signed by Burnley in December 1911, to fill the problem left-back spot. He joined the club from Bradford City, where he had won an FA Cup winners' medal the previous April as the Yorkshiremen beat Newcastle United in the Final after a 1-0 win against Burnley in the fourth round. He was born in Bannockburn and, after playing for Motherwell, joined Glasgow Rangers. He left them for Bradford City in October 1910. Taylor enjoyed a reputation as a sprinter on both sides of the border and was widely acknowledged as the fastest full-back in the Football League. He was a regular in the first team before the war and won his second FA Cup winners' medal in 1914. He was unable to command a regular first-team place after the war, however, and, after starting the Championship season partnering Len Smelt, he lost the left-back position to Clifford Jones. He re-established himself in 1922, but in 1924 decided to end his playing career and went back to his native Scotland, joining St Johnstone as manager. Later in his career he had a brief spell as a coach with Blackburn Rovers and came on the management scene again in 1938 when he spent two years with Carlisle United. He retired to his beloved Scotland and died at his home in Bridge of Allan, near Stirling, on 6 August 1949.

	LEAGUE		*FA CUP*		*OTHERS*		*TOTAL*	
	App	*Gls*	*App*	*Gls*	*App*	*Gls*	*App*	*Gls*
1911-12	21	0	1	0	0	0	22	0
1912-13	30	1	6	0	0	0	36	1
1913-14	30	1	8	0	0	0	38	1
1914-15	34	1	3	0	0	0	37	1
1919-20	3	0	0	0	0	0	3	0
1920-21	11	0	0	0	0	0	11	0
1921-22	15	0	2	0	1	0	18	0
1922-23	40	1	1	0	0	0	41	1
1923-24	37	1	7	0	0	0	44	1
	221	5	28	0	1	0	250	5

Burnley-born Joseph Taylor was a one-club man throughout his Football League career and was the first Claret to make 300 League appearances for the club. In his early days in local football, Taylor was a prolific goalscorer and once scored 26 goals in a match in his side's 42-0 win. Much to his chagrin, the game had to be replayed as the opposition 'did not try'. He joined Bacup Borough in 1892 and signed for Burnley in November 1893. By now his recognized position was as a half-back and it was here, alongside John Espie and Archie Livingstone, that he made his League debut in a 4-0 defeat at Preston on 26 January 1895. His goals were quite rare from his defensive position, only 12 in his entire League career. He scored half of these in the Clarets' Second Division championship season of 1897-8, when he was an ever-present in League, Cup and Test matches, at centre-half. He retired at the end of the 1906-07 season and severed his connection with the game.

JOE TAYLOR

	LEAGUE		*FA CUP*		*OTHERS*		*TOTAL*	
	App	*Gls*	*App*	*Gls*	*App*	*Gls*	*App*	*Gls*
1894-95	6	0	0	0	0	0	6	0
1895-96	21	1	3	0	0	0	24	1
1896-97	30	1	1	0	4	0	35	1
1897-98	30	6	3	1	4	0	37	7
1898-99	26	0	1	0	0	0	27	0
1899-1900	34	1	1	0	0	0	35	1
1900-01	34	0	3	1	0	0	37	1
1901-02	32	2	2	0	0	0	34	2
1902-03	33	0	1	0	0	0	34	0
1903-04	19	0	2	0	0	0	21	0
1904-05	30	0	2	0	0	0	32	0
1905-06	17	0	1	0	0	0	18	0
1906-07	11	1	1	0	0	0	12	1
	323	12	21	2	8	0	352	14

Steve Taylor has a goalscoring record that any player would be proud of, but it was a penalty he missed that will always stick in the minds of Burnley fans. Taylor scored 43 goals in 118 games during two spells with the Clarets, but his penalty miss against Sheffield Wednesday in an FA Cup quarter-final cost Burnley dearly as they were thrashed in the replay. A goalscorer wherever he played, the much-travelled Taylor first came to Burnley in the summer of 1980. He moved on three years later after losing his place to Terry Donavon. Royton-born Taylor started his career with Bolton Wanderers and played for Port Vale, Oldham Athletic, Luton Town and Mansfield Town before arriving at Turf Moor. When he left Burnley, he played for Wigan Athletic, Stockport County, Rochdale and Preston before re-signing for the Clarets. After a full season and an appearance at Wembley in the Sherpa Van Trophy Final, Taylor was again displaced, and again sought solace at Spotland. A tireless campaigner who was either loved or hated by the crowd, Taylor has scored more than 100 goals in the Football League.

STEVE TAYLOR

	LEAGUE		*FA CUP*		*FL CUP*		*OTHERS*		*TOTAL*	
	App	*Gls*	*App*	*Gls*	*App*	*Gls*	*App*	*Gls*	*App*	*Gls*
1980-81	37/1	16	2	0	4	0	3	1	46/1	17
1981-82	21/1	9	4	3	1	0	4	2	30/1	14
1982-83	22/4	12	7	2	6/2	1	3	0	38/6	15
1987-88	38/4	6	1	0	3	0	8	0	50/4	6
1988-89	0/3	0	0	0	0	0	0/2	0	0/5	0
	118/13	43	14	5	14/2	1	18/2	3	164/17	52

DAVID THOMAS

In a club renowned for the excellence of its wing play, Dave Thomas was another shining example of the winger's art at its very best. Burnley's youngest-ever First Division player — only the legendary Tommy Lawton has played at a younger age, in a Second Division game — Thomas was already on his way to securing a first-team place on a regular basis when he helped Burnley win the FA Youth Cup in 1967-8. After over 150 games for Burnley, a number of clubs started to show interest in Thomas. But, despite the attentions of clubs like Manchester United, Everton and Leeds United, he was surprisingly sold to Burnley's biggest Second Division rivals, Queen's Park Rangers, for £165,000. In his first season at Loftus Road, 1972-3, he played in a side which finished second — runners-up to Burnley. Almost five years and eight England caps followed before Thomas was transferred to Everton for £200,000. He played over 70 games for them before being one of the many victims of a wholesale clear-out in 1979. Brief spells with Wolves, Vancouver Whitecaps and Middlesbrough followed before Thomas became a player-coach and youth-team manager at Portsmouth. Since then he has been involved in senior non-League football in the south of England.

	LEAGUE		*FA CUP*		*FL CUP*		*OTHERS*		*TOTAL*	
	App	*Gls*	*App*	*Gls*	*App*	*Gls*	*App*	*Gls*	*App*	*Gls*
1966-67	1	0	0	0	0	0	0	0	1	0
1967-68	3	0	0	0	0	0	0	0	3	0
1968-69	37/2	4	2	0	8	3	0	0	47/2	7
1969-70	34/2	4	0	0	3	1	0	0	37/2	5
1970-71	34	3	1	0	1	0	2	0	38	3
1971-72	33	4	1	0	3	0	0	0	37	4
1972-73	11	4	0	0	1	0	0	0	12	4
	153/4	19	4	0	16	4	2	0	175/4	23

HARRY THOMSON

Not big for a goalkeeper at 5ft 9in, what Harry Thomson lacked in inches he made up for with supreme confidence, ability and agility. Signed in the summer of 1959, Thomson spent almost six years as understudy to Adam Blacklaw before making his debut in a 2-0 win at Leicester in March 1965 during which he saved a penalty, a feat he performed on many occasions. Thomson's most famous game came in February 1967 in Naples. He saved a penalty and made a string of remarkable saves as the Clarets overcame the challenge of Napoli in the European Fairs Cup, a performance after which he was likened to 'A God in a green jersey' by one national newspaper reporter. Five months later, the battle for the 'keeper's jersey was over as Blacklaw was transferred to Blackburn Rovers. Thomson had the position to himself for a couple of seasons but was then transferred to Blackpool following the arrival at Burnley of Peter Mellor from Witton Albion. He played almost 60 games for the Seasiders before moving on again, this time to Barrow where he finished his career.

	LEAGUE		*FA CUP*		*FL CUP*		*OTHERS*		*TOTAL*	
	App	*Gls*	*App*	*Gls*	*App*	*Gls*	*App*	*Gls*	*App*	*Gls*
1964-65	8	0	0	0	0	0	0	0	8	0
1965-66	15	0	0	0	2	0	0	0	17	0
1966-67	19	0	2	0	1	0	4	0	26	0
1967-68	41	0	1	0	5	0	0	0	47	0
1968-69	34	0	2	0	7	0	0	0	43	0
	117	0	5	0	15	0	4	0	141	0

Very few players have enjoyed Burnley careers which have spanned three decades, but defender Jim Thomson is one of that select band. A Glaswegian, Thomson went from club football in Scotland to Chelsea. After 33 games with the Stamford Bridge club he moved to Turf Moor for £40,000, a considerable fee in 1968. Originally playing for the Clarets at full-back, Thomson — he later captained the side to an Anglo-Scottish Cup Final — soon moved to his preferred position in the heart of the defence where he formed a formidable partnership with Colin Waldron and later with Billy Rodaway. His almost 300 League appearances for Burnley included an ever-present role in the 1972-3 Second Division championship campaign; he was one of six players to feature in all 42 games that season. He was finally released in 1981 and after a spell with non-League Morecambe worked in the brewery trade as a representative. In 1986, Thomson returned to Turf Moor as commercial manager but after a year he was on the move again, first to a soft drinks company and then back into the brewery business. Still a regular visitor to matches at Turf Moor, Thomson is fondly remembered for his utter loyalty to the Burnley cause.

	LEAGUE		*FA CUP*		*FL CUP*		*OTHERS*		*TOTAL*	
	App	*Gls*	*App*	*Gls*	*App*	*Gls*	*App*	*Gls*	*App*	*Gls*
1968-69	7/1	0	1	0	1	0	0	0	9/1	0
1969-70	13/1	0	3	0	0	0	0	0	16/1	0
1970-71	12	0	0	0	1	0	1	0	14	0
1971-72	14	1	1	0	0	0	0	0	15	1
1972-73	42	1	2	0	1	0	2	0	47	1
1973-74	31	0	4	0	3	0	5	0	43	0
1974-75	13/1	0	1	0	0	0	0	0	14/1	0
1975-76	40	0	1	0	5	0	0	0	46	0
1976-77	27	0	3	0	1	0	3	0	34	0
1977-78	31	0	2	0	1	0	0	0	34	0
1978-79	41	1	4	1	3	0	9	1	57	3
1979-80	20	0	0	0	2	0	2	0	24	0
1980-81	3	0	0	0	3	1	1	0	7	1
	294/3	3	22	1	21	1	23	1	360/3	6

JIM THOMSON

A victim of Burnley's strength in depth, Sammy Todd never really fulfilled his potential at Turf Moor. A versatile player who functioned either in midfield or defence, Todd was a tall, blond-haired figure who faced a continual scrap for a first-team place with players like Brian Miller, John Talbut and Dave Merrington. Born in Belfast, Todd came to Burnley from Glentoran in 1962 and made his League debut on the last day of the 1963-4 season, at right-back in Burnley's 7-2 win over Spurs. Although never really establishing himself as a first-team regular, Todd did enough to earn international recognition at Under-23 level in 1965 and the following season gained the first of his 11 full caps for Northern Ireland. After just over 100 appearances for Burnley in seven seasons, Todd was transferred to Sheffield Wednesday in May 1970 and also had a loan spell with Mansfield Town during his time at Hillsborough. In May 1974, after 22 full League appearances for the Owls, he was released and joined Great Harwood.

	LEAGUE		*FA CUP*		*FL CUP*		*OTHERS*		*TOTAL*	
	App	*Gls*	*App*	*Gls*	*App*	*Gls*	*App*	*Gls*	*App*	*Gls*
1963-64	1	0	0	0	0	0	0	0	1	0
1964-65	17	1	0	0	0	0	0	0	17	1
1965-66	17/2	0	0	0	0	0	0	0	17/2	0
1966-67	23/3	0	0/1	0	3	1	3	0	29/4	1
1967-68	19	0	0	0	0	0	0	0	19	0
1968-69	6/1	0	0	0	1/1	0	0	0	7/2	0
1969-70	25/2	0	0	0	3	0	0	0	28/2	0
	108/8	1	0/1	0	7/1	1	3	0	118/10	2

SAMMY TODD

DAVID WALDERS

When David Walders arrived from Barrow in July 1903, his reputation as a fine young centre-half had come before him. He went straight into Burnley's first team at the heart of the defence, Joe Taylor, who had filled the position for almost two seasons, moving to left-half to accommodate him. Walders was born in Barrow-in-Furness in 1884 and in his early teens became something of a hot property in this somewhat out of the way part of the country. He was tall, commanding and exceptionally good in the air and chose to come to Burnley aged only 19. His brother Jonathon, known as Jack, followed him from Barrow to Turf Moor in 1904 and when the two lined up together in the opening game of the season on 3 September 1904, it was the first occasion that two brothers had played in the same Burnley side. After three years as almost a permanent fixture, David Walders was surprisingly transferred to Oldham in May 1906 as the Latics were building a side strong enough to win election to the Football League. David was immediately followed to Boundary Park by brother Jack and the two were instrumental in Oldham's election to Division Two the following summer. David Walders later had a spell coaching in Holland with Sparta Rotterdam and, after serving his country with distinction in World War One, returned to live in Burnley and acted as a talent scout for the Clarets.

	LEAGUE		*FA CUP*		*TOTAL*	
	App	*Gls*	*App*	*Gls*	*App*	*Gls*
1903-04	33	2	2	3	35	5
1904-05	32	1	2	0	34	1
1905-06	28	0	0	0	28	0
	93	3	4	3	97	6

In the 1960s, spending money on players was not a usual custom at Turf. Yet within four months of 1967 it happened twice and both players went on to serve the club with distinction. Frank Casper was the first to arrive and four months later Colin Waldron came on the Turf Moor scene. Waldron went on to play over 300 games for Burnley and score 16 goals, none of them more important than the one he netted at Deepdale in April 1973. There were only 35 minutes of the 1972-3 season remaining when the central defender collected the ball on the edge of the area and crashed an unstoppable shot which earned the Clarets the Second Division championship. An ever-present in that season, Waldron started his career with Bury. Twenty games for the Gigg Lane club were followed by nine at Chelsea before he moved to Burnley, being followed on the path from Stamford Bridge to Turf Moor 11 months later by Jim Thomson. Having played his first two games at full-back, Waldron switched to the number-five shirt and, despite the Clarets losing 8-1 at West Brom in his first game in that shirt, he made the position his own until he left Burnley for Old Trafford towards the end of the 1975-6 season. A very young club captain in the late 1960s and early '70s, Waldron lost the captaincy to Martin Dobson but regained it when the gifted midfielder was transferred to Everton. Waldron never settled at United and after nine months was transferred to Sunderland. But after only 20 games with the Rokerites he crossed the Atlantic and spent two years with Atlanta Chiefs in the NASL. He returned to the North-West and played for Rochdale before joining his father in a bookmaker's business in Nelson. Waldron's brother, Alan, was a midfielder who played over 100 times for Bolton Wanderers and also appeared for Blackpool, Bury and York City.

COLIN WALDRON

	LEAGUE		*FA CUP*		*FL CUP*		*OTHERS*		*TOTAL*	
	App	*Gls*	*App*	*Gls*	*App*	*Gls*	*App*	*Gls*	*App*	*Gls*
1967-68	24	0	1	0	0	0	0	0	25	0
1968-69	37	2	2	0	6	0	0	0	45	2
1969-70	15	0	0	0	1	0	0	0	16	0
1970-71	35	2	1	0	1	0	2	0	39	2
1971-72	40	2	1	0	3	0	0	0	44	2
1972-73	42	4	2	0	1	0	2	0	47	4
1973-74	40	4	5	0	3	0	7	2	55	6
1974-75	39	1	1	0	3	0	0	0	43	1
1975-76	36	1	1	0	5	0	0	0	42	1
	308	16	14	0	23	0	11	2	356	18

George Smith Waterfield was signed by Burnley from Mexborough Town in October 1923. He was originally a left winger and was to alternate with Walt Weaver for that position for the first year or so of his time at Turf Moor. On Boxing Day 1924, for a difficult away match at defending League Champions Huddersfield Town, Waterfield was moved to left-back, a position that had never been adequately filled since the departure of David Taylor. Although Burnley lost that day, George Waterfield was a revelation, his future role assured. He was born in Swinton in 1901 and played for his home-town team in his teens, then Mexborough Town, whilst earning his living down the pit. He was somewhat of a late developer and had resigned himself to part-time football as a relief from the coalface when Burnley stepped in to secure his signature. It was a time of change at Turf Moor, wholesale rebuilding going on as the Clarets sought to recapture former glories. Among the new faces in 1925 was right-back Andy McCluggage and the two players were to form Burnley's full-back pairing for the next six years. Waterfield's consistency brought him international recognition in February 1927, when he won his only England cap in a 3-3 draw with Wales in Wrexham. Louis Page played on England's left wing in that match. In 1934-5, his 12th season in claret and blue, he became only the third Burnley player to complete 350 League games following stalwarts Fred Barron and Jerry Dawson. He left Turf Moor in June 1935 to spend a season with Crystal Palace before retiring from the game in 1936. George Waterfield died in 1988 in Bamber Bridge, aged 87.

	LEAGUE		*FA CUP*		*TOTAL*	
	App	*Gls*	*App*	*Gls*	*App*	*Gls*
1923-24	17	1	0	0	17	1
1924-25	27	0	1	0	28	0
1925-26	32	0	2	0	34	0
1926-27	32	0	3	0	35	0
1927-28	42	0	1	0	43	0
1928-29	29	0	3	0	32	0
1929-30	39	0	1	0	40	0
1930-31	34	0	2	0	36	0
1931-32	37	2	1	0	38	2
1932-33	36	0	3	0	39	0
1933-34	20	2	0	0	20	2
1934-35	26	0	6	0	32	0
	371	5	23	0	394	5

GEORGE WATERFIELD

Apart from Jerry Dawson, William Watson was the first member of the FA Cup winning side of 1914 to establish himself in Burnley's first team and, again apart from Dawson, played more games for the club than any other member of either the Cup team or League Championship side of 1921. Watson was born in Birkdale, Southport, in 1890 and was spotted playing junior football, signing for his home-town club, Southport Central, in 1907. It was not long before his mature play attracted the attention of League clubs and Burnley were quickest off the mark, securing his signature in March 1909. It took him some time to make the left-half position his own, but when he did, his consistency over a decade and a half contributed enormously to his club's success and brought him international honours. He won the first of three England caps in a 1-0 win for his country against Scotland at Stamford Bridge in April 1913. His third and final international appearance was not until 1919 and, but for the intervention of war, he would undoubtedly have graced the England scene much more often, although he did appear five times for the Football League. After the war, Billy Watson carried on performing with his usual level of skill and effectiveness. His consistency was unequalled and he was the only ever-present in the Championship side of 1920-21. He retired from League football in 1925 and moved to Accrington as a coach, then to Blackburn, also coaching but, in addition, captaining Rovers 'A' team in 1927. In later life he went into business as an ironmonger, then as a painter and decorator. He subsequently returned to Southport and entered politics as a local councillor. Billy Watson died in his home town on 1 September 1955. He will always be remembered as a courteous man, a modest player who was a model of consistency, and a member of what was arguably one of the greatest half-back lines of all time — Halley, Boyle and Watson.

	LEAGUE		*FA CUP*		*OTHERS*		*TOTAL*	
	App	*Gls*	*App*	*Gls*	*App*	*Gls*	*App*	*Gls*
1908-09	1	0	0	0	0	0	1	0
1909-10	4	0	0	0	0	0	4	0
1910-11	32	2	4	1	0	0	36	3
1911-12	38	0	1	0	0	0	39	0
1912-13	32	2	6	0	0	0	38	2
1913-14	32	1	8	0	0	0	40	1
1914-15	36	0	3	1	0	0	39	1
1919-20	39	5	4	0	0	0	43	5
1920-21	42	2	3	0	0	0	45	2
1921-22	31	2	2	0	1	0	34	2
1922-23	39	4	1	0	0	0	40	4
1923-24	19	0	1	0	0	0	20	0
1924-25	1	0	0	0	0	0	1	0
	346	18	33	2	1	0	380	20

BILLY WATSON

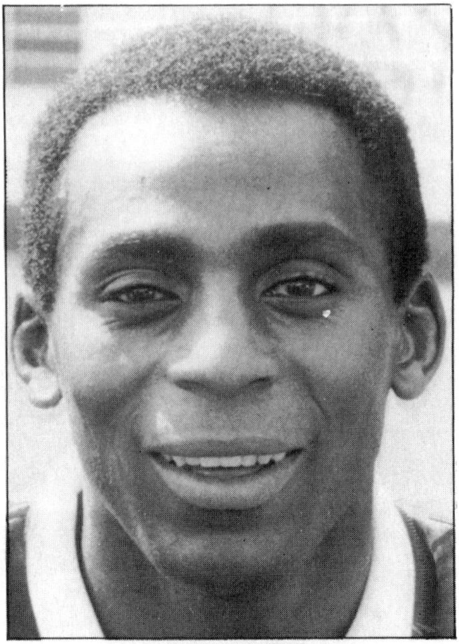

WINSTON WHITE

Signed in the 1988-9 season, Winston White proved to be a highly versatile player. Equally at home on either wing or in midfield, White made an instant hit with a number of spectacular goals, most of his Burnley goals coming from outside the area. Let down by weakness in the air, White was transferred to West Bromwich Albion in March 1991, just two days after what was undoubtedly his finest Burnley performance in a 1-0 win against Scarborough at Seamer Road. With almost 500 Football League appearances and around 60 goals to his credit, White hopes for a career in radio when he retires. He started his career at Leicester City but left Filbert Street for Hereford United. After 175 games for the Edgar Street club he went to play in Hong Kong before returning to England and a career with Chesterfield. Short spells at Port Vale and Stockport County followed before White settled at Bury, where he played over 100 games. He left Gigg Lane for Colchester United and it was from Layer Road that he came to Turf Moor.

	LEAGUE		*FA CUP*		*FL CUP*		*OTHERS*		*TOTAL*	
	App	*Gls*	*App*	*Gls*	*App*	*Gls*	*App*	*Gls*	*App*	*Gls*
1988-89	30/5	5	1	0	0	0	2	1	33/5	6
1989-90	37/3	7	6	1	2	1	4/1	0	49/4	9
1990-91	26/3	2	3	2	4	0	4/2	2	37/5	6
	93/11	14	10	3	6	1	10/3	3	119/14	21

JOCK WINTON

Douglas 'Jock' Winton came to Burnley as a winger but was converted to a full-back who was ice-cool under pressure, particularly in his own goal-area. Born in Perth in 1929, Winton came to Burnley in September 1947 from the Scottish Junior club, Jeanfield Swifts. After he had been tried as a full-back in the Reserves, the club felt that was his best position, but he still had to wait more than five years for his first-team chance, such was the strength in depth at the club. He first of all deputized for Jock Aird at right-back in 1952, but then began to take over from the great Harold Mather at left-back the following season. He was a first-team regular until 1958, but then lost his place to David Smith, who was moved from right-back to accommodate John Angus. Winton joined Aston Villa in January 1959 and moved to Rochdale in June 1961. He reached the League Cup Final with the Spotland Club in 1962, when Rochdale were beaten on aggregate by Norwich City. When his playing days were over in 1964, Winton left football completely and worked as a driver before buying a coal round in Burnley which he still has. These days left-hander Winton is a keen golfer and regularly partners his good friend Jimmy McIlroy in club competitions.

	LEAGUE		*FA CUP*		*TOTAL*	
	App	*Gls*	*App*	*Gls*	*App*	*Gls*
1952-53	6	0	0	0	6	0
1953-54	19	0	0	0	19	0
1954-55	36	0	1	0	37	0
1955-56	35	1	6	0	41	1
1956-57	38	0	5	0	43	0
1957-58	39	0	3	0	42	0
1958-59	10	0	0	0	10	0
	183	1	15	0	198	1

A hard Yorkshireman, Arthur Woodruff came to Burnley in July 1936, from Bradford City, and soon set about replacing Bob Johnson as the Clarets' first-choice centre-half. He was born in Barnsley in 1913 and, like many players, lost a large part of his potential playing career because of the war. He played for Burnley during most of the wartime period, excelling at the heart of the defence, but in 1945 he was moved to the right-back position he was to make his own. Woodruff and his left-flank partner, Harold Mather, were an integral part of the 'Iron Curtain' defence in 1946-7 and Woodruff excelled at the cover game introduced by manager Cliff Britton. He missed only two games that season and his blond locks made him stand out as the Clarets reached Wembley and the First Division. His only representative honours were two appearances for the Football League, but this very quiet man, with never a lot to say, performed with distinction for his club week in and week out. He fought off a challenge from Joe Loughran for his number-two shirt in 1948-9, but in 1951, at the age of 38, he lost his place to Jock Aird and moved to Workington where he ended his League career. He eventually returned to live in Burnley, where he kept a newsagent's shop for many years and on match days could be seen around Turf Moor. He died on 5 January 1983, aged 69.

	LEAGUE		*FA CUP*		*TOTAL*	
	App	*Gls*	*App*	*Gls*	*App*	*Gls*
1936-37	37	0	3	0	40	0
1937-38	21	0	0	0	21	0
1938-39	37	0	1	0	38	0
1945-46	0	0	2	0	2	0
1946-47	40	0	9	0	49	0
1947-48	35	0	1	0	36	0
1948-49	19	0	1	0	20	0
1949-50	32	0	3	0	35	0
1950-51	37	0	1	0	38	0
1951-52	13	0	0	0	13	0
	271	0	21	0	292	0

ARTHUR WOODRUFF

Although he played only 29 League games for Burnley, Jack Yates was a key figure in the development of League football at Turf Moor and also when the face of football was changed for ever in the early 1880s. He was born in Blackburn in 1861 and, in the days when there were two major footballing powers in the town, was instrumental in the formation of Blackburn Olympic as they rose to challenge the supremacy of the more established Rovers. Olympic battled their way to the FA Cup Final of 1883, at Kennington Oval. Their opponents were Old Etonians, FA Cup holders and the cream of British football which was dominated by public schools teams, varsity teams and the Old Boys' network. Jack Yates was a member of the Olympic team. He was a weaver and the team was an assortment of spinners, cottonworkers, blacksmiths, a team of working men. Olympic triumphed after extra-time and changed the course of football history. The reign of the common man in football had begun. Jack Yates went on to play for Accrington and joined Burnley in the summer of 1888. He missed only one game in that first League season and his skill was rewarded with an England cap in the game against Ireland at Goodison Park on 2 March 1889. England won 6-1 and Yates scored a hat-trick, yet, strangely, he was never picked for his country again. He was reinstated as an amateur in 1890 but he stayed with Burnley until 1894, when he became the licensee at one of the pubs close to Turf Moor. After a long illness he died at his home in Burnley on 1 June 1917, aged 55.

	LEAGUE		*FA CUP*		*TOTAL*	
	App	*Gls*	*App*	*Gls*	*App*	*Gls*
1888-89	21	5	2	0	23	5
1889-90	6	1	0	0	6	1
1890-91	1	1	0	0	1	1
1891-92	0	0	0	0	0	0
1892-93	0	0	0	0	0	0
1893-94	1	0	0	0	1	0
	29	7	2	0	31	7

JACK YATES

KEVIN YOUNG

When Kevin Young broke into the Burnley first team as a 17-year-old in April 1979, he was rated as one of the most promising players to appear on the Turf Moor scene for a number of years. Surprisingly, it took him two full seasons to establish himself as a regular component of the Burnley midfield, his first full campaign being the one that brought Burnley the Third Division championship in season 1981-2. For Sunderland-born Young, who joined the Clarets as an apprentice, the final game of the season saw him score the goal which effectively sealed the title. On a night of torrential rain he cut in from the left on a waterlogged pitch and fired a low, hard shot into the far corner to equalize against Chesterfield. Young featured prominently in the FA Cup and League Cup runs the following season, but back in the Third Division the season afterwards he began to lose his place and, after spells on loan to Torquay United and Port Vale, he was transferred to Bury in the summer of 1984. At Gigg Lane he teamed up with former Clarets like Leighton James, Terry Pashley, Joe Jakub and Wayne Entwistle. Another former Burnley favourite, Martin Dobson, was player-manager, whilst Frank Casper and Ray Pointer were on the coaching staff as Bury won promotion from the Fourth Division. In late 1986, Young became one of the very few former Clarets to play in European club football when he went to Dutch club side DOS Utrecht.

	LEAGUE		*FA CUP*		*FL CUP*		*OTHERS*		*TOTAL*	
	App	*Gls*	*App*	*Gls*	*App*	*Gls*	*App*	*Gls*	*App*	*Gls*
1978-79	1	0	0	0	0	0	0	0	1	0
1979-80	22/3	0	2	0	0	0	0	0	24/3	0
1980-81	28/1	3	2/1	0	2/1	0	0/2	0	32/5	3
1981-82	37/2	7	6	0	1	0	3	0	47/2	7
1982-83	24	1	7	0	7	1	2	0	40	2
1983-84	2	0	0	0	0	0	0	0	2	0
	114/6	11	17/1	0	10/1	1	5/2	0	146/10	12

Bathtime celebrations after Kevin Young's goal which effectively sealed the Third Division championship in 1982.

Paul Comstive sends in a header which shaved the Wolves crossbar during the Sherpa Van Trophy Final at Wembley.

Match to Remember 1 — 8 September 1888

Preston North End 5 Burnley 2

Dewhurst 2, Gordon, Ross 2 — *Gallocher, Poland*

A NEW era dawned in September 1888 with the advent of the Football League. The FA Cup and county competitions were the main prizes on offer until the now-famous 12 founder members of the League got together, but Burnley's first game in the new competition saw them lose to the team who went on to claim the inaugural Championship, Preston North End.

Burnley no doubt hoped for great things from their involvement in organized League football. Indeed, there was such interest generally in this first game that it kicked-off 20 minutes late to allow all the 6,000 crowd to take their places at Deepdale.

Fred Dewhurst scored for Preston after only two minutes and Gordon added another early in the game as North End got their League career off to a flying start, but Burnley responded with a Tait effort which was cleared off the line before Pat Gallocher scored the club's first League goal.

Danny Friel then had a long shot well saved as Burnley fought hard to get back into the game, but Preston continued to dominate and had a goal disallowed.

The score was still 2-1 at the interval and the *Burnley Express* described the start of the second half thus: 'Soon after the restart a little roughness was imported into the game, both sides being to blame'.

Jimmy Ross then scored twice in fairly quick succession for North End, but Burnley continued to fight back bravely and, according to the *Burnley Express,* 'The visitors then showed up strongly, their play being characterized by great dash and several times Alec Brady and Tait gave trouble to the home backs'. The paper added: 'The Burnley men were in splendid trim and as frisky as colts right up to the finish'.

The fight-back was to be in vain, however, and the Preston responded when Dewhurst snatched his second and Preston's fifth goal of the game.

As full time approached, Fred Poland scored a great goal for Burnley, who later in the season were to snatch a crumb of comfort by drawing 2-2 with Preston at Turf Moor to become one of only four teams in that first League season to take a point from the Champions and FA Cup winners.

Preston North End: Trainer; Howarth, Holmes, Robertson, W.Graham, J.Graham, Gordon, Ross, Goodall, Dewhurst, Drummond.
Burnley: Smith; Lang, Bury, Abrams, Friel, Keenan, A.Brady, Tait, Poland, Gallocher, Yates.
Referee: Mr Brownlow — *Attendance: 6,000*

Match to Remember 2 — 12 December 1891

Burnley 3 Blackburn Rovers 0

Nicol, Galbraith, Bowes

FEW could doubt that this was one of the most remarkable games ever to take place between two Football League clubs, never mind between two such fierce rivals.

Trailing 3-0 at half-time, it appeared that the Rovers were not going to come out again for the second half. Eventually they did, but when their captain was sent off, they simply walked off and refused to continue!

The weather was so bad that football was almost impossible. Snow had fallen for more than two hours before the kick-off and matters were made worse for the visiting Rovers, the FA Cup holders, by the fact that they had three players on the injured list.

Burnley started well and after only seven minutes, James Matthew crossed the ball and a goalmouth scramble ensued before Tom Nicol forced the ball home to put Burnley on their way to a great victory over famous rivals.

Some 15 minutes later, a 'rush' by Nicol and Hugh Galbraith led to the latter scoring. And on 35 minutes, a Billy Bowes shot led to the game's first controversial moment.

Herbie Arthur, the Rovers 'keeper, appeared to pick the ball from under the net from the outside and placed the ball for a goal-kick, but the referee had no hesitation in awarding the goal.

Burnley needed the three-goal advantage as they would be playing against the wind and driving snow in the second half, but the Rovers only had seven men on the field when that second half got underway and an already extraordinary game took several more strange twists before the referee had to abandon matters.

Joe Lofthouse fouled Alex Stewart, the Burnley skipper, and the two had a brief fight. They had to be separated and both were sent off, an action which caused the remaining Rovers players, with the exception of goalkeeper Arthur, to walk off.

After waiting a few moments for them to reappear, the referee threw the ball into the air and the Burnley players rushed at goal. But when Nicol scored, Arthur's appeal for offside was successful and the game was abandoned.

At half-time, apparently, the Rovers had said that they did not want to continue and would give Burnley the points. Afterwards they claimed to have 'given up' purely because of the weather, a claim which caused a *Burnley Express* reporter to ask them: 'Why then did you play against the wind and the storm in the first half and leave the field when you had the wind at your backs?'

Burnley: Hillman; Walker, Lang, McFettridge, Matthew, Stewart, Nicol, Bowes, Galbraith, McLardie, Graham.
Blackburn Rovers: Arthur; Forest, Forbes, Smith, Almond, Campbell, Lofthouse, Hall, Southworth, Walton, Townley.
Referee: J.C.Clegg (Sheffield) *Attendance: 5,500*

Match to Remember 3 — 28 March 1898

Burnley 9 Loughborough Town 3

Ross 5, Morrison, Toman, Taylor, Ferguson — *Scrimmage, Pegg 2*

THE highest number of goals ever scored in Football League match involving Burnley, 12, came in the season when Burnley claimed their first-ever Second Division title.

Jimmy Ross had a hat-trick under his belt inside 14 minutes and went on to become one of the very few Burnley players to score five goals in a game.

Tom Morrison made it 4-0 after 15 minutes and Burnley, in their last home game of the season, were on their way to a five-point lead at the top of the table and the championship title.

On the half-hour, a clearance by Jack Hillman hit two Loughborough forwards and rebounded past the Burnley 'keeper and into the net. But five minutes later, good work by Billy Bowes led to Ross getting his fourth goal.

Towards the end of the first half, during which Burnley played up the hill with the wind at their backs, the Loughborough team which was to finish bottom of the Second Division, conceded two more, one from Wilf Toman and the other from Joe Taylor, and Burnley started the second half 7-1 in front.

In the second half, William Ferguson got his name on the score-sheet before Ross scored his fifth and Loughborough managed to salvage some degree of respectability when Pegg scored twice for them late in the game.

There are, of course, other games in which Burnley have scored nine goals but it was a great shame that interest in the Second Division was such that there was only a 'small' attendance for this game.

Burnley: Hillman; Place snr, McLintock, Beveridge, Taylor, Place jnr, Morrison, Ross, Toman, Bowes, Ferguson.
Loughborough Town: Foulds; Ward, Mumford, Smith, Hodgkin, White, Hall, Roulston, Pegg, Lakin, Pike.
Referee: Mr Ashmole (Sheffield) *Attendance: 'small'*

Match to Remember 4 25 April 1914

Burnley 1 Liverpool 0

Freeman

WHEN Burnley skipper Tom Boyle received the 'English Cup', as it was then inscribed, from King George V he became the first footballer to be handed the famous trophy by a reigning monarch.

Burnley's first and only FA Cup success saw them become the the first team to lay claim to the trophy by beating five First Division clubs on the way, Derby County, Bolton Wanderers, Sunderland, Sheffield United and, of course, Liverpool in the Final at the Crystal Palace.

A very sporting Final, played in the best of spirits, was decided by a goal commonly regarded as 'one of the very finest ever scored in a Cup Final,' according to the *Burnley News*.

Bert Freeman scored that goal in the 58th minute. Teddy Hodgson jumped to a great height to head the ball down and when it bounced knee-high, Freeman glanced it into the net before anyone realized what had happened. It was a great reward for Freeman's father, who had just sailed 13,000 miles from Australia to watch the Cup Final.

In a game in which both teams were fighting as much against nerves as against each other, the second half of the 'Royal Cup Final' was much better than the first and, although Liverpool supporters would probably have disagreed at the time, few would have argued that Burnley, promoted to the First Division the season before, were worthy of their win.

The very first minute of the game had seen Dick Lindley shoot against the crossbar,

Above: Bert Freeman's goal that clinched the 1914 FA Cup Final for Burnley. Below: The Clarets return home with the Cup.

whilst in the 20th minute, Liverpool's Tom Miller found the back of the net, but his effort was disallowed for offside.

Whilst Freeman emerged as the goalscoring hero, much credit must also rest with Burnley goalkeeper Jerry Dawson — and he never even kicked a ball.

Dawson chose to give up his chance of a winners' medal because he had been injured shortly before the Final. He did not feel certain of himself and did not want to inhibit his team's chances, so he let Ronnie Sewell play in his place.

Attendance figures for the 1914 FA Cup Final vary greatly. 'Gates' of anything from 72,000 to 100,000 are often quoted, but the most common figure for the match is 72,778 and Burnley was almost a 'ghost town' for the Cup Final weekend.

Burnley: Sewell; Bamford, Taylor, Halley, Boyle, Watson, Nesbitt, Lindley, Freeman, Hodgson, Mosscrop.
Liverpool: Campbell; Longworth, Pursell, Fairfoul, Ferguson, McKinley, Sheldon, Metcalf, Miller, Lacey, Nicholl.
Referee: H.S.Bamlett (Gateshead) *Attendance: 72,778*

Aston Villa's Billy Walker scores his side's eighth goal against Burnley as goalkeeper Jerry Dawson can only watch.

Match to Remember 5 — 29 August 1925

Aston Villa 10 Burnley 0

Capewell 5, Walker 3, York, Stephenson

THE 1925-6 season started with a change in the offside law. It was just a shame that nobody told Burnley! The opening game of that season saw them visit Aston Villa and return home with a goals-against column already showing double-figures.

Burnley were missing key players through injury, whilst Villa had a plan of how to tackle the new offside situation. And such was the effectiveness of that plan that they were caught offside only three times in the whole game (twice goals were disallowed for it) and each time a Villa player scored he was unguarded by a Burnley player.

Len Capewell netted after only 25 seconds and had completed a hat-trick before the interval. The second half was almost farcical and the game dissolved into target practice against the unprotected Jerry Dawson. Capewell ended with five goals and the great Billy Walker hit a hat-trick.

Villa, as well as having two goals disallowed, also hit the woodwork twice, whilst the closest Burnley came to scoring was a George Beel effort which rattled against the woodwork just before the interval.

Burnley's misery was made complete when their skipper, Jack Hill, had to leave the field injured in the first half. He needed three stitches in a wound over his left eye, and could not resume for the second half.

Burnley's Bob Kelly summed things up more than adequately after the game when he was quoted as saying, "If it had been 20 we could not have grumbled."

The Clarets avoided relegation by only one point at the end of the season but conceded 108 goals — the worst defensive performance in the club's history.

Aston Villa: Spiers; Smart, Mort, Moss, Talbot, Muldoon, York, Stephenson, Capewell, Walker, Dorrell.
Burnley: Dawson; McCluggage, Waterfield, Bassnett, Hill, Parkin, Kelly, Freeman, Roberts, Beel, Page.
Referee: G.N. Watson (Nottingham) *Attendance: 37,025*

Match to Remember 6 10 April 1926

Birmingham 1 Burnley 7

Bradford *Page 6, Bruton*

THE only player to score a double hat-trick in a League game for Burnley was gifted left-winger Louis Page. In a last-ditch effort to avoid relegation, Page was switched to centre-forward for the trip to Birmingham, and what a wise decision that turned out to be.

He scored three goals in each half as well as rattling another fierce shot against the crossbar. It was his positional play that did the trick as he was always ready to go through quickly and controlled the ball with unerring judgement.

If a newspaper account of the match can be believed in its entirety, Page was none too pleased with his 'promotion' to centre-forward. According to the *Burnley Express*, when wished luck by his colleagues just before leaving the dressing-room, he said, somewhat facetiously, "I will score six and stop at that number."

His first goal came after 22 minutes, when a pass from Billy Dougal saw Page slip between the defenders and shoot past the advancing Dan Tremelling. Seven minutes later he made it 2-0 when Jack Hill ran from the halfway line, beat three opponents and lifted a neat centre into the area which Page converted into the top corner.

A minute before the interval, Page completed his first hat-trick when cashing in on clever play by Henry Hargreaves, and in the second half the floodgates really opened.

In the 58th minute, Jack Bruton, who also hit an upright, interrupted Page's one-man show with a shot so hard that Tremelling could only fist it into his own goal, and then Page scored a hat-trick in the next three minutes.

His fourth strike came when he dashed on to a pass from Hill to leave Tremelling helpless; his fifth came when Tremelling knocked down a John Steel free-kick and Page was in the right place at the right time; and he completed his personal demolition of Birmingham in the 62nd minute when he headed home James Tonner's centre.

Birmingham's consolation goal came in the 86th minute when Joe Bradford found his way through a Burnley defence which had found little employment during the rest of the game.

Birmingham: Tremelling; Womack, Jones, Liddell, Hunter, Dale, Harris, Crosbie, Briggs, Bradford, Linley.
Burnley: Hampson; McCluggage, Blinkhorn, Steel, Hill, Dougall, Bruton, Cross, Page, Hargreaves, Tonner.
Referee: R.J.Kelsoe (Sheffield) *Attendance: 16,616*

Charlton Athletic 1 Burnley 0

Duffy

CHARLTON Athletic won the first FA Cup Final to be televised 'live' full-length, when they snatched one late chance at Wembley.

Burnley, meanwhile, lost it by wasting at least four golden opportunities in front of goal.

Throughout the competition, Charlton had been dubbed 'lucky', and they showed why in this second post-war Cup Final.

Peter Kippax was the 'golden boy' of Burnley football at the time, but the talented amateur chose the wrong day to miss out on top form and was responsible for some of the worst misses in an otherwise drab match.

Early in the game, Billy Morris lifted the ball over the bar when it seemed easier to score, and then Harold Mather cleared a Chris Duffy shot off the line.

Kippax's first scoring chance saw him take too long over the ball and by the time he brought it under control, the Charlton defence had consolidated and the chance was wasted.

From an Arthur Woodruff free-kick, Kippax showed some of his international form and forced his way into the area. A prompt shot would, surely, have brought a goal but again Kippax took too long.

The shot of the match (apart from the goal) came when Harry Potts emerged from a ruck of players and unleashed a rocket from 20 yards out. The crowd roared 'goal' but the ball crashed against the crossbar and bounced safely away.

The first period of extra-time came and went. Then, with only six minutes remaining,

Burnley's players are introduced to the Duke of Gloucester before the 1947 FA Cup Final.

Burnley's 1947 Cup Final line-up (from left to right): Kippax, Chew, Mather, Potts, Strong, Brown, Attwell, Bray, Woodruff, Harrison, Morris.

Robinson centred hard and Walsh glanced it on with his head. The ball fell to Duffy's feet and he unleashed a shot into the roof of the Burnley net. Poor Jim Strong probably did not see the ball until he picked it out of the net.

Two minutes later there was a chance of an equalizer when Reg Attwell put the ball into the goalmouth and Morris rose above the defence, but saw his header graze the wrong side of the crossbar.

Throughout the second period of extra-time, Charlton had been performing like a punch drunk boxer whilst Burnley did everything but score. Extra-time saw a move talked about in Burnley for years afterwards.

Ray Harrison collected a pass and burst into the penalty area after beating Phipps. Harrison slowed to steady himself for a shot when he was tackled from behind by Phipps, but no penalty was awarded, despite the fact that the ball was two yards in front of the Burnley centre-forward when he was tackled.

Consolation for the Clarets came within weeks of Wembley when they were promoted to the First Division as runners-up to Manchester City.

Charlton Athletic: Bartram; Croker, Shreeve, Johnson, Phipps, Whitaker, Hurst, Dawson, Robinson, Walsh, Duffy.
Burnley: Strong; Woodruff, Mather, Attwell, Brown, Bray, Chew, Morris, Harrison, Potts, F.P.Kippax.
Referee: J.M.Wiltshire (Dorset) *Attendance: 98,215*

Match to Remember 8 — 9 January 1954

Burnley 5 Manchester United 3

Shannon 2, Holden, McIlroy, Gray *Viollet, Aird (og), Taylor*

IF THERE was ever a match to rouse enthusiasm for the FA Cup, this eight-goal thriller was it.

Burnley line-up in the early part of 1953-4. Back row (left to right): Aird, Adamson, Holden, Thompson, Brown, Winton. Front row: McIlroy, Gray, Cummings, Morris, Pilkington.

Before the third-round tie, Burnley supporters had not given their team any hope whatsoever, but how wrong they were.

The Clarets started in sensational manner with Les Shannon, alone in the penalty area, gliding the ball wide of Ray Wood and into the corner of the goal.

United attacked from the restart but Harold Mather intercepted and sent a long ball to Bill Holden, whose cross-cum-shot brought another roar from the crowd as it nestled just inside the post.

Almost immediately, though, United were back on level terms. Ernie Taylor whipped across a hard centre and Dennis Viollet revived the Reds' dropping spirits by turning it past Des Thompson. Straight afterwards, Burnley checked in midfield and United took the ball upfield.

Jock Aird, the Burnley defender, was hot in pursuit of Jackie Blanchflower. Aird tried to push the ball to Thompson, hit it harder than intended and the 'keeper could do nothing about it. Just over five minutes had been played and the score was already 2-2!

The game continued at the same furious pace with both Shannon and Jimmy McIlroy working flat out to impress. The struggle for ascendancy continued and, following a throw-in near the left corner-flag, Shannon sent in a corner rather more than head high which clipped a United defender, grazed the underside of the bar and Burnley were back in front.

Seven minutes into the second half, United were again level, this time when Taylor scored with a brilliant control and turn movement which led to him snapping the ball past Thompson.

United then enjoyed their best spell but, before they could take the lead, the pendulum swung back in Burnley's favour when the ball emerged from a ruck of players and McIlroy toe-poked it home.

Eighteen minutes from time, Billy Gray made it 5-3 when the ball found him unmarked in the area. Despite again trailing by two goals, though, United were still full of fight and the game was not won until the final whistle.

Afterwards, the legendary Matt Busby said, "Best wishes to Burnley for the Cup. If we have to lose there is no club we would rather be beaten by than Burnley. Believe me, I mean that."

Burnley: Thompson; Aird, Mather, Adamson, Cummings, Attwell, Gray, McIlroy, Holden, Shannon, Pilkington.
Manchester United: Wood; Foulkes, Byrne, Whitefoot, Chilton, Edwards, Berry, Blanchflower, Taylor, Viollet, Rowley.
Referee: A. W. Luty (Leeds) *Attendance: 52,847*

Match to Remember 9 — 2 May 1960

Manchester City 1 Burnley 2

Colbridge — *Pilkington, Meredith*

BURNLEY travelled to Maine Road, Manchester, needing to beat City to claim the First Division title which had eluded them for 39 years.

They had to fight every inch of the way and for every second of the game to deny Wolves the title and deprive the Molineux club of a Championship hat-trick.

The Clarets made a sensational start when, after only four minutes, Alex Elder and Jimmy Robson combined to push the ball along to Brian Pilkington. He cut

Ray Pointer celebrates Brian Pilkington's goal which gave the Clarets a sensational start at Maine Road.

inside and blasted a hard, low centre across the face of goal which appeared to touch Bert Trautmann before it ended up in the back of the net.

City, cheered on by a large contingent of Wolves fans as well as their own partisan supporters, hit back hard and a free-kick was played forward to Denis Law. He chipped it through to the penalty area and Clive Colbridge blasted the ball past Adam Blacklaw.

Just after the half-hour, a heavy foul on Ray Pointer led to a free-kick by Tommy Cummings. Ken Branagan sliced the ball into his own area, and Trevor Meredith found himself in the middle of the fray and smacked the ball home.

From then, Burnley, with one hand already on the Championship trophy, had to cling on for 59 agonizing minutes.

City threw everything they had at the Clarets and Burnley defended stoutly whilst always looking for a way in which to increase their lead and put a stranglehold on the title.

As time ticked away, both goalkeepers performed heroics and the game proved to be a tremendous climax to a tremendous season and, most important for the thousands who made the short trip to Manchester from Burnley, the League Championship trophy was back in residence at Turf Moor for the first time in 39 years.

Manchester City: Trautmann; Branagan, Sear, Barnes, Ewing, Oakes, Barlow, Hannah, Hayes, Law, Colbridge.

Burnley: Blacklaw; Angus, Elder, Adamson, Cummings, Miller, Meredith, McIlroy, Pointer, Robson, Pilkington.

Referee: T.H. Gerrard (Preston) *Attendance: 65,981*

Match to Remember 10 — 16 November 1960

Burnley 2 Stade de Reims 0

Robson, McIlroy

A TYPICAL November evening in East Lancashire? Not if you were at Turf Moor, for European football had arrived for the first time.

League Champions Burnley were in the second round of the European Cup and drawn to play the French Champions, Reims, at home in the first leg.

Reims, having done their homework, targeted Jimmy McIlroy as their danger man and closed him down right from the start. But all they really succeeded in doing was transferring Burnley's firepower to Ray Pointer and he did much of the damage.

The game was another that got off to a dream start for the Clarets and they scored within a minute of the kick-off. A long, diagonal pass by Brian Miller was headed out by Rodzic and fell to John Connelly. He hooked the ball forward to Jimmy Robson, who wasted no time in scoring Burnley's first goal in a European competition.

In the 22nd minute the mercurial McIlroy made it 2-0. His shot had the sting taken out of it when it was deflected off Siatka, but Jacquet in the Reims goal was covering the ball's original 'flight path' and could only watch as it rolled over the line at the far post.

For the rest of the game, Burnley played well enough to deserve the two-goal advantage they took to France for the return leg. The defence had a couple of

Burnley skipper Jimmy Adamson exchanges pennants before the second leg of the European Cup tie against Reims. The Clarets had the cushion of a 2-0 lead.

moments they would have wanted to forget in a hurry, but at the other end McIlroy hit an upright.

In the second leg, Burnley lost 3-2 but had earned a place in the quarter-finals at their very first attempt.

Burnley: Blacklaw; Angus, Elder, Joyce, Adamson, Miller, Connelly, McIlroy, Pointer, Robson, Pilkington.
Stade de Reims: Jacquet; Wendling, Rodzik, Lebland, Siatka, Moreau, Rustichelle, Muller, Kopa, Piantoni, Vincent.
Referee: D.J.G.Echevarria (Spain) *Attendance: 36,742*

Tottenham Hotspur 4 Burnley 4

Norman, Jones 2, Mackay *Connelly 2, Robson, Pointer*

AS DON Smith wrote in the *Burnley Express:* 'If there were a roll of honour whereon could be inscribed in golden letters the most meritorious deeds of any club . . .then the performance of Burnley at White Hart Lane would be given most careful and special recognition'.

Fine words indeed, but consider the scenario. Away from home and trailing 4-0 is bad enough by anyone's standards. Doing it when playing against the all-conquering Spurs presented Burnley with the toughest of tasks.

The eyes of the football world were on Burnley, reigning First Division champions, as they went 4-0 down to goals by Maurice Norman, Cliff Jones (two) and Dave Mackay.

However, a sign of things to come arrived not long before the interval when John Connelly snatched one back by adding the finishing touches to a Jimmy McIlroy/Brian Pilkington move in the 38th minute.

But, as the second half got underway, they were still three goals adrift and, to

Alex Elder looks a little perplexed as the ball spins by. Bobby Smith of Spurs is in the background.

all intents and purposes, out for the count. It was a shame for Spurs that nobody bothered to show the Clarets the script.

Both Jimmy Robson and Ray Pointer netted to reduce the arrears to one goal and a grandstand finale was in the offing.

Spurs hit an upright and Connelly did likewise. Bill Brown made a great save from Brian Miller, and then came the equalizer. A one-two between Connelly and Robson saw Connelly slam the ball into the far corner and the Tottenham crowd were stunned.

Even then, one of the greatest fight-backs in League football history nearly counted for nothing when, in the dying minutes, John White was presented with a great chance but missed an open goal.

It was the match of the season played in horrible conditions on a difficult pitch as Burnley covered themselves in mud as well as pride. Their large contingent of fans enjoyed a happy trip home.

Tottenham Hotspur: Brown; Baker, Henry, Blanchflower, Norman, Mackay, Jones, White, Smith, Allen, Dyson.
Burnley: Blacklaw; Angus, Elder, Joyce, Cummings, Miller, Connelly, McIlroy, Pointer, Robson, Pilkington.
Referee: R.H. Windle (Chesterfield) *Attendance: 58,737*

Match to Remember 12 — 5 May 1962

Burnley 1 Tottenham Hotspur 3

Robson *Greaves, Smith, Blanchflower (pen)*

UNDOUBTEDLY two of the great English sides of the time, Burnley and Spurs clashed in a great Wembley Cup Final and once again the Clarets, despite losing, maintained their place as one of the most-feared clubs in English football.

They got off to the worst possible start when Jimmy Greaves put Spurs in front in the third minute. Bill Brown punted a long ball into Burnley's half and Bobby Smith headed it on to Greaves. The Spurs striker seemed to have lost possession as Tommy Cummings came in for a tackle, but he recovered and snapped a half-hit shot just inside the post.

Burnley fought hard to reply and they equalized in thrilling fashion in the 49th minute, when an attack seemed about to be repelled until Ray Pointer whipped the ball off a defender's foot and squared it to Gordon Harris. The winger flew past Peter Baker and centred to Jimmy Robson, who cleverly stabbed the ball past Brown.

But as the Burnley cheers still filled the famous stadium, Spurs dealt the Clarets a sickening blow by restoring their lead within a minute. John White moved down the left flank and evaded challenges from Jimmy McIlroy and John Angus. He floated one of his best centres into the area and Smith pivoted, beat Brian Miller to the ball and smashed a fierce shot into the net.

If that goal was a sickener, events which unfolded in the 82nd minute really knocked the stuffing out of Burnley. Cummings clearly handled on the line but, in the opinion of many, the penalty should never have been awarded.

As White had crossed the ball, the linesman flagged for a Cliff Jones foul on Adam Blacklaw. But as the ball ran to Medwin, the linesman suddenly stopped trying to attract the referee's attention and the penalty, which Danny Blanchflower converted, was awarded moments later.

Bobby Smith restores Tottenham's lead at Wembley with a fierce shot past Adam Blacklaw.

A number of the players taking part in this Wembley game were likely to be heading for Chile for the World Cup finals within weeks, and many thought that Jimmy Adamson, the Burnley captain, Player of the Year and England assistant manager, would hold the key to the Cup Final.

He was immaculate throughout and, just as England honours passed him by, he was to miss out on a Cup winners' medal. Pointer worked tirelessly throughout, Harris and Connelly showed plenty of determination and, but for the stylish performance of Adamson, Miller would have been the man of the match.

Burnley: Blacklaw; Angus, Elder, Adamson, Cummings, Miller, Connelly, McIlroy, Pointer, Robson, Harris.
Tottenham Hotspur: Brown; Baker, Henry, Blanchflower, Norman, Mackay, Medwin, White, Smith, Greaves, Jones.
Referee: J.Finney (Hereford) *Attendance: 100,000*

Match to Remember 13 8 February 1967

Napoli 0 Burnley 0

CREDIT for success in certain matches has often been given to individual players, but if ever a football match belonged to one man, this was it.

After the game, the *Daily Express* said of Harry Thomson, the man who made 13 breathtaking saves, including one from a penalty: 'He was a god in a green jersey. Burnley's little Scot had one of those goalkeeping hours when the impossible seemed to have happened, not once, but frequently. Burnley survived the most one-sided game I have ever seen. And throughout it Thomson was brave, brilliant, lucky and, as 60,000 Neopolitan fans will confirm, sometimes fantastico!'

But the main story of this Inter-Cities Fairs Cup encounter had nothing to do with football. Burnley led 3-0 from the Turf Moor leg and, barring a complete disaster, were already into the quarter-finals.

Before arriving at the San Paolo Stadium, the Italian Press had whipped up something of a campaign against the Clarets with paragraphs like: 'From Lancashire, where studs are made out of rose petals . . .to Naples where visiting players are put through a mincing machine at the end of the game and their remains are roasted on a spit'.

And throughout the game, Burnley had to endure the shoes, cushions, rotten eggs, fruit and abuse that was hurled at them from the other side of the deep moat which separated the fans from the pitch.

The game, later to be dubbed 'The Battle of Naples', was a living nightmare for the players, but the real problems did not start until about four minutes from time. It was then that Omar Sivori viciously elbowed Dave Merrington in the stomach and then left the ball to have a go at Les Latcham, already bandaged and stitched following an accidental clash of heads with Jośe Altafini in the first half.

At the final whistle, Thomson offered a sporting hand of friendship to Orlando, who promptly spat in his face. Substitute goalkeeper Adam Blacklaw dived between them to prevent further trouble and, as the rest of the Burnley players ran for safety down the players' tunnel, Blacklaw was flattened by no fewer than a dozen men, many of them members of the stadium staff.

While he was on the floor, he was kicked in the head and, whilst making good his escape, threw one of the 'dirty dozen' down some stone stairs where he cracked his head on a concrete floor.

Adam Blacklaw is the victim of a mob attack in one of the many distressing scenes at the end of the 'Battle of Naples'.

Just as Blacklaw reached the dressing-room, a man in plain clothes appeared, drew back his coat to reveal a gun and tried to take the Burnley goalkeeper away. A fantastic scene followed, during which several players, including Colin Blant, tried to keep Blacklaw in the dressing-room as officials tried to take him away.

A glass door was shattered and eventually Blacklaw was taken away, quickly followed by team manager Harry Potts.

All the while an angry group of spectators surrounded the exit which the Burnley team coach would have been using. They dispersed only when police drew their guns. A group of six English sports reporters had to be taken into police custody for their own safety.

Napoli: Bandoni; Nasdin, Micelli, Ronzon, Gisardo, Bianchi, Orlando, Juliano, Altafini, Sivori, Braca.
Burnley: Thomson; Smith, Todd, O'Neil, Miller, Merrington, Morgan, Lochhead, Coates, Harris, Latcham.
Referee: G.Emsberger (Hungary) *Attendance: 60,000*

Match to Remember 14 19 October 1968

Burnley 5 Leeds United 1

Coates, Casper 2, Murray, Kindon *Bremner*

FOR six weeks of the 1967-8 First Division season, the 'Burnley babes' ruled English soccer.

Winning eight consecutive games, six in the First Division and another two in the League Cup, when the average age of your team is only 22 is one thing.

Doing it by dropping half your regular first team is quite another, but that is exactly what Burnley achieved early in this campaign.

On 5 October they were beaten 4-0 at home by Liverpool. Then drastic changes followed. The youngsters were left in charge up until a draw with Wolves, and then the 'old guard' was largely recalled and Burnley went out of the Cup to Swindon Town and slipped back into League obscurity.

The undisputed highlight of their eight-match winning streak was the 5-1 thrashing of Leeds United. It was the worst defeat that Leeds, then First Division leaders, had suffered in two years.

Forced on by the eager captaincy of Colin Waldron, fired by the dash of Ralph Coates and Dave Thomas and steeled by the midfield domination of Martin Dobson, Burnley recorded the most astonishing result of the season.

The *Daily Telegraph* said of the game: 'Burnley's capacity for producing the goods just when they seem about to join the other Lancashire teams in the Second Division is enough to send rich clubs flocking to see what the Turf Moor boffins do in their mysterious laboratories.'

To which the *Daily Mirror* added: 'The best defence in England was thrown into confusion by players who have not yet achieved the status of household names in Burnley, never mind the country. Who ever heard of David Thomas, Steve Kindon and John Murray for instance.'

In truth, Burnley's cause on this October day was helped by Leeds goalkeeper Gary Sprake. The Clarets were 2-0 in front by the 21st minute and both goals appeared to be Sprake's fault.

On 18 minutes, Thomas launched a 50-yard pass to Frank Casper, who held

Burnley in 1968-9. Back row (left to right): Angus, Todd, Waldron, Merrington, Thomson, Lochhead, Latcham, Blant. Front row: O'Neil, Casper, Coates, Bellamy, Dobson, Morgan.

off two challengers before passing into the path of Coates, whose shot seemed to pass underneath the diving Sprake.

Three minutes later, Coates returned the compliment when he crossed over Gary Sprake's head and Casper headed home. Billy Bremner pulled a goal back for United late in the first half, but the second half was only seconds old when Paul Madeley and Eddie Gray got themselves in a dither and Murray nipped between them to score.

After 77 minutes, Colin Blant collected a Johnny Giles free-kick and fed the ball to Murray, who raced into Leeds territory and then released a pass to Steve Kindon. The 17-year-old had a lot to do, but he flew past the tenacious Paul Reaney, rode another tackle and thumped a brilliant ball through the defence and past Sprake.

The rout was complete three minutes later when Casper found possession just outside the penalty area and chipped the ball over everyone, easily beating the stranded Sprake.

Leeds, one of the most complete sides since the war, went on to win the Championship by six points. Their only other defeat that season was a 3-1 reverse at Maine Road and they only conceded more than one goal on two other occasions.

Burnley: Thomson; Smith, Latcham, Dobson, Waldron, Blant, Thomas, Murray, Casper, Coates, Kindon.
Leeds United: Sprake; Reaney, Cooper(Lorimer), Bremner, Charlton, Hunter, O'Grady, Giles, Jones, Madeley, Gray.
Referee: K.Howley (Billingham) *Attendance: 26,434*

Match to Remember 15 — 28 April 1973

Preston North End 1 Burnley 1

Bruce *Waldron*

TOO much was at stake for this game to be a classic. The Clarets needed a point to beat Queen's Park Rangers in the race for the Second Division title and return to the top flight after a break of two years. North End, meanwhile, needed a point to avoid relegation to Division Three.

On a sunny afternoon it turned out to be an absorbing clash between two teams of contrasting styles and ambitions.

North End had decided that they could not match Burnley for skill. The Deepdale pitch was narrowed by six yards for the game, the middle of the playing surface was heavily watered and Preston packed eight defenders between Burnley and the goal.

Burnley had by far the greater share of possession, but when they had the ball they found they had little room to manoeuvre and were restricted to attacks which pounded against a human barrier.

Throughout the first half, North End employed only two forwards, but there was always the chance that Burnley might overstretch themselves in their search for goals.

And so it proved. The ball fell just right for Alan Lamb, who was well clear of the defence. He ran 40 yards and then pushed the ball to his striking partner, Alec Bruce, and he shot past Alan Stevenson to give North End a sensational lead.

Leighton James drives a left-foot volley at the Preston goal as Burnley strive to return to the First Division as champions.

And they did it! The Clarets' players celebrate in the Deepdale dressing-room.

Early in the second half, Burnley's Paul Fletcher had a header cleared off the line and other chances went begging.

It appeared that Queen's Park Rangers were going to steal the title from under Burnley's noses. Then in the 55th minute, Waldron got in a header and when the ball rebounded to him, he cracked a 25-yard left-foot volley into the top corner and both teams were back on course for the point they needed.

Burnley had earned the title. Beaten only four times all season, they collected 30 points away from home (two points for a win in those days), equalled a Second Division record and returned to the top flight in some style.

Preston North End: Kelly; McMahon, Snookes, Bird, Hawkins, Baxter, Connor, Bruce, Lamb, Spark, Young.
Burnley: Stevenson; Ingham, Newton, Dobson, Waldron, Thomson, Nulty, Casper, Fletcher, Collins, James.
Referee: J.Hunting (Leicester) *Attendance: 21,550*

Match to Remember 16 — 23 March 1974

Leeds United 1 Burnley 4

Clarke — *Fletcher 2, Collins, Nulty*

LONG will Burnley fans remember this day in March 1974, when their team went to Elland Road and gave Leeds United a thrashing.

The match featured one of the most spectacularly stunning goals ever scored by a Burnley player, but also marked the end of a fine career which had included some 'rasping' goals.

It was Paul Fletcher who scored that great goal — an overhead kick to give the Clarets a 2-1 lead just before the interval.

Alas, eight minutes from time Frank Casper was fouled by Norman Hunter when the ball was yards away. Casper was on the running track which surrounds the Elland Road pitch and Burnley were already 4-1 in front. The free-scoring striker did play again for Burnley, but he never rediscovered the form that he possessed before that fateful challenge.

Throughout the match, Burnley defended stubbornly, attacked brilliantly and finished in devastating fashion. They took the lead after 16 minutes, when Paul Reaney fouled Leighton James. Dougie Collins hit a floated free-kick which was half-cleared by Hunter, and Casper headed the ball back across the face of goal for Fletcher to finish from close range.

On 39 minutes, Peter Noble half-cleared a Billy Bremner corner and Allan Clarke nodded the scores level, but within a minute Burnley regained their lead in scintillating style.

A Noble centre was chipped up by Geoff Nulty to Fletcher. With his back to goal the centre-forward leapt into the air, performed a bicycle kick and volleyed the ball at great pace past David Harvey. The normally placid Jimmy Adamson danced on the touch-line.

The second half was 17 minutes old when Martin Dobson tackled Paul Madeley in midfield and left Leeds exposed. Casper passed to Fletcher and he swung the ball to Collins, who placed a perfect lob over Harvey and Burnley were 3-1 in front.

And in the 70th minute, another free-kick paid off when Collins floated the ball to Waldron, who headed across the face of goal and Nulty got down on all fours to head the ball home.

Leeds had plenty of possession throughout the game but failed to make the most

Burnley grab their fourth goal against Leeds as Nulty gets home a low header.

of their chances and few could deny that Burnley deserved their thumping triumph at Elland Road.

It was just the tonic the players needed to set them up for an FA Cup semi-final the following weekend, but on that occasion a trip across the Pennines was to come unstuck for the Clarets, due largely to the efforts of Malcolm Macdonald.

Leeds United: Harvey; Reaney, McQueen, Hunter, Cherry, Bremner, Yorath, Madeley, Lorimer, Jordan, Clarke.
Burnley: Stevenson; Noble, Newton, Dobson, Waldron, Thomson, Nulty, Casper, Fletcher, Collins(Ingham), James.
Referee: R.Capey (Madeley Heath) *Attendance: 39,453*

Match to Remember 17 — 4 January 1975

Burnley 0 Wimbledon 1

Mahon

BURNLEY, expecting a 'free passage' into the fourth round of the FA Cup, became the first Division One club to lose to a non-League outfit on their own ground since the Football League was extended to four divisions in the 1920s.

At 16/1, the Clarets were fifth favourites for the Cup but they were beaten by a bunch of part-timers, only one of whom had played in the Football League. On the day, though, there could be no argument — the Southern League team deserved their victory.

Wimbledon's defence shackled Leighton James as Burnley had to resort to long, high balls. But the visitors' back four — and often they had as many as eight

Wimbledon's Dickie Guy makes a fine save from Ray Hankin as the Dons cause a Cup upset.

men strung across the back — dealt with everything that the First Division's leading scorers threw at them.

Dickie Guy had one of those games which every goalkeeper enjoys at least once in his career. In the first half, Jim Thomson missed a golden chance from inside the six-yard box, whilst Guy clawed away a Ray Hankin header and then saved a Keith Newton half-volley from 15 yards at the second attempt.

In the 49th minute, Wimbledon turned the match upside-down when Mick Mahon hit a crisp shot from 12 yards and Peter Noble, on the line, had no chance of keeping it out.

Burnley launched an all-out attack and appeared to be trying to equalize in five seconds rather than patiently using the 41 minutes they had at their disposal.

Paul Fletcher hit a volley from eight yards which Guy somehow managed to keep out. James lashed at a shot from 12 yards that went agonizingly over the top and Fletcher poked the ball over the bar from six yards after Guy dropped Dougie Collins' free-kick.

But the chances dried up and Burnley became victims of one of the greatest Cup upsets of all time.

A couple of days after the game, manager Jimmy Adamson said, "There were many broken hearts in Burnley on Saturday night. But believe me there were no more disappointed people than the players. It hurt their professional pride, but it's no good feeling sorry for ourselves. The players gave everything, but their skills were off."

Burnley: Stevenson; Newton, Thomson(Morris), Ingham, Waldron, Noble, Flynn, Hankin, Fletcher, Collins, James.
Wimbledon: Guy; Stockley, Bryant, Donaldson, Edwards, Cooke, Rice, Bassett, Mahon, Connell, Somers.
Referee: R.Lee (Cheadle) *Attendance: 19,683*

Match to Remember 18 — 13 September 1975

Burnley 4 Norwich City 4

Noble 4 (2 pens) — *MacDougall 2 (1 pen), Peters, Boyer*

AFTER this match the Burnley team was criticized for losing the advantage so many times, but it is a game which will stand out in many people's memories as the day Peter Noble scored four times and yet failed to finish on the winning side.

It was the only time in his playing career that Noble scored four goals in a game, but to the player's eternal credit he said afterwards that he would rather have scored two and finished on the winning side.

The game was only 30 seconds old when Ian Brennan hit a huge clearance, Noble ran clear of the defence and hammered the ball past Kevin Keelan from 12 yards out.

He had to wait 25 minutes before doubling his tally. Brian Flynn was fouled in the penalty area by Colin Suggett when lining up a shot and Noble's spot-kick beat Keelan's dive.

Five minutes later, Mike Summerbee fouled Martin Peters and Norwich pulled a goal back when Ted MacDougall sent Alan Stevenson the wrong way from the penalty-spot. But only two minutes before half-time the Clarets were two goals clear again when the game's third penalty was conceded.

Peter Noble's powerful header finds the back of the Norwich net for one of his four goals.

The Norwich goal was under a lot of pressure and Leighton James beat Mel Machin to the ball and sent in a cross which Geoff Butler handled away from Noble and Ray Hankin. Noble completed his hat-trick by sending Keelan the wrong way.

On 66 minutes, Norwich started their fight-back. Burnley failed to clear properly, Machin mis-hit a speculative shot and, as the defence 'froze', MacDougall nipped in to tip the ball past Stevenson.

Ten minutes later, MacDougall's first-time pass found Peters in yards of room and he powered a low shot just wide of Stevenson.

Only three minutes remained when Noble, risking everything, plunged between two defenders to meet Summerbee's free-kick and steer a magnificent header into the top corner of the goal.

The points looked safe but, with seconds remaining, Norwich, managed at the time by John Bond, came back from the dead when Phil Boyer headed home from five yards out.

Noble had scored a hat-trick in the previous home game and afterwards Peter Higgs of the *Burnley Express* asked when a Burnley player had last scored successive hat-tricks in Turf Moor matches. A young statistician called Ray Simpson answered in the next issue: it had never happened before!

Burnley: Stevenson; Brennan, Newton, Noble, Waldron, Thomson, Flynn, Hankin, Summerbee, Collins, James.
Norwich City: Keelan; Machin, Forbes, Powell, Butler, Morris, Suggett(Stringer), Peters, McQuire, Boyer, MacDougall.
Referee: K.McNally (Cheshire) *Attendance: 15,513*

The Burnley playing staff at the start of the 1978-9 season.

Match to Remember 19 — 5 December 1978

Oldham Athletic 1 Burnley 4

Young — *Kindon 2, Noble, Thomson*

STEVE Kindon had a night to remember as Burnley gave themselves an almost unassailable lead in the Anglo-Scottish Cup Final.

Kindon scored twice, once in the very first minute, and was in scintillating form throughout the match. Burnley's success was also down to the fact that eight of their players wore training boots instead of studs on the frozen surface, whilst all the home side were in studs.

Burnley moved straight on to the attack and pumped long balls down the middle of the park for the courageous Kindon to chase on the treacherous Boundary Park surface.

The game was less than 60 seconds old when Paul Fletcher hit a through ball to Kindon and he rounded Peter McDonnell to slot the ball into an empty net. Within two minutes the Clarets were two ahead in the away leg. Leighton James hit a great cross, Kindon chested it down and Peter Noble made no mistake with the easiest of chances.

The rest of the first half was a real 'ding-dong' battle, but the Clarets preserved their lead. Early in the second half, Athletic fought hard to get back into things and Alan Stevenson made a couple of outstanding saves.

The issue was put beyond any reasonable doubt midway through that second period when a corner was only partially cleared, Kindon crossed and Jim Thomson side-footed the Clarets into a 3-0 lead.

On 75 minutes, Kindon crowned a fine personal contribution to the game when Tony Arins played the ball to Billy Ingham, who then fed it to Kindon. He blasted a shot across the face of McDonnell which bounced into the net off the far post.

The Latics pulled a goal back, Young scoring with six minutes to go, and went on to win the Turf Moor leg 1-0.

But the Clarets had done enough at Boundary Park for skipper Peter Noble to be presented with the Anglo-Scottish Cup by Tom Fagan, the senior member of the Scottish Football League management committee, Scottish FA councillor and chairman of Albion Rovers.

Oldham Athletic: McDonnell; Wood, Blair, Bell, Hicks, Hurst, Valentine, Taylor, Young, Chapman, Steele.
Burnley: Stevenson; Arins, Brennan, Rodaway, Thomson, Noble, Hall, Ingham, Fletcher, Kindon, James.
Referee: P.G.Reeves (Leicester) *Attendance: 10,446*

Match to Remember 20 19 January 1983

Tottenham Hotspur 1 Burnley 4

Gibson *Roberts 2 (2 og's), Hamilton 2*

HAVING already disposed of First Division clubs Coventry City and Birmingham City, the Clarets pulled off one of the biggest shocks in football when they humbled mighty Spurs 4-1 under the White Hart Lane floodlights in this Milk Cup quarter-final tie.

In their 100-year history, Burnley had never produced a more unlikely victory. They had parted company with manager Brian Miller on the morning of the match and, although they were progressing well in both Cup competitions, their slide down the Second Division was bad enough for the alarm bells to have started to sound with more than three months of the season remaining.

Against all the odds it was typical 'Roy of the Rovers' stuff. The main focus of attention before the game was on the midfield. How would Trevor Steven cope with Ossie Ardíles? What chance had Kevin Young against Glenn Hoddle? Would little Brian Flynn be able to hold off Ricky Villa? What could Derek Scott do to quieten Gary Mabbutt?

But by the end of the day, a remarkable display of courage, skill and character, helped along by a little luck in the shape of two own-goals from Spurs' Graham Roberts, saw Burnley earn a plum two-leg semi-final tie with Liverpool.

A goalless first half gave the Clarets plenty of confidence, but gave no indication of the sensational stuff to follow.

The second half was only 45 seconds old when Chris Hughton's long throw-in skidded off Mick Phelan's head. Willie Donachie got a toe to the ball, but it dropped to Terry Gibson who scored from six yards out.

Roberts gifted Burnley an equalizer when he leapt to meet Young's curling cross, but only succeeded in diverting the ball into the roof of the net beyond the grasp of Ray Clemence.

Within moments the Clarets were in front when Young's free-kick deflected off the Spurs wall. Taylor rushed in, skipped over the ball, and Billy Hamilton was on hand to score from four yards out.

Steve Archibald and Hoddle both found time to trouble the Burnley defence, but the Clarets booked their place in the semi-final when Taylor raced 50 yards down the right wing with the ball before seeing Roberts, stretching to clear his cross, divert it into his own goal.

The large following of Burnley supporters in the White Hart Lane crowd were urging the referee to blow the final whistle when Hamilton completed a great night out. Young chipped the ball forward and Hamilton shrugged off a challenge from

Billy Hamilton watches the second of his two goals fly past Ray Clemence.

Gary O'Reilly, surged towards goal and cracked a shot past Clemence from 20 yards out.

Tottenham Hotspur: Clemence; Perryman, O'Reilly, Roberts, Hughton, Hoddle, Villa(Brooke), Ardíles, Mabbutt, Gibson, Archibald.
Burnley: Stevenson; Brennan, Donachie, Dobson, Phelan, Flynn, Scott, Steven, Hamilton, Taylor, Young.
Referee: A. Grey (Norfolk) *Attendance: 30,771*

Match to Remember 21 9 May 1987

Burnley 2 Orient 1

Grewcock, Britton *Comfort*

IT WAS the day they came to bury Burnley. The unbelievable had happened and Burnley, a founder member of the Football League, were on the verge of losing that proud League status.

A crowd of 17,600 crammed into Turf Moor for the last match of the season and the good luck messages flooded in from just about everywhere in the football world.

Burnley had to win to have a chance of staying in the Fourth Division; Lincoln City had to lose if they were to take Burnley's place in the Vauxhall Conference. And to compound matters further, visitors Orient needed victory to get into the promotion play-offs.

On police advice the game kicked-off 15 minutes late so that everyone could

Ian Britton, the smallest man on the field, heads Burnley's second goal and throws the Clarets a Football League lifeline.

get into the ground and within two minutes of the start both sides had efforts cleared off the line.

Play began at a furious tempo and Peter Leebrook bundled Terry Howard's header off the line to deny Orient a great start; within seconds, Kevin Hales did likewise at the other end to stop Joe Gallagher's effort giving Burnley breathing space.

Play continued to swing from end to end with both 'keepers busy until Neil Grewcock latched on to an Ian Britton pass on the right, cut inside and sent a 20-yard left-foot drive just inside the far post.

With news coming through that Swansea were beating Lincoln, the Clarets seemed to have won their battle three minutes into the second half when Grewcock's perfect free-kick was headed in by Britton, the smallest player on the pitch.

But Orient still had an eye on a place in the play-offs and the home fans had to endure a nerve-jangling finale, especially after Allan Comfort cut back Burnley's lead with a volley into the roof of the net after 56 minutes.

Britton could have relieved the tension, but he swept Phil Devaney's cross just wide of the net.

Now every catch by Joe Neenan was greeted with resounding applause, every tackle by a Burnley player met with roars of approval. The emotional fans — there were three times as many spectators as there had been for any previous game that season and the attendance was the biggest at Turf Moor for three years — willed the ball out of the Burnley half and into Orient territory.

Phil Malley hurled himself at the ball to block a goal-bound effort from John Cornwell and Neenan dropped on to the shot from the rebound. Grewcock hit an upright as the time ticked away and within seconds of the final whistle, the

The eyes and lenses of the football world are on Burnley manager Brian Miller as the Clarets fight for their survival as a League club.

famous pitch was engulfed in a sea of claret and blue as the supporters celebrated their club's survival.

Burnley: Neenan; Leebrook, Hampton, Rodaway, Gallagher, Deakin, Grewcock, Malley, James, Devaney, Britton.
Orient: Cass; Cunningham, Hales, Smalley, Howard, Cornwell, Hughton, Brooks, Jones, Godfrey, Comfort.
Referee: G.Courtney (Spennymoor) *Attendance: 17,600*

Match to Remember 22 29 May 1988

Wolverhampton Wanderers 2 Burnley 0

Mutch, Dennison

THE walk along Wembley Way could not have been friendlier. The good times had returned for both Burnley and Wolverhampton Wanderers, and the Sherpa Van Trophy Final saw the meeting of two famous old clubs, a prospect which attracted an attendance of more than 80,000.

The game was also televised live throughout the Continent, although not in Britain, and the armchair audience saw a game of contrasting fortunes, during which Burnley dominated for probably half the proceedings, but never got the goals they deserved.

At the end of the day, victory for Wolves was a fair result, but Burnley, gracious losers who gave their all, deserved special accolades.

Neither team was as skilful as their illustrious predecessors, but in terms of old-fashioned blood-and-guts Cup-tie spirit, the game had everything and the sportsmanship displayed by both sides equalled anything seen previously at Wembley.

For the first 20 minutes, Burnley were in the driving seat and Andy Farrell saw a first-minute diving header go just wide from the best of the early exchanges.

Burnley and Wolves step out at Wembley for the 1988 Sherpa Van Trophy Final.

Wolves, who in winning at Wembley completed a remarkable Fourth Division title and Cup double, fought their way back into the game and there were chances for Gary Bellamy and Steve Bull before Andy Mutch headed them into a 22nd-minute lead.

Ray Deakin had a shot blocked on the half-hour as the Clarets fought hard to make an impression and, by half-time, the crowd knew that Wolves deserved their lead but that Burnley still had plenty to offer.

Three minutes into the second half, Deakin hit a free-kick which Steve Davis headed goalwards, but Mark Kendall was equal to the challenge.

In the 51st minute, Wolves thought they had sealed things when Robbie Dennison chipped a free-kick over the wall and left Chris Pearce clutching at thin air, but Burnley refused to lie down and accept defeat.

On the hour, Steve Taylor headed Shaun McGrory's cross over the bar when a downward header might easily have sparked a revival; and two minutes later, Leighton James came on as a substitute to grace the Wembley stage for the eighth time in a great career, the other seven appearances all being for Wales.

He added a new dimension to the game and had the previously confident Wolves defence back-pedalling for long periods.

Burnley battled back and George Oghani hit a great cross for Paul Comstive, but his header grazed the crossbar. Five minutes later, James crossed and Comstive's shot went wide of Kendall before Andy Thompson cleared off the line.

Fifteen minutes remained when Oghani and Taylor played a delightful one-two and Oghani's shot went just over the bar; three minutes later the same striker headed a cross over the top.

In the 82nd minute, Comstive powered another header from a Daniel cross, and again the ball grazed the crossbar. That signalled the end of Burnley's chances and Wolves fought back, piled on the pressure and went close to adding to their tally.

Two great clubs had combined to produce a great Cup Final and, despite the result, the Burnley fans went home happy indeed.

Wolverhampton Wanderers: Kendall; Bellamy, Thompson, Streete, Robertson (Gallagher), Robinson, Dennison, Downing, Bull, Mutch, Holmes(Vaughan).
Burnley: Pearce; Daniel, Deakin, Britton, Davis, Gardner, Farrell, Oghani, Taylor, Comstive, McGrory(James).
Referee: R.G.Milford (Bristol) *Attendance: 80,841*

Burnley Against Other League Clubs

Burnley have played 102 clubs in the Football League since 1888-89. Below is their record against each club. Some clubs changed their names (eg Clapton Orient became Leyton Orient then Orient and then Leyton Orient again) and some clubs modified their titles (eg Swansea Town became Swansea City). In all cases the current name used by each club covers all games under previous names.

		HOME					AWAY				
	P	W	D	L	F	A	W	D	L	F	A
Accrington	10	2	2	1	9	8	1	2	2	8	9
AFC Bournemouth	4	1	1	0	6	2	0	1	1	1	2
Aldershot	8	1	1	2	4	3	2	1	1	5	4
Arsenal	86	21	10	12	67	50	9	9	25	46	94
Aston Villa	94	28	8	11	113	71	7	12	28	47	109
Barnsley	44	14	5	3	51	21	8	7	7	27	33
Birmingham City	74	24	9	4	76	36	11	6	20	44	63
Blackburn Rovers	80	20	7	13	70	58	13	6	21	71	91
Blackpool	90	27	9	9	83	44	13	16	16	48	51
Bolton Wanderers	104	29	11	12	94	51	13	15	24	54	91
Bradford	36	9	6	3	33	24	6	4	8	25	34
Bradford City	38	8	6	5	31	21	5	4	10	23	31
Brentford	12	3	2	1	10	7	0	3	3	4	13
Brighton & Hove Albion	6	2	1	0	6	0	1	0	2	3	4
Bristol City	26	3	5	5	21	20	5	3	5	19	20
Bristol Rovers	14	3	4	0	11	3	0	3	4	5	13
Burton Swifts	2	1	0	0	2	0	1	0	0	2	0
Burton United	14	5	2	0	14	4	3	1	3	9	11
Bury	40	8	7	5	30	21	2	8	10	25	42
Cambridge United	18	4	2	3	14	13	3	1	5	13	16
Cardiff City	50	13	5	7	44	29	4	8	13	27	50
Carlisle United	22	8	2	1	22	13	2	5	4	16	17
Charlton Athletic	42	12	4	5	37	19	2	7	12	21	41
Chelsea	78	21	11	7	79	35	15	5	19	50	61
Chester City	6	3	0	0	3	0	1	1	1	1	4
Chesterfield	38	5	10	4	22	17	6	3	10	18	37
Colchester United	12	3	1	2	5	6	2	2	2	8	8
Coventry City	22	4	6	1	16	11	4	3	4	14	17
Crewe Alexandra	8	2	1	1	5	1	1	0	3	2	8
Crystal Palace	10	4	1	0	11	6	2	1	2	5	5
Darlington	6	2	0	1	5	3	0	1	2	4	8
Darwen	6	3	0	0	20	2	2	1	0	7	2
Derby County	72	17	7	12	66	48	7	7	22	40	75
Doncaster Rovers	20	5	2	3	20	8	3	0	7	8	15
Everton	98	21	14	14	86	64	8	14	27	61	97
Exeter City	16	6	2	0	18	4	2	2	4	7	12
Fulham	70	24	6	5	74	28	8	9	18	44	62
Gainsborough Trinity	26	10	2	1	29	11	4	2	7	9	18
Gillingham	12	2	1	3	9	10	1	3	2	5	7
Glossop	28	9	3	2	28	14	4	4	6	14	21
Grimsby Town	36	14	4	0	42	9	4	1	13	15	31
Halifax Town	12	5	0	1	12	6	2	3	1	9	8
Hartlepool United	12	3	3	0	8	1	0	3	3	6	12
Hereford United	14	3	3	1	12	14	1	2	4	4	12
Huddersfield Town	50	12	5	8	39	32	9	2	14	20	35
Hull City	36	8	5	5	30	18	5	5	8	22	33

		HOME					AWAY				
	P	W	D	L	F	A	W	D	L	F	A
Ipswich Town	18	5	1	3	14	10	1	1	7	7	21
Leeds United	58	13	7	9	53	39	6	9	14	38	56
Leicester City	80	24	11	5	91	42	9	13	18	60	75
Leyton Orient	42	12	4	5	42	17	8	2	11	19	32
Lincoln City	42	15	3	3	42	19	5	3	13	22	40
Liverpool	74	18	9	10	61	51	8	10	19	34	66
Loughborough Town	2	1	0	0	9	3	1	0	0	2	0
Luton Town	32	10	4	2	32	16	5	3	8	23	32
Maidstone United	4	1	1	0	3	2	1	0	1	2	2
Manchester City	80	20	11	9	72	53	7	10	23	43	87
Manchester United	102	26	8	17	91	64	13	8	30	66	116
Mansfield Town	4	2	0	0	4	1	0	1	1	1	4
Middlesbrough	46	14	7	2	59	21	4	7	12	28	54
Millwall	30	9	3	3	26	12	1	7	7	15	25
New Brighton	2	1	0	0	2	1	0	0	1	1	2
Newcastle United	94	27	6	14	77	60	14	10	23	60	83
Newport County	12	5	1	0	12	4	3	1	2	7	4
Northampton Town	8	4	0	0	12	4	1	1	2	4	7
Norwich City	16	6	2	0	17	5	1	1	6	6	18
Nottingham Forest	78	20	13	6	81	41	8	9	22	38	79
Notts County	40	12	6	2	32	11	2	4	14	17	57
Oldham Athletic	38	10	3	6	38	23	3	5	11	17	34
Oxford United	10	1	4	0	6	5	2	2	1	7	4
Peterborough United	12	1	3	2	8	7	0	2	4	4	16
Plymouth Argyle	30	6	5	4	18	17	4	5	6	16	25
Portsmouth	38	15	2	2	42	17	5	2	12	23	37
Port Vale	30	7	5	3	40	17	3	8	4	23	25
Preston North End	94	26	13	8	86	56	10	8	29	61	110
Queen's Park Rangers	16	5	2	1	12	8	2	0	6	7	18
Reading	8	2	0	2	12	5	1	1	2	6	10
Rochdale	12	4	0	2	8	5	1	1	4	5	7
Rotherham United	10	2	2	1	12	5	0	2	3	5	9
Scarborough	8	2	0	2	8	5	1	0	3	3	6
Scunthorpe United	14	2	2	3	9	6	1	2	4	7	14
Sheffield United	88	26	9	9	93	52	4	15	25	32	81
Sheffield Wednesday	72	25	4	7	88	36	9	6	21	37	70
Shrewsbury Town	4	0	1	1	1	2	1	0	1	2	3
Southampton	36	13	2	3	39	17	1	7	10	12	34
Southend United	10	2	1	2	9	9	2	1	2	12	10
Stockport County	38	13	4	2	44	17	5	5	9	23	33
Stoke City	68	18	7	9	62	39	5	6	23	40	82
Sunderland	88	24	9	11	85	42	8	12	24	58	92
Swansea City	28	7	6	1	25	11	3	3	8	12	28
Swindon Town	10	1	1	3	3	7	4	0	1	8	4
Torquay United	12	4	2	0	9	3	2	1	3	5	8
Tottenham Hotspur	88	24	13	7	87	50	10	9	25	51	109
Tranmere Rovers	10	2	3	0	11	7	2	0	3	7	6
Walsall	14	3	2	2	9	6	2	2	3	8	11
Watford	4	2	0	0	4	0	0	0	2	1	6
West Bromwich Albion	108	25	11	18	98	68	16	11	27	65	110
West Ham United	66	22	8	3	82	45	7	6	20	41	61
Wigan Athletic	4	1	0	1	4	2	0	0	2	0	3
Wimbledon	4	0	1	1	2	4	1	1	0	4	1
Wolverhampton Wanderers	98	20	13	16	85	78	9	9	31	47	115
Wrexham	16	4	2	2	12	8	4	1	3	13	11
York City	8	1	3	0	8	2	1	1	2	3	7

Burnley in the Football League 1888-89 to 1990-91

	P	W	D	L	F	A	Pts	Pos
FOOTBALL LEAGUE								
1888-89	22	7	3	12	42	62	17	9th
1889-90	22	4	5	13	36	65	13	11th
1890-91	22	9	3	10	52	63	21	8th
1891-92	26	11	4	11	49	45	26	7th
DIVISION ONE								
1892-93	30	13	4	13	51	44	30	6th
1893-94	30	15	4	11	61	51	34	5th
1894-95	30	11	4	15	44	56	26	9th
1895-96	30	10	7	13	48	44	27	10th
1896-97	30	6	7	17	43	61	19	16th
DIVISION TWO								
1897-98	30	20	8	2	80	24	48	1st
DIVISION ONE								
1898-99	34	15	9	10	45	47	39	3rd
1899-1900	34	11	5	18	34	54	27	17th
DIVISION TWO								
1900-01	34	20	4	10	53	29	44	3rd
1901-02	34	10	10	14	41	45	30	9th
1902-03	34	6	8	20	30	77	20	18th
1903-04	34	15	9	10	50	55	39	5th
1904-05	34	12	6	16	43	52	30	11th
1905-06	38	15	8	15	42	53	38	9th
1906-07	38	17	6	15	62	47	40	7th
1907-08	38	20	6	12	67	50	46	7th
1908-09	38	13	7	18	51	58	33	14th
1909-10	38	14	6	18	62	61	34	14th
1910-11	38	13	15	10	45	45	41	8th
1911-12	38	22	8	8	77	41	52	3rd
1912-13	38	21	8	9	88	53	50	2nd
DIVISION ONE								
1913-14	38	12	12	14	61	53	36	12th
1914-15	38	18	7	13	61	47	43	4th
1919-20	42	21	9	12	65	59	51	2nd
1920-21	42	23	13	6	79	36	59	1st
1921-22	42	22	5	15	72	54	49	3rd
1922-23	42	16	6	20	58	59	38	15th
1923-24	42	12	12	18	55	60	36	17th
1924-25	42	11	12	19	46	75	34	19th
1925-26	42	13	10	19	85	108	36	20th
1926-27	42	19	9	14	91	80	47	5th
1927-28	42	16	7	19	82	98	39	19th
1928-29	42	15	8	19	81	103	38	19th
1929-30	42	14	8	20	79	97	36	21st
DIVISION TWO								
1930-31	42	17	11	14	81	77	45	8th
1931-32	42	13	9	20	59	87	35	19th
1932-33	42	11	14	17	67	79	36	19th
1933-34	42	18	6	18	60	72	42	13th
1934-35	42	16	9	17	63	73	41	12th
1935-36	42	12	13	17	50	59	37	15th
1936-37	42	16	10	16	57	61	42	13th
1937-38	42	17	10	15	54	54	44	6th
1938-39	42	15	9	18	50	56	39	14th
1946-47	42	22	14	6	65	29	58	2nd
DIVISION ONE								
1947-48	42	20	12	10	56	43	52	3rd
1948-49	42	12	14	16	43	50	38	15th
1949-50	42	16	13	13	40	40	45	10th
1950-51	42	14	14	14	48	43	42	10th
1951-52	42	15	10	17	56	63	40	14th
1952-53	42	18	12	12	67	52	48	6th
1953-54	42	21	4	17	78	67	46	7th
1954-55	42	17	9	16	51	48	43	10th
1955-56	42	18	8	16	64	54	44	7th
1956-57	42	18	10	14	56	50	46	7th
1957-58	42	21	5	16	80	74	47	6th
1958-59	42	19	10	13	81	70	48	7th
1959-60	42	24	7	11	85	61	55	1st
1960-61	42	22	7	13	102	77	51	4th
1961-62	42	21	11	10	101	67	53	2nd
1962-63	42	22	10	10	78	57	54	3rd
1963-64	42	17	10	15	71	64	44	9th
1964-65	42	16	10	16	70	70	42	12th
1965-66	42	24	7	11	79	47	55	3rd
1966-67	42	15	9	18	66	76	39	14th
1967-68	42	14	10	18	64	71	38	14th
1968-69	42	15	9	18	55	82	39	14th
1969-70	42	12	15	15	56	61	39	14th
1970-71	42	7	13	22	29	63	27	21st
DIVISION TWO								
1971-72	42	20	6	16	70	55	46	7th
1972-73	42	24	14	4	72	35	62	1st
DIVISION ONE								
1973-74	42	16	14	12	56	53	46	6th
1974-75	42	17	11	14	68	67	45	10th
1975-76	42	9	10	23	43	66	28	21st
DIVISION TWO								
1976-77	42	11	14	17	46	64	36	16th
1977-78	42	15	10	17	56	64	40	11th
1978-79	42	14	12	16	51	62	40	13th
1979-80	42	6	15	21	39	73	27	21st
DIVISION THREE								
1980-81	46	18	14	14	60	48	50	8th
1981-82	46	21	17	8	66	45	80	1st
DIVISION TWO								
1982-83	42	12	8	22	56	66	44	21st
DIVISION THREE								
1983-84	46	16	14	16	76	61	62	12th
1984-85	46	11	13	22	60	73	46	21st
DIVISION FOUR								
1985-86	46	16	11	19	60	65	59	14th
1986-87	46	12	13	21	53	74	49	22nd
1987-88	46	20	7	19	57	62	67	10th
1988-89	46	14	13	19	52	61	55	16th
1989-90	46	14	14	18	45	55	56	16th
1990-91	46	23	10	13	70	51	79	6th

ANALYSIS

	Sns	P	W	D	L	F	A	Pts
Division One	51	1982	784	447	751	3163	3157	2015
Division Two	31	1218	477	293	448	1787	1756	1259
Division Three	4	184	66	58	60	262	227	238
Division Four	6	276	99	68	109	337	368	365
TOTAL	92	3660	1426	866	1368	5549	5508	3877

Burnley in the Central League 1911-12 to 1990-91

Burnley were founder members of the Central League in 1911 and enjoyed continuous membership until 1986. The championship has been secured on three occasions, 1948-49, and in two successive seasons in the clubs' post-war heyday, 1961-62 and 1962-63. Following the decline in the fortunes in the 1980's, and two finishes in the bottom two positions, re-election was not sought in 1986. After three seasons an application for re-election was successful and the club replaced Darlington in the newly-sponsored Pontins League in 1989.

	P	*W*	*D*	*L*	*F*	*A*	*Pts*	*Pos*
1911-12	32	13	5	14	66	62	31	12th
1912-13	38	22	4	12	87	47	48	3rd
1913-14	38	16	6	16	57	72	38	11th
1914-15	38	21	5	12	80	41	47	4th
1919-20	42	15	5	22	66	71	35	18th
1920-21	42	18	7	17	84	73	43	9th
1921-22	42	21	6	15	77	79	48	4th
1922-23	42	18	10	14	70	63	46	6th
1923-24	42	8	13	21	41	81	29	21st
1924-25	42	8	9	25	62	95	25	22nd
1925-26	42	17	8	17	87	77	42	13th
1926-27	42	14	6	22	71	99	34	19th
1927-28	42	15	5	22	71	115	35	19th
1928-29	42	19	9	14	88	76	47	6th
1929-30	42	14	8	20	80	109	36	16th
1930-31	42	12	10	20	66	95	34	18th
1931-32	42	12	4	26	68	140	28	21st
1932-33	42	15	7	20	78	94	37	17th
1933-34	42	10	11	21	73	102	31	18th
1934-35	42	18	3	21	84	109	39	15th
1935-36	42	12	14	16	58	73	38	15th
1936-37	42	24	5	13	97	71	53	3rd
1937-38	42	16	11	15	71	68	43	7th
1938-39	42	15	4	23	60	85	34	21st
1946-47	42	22	8	12	77	50	52	3rd
1947-48	42	18	7	17	57	50	43	9th
1948-49	42	24	12	6	72	32	60	1st
1949-50	42	21	11	10	78	53	53	3rd
1950-51	42	19	14	9	62	32	52	2nd
1951-52	42	18	5	19	63	61	41	8th
1952-53	42	23	5	14	70	62	51	5th
1953-54	42	24	8	10	68	48	56	2nd
1954-55	42	22	8	12	94	59	52	4th
1955-56	42	15	11	16	72	76	41	11th
1956-57	42	13	9	20	58	78	35	17th
1957-58	42	15	7	20	58	77	37	16th
1958-59	42	14	7	21	58	72	35	16th
1959-60	42	18	7	17	66	68	43	11th
1960-61	42	23	7	12	91	64	53	4th
1961-62	42	30	7	5	113	40	67	1st
1962-63	42	27	7	8	101	34	61	1st
1963-64	42	23	9	10	77	42	55	4th
1964-65	42	19	13	10	76	50	51	6th
1965-66	42	18	9	15	70	71	45	9th
1966-67	42	13	14	15	60	60	40	13th
1967-68	42	17	12	13	52	51	46	10th
1968-69	42	15	13	14	64	58	43	10th
1969-70	42	23	9	10	76	51	55	4th
1970-71	42	18	15	9	77	61	51	5th
1971-72	42	16	8	18	61	73	40	12th
1972-73	42	15	8	19	57	60	38	16th
1973-74	42	12	5	25	38	65	29	20th
1974-75	42	13	13	16	64	68	39	14th
1975-76	42	15	10	17	64	71	40	13th
1976-77	42	11	14	17	55	64	36	16th
1977-78	42	11	12	19	51	67	34	19th
1978-79	42	15	9	18	42	56	39	14th
1979-80	42	18	10	14	46	49	46	9th
1980-81	42	16	12	14	45	45	44	9th
1981-82	42	7	11	24	42	88	25	21st
		DIVISION TWO						
1982-83	30	14	8	8	49	41	36	4th
		DIVISION ONE						
1983-84	30	5	9	16	19	45	24	16th
		DIVISION TWO						
1984-85	34	6	4	24	41	74	22	17th
1985-86	34	6	6	22	36	74	24	17th
1986-89		did not compete						
1989-90	34	7	3	24	30	69	24	18th
1990-91	34	13	11	10	53	48	50	8th

1888-89

Manager: None

1	Sep	8	(a)	Preston NE	L 2-5	Gallocher, Poland	6,000
2		15	(a)	Bolton W	W 4-3	Tait 2, Poland, Scrimmage	
3		22	(a)	Wolves	L 1-4	A.Brady	4,000
4		29	(a)	West Brom A	L 3-4	Gallocher 2, Tait	2,100
5	Oct	6	(h)	Bolton W	W 4-1	Poland 2, A.Brady, Tait	
6		13	(h)	Wolves	L 0-4		4,000
7		20	(a)	Stoke	L 3-4	Poland, Opp own-goal, Scrimmage	
8		27	(a)	Notts C	L 1-6	Yates	
9	Nov	3	(h)	Blackburn R	L 1-7	McKay	3,000
10		10	(h)	West Brom A	W 2-0	McKay, Scrimmage	5,000
11		17	(h)	Everton	D 2-2	Gallocher, McKay	
12		24	(a)	Everton	L 2-3	A.Brady, McKay	
13	Dec	1	(a)	Accrington	L 1-5	Opp own-goal	5,000
14		8	(h)	Stoke	W 2-1	W.Brady, Yates	
15		15	(h)	Preston NE	D 2-2	McKay, W.Brady	
16		22	(a)	Aston Villa	L 2-4	A.Brady, Scrimmage	2,000
17		29	(h)	Notts C	W 1-0	Abrams	
18	Jan	5	(h)	Aston Villa	W 4-0	A.Brady, Yates 2, Gallocher	6,000
19		12	(h)	Accrington	D 2-2	A.Brady, Yates	6,000
20		19	(h)	Derby C	W 1-0	McKay	3,000
21	Feb	4	(a)	Blackburn R	L 2-4	A.Brady, Gallocher	2,000
22	Mar	2	(a)	Derby C	L 0-1		3,000
	FINAL LEAGUE POSITION: 9th in the Football League (Re-elected)						Appearances
							Goals

FA Cup

1	Feb	2	(h)	Old Westminsters	W 4-3	Gallocher 2, Lang, W.Brady	
2		16	(a)	West Brom A	L 1-5	Gallocher	5,104
							Appearances
							Goals

Smith W	Lang A	Bury W	Abrams J	Friel D	Keenan J	Brady A	Tait W	Poland F	Gallocher P	Yates J	McFettridge W	Ridsdale J	Duckworth R	Kay R	Midgeley T	Hibbert J	McKay W	McRae R	Cox W	McMahon R	Kavanagh	Woods J	Brady W	Mudie	Hargreaves	
1	2	3	4	5	6	7	8	9	10	11																1
1		3	4	5	6	7	8	9	10	11	2															2
1	2			5	6	7		9	10	11	3	4	8													3
	2	3	6	5	4	10	11	9	8	7				1												4
	2	3	6	5	4	10	11	9	8	7				1												5
	2	3	4	5	6	7	8	9	10	11				1												6
	3	2	4	5	6	7		9	11	10				1	8											7
	3	2		5	6	8		9	10	11	4			1		7										8
	2	3	6	5	4			1	11	10	9						7	8								9
	3	2	4	5	6	7			10	11							8		1	9						10
	3	2	4	5	6	7			10	11	9						8		1							11
	3	2	6	5	4	7			10	11	9						8		1							12
	3		6	5		7				11	4						8		1	9	2	10				13
	3	2		5	6	7				11	4						10		1				8	9		14
	3	2		4	5	7			9	11	6						10		1				8			15
	2	3		5	4	7			9	11	6						10		1				8			16
	2	3	4	5		7			9	10	6						11		1				8			17
	2	3		4	5	7			9	10	6						11		1				8			18
	3	2		5	6	7			9	11	4						10		1				8			19
	2	3		5	4	7			9	10	6						11		1				8			20
	2	3		5	4	8			9	11	6						10		1				7			21
	3	2	5	11	6				10		4						9	8	1				7			22
3	21	20	13	22	20	20	5	9	20	21	16	1	1	5	1	1	14	2	13	2	1	1	9	1		
			1			7	4	5	6	5							6						2			

2 own-goals, 4 scrimmages

Smith W	Lang A	Bury W	Abrams J	Friel D	Keenan J	Brady A	Tait W	Poland F	Gallocher P	Yates J	McFettridge W	Ridsdale J	Duckworth R	Kay R	Midgeley T	Hibbert J	McKay W	McRae R	Cox W	McMahon R	Kavanagh	Woods J	Brady W	Mudie	Hargreaves	
	2		4	5	6				8	11	10								1	9			7		3	1
	3	2		5	6				10	11	4							7	1	9			8			2
	2	1	1	2	2				2	2	2							1	2	2			2		1	
	1								3														1			

1889-90

Manager: None

1	Sep	7	(a)	Aston Villa	D 2-2	Heyes, Haresnape	4,000
2		14	(a)	Everton	L 1-2	Ashworth	
3		21	(h)	Accrington	D 2-2	Campbell, Duckworth	3,000
4		28	(h)	Preston NE	L 0-3		
5	Oct	5	(h)	Aston Villa	L 2-6	Friel, Scrimmage	8,000
6		12	(h)	West Brom A	L 1-2	Yates	6,000
7		19	(a)	Accrington	D 2-2	McFettridge, Haresnape	
8		26	(a)	Blackburn R	L 1-7	Campbell	4,000
9	Nov	2	(a)	Notts C	D 1-1	Heyes	
10		9	(h)	Wolves	L 1-2	Murray	4,000
11		23	(a)	West Brom A	L 1-6	Crabtree	7,100
12		30	(a)	Preston NE	L 0-6		
13	Dec	7	(a)	Wolves	L 1-9	Opp own-goal	2,000
14	Jan	4	(a)	Derby C	L 1-4	Campbell	3,000
15		11	(h)	Stoke	L 1-3	Ashworth	
16	Feb	8	(h)	Everton	L 0-1		
17		22	(h)	Blackburn R	L 1-2	Stewart	7,000
18	Mar	1	(h)	Bolton W	W 7-0	Lambie 3, Stewart, Hill, Haresnape, McColl	
19		8	(h)	Derby C	W 2-0	McColl, Hill	2,000
20		10	(a)	Stoke	W 4-3	Haresnape 2, Lambie 2	
21		15	(h)	Notts C	W 3-0	Stewart 2, Scrimmage	
22		17	(a)	Bolton W	D 2-2	Hill, McFettridge	

FINAL LEAGUE POSITION: 11th in the Football League (Re-elected)

Appearances
Goals

FA Cup

1	Jan	18	(a)	Sheffield U	L 1-2	Bury

Appearances
Goals

Cox W	Bury W	White E	McFettridge W	Lang A	Keenan J	Campbell J	Haresnape R	Caldow G	Heyes L	Yates J	Friel D	Ashworth J	Duckworth R	Crabtree J	Murray T	Smith W	Spiers D	McColl W	Stewart A	McConnell J	Hill J	Lambie C	Kaye A	McLardie A	Coyle B	
1	2	3	4	5	6	7	8	9	10	11																1
1	2	3		5	6	8	7	9	10		4	11														2
1	3	2	6	5	4	9	8		10				7	11												3
1	2	3	4	5	6	8	7	9	10	11																4
1	2	3	4		6	9	7		10	11	5		8													5
1	3	2	6	5	4	9	7		10	11			8													6
1	3	2	6	5		7	8	11		10	4				9											7
1	2	3	4	5	6	8	7			11	10				9											8
1	2	6	4	3		8	7	10	11		5				9											9
1	2	5	6	3	4	8	7	10	11						9											10
1	3	4	6	2	5	8	7		11					10	9											11
	2	5	4	3	6		7		10				8	11	9	1										12
1	2	5	4	3	6	11	7		10						9										8	13
1	2		4	3	6	9	7										5	8	10						11	14
	2	5	4	3	6	9						7						8	10	1	11					15
	3	5	6	2	4		7									1		8	10		11	9				16
	2	5	4	3	6		7											8	11		10	9	1			17
	2	5	6	3	4		7											8	10		11	9	1			18
	2	5	6	3			7										4	8	10		11	9	1			19
	2	5	4	3			7										6	8	10		11	9	1			20
	3	5	6	2	4													7	10		11	9	1	8		21
	2	5	4	3	6													7	10		11	9	1	8		22
13	22	21	21	21	18	14	19	6	11	6	5	2	4	3	7	2	3	9	9	1	8	7	6	2	2	
			2			3	5		2	1	1	2	1	1	1			2	4		3	5				

1 own-goal, 2 scrimmages

Cox W	Bury W	White E	McFettridge W	Lang A	Keenan J	Campbell J	Haresnape R	Caldow G	Heyes L	Yates J	Friel D	Ashworth J	Duckworth R	Crabtree J	Murray T	Smith W	Spiers D	McColl W	Stewart A	McConnell J	Hill J	Lambie C	Kaye A	McLardie A	Coyle B	
	2	5	4	3	6	11	7		10					9				8		1						1
	1	1	1	1	1	1	1		1					1				1		1						
	1																									

1890-91

Manager: None

1	Sep	6	(a)	Accrington	D	1-1	Lambie	8,000
2		13	(a)	Sunderland	W	3-2	Lambie, McLardie, Stewart	
3		20	(h)	Aston Villa	W	2-1	McLardie, Lambie	10,000
4		27	(h)	Sunderland	D	3-3	McLardie, Spiers, Lambie	
5	Oct	4	(a)	West Brom A	L	1-3	Yates	6,000
6		11	(h)	Bolton W	L	1-2	Scrimmage	
7		18	(h)	Blackburn R	L	1-6	McLardie	10,000
8		25	(a)	Wolves	L	1-3	Scrimmage	3,000
9	Nov	1	(h)	Wolves	W	4-2	McLardie 2, Lambie, Place (Snr)	3,500
10		8	(a)	Aston Villa	D	4-4	Lambie 3, McLardie	5,000
11		15	(h)	Derby C	W	6-1	Lambie 4, Marr, McLardie	6,000
12		22	(a)	Blackburn R	L	2-5	Place (Snr), McLardie	4,000
13		29	(h)	Accrington	W	2-0	Lambie, McLardie	6,000
14	Dec	6	(h)	West Brom A	W	5-4	Hill, McLardie 2, Marr, Oswald	5,500
15		20	(h)	Notts C	L	0-1		
16		27	(a)	Everton	L	3-7	McLardie 2, Hill	
17	Jan	24	(a)	Derby C	W	4-2	Lambie 3, Scrimmage	2,500
18	Feb	2	(a)	Preston NE	L	0-7		
19		10	(a)	Notts C	L	0-4		
20	Mar	7	(h)	Preston NE	W	6-2	Nicol 3, Marr 2, Hill	
21		14	(h)	Everton	W	3-2	Stewart, Haresnape, Bowes	
22		21	(a)	Bolton W	L	0-1		

FINAL LEAGUE POSITION: 8th in the Football League

Appearances
Goals

FA Cup

1	Jan	17	(h)	Crewe A	W	4-2	Lambie, Oswald, McLardie, Hill
2		31	(a)	Notts C	L	1-2	McLardie

Appearances
Goals

Kaye A	Walker J	Lang A	McFettridge W	Spiers D	Keenan J	Oswald J	McLardie A	Lambie C	Stewart A	Hill J	Yates J	Carr Z	Haresnape R	Duerden J	Place W (Snr)	Nash J	Patterson T	Marr R	Brodie J	Crossley T	Bowes W	Nicol T	Bury W	
1	2	3	4	5	6	7	8	9	10	11														1
1	2	3	4	5	6	7	8	9	11	10														2
1	2	3	4	5	6	7	8	9	10	11														3
1	2	3	4	5	6	7	8	9	11	10														4
1	2	3	4	5	6	7	8	9	11		10													5
1	2		6	5	4	7	8	9	10	11		3												6
1	2	3	4	5	6	8	9		10	11			7											7
1	3		4	5	6		8	9	10				7	2	11									8
1	2		4	5	6	7	8	9	10					3	11									9
1	3			5	6	7	8	9	10					2	11	4								10
1	2	3	4		6	7	8	9							11		5	10						11
1	2	3	4	5	6	7	8	9							11			10						12
1	2	3	4	5	6	7	8	9		11								10						13
1	2	3	4	5	6	7	8	9		11								10						14
1	2	3	4	5	6	7	8	9		11								10						15
1	3	2	4		6	7	8	9	10	11							5							16
1		2	6		4		10	9	8	7			11			5							3	17
1	2	3	4		6			9	10	11			7			5			8					18
1	2	3	6	5				9		11						4		10	8	7				19
1	2	3	4	5					6	11			7					10			8	9		20
1	2	3	4	5					6	11			7					10			8	9		21
1	2	3	4	5					6	11			7					10			8	9		22
22	21	18	21	18	18	15	17	18	16	16	1	1	7	3	5	4	2	9	2	1	3	3	1	
				1		1	14	16	2	3	1		1		2			4			1	3		

3 scrimmages

Kaye A	Walker J	Lang A	McFettridge W	Spiers D	Keenan J	Oswald J	McLardie A	Lambie C	Stewart A	Hill J	Yates J	Carr Z	Haresnape R	Duerden J	Place W (Snr)	Nash J	Patterson T	Marr R	Brodie J	Crossley T	Bowes W	Nicol T	Bury W	
1		3	4		6	7	8	9	10	11						5							2	1
1		3	4		6		8	9	10	11			7			5							2	2
2		2	2		2	1	2	2	2	2			1			2							2	
						1	2	1		1														

1891-92

Manager: None

1	Sep	5	(a)	Accrington	L 0-1		7,000
2		7	(h)	Preston NE	W 2-0	Bowes, Haresnape	
3		19	(h)	Stoke	W 4-1	Bowes 2, Nicol, Place (Snr)	
4		21	(a)	Preston NE	L 1-5	Nicol	
5		26	(a)	Blackburn R	D 3-3	McLardie, Lang, Nicol	4,000
6	Oct	10	(a)	Stoke	L 0-3		
7		17	(h)	Aston Villa	W 4-1	Nicol 2, Matthew, Bowes	5,000
8		24	(a)	Bolton W	L 0-2		
9	Nov	7	(a)	Wolves	D 0-0		1,200
10		14	(h)	Accrington	W 2-1	McLardie, Graham	7,000
11		21	(a)	Sunderland	L 1-2	Nicol	
12		23	(h)	West Brom A	W 3-2	Nicol 2, Lang (pen)	8,000
13	Dec	5	(a)	Aston Villa	L 1-6	Hill	5,000
14		12	(h)	Blackburn R	W 3-0	Nicol, Bowes, Galbraith	5,000
15		19	(a)	Derby C	W 1-0	Galbraith	4,000
16		26	(a)	West Brom A	L 0-1		5,000
17	Jan	2	(a)	Everton	D 1-1	McLardie	
18		9	(h)	Darwen	W 9-0	Nicol 3, McLardie 3, Hill 2, Espie	
19	Feb	13	(h)	Everton	W 1-0	Hill	
20		27	(a)	Notts C	L 1-5	Espie	
21	Mar	5	(h)	Bolton W	L 1-2	Nicol	
22		26	(h)	Wolves	D 1-1	Nicol	4,000
23	Apr	2	(a)	Darwen	W 6-2	McLardie 2, Hill, Nicol 2, Bowes	
24		15	(h)	Notts C	W 1-0	Nicol	
25		16	(h)	Derby C	L 2-4	Graham, McLardie	6,000
26		30	(h)	Sunderland	L 1-2	McLardie	

FINAL LEAGUE POSITION: 7th in the Football League

Appearances
Goals

FA Cup

1	Jan	23	(a)	Everton	W 3-1	Hill 2, Nicol	
2		30	(h)	Stoke	L 1-3	Hill	

Appearances
Goals

Hillman J	Jeffrey W	Lang A	McFettridge W	Spiers D	Stewart A	Bowes W	McLardie A	Nicol T	Graham W	Hill J	Haresnape R	Place W (Snr)	Walker J	Matthew J	Galbraith H	Keenan J	Espie J	Match
1	2	3	4	5	6	7	8	9	10	11								1
1	2	3	4	5	6	9	8			11	7	10						2
1	2	3	4	5	6	9	8	7		11		10						3
1	2	3	4	5	6	9	8	7		11		10						4
1		3	4	5	6	9	8	7		11		10	2					5
1		3	4	5	6	9	8	7		11		10	2					6
1		3	4		6	9	8	7		11		10	2	5				7
1		3	4		6	9	8	7		11		10	2	5				8
1	2	3	4		6		8	9	7	11		10		5				9
1		3	4		6	8	10	7	9	11			2	5				10
1		3	4		6	8	10	7	9	11			2	5				11
1		3	4		6	8	10	7	9	11			2	5				12
1		3	4		6	8	10	7	9	11			2	5				13
1		3	4		6	8	10	7	11				2	5	9			14
1		3	4		6	8	10	7	11				2	5	9			15
1		3	4			8	10	7	11				2	5		6	9	16
1		3	4			8	10	7	11	9			2	5		6		17
1		3	4			8	10	7		11			2	5		6	9	18
1	2	3	4		6		10	7	11	8				5			9	19
1		3	4			8		7	11	10			2	5		6	9	20
1	2	3	4			8		7	11	10				5		6	9	21
1		3	4			8	10	9		11			2		7	6	5	22
1		3	4		6	8	10	7	11	9			2				5	23
1		3	4			8	10	9	11				2		7	6	5	24
1		3	4			8	10	9	11				2		7	6	5	25
1		3			4	8	10	7	11	9			2			6	5	26
26	7	26	25	6	18	24	24	25	17	21	1	8	19	15	5	9	10	
		2				6	10	17	2	5	1	1		1	2		2	

Hillman J	Jeffrey W	Lang A	McFettridge W	Spiers D	Stewart A	Bowes W	McLardie A	Nicol T	Graham W	Hill J	Haresnape R	Place W (Snr)	Walker J	Matthew J	Galbraith H	Keenan J	Espie J	Match
1		3	4			8	10	7	11	9			2	5		6		1
1		3	4			8	10	7	11	9			2	5		6		2
2		2	2			2	2	2	2	2			2	2		2		
								1		3								

1892-93

Manager: None

1	Sep	3	(a)	Wolves	L 0-1		10,000
2		5	(h)	Aston Villa	L 0-2		8,000
3		10	(a)	Newton Heath	D 1-1	Boyd	10,000
4		17	(h)	Newton Heath	W 4-1	Hill 2, Crabtree, Bowes	6,500
5		24	(h)	Stoke	W 3-2	Espie, Buchanan, Stewart	5,500
6	Oct	1	(a)	Sheffield W	L 0-2		12,000
7		3	(h)	Derby C	W 2-1	McNab, Crabtree	7,000
8		15	(a)	Preston NE	L 0-2		4,000
9		22	(h)	Notts C	W 3-0	Bowes, Hill, McNab	
10		29	(h)	Accrington	L 1-3	Buchanan	7,000
11	Nov	5	(a)	Sunderland	L 0-2		
12		12	(a)	Derby C	L 0-1		5,000
13		19	(a)	Stoke	L 1-4	Chambers	
14		26	(h)	Nottingham F	D 1-1	Crabtree	4,000
15	Dec	3	(h)	Blackburn R	D 0-0		10,000
16		8	(a)	Notts C	L 1-3	Crabtree	4,000
17		10	(a)	Nottingham F	D 2-2	Crabtree, Graham	8,000
18		17	(a)	Blackburn R	L 0-2		7,500
19		24	(a)	Everton	W 1-0	McNab	10,000
20		31	(h)	West Brom A	W 5-0	Buchanan, Nicol, Chambers, Hill, McNab	4,500
21	Jan	7	(a)	West Brom A	L 1-7	Chambers	1,000
22		14	(a)	Accrington	W 4-0	Buchanan 2, Chambers, Bowes	6,000
23	Feb	11	(h)	Bolton W	W 3-0	King, Bowes, Hill	5,000
24		25	(a)	Bolton W	L 0-1		
25	Mar	18	(h)	Preston NE	W 4-2	Brady, Turnbull, McNab, Bowes	
26		31	(h)	Sheffield W	W 4-0	Buchanan, Turnbull, Bowes, Livingstone	9,500
27	Apr	1	(h)	Wolves	W 2-0	Turnbull, Scrimmage	8,000
28		4	(a)	Aston Villa	W 3-1	Buchanan, Turnbull, Bowes	8,000
29		8	(h)	Everton	W 3-0	Buchanan, Brady, Bowes	7,000
30		15	(h)	Sunderland	L 2-3	Crabtree, Hill	10,000

FINAL LEAGUE POSITION: 6th in Division One

Appearances

Goals

FA Cup

1	Jan	21	(h)	Small Heath	W 2-0	McNab, Hill	7,500
2	Feb	4	(a)	Sheffield W	L 0-1		9,500

Appearances

Goals

Hillman J	Nicol T	Lang A	King G	Matthew J	Stewart A	Crabtree J	Bowes W	Boyd H	Hill J	Graham W	Mullineux J	Buchanan R	Espie J	Keenan J	Smith W	Ryan W	Chambers T	McNab W	McFettridge W	Lambie C	Nash J	Place W (Snr)	Sawers A	Brady A	Turnbull P	Livingstone A	
1	2	3	4	5	6	7	8	9	10	11																	1
1	2	3		5	6	7	8	9	10	11	4																2
1	2	3	4	5	6	7	8	9	10	11																	3
1	2	3	4	5	6	7	10	9	11			8															4
1	2	3		4	10	7	9		11			8	5	6													5
	2	3		4	10	7	9		11			8	6	5	1												6
	2	3		4	6	7			11			8	5			1	9	10									7
1	2	3		4	6		10		11			7	5				8	9									8
1	2	3			6		10		11			7	5				8	9	4								9
1	2	3			6		10		11			7	5				8	9	4								10
1	2	3	4		6	10	11					7	5				8	9									11
1	3	2	6		4	10	11					8	5				7	9									12
1	2	3	4		10	7				11		8	5	6			9										13
1	2	3	4		10	7	6		11			8	5				9										14
1	2	3	4	5		7	6		10	11							8			9							15
1	2	3	4	5		7	6		10	11							8			9							16
1	2	3	4			7	6		10	11							8			9	5						17
1	2	3	4	5		7	6		10								8			9		11					18
1	2	3	4			7	10		11		6	8	5					9									19
1	2	3	4			5	10		11		6	8					7	9									20
1	2		4			5	10		11		6	8					7	9					3				21
1	2	3	4			5	10		11		6	8					7	9									22
1	2		4			5	10		11		6	8					7	9					3				23
1	2	3	4			5	10		11			8	6					9				7					24
1	2	3	4			5	10		11				6					9						7	8		25
1	2	3	4				10		11			8	5											7	9	6	26
1	2	3					10		11		4	8	5											7	9	6	27
1	2	3					10		11		4	8	5											7	9	6	28
1	2	3					10		11		4	8	5											7	9	6	29
1	2	3				7	10		11		4	8	5												9	6	30
28	30	28	19	11	14	23	28	4	27	7	10	22	18	3	1	1	16	13	2	4	1	2	2	5	6	5	
	1		1		1	6	8	1	6	1		8	1				4	5						2	4	1	

1 scrimmage

Hillman J	Nicol T	Lang A	King G	Matthew J	Stewart A	Crabtree J	Bowes W	Boyd H	Hill J	Graham W	Mullineux J	Buchanan R	Espie J	Keenan J	Smith W	Ryan W	Chambers T	McNab W	McFettridge W	Lambie C	Nash J	Place W (Snr)	Sawers A	Brady A	Turnbull P	Livingstone A	
1	2	3	4			5	10		11		6	8					7	9									1
1	2		4			5	10		11		6	8					7	9					3				2
2	2	1	2			2	2		2		2	2					2	2					1				
									1									1									

1893-94

Manager: Arthur F.Sutcliffe

1	Sep	2	(a)	Newton Heath	L 2-3	Brady, Hill	10,000
2		4	(h)	Darwen	W 5-1	Bowes, Turnbull, King, 2 Scrimmages	6,500
3		9	(h)	Preston NE	W 4-1	Buchanan, Brady 2, Turnbull	9,000
4		16	(a)	Nottingham F	L 0-5		7,000
5		23	(a)	West Brom A	D 1-1	Brady	3,000
6		30	(h)	Stoke	W 4-0	Turnbull 2, Espie, Scrimmage	6,000
7	Oct	7	(h)	Everton	W 2-1	Hill, Scrimmage	10,000
8		14	(a)	Preston NE	W 2-1	Hill, Bowes	6,000
9		21	(h)	Newton Heath	W 4-1	Turnbull 2, Espie, Hill	7,000
10		28	(a)	Aston Villa	L 0-4		10,000
11	Nov	4	(h)	Nottingham F	W 3-1	Bowes, Nicol, Brady	6,000
12		11	(a)	Stoke	L 2-4	Bowes, Hill	5,000
13		18	(a)	Blackburn R	L 2-3	Hill, Scrimmage	5,000
14		25	(a)	Everton	L 3-4	Hill (pen), Turnbull, Brady	10,000
15	Dec	2	(h)	Sunderland	W 1-0	Hill (pen)	9,500
16		9	(h)	West Brom A	W 3-0	Turnbull, Espie, Hill	4,500
17		16	(a)	Sunderland	D 2-2	Turnbull 2	7,000
18		23	(h)	Blackburn R	W 1-0	Hill	13,000
19		25	(h)	Sheffield U	W 4-1	Buchanan 2, Bowes, Espie	8,000
20		26	(a)	Sheffield W	W 1-0	Bowes	10,000
21	Jan	6	(a)	Bolton W	L 0-2		
22	Feb	3	(h)	Bolton W	W 2-1	Place (Jnr), Turnbull	6,000
23		6	(a)	Darwen	D 0-0		3,000
24	Mar	3	(a)	Wolves	L 0-1		
25		10	(h)	Derby C	W 3-1	Egan, Hill, Morrison	4,500
26		23	(h)	Sheffield W	L 0-1		10,000
27		26	(a)	Sheffield U	L 0-1		8,000
28	Apr	2	(a)	Derby C	D 3-3	Turnbull, 2 Scrimmages	3,000
29		7	(h)	Aston Villa	L 3-6	Turnbull, Buchanan, Place (Jnr)	6,000
30		14	(h)	Wolves	W 4-2	Turnbull 2, Place (Jnr), Espie	5,000

FINAL LEAGUE POSITION: 5th in Division One

Appearances
Goals

FA Cup

1	Jan	27	(a)	Notts C	L 0-1		8,000

Appearances
Goals

Hillman J	Nicol T	McLintock T	Mullineux J	Espie J	Livingstone A	Brady A	Buchanan R	Turnbull P	Bowes W	Hill J	King G	Crabtree J	Lang A	McNab W	Place W (Snr)	Watson D	Place W (Jnr)	Morrison T	Egan W	Johnson E	Yates J	
1	2	3	4	5	6	7	8	9	10	11												1
1	2	3		5	6	7	8	9	10	11	4											2
1	2	3		5	6	7	8	9	10	11	4											3
1	2	3		5	6	7	8	9	10	11	4											4
1	2	3	4	5	6	7	8	9	10	11												5
1		2	4	5	6	7	8	9	10	11		3										6
1		3	4	5	6	7	8	9	10	11		2										7
1		2	6	5	4	7	8	9	10	11		3										8
1		3	4	5	6	7	8	9	10	11		2										9
1		3	4	5	6	7	8	9	10	11		2										10
1	2	3		5	6	7	8	9	10	11		4										11
1		2		5	6	7	8		10	11	4		3	9								12
		2		5	6	7	8	10	9	11	4		3		1							13
	2	3		9	6	7		8	10	11	4	5			1							14
1	2	3	4	9	6			8	10	11		5				7						15
1	2	3	4	9	6			8	10	11		5				7						16
1	2	3	4	9		7		8	10	11	6	5										17
1	2	3	4	9	6	7		8	10	11		5										18
1	2	3	4	9	6	7	8		10	11		5										19
1	2	3	4	9	6	7		8	10	11		5										20
1	2		4	9	6	7		8		11		5	3				10					21
1	2	3	4	9	6			8	10	11		5					7					22
1	2	3		9	6			8	10	11	4	5					7					23
1	2	3		9	6					11	4		5				8	7	10			24
1	2	3		9	6			8		11	4		5					7	10			25
	2	3		5	6			8			4						11	7	9	1	10	26
1		3		5	6		8	9			4	2					10	7	11			27
1	2	3		9	6		7	8					5		4		10		11			28
1	2	3		9	6		7	8			4		5				10		11			29
1	2	3		9			7	8			4	6	5				10		11			30
27	22	29	15	30	28	19	18	27	22	25	14	18	8	1	3	2	9	4	7	1	1	
	1			5		6	4	15	6	11	1						3	1	1			

7 scrimmages

Hillman J	Nicol T	McLintock T	Mullineux J	Espie J	Livingstone A	Brady A	Buchanan R	Turnbull P	Bowes W	Hill J	King G	Crabtree J	Lang A	McNab W	Place W (Snr)	Watson D	Place W (Jnr)	Morrison T	Egan W	Johnson E	Yates J	
1	7	3	4	9	6			8	10	11		2	5									1
1	1	1	1	1	1			1	1	1		1	1									

1894-95

Manager: Arthur F.Sutcliffe

1	Sep	1	(a)	Nottingham F	L 1-2	McKnight	9,000
2		3	(h)	Liverpool	D 3-3	Crabtree, Hill, Scrimmage	10,000
3		8	(a)	Sunderland	L 0-3		
4		15	(a)	Sheffield U	D 2-2	Nicol 2	
5		22	(h)	Wolves	W 2-1	Nicol 2	6,000
6		29	(h)	Derby C	W 2-0	Espie, Nicol	6,000
7	Oct	6	(a)	Sheffield W	L 3-4	Place (Jnr), Hill, Nicol	
8		13	(h)	Small Heath	W 3-1	Place (Jnr), Nicol, Bowes	5,000
9		20	(a)	Bolton W	D 1-1	Paton (og)	
10		27	(h)	Nottingham F	L 0-1		4,000
11	Nov	3	(a)	Liverpool	W 3-0	Nicol, Turnbull, Scrimmage	8,000
12		10	(h)	Sheffield W	W 3-0	McKnight 2, Bowes	
13		17	(a)	Blackburn R	L 0-1		7,000
14		24	(h)	West Brom A	W 2-0	Bowes, McKnight	6,000
15	Dec	8	(h)	Preston NE	W 2-1	Bowes, Crabtree	
16		12	(a)	Derby C	W 2-0	Turnbull, McKnight	1,750
17		22	(h)	Sheffield U	L 2-4	Nicol, Scrimmage	
18		26	(a)	Wolves	L 0-1		5,000
19		29	(a)	West Brom A	W 1-0	Nicol	2,535
20	Jan	5	(h)	Bolton W	W 1-0	Bowes	
21		12	(h)	Blackburn R	W 2-1	Bowes, Scrimmage	10,000
22		26	(a)	Preston NE	L 0-4		
23	Feb	23	(h)	Aston Villa	D 3-3	Nicol, Place (Jnr), Scrimmage	7,000
24	Mar	16	(h)	Everton	L 2-4	Bowes, Place (Jnr)	
25		21	(a)	Everton	L 2-3	McKnight, Bowes	
26		23	(a)	Small Heath	L 0-1		5,500
27		30	(a)	Stoke	L 1-5	Place (Jnr)	
28	Apr	6	(a)	Aston Villa	L 0-5		4,000
29		13	(h)	Sunderland	L 0-3		
30		20	(h)	Stoke	L 1-2	Hill (pen)	

FINAL LEAGUE POSITION: 9th in Division One

Appearances
Goals

FA Cup

1	Feb	2	(a)	Newcastle U	L 1-2	Bowes	8,000

Appearances
Goals

Hillman J	Nicol T	McLintock T	Munn S	Crabtree J	Livingstone A	Morrison T	Egan W	McKnight J	Bowes W	Sutherland M	Place W (Jnr)	Hill J	Mullineux J	Espie J	Turnbull P	Johnson E	Place W (Snr)	Parker S	Taylor J	Lang A	Hargreaves A	Smith W	Tattersall W	Porterfield A	Lindsay N	
1	2	3	4	5	6	7	8	9	10	11																1
1	2	3	4	5	6	7	9		10		8	11														2
1		3		2	6	7	8		10			11	4	5	9											3
	7	3		2	6			8	10		11			5	9	1	4									4
1	7	3		2	6			8	10		11			5	9		4									5
1	7	3		2	6			9	10		11	8		5			4									6
1	7	3		2	6			9	10		11	8		5			4									7
1	7	3		2	6			9	10		11			5			4	8								8
1	7	3		2	6			9	10		11			5			4	8								9
1	7	3		2	6			9	10		11			5			4	8								10
1	7	3		2	6				10		11	8		5	9		4									11
	7	3		2	6			8	10			11		5	9	1	4									12
1	7	3		2	6			8	10			11		5	9		4									13
1	7	3		2	6			9	10		11	8		5			4									14
1	7	3		2	6			9	10		11			5	8		4									15
1		3		2	6			9	10		11			5	8		4	7								16
1	7	3		2	6			9	10		11			5	8		4									17
1	7	3		2	6			9	10		11	8		5			4									18
1	7	3		2	6				8		10	11		5	9		4									19
1	7	3		2	6				8		11	10		5	9		4									20
1	7	3		2	6				8		11	10		5	9		4									21
		3		2	6				8		11	10		5	9	1		7	4							22
	7	3		2	6			9	10		11	8		5		1	4									23
		3		2	6			9	10		11	7		5		1	4		8							24
		3		2	6			9	10		11	8		5		1	7		4							25
		3		2	6			9	10		11					1	7		4	5	8					26
		3		2	6			9	10		11	8		5		1	7		4							27
		3			5			9	10		11	8					4		6		7	1	2			28
	7	3			6			8	10			11		5			4						2	1	9	29
	7	3		2	6				10		11	8		5			4							1	9	30
19	22	30	2	28	30	3	3	22	30	1	25	20	1	26	13	8	26	5	6	1	2	1	2	2	2	
	11			2				6	8		5	3		1	2											

1 own-goal, 5 scrimmages.

Hillman J	Nicol T	McLintock T	Munn S	Crabtree J	Livingstone A	Morrison T	Egan W	McKnight J	Bowes W	Sutherland M	Place W (Jnr)	Hill J	Mullineux J	Espie J	Turnbull P	Johnson E	Place W (Snr)	Parker S	Taylor J	Lang A	Hargreaves A	Smith W	Tattersall W	Porterfield A	Lindsay N	
	7	3		2	6				10		11	8		5	9	1	4									1
	1	1		1	1				1		1	1		1	1	1	1									
									1																	

1895-96

Manager: Arthur F.Sutcliffe

1	Sep	2	(a)	Wolves	L	1-5	Hill	6,000
2		7	(a)	West Brom A	W	2-0	Bowes, Place (Jnr)	5,000
3		9	(h)	Sunderland	D	0-0		10,000
4		14	(h)	Bury	W	3-0	Nicol, Bowes, Place (Jnr)	5,500
5		21	(a)	Bolton W	L	0-1		7,000
6		28	(h)	Preston NE	W	1-0	Bowes	6,000
7	Oct	5	(a)	Blackburn R	L	0-1		3,500
8		12	(h)	Bolton W	L	1-2	Place (Jnr)	5,000
9		19	(a)	Preston NE	D	1-1	Place (Jnr)	7,000
10		26	(h)	Everton	D	1-1	Robertson	8,000
11	Nov	2	(a)	Aston Villa	L	1-5	Robertson	6,500
12		9	(a)	Derby C	L	1-5	Robertson	6,000
13		23	(h)	Aston Villa	L	3-4	Paterson, Bowes, Nicol	7,000
14		30	(a)	Everton	L	1-2	McEleny	14,000
15	Dec	7	(a)	Stoke	L	1-2	Paterson	2,500
16		14	(a)	Sheffield W	L	0-1		5,000
17		21	(h)	Nottingham F	D	0-0		4,500
18		26	(a)	Small Heath	L	0-1		5,000
19	Jan	1	(a)	Bury	W	4-3	Hill 3, Bowes	
20		4	(h)	Sheffield W	W	2-0	Robertson 2	6,000
21		11	(h)	West Brom A	W	3-0	Davidson, Nicol, Scrimmage	6,000
22	Feb	3	(h)	Sheffield U	W	5-0	Paterson, Davidson, Place (Jnr), Place (Snr), Bowes	3,000
23		18	(a)	Sunderland	L	1-3	Scrimmage	3,000
24		22	(h)	Wolves	W	3-1	Robertson, Taylor, McLintock (pen)	4,000
25	Mar	7	(a)	Nottingham F	L	1-2	Nicol	5,000
26		16	(h)	Stoke	W	2-0	Robertson, Opp own-goal	1,500
27		30	(a)	Sheffield U	D	1-1	Place (Jnr)	2,000
28	Apr	3	(h)	Small Heath	D	1-1	Robertson	5,000
29		4	(h)	Derby C	D	2-2	Place (Jnr), Nicol	6,000
30		13	(h)	Blackburn R	W	6-0	Nicol 3, Robertson 2, Place (Snr)	5,000

FINAL LEAGUE POSITION: 10th in Division One — Appearances

Goals

FA Cup

1	Feb	1	(h)	W Arsenal	W	6-1	Place (Jnr) 2, Robertson 2, Nicol, Place (Snr)	6,000
2		15	(h)	Stoke	D	1-1	Scrimmage	13,000
R		20	(a)	Stoke	L	1-7	Bowes	10,915

Appearances

Goals

Napier W	Reynolds J	McLintock T	Place W (Snr)	Espie J	Livingstone A	Davidson J	Stirling J	Provan J	Place W (Jnr)	Hill J	Tatham W	Nicol T	Bowes W	Robertson H	Taylor J	Robertson P	McEleny C	Paterson T	Tattersall W	Haddow D	
1	2	3	4	5	6	7	8	9	10	11											1
	2	3	4	5	6				10	11	1	7	8	9							2
	2	3	4	5	6				10	11	1	7	8	9							3
	2	3	4	5	6				10	11	1	7	8	9							4
	2	3	5		6		8		10	11	1	7		9	4						5
	2	3	5		6	9			10		1	7	8	11	4						6
	2	3	5		6	9			10		1	7	8	11	4						7
	2	3	5		6	8			11	9	1	7	10		4						8
	2	3	4		6	8			11		1	7	10	9	5						9
	2	3	4		6	8			11		1	7	10	9	5						10
	2	3	4		6			8	11		1	7	10	9	5						11
	2	3			6	7		9	11		1		10	8	5	4					12
	2	3			6				10	11	1	9	8		5		4	7			13
	2	3		5		8			10	11	1		9		6		4	7			14
	2	3		5					10	11	1	9	8		6		4	7			15
	2	3		5					10	11	1	9	8		6		4	7			16
	2	3		5	6				10	11	1	9	8				4	7			17
		3			6	8				11	1	9	10		5		4	7	2		18
		3			6				11	8	1	7	10	9	5		4		2		19
	2	3	4		6				11	8	1	7	10	9	5						20
	2	3	4			8			11		1	7	10	9	6		5				21
	2	3	4			8			11		1		10	9	6		5	7			22
	2	3	4	5	6	8			11			7	10	9						1	23
	2	3			6	10		9		11	1	7		8	5		4				24
		3	4		6				11	8	1	7	10	9	5				2		25
	2	3	4		6	8			11		1	7	10	9			5				26
	2	3	4		6	8			10	11		7		9			5			1	27
	2	3	4		6	10			11	8		7		9			5			1	28
	2	3	4			10			11	8		7		9	6		5			1	29
	2	3	4			10			11	8	1	7		9	6		5				30
1	27	30	21	9	23	18	2	4	28	20	25	26	23	22	21	1	15	7	3	4	
		1	2			2			7	4		8	6	10	1		1	3			

1 own-goal, 2 scrimmages.

Napier W	Reynolds J	McLintock T	Place W (Snr)	Espie J	Livingstone A	Davidson J	Stirling J	Provan J	Place W (Jnr)	Hill J	Tatham W	Nicol T	Bowes W	Robertson H	Taylor J	Robertson P	McEleny C	Paterson T	Tattersall W	Haddow D	
	2	3	4						11	8	1	7	10	9	6		5				1
	2	3	4						11	8		7	10	9	6		5			1	2
	2	3	4						11	8		7	10	9	6		5			1	R
	3	3	3						3	3	1	3	3	3	3		3			2	
			1						1			1	1	2							

1 scrimmage

1896-97

Manager: Harry Bradshaw

1	Sep	5	(a)	Sheffield U	L 0-1		
2		7	(h)	Sunderland	D 1-1	Bowes	
3		12	(h)	Bury	W 1-0	Chambers	
4		19	(h)	Nottingham F	D 2-2	Nicol, Bowes	4,000
5		26	(a)	Preston NE	L 3-5	Robertson, Hill, Chambers	
6	Oct	3	(a)	Blackburn R	L 2-3	Bowes, McLintock (pen)	9,000
7		10	(h)	Everton	W 2-1	Chambers, Bowes	
8		17	(h)	Preston NE	D 2-2	Bowes, Chambers	
9		24	(a)	Nottingham F	L 1-4	Scrimmage	4,000
10	Nov	7	(h)	Blackburn R	L 0-1		5,000
11		14	(a)	Derby C	L 2-3	Robertson, Place (Jnr)	6,000
12		21	(a)	Wolves	L 0-2		4,000
13		28	(a)	Everton	L 0-6		
14	Dec	19	(h)	Sheffield W	D 1-1	Scrimmage	
15		26	(h)	Liverpool	W 4-1	Bowes 2, Toman, Chambers	9,000
16	Jan	1	(a)	Bury	D 1-1	Black	
17		2	(a)	Aston Villa	W 3-0	Black 2, Bowes	14,000
18		9	(h)	Stoke	L 1-3	Toman	
19		16	(h)	Sheffield U	D 1-1	Taylor	
20	Feb	6	(h)	Bolton W	L 0-2		
21		8	(h)	Aston Villa	L 3-4	Robertson, Black, Toman	4,000
22		27	(a)	Stoke	L 2-3	Scrimmage, Black	
23	Mar	2	(a)	Sunderland	D 1-1	Bowes	
24		6	(a)	Sheffield W	L 0-1		
25		13	(a)	Bolton W	L 1-2	Place (Jnr)	
26		20	(h)	Wolves	L 0-3		3,000
27		27	(a)	Liverpool	W 2-1	Toman, Brown	12,000
28	Apr	3	(a)	West Brom A	L 0-3		3,100
29		5	(h)	Derby C	L 2-3	Bowes, Morrison	3,000
30		10	(h)	West Brom A	W 5-0	Robertson 2, Bowes, Ferguson, Ross	4,900

FINAL LEAGUE POSITION: 16th in Division One (Relegated after Test Matches)

Appearances
Goals

FA Cup

1	Jan	30	(a)	Sunderland	L 0-1	

Appearances
Goals

Test Matches

1	Apr	19	(h)	Newton Heath	W 2-0	Bowes, Ferguson	10,000
2		21	(a)	Newton Heath	L 0-2		7,000
3		24	(a)	Notts C	D 1-1	Brown	15,000
4		26	(h)	Notts C	L 0-1		11,000

Appearances
Goals

Tatham W	Nicol T	McLintock T	Place W (Snr)	Brae J	Taylor J	Hill J	Chambers T	Brown D	Bowes W	Place W (Jnr)	Reynolds J	Robertson H	Haddow D	Warburton T	Davidson J	Longair W	Black D	Hartley J	Dunn T	Beveridge D	Toman W	Hargreaves E	Almond J	Ferguson W	Ross J	McVean M	Morrison T	Brown R	
1	2	3	4	5	6	7	8	9	10	11																			1
1	2	3	4	5	6	7	8	9	10	11																			2
1	2	3	4	5	6	7	8	9	10	11																			3
1	7	3	4	5	6	8			10	11	2	9																	4
1	2	3	4	5	6	8	7		10	11		9																	5
	2	3	4	5	6	8			10	11		9	1	7															6
1	5	3	4		6	8	7		10	11	2	9																	7
1	5	3	4		6	8	7		10	11	2	9																	8
1	5	3	4		6	8	7		10	11	2	9																	9
1	5	3	4		6	8			10	11	2	9			7														10
1	7	3	4		6	5	8		10	11	2	9																	11
1	7	3	4		6	5	8		10	11	2	9																	12
1		3	4		6	5		8	10	11	2	9			7														13
		3	4		6	8			10	11	2		1			5	7	9											14
1		3	4		6		8		10	11						5			2	7	9								15
1		3	4		6				10	11	2					5	8			7	9								16
1		3	4		6				10	11						5	8		2	7	9								17
1		3	4		6				10	11						5	8		2		9	7							18
1		3	4		5				10	11	2	7					8				9		6						19
1			4		6				10	11	2					5	8		3	7	9								20
1		3	4		6				10	11	2	9				5	8				7								21
1		3	4		6				8	10	2	9				5	11										7		22
		3	4		6				8	10	2	9	1			5	11										7		23
		3	4		6				10	11	2	9	1			5	8										7		24
		3	4		6				10	11	2	9	1			5	8										7		25
		3	4		6					10	2	9	1			5	8							11			7		26
		3	4		6					10	2		1								9			11	8	7		5	27
		3	4		6				9	10	2		1											11	8	7		5	28
			4		6				10	11	2		1						3						9	8	7	5	29
			4		6				10		2	9	1						3					11	8	7		5	30
20	12	27	30	6	30	14	10	4	28	29	22	18	10	1	2	12	12	1	6	4	8	1	1	4	4	4	6	4	
	1	1			1	1	5	1	11	2		5					5				4			1	1		1		

3 scrimmages

Tatham W	Nicol T	McLintock T	Place W (Snr)	Brae J	Taylor J	Hill J	Chambers T	Brown D	Bowes W	Place W (Jnr)	Reynolds J	Robertson H	Haddow D	Warburton T	Davidson J	Longair W	Black D	Hartley J	Dunn T	Beveridge D	Toman W	Hargreaves E	Almond J	Ferguson W	Ross J	McVean M	Morrison T	Brown R	
1		3	4		6				10	11	2					5	8			7	9								1
1		1	1		1				1	1	1					1	1			1	1								

Tatham W	Nicol T	McLintock T	Place W (Snr)	Brae J	Taylor J	Hill J	Chambers T	Brown D	Bowes W	Place W (Jnr)	Reynolds J	Robertson H	Haddow D	Warburton T	Davidson J	Longair W	Black D	Hartley J	Dunn T	Beveridge D	Toman W	Hargreaves E	Almond J	Ferguson W	Ross J	McVean M	Morrison T	Brown R	
		3	4		6			5	10		2	9	1											11	8	7			1
		3	4		6			5	10		2	9	1											11		8	7		2
		3	4		6			5	10	11	2		1								9				8	7			3
		3	4		6			5	10	11	2	9	1												8	7			4
		4	4		4			4	4	2	4	3	4								1			2	3	4	1		
								1	1															1					

1897-98

Manager: Harry Bradshaw

1	Sep	4	(h)	Blackpool	W 5-1	Ross 2, Bowes 2, Taylor	
2		6	(h)	W Arsenal	W 5-0	Taylor, Livingstone, Toman, Place (Jnr), Opp own-goal	3,000
3		11	(a)	Blackpool	D 1-1	Ross	
4		18	(h)	Walsall	W 4-1	Morrison, Ross, Toman, Taylor	
5		25	(a)	Walsall	W 2-1	Bowes, Place (Jnr)	
6	Oct	2	(h)	Newcastle U	W 3-0	Ross, Place (Jnr), Bowes	8,000
7		9	(a)	Leicester F	W 1-0	Bowes	
8		16	(h)	Burton S	W 2-0	McLintock, Scrimmage	
9		23	(a)	Grimsby T	L 1-2	Bowes	4,000
10		30	(h)	Manchester C	W 3-1	Toman 2, Ross	10,000
11	Nov	6	(a)	Darwen	W 1-0	Ross	
12		13	(h)	Luton T	W 4-0	Toman, Bowes, Place (Jnr), Opp own-goal	
13		20	(a)	Manchester C	D 1-1	Opp own-goal	20,000
14		27	(h)	Darwen	W 6-1	McLintock (pen), O'Rourke, Morrison, Ross, Place (Jnr), Toman	
15	Dec	11	(h)	Grimsby T	W 6-0	Ross 2, Toman 2, Place (Jnr), Morrison	4,000
16		27	(a)	Newcastle U	W 1-0	Toman	24,959
17	Jan	1	(h)	Lincoln C	W 2-1	Bowes, Toman	
18		8	(a)	Small Heath	D 2-2	Place (Jnr), Morrison	12,000
19		12	(a)	Newton Heath	D 0-0		7,000
20		19	(h)	Leicester F	W 4-0	Ross 3 (1 pen), Opp own-goal	
21		22	(a)	Loughborough	W 2-0	Toman, Morrison	
22	Feb	5	(h)	Small Heath	W 4-1	Ferguson, Ross, Taylor, McLintock	4,000
23	Mar	5	(h)	Burton Swifts	W 2-0	Ross, Toman	
24		7	(h)	Newton Heath	W 6-3	Ross 2, Toman 2, Ferguson, Scrimmage	3,000
25		12	(h)	Gainsborough T	D 1-1	Ross	
26		19	(a)	Luton T	L 0-2		
27		28	(h)	Loughborough	W 9-3	Ross 5, Ferguson, Toman, Taylor, Morrison	
28	Apr	2	(a)	W Arsenal	D 1-1	McInnes	12,000
29		8	(a)	Lincoln	D 1-1	Taylor	
30		9	(a)	Gainsborough T	D 0-0		

FINAL LEAGUE POSITION: 1st in Division Two (Promoted after Test Matches) — Appearances

Goals

FA Cup

1	Jan	29	(h)	W Arsenal	W 3-1	Taylor, Place (Jnr), Ferguson	6,000
2	Feb	12	(h)	Burslem Port Vale	W 3-0	Bowes, Beveridge, Ross	
3	Mar	26	(h)	Everton	L 1-3	Place (Jnr)	

Appearances

Goals

Test Matches

1	Mar	21	(a)	Blackburn R	W 3-1	Toman 3	8,000
2		23	(h)	Blackburn R	W 2-0	Toman, Ross	12,000
3		26	(h)	Stoke	L 0-2		9,000
4		30	(a)	Stoke	D 0-0		

Appearances

Goals

Haddow D	Reynolds J	McLintock T	O'Rourke P	Taylor J	Livingstone A	Morrison T	Ross J	Toman W	Bowes W	Place W (Jnr)	Dunn T	Place W (Snr)	Beveridge D	Ferguson W	Arnott J	Hillman J	McInnes A	
1	2	3	4	5	6	7	8	9	10	11								1
1	2	3	4	5	6	7	8	9	10	11								2
1	2	3	4	5	6	7	8	9	10	11								3
1	2	3	4	5	6	7	8	9	10	11								4
1	2	3	4	5	6	7	8	9	10	11								5
1	2	3	4	5	6	7	8	9	10	11								6
1	2	3	4	5	6	7	8	9	10	11								7
1	2	3	4	5		7	8	9	10	11	6							8
1	2	3	4	5	6	7	8	9	10	11								9
1	2	3	4	5	6	7	8	9	10	11								10
1	2	3	4	5	6	7	8	9	10	11								11
1	2	3	4	5	6	7	8	9	10	11								12
1	2	3	4	5	6	7	8	9	10	11								13
1	2	3	4	5	6	7	8	9	10	11								14
1	2	3	4	5	6	7	8	9	10	11								15
1	2	3		5	6	7	8	9	10	11		4						16
1	2	3		5	6	7	8	9	10	11		4						17
1	2	3		5	6	7	8	9	10	11			4					18
1	2	3		5	6	7	8	9	10	11			4					19
1	2	3		5	6	7	8	9	10	11			4					20
1	2	3		5	6	7	8	9		11			4	10				21
1	2	3		5	6	7	8	9		10			4	11				22
1	2	3		5		7	8	9	10			6	4	11				23
	2	3		5		7	8	9	10			6	4	11	1			24
1	2	3	6	5			8	9	10	7			4	11				25
	2	3		5		7	9		10	11		6	4	8		1		26
		3		5		7	8	9	10	6		2	4	11		1		27
	2			5		7		9	10	6		3	4	11		1	8	28
	2	3		5		7		9	10	6		4		11		1	8	29
	2	3		5		7		9	10	6		4		11		1	8	30
24	29	29	16	30	21	29	27	29	28	28	1	9	11	10	1	5	3	
		3	1	6	1	6	23	15	8	7				3			1	

4 own-goals, 2 scrimmages.

1	2	3		5	6	7	8	9		10			4	11				1
1	2	3		5	6	7	8	9	10	11			4					2
1	2	3		5	6	7	8	9	10	11			4					3
3	3	3		3	3	3	3	3	2	3			3	1				
				1			1		1	2			1	1				

	2	3		5	6	7	8	9	10	11			4			1		1
	2	3		5	6	7	8	9	10	11			4			1		2
	2	3		5	6	7	8	9	10	11			4			1		3
	2	3		5	6	7	8	9	10	11			4			1		4
	4	4		4	4	4	4	4	4	4			4			4		
							1	4										

1898-99

Manager: Harry Bradshaw

1	Sep	3	(h)	Notts C	D 1-1	Toman	
2		5	(h)	Preston NE	W 3-1	Morrison 2, Place (Jnr)	
3		10	(a)	Stoke	L 1-4	Morrison	
4		17	(h)	Aston Villa	L 2-4	Toman, Bowes	8,000
5		24	(a)	Bury	D 1-1	Place (Jnr)	
6	Oct	1	(a)	Sheffield U	D 1-1	Bowes	
7		8	(h)	Newcastle U	W 2-1	Toman 2	6,000
8		15	(a)	Preston NE	D 1-1	Toman	
9		22	(h)	Liverpool	W 2-1	Toman, Opp own-goal	10,000
10		29	(a)	Nottingham F	W 1-0	Place (Jnr)	5,000
11	Nov	5	(h)	Bolton W	W 2-0	Freebairn (og), Lee (og)	
12		12	(a)	Derby C	L 1-2	Toman	8,000
13		19	(h)	West Brom A	D 1-1	Toman	7,500
14		26	(h)	Blackburn R	W 2-0	Toman, McLintock (pen)	12,000
15	Dec	3	(h)	Sheffield W	W 5-0	Ross 4, Toman	
16		10	(a)	Sunderland	W 1-0	Bowes	
17		17	(h)	Wolves	W 4-2	Bowes 2, Place (Jnr), McInnes	4,000
18		24	(a)	Everton	L 0-4		
19		26	(a)	Blackburn R	W 2-0	Toman, Ross	20,000
20		31	(a)	Notts C	D 2-2	Bowes, Place (Snr)	
21	Jan	3	(a)	Bolton W	L 0-2		
22		14	(a)	Aston Villa	L 0-4		22,000
23		21	(h)	Bury	W 2-1	Bowes 2	
24	Feb	4	(a)	Newcastle U	L 1-4	Bowes	20,000
25		18	(a)	Liverpool	L 0-2		12,000
26	Mar	6	(h)	Nottingham F	D 1-1	Place (Jnr)	2,000
27		11	(h)	Derby C	W 2-1	Bowes, Place (Jnr)	7,000
28		18	(a)	West Brom A	W 1-0	Ferguson	2,330
29		31	(h)	Sheffield U	W 1-0	McLintock (pen)	
30	Apr	1	(a)	Sheffield W	L 0-1		
31		8	(h)	Sunderland	W 1-0	Ferguson	
32		15	(a)	Wolves	L 0-4		5,000
33		17	(h)	Stoke	D 1-1	Ferguson	
34		22	(h)	Everton	D 0-0		

FINAL LEAGUE POSITION: 3rd in Division One

Appearances
Goals

FA Cup

1	Jan	28	(h)	Sheffield U	D 2-2	Toman, Bowes	
R	Feb	2	(a)	Sheffield U	L 1-2	Ross (pen)	

Appearances
Goals

Pinnell A	Reynolds J	McLintock T	Beveridge D	Taylor J	Livingstone A	Morrison T	Ross J	Toman W	Bowes W	Place W (Jnr)	O'Rourke P	McInnes A	Tatham W	McMillan W	Ferguson W	Arnott J	Barron F	Hillman J	Nunnick W	Place W (Snr)	Jenkinson W	Watkins W	Nicol T	Lester E	Brearley H	
1	2	3	4	5	6	7	8	9	10	11																1
1	2	3	4		6	7		9	10	11	5	8														2
		3	4		6	7		9	10	11	5	8	1							2						3
	2	3		5	6	7	8	9	10				1	4	11											4
1	2	3	4	5	6	7	8	9	10	11																5
	2	3		5	6	7	8	9	10	11						1	4									6
	2	3		5	6	7	8	9	10	11						1	4									7
1	2	3		5	6	7	8	9	10	11							4									8
	2	3		5	6	7	8	9	10	11							4	1								9
	2	3		5	6	7	8	9	10	11							4	1								10
	2	3		5	6	7	8	9	10	11							4	1								11
	2	3		5	6	7	8	9	10	11							4	1								12
	2	3		5		7	8	9	10	11							4	1	6							13
		3		5	6	7	8	9	10	11							4	1		2						14
		3			6	7	8	9	10	11				5			4	1		2						15
	2	3			6	7	8	9	10	11							4	1		5						16
	2	3			6	7			9	10		8			11		4	1		5						17
		3		5	6	7	8	9	10	11							4	1		2						18
	2	3			6	7	8	9	10	11							4	1		5						19
	2	3			6	7	8	9	10	11							4	1		5						20
	2	3			6	7		8	9	11					10		4	1		5						21
		3		2	6	7	8	9	10	11							4	1		5						22
		2		5	6	7	8		9	10					11		4	1			3					23
1	2	3		5	6	7	8	9	10	11							4									24
		3		5	6	7		9	10	8					11	1	4			2						25
	2	3		5	6	7		9	10	8					11		4	1								26
	2	3		5	6	7			9	10					11		4	1				8				27
	2	3		6		7		9	8	10					11		4	1		5						28
	2	3		5	6				9	10					11	1	4					8	7			29
	2	3		5	6					10					11	1	4					8	7	9		30
	2	3	7	5	6			9	8	10					11	1	4									31
	2	3		5	6	7				10					11	1	4				9	8				32
	2	3		5	6				10						11	1	4				9	8			7	33
	2	3		5	6				9	10					11		4	1				8			7	34
5	27	34	5	26	32	29	20	26	32	32	2	3	2	2	14	8	29	19	1	12	3	6	2	1	2	
		2				3	5	11	10	6		1			3					1						

3 own-goals

	2	3		5	6	7	8	9	10	11							4	1			1
1	2	3			6		8	9	10			7			11		4			5	R
1	2	2		1	2	1	2	2	2	1		1			1		2	1		1	
							1	1	1												

1899-1900

Manager: Ernest Mangnall

1	Sep	2	(a)	Glossop	L 0-2		
2		9	(h)	Stoke	D 2-2	Chadwick, Bowes	
3		16	(a)	Sunderland	L 1-2	Chadwick	
4		23	(h)	West Brom A	W 2-0	Morrison, Chadwick	10,027
5		30	(a)	Everton	L 0-2		
6	Oct	7	(h)	Blackburn R	W 1-0	Bowes	12,855
7		14	(a)	Derby C	L 1-4	Chadwick	10,000
8		21	(h)	Bury	W 1-0	Bowes	
9		28	(a)	Notts C	L 1-6	Chadwick	
10	Nov	4	(h)	Manchester C	W 2-0	Taylor, Jenkinson	5,000
11		11	(a)	Sheffield U	D 0-0		
12		18	(h)	Newcastle U	L 1-3	Jenkinson	5,000
13		25	(a)	Aston Villa	L 0-2		10,000
14	Dec	2	(h)	Liverpool	W 2-1	Bowes, Miller	5,000
15		9	(h)	Wolves	L 0-1		5,000
16		16	(a)	Preston NE	D 1-1	Bowes	
17		23	(h)	Nottingham F	D 2-2	Hartley, Miller	5,000
18		26	(a)	Stoke	L 0-3		
19		29	(h)	Glossop	W 3-1	Chadwick 3	
20	Jan	1	(a)	Blackburn R	L 0-2		14,000
21		13	(h)	Sunderland	W 3-1	Hartley, Chadwick, Hannigan	
22		20	(a)	West Brom A	L 0-2		3,427
23	Feb	3	(h)	Everton	W 3-1	Morrison, Hartley, Chadwick	
24		17	(h)	Derby C	L 1-2	Hartley	5,000
25	Mar	3	(h)	Notts C	W 3-0	Hannigan 2, Morrison	
26		10	(a)	Manchester C	L 0-1		13,000
27		14	(a)	Bury	D 1-1	Place (Snr)	
28		24	(a)	Newcastle U	L 0-2		12,000
29		31	(h)	Aston Villa	L 1-2	Bowes	6,000
30	Apr	7	(a)	Liverpool	W 1-0	Hartley	10,000
31		14	(a)	Wolves	L 0-3		5,000
32		21	(h)	Preston NE	L 0-1		
33		23	(h)	Sheffield U	W 1-0	Davidson	
34		28	(a)	Nottingham F	L 0-4		3,000

FINAL LEAGUE POSITION: 17th in Division One (Relegated)

Appearances
Goals

FA Cup

1	Jan	27	(h)	Bury	L 0-1		

Appearances
Goals

Hillman J	Reynolds J	McLintock T	Barron F	Taylor J	Livingstone A	Morrison T	Chadwick E	Bowes W	Fairburn J	Ferguson W	Woolfall T	Place W (Snr)	Greenwood T	Bannister W	Arnott J	Swainston H	Jenkinson W	McMillan W	Ross H	Watkins W	Miller J	Hartley J	Hannigan R	Sutherland J	Davidson J	Place W (Jnr)	No.
1	2	3	4	5	6	7	8	9	10	11																	1
1		3	4	5	6	7	8	9		11	2	10															2
1		3	4	5	6	7	9	8		11	2	10															3
1		3	4	5	6	7	9	8		11	2	10															4
1		3	4	5	6		9	8		11	2	10	7														5
1		3	4	9	6	7	10	8			2	11		5													6
		3	4	5	6	7	10	8			2	11			1	9											7
1		3	4	9	6	7	10	8			2	11		5													8
		3	4	5	6	7	10	8			2				1		9	11									9
1		3	4	5	6	7	10	8			2	11					9										10
		3	4	5	6	7	10	8			2	11			1		9										11
1		3	4	5	6		10	8			2	11					9		7								12
1		3	4	5	6	7		10			2	11				9				8							13
1		3	4	5	6	7	8	9			2	10									11						14
1		3		5	6	7	8	9			2	10					4				11						15
1	2	3		5	6	7	9	10			4									8	11						16
1		3	4	5	6	7	8	10			2										11	9					17
1		3	4	5	6	7	8	10			2										11	9					18
1		3	4	5	6	8	9	10			2										11		7				19
1		3	4	5	6	8	9				2	10									11		7				20
1		3	4	5	6	8	10				2										11	9	7				21
1		3	4	5		8	10	6			2										11	9	7				22
1		3	4	6		8	10				2			5							11	9	7				23
1		3	4	6		8	10				2			5							11	9	7				24
1		3	4	5	6	7	10				2											9	8	11			25
1		3	4	5	6	7	10	8			2	11										9					26
1		3	4	5	6	7	10	8			2	11										9					27
1		3	4	5	6		10	8			2	11										9	7				28
1		3	4	6		7	9	8			2	10		5							11						29
1		3	4	5	6	7		8			2	10									11	9					30
1		3	4	5	6	7		8			2	10									11	9					31
1		3	4	5	6	7	10	8			2										11	9					32
1		3		5	6	7	10	9			2						4				11				8		33
1		3		5	6	7	10	9			2						4								8	11	34
31	2	34	30	34	30	31	31	29	1	5	33	20	1	5	3	2	7	1	1	2	16	13	8	1	2	1	
				1		3	10	6				1					2				2	5	3		1		

Hillman J	Reynolds J	McLintock T	Barron F	Taylor J	Livingstone A	Morrison T	Chadwick E	Bowes W	Fairburn J	Ferguson W	Woolfall T	Place W (Snr)	Greenwood T	Bannister W	Arnott J	Swainston H	Jenkinson W	McMillan W	Ross H	Watkins W	Miller J	Hartley J	Hannigan R	Sutherland J	Davidson J	Place W (Jnr)	No.
1		3	4	5	6	8	10	9			2	7									11						1
1		1	1	1	1	1	1	1			1	1									1						

1900-01

Manager: Ernest Mangnall

1	Sep	1	(h)	Grimsby T	W 3-0	Davidson, Bowes, Morrison	
2		3	(h)	Burton S	W 2-1	Morrison (pen), Scrimmage	
3		8	(a)	Lincoln C	L 0-2		
4		15	(h)	Newton Heath	W 1-0	Bowes	4,000
5		22	(a)	Glossop	W 1-0	Sutherland	
6		29	(h)	Middlesbrough	W 2-0	Morrison, Bannister	
7	Oct	6	(a)	Chesterfield	W 3-1	Scrimmage, Hancock (og), Bowes	
8		13	(a)	Burslem Port Vale	L 0-1		
9		20	(h)	Leicester F	D 0-0		
10		27	(a)	New Brighton T	L 1-2	Savage	
11	Nov	3	(h)	New Brighton T	W 2-1	Watkins, Mole	
12		10	(a)	Walsall	L 0-2		
13		17	(a)	Leicester F	D 1-1	Savage	
14	Dec	1	(h)	W Arsenal	W 3-0	Jenkinson, Watkins, Morrison	4,000
15		8	(a)	Blackpool	W 1-0	Watkins	
16		15	(h)	Stockport C	W 3-1	Watkins 2, Jenkinson	
17		22	(a)	Small Heath	W 1-0	Savage	10,000
18		25	(h)	Gainsborough T	W 2-1	Savage, Jenkinson	
19		29	(a)	Grimsby T	L 1-2	Savage	7,000
20	Jan	5	(h)	Lincoln C	W 1-0	Bannister	
21		12	(a)	Newton Heath	W 1-0	Jenkinson	10,000
22		19	(h)	Glossop	W 5-1	Bowes 3, Jenkinson, Mole	
23		26	(h)	Chesterfield	W 5-1	Jenkinson 2, Bowes, Savage, Barron	
24	Feb	16	(h)	Burslem Port Vale	W 1-0	Savage	
25	Mar	9	(a)	Gainsborough T	L 0-3		
26		16	(h)	Walsall	D 0-0		
27		23	(a)	Burton S	L 0-1		
28		30	(h)	Barnsley	W 4-0	Bowes, McLintock (pen), Jenkinson, Watkins	
29	Apr	5	(a)	Barnsley	L 1-2	Barron	
30		6	(a)	W Arsenal	L 1-3	Bowes	7,000
31		9	(a)	Middlesbrough	D 0-0		6,000
32		13	(h)	Blackpool	W 4-0	McLintock 4 (2 pens)	
33		20	(a)	Stockport C	L 2-3	Jenkinson, Bannister	
34		27	(h)	Small Heath	W 1-0	McLintock	5,000

FINAL LEAGUE POSITION: 3rd in Division Two

Appearances
Goals

FA Cup

1	Feb	9	(a)	Newton Heath	D 0-0		8,000
R		13	(h)	Newton Heath	W 7-1	Morrison 2, Jenkinson 2, Mole, Bannister, Taylor	4,000
2		23	(a)	Small Heath	L 0-1		11,000

Appearances
Goals

Tatham W	Lindsay J	Lockhart G	Barron F	Bannister W	Taylor J	Morrison T	Davidson J	Mole G	Bowes W	Sutherland J	Jenkinson W	Miller J	Watkins W	McLintock T	Collins H	Howarth W	Savage J	Ross H	Parkinson W	Driver F	Sawley A	
1	2	3	4	5	6	7	8	9	10	11												1
1	2	3	4	5	6	7	8	9	10	11												2
1	2	3	4	5	6	7	8		10		9	11										3
1	2	3	4	5	6	7			10			11	8	9								4
	2	3	4	5	6	7			9	11			8		1	10						5
	2	3	4	5	6	7			9	11			8		1	10						6
	2	3	4	5	6	7	8		9	11					1	10						7
	2	3	4	5	6	7	8		9	11					1	10						8
	2	3	4	5	6	7			9	11			8		1	10						9
	2	3	4	5	6	7			9	10			8		1		11					10
	2	3	4	5	6	9		7		10			8		1		11					11
	2	3	4	5	6	7	10				9		8		1		11					12
	2	3	4	5	6	7	10				9		8		1		11					13
	2		4	5	6	7	10				9		8		1		11	3				14
	2	3	4	5	6	7	10				9		8		1		11					15
	2	3	4	5	6		10	7			9		8		1		11					16
	2	3	4	5	6	7	10				9		8		1		11					17
	2	3	4	5	6	7	10				9		8		1		11					18
	2	3	4	5	6	7				10	9		8		1		11					19
	2	3	4	5	6	7			10		9		8		1		11					20
	2	3	4	5	6	7			10		9		8		1		11					21
		3	4	5	6	8		7	10		9				1		11	2				22
		3	4	5	6	8		7	10		9				1		11	2				23
	2	3	4	5	6	8		7	10		9				1		11					24
	2	3	4	5	6	8	10	7			9				1		11					25
	2	6	4		5		10	7			9		8		1		11	3				26
	2	3	4	5	6						9		8		1		11		7	10		27
	2	3	4	5	6	7			10		9		8	11	1							28
	2	3	4	5	6	7			10		9		8	11	1							29
	2	3	4	5	6	7			10		9		8	11	1							30
	2	3	4	5	6	7			10		9		8	11	1							31
	2	3	4	5	6				10		9		8	11	1				7			32
		3	4	5	6	7			10		9		8	11	1			2				33
		3	4	5	6	7			10				8	11	1			2			9	34
4	30	33	34	33	34	30	14	9	22	10	23	2	25	8	30	5	18	6	2	1	1	
			2	3		4	1	2	9	1	9		6	6			7					

1 own-goal, 2 scrimmages.

Tatham W	Lindsay J	Lockhart G	Barron F	Bannister W	Taylor J	Morrison T	Davidson J	Mole G	Bowes W	Sutherland J	Jenkinson W	Miller J	Watkins W	McLintock T	Collins H	Howarth W	Savage J	Ross H	Parkinson W	Driver F	Sawley A	
	2	3	4	5	6	8		7	10		9				1		11					1
	2	3	4	5	6	8		7	10		9				1		11					R
	2	3	6	5	4	10		11	8		9				1		7					2
	3	3	3	3	3	3		3	3		3				3		3					
				1	1	2		1			2											

1901-02

Manager: Ernest Mangnall

No	Month	Day	Venue	Opponents	Result	Score	Scorers	Attendance
1	Sep	7	(a)	Lincoln C	L	0-1		
2		9	(h)	Stockport C	W	3-0	Brunton 2, Morrison	
3		14	(h)	West Brom A	D	0-0		4,992
4		21	(a)	W Arsenal	L	0-4		10,000
5		28	(h)	Barnsley	W	2-0	Watkins, Brunton	
6	Oct	5	(a)	Leicester F	L	1-2	Stewart	
7		12	(h)	Preston NE	L	0-3		
8		19	(h)	Burton U	D	0-0		
9		26	(a)	Burslem Port Vale	D	1-1	Davidson	
10	Nov	2	(h)	Chesterfield	D	0-0		
11		9	(a)	Gainsborough T	D	1-1	Sawley	
12		16	(h)	Middlesbrough	D	2-2	Brunton, Davidson	
13		30	(h)	Blackpool	W	2-0	Savage, Brunton	
14	Dec	7	(a)	Stockport C	W	2-1	Morrison, McLintock (pen)	
15		21	(a)	Glossop	D	0-0		
16		28	(h)	Doncaster R	W	7-0	Brunton 3, Hogan 2, Savage 2	
17	Jan	1	(a)	Barnsley	D	2-2	Morrison, Hogan	
18		4	(h)	Lincoln C	W	1-0	Morrison (pen)	
19		11	(a)	West Brom A	L	0-3		9,149
20		18	(h)	W Arsenal	D	0-0		4,000
21	Feb	1	(h)	Leicester F	W	1-0	Taylor	
22		11	(a)	Newton Heath	L	0-2		1,000
23		15	(a)	Burton U	L	2-5	Hogan, Savage	
24		22	(h)	Burslem Port Vale	W	4-1	Morrison 2, Hogan 2	
25	Mar	1	(a)	Chesterfield	L	0-3		
26		8	(h)	Gainsborough T	W	6-0	Morrison, Hogan, Barron, Taylor (pen), Davidson, Birchall	
27		15	(a)	Middlesbrough	L	0-3		10,000
28		22	(h)	Bristol C	L	0-1		1,000
29		28	(h)	Newton Heath	W	1-0	Barron (pen)	3,000
30		29	(a)	Blackpool	L	1-2	Hogan	
31	Apr	7	(a)	Preston NE	L	1-3	Hogan	
32		12	(a)	Bristol C	L	0-1		4,000
33		19	(h)	Glossop	D	1-1	Hogan	
34		26	(a)	Doncaster R	L	0-3		

FINAL LEAGUE POSITION: 9th in Division Two

Appearances
Goals

FA Cup

Round	Month	Day	Venue	Opponents	Result	Score	Scorers
Q	Dec	14	(a)	Bishop Auckland	W	3-2	Barron, Hogan 2
1	Jan	25	(a)	Walsall	L	0-1	

Appearances
Goals

Hillman J	Ross H	Lockhart G	Barron F	Bannister W	Taylor J	Morrison T	Watkins W	Brunton M	Davidson J	McLintock T	Stewart A	Savage J	Sawley A	Dickinson H	Lambie W	Hogan C	Dixon A	Howarth W	Sugden T	Ridsdale G	Birchall J	Brown H	
1	2	3	4	5	6	7	8	9	10	11													1
1	2	3	4	5	6	7	8	9	10	11													2
1	2	3	4	5	6	7	8	9	10	11													3
1	2	3	4	5	6	7	8	9			10	11											4
1	2	3	4	5	6	7	8	9			10	11											5
1	2	3	4	5	6	7		9			10	11	8										6
1	2	3	4	9	5	7		8		6	10			11									7
1	2		4	5	6	8		10		3			9	11	7								8
1	2		4	5		7	8		10	3	6	11	9										9
1	2		4	5		7	8		10	3	6	11	9										10
1	2		4	5	6	7		8	10	3		11	9										11
1	2		4	5	6	7		8	10	3		11				9							12
1	2		4		5	7		8	10	3	6	11				9							13
1	2		4		5	7		8	10	3	6	11				9							14
1	2		4		5	7		8	10	3	6	11				9							15
1	2	3	4		5	7		8	10			11				9	6						16
1	2	3	4		5	7		8	10			11				9	6						17
1	2	3	4		5	7		8	10			11				9	6						18
1	2	3	4		5	7		8	10			11				9	6						19
1		3	4		5	7		8	10			11				9	6	2					20
	2	3			5	7	8		10							9	6		1	4	11		21
	2	3	4		5	7	8		10			11				9	6		1				22
	2	3	4		5	7		8	10			11				9		6	1				23
	2	3	4		5	7		8	10							9	6		1		11		24
	2	3	4		5		8	7	10							9	6		1		11		25
	2	3	4		5	7		8	10							9	6		1		11		26
	2	3			5	7		8	10							9	6		1	4	11		27
	2	3	4		5		7	8	10							9	6				11	1	28
	2	3	4		5	7		8	10			11				9	6					1	29
	2	3	4		5	7		8	10							9	6				11	1	30
	2	3	4		5	7		8	10							9	6				11	1	31
	2	3	4		5	7		8	10							9				6	11	1	32
	2	3	4		5	7		8	10							9	6				11	1	33
	2	3	4		5	7		8	10							9	6				11	1	34
20	33	26	32	12	32	32	11	30	29	12	9	18	5	2	1	23	17	2	7	3	11	7	
			2		2	7	1	8	3	1	1	4	1			10					1		

Hillman J	Ross H	Lockhart G	Barron F	Bannister W	Taylor J	Morrison T	Watkins W	Brunton M	Davidson J	McLintock T	Stewart A	Savage J	Sawley A	Dickinson H	Lambie W	Hogan C	Dixon A	Howarth W	Sugden T	Ridsdale G	Birchall J	Brown H	
1	2		4		5	7		8	10	3	6	11				9							Q
1	2	3	4		5	7		8	10			11				9	6						1
2	2	1	2		2	2		2	2	1	1	2				2	1						
			1													2							

1902-03

Manager: Ernest Mangnall

1	Sep	1	(a)	Burton U	D 0-0		
2		6	(h)	Doncaster R	D 1-1	McInnes	
3		8	(h)	Chesterfield	D 1-1	Hogan	
4		13	(a)	Lincoln C	L 1-4	Scrimmage	
5		20	(h)	Small Heath	W 2-1	Lee, Barron (pen)	3,000
6		27	(a)	Leicester F	L 1-2	Hogan	
7	Oct	4	(h)	Manchester C	D 1-1	McInnes	4,000
8		11	(a)	Chesterfield	L 0-2		
9		18	(a)	Preston NE	L 0-5		
10		25	(h)	Burslem Port Vale	D 3-3	Duckworth, Barron (pen), Lee	
11	Nov	8	(h)	Gainborough T	W 3-2	Barron (pen), Crawford, Morrison	
12		15	(h)	W Arsenal	L 0-3		2,500
13		22	(h)	Bristol C	D 0-0		
14	Dec	2	(a)	Glossop	L 0-2		
15		6	(h)	Manchester U	L 0-2		4,000
16		20	(h)	Blackpool	D 1-1	Hogan	
17		27	(a)	W Arsenal	L 1-5	Opp own-goal	13,000
18	Jan	1	(a)	Barnsley	L 0-3		
19		10	(h)	Lincoln C	W 1-0	Storey	
20		17	(a)	Small Heath	L 0-3		6,000
21		24	(h)	Leicester F	L 1-3	Bell	
22		31	(a)	Manchester C	L 0-6		16,000
23	Feb	7	(a)	Blackpool	L 0-2		
24		14	(h)	Preston NE	D 1-1	Ross (pen)	
25		28	(h)	Barnsley	L 1-2	Duckworth	
26	Mar	7	(a)	Gainsborough T	L 0-3		
27		14	(h)	Burton U	W 4-1	Crawford 2, Hogan, Driver	
28		21	(a)	Bristol C	L 0-3		5,000
29		28	(h)	Glossop	W 2-1	Driver, Hogan	
30		30	(a)	Burslem Port Vale	L 1-3	Lee	
31	Apr	4	(a)	Manchester U	L 0-4		5,000
32		10	(a)	Doncaster R	L 1-2	Scrimmage	
33		11	(h)	Stockport C	W 3-2	Hogan 2, Opp own-goal	
34		18	(a)	Stockport C	L 0-3		

FINAL LEAGUE POSITION: 18th in Division Two (Re-elected)

Appearances
Goals

FA Cup

1	Dec	13	(a)	Reading	L 0-1		

Appearances
Goals

Wynne F	Ross H	Lockhart G	Barron F	Taylor J	Dixon A	Morrison T	Sawley A	Crawford J	McInnes A	Birchall J	Lee E	Hogan C	Duckworth H	Welsh F	Whittaker E	Howarth W	Driver F	Towler E	Storey C	Bell A	Edmondson W	
1	2	3	4	5	6	7	8	9	10	11												1
1	2	3	4	5	6	7	10	9	8		11											2
1	2	3	4	5	6	7		9	8		11	10										3
1	2	3	4	5	6			10	8		11	9	7									4
1	2	3	4	5	6	7		10	8		11	9										5
1	2	3	4	5	6	7		10	8		11	9										6
1	2	3	4	5	6	7		10	8		11	9										7
1	2	3	4	5	6	7		10	8		11	9										8
1	2	3	4	5	6	7		10	8		11	9										9
	2	3	4	5	6	7	8	10			11		9	1								10
	2	3	4		6	7		9	8		11				1	5	10					11
1	2	3	4	5	6	7		9	8		11						10					12
	2	3	4	5	6	7		9	8		11						10	1				13
	2	3	4	5	6	7		9	8		11						10	1				14
	2	3	4	5	6	7		10	8			9					11	1				15
	2	3	4	5	6			10	8		11	7				9		1				16
	2	3	7	5	6			10	8		11		9			4		1				17
	2	3	7	5	6		9	10	8		11					4		1				18
	2	3	7	5	6			9			11					4		1	8	10		19
	2	3	4	5	6			9	7		11						10	1	8			20
	2	3	4	5	6		7	9	8									1		10	11	21
	2	3	4	5	6			9	7								10	1	8		11	22
	2	3	4	5	6			7	11		10	9					8	1				23
	2	3	4	5	6			7	11			9					10	1	8			24
	2	3	4	5	6		8	7	11				9				10	1				25
	2	3	4	5	6			7	11			9	8				10	1				26
	2	3	4	5	6			7	11		8	9					10	1				27
	2	3	4	5	6			7	11		8	9					10	1				28
	2	3	4	5	6			7	11		8	9					10	1				29
	2	3	4	5	6			7	11		8	9					10	1				30
	2	3	4	5	6			8	11		7	9	10					1				31
	2	3	4	5	6			8	11		7	9	10					1				32
	2	3	4	5				8	11		7	9	10			6		1				33
	2	3	4	5			7	8	11			9	10			6		1				34
10	34	34	34	33	32	14	7	34	32	1	26	20	9	1	1	7	15	22	4	2	2	
	1		3			1		3	2		3	7	2				2		1	1		

2 own-goals, 2 scrimmages.

Wynne F	Ross H	Lockhart G	Barron F	Taylor J	Dixon A	Morrison T	Sawley A	Crawford J	McInnes A	Birchall J	Lee E	Hogan C	Duckworth H	Welsh F	Whittaker E	Howarth W	Driver F	Towler E	Storey C	Bell A	Edmondson W	
	2	3	4	5	6	7		10	8		11	9						1				1
	1	1	1	1	1	1		1	1		1	1						1				

1903-04

Manager: Spen Whittaker

1	Sep	5	(a)	Chesterfield	D 0-0		
2		7	(h)	Manchester U	W 2-0	McFarlane, Dixon	5,000
3		12	(h)	Bolton W	D 0-0		
4		19	(h)	Burslem Port Vale	W 1-0	Crawford	
5		26	(a)	Preston NE	L 0-2		
6	Oct	3	(h)	Grimsby T	W 2-0	Aspden, Jackson	5,000
7		10	(a)	Leicester F	D 0-0		
8		17	(h)	Blackpool	L 1-4	Jackson	
9		24	(a)	Gainsborough T	W 2-1	Jackson, Jenkinson	
10	Nov	7	(a)	Bristol C	L 0-6		6,000
11		21	(a)	Glossop	L 2-6	Williams, D.Walders	
12		28	(h)	Bradford C	W 3-2	Whittam, Jackson, D.Walders	1,000
13	Dec	19	(a)	Lincoln C	L 1-3	Williams	
14		25	(h)	Burton U	W 2-1	McFarlane, Dixon	
15		26	(h)	Stockport C	W 2-0	McFarlane, Jackson	
16	Jan	2	(h)	Chesterfield	W 2-1	Aspden, Dixon	
17		9	(a)	Bolton W	D 1-1	Williams	
18		16	(a)	Burslem Port Vale	D 2-2	Williams, Hogan	
19		23	(h)	Preston NE	W 2-1	Aspden 2	
20		30	(a)	Grimsby T	D 0-0		4,000
21	Feb	6	(h)	Leicester F	W 2-1	Dixon (pen), Williams	
22		13	(a)	Blackpool	W 5-0	McFarlane 2, Dixon 2 (1 pen), Hogan	
23		20	(h)	Gainsborough T	W 2-0	Bell, Williams	
24		27	(a)	Burton U	W 2-1	Hogan, Bell	
25		29	(a)	W Arsenal	L 0-4		4,000
26	Mar	5	(h)	Bristol C	L 2-3	Williams, Hogan	4,000
27		12	(a)	Manchester U	L 1-3	Bell	14,000
28		19	(h)	Glossop	L 2-4	Hogan, Williams	
29		26	(a)	Bradford C	L 0-3		10,000
30	Apr	1	(h)	Barnsley	D 2-2	Barron, Jackson	
31		2	(h)	W Arsenal	W 1-0	Ross (pen)	5,000
32		9	(a)	Barsley	D 1-1	McFarlane	
33		16	(h)	Lincoln C	W 3-1	McFarlane, Bell, Moffat	
34		23	(a)	Stockport C	D 2-2	McFarlane, Hall (og)	

FINAL LEAGUE POSITION: 5th in Division Two

Appearances
Goals

FA Cup

Q3	Oct	31	(a*)	Keswick	W 8-0	Jackson 4, D.Walders 3, Crawford	
Q4	Nov	14	(a)	Darwen	L 0-2		

*Played at Turf Moor, Burnley.

Appearances
Goals

Green W	Ross H	Jenkinson W	Barron F	Walders D	Dixon A	Aspden T	Crawford J	McFarlane D	Jackson W	Williams H	Taylor J	Booth J	Towler E	Hogan J	Whittam A	Bell A	Swain J	Moffat H	Lowe R	
1	2	3	4	5	6	7	8	9	10	11										1
1	2	3	4	5	6	7	8	9	10	11										2
1	2	3	4	5	6	7	8	9	10	11										3
1	2	3	4		6	7	8	9	10	11	5									4
1	2	3	4	5	6	7	8	9	10	11										5
1	2	3	4	5	6	7	8	9	10	11										6
1	2	3	4	5	6	7	8	9	10	11										7
1		3	4	5	6	7	8	9	10	11		2								8
1	2	8	4	5	3		7	9	10	11	6									9
	2	9	4	5	3		7		10	11	6		1	8						10
1	2		4	5	3		10	9	7	11	6			8						11
1	2		4	5	3			9	7	11	6			8	10					12
1		3	4	5	2	7		10		11	6			8	9					13
1	2		4	5	3	7		10		11	6			8	9					14
1	2		4	5	3	7		9	10	11	6			8						15
1	2		4	5	3	7		9	10	11	6			8						16
1	2		4	5	3	7		9	10	11	6			8						17
1	2		4	5	3	7		9	10	11	6			8						18
1	2		4	5	3	7		9	10	11	6			8						19
1	2	9	4	5	3	7				11	6			8		10				20
1	2		4	5	3	7		9		11	6			8		10				21
1	2		4	5	3	7		9		11	6			8		10				22
1	2		4	5	3	7		9		11	6			8		10				23
1	2		4	5	3	7		9		11	6			8		10				24
1	2		4	5	3	7		9		11	6			8		10				25
1	2	6	4	5	3	7				11				8	9	10				26
1	2	6	4	5	3	7		9	11					8		10				27
1	2		4	5	3	7		9		11				8		10	6			28
1	2		4	5	3	7		9		11	6			8		10				29
1	2	10	4	5	7			9	6	11				8				3		30
1	2	10	4	5		7		9	6	11				8				3		31
1	2	10	4	5	3	7		9	6	11				8						32
1	2		4	5	3	7		9						8		11		6	10	33
1	2		4	5	3	7		9		11				8				6	10	34
33	32	17	34	33	33	29	11	31	21	32	19	1	1	25	4	11	1	4	2	
	1	1	1	2	6	4	1	8	6	8				5	1	4		1		

1 own-goal

Green W	Ross H	Jenkinson W	Barron F	Walders D	Dixon A	Aspden T	Crawford J	McFarlane D	Jackson W	Williams H	Taylor J	
1	2	9	4	5	3	7	8		10	11	6	Q3
1	2		4	5	3	7	8	9	10	11	6	Q4
2	2	1	2	2	2	2	2	1	2	2	2	
				3			1		4			

1904-05

Manager: Spen Whittaker

1	Sep	3	(h)	West Brom A	L 1-4	Moffat	5,389
2		5	(h)	Chesterfield	W 2-0	J.Smith, Hogan	
3		10	(a)	Bolton W	L 0-4		
4		17	(a)	Grimsby T	L 0-1		5,000
5		24	(h)	Blackpool	L 0-1		
6	Oct	1	(a)	Doncaster R	W 2-0	R.Smith, McFarlane	
7		8	(h)	Gainsborough T	L 1-3	Ross	
8		15	(a)	Burton U	L 1-3	McFarlane	
9		22	(h)	Liverpool	L 0-2		9,000
10		26	(a)	Gainsborough T	L 1-3	Barron	
11		29	(a)	Burslem Port Vale	L 1-3	McFarlane	
12	Nov	5	(h)	Bristol C	L 2-3	McFarlane, Barron (pen)	3,000
13		12	(a)	Manchester U	L 0-1		15,000
14		19	(h)	Glossop	W 3-1	McFarlane 2, Hogan	
15		26	(a)	Chesterfield	D 1-1	Hogan	
16	Dec	3	(h)	Bradford C	W 2-1	Ross (pen), Marshall	3,000
17		17	(h)	Leicester F	W 2-0	Marshall, McFarlane	
18		24	(a)	Barnsley	W 2-1	R.Smith, McFarlane	
19		26	(h)	Grimsby T	W 1-0	Dixon (pen)	
20		31	(a)	West Brom A	D 1-1	McFarlane	7,374
21	Jan	7	(h)	Bolton W	L 0-1		
22		21	(a)	Blackpool	L 0-2		
23		28	(h)	Doncaster R	W 4-3	Hogan 2, McFarlane, D.Walders	
24	Feb	11	(h)	Burton U	D 1-1	Marshall	
25		25	(h)	Burslem Port Vale	W 5-0	R.Smith 3, McFarlane, Marshall	
26	Mar	4	(a)	Bristol C	D 0-0		4,000
27		11	(h)	Manchester U	W 2-0	J.Walders, Hogan	7,000
28		18	(a)	Glossop	D 0-0		
29	Apr	1	(a)	Bradford C	L 1-4	McFarlane	8,000
30		8	(h)	Lincoln C	W 2-1	R.Smith, McFarlane	
31		15	(a)	Leicester F	D 2-2	Hogan, R.Smith	
32		21	(a)	Lincoln C	L 0-2		
33		22	(h)	Barnsley	W 3-0	McFarlane, R.Smith, Barron	
34		29	(a)	Liverpool	L 0-3		10,000

FINAL LEAGUE POSITION: 11th in Division Two

Appearances
Goals

FA Cup

Q	Jan	14	(h)	Lincoln C	D 1-1	Marshall	
R		18	(a)	Lincoln C	L 2-3	J.Smith, Marshall	

Appearances
Goals

Green W	Dixon A	Walders J	Barron F	Walders D	Moffat H	Atkinson G	Hogan J	McFarlane D	Bell A	Lowe R	Taylor J	Smith J	Beard A	Hutchinson W	Henderson R	Ross A	Driver F	Smith R	Jackson W	Marshall T	
1	2	3	4	5	6	7	8	9	10	11											1
1	3		4	5	2	7	8	9	10		6	11									2
1	2		4	5	3	8		9			6	11	7	10							3
1	2	8	4	5		7		9			6	11			3	10					4
1	2		4	5		7		9			6	11			3	10	8				5
1	2		4	5		7		9			6	11			3	10		8			6
1	2	3	4	5		7		10			6	11				9		8			7
1	2		4	5		7		10			6	11			3	9		8			8
1	3		4	5	6	7			10			11			2	9		8			9
1	3	8	4	5	6	7						11			2	10		9			10
1	3		4	5	6	7	8	10			2	11						9			11
1	2		4	5	3	7	8	10			6	11						9			12
1			4	5	3	7	8	10			6				2			9	11		13
1	2		4	5	3	7	8	10			6	11						9			14
1	2		4	5			8	10			6					3		9		7	* 15
1	2		4	5	3		8	10			6					11		9		7	16
1	2	6	4		3		8	10			5					11		9		7	17
1	2		4	5	3		8	10			6					11		9		7	18
1	2		4	5	3		8	10			6					11		9		7	19
1	2	6	4		3		8	10			5					11		9		7	20
1	2		4	5	3		8	10	11		6							9		7	21
1	2	6		4	3			9	10		5	11						8		7	22
1	2		4	5	3		8	10			6	11						9		7	23
1	2	6	4	5	3		8	10								11		9		7	24
1	2		4	5	3		8	10			6					11		9		7	25
1	2	11	4	5	3		8	9			6					10				7	26
1	2	7	4	5			8	10			6				3	11		9			27
1	2	7	4	5			8	10			6				3	11		9			28
1	2	7	4	5			8	9			6	11			3	10					29
1	2	7	4	5	3		8	10			6					11		9			30
1	2	7	4	5	3		8	10			6					11		9			31
1	2	7	4	5	3		8	10			6					11		9			32
1	2	7	4	5	3		8	10			6					11		9			33
1	2	7	4	5	3		8	10			6					11		9			34
34	33	17	33	32	25	14	25	32	5	1	30	15	1	1	10	24	1	27	1	12	
	1	1	3	1	1		7	14				1				2		8		4	

*In Match 15 Burnley only had 10 players

Green W	Dixon A	Walders J	Barron F	Walders D	Moffat H	Atkinson G	Hogan J	McFarlane D	Bell A	Lowe R	Taylor J	Smith J	Beard A	Hutchinson W	Henderson R	Ross A	Driver F	Smith R	Jackson W	Marshall T	
1	2		4	5	3		8	10			6					11		9		7	Q
1	2		4	5	3		8	9			6	11				10				7	R
2	2		2	2	2		2	2			2	1				2		1		2	
												1								2	

1905-06

Manager: Spen Whittaker

1	Sep	2	(a)	West Brom A	W 2-1	McFarlane, Murphy	7,223
2		4	(h)	Bradford C	D 0-0		8,000
3		11	(h)	Chesterfield	D 1-1	A.Smith	
4		16	(a)	Hull C	D 1-1	Cretney	6,000
5		23	(h)	Lincoln C	W 2-1	Murphy, Barron	
6		30	(a)	Chesterfield	L 0-3		
7	Oct	2	(h)	Leicester F	L 0-2		
8		7	(h)	Burslem Port Vale	L 1-3	R.Smith	
9		14	(a)	Barnsley	W 2-1	Davidson, R.Smith	
10		21	(h)	Clapton O	W 3-0	Cretney 2, R.Smith	
11		28	(h)	Grimsby T	D 0-0		4,000
12	Nov	11	(h)	Burton U	W 1-0	A.Smith	
13		18	(a)	Chelsea	L 0-1		8,000
14		25	(h)	Gainsborough T	W 1-0	McFarlane	
15	Dec	2	(a)	Bristol C	L 0-2		8,000
16		9	(h)	Manchester U	L 1-3	Cretney	8,000
17		16	(a)	Glossop	D 1-1	R.Smith	
18		23	(h)	Stockport C	L 0-1		
19		25	(h)	Blackpool	W 4-1	Wood, McFarlane 2, J.Walders	
20		30	(h)	West Brom A	L 0-2		6,500
21	Jan	6	(a)	Leicester F	L 0-2		
22		20	(h)	Hull C	L 1-3	McFarlane	3,000
23		27	(a)	Lincoln C	L 0-5		
24	Feb	3	(a)	Leeds C	D 1-1	McFarlane	7,129
25		10	(a)	Burslem Port Vale	D 2-2	McFarlane, Bell	
26		17	(h)	Barnsley	W 2-1	Davidson 2	
27		24	(a)	Clapton O	L 0-3		
28		27	(a)	Bradford C	W 1-0	Moffat	4,000
29	Mar	3	(a)	Grimsby T	L 0-2		4,000
30		10	(h)	Leeds C	W 4-3	Davidson 2, Bell, A.Smith	5,000
31		17	(a)	Burton U	W 3-1	McFarlane 3	
32		24	(h)	Chelsea	W 2-0	Bell, R.Smith	8,000
33		31	(a)	Gainsborough T	W 1-0	R.Smith	
34	Apr	7	(h)	Bristol C	D 2-2	Davidson, R.Smith	10,000
35		13	(a)	Blackpool	W 1-0	Davidson	
36		14	(a)	Manchester U	L 0-1		12,000
37		21	(h)	Glossop	W 1-0	A.Smith	
38		28	(a)	Stockport C	L 1-3	Moffat (pen)	

FINAL LEAGUE POSITION: 9th in Division Two

Appearances
Goals

FA Cup

1	Jan	13	(a)	Tottenham H	L 0-2		20,000

Appearances
Goals

Green W	Dixon A	Moffat H	Barron F	Walders D	Cretney J	Walders J	Davidson A	Smith R	McFarlane D	Murphy B	Marshall T	Smith A	Taylor J	Parker J	Greenwood J	Campbell T	Bell A	Wood A	Lovett J	Riley J	Whiteley C	Mooney J	Hargreaves A	Whittaker F	McNab	
1	2	3	4	5	6	7	8	9	10	11																1
1	2	3	4	5	6	7	8	9	10	11																2
1	2	3	4	5	6	11	8	9			7	10														3
1	2	3	4	5	10	7	8	9		11			6													4
1	2	3	4		10	7	11	9		8			6	5												5
1	2	3	4		10	7	11	9		8			6	5												6
1	2	3	4		10	7	11	9		8			6	5												7
1	2	3	4	5	6		8	9	10		7	11														8
1	3	6	4	5			8	9	10		7	11			2											9
1	3	6	4	5	10		8	9			7	11			2											10
1		6	4	5	10		8	9	11		7				2	3										11
1	3	6	4	5		7	8	9	10			11				2										12
1	3	6	4	5		7	8	9	10							2	11									13
1	3	6	4	5		7	8	9	10							2	11									14
1	3	6	4	5	10	7	8	9								2	11									15
1	3	6	4	5	10	7	8	9								2	11									16
1	3	6	4	5	9		8	10			7				2		11									17
1	3	6	4	5	9	7		10	8						2		11									18
1	3	6	4	5		7	10		8						2		11	9								19
1	3	6	4	5		7	10		8						2		11	9								20
1	3	6	4		10	7		11	8				5		2			9								21
	3	6	4		8	7		9	10				5			2	11		1							22
1	3	6			4		8		9		7	11		5		2	10									23
1	3	6	4		5	11	8		9		7					2	10									24
1	3	6	4		5	11	8		9		7						10			2						25
1	3	6	4		5	11	8		9		7				2		10									26
1		3	4		5	11	8	10			7		6		2			9								27
1		3	4	5		11	8	9				10	6		2										7	28
1	2	3	4	5		11	8	9				10	6								7					29
1		3	2	5	4	7	8	9				11	6				10									30
1		3	2	5	4	7	8	9	10			11	6													31
1		3	2	5	4	7	8	9				11	6				10									32
1		3	2	5	4	7	8	9				11	6				10									33
1		3	2	5	4	7	8	9				11	6				10									34
1	3	6	2	5		7	8	9				11	4				10									35
1	3	6	2	5		7	8	9				11	4				10									36
1	3	6		5		7	8	9	10			11	4							2						37
1	3	6	4	5			10					11						9				2	7	8		38
37	30	38	36	28	26	31	35	31	19	6	11	17	17	4	11	9	19	5	1	2	1	1	1	1	1	
		2	1		4	1	7	7	10	2		4					3	1								

Green W	Dixon A	Moffat H	Barron F	Walders D	Cretney J	Walders J	Davidson A	Smith R	McFarlane D	Murphy B	Marshall T	Smith A	Taylor J	Parker J	Greenwood J	Campbell T	Bell A	Wood A	Lovett J	Riley J	Whiteley C	Mooney J	Hargreaves A	Whittaker F	McNab	
1	3	6	4		10	7			8				6			2	11	9								1
1	1	1	1		1	1			1				1			1	1	1								

1906-07

Manager: Spen Whittaker

1	Sep	1	(h)	West Brom A	L 0-1		7,500
2		3	(h)	Bradford C	L 0-1		5,000
3		8	(a)	Leicester F	L 0-2		
4		15	(h)	Nottingham F	W 2-1	Whittaker 2	
5		22	(a)	Lincoln C	W 2-1	R.Smith 2	
6		29	(h)	Burton U	W 4-0	Moffat 2, Bell 2	
7	Oct	6	(a)	Grimsby T	L 0-1		4,000
8		13	(h)	Burslem Port Vale	W 6-0	R.Smith 3, Bell, Taylor, A.Smith	
9		20	(a)	Chesterfield	W 1-0	Whittaker	
10		27	(a)	Leeds C	W 1-0	Bell	14,000
11	Nov	3	(h)	Barnsley	D 2-2	R.Smith, Bell	
12		10	(a)	Chelsea	L 0-2		10,000
13		17	(h)	Wolves	W 3-0	Bell, Barron, Whittaker	4,000
14		24	(a)	Clapton O	L 1-2	R.Smith	
15	Dec	1	(h)	Gainsborough T	W 1-0	R.Smith (pen)	
16		8	(a)	Stockport C	L 1-2	Whittaker	
17		15	(h)	Hull C	W 4-2	Whittaker 2, Bell 2	6,000
18		22	(a)	Glossop	L 0-1		
19		25	(h)	Blackpool	W 2-1	Whittaker, R.Smith	
20		29	(a)	West Brom A	L 2-3	R.Smith, Whittaker	12,000
21	Jan	1	(a)	Bradford C	L 1-3	Davidson	13,000
22		5	(h)	Leicester F	W 5-0	Whittaker 2, R.Smith 2, Ogden	
23		19	(a)	Nottingham F	L 0-2		
24		26	(h)	Lincoln C	W 5-1	R.Smith 2, Bell, A.Smith, Whittaker	
25	Feb	2	(a)	Burton U	W 1-0	A.Smith	
26		9	(h)	Grimsby T	W 2-0	Ogden 2	
27		16	(a)	Burslem Port Vale	D 4-4	R.Smith 2, Bell, Ogden	
28		23	(h)	Chesterfield	D 0-0		
29	Mar	2	(h)	Leeds C	L 1-2	Moffat (pen)	5,000
30		16	(h)	Chelsea	D 1-1	Bell	7,000
31		23	(a)	Wolves	L 0-3		6,500
32		29	(a)	Blackpool	L 0-2		
33		30	(h)	Clapton O	W 3-0	McFarlane, A.Smith 2	
34	Apr	6	(a)	Gainsborough T	W 2-0	Ogden, R.Smith	
35		13	(h)	Stockport C	W 3-0	Whittaker, Bell, Moffat (pen)	
36		18	(a)	Barnsley	L 0-5		
37		20	(a)	Hull C	D 1-1	Davidson	7,000
38		27	(h)	Glossop	D 1-1	Davidson	

FINAL LEAGUE POSITION: 7th in Division Two

Appearances
Goals

FA Cup

1	Jan	12	(h)	Aston Villa	L 1-3	Whittaker	16,242

Appearances
Goals

Green W	Barron F	Dixon A	Cawthorne R	Cretney J	Moffat H	Trainer S	Davidson A	Smith R	McFarlane D	Smith A	Parker J	Taylor J	Kenyon J	Morrison T	Whittaker F	Bell A	Goodwin F	Ogden A	Dawson Jon	Whiteley C	Johnson D	Riley J	Dawson Jer	Holden P	
1	2	3	4	5	6	7	8	9	10	11															1
1	2	3		4			8	9	10	11	5	6	7												2
1	2	3	5	4	6			9	10	11			7	8											3
1	2	3		4	6			9		11		5	7		8	10									4
1	2	3	5	4	6			9		11			7		8	10									5
1	2	3	5	4	6			9		11			7		8	10									6
1	2	3	5	4	6			10	9	11			7		8										7
1	2	3	5	4				9		11		6	7		8	10									8
1	2	3	5	4				9		11		6	7		8	10									9
1	2	3	5	4				9		11		6	7		8	10									10
1	2	3	5	4				9		11		6	7		8	10									11
1	2	3	5	4				9		11		6	7		8	10									12
1	2		5	4	3		6	9		11			7		8	10									13
1	2	3	5	4	6			9		11			7		8	10									14
1	2	3	5	4	6			9		11			7		8	10									15
1	2	3	5	4	6			9					7		8	10	11								16
1	2	3	5	4	6			9		11			7		8	10									17
1	2		5	4	3		6	9		11			7		8	10									18
1	2		5	4	3		6	9		11			7		8	10									19
1	2		5		3		4	9		11		6			8			7	10						20
1	2		5		3		4	9		11		6	7		8			10							21
1	2	3		4	6		5	9		11			7		8			10							22
1	2	3			6		4	9		11	5		7		8			10							23
1	2	3		4	6			9		11	5		7		8	10									24
1	2	3		4	6			9		11	5		7		8			10							25
1	2	3		4	6			9		11	5					10		8		7					26
1	2	3			6			9		11	5		7			10		8			4				27
1	2	3		4	6			9		11	5		7			10		8							28
1	2	3	5	4	6					11			7		8	10		9							29
1	2	3		4	6			9		11	5		7		8	10									30
1	2	3		4	6	7		9		11	5				8	10									31
1	2	3		4	6			9	10	11	5		7		8										32
1	2	3		4	5			9	10	11			7		8							6			33
1	2			4	3	7		9	5	11		6			8			10							34
	2	6		4	3				5	11					8	10		9		7			1		35
1	2				3		10	9		11	5	6			8						4			7	36
1	2			4	3		10	9	5	11					8			7			6				37
1	2	6		4			10	9		11	5				8			7			3				38
37	38	30	20	33	31	3	12	36	9	37	12	11	29	1	32	23	1	13	1	2	4	1	1	1	
	1				4		3	17	1	5		1			13	12		5							

Green W	Barron F	Dixon A	Cawthorne R	Cretney J	Moffat H	Trainer S	Davidson A	Smith R	McFarlane D	Smith A	Parker J	Taylor J	Kenyon J	Morrison T	Whittaker F	Bell A	Goodwin F	Ogden A	Dawson Jon	Whiteley C	Johnson D	Riley J	Dawson Jer	Holden P	
1	2	3			6		4	9		11		5	7		8	10									1
1	1	1			1		1	1		1		1	1		1	1									
															1										

1907-08

Manager: Spen Whittaker

1	Sep	7	(a)	West Brom A	L 0-5		16,032
2		9	(h)	Stoke	W 3-1	Beddows 2, Whittaker	
3		14	(h)	Bradford C	W 2-1	R.Smith 2	8,000
4		16	(h)	Lincoln C	L 1-2	R.Smith	
5		21	(a)	Hull C	L 1-3	Valentine	8,000
6		28	(h)	Derby C	D 2-2	Bell, R.Smith	10,000
7	Oct	5	(a)	Lincoln C	W 3-1	R.Smith 2, Bell	
8		12	(h)	Fulham	L 0-1		8,000
9		19	(a)	Barnsley	W 3-2	Beddows 2, R.Smith	
10		26	(h)	Chesterfield	D 1-1	Ogden	
11	Nov	2	(h)	Grimsby T	W 5-1	Bell 2, R.Smith 2, Beddows	4,000
12		9	(a)	Oldham A	D 1-1	Beddows	14,000
13		16	(h)	Clapton O	W 3-0	Bradshaw, R.Smith, A.Smith	
14		23	(a)	Leeds C	D 2-2	R.Smith 2	7,000
15		30	(h)	Wolves	W 1-0	Beddows	5,000
16	Dec	7	(a)	Gainsborough T	L 0-2		
17		14	(h)	Stockport C	W 4-0	Ogden, Moffat, Bell, A.Smith	
18		21	(a)	Glossop	L 1-3	R.Smith	
19		25	(h)	Blackpool	W 2-1	A.Smith, R.Smith	
20		26	(a)	Stoke	D 0-0		
21		28	(h)	Leicester F	W 4-1	Parker, Donaghey 2, A.Smith	
22	Jan	4	(h)	West Brom A	D 1-1	A.Smith	10,146
23		18	(h)	Hull C	W 5-0	McFarlane 2, Mayson, Cretney, A.Smith	7,000
24		25	(a)	Derby C	L 0-1		10,000
25	Feb	8	(a)	Fulham	L 1-2	Leake	15,000
26		15	(h)	Barnsley	W 4-1	R.Smith 3, Bell	
27		22	(a)	Chesterfield	W 4-2	R.Smith 3, A.Smith	
28		29	(a)	Grimsby T	W 1-0	A.Smith	3,000
29	Mar	7	(h)	Oldham A	W 2-1	Mayson, Whittaker	16,000
30		14	(a)	Clapton O	W 1-0	Whittaker	
31		16	(a)	Wolves	L 1-5	R.Smith	16,000
32		21	(h)	Leeds C	W 1-0	R.Smith	7,000
33	Apr	4	(h)	Gainsborough T	W 2-0	Leake, A.Smith	
34		11	(a)	Stockport C	W 3-1	R.Smith, Bell, Whittaker	
35		17	(a)	Blackpool	L 0-1		
36		18	(h)	Glossop	W 1-0	A.Smith	
37		20	(a)	Bradford C	L 0-2		27,000
38		25	(a)	Leicester F	L 1-3	R.Smith	

FINAL LEAGUE POSITION: 7th in Division Two

Appearances
Goals

FA Cup

1	Jan	11	(a)	Southampton	L 1-2	Bell	14,000

Appearances
Goals

Green W	Barron F	Moffat H	Cretney J	McFarlane D	Wolstenholme T	Bradshaw W	Beddows J	Smith R	Short W	Smith A	Whittaker F	Dawson J	Wright R	Valentine F	Bell A	Heys S	Wilcox H	Parker J	Ogden A	Smethams C	Leake A	Donaghey B	Mayson T	
1	2	3	4	5	6	7	8	9	10	11														1
1	2	3	4	5	6	7	8	9		11	10													2
1	2	3	4	5	6	7	8	9		11	10													3
1	2	3	4	5	6	7	8	9		11	10													4
	2	3		5	6		8	9		11	10	1	4	7										5
	2	3		5	6			9		11	8	1	4	7	10									6
	2	3	4	5	6			9		11	8	1		7	10									7
	2		4	5	6			9		11	8	1		7	10	3								8
	2		4		6	7	8	9		11		1					3	5	10					9
	2	3	4		6	7	8	9		11		1						5	10					10
	2	3		4	6	7	8	9		11		1			10			5						11
	2	3		4	6	7	8	9		11		1			10			5						12
	2	3		4	6	7	8	9		11		1			10			5						13
	2	3		4	6	7	8	9		11		1			10			5						14
	2	3	4	5	6		8	9		11		1		7	10									15
	2	3	4	5	6		8	9		11		1		7	10									16
	2	3	4	5	6				8	11		1			10				9	7				17
	2	3	4		6			9		11		1							8	7	5	10		18
	2	3	4		6			9		11		1			10					7	5	8		19
	2	3	4		6			9		11		1								7	5	8	10	20
		3	4		6			9		11		1			10			5		7	2	8		21
	2	3	4		6			9		11		1			10					7	5	8		22
	2	3	4	7	6			8		11		1			10						5		9	23
	2	3	4	7	6			8		11		1			10						5		9	24
	2	3	4	7	6			9		11	8	1			10						5			25
	2	3		7	6			9			8	1			10				4	11	5			26
	2	3	4	7	6			9		11	8	1									5		10	27
	2	3	4	7	6			9		11	8	1									5		10	28
	2	3	4	7	6					11	8	1			10						5		9	29
	2	3	4	7	6			9		11	8	1			10						5			30
	2	3	4	7	6			9		11	8	1			10						5			31
	2	3	4	7	6			9		11	8	1			10						5			32
	2	3	4	7	6			9		11	8	1			10						5			33
	2	3	4	7	6			9		11	8	1			10						5			34
	2	3	4	7	6			9		11	8	1			10						5			35
	2		4		6	7		9		11	8	1			10			5			3			36
	2		4	7	6			9		11	8	1			10			5			3			37
	2	3	4	7	6			9	10	11	8	1									5			38
4	37	34	31	30	38	11	13	36	3	37	21	34	2	6	26	1	1	9	5	7	21	5	6	
		1	1	2		1	7	24		10	4			1	7			1	2		2	2	2	

Green W	Barron F	Moffat H	Cretney J	McFarlane D	Wolstenholme T	Bradshaw W	Beddows J	Smith R	Short W	Smith A	Whittaker F	Dawson J	Wright R	Valentine F	Bell A	Heys S	Wilcox H	Parker J	Ogden A	Smethams C	Leake A	Donaghey B	Mayson T	
	2	3	4		6			9		11		1			10				8	7	5			1
	1	1	1		1			1		1		1			1				1	1	1			
															1									

1908-09

Manager: Spen Whittaker

1	Sep	1	(h)	Chesterfield	L 0-1		
2		5	(h)	Glossop	W 3-2	A.Smith, Morley, Whittaker	
3		7	(h)	Derby C	W 2-0	R.Smith, Lindley	12,000
4		12	(a)	Stockport C	L 1-2	Lindley	
5		19	(h)	West Brom A	L 0-2		11,340
6		26	(a)	Birmingham	L 0-2		20,000
7	Oct	3	(h)	Gainsborough T	W 5-2	R.Smith 4, Morley	
8		10	(a)	Grimsby T	W 1-0	Valentine	
9		17	(h)	Fulham	L 1-3	A.Smith	7,000
10		24	(a)	Bolton W	L 1-2	Morley	
11		31	(a)	Bradford	W 3-2	R.Smith 2 (1 pen), Whittaker	
12	Nov	7	(h)	Wolves	L 3-5	Whittaker 2, R.Smith, (pen)	6,000
13		14	(a)	Oldham A	L 1-4	Bell	10,000
14		21	(h)	Clapton O	L 0-1		
15		28	(a)	Leeds C	D 1-1	Watson (og)	14,000
16	Dec	5	(h)	Barnsley	W 3-2	Lindley, Bell, Mayson	
17		12	(a)	Tottenham H	L 2-4	Moffat, R.Smith	10,000
18		19	(h)	Hull C	W 1-0	Morley	7,000
19		25	(h)	Blackpool	D 1-1	Morley	
20		26	(a)	Derby C	L 0-1		12,000
21	Jan	2	(a)	Glossop	W 2-1	R.Smith, Abbott	
22		9	(h)	Stockport C	W 5-1	Abbott, R.Smith, Ogden 2, Cretney	
23		23	(a)	West Brom A	D 0-0		18,220
24		30	(h)	Birmingham	D 1-1	Morley	8,000
25	Feb	13	(h)	Grimsby T	W 2-0	Abbott 2 (1 pen)	
26		27	(h)	Bolton W	L 1-2	Mayson	
27	Mar	13	(a)	Wolves	L 1-2	Abbott	7,500
28		16	(h)	Bradford	D 3-3	Mayson 2, Ogden	
29		20	(h)	Oldham A	W 1-0	R.Smith (pen)	7,000
30		27	(a)	Clapton O	W 1-0	Abbott	
31		31	(a)	Fulham	L 0-3		8,000
32	Apr	3	(h)	Leeds C	D 0-0		5,000
33		9	(a)	Blackpool	D 0-0		
34		12	(a)	Chesterfield	L 0-1		
35		13	(a)	Barnsley	W 2-1	Little (og), Morley	
36		14	(a)	Gainsborough T	L 0-1		
37		17	(h)	Tottenham H	L 1-2	Mayson	8,000
38		24	(a)	Hull C	L 2-3	R.Smith, Browell (og)	6,000

FINAL LEAGUE POSITION: 14th in Division Two

Appearances
Goals

FA Cup

1	Jan	16	(a)	Bristol R	W 4-2	Ogden 3, R.Smith	6,000
2	Feb	6	(a)	Crystal P	D 0-0		17,076
R		10	(h)	Crystal P	W 9-0	Abbott 2, R.Smith 3, Cretney 2, Smethams, Opp own-goal	14,000
3		20	(a)	Tottenham H	D 0-0		21,838
R		24	(h)	Tottenham H	W 3-1	Ogden, R.Smith, Abbott	30,000
4	Mar	10	(h)	Manchester U*	L 2-3	Ogden 2	16,850

*Following an abandoned game (72 minutes) on 6 March with Burnley leading 1-0.

Appearances
Goals

Dawson J	Barron F	Moffat H	Cretney J	Parker J	Abbott W	Morley J	Brewis R	Smith R	Mayson T	Smith A	Whittaker F	Howarth W	Ogden A	Lindley R	Leake A	Bell A	Beddows J	Green W	Valentine F	Dawson A	McLean J	Cawthorne R	Smethams C	Wilcox H	Woodward H	Minion F	Clarke G	Watson W	McLoughlin W	
1	2	3	4	5	6	7	8	9	10	11																				1
1	2	3	4	5	6	7		9	10	11	8																			2
1	2			5	6	7		9		11	10	3	4	8																3
1	2		4	5	6	7		9		11	10	3		8																4
1	2		4		6	7		9		11	8	3			5	10														5
1	2		4		6	7		8		11		3			5	10	9													6
1	2		4		6	7		9		11		3		8	5	10														7
	2	3	4		6	7		9		11				8	5			1	10											8
	2	3	4		6	7		9		11				8	5	10		1												9
1	2		4	5	6	7		9		8					3	10				11										10
1		3	4	5	6	7		9		11	8				2	10														11
1	2		4	5	6	7		9		11	8				3	10														12
1		3	4		6	7				11				8	5	10	9				2									13
1		6	4			7		9		11		2		8		10					3	5								14
1	2	6				7		9	10				4	8	5	11					3									15
1	2	6				7		9	10				4	8	5	11					3									16
1	2	6				7		9	10				4		5	11			8		3									17
1	2	6				7		9	10				4		5	11			8		3									18
1	2	6				7		9	10				4		5	11			8		3									19
1	2	6				7		9	10				4		5	11			8		3									20
1	2	6	4		10	7		9					8		5						3		11							21
1	2	6	4		10	7		9					8		5						3		11							22
1	2	6	4		10	7		9					8		5						3		11							23
1	2	6	4		10	7		9					8		5						3		11							24
1	2	6	4		10	7		9					8		5						3		11							25
1	2	6	4		10	7			9				8		5								11	3						26
1		6	4		10	7			9				8		5						3		11		2					27
1			4			7		9	10			2	8		5						3		11			6				28
1	2		4		10			9	7				8		5						3	6	11							29
1			4		10			9	7			2	8		5						3		11			6				30
1			4		10			9				2	8		5						3	6	11				7			31
1	2	3	4		10	7		9					8		5								11					6		32
1	2	6	4		10			9	7					8	5								11	3						33
1	2	6			10	7		9	8						5						3		11						4	34
1	2	6			10	7		9	8						5						3		11						4	35
1	2	6				7	10	9	8						5						3		11						4	36
1	2	6			10	7		9	8						5						3		11						4	37
1	2	6			10	7		9	8						5						3		11						4	38
36	31	27	26	7	29	34	2	35	19	14	6	9	19	10	33	15	2	2	5	1	23	3	18	2	1	2	1	1	5	
		1	1		6	7		13	5	2	4		3	3		2			1											

3 own-goals

Dawson J	Barron F	Moffat H	Cretney J	Parker J	Abbott W	Morley J	Brewis R	Smith R	Mayson T	Smith A	Whittaker F	Howarth W	Ogden A	Lindley R	Leake A	Bell A	Beddows J	Green W	Valentine F	Dawson A	McLean J	Cawthorne R	Smethams C	Wilcox H	Woodward H	Minion F	Clarke G	Watson W	McLoughlin W	
1	2	6	4		10	7		9					8		5						3		11							1
1	2	6	4		10	7		9					8		5						3		11							2
1	2	6	4		10	7		9					8		5						3		11							R
1	2	6	4		10	7		9					8		5						3		11							3
1	2	6	4		10	7		9					8		5						3		11							R
1		6	4		10	7		9				2	8		5						3		11							4
6	5	6	6		6	6		6				1	6		6						6		6							
			2		3			5					6										1							

1 own-goal

1909-10

Manager: Spen Whittaker until April, then R.H.Wadge

1	Sep	4	(a)	Derby C	L 2-5	Lindley, Abbott (pen)	5,000
2		6	(h)	Hull C	L 0-1		7,000
3		11	(h)	Stockport C	D 2-2	Abbott (pen), Lomas	
4		18	(a)	Glossop	L 0-2		
5		25	(h)	Birmingham	W 2-0	Abbott (pen), Ogden	5,000
6	Oct	2	(a)	West Brom A	W 2-1	Ogden, Abbott	15,175
7		9	(h)	Oldham A	L 1-2	Abbott	9,000
8		16	(a)	Barnsley	D 0-0		
9		23	(h)	Fulham	W 2-0	Mayson, Morley	3,000
10		30	(h)	Bradford	W 1-0	Smethams	
11	Nov	6	(a)	Leeds C	L 0-1		7,000
12		13	(h)	Wolves	W 4-2	Abbott 3 (1 pen), Smethams	6,000
13		20	(a)	Gainsborough T	L 0-2		
14		27	(h)	Grimsby T	W 3-1	Green, Morley, Opp own-goal	
15	Dec	4	(a)	Manchester C	L 0-4		12,000
16		11	(h)	Leicester F	W 5-2	Green 2, Chadburn, Abbott, Morley	
17		18	(a)	Lincoln C	D 0-0		
18		25	(h)	Blackpool	W 5-1	Green 3, Chadburn 2	
19		27	(a)	Clapton O	L 1-2	Green	
20	Jan	1	(h)	Clapton O	W 2-0	Chadburn, Morley	
21		8	(h)	Derby C	L 1-2	Green	8,000
22		19	(a)	Oldham A	L 0-1		6,000
23		22	(a)	Stockport C	D 1-1	Green	
24	Feb	12	(h)	West Brom A	L 2-3	R.Smith, Green	6,000
25		26	(h)	Barnsley	W 2-0	Lomas, Smethams	
26		28	(a)	Birmingham	L 1-2	R.Smith (pen)	1,000
27	Mar	5	(a)	Fulham	L 1-2	Lomas	12,000
28		12	(a)	Bradford	L 1-3	Lomas	
29		19	(h)	Leeds C	W 3-0	Lomas 2, Green	4,000
30		25	(a)	Blackpool	W 3-2	Valentine, Green, Lomas	
31		26	(a)	Wolves	L 1-3	Lomas	5,000
32		28	(a)	Hull C	L 2-3	Moffat, Green	10,000
33	Apr	2	(h)	Gainsborough T	W 2-1	Lomas, Moffat	
34		9	(a)	Grimsby T	L 3-5	Green 2, Smethams	
35		16	(h)	Manchester C	D 3-3	Green 2 (1 pen), Lomas	7,000
36		18	(h)	Glossop	L 0-1		
37		23	(a)	Leicester F	D 1-1	Lomas	
38		30	(h)	Lincoln C	W 3-0	Moffat, Morley, Green	

FINAL LEAGUE POSITION: 14th in Division Two

Appearances
Goals

FA Cup

1	Jan	15	(h)	Manchester U	W 2-0	Green, Smethams	16,628
2	Feb	5	(a)	Sunderland	L 0-2		

Appearances
Goals

Dawson J	Barron F	McLean J	Cretney J	Leake A	Moffat H	Morley J	Lindley R	Lomas W	Abbott W	Smethams C	Beddows J	Watson W	Clarke G	Green B	Smith R	Mayson T	Ogden A	Valentine F	Cawthorne R	Tillotson S	Chadburn J	Weightman D	Splitt T	Dollins J	Woodward H	McLoughlin W	Bamford T	Boden R	Dougan P	Swift H	
1	2	3	4	5	6	7	8	9	10	11																					1
1	2	3	4	5	6		8	9	10	11	7																				2
1	2	3	4	5				8	10	11		6	7	9																	3
1	2	3	4	5					10			6	7	8	9	11															4
1	2	3	4	5	6		8	9	10	11							7														5
1	2	3	4	5	6				10	11				8			9	7													6
1	2	3	4						10	11		6			9		8	7	5												7
1	2	3	4	5		7			10	11		6		8			9														8
1	2	3	4	5	6	7			10	11				8		9															9
1	2	3	4	5	6	7	8		10	11				9																	10
1	2	3	4	5	6	7			10	11				8		9															11
	2	3	4	5	6	7			10	11				8			9			1											12
	2	3	4	5	6	7			10	11				8			9			1											13
1	2	3	4	5	6	7			10	11				8							9										14
1	2	3	4	5	6	7			10	11				8								9									15
1	2		4	5	6	7			10	11				8							9		3								16
1	2		4		6	7			10					8				11			9		3	5							17
1	2		4	5	6	7			10	11				8							9		3								18
1	2			5	6	7			10	11				8			4				9		3								19
1	2		4	5	6	7			10	11				8							9		3								20
1	2		4	5	6	7			10	11				8							9		3								21
1	2		4	5	6	7			10	11				8	9										3						22
1	2		4	5	6	7			10	11				8	9								3								23
1	2		4	5	6	7			10	11				8	9								3								24
	2		4		6	7		10		11				8	9					1			3	5							25
1	2		4	5	6	7		10		11				8	9								3								26
1	2			5	6	7		9	10	11				8									3			4					27
1			4		6	7		9	10	11				8			5						3		2						28
1	2	3	4		6	7		10		11				8	9									5							29
1			6		4			10		11				8				7				9		5			2	3			30
1			4		6			10		11				8				7				9		5			2	3			31
1			4		6			9	10					8				7						5			2	3	11		32
1		3	4		6			10		11				8				7			9			5			2				33
1		3	4		6			9		11				8							10			5			2	7			34
1			4	5	6	7		9		11				8		10							3				2				35
1			4		6			9		11				8		10							3				2	7		5	36
1			4	5	6	7		9	10	11				8									3				2				37
1			4	5	6	7		9		11				8	10								3				2				38
35	28	18	36	27	34	26	4	18	28	35	1	4	2	34	9	5	8	7	1	3	9	3	16	8	2	1	9	5	1	1	
					3	5	1	11	9	4				18	2	1	2	1			4										

1 own-goal

Dawson J	Barron F	McLean J	Cretney J	Leake A	Moffat H	Morley J	Lindley R	Lomas W	Abbott W	Smethams C	Beddows J	Watson W	Clarke G	Green B	Smith R	Mayson T	Ogden A	Valentine F	Cawthorne R	Tillotson S	Chadburn J	Weightman D	Splitt T	Dollins J	Woodward H	McLoughlin W	Bamford T	Boden R	Dougan P	Swift H	
1	2	3	4	5	6	7			10	11				8	9																1
1	2	3	4	5	6	7			10	11				8	9																2
2	2	2	2	2	2	2			2	2				2	2																
										1				1																	

1910-11

Manager: John Haworth

1	Sep	3	(h)	Lincoln C	W 3-1	Lomas 2, Green	
2		5	(h)	Glossop	D 0-0		
3		10	(a)	Huddersfield T	W 1-0	Lomas	7,371
4		17	(h)	Birmingham	D 2-2	Green 2	10,000
5		24	(a)	West Brom A	L 1-2	Lomas	15,280
6	Oct	1	(h)	Hull C	D 0-0		10,500
7		8	(a)	Fulham	L 0-3		10,000
8		15	(h)	Bradford	D 1-1	Green (pen)	
9		22	(a)	Bolton W	D 1-1	Lomas	
10		29	(a)	Gainsborough T	W 2-1	Lomas 2	
11	Nov	5	(h)	Leeds C	W 4-1	Lomas 2, Cretney, Mayson	8,000
12		12	(a)	Stockport C	L 2-4	Green 2	
13		19	(h)	Derby C	W 2-1	Green, Mayson	8,000
14		26	(a)	Barnsley	W 1-0	Mayson	
15	Dec	3	(h)	Leicester F	W 2-1	Watson (pen), Green	
16		10	(a)	Wolves	L 0-1		8,000
17		17	(h)	Chelsea	D 1-1	Morley	7,000
18		24	(a)	Clapton O	W 2-0	Morley, Lomas	
19		26	(h)	Blackpool	D 1-1	Morley	
20		27	(a)	Hull C	L 0-3		10,000
21		31	(a)	Lincoln C	L 0-1		
22	Jan	2	(a)	Glossop	D 1-1	Bates	
23		7	(h)	Huddersfield T	W 2-1	Bates 2 (1 pen)	7,000
24		21	(a)	Birmingham	D 1-1	Swift	6,000
25		28	(h)	West Brom A	W 2-0	Green 2	8,300
26	Feb	11	(h)	Fulham	W 1-0	Newton	10,000
27		18	(a)	Bradford	D 1-1	Green	
28	Mar	4	(h)	Gainsborough T	D 1-1	Mayson (pen)	
29		18	(h)	Stockport C	W 5-3	Bates 2, Goodwin (og), Mayson, Watson	
30		20	(h)	Bolton W	L 1-3	Mayson	
31		25	(a)	Derby C	L 0-3		3,500
32		27	(a)	Leeds C	D 0-0		5,500
33	Apr	1	(h)	Barnsley	D 0-0		
34		8	(a)	Leicester F	D 1-1	Newton	
35		14	(a)	Blackpool	L 0-1		
36		15	(h)	Wolves	D 1-1	Mountford	5,000
37		22	(a)	Chelsea	L 0-3		36,000
38		29	(h)	Clapton O	W 2-0	Mountford, Bannister (pen)	

FINAL LEAGUE POSITION: 8th in Division Two

Appearances
Goals

FA Cup

1	Jan	14	(h*)	Exeter C	W 2-0	Morley, Mayson	16,000
2	Feb	4	(h)	Barnsley	W 2-0	Morley, Green	
3		25	(h)	Coventry C	W 5-0	Green 2, Mayson 2, Watson	11,714
4	Mar	11	(a)	Bradford C	L 0-1		39,146

*Drawn away but transferred to Turf Moor following an objection to the St James' Park pitch.

Appearances
Goals

Dawson J	Reid R	Splitt T	Cretney J	Bannister W	Moffat H	Morley J	Green B	Seeburg M	Lomas W	Mayson T	Swift H	Smith P	Watson W	Harris J	Bates C	Dodd R	Bamford T	Barron F	McCallum C	McLaren W	Newton F	Tillotson S	Woods J	Lindley R	Freeman B	Mountford H	
1	2	3	4	5	6	7	8	9	10	11																	1
1	2	3	4	5	6	7	8	9	10	11																	2
1	2	3	4		6	7	8	9	10	11	5																3
1	2	3	4		6	7	8		10	11	5	9															4
1	2	3	4		6	7	8		10	11	5	9															5
1	2	3	4			7	8		10	11	5	9	6														6
1	2	3	4		5	7	8		10			9	6	11													7
1	2	3	4			7	8			10	5	9	6	11													8
1	2	3	4				8	7	9	10	5		6	11													9
1	2	3	4				8	7	9	10	5		6	11													10
1	2	3	4				8	7	9	10	5		6	11													11
1	2	3	4				8	7	9	10	5		6	11													12
1	2	3	4				8	7	9	10	5		6	11													13
1	2	3	4				8	7	9	10	5		6	11													14
1	2	3			4		8	7			5	9	6	11	10												15
1	2	3			4		8	7			5	9	6	11	10												16
1	2	3	4			7	8		9		5		6	11	10												17
1	2	3				7	8		9	10	5		6	11		4											18
1	2	3				7	8		9	10	5		6	11		4											19
1	2					7	8		9	10	5		6	11		4	3										20
1	2					7	8		9	10	5		6	11		4	3										21
1	2					7	8	4		10	5		6		9			3	11								22
1	3					7	8	4		10	5		6	11	9			2									23
1	2	3				7	8				5		6	11	10					4	9						24
	2					7	8	4		10	5			11			3			6	9	1					25
1	2					7	8			10	5		6	11			3			4	9						26
1	2					7	8				5		6	11	10		3			4	9						27
	2						8	7		10	5		6				3		11	4	9	1					28
1	2					7	8			10	5		6	11	9		3			4							29
	2			5		7	8			10			6	11			3			4		1	9				30
1		2				7	8			10	5		6	11	9		3			4							31
						7	8			10	5		6	11	9		3	2		4		1					32
							8	7		10	5		6		9		3	2	11	4		1					33
		2						7		10	5		6				3		11	4	9	1		8			34
1		2				7	8			10	5		6		9	11	3			4							35
1		2				7	8			11	5		6				3			4					9	10	36
1		3				7	8			11	5		6		10		2			4					9		37
1	2	3		5		7	9			11			6							4				8		10	38
32	31	26	15	4	8	27	37	17	18	32	33	7	32	24	13	5	15	4	4	15	6	6	1	2	2	2	
			1	1		3	11		10	6	1		2		5						2					2	

1 own-goal

Dawson J	Reid R	Splitt T	Cretney J	Bannister W	Moffat H	Morley J	Green B	Seeburg M	Lomas W	Mayson T	Swift H	Smith P	Watson W	Harris J	Bates C	Dodd R	Bamford T	Barron F	McCallum C	McLaren W	Newton F	Tillotson S	Woods J	Lindley R	Freeman B	Mountford H	
1	2	3				7	8	4	9	10	5		6	11													1
1	2					7	8			10	5		6	11			3			4	9						2
1	2					7	8			10	5		6	11			3			4	9						3
1	2					7	8			10	5		6	11			3			4	9						4
4	4	1				4	4	1	1	4	4		4	4			3			3	3						
						2	3			3			1														

1911-12

Manager: John Haworth

1	Sep	2	(a)	Glossop	W 3-1	Mountford 2, Freeman	
2		4	(h)	Leeds C	W 4-2	Lindley, Freeman, Mountford 2	15,000
3		9	(h)	Gainsborough T	W 2-0	Lindley, Freeman	
4		11	(h)	Leicester F	W 3-0	Mountford (pen), Freeman, Lindley	
5		16	(a)	Hull C	L 1-4	Freeman	10,000
6		23	(h)	Grimsby T	D 1-1	Freeman	
7		30	(a)	Barnsley	D 1-1	Mountford (pen)	
8	Oct	7	(h)	Nottingham F	W 2-0	Freeman 2	
9		14	(a)	Bradford	L 1-2	Boyle	
10		21	(h)	Chelsea	D 2-2	Freeman, Harris	12,000
11		28	(a)	Fulham	W 4-3	Freeman 3, Lindley	16,000
12	Nov	4	(h)	Clapton O	W 1-0	Freeman	
13		18	(h)	Bristol C	W 4-2	Hodgson, Freeman 2 (1 pen), Harris	11,000
14		25	(a)	Stockport C	W 1-0	Freeman	
15	Dec	2	(h)	Birmingham	D 1-1	Freeman	13,000
16		6	(a)	Derby C	L 0-2		12,000
17		9	(a)	Leeds C	W 5-1	Freeman 2, Harris 2, Lindley	10,000
18		16	(a)	Huddersfield T	D 1-1	Boyle	8,000
19		23	(h)	Wolves	W 2-1	Picken, Freeman	7,000
20		25	(h)	Blackpool	D 1-1	Lindley	
21		30	(h)	Glossop	W 4-0	Freeman 3, Lindley	
22	Jan	6	(a)	Gainsborough T	L 0-1		
23		20	(h)	Hull C	W 5-1	Lindley 3, Picken, Boyle	10,000
24		27	(a)	Grimsby T	L 0-1		
25	Feb	10	(a)	Nottingham F	W 1-0	Picken	
26		12	(h)	Barnsley	W 3-0	Hodgson 2, Freeman	
27		17	(h)	Bradford	W 3-1	Picken, Lindley 2	
28		24	(a)	Chelsea	W 2-0	Freeman, Lindley	30,000
29	Mar	2	(h)	Fulham	W 5-1	Freeman 3, Harris, Lindley	16,000
30		9	(a)	Clapton O	W 2-1	Freeman, Nesbitt	
31		16	(h)	Derby C	D 0-0		30,000
32		23	(a)	Bristol C	W 3-0	Picken 2, Nesbitt	10,000
33		30	(h)	Stockport C	W 4-1	Hodgson 3, Freeman	
34	Apr	5	(a)	Blackpool	D 0-0		
35		6	(a)	Birmingham	L 0-4		35,000
36		8	(a)	Leicester F	L 2-3	Hodgson, Freeman	
37		20	(h)	Huddersfield T	W 3-0	Lindley, Boyle, Freeman	15,000
38		27	(a)	Wolves	L 0-2		18,500

FINAL LEAGUE POSITION: 3rd in Division Two — Appearances / Goals

FA Cup

1	Jan	13	(a)	Fulham	L 1-2	Freeman	13,100

Appearances

Goals

Dawson J	Reid R	Bamford T	McLaren W	Swift H	Watson W	Morley J	Lindley R	Freeman B	Mountford H	Mayson T	Harris J	Hodgson E	Snowden T	Bates C	Splitt T	Goodison P	Taylor D	Lowe L	Picken J	Boyle T	Woods J	Bradshaw E	Nesbitt W	Bannister W	Weightman D	
1	2	3	4	5	6	7	8	9	10	11																1
1	2	3	4	5	6	7	8	9	10		11															2
1	2	3	4	5	6	7	8	9	10		11															3
1	2	3	4	5	6	7	8	9	10		11															4
1	2	3	4	5	6		8	9	10	11	7															5
1	2	3	4	5	6	7	8	9	10	11																6
1	2	3		4	6	7		9	10	11		8								5						7
1	2	3		4	6	7	8	9	10		11									5						8
1	2	3		4	6		8	9		10	11		7							5						9
1	2	3		4	6		8	9			11		7	10						5						10
1	2	3		4	6		8	9			11	10	7							5						11
1	2	3		4	6		8	9			11	10	7							5						12
1	2	3		4	6		8	9			11	10	7							5						13
1	2		4		6		8	9			11	10	7		3					5						14
1	2		4		6		8	9			11	10	7		3					5						15
1	2			4	6		8	9			11		7		3	10				5						16
1	2		4		6		8	9			11		7	10	3					5						17
1	2		4		6		8	9			10		7				3	11		5						18
1	2		4		6		8	9			11		7				3		10	5						19
1	2		4	5	6		8	9			11		7				3		10							20
1	2		4	5	6	7	8	9			11						3		10							21
1	2		4		6	7	8				10						3		9	5	11					22
1	2		4		6		8	9			11		7				3		10	5						23
1	2		4		6		8				11	10	7				3		9	5						24
1	2		4		6		8				7	9					3		10	5		11				25
1	2		4		6		8	9			11	10					3			5			7			26
1	2			4	6		8				11	10					3		9				7	5		27
1	2		4		6		8	9			11	10					3			5			7			28
1	2		4		6		8	9			11	10					3			5			7			29
1	2		4		6		8	9			11	10					3			5			7			30
1	2		4		6		8	9			11	10					3			5			7			31
1	2		4		6		8				11	10					3		9	5			7			32
1	2		4		6		8	9			11	10					3			5			7			33
1	2		4		6			9			11	8					3		10	5			7			34
1	2		4		6			9			11	8					3			5			7		10	35
1	2		4		6			9			11	8					3		10	5			7			36
1	2		4		6		8	9	11			10					3			5			7			37
1	2		4		6		8	9	11								3		10	5			7			38
38	38	13	29	17	38	9	34	33	10	5	33	20	14	2	4	1	21	1	12	29	1	1	13	1	1	
							15	32	6		5	7							6	4			2			

Dawson J	Reid R	Bamford T	McLaren W	Swift H	Watson W	Morley J	Lindley R	Freeman B	Mountford H	Mayson T	Harris J	Hodgson E	Snowden T	Bates C	Splitt T	Goodison P	Taylor D	Lowe L	Picken J	Boyle T	Woods J	Bradshaw E	Nesbitt W	Bannister W	Weightman D	
1	2		4		6		8	9			11		7				3		10	5						1
1	1		1		1		1	1			1		1				1		1	1						
								1																		

1912-13

Manager: John Haworth

No	Month	Day	Venue	Opponent	Result	Score	Scorers	Attendance
1	Sep	7	(h)	Glossop	W	2-1	Mountford (pen), Taylor	
2		9	(h)	Hull C	D	0-0		20,000
3		14	(a)	Clapton O	L	0-2		
4		16	(h)	Preston NE	D	2-2	Swift, Freeman	
5		21	(h)	Lincoln C	W	3-1	Lindley 2, Freeman	
6		26	(a)	Hull C	D	0-0		8,000
7		28	(a)	Nottingham F	L	1-2	Nesbitt	
8	Oct	5	(h)	Bristol C	D	2-2	Boyle, Husband	15,000
9		12	(a)	Birmingham	L	0-3		15,000
10		19	(h)	Huddersfield T	W	4-0	Bellamy, Freeman, Picken, Husband	13,000
11		26	(a)	Leeds C	L	1-4	Picken	10,000
12	Nov	2	(h)	Grimsby T	W	3-2	Watson, Picken, Freeman	12,000
13		9	(a)	Bury	D	1-1	Picken	
14		16	(h)	Fulham	W	5-0	Freeman 2, Hodgson, Husband, Watson	13,000
15		23	(a)	Barnsley	W	4-1	Freeman 2, Lindley, Husband	
16		30	(h)	Bradford	W	5-1	Hodgson 2, Lindley, Freeman 2	
17	Dec	7	(a)	Wolves	W	2-0	Hodgson, Boyle	6,000
18		14	(h)	Leicester F	W	5-1	Freeman 4, Hodgson	
19		21	(a)	Stockport C	W	1-0	Freeman	
20		25	(h)	Blackpool	W	4-0	Hodgson 2, Bellamy, Husband	
21		28	(a)	Glossop	W	3-1	Freeman, Boyle (pen), Hodgson	
22	Jan	4	(h)	Clapton O	W	5-0	Lindley 3, Hodgson, Boyle	
23		18	(a)	Lincoln C	W	3-1	Freeman 2, Riley	
24		25	(h)	Nottingham F	L	3-5	Freeman, Hodgson, Boyle (pen)	
25	Feb	8	(a)	Bristol C	D	3-3	Mosscrop, Freeman 2	11,000
26		15	(h)	Birmingham	W	3-0	Freeman 2, Lindley	2,000
27		26	(a)	Huddersfield T	L	0-1		4,500
28	Mar	1	(h)	Leeds C	D	2-2	Lindley, Riley	12,000
29		11	(a)	Grimsby T	L	0-2		
30		15	(h)	Bury	W	3-1	Freeman 2, Boyle	
31		21	(a)	Blackpool	W	2-0	Freeman, Mosscrop	
32		22	(a)	Fulham	L	2-4	Mosscrop, Freeman	25,000
33	Apr	5	(a)	Bradford	W	3-2	Freeman, Husband 2	
34		10	(a)	Preston NE	D	1-1	Hodgson	
35		12	(h)	Wolves	W	4-2	Mosscrop, Freeman, Halley (pen), Hodgson	5,000
36		19	(a)	Leicester F	W	3-2	Hodgson 2, Freeman	
37		23	(h)	Barnsley	L	0-1		
38		26	(h)	Stockport C	W	3-2	Lindley, Freeman, Hodgson	

FINAL LEAGUE POSITION: 2nd in Division Two (Promoted)

Appearances
Goals

FA Cup

Round	Month	Day	Venue	Opponent	Result	Score	Scorers	Attendance
1	Jan	15	(a)	Leeds C	W	3-2	Boyle (pen), Lindley, Freeman	13,109
2	Feb	1	(h)	Gainsborough T	W	4-1	Hodgson 2, Freeman, Boyle (pen)	
3		22	(h)	Middlesbrough	W	3-1	Freeman 2, Hodgson	27,824
4	Mar	8	(a)	Blackburn R	W	1-0	Boyle (pen)	42,778
SF		29	(n*)	Sunderland	D	0-0		
R	Apr	2	(n†)	Sunderland	L	2-3	Freeman, Boyle	

*Played at Bramall Lane, Sheffield. †Played at St Andrew's, Birmingham.

Appearances
Goals

Dawson J	Reid R	Taylor D	Bradshaw E	Boyle T	Watson W	Mosscrop E	Lindley R	Freeman B	Picken J	Mountford H	Bamford T	Swift H	Nesbitt W	Hodgson E	McLaren W	Husband W	Splitt T	Bellamy J	Drabble F	Riley R	Sewell R	Gunton S	Jones C	Halley G	Charlton T	
1	2	3	4	5	6	7	8	9	10	11																1
1	2	5			6		8	9		11	3	4	7	10												2
1	2	3			6			9		10		5	7	8	4	11										3
1	2	3		5	6			9		10		4	7	8		11										4
1	2	3		5	6		8	9		11		4	7	10												5
1	2	3		5	6		8	9		11		4	7	10												6
1	2	3		5	6		8	9		11		4	7	10												7
1	2	3		5	6	7	8	9				4		10		11										8
1	2			5	6		8	9				4		10		11	3	7								9
		3		5	6			9	10	8	2	4				11		7	1							10
		3		5	6			9	10	8	2	4				11		7	1							11
1		3			6	7		9	10	8	2	4			5	11										12
1	2	5			6		8	9	10		3				4	11		7								13
1	2				6	7	8	9			3			10	5	11		4								14
1	2				6	7	8	9			3			10	5	11		4								15
1		3			6	7	8	9			2			10	5	11		4								16
1		3		5	6	7	8	9			2			10		11		4								17
1		3		5	6	7	8	9			2			10		11		4								18
1		3		5	6	7	8	9			2			10		11		4								19
1		3		5	6	7	8	9			2			10		11		4								20
1		3		5	6	7	8	9			2			10		11		4								21
1		3		5	6	7	8	9						10	2	11		4								22
1		3		5	6		8	9				4	7		2	10				11						23
1		3		5	6		8	9			2	4	7	10						11						24
				5	6	7	8	9						10	4	11					1	2	3			25
		4			6		8	9		7	2			10	5	11					1		3			26
				5	6		8		9	7	2			10	4	11					1		3			27
		4			6		8	9			2		7	10	5					11	1		3			28
1		3		5	6		8	9		7	2			10	4	11										29
				5	6	7	8	9		11	2			10							1		3	4		30
1		3		5	6	7	8	9			2			10		11								4		31
1		3		5	6	7	8	9			2			10				4							11	32
			6			7	8	9			2			10	5	11					1		3	4		33
1		3				7	8	9						10	5	11							2	4	6	34
1		3	6			7	8	9						10	5	11							2	4		35
1		3	6			7	8	9						10		11		4					2	5		36
1		3	6			7	8	9			2			10		11		4						5		37
1			6			7	8	9			3			10	2	11		4						5		38
30	12	30	6	23	32	22	33	37	6	14	24	13	9	32	17	29	1	17	2	3	6	1	9	8	2	
		1		6	2	4	10	31	4	1		1	1	15		7		2		2				1		

Dawson J	Reid R	Taylor D	Bradshaw E	Boyle T	Watson W	Mosscrop E	Lindley R	Freeman B	Picken J	Mountford H	Bamford T	Swift H	Nesbitt W	Hodgson E	McLaren W	Husband W	Splitt T	Bellamy J	Drabble F	Riley R	Sewell R	Gunton S	Jones C	Halley G	Charlton T	
1		3		5	6	7	8	9			2			10	4	11										1
1		3		5	6	7	8	9			2			10	4	11										2
1		3		5	6		8	9		7	2			10	4	11										3
1		3		5	6	7	8	9			2			10	4	11										4
1		3		5	6	7	8	9			2			10	4	11										SF
1		3		5	6		8	9			2			10	4	11		7								R
6		6		6	6	4	6	6		1	6			6	6	6		1								
				4			1	5						3												

1913-14

Manager: John Haworth

1	Sep	1	(a)	Everton	D 1-1	Bellamy	
2		6	(a)	West Brom A	L 1-4	Freeman	27,014
3		8	(h)	Blackburn R	L 1-2	Freeman	36,000
4		13	(h)	Sheffield W	W 3-0	Hodgson, Mountford, Freeman	
5		20	(a)	Bolton W	D 0-0		
6		27	(h)	Chelsea	W 6-1	Hodgson 3, Charlton, Freeman, Halley	30,000
7	Oct	4	(a)	Oldham A	D 1-1	Boyle	20,000
8		11	(h)	Manchester U	L 1-2	Freeman	30,000
9		18	(h)	Tottenham H	W 3-1	Charlton 2, Boyle (pen)	22,000
10		25	(a)	Preston NE	L 1-2	Hodgson	
11	Nov	1	(h)	Newcastle U	W 1-0	Lindley	25,000
12		8	(a)	Liverpool	D 1-1	Freeman	18,000
13		15	(h)	Aston Villa	W 4-0	Freeman, Kelly, Lindley, Watson	20,000
14		22	(a)	Middlesbrough	L 1-2	Freeman	15,800
15		29	(h)	Sheffield U	L 0-1		
16	Dec	6	(a)	Derby C	L 1-3	Boyle (pen)	12,000
17		13	(h)	Manchester C	W 2-0	Hodgson, Lindley	20,000
18		20	(a)	Bradford C	D 1-1	Freeman	16,000
19		25	(h)	Sunderland	L 0-1		
20		26	(a)	Sunderland	D 1-1	Hodgson	
21		27	(h)	West Brom A	D 0-0		15,100
22	Jan	1	(a)	Blackburn R	D 0-0		48,000
23		3	(a)	Sheffield W	W 6-2	Lindley 2, Freeman, Hodgson, Nesbitt, Halley	
24		17	(h)	Bolton W	D 2-2	Hodgson 2	
25		24	(a)	Chelsea	D 0-0		35,000
26	Feb	7	(h)	Oldham A	W 2-0	Hodgson, Lindley	20,000
27		14	(a)	Manchester U	W 1-0	Freeman	35,000
28		23	(a)	Tottenham H	L 0-2		15,000
29		28	(h)	Preston NE	L 3-4	Mosscrop, Boyle 2 (1 pen)	
30	Mar	14	(h)	Liverpool	W 5-2	Pickering, Lindley, Boyle (pen), Mosscrop, Thorpe	16,000
31		18	(a)	Newcastle U	L 1-3	Nesbitt	15,000
32		21	(a)	Aston Villa	L 0-1		30,000
33	Apr	4	(a)	Sheffield U	L 0-5		
34		6	(h)	Middlesbrough	L 1-2	Freeman	6,000
35		10	(h)	Everton	W 2-0	Lindley, Freeman	
36		11	(h)	Derby C	W 5-1	Freeman 3, Lindley 2	18,000
37		18	(a)	Manchester C	L 1-4	Hodgson	18,000
38		27	(h)	Bradford C	D 2-2	Boyle (pen), Taylor	40,000

FINAL LEAGUE POSITION: 12th in Division One

Appearances

Goals

FA Cup

1	Jan	10	(h)	South Shields	W 3-1	Lindley 2, Freeman	
2		31	(h)	Derby C	W 3-2	Hodgson 3	30,000
3	Feb	21	(h)	Bolton W	W 3-0	Freeman, Hodgson, Halley	32,734
4	Mar	7	(a)	Sunderland	D 0-0		
R		11	(h)	Sunderland	W 2-1	Lindley, Hodgson	
SF		28	(n*)	Sheffield U	D 0-0		
R	Apr	1	(n†)	Sheffield U	W 1-0	Boyle	
F		25	(n‡)	Liverpool	W 1-0	Freeman	72,778

*Played at Old Trafford, Manchester. †Played at Goodison Park, Liverpool. ‡Played at the Crystal Palace, London.

Appearances

Goals

Dawson J	Bamford T	Taylor D	Halley G	Boyle T	Watson W	Bellamy J	Lindley R	Freeman B	Hodgson E	Husband W	Nesbitt W	Jones C	Mosscrop E	Mountford H	McLaren W	Charlton T	Thorpe L	Kelly R	Milligan G	Reid R	Pickering W	Sewell R	Tranter R	Bradshaw E	
1	2	3	4	5	6	7	8	9	10	11															1
1	2	3	4	5	6	7	8	9	10	11															2
1	2	3	4	5	6		8	9	10	11	7														3
1	2		4	5	6		8	9	10			3	7	11											4
1	2	3	4	5	6		8	9	10				7	11											5
1	2	3	4		6		8	9	10				7		5	11									6
1	2		4	5	6		8	9	10			3	7			11									7
1	2	3	4	5	6		8	9	10				7			11									8
1	2		4	5	6			9	10	11		3	7			8									9
1	2	3		5	6			9	10		11		7		4	8									10
1	2	3		5	6		8	9	10		11		7				4								11
1	2	3		5	6		8	9	10		11		7				4								12
1	2			5	6		8	9		11		3	7				4	10							13
1	2		4	5	6		8	9		11		3	7					10							14
1	2	3	4	5			8	9		11			7				6	10							15
1	2	3	4	5			8	9	10		11		7				6								16
1	2	3	4	5			8	9	10		11		7				6								17
1	2	3	4		6		8	9	10		11		7				5								18
1	2	3	4	5	6	7	8	9	10				11												19
1	2	3	4	9	6		8		10				7				5	11							20
1	2	3	4	9	6		8		10				7				5	11							21
1	2	3	4	5	6		8	9	10		7		11												22
1	2	3	4	5	6		8	9	10		7		11												23
1	2	3	4	5	6		8	9	10		7		11												24
1	2	3	4	5	6		8	9	10		7		11												25
1	2	3	4	5	6		8	9	10		7		11												26
1	2	3	4	5			8	9	10		7		11				6								27
1	2	3		5	6	11	8	9	10		7						4								28
1	2	3	4	5	6		8	9			7		11						10						29
1	2		4	5			8		10		7		11				6			3	9				30
1	2		4						10	11	7						5		8	3	9			6	31
	2		4		6					11	7						5	8		3	9	1	10		32
	2	3	4	5	6		8		10	11	7											1	9		33
	2	3	4		6		8	9			7						5	11				1	10		34
	2	3	4	5	6		8	9	10		7		11									1			35
	2	3	4	5	6		8	9	10		7		11									1			36
1	2	3	4	5	6		8		10		7		11				9								37
	2	3	4	5	11		8	9	10		7						6					1			38
32	38	30	33	33	32	4	34	31	32	10	24	5	29	2	2	5	17	7	2	3	3	6	3	1	
		1	2	7	1	1	10	16	12		2		2	1		3	1	1			1				

Dawson J	Bamford T	Taylor D	Halley G	Boyle T	Watson W	Bellamy J	Lindley R	Freeman B	Hodgson E	Husband W	Nesbitt W	Jones C	Mosscrop E	Mountford H	McLaren W	Charlton T	Thorpe L	Kelly R	Milligan G	Reid R	Pickering W	Sewell R	Tranter R	Bradshaw E	
1	2	3	4	5	6		8	9	10		7		11												1
1	2	3	4	5	6		8	9	10		7		11												2
1	2	3	4	5	6		8	9	10		7		11												3
1	2	3	4	5	6		8	9	10		7		11												4
1	2	3	4	5	6		8	9	10		7		11												R
1	2	3	4	5	6		8	9	10		7		11												SF
	2	3	4	5	6		8	9	10		7		11									1			R
	2	3	4	5	6		8	9	10		7		11									1			F
6	8	8	8	8	8		8	8	8		8		8									2			
			1	1			3	3	5																

1914-15

Manager: John Haworth

1	Sep	5	(h)	Bradford C	L	0-1		10,000
2		7	(h)	Everton	W	1-0	Thorpe	
3		12	(a)	Manchester C	L	0-1		10,000
4		19	(a)	Tottenham H	W	3-1	Freeman 2, Hodgson	25,000
5		26	(h)	Newcastle U	W	2-0	Boyle, Lindsay	15,000
6	Oct	3	(a)	Middlesbrough	D	1-1	Lindsay	15,000
7		10	(h)	Sheffield U	L	1-2	Freeman	
8		17	(a)	Aston Villa	D	3-3	Freeman 2, Lindsay	16,000
9		24	(h)	Liverpool	W	3-0	Freeman 2, Hodgson	18,000
10		31	(a)	Bradford	D	2-2	Freeman 2	
11	Nov	7	(h)	Oldham A	L	2-3	Freeman, Hodgson	
12		14	(a)	Manchester U	W	2-0	Hodgson 2	12,000
13		21	(h)	Bolton W	W	5-0	Lindley 2, Hodgson, Kelly, Boyle (pen)	
14		28	(a)	Blackburn R	L	0-6		21,700
15	Dec	5	(h)	Notts C	D	0-0		
16		12	(a)	Sunderland	L	1-2	Kelly	
17		19	(h)	Sheffield W	L	2-3	Hodgson, Lindsay	
18		25	(h)	West Brom A	L	0-2		10,000
19		26	(a)	West Brom A	L	0-3		15,853
20		28	(a)	Chelsea	W	4-1	Kelly, Hodgson, Freeman, Pickering	20,000
21	Jan	2	(a)	Bradford C	D	0-0		15,000
22		18	(h)	Manchester C	L	1-2	Hodgson	8,000
23		23	(a)	Tottenham H	W	3-1	Kelly, Hodgson, Taylor	4,000
24	Feb	6	(h)	Middlesbrough	W	4-0	Hodgson 2, Boyle, Kelly	9,000
25		13	(a)	Sheffield U	L	0-1		
26		22	(h)	Aston Villa	W	2-1	Kelly, Pickering	8,000
27		27	(a)	Liverpool	L	0-3		22,000
28	Mar	6	(h)	Bradford	W	2-0	Thorpe, Hodgson	
29		13	(a)	Bolton W	L	1-3	Hodgson	
30		20	(h)	Manchester U	W	3-0	Pickering 2, Hodgson	12,000
31	Apr	2	(a)	Everton	W	2-0	Hodgson, Kelly	
32		3	(h)	Blackburn R	W	3-2	Freeman, Hodgson, Mosscrop	14,000
33		5	(h)	Chelsea	W	2-0	Hodgson, Nesbitt	10,000
34		10	(a)	Notts C	D	0-0		
35		14	(a)	Newcastle U	W	2-1	Boyle, Kelly	6,000
36		17	(h)	Sunderland	W	2-1	Pickering, Hodgson	
37		20	(a)	Oldham A	W	2-1	Kelly 2	9,185
38		24	(a)	Sheffield W	D	0-0		

FINAL LEAGUE POSITION: 4th in Division One — Appearances / Goals

FA Cup

1	Jan	9	(h)	Huddersfield T	W	3-1	Freeman, Kelly, Thorpe	14,423
2		30	(h)	Southend U	W	6-0	Freeman 2, Kelly, Watson, Boyle (pen), Thorpe	
3	Feb	20	(a)	Bolton W	L	1-2*	Hodgson	42,932

*After extra-time — Appearances / Goals

Dawson J	Bamford T	Taylor D	Halley G	Thorpe L	Watson W	Mosscrop E	Lindley R	Freeman B	Hodgson E	Grice R	Hampson W	Lindsay J	Boyle T	Wilde J	Kelly R	Pickering W	Nesbitt W	Tranter R	Sewell R	Jones C	Brown J	Bolton W	
1	2	3	4	5	6	7	8	9	10	11													1
1	2	3	4	5			8	9	10	11	6	7											2
1	2	3	7	4	6	11	8	9	10				5										3
1	2	3	7	4	6	11	8	9	10				5										4
1	2	3	7	4	6	11		9	10			8	5										5
1	2	3	7	4	6	11		9	10			8	5										6
1	2	3	7	4	6	11		9	10			8	5										7
1	2	3		4	6	11	7	9	10			8	5										8
1	2			4	6	11	7	9	10			8	5	3									9
1	2	3		4	6	11	7	9	10			8	5										10
1	2	3		4	6	11	7	9	10			8	5										11
1	2	3		4	6	11	8		10				5		7	9							12
1	2	3		4	6	11	8		10				5		7	9							13
1	2	3	4		6	11	8	9	10				5		7								14
1	2	3		4	6	11	8	9	10				5		7								15
1	2	3		4	6			9	10		5	8			7		11						16
1	2	3	4	5	6			9	10			8			7		11						17
1	2	3		4	6	11		9				8	5		7			10					18
	2	3		4	6	11		8					5		7	9		10	1				19
	2	3		4	6	11		9	10				5		7	8			1				20
1	2	3		4	6	11		9	10				5		7	8							21
1	2	3		4	6			9	10			8	5		7		11						22
1	2	5		4	6	11		9	10						8		7			3			23
1	2			4	6	11		9	10				5		8		7			3			24
1	2			4	6	11		9	10				5		8		7			3			25
1	2	3		4				11	10				5		8	9	7				6		26
1	2	3		4	6			11	10			8	5		9		7						27
1	2	3		4	6	11		9	10				5		8		7						28
1	2		5	4	6	11		9	10						8		7			3			29
1	2	3			6	11			10		4		5		8	9	7						30
1	2	3			6	11		9	10		4		5		8		7						31
1	2	3		4	6	11		9	10				5		8		7						32
1	2	3		4	6	11		9	10				5		8		7						33
1	2	3		4	6	11		9	10				5		8		7						34
1	2	3		4	6			9	10				5		8		7					11	35
1	2	3		4	6		11		10				5		8	9	7						36
1	2	3		4	6		11		10				5		8	9	7						37
	2	3		4	6	11			10				5		8	9	7		1				38
35	38	34	10	35	36	29	14	32	36	2	4	13	32	1	27	10	19	2	3	4	1	1	
		1		2		1	2	12	19			4	4		10	5	1						

Dawson J	Bamford T	Taylor D	Halley G	Thorpe L	Watson W	Mosscrop E	Lindley R	Freeman B	Hodgson E	Grice R	Hampson W	Lindsay J	Boyle T	Wilde J	Kelly R	Pickering W	Nesbitt W	Tranter R	Sewell R	Jones C	Brown J	Bolton W	
1	2	3		4	6	11		9	10				5		7	8							1
1	2	3		4	6	11		9	10				5		8		7						2
1	2	3		4	6	11		9	10				5		8		7						3
3	3	3		3	3	3		3	3				3		3	1	2						
				2	1			3	1				1		2								

1915-16

Manager: None

1	Sep	4	(h)	Rochdale	W 6-1	Nesbitt 2, Orr, Kelly, Mosscrop, Hodgson	3,000
2		11	(a)	Preston NE	W 5-0	Freeman 2, Boyle, Kelly, Hodgson	5,000
3		18	(h)	Stockport C	D 1-1	Hodgson	4,000
4		25	(a)	Liverpool	L 2-5	Nesbitt, Hodgson	15,000
5	Oct	2	(h)	Bury	D 2-2	Boyle 2 (2 pens)	3,200
6		9	(a)	Manchester U	W 7-3	Lindley 2, Nesbitt 2, Hodgson, Mosscrop, Hampson	12,000
7		16	(h)	Blackpool	W 5-2	Nesbitt 2, Lindley, Taylor (pen), Hodgson	6,000
8		23	(a)	Southport Cen	D 1-1	Nesbitt	4,000
9		30	(h)	Oldham A	W 4-0	Hodgson 3, Lindley	5,000
10	Nov	6	(a)	Everton	W 2-1	Freeman, Hodgson	18,000
11		13	(h)	Bolton W	W 3-0	Nesbitt 2, Kelly	4,000
12		20	(a)	Manchester C	L 0-1		15,000
13		27	(h)	Stoke	W 3-2	Watson, Lindley, Hodgson	4,000
14	Dec	4	(a)	Rochdale	L 0-1		1,500
15		11	(h)	Preston NE	W 4-1	Kelly, Lindley, Nesbitt, Hodgson	1,000
16		18	(a)	Stockport C	W 2-0	Freeman, Watson	10,000
17		25	(h)	Liverpool	D 3-3	Nesbitt, Hodgson, Walmsley	15,000
18	Jan	1	(a)	Bury	L 0-3		3,000
19		8	(h)	Manchester U	W 7-4	Hodgson 3, Mosscrop 2, Nesbitt, Boyle	7,000
20		15	(a)	Blackpool	L 1-2	Nesbitt	7,000
21		22	(h)	Southport Cen	W 5-0	Boyle 2, Nesbitt 2, Lindley	5,000
22		29	(a)	Oldham A	L 1-3	Hodgson	5,000
23	Feb	5	(h)	Everton	W 2-1	Nesbitt, Mosscrop	11,000
24		12	(a)	Bolton W	L 0-3		10,000
25		19	(h)	Manchester C	W 3-1	Orr 2, Hodgson	13,000
26		26	(a)	Stoke	D 2-2	Freeman, Hodgson	

FINAL LEAGUE POSITION: 2nd in Lancashire Section (Principal Tournament, 14 clubs competed)

27	Mar	4	(h)	Bolton W	W 3-1	Hodgson, Halley, Watson (pen)	6,000
28		11	(a)	Blackpool	W 2-1	Hastie 2	5,000
29		18	(h)	Bury	L 1-2	Hastie	5,000
30		25	(h)	Southport Cen	W 6-1	Chapman 2, Lindley 3, Boyle	2,000
31	Apr	1	(a)	Preston NE	W 2-1	Boyle (pen), Lindley	5,000
32		8	(a)	Bolton W	L 0-2		4,000
33		15	(h)	Blackpool	W 2-1	Hodgson, Chapman	4,000
34		21	(a)	Preston NE	W 4-0	Kelly, Nesbitt, Hodgson, Ellis	8,000
35		22	(a)	Bury	W 5-1	Lindley, Freeman, Hodgson, Watson, Kelly	4,000
36		29	(h)	Southport Cen	W 4-2	Kelly, Thorpe, Nesbitt, Lindley	

FINAL LEAGUE POSITION: 1st in Lancashire Section (Subsidiary Tournament) Northern Group (6 clubs competed)

1	2	3	4	5	6	7	8	9	10	11	
Dawson	Bamford	Taylor	Walmsley	Boyle	Watson	Nesbitt	Kelly	Orr	Hodgson	Mosscrop	1
..	Cowell	..	..	..	..	Lindley	..	Freeman	..	Nesbitt	2
..	Bamford	..	Hampson	..	..	Nesbitt	..	..	..	Mosscrop	3
..	..	Cowell	Walmsley	..	..	..	Lindley	..	..	..	4
..	Cowell	Taylor	..	..	..	..	..	Kelly	..	..	5
..	Bamford	Cowell	..	Taylor	Hampson	Kelly	..	Nesbitt	..	..	6
..	..	Taylor	..	Hampson	Watson	..	..	..	..	..	7
..	..	..	..	..	..	Nesbitt	..	Freeman	..	..	8
..	..	..	..	Boyle	..	Freeman	..	Nesbitt	..	..	9
..	..	..	Hampson	..	..	..	..	..	..	..	10
..	..	..	Walmsley	..	..	Kelly	..	..	..	..	11
..	..	..	..	..	..	..	..	..	..	..	12
..	..	..	..	..	..	Nesbitt	..	Orr	..	..	13
..	..	..	..	..	..	..	Kelly	..	..	..	14
..	..	Cowell	..	Taylor	..	Kelly	Lindley	Nesbitt	..	..	15
..	..	Taylor	Nesbitt	Boyle	..	..	..	Freeman	..	..	16
..	..	..	Walmsley	..	Nesbitt	..	..	..	..	..	17
..	..	Clarkson	..	..	Watson	..	..	..	..	Nesbitt	18
..	..	Taylor	..	..	..	..	Percival	Nesbitt	..	Mosscrop	19
..	..	..	..	..	..	..	Lindley	..	..	Tranter	20
Hillman	..	..	..	..	..	..	..	..	..	Mosscrop	21
..	..	..	..	..	..	..	..	Mitton	..	..	22
Dawson	..	..	..	..	..	..	..	Nesbitt	..	..	23
..	..	..	..	..	..	..	..	Orr	..	..	24
..	..	..	Brown	..	..	..	..	..	..	..	25
..	..	..	..	..	..	..	..	Freeman	..	..	26

Dawson	Bamford	Taylor	Halley	Boyle	Brown	Kelly	Lindley	Watson	Hodgson	Mosscrop	27
..	..	..	Brown	..	Watson	..	..	Hastie	..	..	28
..	..	..	..	..	..	..	..	..	..	Nesbitt	29
..	..	..	Hastie	..	Brown	..	..	Chapman	..	Watson	30
..	..	..	D.Walders	..	..	..	..	Hastie	..	..	31
..	..	..	Hastie	..	..	..	..	Chapman	..	Bradshaw	32
..	..	..	Lindley	..	..	..	Hastie	..	..	Ellis	33
..	..	..	Thorpe	..	..	..	Lindley	Nesbitt	..	..	34
..	..	..	..	..	Watson	..	..	Freeman	..	..	35
..	..	Boyle	Hastie	Thorpe	Brown	..	..	Nesbitt	..	..	36

Appearances (goals scored in brackets): T.Bamford 34, T.Boyle 32 (8), E.Bradshaw 1, W.Brown 11, G.Chapman 3 (3), W.Clarkson 1, A.Cowell 5, J.Dawson 34, W.Ellis 4 (1), B.Freeman 11 (6), G.Halley 1 (1), W.Hampson 5 (1), H.Hastie 7 (3), J.Hillman 2, E.Hodgson 36 (23), R.Kelly 31 (7), R.Lindley 32 (13), J.Mitton 1, E.Mosscrop 25 (5), W.Nesbitt 25 (19), Orr 5 (3), Percival 1, D.Taylor 33 (1), L.Thorpe 3 (1), R.Tranter 1, D.Walders 1, Walmsley 21 (1), W.Watson 30 (4).

1916-17

Manager: None

1	Sep	2	(h)	Oldham A	W 3-2	Norman 2, Freeman	3,500
2		9	(a)	Preston NE	W 5-4	Kellock 3, Barber, Kelly	1,500
3		16	(a)	Blackpool	D 1-1	Kellock	4,000
4		23	(h)	Manchester U	W 7-1	Kellock 2, Hancock 2, Lindley, Halley (pen), Kelly	4,000
5		30	(a)	Liverpool	D 0-0		20,000
6	Oct	7	(h)	Stockport C	W 4-3	Kellock 2, Hodgson, Barber	1,000
7		14	(a)	Bury	W 2-1	Freeman, Kelly	
8		21	(h)	Stoke	W 4-1	Halley, Kellock 2, Lindley	3,000
9		28	(a)	Southport Cen	L 0-3		
10	Nov	4	(h)	Blackburn R	W 2-0	Lindley, Kelly	9,000
11		11	(a)	Manchester C	L 1-2	Lindley	16,000
12		18	(h)	Everton	D 2-2	Halley, Johnson	1,000
13		25	(a)	Rochdale	W 2-1	Kellock, Kelly	2,000
14	Dec	2	(h)	Bolton W	D 2-2	Mosscrop, Hodgson	2,000
15		9	(a)	Port Vale	W 6-2	Kelly 2, Johnson, Cook (pen), Boyle, Kellock	4,000
16		16	(a)	Oldham A	L 1-2	Lindley	703
17		23	(h)	Preston NE	W 3-1	Boyle 2 (1 pen), Kellock	1,000
18		30	(h)	Blackpool	W 7-0	Lindley 4, Yates, Jos Wilde 2	2,000
19	Jan	1	(a)	Blackburn R	W 4-1	Lindley, Hastie, Jos Wilde 2	2,000
20		6	(a)	Manchester U	L 1-3	Lindley	7,000
21		13	(h)	Liverpool	L 0-1		5,000
22		20	(a)	Stockport C	L 0-1		
23		27	(h)	Bury	L 3-4	Lindley 2, Kellock	1,200
24	Feb	3	(a)	Stoke	L 0-6		5,000
25		10	(h)	Southport Cen	W 7-0	Lindley 2, Hastie, Lawson, Roberts, Thomas, Lockett	1,000
26		24	(h)	Manchester C	L 0-1		4,000
27	Mar	3	(a)	Everton	L 0-5		12,000
28		10	(h)	Rochdale	W 4-3	Hancock 2, Johnson, Halley (pen)	1,000
29		17	(a)	Bolton W	L 1-3	Johnson	
30		24	(h)	Port Vale	W 1-0	Hodgson	1,000

FINAL LEAGUE POSITION: 6th in Lancashire Section (Principal Tournament, 16 clubs competed)

31	Dec	25	(h)	Blackpool	W 4-0	Kelly 2, Lindley 2	5,000
32	Mar	31	(a)	Blackburn R	L 0-4		2,000
33	Apr	6	(a)	Blackpool	W 3-2	Hodgson 2, Nesbitt	5,000
34		7	(h)	Preston NE	D 0-0		3,000
35		14	(h)	Blackburn R	W 4-1	Woodward 2, Freeman, Jos Wilde	1,500
36		21	(a)	Preston NE	W 3-2	Freeman 2, Woodward	2,000

FINAL LEAGUE POSITION: 3rd in Lancashire Section (Subsidiary Tournament, 16 clubs competed)

1	2	3	4	5	6	7	8	9	10	11	
Dawson	Jas Wilde	Hastie	Lindley	Boyle	Nesbitt	Kelly	Norman	Freeman	Hodgson	Kellock	1
Dutton	Wareing	..	..	..	D.Walders	..	..	Barber	..	..	2
Dawson	H.Wilde	..	Yates	..	Jos Wilde	..	Lindley	Nesbitt	..	..	3
..	Halley	..	..	..	Nesbitt	..	Hancock	Lindley	..	..	4
..	Jas Wilde	..	..	..	Jos Wilde	..	Lindley	Freeman	..	..	5
..	Wareing	..	..	..	..	..	Johnson	Barber	..	..	6
..	Cook	..	..	..	..	..	Lindley	Freeman	Johnson	..	7
..	Jas Wilde	..	..	..	..	..	..	Halley	Hodgson	..	8
..	..	..	..	..	..	..	..	Lord	Johnson	..	9
..	Wareing	D.Taylor	..	..	..	..	..	Freeman	Hodgson	..	10
..	Jas Wilde	Cook	Thorpe	Jos Wilde	Hastie	..	..	Johnson	Kellock	Bolton	11
..	Wareing	..	Yates	Boyle	Jos Wilde	Halley	..	Hastie	Johnson	Kellock	12
..	Jas Wilde	..	Hastie	..	..	Kelly	..	Barber	Hodgson	..	13
..	Wareing	Hastie	Yates	Freeman	Nesbitt	Glendinning	..	..	..	Mosscrop	14
Pickles	..	Cook	..	Boyle	Jos Wilde	Kelly	..	Johnson	..	Kellock	15
..	..	..	..	..	Hastie	..	..	Barber	Kellock	Nesbitt	16
Dawson	..	Hastie	..	..	Clarkson	..	..	Freeman	..	..	17
..	Williams	..	Thorpe	Thomas	Brown	Roberts	Yates	Jos Wilde	Lindley	..	18
..	Hendry	Jas Wilde	Nesbitt	Jos Wilde	Broom	Yates	Barber	Hastie	..	Kehoe	19
..	Thomas	Hastie	Yates	..	Nesbitt	Roberts	..	Hancock	..	Lockett	20
..	Wareing	..	..	Boyle	Jos Wilde	Kelly	..	Nesbitt	..	Kellock	21
..	A.Newton	..	..	..	..	..	Brown	Adamson	Johnson	..	22
..	Wareing	..	..	..	..	..	Stewart	Johnson	Lindley	..	23
Wilcox	..	Green	..	..	..	..	Lindley	Adamson	Hastie	..	24
Pickles	Hendry	Johnson	Hastie	Thomas	..	Yates	..	Lawson	Roberts	Lockett	25
..	..	Hastie	Nesbitt	Boyle	..	..	..	Freeman	..	..	26
Dawson	Jas Wilde	..	Yates	Freeman	..	Roberts	..	Adamson	Lockett	Jones	27
Wilcox	Halley	..	..	..	Nesbitt	Barber	..	Hancock	Johnson	Jos Wilde	28
..	Smelt	Jas Wilde	Hastie	Jos Wilde	Heslop	Nesbitt	..	Hibbert	..	Freeman	29
Dawson	Nesbitt	Hastie	Lindley	..	..	H.Watson	Johnson	Hancock	Hodgson	..	30

Dawson	Hastie	Clarkson	Yates	Boyle	Nesbitt	Kelly	Lindley	Freeman	Barber	Kellock	31
..	A.Newton	Duckworth	Nesbitt	Freeman	Heslop	Birch	Hastie	Hancock	Johnson	Cocker	32
..	Smelt	Jas Wilde	Thorpe	Jos Wilde	..	Hastie	Lindley	Hibbert	Hodgson	Nesbitt	33
..	..	..	Hastie	..	..	Nesbitt	..	..	..	Freeman	34
..	Jas Wilde	Hastie	Lindley	..	Johnson	Birch	Woodward	Freeman	Hibbert	Cawtherley	35
..	Cook	Jas Wilde	Roberts	Nesbitt	Hastie	Dickinson	Lindley	..	Woodward	Heslop	36

Appearances (goals scored in brackets): Adamson 3, Barber 10 (2), J.Birch 2, W.Bolton 1, T.Boyle 21 (3), Broom 1, W.Brown 2, P.Cawtherley 1, W.Clarkson 2, Cocker 1, W.Cook 7 (1), J.Dawson 28, Dickinson 1, Duckworth 1, Dutton 1, B.Freeman 16 (5), Glendinning 1, Green 1, G.Halley 4 (4), Hancock 5 (4), H.Hastie 34 (2), Hendry 3, T.Heslop 6, W.Hibbert 4, E.Hodgson 14 (5), G.Johnson 14 (4), R.Jones 1, Kehoe 1, W.Kellock 21 (14), R.Kelly 20 (9), Lawson 1 (1), R.Lindley 33 (17), Lockett 4 (1), Lord 1, E.Mosscrop 1 (1), W.Nesbitt 19 (1), A.Newton 2, Norman 2 (2), G.Pickles 4, K.Roberts 6 (1), L.Smelt 3, A.Stewart 1, D.Taylor 1, B.Thomas 3 (1), L.Thorpe 3, D.Walders 1, H.Watson 1, Wareing 11, Wilcox 3, H.Wilde 1, Jas Wilde 13, Jos Wilde 27 (5), Williams 1, F.Woodward 2 (3), J.Yates 25 (1).

1917-18

Manager: None

1	Sep	1	(a)	Rochdale	L 0-9		1,000
2		8	(h)	Rochdale	D 2-2	Hodgson, Nesbitt (pen)	1,500
3		15	(a)	Everton	L 0-9		12,000
4		22	(h)	Everton	L 0-5		1,500
5		29	(a)	Blackburn R	L 1-3	Kehoe	700
6	Oct	6	(h)	Blackburn R	W 6-1	Freeman 3, Woodward, Heslop, Woods	1,000
7		13	(a)	Port Vale	L 2-5	Freeman, Adamson	
8		20	(h)	Port Vale	D 2-2	Woodward, Edwards	
9		27	(h)	Bolton W	W 2-1	Johnson, Woodward	1,000
10	Nov	3	(a)	Bolton W	L 0-8		
11		10	(h)	Preston NE	L 1-2	Cornthwaite	
12		17	(a)	Preston NE	D 0-0		
13	Dec	8	(h)	Manchester C	L 0-4		1,000
14		15	(a)	Manchester C	L 1-4	Freeman	6,000
15		22	(h)	Manchester U	L 0-5		1,000
16		25	(h)	Blackpool	D 1-1	Booth (og)	3,000
17		29	(a)	Manchester U	L 0-1		6,000
18	Jan	5	(h)	Bury	W 5-1	Woods 2, Edwards, Whittaker, Freeman	700
19		12	(a)	Bury	L 1-2	Edwards	
20		19	(h)	Southport Cen	W 1-0	Freeman	500
21		26	(a)	Southport Cen	L 0-2		1,000
22	Feb	2	(h)	Oldham A	L 0-3		1,000
23		9	(a)	Oldham A	L 2-6	Thompson, Grundy (og)	1,130
24		16	(a)	Liverpool	L 1-7	Cross	16,000
25		23	(h)	Liverpool	L 1-3	Adamson	2,000
26	Mar	2	(a)	Stockport C	D 0-0		
27		9	(h)	Stockport C	L 0-2		2,000
28		16	(a)	Stoke	L 0-9		6,000
29		23	(h)	Stoke	L 0-2		4,000
30		29	(a)	Blackpool	L 0-1		

FINAL LEAGUE POSITION: 15th in Lancashire Section (Principal Tournament, 16 clubs competed)

31	Nov	24	(h)	Blackpool	W 3-1	Heslop 2, Freeman	500
32	Dec	1	(a)	Blackpool	L 1-5	Edwards	1,000
33	Mar	30	(a)	Preston NE	L 1-2	W.Newton	
34	Apr	6	(h)	Preston NE	D 1-1	Freeman	500
35		13	(h)	Blackburn R	W 3-0	Edwards, Woods, Riley	800
36		20	(a)	Blackburn R	L 1-2	Briggs	

FINAL LEAGUE POSITION: 11th in Lancashire Section (Subsidiary Tournament, 16 clubs competed)

1	2	3	4	5	6	7	8	9	10	11	
Ewart	Aunger	Hastie	Lindley	Johnson	Heslop	E.Woods	Edwards	Mitton	Woodward	Cawtherley	1
Wilcox	Nesbitt	..	..	Thorpe	..	..	Woodward	..	Hodgson	Kehoe	2
Kelly	Kempster	..	..	Heslop	Johnson	..	Dunn	..	Edwards	Woodward	3
Lovett	Bamford	..	Thorpe	..	..	..	Lindley	Freeman	Woodward	Nesbitt	4
Wilcox	Johnson	..	Lindley	Duxbury	Heslop	..	Ewart	Mitton	Duckworth	Kehoe	5
Quinn	Nesbitt	..	..	..	..	..	Edwards	Freeman	Woodward	Johnson	6
..	Hinton	..	..	W.Taylor	..	Wellings	Malkin	..	Adamson	Willetts	7
H.Spencer	Nesbitt	..	..	J.Spencer	..	E.Woods	Edwards	Pollitt	Woodward	Johnson	8
..	Hastie	Hampson	J.Spencer	Duxbury	..	..	Lindley	Edwards	..	..	9
..	..	..	..	..	..	..	..	..	..	Cornthwaite	10
..	Pollard	Finney	..	Halstead	..	..	..	Hastie	Robinson	..	11
Wilcox	Finney	Hastie	Lindley	Nesbitt	Pollard	..	Edwards	Woodward	Heslop	..	12
Tillotson	..	..	A.Spencer	Lindley	Heslop	..	..	Freeman	Woodward	Garnett	13
..	..	Hinton	Lindley	Heslop	Hastie	..	..	..	Adamson	Nesbitt	14
..	..	Nesbitt	..	..	..	..	..	..	Benson	Cornthwaite	15
Dawson	Hargreaves	Finney	Hastie	Freeman	Heslop	..	Lindley	Pollitt	..	Nesbitt	16
..	Finney	Hinton	..	Lindley	Jones	Nesbitt	Adamson	Freeman	Heslop	Benson	17
Tillotson	..	..	Lindley	Hobson	..	E.Woods	Edwards	..	Whittaker	Hastie	18
..	..	..	Hastie	Lindley	..	..	..	..	Heslop	Garnett	19
..	..	..	..	Hobson	..	..	Lindley	..	..	Cornthwaite	20
..	Tattersall	Finney	..	Watson	..	..	Edwards	Lindley	..	..	21
..	..	Hinton	J.Spencer	..	..	..	Lindley	Hastie	..	..	22
Henshaw	..	Hastie	Lindley	Hobson	..	..	Edwards	Adamson	Thompson	Johnson	23
Pritchard	Finney	..	..	..	..	R.Woods	..	..	Moorcroft	Cross	24
Dawson	..	..	..	..	..	E.Woods	Kelly	Freeman	Adamson	Pollard	25
Spencer	..	..	..	..	..	..	Edwards	..	..	Booth	26
..	..	..	Hobson	Boyle	..	..	..	..	Lindley	Clarkson	27
Smallwood	A.Newton	H.Newton	Lindley	Hobson	..	Chatto	E.Woods	Adamson	Jenkins	Lees	28
Hillman	Smelt	D.Taylor	Thorpe	..	..	E.Woods	Lindley	Freeman	Hodgson	O'Brien	29
Monaghan	Finney	W.Newton	Lindley	..	..	..	Edwards	A.Newton	..	..	30
Spencer	Finney	Hastie	Lindley	Jos Wilde	Marr	Brown	E.Woods	Freeman	Heslop	Cornthwaite	31
..	..	..	..	Thorpe	Heslop	E.Woods	Edwards	..	Woodward	..	32
Hayes	..	W.Newton	..	Hobson	Jones	..	..	Atkinson	G.Newton	O'Brien	33
Pollard	..	..	A.Newton	Lindley	..	..	Freeman	Pollitt	Edwards	Marr	34
..	..	..	..	..	..	..	Edwards	Riley	Adamson	F.Newton	35
..	..	..	..	..	..	Hastie	..	Briggs	F.Newton	Kehoe	36

Appearances (goals scored in brackets): Adamson 9 (2), Atkinson 1, Aunger 1, T.Bamford 1, Benson 3, Booth 1, T.Boyle 1, Briggs 1 (1), W.Brown 1, P.Cawtherley 1, Chatto 1, W.Clarkson 1, Cornthwaite 9 (1), Cross 1 (1), J.Dawson 3, Duckworth 1, Dunn 1, Duxbury 4, Edwards 23 (5), Ewart 2, W.Finney 22, B.Freeman 18 (9), Garnett 2, Halstead 1, W.Hampson 2, Hargreaves 1, H.Hastie 30, Hayes 1, Henshaw 1, T.Heslop 23 (3), J.Hillman 1, Hinton 7, Hobson 11, Hodgson 2, E.Hodgson 1 (1), Jenkins 1, G.Johnson 8 (1), R.Jones 18, Kehoe 3 (1), Kelly 1, R.Kelly 1, Kempster 1, Lees 1, R.Lindley 36, Lovatt 1, Malkin 1, Marr 2, J.Mitton 4, Moorcroft 1, Monaghan 1, W.Nesibtt 9 (1), A.Newton 5, F.Newton 2, G.Newton 1, H.Newton 1, W.Newton 5 (1), O'Brien 3, Pollard 6, Pollitt 3, Pritchard 1, Quinn 2, Riley 1 (1), Robinson 1, Smallwood 1, L.Smelt 1, A.Spencer 1, H.Spencer 8, J.Spencer 5, Tattersall 3, D.Taylor 1, W.Taylor 1, Thompson 1 (1), L.Thorpe 4, Tillotson 8, W.Watson 2, Wellings 1, Whittaker 1 (1), Wilcox 3, Jos Wilde 1, Willetts 1, E.Woods 32 (4), R.Woods 1, F.Woodward 11 (3). Own Goals 2.

1918-19

Manager: None

1	Sep	7	(h)	Everton	L 0-6		1,500
2		14	(a)	Everton	L 1-6	Freeman	
3		21	(h)	Rochdale	L 2-4	Freeman, Cliff	1,000
4		28	(a)	Rochdale	L 1-2	Grant	2,000
5	Oct	5	(h)	Blackburn R	L 0-1		1,000
6		12	(a)	Blackburn R	W 4-3	Freeman 3, Cunningham	1,500
7		19	(h)	Preston NE	L 2-5	Yates (pen), Lindley	2,000
8		26	(a)	Preston NE	L 2-4	Johnson, Cunningham	
9	Nov	2	(a)	Bolton W	L 1-2	Clarkson	5,000
10		9	(h)	Bolton W	L 0-4		1,000
11		16	(a)	Port Vale	L 2-4	Freeman, Lindley	4,000
12		23	(h)	Port Vale	W 4-1	Hodgson 3, A.Newton	4,000
13		30	(a)	Manchester C	L 1-2	Broome	9,000
14	Dec	7	(h)	Manchester C	W 2-1	Freeman, Bellamy	6,000
15		14	(a)	Oldham A	L 1-3	Freeman	3,000
16		21	(h)	Oldham A	D 2-2	Hodgson, Freeman	4,000
17		28	(a)	Liverpool	L 0-7		15,000
18	Jan	11	(a)	Bury	D 0-0		6,000
19		18	(h)	Bury	W 2-1	Freeman, Hodgson	5,500
20		25	(a)	Southport Vulcan	L 1-2	Johnson	
21	Feb	1	(h)	Southport Vulcan	W 4-0	Johnson, Brownhill, Nesbitt (pen), Kelly	6,000
22		8	(a)	Blackpool	D 1-1	Lindley	
23		15	(h)	Blackpool	W 3-0	Hodgson, Freeman, Kelly	6,283
24		22	(h)	Manchester U	W 4-2	Freeman 2, Kelly, Hodgson	10,000
25	Mar	1	(a)	Manchester U	L 0-4		8,000
26		8	(h)	Stockport C	W 4-2	Freeman 3, Hodgson	10,000
27		15	(a)	Stockport C	W 3-0	Freeman, Boyle, Kelly	
28		22	(h)	Stoke	L 1-2	Freeman	15,000
29		29	(a)	Stoke	L 1-2	Kelly	8,000
30	Apr	7	(h)	Liverpool	W 5-3	S.Taylor 2, Kelly, W.Taylor, Lindley	8,500

FINAL LEAGUE POSITION: 13th in Lancashire Section (Principal Tournament, 16 clubs competed)

31	Dec	25	(h)	Blackpool	W 5-1	Lindley 2, Hodgson 2, A.Newton	7,000
32	Apr	5	(a)	Preston NE	L 0-1		7,000
33		12	(h)	Preston NE	L 1-3	Freeman	8,000
34		18	(a)	Blackpool	D 0-0		12,000
35		19	(a)	Blackburn R	W 4-2	Kelly 2, Lindley, Boyle	4,000
36		26	(h)	Blackburn R	W 5-1	Kelly 2, Norris, Clarkson, Nesbitt	18,000

FINAL LEAGUE POSITION: 2nd in Group A, Lancashire Section (Subsidiary Tournament, 4 clubs in each group)

Note: The Subsidiary Tournament also incorporated the Lancashire Cup

1	2	3	4	5	6	7	8	9	10	11	
Greenwood	Finney	Stuttard	Lindley	Hobson	Dixon	Atkinson	A.Newton	Bradshaw	Johnson	Clarkson	1
..	..	..	..	Jas Wilde	A.Newton	Ormerod	Bertinshaw	Freeman	..	..	2
Kite	..	Marrs	..	Cliff	Dixon	Nesbitt	Ormerod	..	Bertinshaw	..	3
..	..	Wood	..	Emmott	A.Newton	Ormerod	Cunningham	..	Johnson	Grant	4
Greenwood	Ormerod	Finney	..	..	..	Grant	..	..	Ormerod	Clarkson	5
Wilcox	Finney	W.Newton	Hastie	Lindley	..	..	..	..	Cowgill	..	6
Lucas	..	..	Lindley	McLoughlin	..	Yates	..	Johnson	Bullen	Birrell	7
Greenwood	Bamford	Finney	..	Emmott	..	Ormerod	..	..	Williams	Clarkson	8
Lee	Emmot	W.Newton	..	Nestor	..	..	..	..	Floyd	..	9
..	Nesbitt	Johnson	..	Emmott	..	..	..	Freeman	Sinclair	..	10
..	..	W.Newton	Johnson	Lindley	..	..	F.Newton	..	Beech	..	11
Pearson	W.Newton	D.Taylor	Nesbitt	Brownhill	..	Bellamy	Lindley	..	Hodgson	..	12
Lee	Johnson	W.Newton	A.Newton	Lindley	Jones	Nesbitt	Lomas	..	Broome	..	13
Mellor	Whittle	..	..	W.Taylor	Nesbitt	Bellamy	McGuire	..	Lindley	..	14
..	Johnson	..	..	..	Littlefair	Kelly	Lindley	..	Nesbitt	..	15
Dawson	Nesbitt	..	Shaw	..	Jones	..	..	..	Hodgson	..	16
Mellor	Johnson	..	Lindley	..	A.Newton	Nesbitt	Barber	..	Benson	..	17
Lee	Splitt	..	Nesbitt	..	..	E.Woods	Kelly	..	..	Grant	18
H.Taylor	..	..	..	..	..	Kelly	Hodgson	..	Bibby	Clarkson	19
..	..	..	..	..	..	..	J.Spencer	..	Johnson	..	20
..	..	..	W.Brown	..	..	Nesbitt	Kelly	Brownhill	Hodgson	Johnson	21
..	..	..	..	..	..	..	Lindley	Freeman	..	..	22
Dawson	..	..	..	..	..	Kelly	..	..	..	..	23
..	..	..	Yates	..	Watson	..	..	..	..	Mosscrop	24
..	..	..	A.Newton	..	..	..	..	..	..	..	25
..	Smelt	W.Brown	W.Taylor	Boyle	..	..	..	..	..	..	26
..	..	Jas Wilde	..	..	..	..	..	..	..	..	27
..	..	D.Taylor	..	..	..	..	..	..	Smith	..	28
..	..	Jas Wilde	..	..	..	..	..	..	Hilton	..	29
..	..	..	..	..	..	Freeman	..	S.Taylor	Kelly	Clarkson	30

1	2	3	4	5	6	7	8	9	10	11	
Mallinson	Hampson	W.Newton	Nesbitt	Brownhill	A.Newton	Kelly	Lindley	Freeman	Hodgson	Clarkson	31
Dawson	Smelt	Jas Wilde	W.Brown	W.Taylor	Watson	Nesbitt	..	..	Kelly	..	32
..	..	..	W.Taylor	Boyle	..	..	..	..	..	Mosscrop	33
..	..	..	..	..	..	..	..	..	..	..	34
..	..	..	..	..	..	..	Kelly	..	Lindley	..	35
Sewell	..	Bamford	Thorpe	..	..	..	..	..	Norris	Clarkson	36

Appearances (goals scored in brackets): Atkinson 1, T.Bamford 2, Barber 1, Beech 1, Bellamy 2 (1), Benson 2, Bertinshaw 2, Bibby 1, Birrell 1, T.Boyle 9 (2), E.Bradshaw 1, Broome 1 (1), W.Brown 5, W.Brownhill 3 (1), Bullen 1, J.Clarkson 21 (2), Cliff 1 (1), Cowgill 1, Cunningham 7 (2), J.Dawson 13, Dixon 2, Emmott 5, W.Finney 8, Floyd 1, B.Freeman 31 (19), Grant 4 (1), Greenwood 4, W.Hampson 1, H.Hastie 1, Hilton 1, Hobson 1, E.Hodgson 11 (10), G.Johnson 15 (3), R.Jones 2, R.Kelly 20 (10), Kite 2, A.Lee 5, R.Lindley 31 (7), Littlefair 1, Lomas 1, Lucas 1, McGuire 1, McLoughlin 1, J.Mallinson 1, Marrs 1, W.Mellor 3, E.Mosscrop 9, W.Nesbitt 20 (2), Nestor 1, A.Newton 23 (2), F.Newton 1, W.Newton 19, P.Norris 1 (1), J.Ormerod 1, M.Ormerod 8, F.Pearson 1, W.Sewell 1, H.Shaw 1, Sinclair 1, L.Smelt 10, A.Smith 1, J.Spencer 1, T.Splitt 8, H.Stuttard 2, D.Taylor 2, H.Taylor 4, S.Taylor 1 (2), W.Taylor 21 (1), L.Thorpe 1, W.Watson 12, W.Whittle 1, Wilcox 1, Jas Wilde 8, Williams 1, Wood 1, E.Woods 1, J.Yates 2 (1).

1919-20

Manager: John Haworth

1	Aug	30	(a)	Notts C	L 0-2		13,000
2	Sep	1	(a)	Bolton W	D 1-1	Boyle	10,000
3		6	(h)	Notts C	W 2-1	Freeman, Kelly	13,000
4		8	(h)	Bradford C	D 1-1	Nesbitt	18,000
5		10	(h)	Bolton W	W 2-1	Cragg, Nesbitt	14,000
6		13	(a)	Blackburn R	W 3-2	Boyle, W.Taylor, Mosscrop	20,000
7		20	(h)	Blackburn R	W 3-1	Nesbitt, Freeman, Kelly	20,000
8		27	(a)	Chelsea	W 1-0	Kelly	35,000
9	Oct	4	(h)	Chelsea	L 2-3	W.Taylor, Freeman	20,000
10		11	(h)	Sheffield U	D 2-2	Freeman, Boyle	16,000
11		18	(a)	Sheffield U	W 3-1	Kelly, Freeman, Lindsay	25,000
12		25	(h)	Liverpool	L 1-2	Lindsay	14,000
13	Nov	1	(a)	Liverpool	W 1-0	Freeman	30,000
14		8	(h)	Manchester U	W 2-1	Watson, Cragg	18,000
15		15	(a)	Manchester U	W 1-0	Nesbitt	25,000
16		22	(h)	Bradford	L 2-6	Lindsay, Cragg	14,000
17		29	(a)	Bradford	W 1-0	Nesbitt	15,000
18	Dec	6	(a)	Oldham A	L 0-1		7,000
19		13	(h)	Oldham A	W 2-1	Boyle, Nesbitt	12,500
20		20	(a)	Preston NE	W 1-0	Cragg	10,000
21		25	(h)	Middlesbrough	W 5-3	Lindsay 2, Mosscrop 2, Twiss	25,000
22		26	(a)	Newcastle U	D 0-0		50,000
23		27	(h)	Preston NE	D 1-1	Freeman	20,000
24	Jan	1	(a)	Middlesbrough	L 0-4		25,000
25		3	(a)	Aston Villa	D 2-2	Kelly, Cragg	30,000
26		17	(h)	Aston Villa	D 0-0		29,500
27		24	(a)	Sheffield W	L 1-3	Lindley	20,000
28	Feb	7	(a)	Manchester C	L 1-3	Freeman	30,000
29		14	(h)	Manchester C	W 2-0	Kelly, Watson	20,000
30		17	(h)	Sheffield W	W 2-0	Watson 2	15,000
31		21	(a)	Derby C	W 2-0	Kelly, Freeman	12,000
32		28	(h)	Derby C	W 2-0	Bassnett, Freeman	18,000
33	Mar	6	(h)	West Brom A	D 2-2	Freeman, Boyle	30,000
34		13	(a)	West Brom A	L 1-4	Mosscrop	30,000
35		20	(h)	Sunderland	W 2-1	Freeman, Lindsay	27,500
36		27	(a)	Sunderland	L 0-3		30,000
37	Apr	2	(h)	Newcastle U	W 1-0	Kelly	30,000
38		3	(h)	Arsenal	W 2-1	Anderson, Weaver	20,000
39		10	(a)	Arsenal	L 0-2		40,000
40		17	(h)	Everton	W 5-0	Anderson 3, Watson, Kelly	25,000
41		24	(a)	Everton	D 2-2	Weaver, Anderson	35,000
42	May	1	(a)	Bradford C	L 1-2	Anderson	25,000

FINAL LEAGUE POSITION: 2nd in Division One — Appearances / Goals

FA Cup

1	Jan	10	(a*)	Thorneycrofts	D 0-0		14,261
R		13	(h)	Thorneycrofts	W 5-0	Lindsay 3, Nesbitt, Cragg	19,000
2		31	(h)	Sunderland	D 1-1	Kelly	33,222
R	Feb	4	(a)	Sunderland	L 0-2		44,618

*Played at Fratton Park, Portsmouth. — Appearances / Goals

Dawson J	Smelt L	Jones C	Taylor W	Boyle T	Watson W	Kelly R	Lindsay J	Freeman B	Norris P	Mosscrop E	Nesbitt W	Cragg R	Clarkson W	Thorpe L	Hastie H	Lindley R	Halley G	Thompson G	Sewell R	Twiss J	Roberts L	Gallacher W	Bassnett A	Jackson T	Anderson J	Weaver W	Taylor D	
1	2	3	4	5	6	7	8	9	10	11																		1
1	2	3	4	5	6	7	8	9	10	11																		2
1	2	3	4	5	6	8	10	9		11	7																	3
1	2	3	4	5	6	8		9			7	10	11															4
1	2	3	5		6	8		9			7	10	11	4														5
1	2	3	9	5	6	8	10			11	7			4														6
1	2	3		5	6	8	10	9		11	7			4														7
1	2	3	5		6	8	10	9		11	7			4														8
1	2	3	5		6	8	10	9		11	7			4														9
1	2			5	6	8	10	9		11	7			4	3													10
1	2	3	6	5		7	10	9		11				4		8												11
1	2	3		5		7	10	9		11				4		8	6											12
1	2	3			6		10	9		11	7	8		4				5										13
1	2	3			6	7	10			11	9	8		4				5										14
1	2	3			6	7	10			11	9	8		4				5										15
1	2	3			6	7	10	9			11	8		4				5										16
1	2	3		5	6	7	10			11	9	8					4											17
1	2	3		5	6	7	10			11	9	8		4														18
1	2			5	6	7	10			11	9	8			3		4											19
	2			5	6	7	10			11	9	8			3		4		1									20
	2			5	6	7	10			11		8			3		4		1	9								21
	2			5	6	7	10			11		8			3		4		1	9								22
	2			5	6	7	10	9		11		8			3		4		1									23
	2			5	6	7	10			11		8			3		4		1	9								24
	2			5	6	7	10	9			11	8		4			3		1									25
	2			5	6	7	10			11	9			4		8	3		1									26
	2			5	6	7	10			11	9			4		8	3		1									27
1	2		5		6	10		9		11	7			4		8	3											28
1	2				6	8				11	7			4			3	5			9	10						29
1	2		5		6	8				11	7			4			3			9		10						30
1	2		5		6	8		9		11	7			4			3					10						31
1	2		6	5		8		9		11	7						3					10	4					32
1	2			5	6	8		9		11	7						3						4	10				33
1	2	3		5	6	8		9		11	7					10	4											34
1	2			5	6		10	8		11	7						3						4		9			35
1	2			5	6		10	8			7						3						4		9	11		36
1	2		5		6	8		10			7						3						4		9	11		37
1	2		5		6	8	10	7									3						4		9	11		38
1	2			5	6		10	8			7						4								9	11	3	39
1	2			5	6	8	10	7									4								9	11	3	40
1	2			5	6	8	10	7									4								9	11	3	41
1	2	3		5	6	8	10	7									4								9	11		42
34	42	19	15	29	39	38	32	28	2	31	30	15	2	20	7	6	26	5	8	4	1	4	6	1	8	7	3	
			2	5	5	9	6	12		4	6	5				1				1			1		6	2		

Dawson J	Smelt L	Jones C	Taylor W	Boyle T	Watson W	Kelly R	Lindsay J	Freeman B	Norris P	Mosscrop E	Nesbitt W	Cragg R	Clarkson W	Thorpe L	Hastie H	Lindley R	Halley G	Thompson G	Sewell R	Twiss J	Roberts L	Gallacher W	Bassnett A	Jackson T	Anderson J	Weaver W	Taylor D	
	2			5	6	7	10	9			11	8		4			3		1									1
	2			5	6	7	10	9			11	8		4			3		1									R
1	2		5		6	8	10	9		11	7			4			3											2
1	2		5		6	8	10	9		11	7			4			3											R
2	4		2	2	4	4	4	4		2	4	2		4			4		2									
						1	3				1	1																

1920-21

Manager: John Haworth

1	Aug	28	(h)	Bradford C	L 1-4	Anderson	30,000
2		30	(a)	Huddersfield T	L 0-1		22,500
3	Sep	4	(a)	Bradford C	L 0-2		26,000
4		6	(h)	Huddersfield T	W 3-0	Boyle, Nesbitt, Kelly	30,000
5		11	(h)	Middlesbrough	W 2-1	Anderson, Cross	28,000
6		18	(a)	Middlesbrough	D 0-0		30,000
7		25	(h)	Chelsea	W 4-0	Cross, Nesbitt, Boyle, Kelly	30,000
8	Oct	2	(a)	Chelsea	D 1-1	Anderson	45,000
9		9	(a)	Bradford	W 3-1	Kelly 2, Opp own-goal	24,000
10		16	(h)	Bradford	W 1-0	Anderson	25,000
11		23	(a)	Tottenham H	W 2-1	Anderson 2	45,000
12		30	(h)	Tottenham H	W 2-0	Cross, Kelly	35,830
13	Nov	6	(a)	Newcastle U	W 2-1	Boyle, Kelly	50,000
14		13	(h)	Newcastle U	W 3-1	Kelly, Boyle, Cross	38,860
15		20	(a)	Oldham A	D 2-2	Weaver, Anderson	19,273
16		27	(h)	Oldham A	W 7-1	Kelly 4, Cross 2, Boyle	22,569
17	Dec	4	(a)	Liverpool	D 0-0		37,500
18		11	(h)	Liverpool	W 1-0	Weaver	35,860
19		18	(h)	Preston NE	W 2-0	Anderson 2	
20		25	(h)	Sheffield U	W 6-0	Anderson 4, Kelly, Cross	35,912
21		27	(a)	Sheffield U	D 1-1	Kelly	50,000
22	Jan	1	(a)	Preston NE	W 3-0	Cross, Anderson, Kelly	32,000
23		15	(h)	Blackburn R	W 4-1	Cross 2, Kelly, Boyle	41,534
24		22	(a)	Blackburn R	W 3-1	Kelly, Anderson, Mosscrop	43,000
25	Feb	5	(h)	Aston Villa	W 7-1	Anderson 5, Lindsay, Watson	40,000
26		9	(a)	Aston Villa	D 0-0		40,000
27		12	(h)	Derby C	W 2-1	Lindsay, Anderson	30,000
28		23	(a)	Derby C	D 0-0		17,000
29		26	(h)	Bolton W	W 3-1	Kelly, Cross, Nesbitt	42,653
30	Mar	5	(a)	Bolton W	D 1-1	Anderson	57,000
31		12	(h)	Arsenal	W 1-0	Watson	30,000
32		19	(a)	Arsenal	D 1-1	Anderson	45,000
33		25	(h)	Manchester U	W 1-0	Cross	40,000
34		26	(a)	Manchester C	L 0-3		42,000
35		28	(a)	Manchester U	W 3-0	Boyle, Kelly, Anderson	30,000
36	Apr	2	(h)	Manchester C	W 2-1	Nesbitt, Anderson	37,000
37		9	(a)	West Brom A	L 0-2		16,000
38		16	(h)	West Brom A	D 1-1	Kelly	26,422
39		23	(a)	Everton	D 1-1	Cross	40,000
40		30	(h)	Everton	D 1-1	Cross	22,066
41	May	2	(a)	Sunderland	L 0-1		20,000
42		7	(h)	Sunderland	D 2-2	Kelly, Nesbitt	22,000

FINAL LEAGUE POSITION: 1st in Division One

Appearances
Goals

FA Cup

1	Jan	8	(a)	Leicester C	W 7-3	Anderson 4, Kelly, Cross, Opp own-goal	29,149
2		29	(h)	Queen's Park R	W 4-2	Kelly 2, Anderson 2	41,007
3	Feb	19	(a)	Hull C	L 0-3		30,000

Appearances
Goals

Dawson J	Smelt L	Taylor D	Halley G	Boyle T	Watson W	Freeman B	Kelly R	Anderson J	Lindsay J	Mosscrop E	Birchenough F	Taylor W	Weaver W	Nesbitt W	Cross B	McGrory R	Jones C	Brophy T	Bassnett A	Douglas G	Lane J	Moorwood L	
1	2	3	4	5	6	7	8	9	10	11													1
	2	3	4		6	7	8	9	10		1	5	11										2
	2	3	4		6	8		9	10		1	5	11	7									3
1	2	3	4	5	6		8	9					11	7	10								4
1	2	3	4	5	6		8	9					11	7	10								5
1	2	3	4	5	6		8	9					11	7	10								6
1	2	3	4	5	6		8	9					11	7	10								7
1		3	4	5	6		8	9					11	7	10	2							8
1		3	4	5	6		8	9					11	7	10	2							9
1			4	5	6		8	9					11	7	10	2	3						10
1	2	3	4	5	6			9	10				11	7	8								11
1	2		4	5	6		8	9					11	7	10		3						12
1	2		4	5	6		8	9					11	7	10		3						13
1	2		4	5	6		8	9					11	7	10		3						14
1	2		4	5	6		8	9					11	7	10		3						15
1	2		4	5	6		8	9					11	7	10		3						16
1	2		4	5	6		8	9					11	7	10		3						17
1	2		4	5	6		8	9					11	7	10		3						18
1	2		4	5	6		8	9					11	7	10		3						19
1	2		4	5	6		8	9					11	7	10		3						20
1	2		4	5	6		8	9					11	7	10		3						21
1	2		4	5	6		8	9					11	7	10		3						22
1	2		4	5	6		8	9					11	7	10		3						23
1	2		4	5	6		8	9		11				7	10		3						24
1	2		4		6		8	9	10	11				7			3	5					25
1	2		4	5	6		8	9	10	11				7			3						26
1	2			5	6			9	8	11				7	10		3	4					27
1	2			5	6		8						11	7	10		3		4	9			28
1	2			5	6		8	9					11	7	10		3		4				29
1	2			5	6		8	9					11	7	10		3		4				30
1	2			5	6			9	8				11	7	10		3		4				31
1	2				6		8	9		11				7	10		3	5	4				32
1	2			5	6		8	9		11				7	10		3		4				33
1	2			5	6		8	9		11				7	10		3		4				34
1	2			5	6		8	9		11				7	10		3		4				35
1	2			5	6		8	9		11				7	10		3		4				36
1	2			5	6			9						7	10		3		4	11	8		37
1	2			5	6		8	9		11				7	10		3		4				38
1	2			5	6		8	9		11				7	10		3		4				39
1	2			5	6		8	9		11				7	10		3		4				40
1	2			5	6		8	9					11	7	10		3		4				41
	2	3		5	6		8	9		11				7	10				4			1	42
39	39	11	26	38	42	3	37	41	8	14	2	2	27	40	37	3	31	3	15	2	1	1	
				7	2		20	25	2	1			2	5	14								

1 own-goal

Dawson J	Smelt L	Taylor D	Halley G	Boyle T	Watson W	Freeman B	Kelly R	Anderson J	Lindsay J	Mosscrop E	Birchenough F	Taylor W	Weaver W	Nesbitt W	Cross B	McGrory R	Jones C	Brophy T	Bassnett A	Douglas G	Lane J	Moorwood L	
1	2		4	5	6		8	9					11	7	10		3						1
1	2		4	5	6		8	9		11				7	10		3						2
1	2			5	6	9	8			7			11	4	10		3						3
3	3		2	3	3	1	3	2		2			2	3	3		3						
							3	6							1								

1 own-goal

1921-22

Manager: John Haworth

1	Aug	27	(a)	Birmingham	W 3-2	Boyle, Anderson, Mosscrop	50,000
2		31	(a)	Sunderland	L 2-3	Anderson, Kelly	35,000
3	Sep	3	(h)	Birmingham	W 3-1	Anderson, Watson, Boyle	27,000
4		5	(h)	Sunderland	W 2-0	Kelly, Cross	31,000
5		10	(h)	Newcastle U	W 2-0	Anderson 2	28,016
6		17	(a)	Newcastle U	L 1-2	Cross	45,000
7		24	(h)	Bradford C	W 4-0	Boyle, Mosscrop, Anderson, Kelly	35,000
8	Oct	1	(a)	Bradford C	W 4-0	Cross 2, Anderson, Kelly	30,000
9		8	(h)	Sheffield U	W 2-1	Cross, Kelly	25,000
10		15	(a)	Sheffield U	W 1-0	Kelly	35,000
11		22	(h)	Chelsea	W 5-0	Anderson 2, Cross 2, Kelly	10,000
12		29	(a)	Chelsea	L 1-4	Anderson	50,000
13	Nov	5	(h)	Preston NE	D 3-3	Anderson 2, Cross	30,000
14		12	(a)	Preston NE	L 1-2	Cross	34,144
15		19	(a)	Tottenham H	D 1-1	Anderson	45,000
16		26	(h)	Tottenham H	W 1-0	Kelly	29,308
17	Dec	3	(a)	Huddersfield T	L 0-1		26,000
18		10	(h)	Huddersfield T	W 1-0	Nesbitt	25,297
19		17	(a)	Middlesbrough	L 1-4	Weaver	20,000
20		24	(h)	Middlesbrough	W 3-1	Kelly 3	25,000
21		26	(a)	Manchester U	W 1-0	Lindsay	50,000
22		27	(h)	Manchester U	W 4-2	Mosscrop 2, Kelly, Lindsay	25,000
23		31	(h)	Aston Villa	W 2-1	Mosscrop, Watson	30,000
24	Jan	14	(a)	Aston Villa	L 0-2		40,000
25		21	(a)	Arsenal	D 0-0		25,000
26	Feb	4	(a)	Blackburn R	L 2-3	Anderson 2	20,000
27		11	(h)	Blackburn R	L 1-2	Anderson	40,919
28		18	(a)	Bolton W	W 1-0	Anderson	
29		20	(h)	Arsenal	W 1-0	Kelly	16,000
30		25	(h)	Bolton W	W 2-0	Lindsay, Halley	29,412
31	Mar	4	(a)	Oldham A	W 1-0	Kelly	17,436
32		11	(h)	Oldham A	L 0-1		20,438
33		18	(h)	Cardiff C	D 1-1	Anderson	30,000
34		25	(a)	Cardiff C	L 2-4	Bassnett, Mosscrop	
35	Apr	1	(a)	West Brom A	L 0-2		15,000
36		8	(h)	West Brom A	W 4-2	Richardson 3, Anderson	12,000
37		14	(h)	Liverpool	D 1-1	Anderson	30,000
38		15	(h)	Manchester C	W 5-2	Kelly, Fisher, Richardson, Mosscrop, Opp own-goal	16,000
39		17	(a)	Liverpool	L 1-2	Richardson	50,000
40		22	(a)	Manchester C	L 0-2		25,000
41		29	(h)	Everton	W 2-0	Fisher, Kelly	
42	May	6	(a)	Everton	L 0-2		

FINAL LEAGUE POSITION: 3rd in Division One

Appearances
Goals

FA Cup

1	Jan	7	(h)	Huddersfield T	D 2-2	Anderson, Mosscrop	39,103
R		11	(a)	Huddersfield T	L 2-3	Kelly, Boyle	35,355

Appearances
Goals

Dawson J	Smelt L	Jones C	Halley G	Boyle T	Watson W	Nesbitt W	Kelly R	Anderson J	Cross B	Mosscrop E	Weaver W	Morgan W	Moorwood L	Bassnett A	Taylor D	Lindsay J	Lane J	Astin J	Dobinson H	Douglas G	Emerson W	Fisher J	Richardson G	
1	2	3	4	5	6	7	8	9	10	11														1
1	2	3	4	5	6	7	8	9	10		11													2
1	2	3	4	5	6	7	8	9	10	11														3
1	2	3	4	5	6	7	8	9	10	11														4
1	2	3	4	5	6	7	8	9	10	11														5
1	2	3	4	5	6	7	8	9	10	11														6
1	2	3	4	5	6	7	8	9	10	11														7
	2	3	4	5		7	8	9	10	11		6	1											8
1	2	3	4	5	6	7	8	9	10	11														9
1	2	3	4	5	6	7	8	9	10	11														10
	2	3	4	5	6	7	8	9	10	11			1											11
1	2	3	4	5		7	8	9	10	11		6												12
1	2	3	4		6	7	8	9	10	11				5										13
1	2	3	4		6	7	8	9	10	11				5										14
1	2		4			7	8	9		11		6		5	3	10								15
1	2		4	5	6	7	8	9		11					3		10							16
1	2		4	5	6	7	8	9	10	11					3									17
1			4	5	6	7	8	9	10		11				3			2						18
1	2		4	5	6	7	8	9	10		11				3									19
1	2		4	5	6	7	8	9		11					3	10								20
1	2		4	5	6	7	8	9		11					3	10								21
1	2		4	5	6	7	8	9		11					3	10								22
1	2		4	5	6	7	8	9		11					3	10								23
1	2			5	6	7	8			11				4	3	10			9					24
1	2			5	6	7	8			11				4	3	10			9					25
1	2			5	6	7	8	9	10	11				4	3									26
1	2		4	5	6	7	8	9	10		11				3									27
1	2		4	5		7	8	9	10	11				6				3						28
1	2		4	5		7	8	9	10		11			6				3						29
1	2		4				8	9		11		6		5		10		3		7				30
1	2		4				8	9		11		6		5		10		3		7				31
1	2		4				8	9		11		6		5		10		3		7				32
	2		4					9	10	11			1	5			8	3			6	7		33
1	2		4				8	9	10	11				5				3			6	7		34
	2		4		6		8		10	11			1	5				3				7	9	35
	2				6			10		11			1	5		8		3			4	7	9	36
1	2				6		8	10		11				5				3			4	7	9	37
1	2		4				8	10		11				5				3			6	7	9	38
1	2				6		8	10			11			5				3			4	7	9	39
1	2				6		8		10		11			5	3						4	7	9	40
1	2				6		8			11				5	3	10					4	7	9	41
1	2		3		6		8			11				5		10					4	7	9	42
37	41	14	34	26	31	29	40	36	25	35	7	6	5	21	15	13	2	13	2	3	9	10	8	
			1	3	2	1	16	20	9	7	1			1		3						2	5	

1 own-goal

Dawson J	Smelt L	Jones C	Halley G	Boyle T	Watson W	Nesbitt W	Kelly R	Anderson J	Cross B	Mosscrop E	Weaver W	Morgan W	Moorwood L	Bassnett A	Taylor D	Lindsay J	Lane J	Astin J	Dobinson H	Douglas G	Emerson W	Fisher J	Richardson G	
1	2		4	5	6	7	8	9		11					3	10								1
1	2		4	5	6	7	8		9	11					3	10								R
2	2		2	2	2	2	2	1	1	2					2	2								
				1			1	1		1														

1922-23

Manager: John Haworth

1	Aug	26	(h)	West Brom A	W 3-0	Cross 2, Kelly	24,472
2		28	(a)	Arsenal	D 1-1	Taylor	25,000
3	Sep	2	(a)	West Brom A	L 1-2	Anderson	23,561
4		4	(h)	Arsenal	W 4-1	Anderson 2, Kelly, Opp own-goal	20,000
5		9	(a)	Tottenham H	W 3-1	Kelly, Watson, Cross	40,000
6		16	(h)	Tottenham H	L 0-1		24,586
7		23	(a)	Liverpool	L 0-3		40,000
8		30	(h)	Liverpool	W 2-0	Cross, Weaver	35,000
9	Oct	7	(a)	Newcastle U	W 2-0	Kelly 2	35,000
10		14	(h)	Newcastle U	D 0-0		25,000
11		21	(h)	Blackburn R	W 3-1	Kelly 2, Cross	29,000
12		28	(a)	Blackburn R	L 1-2	Anderson	23,000
13	Nov	4	(h)	Nottingham F	W 8-2	Cross 3, Kelly 2, Weaver, Watson 2	
14		11	(a)	Nottingham F	L 0-1		20,000
15		18	(h)	Chelsea	W 1-0	Kelly	17,000
16		25	(a)	Chelsea	W 1-0	Anderson	25,000
17	Dec	2	(a)	Middlesbrough	L 1-4	Kelly	25,000
18		9	(h)	Middlesbrough	W 3-0	Kelly, Cross, Weaver	15,000
19		16	(h)	Oldham A	D 1-1	Weaver	12,000
20		23	(a)	Oldham A	D 1-1	Cross	9,162
21		25	(h)	Aston Villa	D 1-1	Watson	27,000
22		26	(a)	Aston Villa	L 1-3	Cross	40,000
23		30	(a)	Sheffield U	L 1-2	Anderson	20,000
24	Jan	6	(h)	Sheffield U	L 1-4	Bassnett	
25		20	(h)	Preston NE	W 2-0	Anderson, Bassnett	16,033
26		27	(a)	Preston NE	L 1-3	Weaver	
27	Feb	10	(a)	Bolton W	L 1-2	Kelly	
28		17	(h)	Manchester C	W 2-0	Lindsay, Weaver	14,000
29		24	(a)	Manchester C	L 0-1		22,000
30	Mar	3	(h)	Stoke	W 3-2	Weaver, Cross, Fisher	
31		10	(a)	Stoke	W 1-0	Kelly	20,000
32		12	(h)	Bolton W	W 2-1	Nesbitt, Anderson	
33		17	(a)	Huddersfield T	L 0-2		14,000
34		24	(h)	Huddersfield T	L 0-2		9,100
35		30	(h)	Cardiff C	L 1-5	Kelly	20,000
36		31	(a)	Everton	L 0-1		25,000
37	Apr	2	(a)	Cardiff C	D 2-2	Lindsay, Kelly	30,000
38		7	(h)	Everton	L 0-1		
39		14	(a)	Sunderland	L 1-3	Lindsay	
40		21	(h)	Sunderland	W 2-0	Kelly, Freeman	12,000
41		28	(a)	Birmingham	L 0-1		19,400
42	May	5	(h)	Birmingham	L 0-2		8,000

FINAL LEAGUE POSITION: 15th in Division One

Appearances
Goals

FA Cup

1	Jan	13	(a)	Sunderland	L 1-3	Anderson	40,000

Appearances
Goals

Dawson J	Smelt L	Taylor D	Emerson W	Sims S	Watson W	Fisher J	Kelly R	Anderson J	Cross B	Mosscrop E	Bassnett A	Weaver W	Gee H	Richardson G	Nesbitt W	Chambers R	Pearson J	Lindsay J	Moorwood L	Morgan W	Lane J	Freeman A	Waller W	Evans J	Greenhalgh J	Beel G	
1	2	3	4	5	6	7	8	9	10	11																	1
1	2	3	4	5	6	7	8	9	10	11																	2
1	2	3	4		6	7	8	9	10	11	5																3
1	2	3	4		6	7	8	9	10	11	5																4
1	2	3	4		6	7	8	9	10	11	5																5
1	2	3	4		6	7	8	9	10	11	5																6
1	2	3	6	5		7	8	9	10	11	4																7
1	2	3	4		6		8	9	10	11	5	7															8
1	2	3	4		6		8	9	10	11	5	7															9
1	2	3	4		6		8	9	10	11	5	7															10
1	2	3			6		8	9	10	11	5	7	4														11
1	2	3	4		6		8	9	10	11	5	7															12
1	2	3	4		6		8	9	10	11	5	7															13
1	2	3	4		6		8	9	10	11	5	7															14
1	2	3	4		6	7	8		10	11	5			9													15
1	2	3	4		6	7	8	9	10	11	5																16
1	2	3			6	7	8	9	10		5	11	4														17
1	2	3			6	7	8	9	10		5	11	4														18
1	2	3			6	7	8	9	10		5	11	4														19
1	2	3	4		6	7	8	9	10		5	11															20
1	2	3	4		6		8		10		5	11			7	9											21
1	2	3	4		6		8		10		5	11			7	9											22
1	2	3	4		6	7	8	9	10		5	11															23
1	2	3	4		6	7	8	9	10		5	11															24
1	2			5	6	7	8	9	10		4	11					3										25
1	2	3		5	6	7	8	9	10		4	11															26
1	2	3	4	5	6	7	8	9	10			11															27
1	2	3	6	5	4	7	8		9			11						10									28
1	2	3	6	5	4	7	8		9			11						10									29
	2	3		5	6	7	8		10			11	4			9			1								30
	2	3	4		6		8	9	10		5	11			7				1								31
	2	3	4		6		8	9	10		5	11			7				1								32
	2	3	4		6		8		10		5	11			7	9			1								33
	2	3	4		6		8	9	10		5	11			7				1								34
1	2	3	4		6		7	9	10		5	11						8									35
	2	3	4				9		10		5	11			7			8	1	6							36
	2	3			4		9		10		5	11			7			8	1	6							37
	2	3	4			7	9		10		5	11						8	1	6							38
	2	3			4				10		5	11						8	1	6	7	9					39
	2	3	6		4		8		10		5	11							1		7	9					40
	2	3	6		4				10		5	11						8	1			9	7				41
	2		6		4		8		10		5	11							1					3	7	9	42
30	42	40	33	9	39	22	40	28	42	16	36	33	5	1	8	4	1	8	12	4	2	3	1	1	1	1	
		1			4	1	17	8	12		2	7			1			3				1					

1 own-goal

Dawson J	Smelt L	Taylor D	Emerson W	Sims S	Watson W	Fisher J	Kelly R	Anderson J	Cross B	Mosscrop E	Bassnett A	Weaver W	Gee H	Richardson G	Nesbitt W	Chambers R	Pearson J	Lindsay J	Moorwood L	Morgan W	Lane J	Freeman A	Waller W	Evans J	Greenhalgh J	Beel G	
1	2	3	4		6	7	8	9	10		5	11															1
1	1	1	1		1	1	1	1	1		1	1															
								1																			

1923-24

Manager: John Haworth

1	Aug	25	(a)	Notts C	L 1-2	Beel	18,000
2		27	(h)	Everton	D 2-2	Hill, Bennie	16,000
3	Sep	1	(h)	Notts C	D 1-1	Beel	17,000
4		3	(a)	Everton	D 3-3	Anderson 2, Kelly	25,000
5		8	(h)	Nottingham F	L 2-4	Freeman, Anderson	
6		15	(a)	Nottingham F	D 0-0		20,000
7		22	(h)	Liverpool	W 2-0	Anderson 2	17,765
8		29	(a)	Liverpool	L 0-1		40,000
9	Oct	6	(h)	Aston Villa	L 1-2	Cross	17,000
10		13	(a)	Aston Villa	D 1-1	Opp own-goal	20,000
11		20	(a)	Sheffield U	L 1-2	Bennie	15,000
12		27	(h)	Sheffield U	W 2-0	Kelly, Cross	12,000
13	Nov	3	(a)	Blackburn R	D 1-1	Kelly	20,000
14		10	(h)	Blackburn R	L 1-2	Beel	30,000
15		17	(h)	West Ham U	W 5-1	Beel 3, Bennie 2	9,000
16		24	(a)	West Ham U	D 0-0		20,000
17	Dec	1	(h)	Newcastle U	W 3-2	Beel 2, Opp own-goal	8,000
18		8	(a)	Newcastle U	L 0-2		25,000
19		15	(h)	Chelsea	W 2-0	Bennie 2	15,000
20		22	(a)	Chelsea	L 2-3	Beel 2	17,500
21		25	(h)	Middlesbrough	D 0-0		25,000
22		26	(a)	Middlesbrough	L 0-3		20,000
23		29	(h)	Preston NE	W 1-0	Beel	12,000
24	Jan	5	(a)	Preston NE	L 0-5		15,000
25		19	(a)	West Brom A	W 3-0	Hill, Beel, Cross	8,527
26		26	(h)	West Brom A	W 4-0	Weaver 2, Beel, Bennie	15,000
27	Feb	9	(h)	Birmingham	L 1-2	Kelly	10,000
28		16	(a)	Manchester C	D 2-2	Beel 2	25,000
29		27	(a)	Birmingham	L 1-2	Kelly	14,500
30	Mar	1	(a)	Bolton W	D 0-0		10,000
31		15	(h)	Sunderland	L 0-3		14,000
32		17	(h)	Manchester C	W 3-2	Beel 2, Cross	12,000
33		22	(a)	Sunderland	W 1-0	Beel	30,000
34	Apr	1	(h)	Bolton W	W 1-0	Taylor	
35		5	(a)	Arsenal	L 0-2		25,000
36		12	(a)	Cardiff C	L 0-2		
37		18	(h)	Huddersfield T	D 1-1	Waterfield	25,000
38		19	(h)	Cardiff C	L 1-2	Kelly	
39		22	(a)	Huddersfield T	L 0-1		33,000
40		26	(h)	Tottenham H	D 2-2	Kelly, Cross	50,000
41		28	(h)	Arsenal	W 4-1	Freeman 2, Beel, Kelly	9,000
42	May	3	(a)	Tottenham H	L 0-1		20,000

FINAL LEAGUE POSITION: 17th in Division One

Appearances
Goals

FA Cup

1	Jan	12	(h)	South Shields	W 3-2	Kelly 2, Cross	20,606
2	Feb	2	(h)	Fulham	D 0-0		23,601
R		7	(a)	Fulham	W 1-0*	Cross	31,000
3		23	(h)	Huddersfield T	W 1-0	Weaver	54,775
4	Mar	8	(a)	Swindon T	D 1-1	Weaver	22,210
R		12	(h)	Swindon T	W 3-1	Beel 2, Weaver	34,089
SF		29	(n†)	Aston Villa	L 0-3		54,531

*After extra-time. †Played at Bramall Lane, Sheffield.

Appearances
Goals

Dawson J	Smelt L	Taylor D	Watson W	Hill J	Emerson W	Bennie P	Kelly R	Beel G	Cross B	Weaver W	Morgan W	Evans J	Anderson J	Freeman A	Bassnett A	O'Beirne J	Gillatt E	Waterfield G	Sims S	Page S	Robinson J	Parkin G	Dixon E	Wheelhouse B	Greenhalgh J	
1	2	3	4	5	6	7	8	9	10	11																1
1	2	3	4	5	6	7	8	9	10	11																2
1	2	3	4	5		7	8	9	10	11	6															3
1	2		4	5		7	8		11		6	3	9	10												4
1	2		4	5		7	8			11	6	3	9	10												5
1	2	3		5		7	8		11		6		9		4	10										6
1	2	3		5		7	8		11		6		9		4	10										7
1	2	3		5				8	11		6		9		4	10	7									8
1	2	3		5		7	8		11		6		9		4	10										9
1	2	3	11	5		7	8		10		6		9		4											10
1	2	3		5		7			10	11	6		9	8	4											11
1	2	3	6	5		7	8	9	10						4			11								12
1	2	3	6	5		7	8		10						4			11	9							13
1	2	3	6	5		7	8	9	10						4			11								14
1	2	3	6	5		7	8	9	10						4			11								15
1	2	3	6	5		7	8	9	10						4			11								16
1	2	3	6	5		7	8	9	10						4			11								17
1	2	3	6	5		7	8	9	10						4			11								18
1	2	3	6	5		7	8	9	10						4			11								19
1	2	3	6	5			8	9	10	7					4			11								20
1	2	3		5		7	8	9	10	11	6				4											21
1	2	3		5		7	8	9	10	11	6				4											22
	2	3		5		7	8	9	10	11	6				4					1						23
1	2	3	6	5		7	8	9	10	11					4											24
	2	3		5		7	8	9	10	11	6				4					1						25
	2	3		5		7	8	9	10	11	6				4					1						26
	2	3				7	8	9	10	11	6				4				5	1						27
	2	3		5		7	8	9		11					4	10				1	6					28
		2		5		7	8	9	10	11	6	3			4					1						29
1		2		5		7	8	9	10	11	6	3			4											30
1	2	3				7		8	10	11	6				5							4	9			31
1		2	6	5		7		8	10	11		3			4								9			32
1		2	6			7	8	9				3			5			11				4	10			33
1		3		5		7	8	9	10	11					4							6		2		34
1	2			5			8	9	10	11		3			4			7				6				35
1		3	2	5		7		9	10					8	4			11				6				36
1	2	3		5		7	8	9	10						4			11				6				37
1		3		5		7	8	9	10						4			11				6		2		38
1		3		5		7	8	9	10									11			6	4		2		39
1		3		5			7	9	8						4			11				6		2	10	40
1				5			7	9	8					10	2			11			4	6		3		41
1				5			7	9	8	11				10	2						6	4		3		42
36	31	37	19	39	2	36	37	34	39	21	18	7	8	6	36	5	1	17	2	6	4	11	3	6	1	
		1		2		7	8	19	5	2			5	3				1								

2 own-goals

Dawson J	Smelt L	Taylor D	Watson W	Hill J	Emerson W	Bennie P	Kelly R	Beel G	Cross B	Weaver W	Morgan W	Evans J	Anderson J	Freeman A	Bassnett A	O'Beirne J	Gillatt E	Waterfield G	Sims S	Page S	Robinson J	Parkin G	Dixon E	Wheelhouse B	Greenhalgh J	
1	2	3		5		7	8	9	10	11	6				4											1
	2	3		5		7	8	9	10	11	6				4					1						2
	2	3		5		7	8	9	10	11	6				4					1						R
1	2	3		5		7	8	9	10	11	6				4											3
1	2	3		5		7	8	9	10	11	6				4											4
1	2	3		5		7	8	9	10	11	6				4											R
1	2	3	6	5		7	8	9	10	11					4											SF
5	7	7	1	7		7	7	7	7	7	6				7					2						
							2	2	2	3																

1924-25

Manager: John Haworth until December, then Albert Pickles

1	Aug	30	(h)	Cardiff C	D 0-0		20,000
2	Sep	6	(a)	Preston NE	W 2-0	Parkin, Kelly	22,000
3		8	(h)	Everton	D 0-0		20,172
4		13	(h)	Blackburn R	L 3-5	Hill 2, Freeman	16,000
5		20	(h)	Leeds U	D 1-1	Beel	23,000
6		27	(a)	Birmingham	L 0-1		20,000
7		29	(h)	Sunderland	L 1-2	Beel	10,000
8	Oct	4	(h)	West Brom A	L 0-1		30,000
9		11	(a)	Tottenham H	D 1-1	Roberts	30,000
10		18	(h)	Bolton W	D 0-0		
11		25	(a)	West Ham U	L 0-2		20,000
12	Nov	1	(h)	Sheffield U	D 1-1	Roberts	10,000
13		8	(a)	Newcastle U	L 0-3		22,000
14		15	(h)	Liverpool	W 2-1	Beel, Roberts	18,000
15		22	(a)	Nottingham F	D 0-0		15,000
16		29	(h)	Bury	W 4-0	Roberts 3, Weaver	20,000
17	Dec	6	(a)	Manchester C	D 3-3	Cross, Beel, Bassnett	15,000
18		13	(h)	Arsenal	W 1-0	Roberts	9,477
19		20	(a)	Aston Villa	L 0-3		25,000
20		25	(h)	Huddersfield T	L 1-5	Cross	26,332
21		26	(a)	Huddersfield T	L 0-2		30,300
22	Jan	1	(a)	Everton	L 2-3	Roberts 2	
23		3	(h)	Preston NE	W 1-0	Roberts	17,988
24		17	(a)	Blackburn R	W 3-0	Cross, Roberts 2	20,000
25		24	(a)	Leeds U	W 2-0	Hill, Roberts	15,000
26	Feb	2	(h)	Birmingham	W 3-2	Kelly, Roberts, Tonner	7,636
27		7	(a)	West Brom A	W 4-1	Cross, Tonner, Beel, Roberts	24,000
28		11	(a)	Cardiff C	L 0-4		5,000
29		14	(h)	Tottenham H	L 1-4	Beel	20,000
30		21	(a)	Bolton W	L 0-5		20,000
31		28	(h)	West Ham U	W 5-4	Williams 2, Beel 2, Cross	10,000
32	Mar	14	(h)	Newcastle U	L 1-3	Bruton	9,000
33		21	(a)	Liverpool	L 0-3		25,000
34		28	(h)	Nottingham F	D 0-0		10,000
35	Apr	4	(a)	Bury	L 0-1		15,000
36		6	(a)	Sheffield U	L 0-4		
37		10	(h)	Notts C	D 1-1	Kelly	13,000
38		11	(h)	Manchester C	W 1-0	Beel	13,000
39		13	(a)	Notts C	L 0-2		
40		18	(a)	Arsenal	L 0-5		20,000
41		25	(h)	Aston Villa	D 1-1	Cross	7,500
42	May	2	(a)	Sunderland	D 1-1	Beel	

FINAL LEAGUE POSITION: 19th in Division One — Appearances / Goals

FA Cup

1	Jan	10	(a)	Everton	L 1-2	Roberts	28,315

Appearances
Goals

Dawson J	Smelt L	Evans J	Bassnett A	Hill J	Parkin G	Kelly R	Cross B	Beel G	Drummond R	Weaver W	Watson W	Freeman A	Waterfield G	Armitage J	Tonner J	Roberts W	Greenhalgh J	Wheelhouse B	Tresadern J	Fergus A	Lancaster W	Williams J	Hughes L	Bruton J	Page S	
1	2	3	4	5	6	7	8	9	10	11																1
1	2	3	4	5	6	7	8	9	10	11																2
1	2	3		5	4	7	8	9	10	11	6															3
1	2	3	4	5	6	7	8	9				10	11													4
1	2	3	4	5	6	7	10	9				8	11													5
1	2	3	4	5	6	8	10	9		7			11													6
1	2	3	4	5	6	8	10	9		7			11													7
1	2	3		5	6	8	10						11	4	7	9										8
1	2	3	4	5	6		10						11		7	9	8									9
1	2		4		6	8	10						11	5	7	9		3								10
1	2		4		6	8	10			11				5	7	9		3								11
1	2	3	4			8	10			11				5	7	9			6							12
1	2	3		5	4	7	10	8					11			9			6							13
1	2		4			10		8					11	5	7	9		3	6							14
1	2		4			10		8					11	5	7	9		3	6							15
1	2		4			7	8	10		11				5		9		3	6							16
1	2		4			7	8	10		11				5		9		3	6							17
1	2		4			7	8	10		11				5		9			6	3						18
1	2		4			7	8	10		11				5		9			6	3						19
1	2		4				8						11	5	7	9	10		6	3						20
1	2		4	5			8	10					3		7	9			6		11					21
1	2		4	5			8	10					3		7	9			6		11					22
1	2		4	5			8	10					11		7	9		3	6							23
1				4	6	7	8	10					3	5	11	9				2						24
1				4	6	7	8	10					3	5	11	9				2						25
1				4	6	7	8	10					3	5	11	9				2						26
1	3			4		7	8	10						5	11	9			6	2						27
1	3			4		7	8	10						5	11	9			6	2						28
1	3			4		7	8	10						5	11	9			6	2						29
1	3			4		7	8	10						5					6	2		9	11			30
1	3		4				8	10						5			7		6	2	11	9				31
1		3					8	10						5	11				6	2		9	4	7		32
1				4	6	7	8	9				10	3	5	11					2						33
1			5	4	6	7	8	9				10	3		11					2						34
	2				4		8	9				10	3	5	11				6					7	1	35
	2				4	7	8	9				10	3	5	11				6						1	36
1	2			4	6	7	8					10	3	5	11							9				37
	2			4	6	7	8	10				9	3	5	11										1	38
	2		4		6	7	8	10				9	3	5			11								1	39
1	2				4	7	8	10				9	3	5	11				6							40
			4		5	8	10	9					3		7				6	2	11				1	41
			4	5	6	7	10	9					3		11		8			2					1	42
36	34	12	25	25	25	34	40	35	3	11	1	10	27	27	27	22	5	7	22	16	4	4	2	2	6	
			1	3	1	3	6	10		1		1			2	15						2		1		

Dawson J	Smelt L	Evans J	Bassnett A	Hill J	Parkin G	Kelly R	Cross B	Beel G	Drummond R	Weaver W	Watson W	Freeman A	Waterfield G	Armitage J	Tonner J	Roberts W	Greenhalgh J	Wheelhouse B	Tresadern J	Fergus A	Lancaster W	Williams J	Hughes L	Bruton J	Page S	
1	2		4	5		7	11	10					3			9			6			8				1
1	1		1	1		1	1	1					1			1			1			1				
																1										

1925-26

Manager: Albert Pickles

1	Aug	29	(a)	Aston Villa	L 0-10		37,025
2	Sep	5	(h)	Leicester C	W 4-0	Roberts 3, Beel	18,372
3		7	(h)	Notts C	D 0-0		13,561
4		9	(h)	Bolton W	D 1-1	Roberts	14,295
5		12	(a)	West Ham U	L 0-2		24,188
6		16	(a)	Bolton W	L 2-4	Pollard, Beel	16,647
7		19	(h)	Arsenal	D 2-2	Roberts, Page	12,334
8		21	(a)	Notts C	W 1-0	Page	8,363
9		26	(a)	Manchester U	L 1-6	Beel	17,259
10	Oct	3	(h)	Liverpool	W 2-1	Kelly, Cross	15,857
11		10	(a)	Huddersfield T	L 1-2	McCluggage	18,963
12		17	(h)	Everton	L 1-3	Roberts	10,343
13		24	(a)	Manchester C	L 3-8	Hill, Kelly, Page	19,740
14		31	(h)	Blackburn R	L 1-3	Page	26,181
15	Nov	7	(a)	Sunderland	D 2-2	Kelly, Roberts	9,366
16		14	(h)	Sheffield U	D 1-1	Page	16,014
17		21	(a)	West Brom A	L 3-5	Page, Roberts, Kelly	15,335
18	Dec	7	(h)	Birmingham	W 3-1	Bruton, Devine, Roberts	5,862
19		12	(h)	Tottenham H	L 1-2	Page	18,592
20		16	(a)	Bury	L 1-8	Bruton	7,921
21		19	(a)	Cardiff C	W 3-2	Page 2, Hughes	17,678
22		25	(a)	Leeds U	D 2-2	Page, Beel	23,325
23		26	(h)	Leeds U	W 6-3	Page 3, Hill, Cross, Beel	22,207
24	Jan	1	(a)	Newcastle U	W 3-1	Beel 2, Armitage	34,903
25		2	(h)	Aston Villa	L 2-3	Bruton, Beel	22,329
26		16	(a)	Leicester C	L 2-3	Roberts, Page	16,423
27		23	(h)	West Ham U	D 2-2	Devine, Roberts	10,304
28	Feb	3	(a)	Arsenal	W 2-1	Cross, Beel	14,800
29		6	(h)	Manchester U	L 0-1		17,141
30		13	(a)	Liverpool	L 2-3	Bruton, Page	29,059
31		20	(h)	Huddersfield T	D 1-1	Beel	21,482
32		27	(a)	Everton	D 1-1	Richards	22,691
33	Mar	13	(a)	Blackburn R	L 3-6	Richards 2, Bruton	26,991
34		20	(h)	Sunderland	W 5-2	Page 2, Hargreaves, Roberts 2	25,077
35	Apr	2	(h)	Newcastle U	W 1-0	McCluggage	27,674
36		3	(h)	West Brom A	L 3-4	McCluggage 2, Beel	25,243
37		6	(h)	Manchester C	L 1-2	Hill	19,966
38		10	(a)	Birmingham	W 7-1	Page 6, Bruton	16,616
39		17	(h)	Bury	D 2-2	Parkin, Page	15,787
40		19	(a)	Sheffield U	L 1-6	Page	10,134
41		24	(a)	Tottenham H	W 2-0	Beel, McCluggage	21,211
42	May	1	(h)	Cardiff C	W 4-1	Bruton, Page, Beel 2	16,381

FINAL LEAGUE POSITION: 20th in Division One

Appearances
Goals

FA Cup

3	Jan	9	(a)	Cardiff C	D 2-2	Beel 2	30,000
R		13	(h)	Cardiff C	L 0-2		26,911

Appearances
Goals

Dawson J	McCluggage	Waterfield G	Bassnett A	Hill J	Parkin G	Kelly R	Freeman A	Roberts W	Beel G	Page L	Armitage J	Hughes L	Devine J	Tonner J	Pollard W	Cross B	Blinkhorn F	Bruton J	Fergus A	Steel J	Ashcroft G	Hampson T	Spargo S	Richards P	Dougall W	Hargreaves H	
1	2	3	4	5	6	7	8	9	10	11																	1
1	2	3		4		7		9	10	11	5	6	8														2
1	2	3		4		7		9	10	11	5	6	8														3
1	2	3		4		8		9	10	11	5	6		7													4
1	2	3		4		8		9	10	11	5	6		7													5
1	2	3		4		7		9	10	11	5	6			8												6
1	2	3	4			7		9	10	11	5	6			8												7
1	2	3	4			7		9	10	11	5	6			8												8
1	2	3		4		7		9	10	11	5	6			8												9
1	2	3		4	6	7		9	10	11	5					8											10
1	2	3		4	6	7		9	10	11	5					8											11
1	3			4	6	7		9	10	11	5					8	2										12
1	2	3		4	6	8			9	11	5					10		7									13
1	2	3	4	5		9			10	11		6				8		7									14
1		3	4	5		8		9		11		6				10		7	2								15
1		3		5		8		9		11		6				10		7	2	4							16
1		3		5		8		9		11		6				10		7	2	4							17
	3	11		5				9				6	8			10		7	2	4	1						18
	3			5				9		11		6	8			10		7	2	4		1					19
	3			5				9		11		6	8			10		7	2	4		1					20
1		3		5					10	11	9	6	8			7			2	4							21
1		3		5					10	11	9	6	8					7	2	4							22
1		3		5					10	11	9	6				8		7	2	4							23
1		3		5					10	11	9	6				8		7	2	4							24
1		3		5					10	11	9	6				8		7	2	4							25
1	3			5				9	10	11		6				8		7	2	4							26
1		3		5	6			9	10	11			8					7	2	4							27
1	2	3		5				9	10	11		6				8		7		4							28
1	2	3		5				9	10	11		6				8		7		4							29
1	2	3							10	11		6		9		8		7		4			5				30
1	2	3		5					10	11		6				8		7		4				9			31
1	2	3		5					8	11		6						7		4				9	10		32
1	2	3						9	10	11								7		4			5	8	6		33
1	2	3		5				9	8	11				7						4					6	10	34
1	2			5				9	8	11				7			3			4					6	10	35
1	2	3		5				9	8	11				7						4					6	10	36
1	2	3		5				9	8	11				7						4					6	10	37
	2			5						9				11		8	3	7		4		1			6	10	38
	2				5					9				11		8	3	7		4		1			6	10	39
	2			5						9				11		8	3	7		4		1			6	10	40
1	2		4	5					10	9			8				3	7							6	11	41
	2		4	5					9	11						8	3	7				1			6	10	42
35	33	32	7	37	7	17	1	27	33	41	17	26	9	10	4	24	7	25	13	25	1	6	2	3	11	9	
	5			3	1	4		13	14	26	1	1	2		1	3		7						3		1	

Dawson J	McCluggage	Waterfield G	Bassnett A	Hill J	Parkin G	Kelly R	Freeman A	Roberts W	Beel G	Page L	Armitage J	Hughes L	Devine J	Tonner J	Pollard W	Cross B	Blinkhorn F	Bruton J	Fergus A	Steel J	Ashcroft G	Hampson T	Spargo S	Richards P	Dougall W	Hargreaves H	
1		3		5			9		10	11		6				8		7	2	4							3
1		3		5			9		8	7		6				10		11	2	4							R
2		2		2			2		2	2		2				2		2	2	2							
									2																		

1926-27

Manager: Albert Pickles

1	Aug	28	(h)	Cardiff C	W 4-3	Hargreaves 2, Beel, Page	19,985
2	Sep	1	(a)	Newcastle U	W 5-1	Beel 3, Bruton, Page	33,069
3		4	(a)	Aston Villa	D 1-1	Beel	30,386
4		6	(h)	Newcastle U	D 3-3	Beel, Steel, Cross	25,374
5		11	(h)	Bolton W	W 4-3	Beel 3, Hargreaves	23,730
6		18	(a)	Manchester U	L 1-2	Cross	32,573
7		25	(h)	Derby C	W 1-0	Bruton	17,674
8	Oct	2	(a)	Sheffield U	D 2-2	Beel, Steel	21,482
9		6	(a)	Sunderland	L 1-7	Page	19,550
10		9	(h)	Arsenal	W 2-0	Steel, Beel	12,709
11		12	(h)	Sunderland	W 4-2	Cross 2, Freeman, Steel	14,590
12		16	(a)	Blackburn R	W 5-1	Page 2, Freeman, Cross, McCluggage	42,289
13		23	(h)	Huddersfield T	D 2-2	Beel, Freeman	33,638
14		30	(a)	West Brom A	L 2-4	Devine, Beel	16,307
15	Nov	6	(h)	Bury	D 0-0		16,002
16		13	(a)	Birmingham	L 0-1		11,208
17		20	(h)	Tottenham H	W 5-0	Pollard 2, Beel 3	17,957
18		27	(a)	West Ham U	L 1-2	Page	19,634
19	Dec	4	(h)	Sheffield W	W 1-0	Page	18,349
20		11	(a)	Leicester C	W 3-0	Beel, Page, Bruton	26,591
21		18	(h)	Everton	W 5-1	Beel 2, Devine, Page, Freeman	18,290
22		25	(h)	Liverpool	W 4-0	Beel 2, Devine 2	31,823
23		27	(a)	Liverpool	D 2-2	Bruton, Beel	46,378
24	Jan	1	(a)	Everton	L 2-3	Freeman 2	44,586
25		15	(a)	Cardiff C	D 0-0		14,647
26		22	(h)	Aston Villa	W 6-3	Bruton 2, Cross, Beel, Devine, Opp own-goal	18,081
27	Feb	5	(h)	Manchester U	W 1-0	Bruton	22,010
28		12	(a)	Derby C	L 1-4	Devine	14,065
29		26	(a)	Arsenal	L 2-6	Hill, Devine	29,970
30	Mar	5	(h)	Blackburn R	W 3-1	Cross, Beel, Page	24,546
31		9	(a)	Bolton W	L 1-3	Page	13,331
32		12	(a)	Huddersfield T	L 0-2		23,893
33		19	(h)	West Brom A	W 2-1	McCluggage, Hargreaves	18,863
34		26	(a)	Bury	D 3-3	Bruton, Devine, Page	9,029
35		29	(h)	Sheffield U	L 2-5	Freeman, Cross	9,056
36	Apr	2	(h)	Birmingham	L 0-2		12,679
37		9	(a)	Tottenham H	L 1-4	Richards	15,481
38		15	(h)	Leeds U	W 3-2	Bruton, Richards, Devine	21,099
39		16	(h)	West Ham U	W 2-1	Richards, Steel	20,333
40		19	(a)	Leeds U	W 2-0	Richards 2	18,740
41		23	(a)	Sheffield W	L 1-2	Earle	16,721
42		30	(h)	Leicester C	D 1-1	Page	11,072

FINAL LEAGUE POSITION: 5th in Division One

Appearances

Goals

FA Cup

3	Jan	8	(h)	Grimsby T	W 3-1	Bruton, Beel, Page	19,556
4		29	(a)	Fulham	W 4-0	Beel 2, Page, Bruton	23,562
5	Feb	19	(a)	Chelsea	L 1-2	Cross	62,238

Appearances

Goals

Sommerville	McCluggage A	Blinkhorn F	Steel J	Hill J	Dougall W	Bruton J	Cross B	Beel G	Hargreaves H	Page L	Bassnett A	Parkin G	Waterfield G	Freeman A	Devine J	Fergus A	Burley G	Pollard W	Earle E	Spargo S	Reid A	Richards P	Dawson J	
1	2	3	4	5	6	7	8	9	10	11														1
1	2	3	4	5	6	7	8	9	10	11														2
1	2	3		5	6	7	8	9	10	11	4													3
1	2	3	4	5		7	8	9	10	11		6												4
1	2	3	4	5	6	7	8	9	10	11														5
1	2	3	4	5	6	7	8	9	10	11														6
1	2	3	4	5	6	7	8	9	10	11														7
1	2	3	4	5	6	7	8	9	10	11														8
1	2		4	5	6	7	8	9	10	11			3											9
1	2		4		6	7	8	9		11		5	3	10										10
1	2		4	5		7	8	9		11		6	3	10										11
1	2		4	5	6	7	8	9		11			3	10										12
1	2		4		6	7	8	9		11		5	3	10										13
1	2		4		6	7		9		11		5	3	10	8									14
1			4	5	6	7	8	10		11			3			2	9							15
1	2		4	5	6	7	8	9		11			3		10									16
1	2		4	5	6	7		9		11			3		10			8						17
1	2		4	5	6	7		9		11			3		10			8						18
1			4	5	6	7		9		11			3		10	2		8						19
1			4	5	6	7		9		11			3	8	10	2								20
1			4	5	6	7		9		11			3	8	10	2								21
1			4	5	6	7		9		11			3	8	10	2								22
1			4	5	6	7		9		11			3	8	10	2								23
1			4	5	6	7		9		11			3	8	10	2								24
1	2			5	6	7		9		11		4	3	8	10									25
1	2			5	6	7	8	9		11		4	3		10									26
1	2		4	5		7	8	9		11		6	3		10									27
1	3		4		6	7	8	9				5			10	2			11					28
1			4	5	6	7	8	9		11			3		10	2								29
1	2		4	5	6	7	8	9		11			3		10									30
1	2		4	5	6	7	8	9		11			3		10									31
1	2		4	5	6	7	8	10		11			3				9							32
1	2		4	5	3	7		9	10	11		6		8										33
1	2		4	5	6	7	9			11			3	8	10									34
1	2		4		6	7	9					5	3	8	10				11					35
1	2		4			7	8	9	11			6	3		10					5				36
1			4			7	8		5	11		6	3		10						2	9		37
1	2		4	5	6	7	8			11			3		10							9		38
	2		4	5	6	7	8		11				3		10							9	1	39
1	2		4	5	6	7		8	11				3		10							9		40
1	2		4	5	6	7							3		10			8	11			9		41
1	2			5	6	7	8	9		11		4	3		10									42
41	33	8	38	35	37	42	29	36	14	36	1	14	32	14	26	9	2	4	3	1	1	5	1	
	2		5	1		9	8	24	4	13				7	9			2	1			5		

1 own-goal

Sommerville	McCluggage A	Blinkhorn F	Steel J	Hill J	Dougall W	Bruton J	Cross B	Beel G	Hargreaves H	Page L	Bassnett A	Parkin G	Waterfield G	Freeman A	Devine J	Fergus A	Burley G	Pollard W	Earle E	Spargo S	Reid A	Richards P	Dawson J	
1				5	6	7		9		11			3	8	10	2				4				3
1	2		4	5	6	7	8	9		11			3		10									4
1	2		4	5	6	7	8	9		11			3		10									5
3	2		2	3	3	3	2	3		3			3	1	3	1				1				
						2	1	3		2														

1927-28

Manager: Albert Pickles

1	Aug	27	(a)	Blackburn R	L 1-2	Hargreaves	32,441
2		31	(a)	Arsenal	L 1-4	Bruton	19,910
3	Sep	3	(h)	Bury	L 2-3	Bruton, Freeman	22,414
4		5	(h)	Arsenal	L 1-2	Beel	14,688
5		10	(a)	Sheffield U	L 2-5	Freeman, Beel	17,479
6		17	(h)	Aston Villa	W 4-2	Beel 2, Hill, Page	19,523
7		24	(a)	Sunderland	W 3-2	Page 2, Hill	22,420
8	Oct	1	(h)	Derby C	W 4-2	Beel 3, Freeman	11,911
9		8	(a)	West Ham U	L 0-2		27,467
10		15	(h)	Portsmouth	W 2-0	Beel, Page	19,492
11		22	(a)	Middlesbrough	W 3-2	Beel 2, Weston	17,803
12		29	(h)	Sheffield W	W 3-1	Page 2, Beel	16,366
13	Nov	5	(a)	Bolton W	L 1-7	Page	14,340
14		12	(h)	Birmingham	W 2-1	Freeman, Beel	14,648
15		19	(a)	Newcastle U	D 1-1	Beel	26,991
16		26	(h)	Manchester U	W 4-0	Beel 2, Devine, Hill	18,509
17	Dec	3	(a)	Tottenham H	L 0-5		20,404
18		10	(h)	Huddersfield T	L 0-1		19,130
19		17	(a)	Everton	L 1-4	Beel	30,180
20		24	(h)	Cardiff C	W 2-1	Beel, W.Dougall	13,159
21		26	(a)	Leicester C	L 0-5		20,063
22		27	(h)	Leicester C	W 5-1	Beel 2, Page 2, P.Dougall	24,824
23		31	(h)	Blackburn R	W 3-1	McCluggage, Page, Beel	28,354
24	Jan	2	(a)	Liverpool	D 2-2	Page 2	26,632
25		7	(a)	Bury	L 0-2		13,161
26		21	(h)	Sheffield U	W 5-3	Beel 3, Bruton 2	12,716
27	Feb	4	(h)	Sunderland	W 3-0	Beel, Page 2	11,442
28		8	(a)	Aston Villa	L 1-3	Mantle	18,602
29		11	(a)	Derby C	W 4-3	Freeman, Beel, Page, P.Dougall	8,503
30		18	(h)	West Ham U	D 0-0		14,663
31		25	(a)	Portsmouth	L 0-1		19,666
32	Mar	3	(h)	Middlesbrough	D 1-1	Beel	18,209
33		10	(a)	Sheffield W	L 0-5		12,401
34		17	(h)	Bolton W	D 2-2	Beel, Page	15,865
35		24	(a)	Birmingham	L 0-4		23,689
36		31	(h)	Newcastle U	W 5-1	Beel 2, Hill, Bruton, Page	12,454
37	Apr	6	(h)	Liverpool	D 2-2	Pollard, Freeman	21,824
38		7	(a)	Manchester U	L 3-4	Beel 2, Bruton	28,311
39		14	(h)	Tottenham H	D 2-2	Page 2	10,906
40		25	(a)	Huddersfield T	W 2-1	Beel, Page	20,643
41		28	(h)	Everton	L 3-5	Page, Beel 2	24,485
42	May	5	(a)	Cardiff C	L 2-3	Beel, Page	8,663

FINAL LEAGUE POSITION: 19th in Division One

Appearances
Goals

FA Cup

3	Jan	14	(h)	Aston Villa	L 0-2		26,150

Appearances
Goals

Sommerville G	Reid A	Waterfield G	Parkin G	Hill J	Dougall W	Bruton J	Devine J	Haddow A	Hargreaves H	Page L	Pollard W	Richards P	Knox W	Freeman A	Beel G	Weston J	Brown J	Steel J	McCluggage A	Forrest A	Down W	Dougall P	Burley G	Heslop A	Mantle J	Cross B	
1	2	3	4	5	6	7	8	9	10	11																	1
1	2	3	4	5	6	7	10			11	8	9															2
1		3	4	5	6	7	10			11			2	8	9												3
1		3	4	5	6	7			10	11			2	8	9												4
1		3	4	5		7			10	11			2	8	9	6											5
1		3	4	5	6	7	10			11			2	8	9												6
1		3	4	5	6	7	10			11			2	8	9												7
1		3	4	5	6	7	10			11			2	8	9												8
1		3	4		6	7	10			11			2	8	9		5										9
1		3	4	5	6	7	10			11			2	8	9												10
1		3	6			7	10						2	8	9	11	5	4									11
1		3	4			7	10			11				8	9		5		2	6							12
1		3	4	5		7	10			11				8	9		6		2								13
		3	6	5		7	10			11				8	9		4		2		1						14
		3	6	5		7	10			11				8	9		4		2		1						15
		3	6	5		7	10			11				8	9		4		2		1						16
		3	6	5		7	10			11				8	9		4		2		1						17
		3	6	5		7	10			11				8	9			4	2		1						18
		3	6	5	10	7				11	8				9			4	2		1						19
		3	6	5	10	7				11				8	9			4	2		1						20
		3	6	5	10	7				11				8	9			4	2		1						21
		3	6			7				11				8	9		5	4	2		1	10					22
		3	6	5		7				11				8	9			4	2		1	10					23
		3	6	5		7				11				8	9			4	2		1	10					24
		3	6	5		7				11				8	9			4	2		1		10				25
		3	6	5		7				11	8			10	9			4	2		1						26
		3	6	5		7				11	8		2	10	9			4			1						27
		3	6	5						11				10			4		2		1		8	7	9		28
		3	6	5		7				11				8	9			4	2		1	10					29
		3	6	5		7				11				8	9			4	2		1	10					30
		3	6	5		7				11	8		2		9			4			1	10					31
		3	6	5		7				11	8			10	9			4	2		1						32
		3	6			7				11	8			10	9		5	4	2		1						33
		3	6	5		7				11				10	9		4	8	2		1						34
		3	6	5		7				11				10	9		4	8	2		1						35
		3	6	5		7				11	8			10	9			4	2		1						36
		3	6	5		7				11	8			10	9			4	2		1						37
		3	6	5		7	10			11				8	9			4	2		1						38
		3	6	5		7				11	8			10	9			4	2		1						39
		3	6	5		7				11	8			10	9			4	2		1						40
		3		5		7				11	8			10	9		6	4	2		1						41
		3	6	5		7				11				10	9			4	2		1					8	42
13	2	42	41	37	12	41	17	1	3	41	12	1	11	38	39	2	14	25	29	1	29	6	2	1	1	1	
				4	1	6	1		1	22	1			6	35	1			1			2			1		

Sommerville G	Reid A	Waterfield G	Parkin G	Hill J	Dougall W	Bruton J	Devine J	Haddow A	Hargreaves H	Page L	Pollard W	Richards P	Knox W	Freeman A	Beel G	Weston J	Brown J	Steel J	McCluggage A	Forrest A	Down W	Dougall P	Burley G	Heslop A	Mantle J	Cross B	
		3	6	5		7				11				8	9		10	4	2		1						3
		1	1	1		1				1				1	1		1	1	1		1						

1928-29

Manager: Albert Pickles

1	Aug	25	(h)	Sunderland	W 3-1	Bruton 2, Devine	21,448
2		29	(a)	Newcastle U	W 7-2	Beel 3, Bruton 2, Page 2	19,648
3	Sep	1	(a)	Cardiff C	L 0-7		20,174
4		3	(h)	West Ham U	D 3-3	Beel, Bruton, Page	17,719
5		8	(h)	Sheffield U	W 2-1	McCluggage, Bruton	14,805
6		10	(h)	Newcastle U	W 4-3	Beel 2, Page, Mantle	19,976
7		15	(a)	Bury	L 1-2	Beel	20,114
8		22	(h)	Aston Villa	W 4-1	Beel 2, Devine, McCluggage	19,147
9		29	(a)	Leicester C	D 1-1	Beel	26,506
10	Oct	6	(h)	Manchester U	L 3-4	McCluggage 2, Beel	17,693
11		13	(a)	Leeds U	L 1-2	Fitton	29,565
12		20	(h)	Blackburn R	D 2-2	Devine, McCluggage	35,694
13		27	(a)	Derby C	L 0-4		13,091
14	Nov	3	(h)	Everton	W 2-0	Bruton, Devine	25,959
15		10	(a)	Huddersfield T	L 1-7	Beel	12,645
16		17	(h)	Manchester C	L 2-3	Page 2	14,021
17		24	(a)	Birmingham	W 6-3	Beel 3, Devine, Page 2	13,071
18	Dec	1	(h)	Portsmouth	W 4-1	Beel 3, Freeman	17,525
19		8	(a)	Bolton W	W 1-0	Page	17,222
20		15	(h)	Sheffield W	L 0-2		16,173
21		22	(a)	Arsenal	L 1-3	Page	14,990
22		25	(h)	Liverpool	W 3-2	Beel 2, Page	25,361
23		26	(a)	Liverpool	L 0-8		42,449
24		29	(a)	Sunderland	L 1-2	Beel	23,678
25	Jan	5	(h)	Cardiff C	W 3-0	Beel 2, Bruton	10,966
26		19	(a)	Sheffield U	L 0-10		23,280
27	Feb	2	(a)	Aston Villa	L 2-4	Wallace, Devine	21,277
28		9	(h)	Leicester C	L 0-1		14,879
29		16	(a)	Manchester U	L 0-1		12,516
30		18	(h)	Bury	D 0-0		6,238
31		23	(h)	Leeds U	W 5-0	Beel 3, Page 2	13,506
32	Mar	9	(h)	Derby C	D 2-2	Devine, Page	19,979
33		16	(a)	Everton	L 0-2		17,810
34		29	(a)	West Ham U	L 0-4		20,926
35		30	(a)	Manchester C	L 1-4	Beel	33,166
36	Apr	6	(h)	Birmingham	W 4-0	Devine 2, Storer, Page	13,730
37		13	(a)	Portsmouth	L 1-3	Page	23,031
38		16	(h)	Huddersfield T	W 3-2	Bruton, Beel, Page	15,426
39		20	(h)	Bolton W	W 3-1	Devine, Beel, Brown	14,584
40		27	(a)	Sheffield W	D 1-1	Storer	33,314
41	May	2	(a)	Blackburn R	D 1-1	Bruton	5,461
42		4	(h)	Arsenal	D 3-3	McCluggage, Beel, Bruton	7,400

FINAL LEAGUE POSITION: 19th in Division One

Appearances
Goals

FA Cup

3	Jan	12	(h)	Sheffield U	W 2-1	Beel, Page	27,865
4		26	(h)	Swindon T	D 3-3	Devine, Page, McCluggage	30,689
R		30	(a)	Swindon T	L 2-3	Beel, Devine	24,730

Appearances
Goals

Down W	McCluggage A	Waterfield G	Steel J	Hill J	Parkin G	Bruton J	Stage W	Beel G	Devine J	Page L	Mantle J	Brown J	Forrest A	Heslop A	Freeman A	Fitton F	Knox W	Hunt P	Dawson J	Sommerville G	Wallace J	Bowsher S	Flack H	Heap C	Storer H	Conway T	
1	2	3	4	5	6	7	8	9	10	11																	1
1	2	3	4	5	6	7	8	9	10	11																	2
1	2	3	4	5	6	7	8	9	10	11																	3
1	2	3	4	5	6	7		8	10	11	9																4
1	2	3	4		6	7		8	10	11	9	5															5
1	2	3	4	5	6	7		8	10	11	9																6
1	2	3	4	5	6	7	8	9	10	11																	7
1	2	3	4	5			8	9	10	11			6	7													8
1	2	3	4	5		7	8	9	10	11			6														9
1	2	3	4	5		7		9	10	11			6		8												10
1	2	3	4	5	6	7		9	10	11						8											11
1	2	3	4	5	6	7		9	10	11						8											12
1	2	3	4		5	7		9	10	11			6			8											13
1		3	4		5	7		9	10	11			6			8	2										14
1		3	4		5	7		9	10	11			6			8	2										15
1	2	3	4		5	7	8	9	10	11			6														16
1	2	3	4		6	7		9	10	11						8		5									17
1	2	3	4		6	7		9	10						11	8		5									18
1	2	3	4		6	7		9	10	11						8		5									19
1	2	3	4		6	7		9	10	11						8		5									20
1		3	4		6	7		9	10	11		5				8	2										21
	2	3	4		5	7		9	10	11			6			8			1								22
	2	3	4		5	7		9	10				6		11	8				1							23
	2	3	4			7	8	9	10	11		5			6					1							24
	2	3	4			7	8	9	10	11			6					5		1							25
	2	3	4		6	7	8	9	10						11			5		1							26
1		3			4	7		9	10	11			6				2	5			8						27
1	2	3			4	7		9	10	11								5			8	6					28
1	2	3	4			7		9	10	11		5									8	6					29
1	2		4			7		10	8	11	9	5										6	3				30
1			4			7	8	9	10	11		5					2							3	6		31
1	2		4			7	8		10	11		5									9			3	6		32
1	2		4			7	8	9	10	11		5												3	6		33
1	2		4			7	8	9	10	11		5												3	6		34
1			4			7		9	10	11		5			8		2							3	6		35
1	2					7	8	9	10	11												5	3		6	4	36
1	2						8	9	10	11				7								5	3		6	4	37
1	3				4	7		9	10	11							2				8	5			6		38
1	3				4	7		9	10	11		5					2				8				6		39
1	3				4	7	8	9	10	11							2					5			6		40
1	3				4	7	8	9	10	11							2					5			6		41
1	3					7	8	9	10	11							2					5			6	4	42
37	36	29	33	11	27	40	19	41	42	39	4	11	11	2	6	12	11	8	1	4	6	9	3	5	12	3	
	6					11		30	10	17	1	1			1	1					1				2		

Down W	McCluggage A	Waterfield G	Steel J	Hill J	Parkin G	Bruton J	Stage W	Beel G	Devine J	Page L	Mantle J	Brown J	Forrest A	Heslop A	Freeman A	Fitton F	Knox W	Hunt P	Dawson J	Sommerville G	Wallace J	Bowsher S	Flack H	Heap C	Storer H	Conway T	
	2	3	4		6	7	8	9	10	11								5		1							3
	2	3				7	8	9	10	11			6					5		1						4	4
1	2	3			4	7	8	9	10	11			6					5									R
1	3	3	1		2	3	3	3	3	3			2					3		2						1	
	1							2	2	2																	

1929-30

Manager: Albert Pickles

1	Aug	31	(a)	Manchester C	D 2-2	Wallace, Fitton	21,196
2	Sep	2	(h)	Everton	D 1-1	Mantle	17,704
3		7	(h)	Portsmouth	W 4-0	Bruton, Page 2, Mantle	15,094
4		10	(h)	Sunderland	W 2-0	Bruton, McCluggage	19,691
5		14	(a)	Arsenal	L 1-6	Bruton	38,556
6		21	(h)	Aston Villa	L 1-4	Page	14,062
7		25	(a)	Derby C	W 3-1	Mantle 2, Wallace	14,413
8		28	(a)	Leeds U	L 0-3		26,676
9	Oct	5	(h)	Sheffield W	L 2-4	Beel, Opp own-goal	17,294
10		12	(a)	Newcastle U	L 1-2	Wallace	33,306
11		19	(h)	Sheffield U	W 5-0	Devine 2, Beel 2, Bruton	12,569
12		26	(a)	Huddersfield T	L 0-3		15,644
13	Nov	2	(h)	Birmingham	W 3-1	Page, Bruton, Devine	11,068
14		9	(a)	Blackburn R	L 3-8	McCluggage 2, Page	22,647
15		16	(h)	Grimsby T	W 3-1	Bruton 2, Page	11,660
16		23	(a)	Manchester U	L 0-1		9,060
17		30	(h)	West Ham U	D 1-1	Bruton	6,640
18	Dec	7	(a)	Liverpool	W 3-1	Beel 2, Page	15,210
19		14	(h)	Middlesbrough	W 4-1	Hutchison, Mantle, Heslop, Devine	8,671
20		21	(a)	Leicester C	L 3-4	McCluggage, Devine, Heslop	16,188
21		25	(a)	Bolton W	D 1-1	Hutchison	21,533
22		26	(h)	Bolton W	D 2-2	Beel, McCluggage	27,515
23		28	(h)	Manchester C	W 4-2	Heslop, Mantle 2, Wallace	20,239
24	Jan	1	(a)	Sunderland	D 3-3	Mantle 2, Wallace	28,615
25		4	(a)	Portsmouth	L 1-7	Mantle	20,366
26		18	(h)	Arsenal	D 2-2	Wallace, Mantle	22,566
27	Feb	1	(h)	Leeds U	L 0-3		12,505
28		5	(a)	Aston Villa	W 2-1	Heslop, Page	13,378
29		8	(a)	Sheffield W	L 1-4	Page	23,864
30		15	(h)	Leicester C	D 1-1	Page	10,717
31		22	(a)	Sheffield U	L 1-3	Beel	18,066
32	Mar	8	(a)	Birmingham	L 0-2		19,485
33		11	(h)	Newcastle U	L 0-3		12,487
34		15	(h)	Blackburn R	W 3-2	Opp own-goal, McCluggage, O'Dowd	16,673
35		22	(a)	Grimsby T	L 0-4		11,262
36		29	(h)	Manchester U	W 4-0	O'Dowd, Beel 2, Forrest	11,659
37	Apr	1	(h)	Huddersfield T	L 1-3	Page	9,418
38		5	(a)	West Ham U	L 0-1		12,092
39		12	(h)	Liverpool	W 4-1	Page 3, Stage	12,693
40		18	(a)	Everton	L 0-3		47,897
41		19	(a)	Middlesbrough	L 1-3	Beel	5,370
42		26	(h)	Derby C	W 6-2	Mantle 3, Page, Wallace, O'Dowd	18,328

FINAL LEAGUE POSITION: 21st in Division One (Relegated)

Appearances
Goals

FA Cup

3	Jan	11	(a)	Sheffield W	L 0-1	

Appearances
Goals

Down W	McCluggage A	Waterfield G	Brown J	Bowsher S	Storer H	Bruton J	Wallace J	Mantle J	Devine J	Fitton F	Forrest A	Page L	Beel G	Wadsworth S	Steel J	Henderson R	Hutchison A	Sommerville G	Stage W	Heslop A	Knox W	Prest T	O'Dowd P	Willighan T	Chambers W	
1	2	3	4	5	6	7	8	9	10	11																1
1	2	3	4	5		7	8	9	10	11	6															2
1	2	3	4	5		7	8	9	10		6	11														3
1	2	3	4	5		7	8	9	10		6	11														4
1	2	3	4	5		7	8		10		6	11	9													5
1	2	3	4	5		7	8	9	10		6	11														6
1	2	11	4	5		7	8	9	10		6			3												7
1	2		4	5	6	7	8	9	10			11		3												8
1	2		4	5		7	8		10		6	11	9	3												9
1	2	3	4	5		7	8		10		11		9		6											10
1	2	3	4	5		7	8		10				9		6	11										11
1	2	3	4	5		7	8		10				9		6		11									12
1	2	3	4	5		7	8		10			11	9		6											13
1	2	3	4	5		7	8	9	10			11			6											14
	2	3	4	5		7	8		10			11	9		6			1								15
	2	3	4	5		7	8			10		11	9		6			1								16
	2	3		5		7	10				6	11	9		4			1	8							17
	2	3		5				9	10		6	11	8		4			1		7						18
	2	3		5				9	10		6		8		4		11	1		7						19
	2	3		5				9	10		6		8		4		11	1		7						20
	2	3		5				9	10		6		8		4		11	1		7						21
	2	3		5				9	10		6		8		4		11	1		7						22
	2	3	4	5			10	9			6	11	8					1		7						23
	2	3	4	5			10	9			6	11	8					1		7						24
	2	3	4	5			10	9			6	11	8					1		7						25
	2	3	5				10	9			6	11	8		4			1		7						26
		3	4	5			10	9			6	11	8					1		7	2					27
	2	3		5			10	9			6	11	8		4			1		7						28
	2	3		5			10	9			6	11	8		4			1		7						29
	2	3		5			10	9			6	11	8		4			1		7						30
	2	3		5			10	9			6	11	8		4			1		7						31
	2	3	4	5			10				6	11	9					1		7		8				32
	2	3		4			8	9			6	11	10					1		7			5			33
	2	3	4				10	7			6	11	9					1				8	5			34
	2	3	4				8	9			6	11	10					1		7			5			35
		3	4				10				6	11	9					1	8				5	2	7	36
	2	3	4				10				6	11	9					1	8				5		7	37
	2	3	4	6				9			10	11	8					1		7			5			38
	2	3									6	11	9		4			1	8	7		10	5			39
	2	3									6	11	9		4			1	8	7		10	5			40
	3										6	11	9		4			1	8	7		10	5	2		41
	2	3			10		7	9			6	11			4			1				8	5			42
14	40	39	27	33	3	17	33	27	20	3	34	32	33	3	22	1	5	28	6	21	1	6	10	2	2	
	6					8	7	14	5	1	1	15	10				2		1	4			3			

2 own-goals

Down W	McCluggage A	Waterfield G	Brown J	Bowsher S	Storer H	Bruton J	Wallace J	Mantle J	Devine J	Fitton F	Forrest A	Page L	Beel G	Wadsworth S	Steel J	Henderson R	Hutchison A	Sommerville G	Stage W	Heslop A	Knox W	Prest T	O'Dowd P	Willighan T	Chambers W	
	2	3	5					9	10		6	11	8		4			1		7						3
	1	1	1					1	1		1	1	1		1			1		1						

1930-31

Manager: Albert Pickles

1	Aug	30	(h)	Bury	L 0-2		13,842
2	Sep	1	(a)	Tottenham H	L 1-8	Page	23,518
3		6	(a)	Southampton	D 1-1	O'Dowd	13,045
4		8	(h)	Nottingham F	W 5-2	Jenkins, Beel, Mantle, Prest, Page	10,393
5		13	(h)	Reading	W 8-1	Page 2, Mantle 2, Brown, O'Dowd, Jenkins, Prest	9,861
6		17	(a)	Nottingham F	D 3-3	Page, Beel, Jenkins	3,824
7		20	(a)	Wolves	W 4-2	Page 2, Jenkins, O'Dowd	18,504
8		27	(h)	Bradford	W 3-2	Beel, Prest, Jenkins	13,132
9	Oct	4	(a)	Stoke C	D 1-1	Mantle	13,140
10		11	(h)	Millwall	W 2-1	Drinnan, Prest	12,440
11		18	(h)	Swansea T	D 2-2	Page 2	11,624
12		25	(a)	Plymouth A	W 2-1	Beel, Mantle	18,494
13	Nov	1	(h)	Bristol C	W 4-2	Prest 2, Beel, Storer	10,207
14		8	(a)	Barnsley	W 1-0	Prest	9,427
15		15	(h)	Port Vale	L 1-2	Mantle	12,277
16		22	(a)	Bradford C	W 3-2	Beel, Page, McCluggage	12,886
17		29	(h)	Charlton A	D 1-1	Prest	11,021
18	Dec	6	(a)	West Brom A	L 0-2		17,050
19		13	(h)	Everton	W 5-2	Beel 2, Storer, Prest, Page	17,849
20		20	(a)	Cardiff C	L 0-4		7,485
21		25	(h)	Preston NE	W 1-0	Beel	31,000
22		26	(a)	Preston NE	L 0-2		28,682
23		27	(a)	Bury	L 1-2	Beel	13,295
24	Jan	3	(h)	Southampton	W 3-2	Prest, McCluggage, Beel	10,712
25		17	(a)	Reading	L 1-3	Opp own-goal	8,141
26		31	(a)	Bradford	L 1-4	Beel	7,954
27	Feb	3	(h)	Wolves	W 4-2	Beel 3, Jenkins	8,652
28		7	(h)	Stoke C	L 1-2	Beel	10,517
29		14	(a)	Millwall	L 1-2	Beel	15,417
30		21	(a)	Swansea T	D 1-1	Beel	10,906
31		28	(h)	Plymouth A	D 2-2	Jenkins, Drinnan	4,986
32	Mar	7	(a)	Bristol C	D 1-1	Beel	8,940
33		14	(h)	Barnsley	D 2-2	Storer, Bowsher	7,877
34		21	(a)	Port Vale	D 0-0		9,185
35		28	(h)	Bradford C	D 1-1	Jenkins	7,082
36	Apr	3	(h)	Oldham A	W 6-1	Jenkins, Jones, Beel 2, Page, Brown	11,563
37		4	(a)	Charlton A	L 1-2	Kelly	12,688
38		6	(a)	Oldham A	L 1-3	Bowsher	12,346
39		11	(h)	West Brom A	W 2-1	Beel, Page	12,109
40		18	(a)	Everton	L 2-3	Beel, Prest	19,144
41		25	(h)	Cardiff C	W 1-0	Beel	4,125
42	May	2	(h)	Tottenham H	W 1-0	Beel	10,077

FINAL LEAGUE POSITION: 8th in Division Two

Appearances
Goals

FA Cup

3	Jan	10	(h)	Manchester C	W 3-0	Prest, McCluggage, Jenkins	25,893
4		24	(a)	Bradford	L 0-2		26,444

Appearances
Goals

Sommerville G	McCluggage A	Waterfield G	Steel J	O'Dowd P	Forrest A	Jenkins E	Mays A	Mantle J	Storer H	Page L	Beel G	Wadsworth S	Brown J	Prest T	Conway H	Drinnan J	Hall J	Henderson R	Bowsher S	Weaver R	Willighan T	Wood WH	Jones T	Kelly J	
1	2	3	4	5	6	7	8	9	10	11															1
1	2	3	4	5	6	7		9	10	11	8														2
1	2			5		7		9	6	11	8	3	4	10											3
1	2			5		7		9	6	11	8	3	4	10											4
1	2			5		7		9	6	11	8	3	4	10											5
1	2			5		7		9	6	11	8	3	4	10											6
	2	3		5		7		9	6	11	8		4	10	1										7
	2	3		5		7		9	6	11	8		4	10	1										8
	2	3		5		7		9	6	11	8		4	10	1										9
	2	3		5		7			6		9		4	8	1	10	11								10
	2	3		5	6	7		9		11	8		4	10	1										11
	3	2		5		7		9	6		8		4	10	1		11								12
	2	3		5		7		9	6		8		4	10	1		11								13
	2	3		5	4	7		9	6		8			10	1		11								14
	2	3		5	4	7		9	6	11	8			10	1										15
	2	3		5		7		9	6	11	8		4	10	1										16
	2	3		5		7			6	11	9		4	10	1			8							17
	2	3		5		7	9		6	11	8		4	10	1										18
	2	3		5		7			6	11	8		4	10	1				9						19
	2	3		5		7			6	11	8		4	10	1				9						20
	2	3		5					6	11	8		4	10	1	9				7					21
	2	3		5					6	11	8		4	10	1	9	7								22
	2			5		7			6		8		4	10	1		11	9			3				23
	3			5					6		8		4	10	1		11		9	7		2			24
	2	3		5		7			6		8		4	10	1		11		9						25
	2	3		5		7		9	6		8		4	10	1								11		26
1	2	3		5	6	7		9	11		8		4	10											27
1	2	3		5	6	7		9	11		8		4	10											28
1				5	6	7			3		9		4			10						2	11	8	29
1	3			5	6	7					9		4	8		10						2	11		30
1	2	3		5	6	7					9		4	8		10							11		31
1	2	3		5		8			6	11	9		4	7									10		32
1	2	3		5		7			6	11	8		4	10					9						33
		3		5		7			6	11	8		4		1				9			2	10		34
		3		5		7			6	11	8		4		1				9			2	10		35
		3		5		7			6	11	8		4		1							2	10	9	36
		3		5					6	11	8		4		1					7		2	10	9	37
	2	3		5					6	11	8		4		1				9	7			10		38
		3		5		7			6	11	9		4	10	1							2		8	39
		3		5		7			6	11	9		4	10	1							2		8	40
		3		5	6	7				11	9		4	8	1							2	10		41
		3		5	6	7				11	9		4	8	1							2	10		42
13	33	34	2	42	12	37	2	18	37	29	41	4	38	34	29	6	8	2	8	4	1	11	12	5	
	2			3		9		6	3	13	25		2	11		2			2				1	1	

1 own-goal

Sommerville G	McCluggage A	Waterfield G	Steel J	O'Dowd P	Forrest A	Jenkins E	Mays A	Mantle J	Storer H	Page L	Beel G	Wadsworth S	Brown J	Prest T	Conway H	Drinnan J	Hall J	Henderson R	Bowsher S	Weaver R	Willighan T	Wood WH	Jones T	Kelly J	
	2	3		5		7			6		8		4	10	1		11		9						3
	2	3		5		7		9	6		8		4	10	1		11								4
	2	2		2		2		1	2		2		2	2	2		2		1						
	1					1								1											

1931-32

Manager: Albert Pickles

1	Aug	29	(a)	Southampton	L 0-3		14,293
2	Sep	5	(h)	Stoke C	W 3-0	Prest, Edwards, Jones	8,710
3		7	(h)	Chesterfield	D 2-2	Waterfield, Brown	9,207
4		12	(a)	Charlton A	W 1-0	Edwards	6,597
5		19	(h)	Wolves	L 1-3	Page	11,286
6		26	(a)	Bradford	L 0-2		15,426
7	Oct	1	(a)	Nottingham F	W 2-1	Jenkins, Beel	7,175
8		3	(h)	Manchester U	W 2-0	Jenkins, Jones	9,719
9		10	(a)	Tottenham H	D 1-1	O'Dowd	28,877
10		17	(a)	Oldham A	L 1-3	Beel	11,564
11		24	(h)	Bury	D 2-2	Beel, Waterfield	12,590
12		31	(a)	Port Vale	W 3-1	Page 2, Hall	9,468
13	Nov	7	(h)	Plymouth A	D 1-1	O'Dowd	9,461
14		14	(a)	Bradford C	W 2-1	Page, Beel	12,859
15		21	(h)	Leeds U	L 0-5		12,767
16		28	(a)	Swansea T	L 1-5	Page	8,051
17	Dec	5	(h)	Barnsley	W 5-3	Brown, Hall, Beel 2, Jones	5,333
18		12	(a)	Notts C	L 0-5		13,198
19		19	(h)	Millwall	D 1-1	Beel	4,751
20		25	(h)	Preston NE	D 2-2	Beel 2	18,105
21		26	(a)	Preston NE	L 1-2	Beel	27,677
22	Jan	1	(a)	Chesterfield	L 1-5	Harker	11,839
23		2	(h)	Southampton	L 1-3	Jenkins	3,135
24		16	(a)	Stoke C	L 0-3		9,045
25		23	(h)	Charlton A	L 0-1		7,273
26		30	(a)	Wolves	L 1-3	Jones	18,463
27	Feb	6	(h)	Bradford	W 3-2	Jenkins, Beel, Jennings	7,942
28		17	(a)	Manchester U	L 1-5	Jennings	11,036
29		20	(h)	Tottenham H	W 2-0	Kelly, Jones	7,517
30		27	(h)	Oldham A	L 1-4	Smith	9,190
31	Mar	5	(a)	Bury	L 0-1		8,422
32		12	(h)	Port Vale	D 2-2	Kelly 2	6,869
33		19	(a)	Plymouth A	L 0-4		16,838
34		25	(h)	Bristol C	L 1-2	Hall	7,297
35		26	(h)	Bradford C	D 1-1	Jenkins	7,355
36		28	(a)	Bristol C	W 6-1	Kelly 3, Forrest, Jenkins, Opp own-goal	8,129
37	Apr	2	(a)	Leeds U	L 1-3	Jenkins	13,037
38		9	(h)	Swansea T	W 4-1	Harker, Fairhurst, Kelly, Jones	5,969
39		16	(a)	Barnsley	W 1-0	Hall	6,991
40		23	(h)	Notts C	D 1-1	Kelly	5,604
41		30	(a)	Millwall	L 0-2		10,600
42	May	7	(h)	Nottingham F	W 1-0	Kelly	6,533

FINAL LEAGUE POSITION: 19th in Division Two — Appearances / Goals

FA Cup

3	Jan	9	(h)	Derby C	L 0-4		16,694

Appearances

Goals

Conway H	Wood WH	Waterfield G	Brown J	O'Dowd P	Forrest A	Jenkins E	Prest T	Beel G	Jones T	Page L	Sommerville G	Edwards R	Bowsher S	Willighan T	Hall J	Merrick C	Hughes A	Kelly J	Twist R	Whitty E	Harker W	Weaver R	Jennings S	Schofield J	Smith E	Fairhurst R	
1	2	3	4	5	6	7	8	9	10	11																	1
	2	3	4	5	6	7	8		10	11	1	9															2
	2	3	4	5	6	7	8		10	11	1	9															3
	2	3	4	5	6	7		8	10	11	1	9															4
	2	3	4	5	6	7		8	10	11	1	9															5
	2	3	4	5		7		8	10	11	1	9	6														6
		3	4	5		7		8	10	11	1	9	6	2													7
		3	4	5		7		8	10	9	1		6	2	11												8
		3	4	5		7		8	10	9	1		6	2	11												9
		3	4	5		7		8	10	9	1		6	2	11												10
		3	4	5				8	10	7	1	9	6	2	11												11
		3	4	5		7			10	8	1	9	6	2	11												12
		3	4	5		7			10	8	1	9	6	2	11												13
		3	4			7		9	10	8	1		6	2	11	5											14
		3	4		6	8		9	10	7	1				11	5	2										15
		3	4			7		8	10	11	1		6	2		5		9									16
	2	3	4				8	9	10	11	1		6		7	5											17
	2	3	4					9	8	11	1	10	6		7	5											18
	2	3	4				8	9	10	11			6		7	5			1								19
	2	3	4				8	9		10			6		11	5			1	7							20
	2		4					9	10	8			6	3	11	5			1	7							21
	2		4		3			9		10			6		11	5			1		8	7					22
	2		4		3	7		9		8		10	6		11	5			1								23
		3	4		6	7		8	10			9	5	2	11				1								24
		3	4			7		8	10				6	2	11	5			1				9				25
		3	5			7		8	10	11			6	2					1				9	4			26
		3	5			7		8	10	11			6	2					1				9	4			27
		3	5			7			10	11			6	2					1				9	4	8		28
		3	5		6				10	11	1			2	7			9						4	8		29
		3	5		6				10	11	1			2	7			9						4	8		30
1		3	5		6				10	11				2	7			9						4	8		31
1		3			6				10	11				2	7			9					8	4		5	32
1		3	4		6	7			10					2	11			9					8			5	33
1			4		6		8		10				5	2	11		3	9				7					34
1			4			7			10				6	2	11		3	9			8					5	35
1		3	4		11	7			10				6	2				9			8					5	36
1		3	4		11	7			10				6	2				9			8					5	37
1		3	4		6	7			10					2	11			9			8					5	38
1		3	4		6		7		10					2	11			9			8					5	39
1		3	4		6	7			10					2	11			9			8					5	40
1		3	4		6	7			10					2	11			9			8					5	41
1		3	4		6	7			10				5	2	11			9			8						42
13	13	37	41	13	22	29	8	23	39	30	19	12	27	29	29	11	3	15	10	2	9	2	6	7	4	9	
		2	2	2	1	7	1	11	6	5		2			4			9			2		2		1	1	

1 own-goal

		3	4		6	7		9	10	8			5	2	11				1								3
		1	1		1	1		1	1	1			1	1	1				1								

1932-33

Manager: Albert Pickles until September, then Tom Bromilow

1	Aug	27	(h)	Chesterfield	D 1-1	Forrest	8,935
2		30	(a)	Preston NE	L 1-6	Crompton	12,732
3	Sep	3	(a)	Bradford	W 4-0	Kelly 2, Mee, Harker	11,020
4		5	(h)	Preston NE	W 4-0	C.Smith 2, Jones, Mee	14,271
5		10	(h)	Plymouth A	D 1-1	Fairhurst	12,438
6		17	(a)	Nottingham F	D 1-1	Harker	9,736
7		24	(h)	Charlton A	L 0-1		10,657
8	Oct	1	(a)	Stoke C	L 0-3		13,056
9		8	(h)	Manchester U	L 2-3	Forrest, Prest	5,314
10		15	(a)	Tottenham H	L 1-4	Prest	26,097
11		22	(h)	Fulham	D 3-3	Fairhurst, Jones, Mee	6,603
12		29	(a)	West Ham U	D 4-4	Jones 4	12,009
13	Nov	5	(h)	Lincoln C	D 0-0		9,046
14		12	(a)	Bradford C	L 1-2	Opp own-goal	11,378
15		19	(h)	Port Vale	D 1-1	Edwards	7,940
16		26	(a)	Millwall	L 1-4	Edwards	10,865
17	Dec	3	(h)	Southampton	W 2-0	Edwards, Jones	7,139
18		10	(a)	Notts C	L 2-4	Crompton 2	8,216
19		17	(h)	Swansea T	L 1-2	Jones	6,637
20		24	(a)	Bury	L 3-5	Reynolds, Jones, Crompton	7,789
21		26	(a)	Grimsby T	W 2-1	Reynolds, Harker	11,186
22		27	(h)	Grimsby T	W 2-0	Harker 2	13,602
23		31	(a)	Chesterfield	L 0-6		8,403
24	Jan	7	(h)	Bradford	W 2-0	Jones, C.Smith	7,640
25		21	(a)	Plymouth A	L 0-4		11,529
26		31	(h)	Nottingham F	D 3-3	Crompton 2, C.Smith	4,845
27	Feb	4	(a)	Charlton A	D 2-2	Crompton, Richmond	7,777
28		11	(h)	Stoke C	L 1-2	C.Smith	12,228
29		22	(a)	Manchester U	L 1-2	C.Smith	18,533
30	Mar	8	(a)	Fulham	L 1-2	Jones	11,506
31		11	(h)	West Ham U	W 4-0	C.Smith 3, Hancock	10,771
32		18	(a)	Lincoln C	W 4-1	Mustard, C.Smith, Jones 2	8,617
33		25	(h)	Bradford C	D 0-0		12,228
34	Apr	1	(a)	Port Vale	D 1-1	C.Smith	7,221
35		8	(h)	Millwall	W 3-0	C.Smith, Mustard, Jones	8,691
36		14	(h)	Oldham A	D 1-1	Mustard	13,787
37		15	(a)	Southampton	L 1-3	C.Smith	7,302
38		17	(a)	Oldham A	D 2-2	Hancock, C.Smith	13,501
39		22	(h)	Notts C	W 2-1	Reynolds, Hancock	7,665
40		24	(h)	Tottenham H	D 1-1	Jones	11,353
41		29	(a)	Swansea T	L 0-2		3,843
42	May	6	(h)	Bury	W 1-0	Jones	5,697

FINAL LEAGUE POSITION: 19th in Division Two

Appearances
Goals

FA Cup

3	Jan	14	(a)	Swindon T	W 2-1	Harker, C.Smith	
4		28	(h)	Sheffield U	W 3-1	C.Smith, Mee 2	25,380
5	Feb	18	(h)	Chesterfield	W 1-0	Hancock	31,699
6	Mar	4	(h)	Manchester C	L 0-1		48,717

Appearances
Goals

Conway H	Willighan T	Waterfield G	Brown J	Fairhurst R	Forrest A	Crompton W	Prest T	Smith C	Jones T	Hall J	Richmond G	Kelly J	Harker W	Mee G	Wood WH	Manns T	Reynolds W	Bowsher S	Hillam C	Schofield J	Edwards R	Merrick C	Jeavons W	Bennion R	Bellis G	Smith E	Hancock E	Mustard J	Wood W	Jenkins E	
1	2	3	4	5	6	7	8	9	10	11																					1
1	2		4	5	6	7	10	9	11		3	8																			2
1	2	3	4	5	6	7			10			9	8	11																	3
1	3			5	6	7		9	10				8	11	2	4															4
1	2	3	4	5	6	7			10			9	8	11																	5
1	2	3		5	6	7			10			9	8	11		4															6
1	2	3		5	6	7			10			9	8	11		4															7
1	2	3		5	6	11		9	10				8			4	7														8
1	2	3			6		8		10			9		11		4	7	5													9
1		3		5	6		8		10			9		11	2	4	7														10
1		3		5	6		8	9	10		2			11		4	7														11
		3		5	6		8	9	10		2			11		4	7		1												12
		3		5	6		8	9	10		2			11		4	7		1												13
		3		5	6	11	8	9	10		2					4	7		1												14
	2	3		5	6	11	8		10								7		1	4	9										15
	2	3			6	11			10				8						1	4	9	5	7								16
	2	3			6	11	7		10										1		9			4	5	8					17
	2	3			6	11	7		10										1		9			4	5	8					18
1	2	3	4		6	11	7		10			9													5	8					19
1	2	3	4		6	11		9	10								7				8				5						20
1	2	3			6	11			10				8				7				9			4	5						21
	2	3			6	11			10			9	8				7		1					4	5						22
	2	3			6	11			10			9	8				7		1					4	5						23
1	2				6	11		9	10		3		8				7							4	5						24
1	2					11		9	10		3		8				7	6						4	5						25
1		3			6	7		9	10		2		8	11				5						4							26
1	2				6	7		9	10		3			11				5						4			8				27
	2				6	7		9	10		3			11				5	1					4			8				28
		3			6			9	10		2		8	11			7		1					4	5						29
		3	6			11		9	10		2						7		1					4	5		8				30
		3	6			11		9	10		2		7						1					4	5		8				31
		3	6					9	10		2								1					4	5		8	7	11		32
		3	6					9	10		2								1					4	5		8	7	11		33
		3	6					9	10		2								1					4	5		8	7	11		34
		3	6					9	10		2								1					4	5		8	7	11		35
		3	6					9	10		2								1					4	5		8	7	11		36
		3	6					9	10		2								1					4	5		8	7	11		37
1		3	6				10	9			2						7							4	5		8		11		38
1		3	6				10	9			2			11			7							4	5		8				39
1		3	6					9	10		2			11										4	5		8	7			40
1		3	6					9	10		2			11										4	5		8	7			41
1		3	6						10		2			11			7							4	5		8	9			42
23	22	36	19	14	28	25	14	27	40	1	24	10	15	18	2	10	19	5	19	2	6	1	1	24	23	3	15	9	7		
				2	2	7	2	14	16		1	2	5	3			3				3						3	3			

1 own-goal

Conway H	Willighan T	Waterfield G	Brown J	Fairhurst R	Forrest A	Crompton W	Prest T	Smith C	Jones T	Hall J	Richmond G	Kelly J	Harker W	Mee G	Wood WH	Manns T	Reynolds W	Bowsher S	Hillam C	Schofield J	Edwards R	Merrick C	Jeavons W	Bennion R	Bellis G	Smith E	Hancock E	Mustard J	Wood W	Jenkins E	
1	2				6	11		9	10		3		8				7							4	5						3
1		3			6	7		9	10		2		8	11				5						4							4
		3			6	7		9	10		2			11					1					4	5		8				5
		3			6			9	10		2			11					1					4	5		8			7	6
2	1	3			4	3		4	4		4		2	3			1	1	2					4	3		2			1	
								2					1	2													1				

1933-34

Manager: Tom Bromilow

1	Aug	26	(a)	Grimsby T	L 0-1		10,501
2		28	(a)	Preston NE	L 2-3	C.Smith, Miller	18,950
3	Sep	2	(h)	Nottingham F	W 1-0	Jones	11,219
4		4	(h)	Preston NE	L 1-4	Sellars	13,543
5		9	(a)	West Ham U	W 2-1	C.Smith, Hancock	22,087
6		16	(h)	Plymouth A	D 2-2	Sellars, C.Smith	11,609
7		23	(a)	Manchester U	L 2-5	Douglas, Mustard	18,411
8		30	(h)	Bolton W	L 1-3	C.Smith	12,672
9	Oct	7	(a)	Brentford	L 2-5	Douglas, C.Smith	14,797
10		14	(h)	Fulham	W 2-1	C.Smith 2	9,878
11		21	(a)	Southampton	L 1-2	C.Smith	10,404
12		28	(h)	Blackpool	W 3-2	Robinson, Hancock, Crompton	18,150
13	Nov	4	(a)	Bradford C	L 1-2	C.Smith	10,594
14		11	(h)	Port Vale	D 0-0		13,445
15		18	(a)	Notts C	L 1-3	O'Grady	7,938
16		25	(h)	Swansea T	W 3-1	Hancock 2, Prest	8,708
17	Dec	2	(a)	Millwall	D 0-0		8,686
18		9	(h)	Lincoln C	W 3-1	O'Grady 3	7,993
19		16	(a)	Bury	D 1-1	Hancock	7,510
20		23	(h)	Hull C	W 3-1	O'Grady 2, Waterfield	10,246
21		25	(h)	Oldham A	L 0-1		19,394
22		26	(a)	Oldham A	L 0-1		15,259
23		30	(h)	Grimsby T	W 2-0	Robinson, Douglas	9,598
24	Jan	6	(a)	Nottingham F	W 2-0	O'Grady 2	8,452
25		20	(h)	West Ham U	W 4-2	C.Smith 2, Douglas, Warburton	9,655
26		27	(a)	Plymouth A	L 0-1		13,952
27	Feb	3	(h)	Manchester U	L 1-4	Warburton	9,906
28		10	(a)	Bolton W	L 1-4	Warburton	13,214
29		17	(h)	Brentford	W 3-1	Hancock, C.Smith 2	11,666
30		24	(a)	Fulham	D 1-1	Weale	15,059
31	Mar	3	(h)	Southampton	W 2-1	Hancock 2	9,177
32		10	(a)	Blackpool	D 1-1	Douglas	13,278
33		17	(h)	Bradford C	W 4-2	Waterfield, C.Smith, Hancock, Warburton	8,624
34		24	(a)	Port Vale	W 2-0	C.Smith 2	7,367
35		30	(h)	Bradford	W 1-0	Hancock	18,721
36		31	(h)	Notts C	W 1-0	Douglas	13,971
37	Apr	2	(a)	Bradford	L 0-5		15,360
38		7	(a)	Swansea T	L 0-3		7,146
39		14	(h)	Millwall	W 2-1	Chedgzoy, Weale	7,157
40		21	(a)	Lincoln C	L 0-4		3,483
41		28	(h)	Bury	L 1-2	Douglas	4,125
42	May	5	(a)	Hull C	W 1-0	C.Smith	3,784

FINAL LEAGUE POSITION: 13th in Division Two

Appearances

Goals

FA Cup

3	Jan	13	(h)	Bury	D 0-0		37,379
R		17	(a)	Bury	L 2-3	C.Smith, Richmond	20,169

Appearances

Goals

Conway H	Richmond G	Waterfield G	Bennion R	Bellis G	Brown J	Sellars W	Hancock E	Meechan J	Jones T	Miller T	Willighan T	Smith C	Chedgzoy S	O'Grady H	Scott R	Mustard J	Douglas T	Robinson A	Prest T	Crompton W	Wood WH	Warburton A	Graham W	Wallace T	Smith W	Hetherington T	Weale T	
1	2	3	4	5	6	7	8	9	10	11																		1
1		3	4	5	6	7	8		10	11	2	9																2
1	3		4	5	6	7	8		10	11	2	9																3
1		3		5	6	7	8	9		11	2		4	10														4
		3	4	5	6	7	8				2	9		10	1	11												5
	2	3	4	5	6	7	8					9		10	1	11												6
		3	4	5	6	7	8				2	9			1	11	10											7
	2	3		5	6	7	8					9		4	1	11	10											8
	2	3		5	4	7	8			11		9			1		10	6										9
1	2	3		5	4		8					9					10	6	7	11								10
1	2	3		5	4	7	8					9					10	6		11								11
1	2	3		5	4	7	8					9					10	6		11								12
1	2	3		5	4	7	8					9				11	10	6										13
1	2	3		5	4		8					9				11	10	6	7									14
1	2	3		5	4	11						9		8			10	6	7									15
	3			5	4		7					9		8	1		10	6	11		2							16
	3			5	4		7								1		10	6	11		2	8	9					17
	3			5	4		7							9	1		10	6	11		2	8						18
	3			5	4		7							9	1		10	6	11		2	8						19
	2	3		5	6		7							9	1		10		11			8		4				20
	3			6	4		7							9	1		10		11		2	8		5				21
1	3			6	4		7							9			10		11		2	8		5				22
1	2			6	4	7								9			10	3		11		8		5				23
1	2				4	7								9			10	6		11		8		5	3			24
1	2			6	4		7					9					10	11				8		5	3			25
1	2			6	4		7					9					10	11				8		5	3			26
1	2			5	4	11	7					9					10	6				8			3			27
	2			5	4		7					9					10	6				8			3	1	11	28
	2			3	4		7					9					10	6				8		5		1	11	29
	2			6	4		7					9					10					8		5	3	1	11	30
			2	6	4		7					9					10					8		5	3	1	11	31
		3		6	4		7					9					10					8		5	2	1	11	32
	2	11		3	4		7					9					10	6				8		5		1		33
	2	11		3	4		7					9					10	6				8		5		1		34
	2	11		3	4		7					9					10	6				8		5		1		35
	2			3	4	7						9					10	6				8		5		1	11	36
	2			3	4							9					10	6		7		8		5		1	11	37
	2			3	4	7						9					10	6				8		5		1	11	38
	2			3	4							9	7				10	6				8		5		1	11	39
	2			3	4							9	7				10	6				8		5		1	11	40
	2			3		7						9	4				10	6				8		5		1	11	41
	2	3		6								9	7				10	4	8					5		1	11	42
16	36	20	7	41	40	19	32	2	3	5	5	32	5	13	11	6	36	28	11	6	6	25	1	21	8	15	12	
		2				2	10		1	1		17	1	8		1	7	2	1	1		4					2	
1	2			6	4	7								9			10	3		11		8		5				3
1	2			3	4		7					9		8			10	6				11		5				R
2	2			2	2	1	1					1		2			2	2		1		2		2				
	1											1																

1934-35

Manager: Tom Bromilow

1	Aug	25	(h)	Southampton	W 3-0	Robinson 2, Douglas	12,995
2		27	(a)	West Ham U	W 2-1	Douglas, Opp own-goal	18,070
3	Sep	1	(a)	Notts C	L 0-1		15,363
4		3	(h)	West Ham U	W 5-2	Douglas 2, C.Smith, Wallace, Robinson	13,562
5		8	(h)	Bradford C	W 2-0	C.Smith, Douglas	14,325
6		15	(a)	Sheffield U	D 0-0		14,040
7		22	(h)	Barnsley	W 4-1	Downes 2, Alderman, Robinson	9,424
8		29	(a)	Port Vale	L 1-3	Downes	7,311
9	Oct	6	(h)	Manchester U	L 1-2	G.Brown	16,757
10		13	(a)	Swansea T	L 0-2		10,076
11		20	(a)	Blackpool	L 0-1		22,096
12		27	(h)	Bury	D 3-3	Hancock, G.Brown, Graham	10,715
13	Nov	3	(a)	Hull C	W 3-1	G.Brown 3	5,896
14		10	(h)	Nottingham F	W 2-1	Robinson, Hancock	12,373
15		17	(a)	Brentford	L 1-6	G.Brown	15,459
16		24	(h)	Fulham	W 3-1	Prest, G.Brown, Alderman	11,263
17	Dec	1	(a)	Bradford	D 1-1	G.Brown	8,803
18		8	(h)	Plymouth A	L 1-2	G.Brown	11,072
19		15	(a)	Norwich C	W 3-2	C.Smith, G.Brown 2	10,634
20		22	(h)	Newcastle U	L 0-3		14,792
21		25	(h)	Bolton W	W 2-1	G.Brown, C.Smith	26,518
22		29	(a)	Southampton	D 0-0		11,257
23	Jan	2	(a)	Bolton W	L 0-7		19,354
24		5	(h)	Notts C	W 4-0	G.Brown 2, Downes, C.Smith	10,409
25		19	(a)	Bradford C	D 1-1	C.Smith	12,048
26		28	(h)	Sheffield U	L 0-2		4,974
27	Feb	2	(a)	Barnsley	D 0-0		5,924
28		9	(h)	Port Vale	D 2-2	Opp own-goal, G.Brown	9,830
29		23	(h)	Swansea T	W 3-0	Hancock, C.Smith 2	9,452
30	Mar	5	(h)	Blackpool	L 1-2	Clacher	8,992
31		9	(a)	Bury	D 0-0		8,151
32		19	(h)	Hull C	L 1-3	Graham	4,256
33		23	(a)	Nottingham F	L 0-5		5,366
34		27	(a)	Manchester U	W 4-3	Rayner, Hornby, G.Brown 2	10,247
35		30	(h)	Brentford	L 0-3		11,206
36	Apr	6	(a)	Fulham	L 0-2		14,173
37		13	(h)	Bradford	L 1-2	G.Brown	5,833
38		19	(h)	Oldham A	W 4-2	G.Brown 2, Rayner, Douglas	4,813
39		20	(a)	Plymouth A	D 2-2	Robinson, Rayner	11,929
40		22	(a)	Oldham A	W 2-1	Rayner, Downes	6,857
41		27	(h)	Norwich C	W 1-0	G.Brown	3,765
42	May	4	(a)	Newcastle U	L 0-2		7,718

FINAL LEAGUE POSITION: 12th in Division Two — Appearances / Goals

FA Cup

3	Jan	12	(h)	Mansfield T	W 4-2	Hancock 2, G.Brown, C.Smith	20,790
4		26	(h)	Luton T	W 3-1	G.Brown, C.Smith, Hancock	26,605
5	Feb	16	(a)	Nottingham F	D 0-0		34,180
R		19	(h)	Nottingham F	W 3-0	Robinson, Hancock, G.Brown	29,520
6	Mar	2	(h)	Birmingham	W 3-2	Hornby 2, Hancock	47,670
SF		16	(n*)	Sheffield W	L 0-3		56,625

*Played at Villa Park, Birmingham. — Appearances / Goals

Scott R	Richmond R	Bellis G	Brown J	Wallace T	Robinson A	Hancock E	Comrie M	Syme R	Douglas T	Downes P	Alderman A	Smith C	Waterfield G	Smith W	Brown G	Hetherington T	Readett H	Prest T	Graham W	Clacher J	Hornby R	Johnson R	Weale T	Rayner F	
1	2	3	4	5	6	7	8	9	10	11															1
1	2	3	4	5	6	7	8	9	10	11															2
1	2	3	4	5	6		8	9	10	11	7														3
1	2	3	4	5	6		8		10	11	7	9													4
1	2	3	4	5	6		8		10	11	7	9													5
1	2	3	4	5	6			7	10	11	8	9													6
1	2	3	4	5	6	7		9	10	11	8														7
1	2	6	4			7		9	10	11	8		3	5											8
1	2	6	4	5		7			10	11	8		3		9										9
		6	4			7				11	8	9	3	5	10	1	2								10
		3	4		6	7				11	8			5	9	1	2	10							11
		3	4	5	6	8				11	7				9	1	2		10						12
			4	5	6	7			10	11			3	2	9	1			8						13
			4	5	6	7			10	11	8		3	2	9	1									14
1		5	4		6	7			10	11	8		3	2	9										15
1			4	5	6	7				11	8		3	2	9			10							16
1			4	5	6	7				11	8		3	2	9			10							17
1			4	5	6	7				11	8		3	2	9			10							18
1			4	5	6			7		11		9	3	2	8			10							19
1			4	5	6			7		11		9	3	2	8			10							20
1	3		4	5		7				11		9		2	8					6	10				21
1	3		4	5					10	11	7	9		2	8					6					22
1	3		4	5					10	11	7	9		2	8					6					23
1			4		6			7		11		9	3	2	8						10	5			24
1	2				6	7				11		9	3	5	8					4	10				25
1	2				6	7				11		9	3	5	8					4	10				26
1	2				6					11	7	9	3	5	8					4	10				27
1	2		4		6	7				11		9	3	5	8						10				28
1	2			5	6	7	8					9	3							4	10		11		29
1	2		4	5		7	8			11		9	3							6	10				30
1	2	5	4				8			11	7		3		9					6	10				31
1	2		4	5	6	7				11			3		9				8		10				32
1	2		4	5	6	7				11		9	3		8						10				33
	2	3	4		10	7									9	1				6	11	5		8	34
	2	3	4	5	6	7						9				1					10		11	8	35
	2	3	4		6									5	9	1		7			10		11	8	36
	3	2	4		6				10	11				5	9	1			7					8	37
	2	5	4		6	7			10	11			3		9	1								8	38
		2	4	5	6	7			10	11			3		9	1								8	39
		2	4	5	6	7			10	11			3		9	1								8	40
		2	4	5	6	7			10	11			3		9	1								8	41
	2		4	5	6	7				11			3		9	1					10			8	42
28	27	22	38	28	34	29	8	9	19	38	19	18	26	21	31	14	3	7	4	10	15	2	3	9	
				1	6	3			6	5	2	8			21			1	2	1	1			4	

2 own-goals

Scott R	Richmond R	Bellis G	Brown J	Wallace T	Robinson A	Hancock E	Comrie M	Syme R	Douglas T	Downes P	Alderman A	Smith C	Waterfield G	Smith W	Brown G	Hetherington T	Readett H	Prest T	Graham W	Clacher J	Hornby R	Johnson R	Weale T	Rayner F	
1	2		4		6	7				11		9	3	5	8						10				3
1	2		4		6	7				11		9	3	5	8						10				4
1	2		4	5	6	7				11		9	3		8						10				5
1	2		4	5	6	7				11		9	3		8						10				R
1	2		4	5	6	7				11		9	3		8						10				6
1	2		4	5	6	7				11		9	3		8						10				SF
6	6		6	4	6	6				6		6	6	2	6						6				
					1	5						2			3						2				

1935-36

Manager: Alf Boland

1	Aug	31	(a)	Charlton A	L 0-4		20,681
2	Sep	2	(a)	Port Vale	D 1-1	Brown	9,450
3		7	(h)	Hull C	W 2-0	Brown, Smith	10,082
4		9	(h)	Port Vale	W 5-1	Hancock 2, Brown, Smith, Hornby	11,268
5		14	(a)	Barnsley	L 1-3	Kilcar	10,921
6		18	(a)	Fulham	D 2-2	Smith, Downes	10,188
7		21	(h)	Plymouth A	L 0-1		10,631
8		28	(a)	Bradford C	D 0-0		7,419
9	Oct	5	(h)	Newcastle U	L 1-2	Kilcar	10,765
10		12	(a)	Tottenham H	L 1-5	Smith	34,483
11		19	(h)	Nottingham F	W 1-0	Hancock	5,226
12		26	(a)	Norwich C	L 0-2		18,030
13	Nov	2	(h)	Southampton	W 2-0	Hornby, Hancock	8,524
14		9	(a)	Sheffield U	L 0-2		11,825
15		16	(h)	Bradford	D 1-1	Liggins	10,047
16		23	(a)	Doncaster R	L 0-1		12,999
17		30	(h)	Swansea T	W 5-2	Hancock 2, Smith 2, Kilcar	6,823
18	Dec	14	(h)	Bury	D 1-1	Kilcar	8,906
19		21	(a)	Leicester C	L 0-2		9,042
20		25	(h)	Blackpool	W 3-2	Storey, Hindmarsh, Smith	19,367
21		26	(a)	Blackpool	L 0-2		15,779
22		28	(h)	Charlton A	L 0-2		11,572
23	Jan	4	(a)	Hull C	W 2-1	Kilcar 2	5,811
24		18	(h)	Barnsley	W 3-0	Smith 3	6,757
25		29	(a)	Plymouth A	L 0-2		8,566
26	Feb	1	(h)	Bradford C	W 3-0	Opp own-goal, Storey, Hancock	8,808
27		3	(a)	West Ham U	D 0-0		12,212
28		8	(a)	Newcastle U	D 1-1	Hornby	17,487
29		22	(a)	Nottingham F	L 0-2		7,513
30		29	(h)	West Ham U	W 1-0	Hornby	7,614
31	Mar	7	(a)	Bradford	L 0-2		5,120
32		14	(h)	Sheffield U	D 1-1	Kilcar	12,920
33		21	(a)	Southampton	L 0-1		5,095
34		28	(h)	Doncaster R	D 1-1	Fletcher	12,350
35	Apr	4	(a)	Swansea T	W 3-1	T.Lawton 2, Fletcher	5,890
36		10	(h)	Manchester U	D 2-2	Hubbick, Fletcher	27,245
37		11	(h)	Norwich C	D 1-1	Fletcher	10,651
38		13	(a)	Manchester U	L 0-4		39,855
39		18	(a)	Bury	W 4-0	T.Lawton 2, Fletcher, Brocklebank	7,093
40		20	(h)	Tottenham H	D 0-0		8,567
41		25	(h)	Leicester C	D 2-2	Brocklebank, T.Lawton	5,543
42	May	2	(h)	Fulham	L 0-2		4,764

FINAL LEAGUE POSITION: 15th in Division Two

Appearances
Goals

FA Cup

3	Jan	11	(h)	Sheffield U	D 0-0		25,444
R		16	(a)	Sheffield U	L 1-2	Hancock	12,802

Appearances
Goals

Hetherington T	Nevin G	Richmond G	Clacher J	Wallace T	Robinson A	Hancock E	Rayner F	Brown G	Hornby R	Downes P	Smith C	Kilcar S	Hindmarsh J	Scott R	Douglas T	Hubbick H	Johnson R	Liggins J	Nisbet G	Storey T	Adams E	Fletcher C	Brocklebank R	Lawton T	Ashbridge E	Lawton J	Oliver J	
1	2	3	4	5	6	7	8	9	10	11																		1
1	2	3	4	5	6	7	8	9	10	11																		2
1	2	3	4	5	6	7		8	10	11	9																	3
1	2	3	4	5	6	7		8	10	11	9																	4
1	2	3	4	5	6	7			10	11	9	8																5
1	2	3	4	5	6	7			8	11	9	10																6
1	2	3	4	5	6	7			8	11	9	10																7
1	2	3		5	6	7			8	11	9	10	4															8
1	2	3		5	6		7		8	11	9	10	4															9
	2	3		5	6	7				11	9	10	4	1	8													10
	2			5	6	7				11	9	10	4	1	8	3												11
	2			5	6	7	8		11		9	10	4	1		3												12
	2				6	7	8		11		9	10	4	1		3	5											13
	2				6	7	8		11			10	4	1		3	5	9										14
		2			6	7	8		11			10	4	1		3	5	9										15
		2				7						11	4	1	10	3	5	9	6	8								16
		2				7				11	9	8	4	1	10	3	5		6									17
		2			6	7				11	9	8	4	1	10	3	5											18
		2			6	7			10	11	9	8	4	1		3	5											19
		2			6				10	11	9	8	4	1		3	5			7								20
		2			6				10	11	9	8	4	1		3	5			7								21
		2			6	7	8			11	9		4	1	10	3	5											22
		2			6				10	11	9	8	4	1		3	5			7								23
		2			6	8			10	11	9		4	1		3	5			7								24
		2			6	8			10	11	9		4	1		3	5			7								25
		2			6	8			10	11	9		4	1		3	5			7								26
	2				6	8			10	11	9		4	1		3	5			7								27
1	2				6	8	11		10		9		4			3	5			7								28
1	2				6	8	11		10		9		4			3	5			7								29
	2				6	8			10		9		4			3	5			7	1	11						30
	2				6	8			10		9		4			3	5			7	1	11						31
		2			6				10			8	4			3	5	9		7	1	11						32
		2			6				10		9		4			3	5			7	1	11	8					33
		2			6	7			10				4			3	5				1	11	8	9				34
		2			6	7			10				4			3	5				1	11	8	9				35
		2			6	7			10				4			3	5				1	11	8	9				36
		2			6	7			10		9		4			3	5				1	11	8					37
		2			6	7			10		9		4			3	5					11	8		1			38
		2			6		4					10				3	5				1	11	8	9		7		39
		2			6		4								10	3	5				1	11	8	9		7		40
	2				5	7	4						6		10	3					1	11	8	9				41
	2				6		4		10	11						3					1		8	9		7	5	42
11	21	31	7	12	40	33	14	4	33	23	29	20	32	18	8	32	28	4	2	14	12	12	10	7	1	3	1	
						7		3	4	1	10	7	1			1		1		2		5	2	5				

1 own-goal

Hetherington T	Nevin G	Richmond G	Clacher J	Wallace T	Robinson A	Hancock E	Rayner F	Brown G	Hornby R	Downes P	Smith C	Kilcar S	Hindmarsh J	Scott R	Douglas T	Hubbick H	Johnson R	Liggins J	Nisbet G	Storey T	Adams E	Fletcher C	Brocklebank R	Lawton T	Ashbridge E	Lawton J	Oliver J	
		2			6	7			10	11	9	8	4	1		3	5											3
		2			6	7			10	11	9	8	4	1		3	5											R
		2			2	2			2	2	2	2	2	2		2	2											
						1																						

1936-37

Manager: Alf Boland

1	Aug	29	(h)	Nottingham F	W 3-0	Lawton 2, Fletcher	11,498
2	Sep	5	(a)	Chesterfield	L 1-4	Lawton	14,762
3		7	(h)	Fulham	L 0-2		9,998
4		12	(h)	Aston Villa	L 1-2	Gastall	16,098
5		14	(h)	Plymouth A	W 2-0	Gastall, Brocklebank	8,725
6		19	(a)	Bradford C	W 3-1	Gastall 2, Fletcher	10,221
7		21	(a)	Fulham	L 0-2		9,967
8		26	(h)	Swansea T	D 0-0		12,131
9	Oct	3	(a)	Southampton	D 1-1	Brocklebank	16,066
10		10	(h)	Tottenham H	W 3-1	Lawton 3	20,447
11		17	(a)	Blackpool	L 0-2		22,529
12		24	(h)	Blackburn R	D 0-0		32,567
13		31	(a)	Bury	L 1-3	Gastall	21,721
14	Nov	7	(h)	Leicester C	D 0-0		10,208
15		14	(a)	West Ham U	W 2-0	Lawton 2	19,464
16		21	(h)	Norwich C	W 3-0	Toll 2, Lawton	9,352
17		28	(a)	Newcastle U	L 0-3		27,465
18	Dec	5	(h)	Bradford	D 2-2	Toll, Lawton	7,360
19		12	(a)	Barnsley	D 1-1	Fletcher	7,086
20		19	(h)	Sheffield U	W 1-0	Lawton	10,905
21		25	(h)	Doncaster R	W 3-0	Miller 2, Fletcher	21,295
22		26	(a)	Nottingham F	W 2-1	Brocklebank, Fletcher	21,340
23		28	(a)	Doncaster R	L 0-2		8,140
24	Jan	2	(h)	Chesterfield	W 3-1	Richardson, Toll, Fletcher	8,476
25		9	(a)	Aston Villa	D 0-0		37,691
26		23	(h)	Bradford C	W 3-0	Stein, Fletcher, Opp own-goal	8,461
27	Feb	6	(h)	Southampton	L 1-3	Toll	13,345
28		11	(a)	Swansea T	L 0-3		6,018
29		13	(a)	Tottenham H	L 0-3		30,288
30		24	(h)	Blackpool	W 3-0	Fletcher 2, Stein	9,051
31		27	(a)	Blackburn R	L 1-3	Stein	18,240
32	Mar	6	(h)	Bury	L 1-2	Brocklebank	9,006
33		13	(a)	Leicester C	L 3-7	Gastall, Brocklebank, Fletcher	19,747
34		20	(h)	West Ham U	W 2-1	Fletcher, Toll	8,455
35		26	(h)	Coventry C	D 3-3	Toll 2, Fletcher	9,982
36		27	(a)	Norwich C	D 2-2	Toll, Pake	15,792
37		30	(a)	Coventry C	W 1-0	Brocklebank	20,240
38	Apr	3	(h)	Newcastle U	L 0-3		10,574
39		10	(a)	Bradford	L 0-2		9,697
40		17	(h)	Barnsley	W 3-0	Brocklebank 2, Rayner	4,919
41		24	(a)	Sheffield U	D 1-1	Brocklebank	12,412
42	May	1	(a)	Plymouth A	W 1-0	Miller	9,915

FINAL LEAGUE POSITION: 13th in Division Two

Appearances
Goals

FA Cup

3	Jan	16	(a)	Aston Villa	W 3-2	Toll 2, Brocklebank	44,000
4		30	(h)	Bury	W 4-1	Stein, Toll, Brocklebank, Fletcher	28,404
5	Feb	20	(h)	Arsenal	L 1-7	Richardson	54,445

Appearances
Goals

Hetherington T	Richmond G	Hubbick H	Hindmarsh J	Johnson R	Robinson A	Carson J	Brocklebank R	Lawton T	Kilcar S	Fletcher C	Hancock E	Gastall J	Woodruff A	Hornby R	Rayner F	Storey T	Pinkerton H	Clacher J	Miller W	Stein J	Smith W	Toll J	Oliver G	Richardson A	Adams E	Nevin G	Pake R	Fisher P	Chester T	
1	2	3	4	5	6	7	8	9	10	11																				1
1	2	3	4	5	6	7	8	9	10	11																				2
1	2	3	4	5	6	7	8	9	10	11																				3
1	2	3	4	5	6		8		10	11	7	9																		4
1	2	3	4		6		8			11	7	9	5	10																5
1	2	3			6		8			11		9	5	10	4	7														6
1	2	3			6		8			11		9	5	10	4	7														7
1	2	3			6		8			11		9	5		4	7	10													8
1	2	3			4		8	9				7	5					6	10	11										9
1	2	3			4		8	9				7	5					6	10	11										10
1	2	3			4		8	9				7	5					6	10	11										11
1	2	3	4		6		8	9				7	5						10	11										12
1	2	3			4		8	9				7	5						10	11	6									13
1	2	3			4		8	9		11	7		5						10		6									14
1	2	3			6			9		11		7	5		4				10			8								15
1	2	3			6			9		11		7	5		4				10			8								16
1	2	3			6			9		11		7	5		4				10			8								17
1	2				6	7		9		11			5		4				10			8	3							18
1	2	3				7		9		11			5		4			6	10			8								19
1	2	3				7	10	9		11			5		4			6				8								20
1	2	3					8	9		11			5		4			6	10	7										21
1	2	3					8	9		11			5		4			6	10	7										22
1	2	3					8	9		11			5		4			6	10	7										23
1	2	3			6		10			11			5		4					7		8		9						24
	2	3			6		10			11			5		4					7		8		9	1					25
	2	3			6		10			11			5		4					7		8		9	1					26
	2	3			6		10			11			5		4					7		8		9	1					27
	3									11			5		4				10	7	6	8		9	1	2				28
	2			5	6		10			11									4	7		8			1	3	9			29
	2				3					11		9	5		4				10	7	6				1			8		30
	2				3					11		9	5		4				10	7	6				1			8		31
1	2				6		10			11			5		4					7			3	9				8		32
1	3						10			11		9	5		4			6		7								8	2	33
	3				6		10			11			5		4					7		8		9	1				2	34
	3						10			11			5		4			6		7		8			1		9		2	35
	3									11			5		4			6	10	7		8			1		9		2	36
	3						10			11			5		4			6		7		8			1	2	9			37
	3						10			11			5		4			6		7		8			1	2	9			38
	3		6							11			5		4				10	7		9			1	2		8		39
	3				2		9			11			5	10	4				8	7	6				1					40
	3				2		9			11			5	10	4				8	7	6				1					41
	3				2		9			11			5	10	4				8	7	6				1					42
26	42	26	7	5	30	6	32	18	4	37	3	16	37	6	30	3	1	13	23	27	8	18	2	7	16	5	5	5	4	
							9	11		12		6			1				3	3		9		1			1			

1 own-goal

Hetherington T	Richmond G	Hubbick H	Hindmarsh J	Johnson R	Robinson A	Carson J	Brocklebank R	Lawton T	Kilcar S	Fletcher C	Hancock E	Gastall J	Woodruff A	Hornby R	Rayner F	Storey T	Pinkerton H	Clacher J	Miller W	Stein J	Smith W	Toll J	Oliver G	Richardson A	Adams E	Nevin G	Pake R	Fisher P	Chester T	
	2	3			6		10			11			5		4					7		8		9	1					3
	2	3			6		10			11			5		4					7		8		9	1					4
	2	3			6		10			11			5		4					7		8		9	1					5
	3	3			3		3			3			3		3					3		3		3	3					
							2			1										1		3		1						

1937-38

Manager: Alf Boland

1	Aug	28	(h)	Bury	W 2-0	Brocklebank, Fletcher	16,221
2		30	(a)	Tottenham H	L 0-4		13,766
3	Sep	4	(a)	Coventry C	L 0-1		25,608
4		6	(h)	Tottenham H	W 2-1	Richardson, Fletcher	11,287
5		11	(h)	Nottingham F	D 0-0		11,161
6		13	(h)	Sheffield U	W 2-0	Fisher, Miller	7,847
7		18	(a)	Newcastle U	D 2-2	Fisher, Brocklebank	14,982
8		20	(a)	Sheffield U	L 1-2	Fletcher	8,270
9		25	(h)	Luton T	W 3-2	Brocklebank, Hornby, Fletcher	14,073
10	Oct	2	(a)	Barnsley	D 2-2	Storey, Miller	15,358
11		9	(h)	Stockport C	D 0-0		16,423
12		16	(a)	Plymouth A	W 3-2	Brocklebank 2, Miller	15,417
13		23	(h)	Chesterfield	L 0-2		9,329
14		30	(a)	Swansea T	L 1-3	Brocklebank	10,111
15	Nov	6	(h)	Norwich C	W 3-0	Taylor 2, Gastall	11,073
16		13	(a)	Aston Villa	D 0-0		37,167
17		20	(h)	Southampton	W 4-0	Stein 3, Miller	11,717
18		27	(a)	West Ham U	L 0-1		21,607
19	Dec	4	(h)	Bradford	D 1-1	Chester	9,453
20		11	(a)	Blackburn R	D 3-3	Storey, Miller, Stein	15,136
21		18	(h)	Sheffield W	D 1-1	Storey	13,722
22		25	(h)	Fulham	W 1-0	Robson	27,584
23		27	(a)	Fulham	L 1-2	Miller	18,008
24	Jan	1	(a)	Bury	L 0-4		21,717
25		15	(h)	Coventry C	W 2-0	Storey, Miller	9,821
26		26	(a)	Nottingham F	D 1-1	Miller	5,761
27		29	(h)	Newcastle U	W 2-1	Miller, Hornby	10,550
28	Feb	5	(a)	Luton T	L 1-3	Miller	14,957
29		12	(h)	Barnsley	W 1-0	Robson	12,178
30		19	(a)	Stockport C	L 1-3	Brocklebank	14,097
31		26	(h)	Plymouth A	L 0-2		9,315
32	Mar	5	(a)	Chesterfield	W 1-0	Brocklebank	12,208
33		12	(h)	Swansea T	W 2-0	Taylor, Miller	9,050
34		19	(a)	Norwich C	L 0-1		10,072
35	Apr	2	(a)	Southampton	D 0-0		15,113
36		5	(h)	Aston Villa	W 3-0	Miller 2, Brocklebank	16,704
37		9	(h)	West Ham U	W 2-0	Brocklebank, Hornby	11,173
38		15	(h)	Manchester U	W 1-0	Brocklebank	28,459
39		16	(a)	Bradford	L 1-3	Brocklebank	10,180
40		18	(a)	Manchester U	L 0-4		35,808
41		23	(h)	Blackburn R	W 3-1	Brocklebank 2, Stein	14,139
42		30	(a)	Sheffield W	L 1-2	Storey	19,571

FINAL LEAGUE POSITION: 6th in Division Two

Appearances
Goals

FA Cup

3	Jan	8	(a)	Sheffield W	D 1-1	Stein	33,006
R		11	(h)	Sheffield W	W 3-1	Brocklebank 2, Hornby	25,933
4		22	(a)	Chesterfield	L 2-3	Miller, Robson	21,620

Appearances
Goals

Adams E	Robinson A	Richmond G	Rayner F	Woodruff A	Smith W	Cunliffe A	Toll J	Brocklebank R	Miller W	Fletcher C	Richardson A	Johnson R	Lumsden F	Fisher P	Storey T	Hornby R	Stein J	Pinkerton H	Chester T	Martindale L	Taylor F	Gastall J	Hetherington T	Robson W	
1	2	3	4	5	6	7	8	9	10	11															1
1	2	3	4	5	6	7	8	9	10	11															2
1	2	3	4	5	6	7		8	10	11	9														3
1	2	3	4	5	6	7		8	10	11	9														4
1	2	3	4	5	6	7		10	8	11	9														5
1		3	4	2	6			9	10	11		5	7	8											6
1	2	3	4	5	6			9						8	7	10	11								7
1	2	3	4	5				9		11				8	7	10		6							8
1	2	3	4	5	6			9	8	11					7	10									9
1	2		4	5	6			9	8	11					7	10			3						10
1	2		4	5	6	7		9	8	11						10			3						11
1	2		4	5	6	7		9	8	11						10			3						12
1	2		4	5	6	7		9	8	11						10			3						13
1	2			5	6			9	8	11					7	10			3	4					14
1	2				6			10	8			5					11		3	4	7	9			15
1	2				6			10	8			5					11		3	4	7	9			16
1	2				6			10	8			5					11		3	4	7	9			17
1	2				6			10	8			5					11		3	4	7	9			18
1	2				6			10	8			5					11		3	4	7	9	1		19
1	2				6			10	8			5			7		11		3	4				9	20
1	2				6			10	8			5			7		11		3	4				9	21
1	2				6			10	8			5					11		3	4	7			9	22
1		2			6			9	8			5			7		11	10	3	4					23
1	2		4		6			10	8		9	5			7		11		3						24
1	2				6			10	8			5			7	11			3	4				9	25
1	2			5	6			10	8							11	7		3	4				9	26
1	2			5	6			10	8							11	7		3	4				9	27
1	2			5	6			10	8							11	7		3	4				9	28
1	2			5	6	7		10	8							11			3	4				9	29
1	2		4	5	6			10	8						7	11			3					9	30
1	2	3		5	6			10	8						7	11				4				9	31
1	2				6			9	8			5		10		11			3	4	7				32
1	2				6			9	8			5		10		11			3	4	7				33
1	2				6			9	8			5		10		11			3	4	7				34
1	2				6			9	8			5		10	7	11			3	4					35
1	2				6			9	8			5		10	7	11			3	4					36
1	2				6			9	8			5		10	7	11			3	4					37
1	2				6			9	8			5		10		11			3	4	7				38
1	2		6					9	8			5		10		11			3	4	7				39
1	2		6	4				9	8			5		10	11				3	7					40
1	2		6					9	8			5		10	7		11		3	4					41
1	2		6					9	8			5		10	7	11			3	4					42
41	40	11	19	21	37	9	2	42	40	13	4	23	1	14	18	24	15	2	32	27	11	5	1	10	
								14	13	4	1			2	5	3	5		1		3	1		2	

Adams E	Robinson A	Richmond G	Rayner F	Woodruff A	Smith W	Cunliffe A	Toll J	Brocklebank R	Miller W	Fletcher C	Richardson A	Johnson R	Lumsden F	Fisher P	Storey T	Hornby R	Stein J	Pinkerton H	Chester T	Martindale L	Taylor F	Gastall J	Hetherington T	Robson W	
1	2				6			10	8		9	5				11	7		3	4					3
1	2				6			10	8			5				11	7		3	4				9	R
1	2				6			10	8			5			7	11			3	4				9	4
3	3				3			3	3		1	3			1	3	2		3	3				2	
								2	1							1	1							1	

1938-39

Manager: Alf Boland

1	Aug	27	(a)	Coventry C	D 1-1	Hornby	25,830
2		30	(h)	Southampton	W 2-1	Brocklebank, F.Taylor	13,334
3	Sep	3	(h)	Nottingham F	W 2-1	Martindale, Hornby	11,534
4		5	(h)	Fulham	W 2-0	Gardner, Brocklebank	13,892
5		10	(a)	Newcastle U	L 2-3	Hornby, Martindale	30,824
6		12	(a)	Fulham	D 0-0		11,966
7		17	(h)	West Brom A	L 0-3		15,990
8		24	(a)	Norwich C	L 0-4		13,345
9	Oct	1	(h)	Luton T	W 3-2	Rayner, Hornby, Miller	11,699
10		8	(a)	Plymouth A	L 0-1		16,996
11		15	(h)	Blackburn R	W 3-2	Clayton 2, Hornby	29,254
12		22	(a)	Millwall	D 1-1	Hornby	33,975
13		29	(h)	Bury	L 0-1		17,719
14	Nov	5	(a)	Bradford	D 2-2	Clayton, F.Taylor	12,408
15		12	(h)	Swansea T	D 1-1	F.Taylor	12,128
16		19	(a)	Chesterfield	L 2-3	F.Taylor, Miller	13,780
17		24	(h)	Tranmere R	W 3-1	Clayton 3	9,354
18	Dec	3	(a)	West Ham U	L 0-1		18,759
19		10	(h)	Manchester C	D 1-1	Gardner	24,096
20		17	(a)	Sheffield W	L 1-4	Clayton	12,251
21		24	(h)	Coventry C	W 1-0	Clayton	12,382
22		26	(h)	Tottenham H	W 1-0	A.Taylor	15,629
23		27	(a)	Tottenham H	L 0-1		30,276
24		31	(a)	Nottingham F	D 2-2	Clayton, Rayner	11,456
25	Jan	2	(a)	Sheffield U	D 1-1	Billingham	20,958
26		14	(h)	Newcastle U	W 2-0	Billingham, Dryden	12,745
27		28	(h)	Norwich C	W 3-0	Hornby, Brocklebank, Billingham	10,345
28	Feb	1	(a)	West Brom A	W 2-1	Gardner, Billingham	7,831
29		4	(a)	Luton T	L 0-1		13,547
30		11	(h)	Plymouth A	W 1-0	Billingham	12,893
31		18	(a)	Blackburn R	L 0-1		30,223
32		25	(h)	Millwall	W 2-0	Brocklebank 2	10,312
33	Mar	4	(a)	Bury	L 0-1		13,950
34		11	(h)	Bradford	D 0-0		8,473
35		18	(a)	Swansea T	L 0-4		10,357
36		25	(h)	Chesterfield	L 1-2	Brocklebank	8,095
37	Apr	1	(a)	Tranmere R	W 3-0	Billingham, Dryden, Knight	6,759
38		7	(h)	Sheffield U	L 2-3	Knight, Billingham	18,104
39		8	(h)	West Ham U	W 1-0	Brocklebank	10,420
40		15	(a)	Manchester C	L 0-2		19,230
41		22	(h)	Sheffield W	L 1-2	Brocklebank	9,953
42		29	(a)	Southampton	L 1-2	Clayton	4,169

FINAL LEAGUE POSITION: 14th in Division Two

Appearances
Goals

FA Cup

3	Jan	7	(a)	Notts C	L 1-3	Brocklebank	14,500

Appearances
Goals

Adams E	Richmond G	Chester T	Gardner T	Johnson R	Smith W	Taylor F	Miller W	Brocklebank R	Fisher P	Hornby R	Woodruff A	Martindale L	Rayner F	Marshall J	Robinson A	Bray G	Clayton J	Taylor A	Billingham J	Dryden J	Morris W	Knight G	
1	2	3	4	5	6	7	8	9	10	11													1
1	2	3	4	5	6	7	8	9	10	11													2
1		3	4	5	6	7	8	9		11	2	10											3
1		3	4	5	6	7	10	9		11	2	8											4
1		3	4	5	6	7	10	9		11	2	8											5
1		3	4	5	6	7		9		11	2	10	8										6
1		3	4	5	6	7		9	10	11	2	8											7
1			4	5	6	7		9		11	2	10	8	3									8
1		3	4	5		7	10	9		11			8		2	6							9
1		3	4	5		7	10	8		11					2	6	9						10
1		3	4	5		7	8	10		11					2	6	9						11
1		3	4			7	10	8		11	5				2	6	9						12
1		3	4			7	10	8		11	5				2	6	9						13
1		3	8			7				11	5	4			2	6	9	10					14
1		3	8			7				11	5	4			2	6	9	10					15
1			8			7	10			11	5	4		3	2	6	9						16
1			8			7		10		11	5	4		3	2	6	9						17
1			8			7		10		11	5	4		3	2	6	9						18
1			8			7		10		11	5	4		3	2	6	9						19
1			8			7		10		11	5	4		3	2	6	9						20
1			8			7		10		11	5	4		3	2	6	9						21
1			8					10		11	5		4	3	2	6	9	7					22
1			8					10		11	5		4	3	2	6	9		7				23
1			8						10	11	5		4	3	2	6	9		7				24
1			8			7		10		11	5		4	3	2	6			9				25
1			8			7		10			5	4		3	2	6			9	11			26
1			4			7		10		11	5			3	2	6			9		8		27
1			4			7		10		11	5			3	2	6			9		8		28
1			4			7		10		11	5			3	2	6			9		8		29
1			4			7		10			5			3	2	6			9	11	8		30
1			4			7		10		11	5			3	2	6			9		8		31
1						7		9		11	5	4		3	2	6					8	10	32
1	3		9			7				11	5	4			2	6					8	10	33
1	3					7		9		11	5	4			2	6					8	10	34
1	3					7		9		11	5	4			2	6					8	10	35
1			8			7		9		11	5	4		3	2	6						10	36
1			4					8		11	5			3	2	6			9	7		10	37
1			4					8		11	5			3	2	6			9	7		10	38
1		2	4			7		8		11	5			3		6			9			10	39
1			4			7		10		11	5			3	2	6			9		8		40
1			4			7		10		11	5			3	2	6			9		8		41
1			2			7		10		11	5	4		3		6	9				8		42
42	5	15	39	11	8	37	11	37	4	40	37	21	7	25	32	34	16	3	14	4	12	8	
			3			4	2	8		7		2	2				10	1	7	2		2	

Adams E	Richmond G	Chester T	Gardner T	Johnson R	Smith W	Taylor F	Miller W	Brocklebank R	Fisher P	Hornby R	Woodruff A	Martindale L	Rayner F	Marshall J	Robinson A	Bray G	Clayton J	Taylor A	Billingham J	Dryden J	Morris W	Knight G	
1			8			7		10		11	5		4	3	2	6			9				3
1			1			1		1		1	1		1	1	1	1			1				
								1															

1939-40

Manager: None

1	Aug	26	(h)	Coventry C	D 1-1	Hornby	11,661
2	Sep	2	(a)	Birmingham	L 0-2		18,001

Above games played in Division Two before Football League closed down upon outbreak of World War Two

3	Oct	21	(h)	Bolton W	D 1-1	Brocklebank	3,300
4		28	(a)	Preston NE	L 1-2	Taylor	5,850
5	Nov	11	(a)	Bury	L 0-5		3,686
6		18	(h)	Carlisle U	W 8-0	Clayton 4, Brocklebank, Knight 2, Taylor	1,665
7		25	(a)	Oldham A	L 1-3	Brocklebank	2,500
8	Dec	2	(h)	Rochdale	W 3-1	Knight 2, Clayton	1,181
9		9	(a)	Blackburn R	L 0-1		1,233
10		23	(h)	Blackpool	D 1-1	Knight	2,668
11	Jan	6	(a)	Barrow	L 2-5	Moir, Knight	3,753
12		20	(h)	Southport	W 7-3	Brocklebank 2, Hornby 2, Knight 2, Taylor	438
13	Feb	24	(h)	Preston NE	W 1-0	Taylor	2,315
14	Mar	9	(h)	Bury	L 1-2	Wood	1,349
15		16	(a)	Carlisle U	W 4-3	Wood 2, Brocklebank, Hornby	
16		23	(a)	Oldham A	W 4-3	Taylor, Wood 2, Brocklebank	4,114
17		30	(a)	Rochdale	D 1-1	Wood	3,000
18	Apr	6	(h)	Blackburn R	D 0-0		2,995
19		10	(a)	Bolton W	L 1-5	Hornby	250
20		13	(a)	Blackpool	L 0-5		5,000
21	May	21	(h)	Barrow	W 2-0	Hornby 2	423
22		25	(a)	Southport	D 1-1	Knight	400
23		29	(a)	Accrington S	W 2-1	Knight 2	
24	Jan	1	(h)	Accrington S	W 7-0	Nuttall 2, Hornby 2, Gardner, Brocklebank, Knight	448

FINAL LEAGUE POSITION: 6th in North West Regional League (12 clubs completed)

League War Cup (North A Group)

25	Apr	20	(a)	Chester	W 3-1	Morris 2, Hornby	2,202
26		27	(h)	Chester	W 3-0	Hornby 2, Brocklebank	2,458
27	May	4	(h)	Blackpool	L 1-2	Morris	7,857
28		11	(a)	Blackpool	L 1-3	Billingham	7,631

1	2	3	4	5	6	7	8	9	10	11	
Adams	Robinson	Marshall	Gardner	Woodruff	Bray	Hays	Brocklebank	Clayton	Dryden	Hornby	1
..	..	..	..	..	..	..	..	..	..	..	2

1	2	3	4	5	6	7	8	9	10	11	
Adams	Marshall	Mather	Martindale	Spencer	Bray	Hays	Gardner	Brocklebank	Knight	Hornby	3
..	..	..	..	T.Smith	..	Taylor	..	..	..	..	4
Bentley	..	..	..	Woodruff	..	..	..	T.Smith	..	..	5
..	..	..	Gardner	..	..	..	Brocklebank	Clayton	..	..	6
..	..	..	..	..	..	..	..	..	..	..	7
..	..	..	..	..	..	..	..	..	..	..	8
..	..	..	..	..	..	..	..	..	..	..	9
Adams	..	..	Martindale	..	..	..	Gardner	Brocklebank	..	..	10
Bentley	Mather	Marshall	Gardner	..	..	..	Brocklebank	Moir	..	..	11
Hetherington	Marshall	Mather	..	..	T.Smith	..	Knight	Brocklebank	Emptage	..	12
Morton	T.Smith	..	..	..	Bray	..	..	..	Wood	..	13
..	Marshall	..	T.Smith	..	..	Martindale	Wood	..	Knight	..	14
..	T.Smith	..	Gardner	..	..	Taylor	..	..	..	McIntosh	15
..	..	..	..	..	..	..	..	..	..	Hornby	16
..	Marshall	..	..	..	..	Martindale	..	..	..	..	17
..	..	..	..	..	..	T.Smith	..	..	..	..	18
Adams	..	..	..	..	T.Smith	Martindale	G.Smith	..	..	..	19
..	..	..	T.Smith	..	Bray	..	Gardner	..	..	..	20
..	T.Smith	..	Gardner	..	Lomax	Knight	Dougall	Kippax	Brocklebank	..	21
..	Marshall	..	..	..	T.Smith	Hulbert	..	Brocklebank	Knight	..	22
..	T.Smith	..	..	..	Lomax	Nuttall	..	..	..	..	23
..	..	..	..	..	..	..	..	Knight	Brocklebank	..	24

1	2	3	4	5	6	7	8	9	10	11	
Adams	T.Smith	Mather	Gardner	Woodruff	Loughran	Hulbert	Morris	Billingham	Brocklebank	Hornby	25
..	..	..	..	..	..	..	..	..	..	..	26
..	..	..	..	..	..	..	..	..	..	..	27
..	..	..	..	..	Johnson	..	Knight	..	..	..	28

Appearances (goals scored in brackets): E.Adams 15, G.Bentley 6, J.Billingham 4 (1), G.Bray 18, R.Brocklebank 27 (9), Clayton 6 (5), N.Dougall 4, Dryden 2, Emptage 1, Gardner 27 (1), J.Hays 3, T.Hetherington 1, R.Hornby 27 (12), Hulbert 5, R.Johnson 1, F.Kippax 1, G.Knight 23 (12), J.Lomax 3, J.Loughran 3, McIntosh 1, J.Marshall 18, L.Martindale 8, H.Mather 26, W.Moir 1 (1), Morton 6, W.Morris 3 (3), Nuttall 2 (2), A.Robinson 2, G.Smith 1, T.Smith 18, H.Spencer 1, F.Taylor 12 (5), Wood 6 (6), A.Woodruff 26.
Note: Totals include two games played before League football was abandoned.

1940-41

Manager: None

1	Aug	31	(h)	Blackburn R	W 2-1	Brocklebank, Hornby	3,731
2	Sep	7	(a)	Rochdale	W 2-1	Cooke, Brocklebank	2,000
3		14	(a)	Bury	D 0-0		2,265
4		21	(h)	Crewe A	W 5-1	Cooke 3, Martindale, Brocklebank	2,631
5		28	(a)	Preston NE	L 2-6	Brocklebank (pen), Martindale	2,000
6	Oct	5	(h)	Stockport C	D 2-2	Wilkinson 2	2,306
7		12	(h)	Manchester U	L 0-1		3,652
8		19	(a)	Oldham A	L 1-6	Hornby	2,000
9		26	(h)	Oldham A	W 2-1	Kippax, Brocklebank	2,402
10	Nov	2	(a)	Manchester U	L 1-4	Kippax	1,000
11		9	(a)	Blackburn R	D 1-1	Gardner	1,100
12		16	(a)	Chester	D 0-0		1,916
13		23	(h)	Rochdale	L 0-1		1,772
14		30	(h)	Bury	W 4-3	Kippax 4	1,620
15	Dec	7	(a)	Stockport C	L 0-1		1,600
16		14	(a)	Chester	W 4-3	Brocklebank 2, Kippax 2	350
17		21	(a)	Southport	W 3-1	Kippax 3	300
18		25	(h)	Manchester C	D 2-2	Kippax, Brocklebank (pen)	8,272
19		28	(h)	Preston NE	W 2-0	Brocklebank, Knight	4,360
20	Jan	25	(h)	Everton	L 2-3	Brocklebank 2	5,216
21	Feb	1	(h)	Blackburn R	W 2-1	Bright, Knight	2,310
22	Mar	1	(a)	Oldham A	L 0-2		2,000
23		8	(h)	Oldham A	W 4-0	Knight 2, Brocklebank 2	1,034
24		15	(a)	Blackburn R	L 2-3	Knight 2	2,000
25		22	(a)	Halifax T	D 2-2	Coates, Bright	2,500
26		29	(a)	Sheffield W	W 2-0	Bright, Hornby	1,500
27	Apr	5	(h)	Sheffield W	W 2-0	Kippax, Bright	1,880
28		12	(h)	Bolton W	D 2-2	Coates, Kippax	3,724
29		14	(a)	Bolton W	W 2-0	Hornby, Coates	2,000
30		19	(h)	Halifax T	W 3-1	Brocklebank, Kippax, Bright	1,802
31		26	(a)	Huddersfield T	W 3-0	Coates, Brocklebank, Kippax	1,001
32	May	3	(a)	Everton	W 2-0	Coates 2	2,500
33		10	(h)	Blackpool	W 1-0	Brocklebank (pen)	5,693
34		17	(h)	Manchester U	L 0-1		9,790
35		24	(a)	Blackpool	L 0-3		2,000

FINAL LEAGUE POSITION: 14th in North Regional League (36 clubs competed)

League War Cup

1	Feb	15	(a)	Bolton W	L 1-3	Brocklebank	3,000
		22	(h)	Bolton W	D 2-2	Hornby, Bright	2,415

Note: League tables for this season were decided on goal-average only. Teams played varying numbers of games and points were not awarded.
Matches 20, 32-34 (4 in all) also counted as Lancashire Cup games.

1	2	3	4	5	6	7	8	9	10	11	
Adams	Marshall	Mather	Gardner	Woodruff	Lomax	Dougall	Cooke	Knight	Brocklebank	Hornby	1
..	..	..	..	..	..	..	..	..	..	..	2
..	..	..	..	..	..	..	..	..	..	..	3
..	..	..	..	..	..	Martindale	Dougall	Brocklebank	Cooke	..	4
..	..	..	..	..	..	..	..	..	..	..	5
..	..	..	..	..	..	Dougall	Taylor	Wilkinson	Brocklebank	..	6
Bentley	..	..	..	..	..	Martindale	Dougall	..	..	..	7
..	..	..	..	..	Loughran	Lomax	..	..	..	..	8
Fairbrother	..	..	Loughran	..	Lomax	Jeavons	..	Kippax	..	..	9
..	..	..	Gardner	..	Loughran	Coates	..	..	..	..	10
..	..	..	Loughran	..	Lomax	Dougall	Gardner	Brocklebank	Knight	..	11
..	..	..	Gardner	..	Loughran	..	Brocklebank	Kippax	..	..	12
..	..	..	Loughran	..	Lomax	Gardner	..	..	..	..	13
..	..	..	..	..	Bray	..	..	..	..	..	14
Holdcroft	..	..	Gardner	..	Lomax	Dougall	..	..	..	Nuttall	15
..	..	..	Loughran	..	..	Gardner	..	..	..	Hornby	16
Conway	..	..	Gardner	..	Loughran	Nuttall	..	..	..	..	17
..	..	..	..	..	..	Jackson	..	..	..	..	18
..	..	..	..	..	..	..	..	..	..	..	19
..	Robinson	..	..	..	..	..	..	..	..	..	20
..	Johnson	..	..	..	..	Hornby	..	..	..	Bright	21
Robinson	Loughran	..	..	..	Lomax	Bright	..	Coates	Kippax	Hornby	22
Holdcroft	Snowden	..	..	..	Loughran	..	..	..	Knight	..	23
..	..	..	..	..	Robinson	..	..	Kippax	..	..	24
Bentley	..	..	..	..	..	..	..	Coates	..	..	25
Conway	..	..	..	..	..	..	..	..	Jackson	..	26
..	..	..	..	..	..	Coates	..	Kippax	Hornby	Bright	27
..	..	..	..	..	Johnson	..	Potts	..	..	..	28
..	..	..	..	..	Robinson	..	Brocklebank	..	..	..	29
..	..	..	..	..	..	..	..	..	..	..	30
..	..	..	..	..	..	..	..	..	..	..	31
..	..	..	..	..	..	..	..	..	..	..	32
..	..	Marshall	..	..	..	..	..	..	..	..	33
..	..	Mather	..	..	..	..	..	..	..	..	34
Holdcroft	..	Kirkman	..	..	Marsden	..	..	..	..	..	35

Conway	Kirkman	Mather	Gardner	Robinson	Loughran	Hornby	Brocklebank	Kippax	Knight	Bright	1
Robinson	Loughran	..	..	Woodruff	Bray	..	..	..	..	..	

Appearances (goals scored in brackets): E.Adams 6, G.Bentley 3, G.Bray 2, Bright 17 (6), R.Brocklebank 36 (17), F.Coates 14 (6), H.Conway 15, Cooke 5 (4), N.Dougall 13, Fairbrother 6, T.Gardner 36 (1), Holdcroft 5, R.Hornby 36 (5), H.Jackson 3, P.Jackson 1, Jeavons 1, R.Johnson 2, F.Kippax 25 (16), Kirkman 2, G.Knight 19 (6), J.Lomax 14, J.Loughran 17, Marsden 1, J.Marshall 20, L.Martindale 3 (2), H.Mather 35, Nuttall 2, H.Potts 1, A.Robinson 14, Snowden 13, F.Taylor 1, Wilkinson 3 (2), A.Woodruff 36.

1941-42

Manager: None

1	Aug	30	(a)	Halifax T	W 3-2	Kippax 2, Brocklebank	2,000
2	Sep	6	(h)	Halifax T	L 0-1		2,863
3		13	(h)	Rochdale	W 3-1	Whalley, Kippax, Gardner	2,271
4		20	(a)	Rochdale	D 1-1	Brocklebank	1,995
5		27	(a)	Preston NE	L 1-2	Kippax	7,000
6	Oct	4	(h)	Preston NE	W 1-0	Brocklebank	4,699
7		11	(h)	Southport	W 4-2	Brocklebank 2, Kippax, Gardner	2,181
8		18	(a)	Southport	D 1-1	Brocklebank	
9		25	(a)	Bury	D 3-3	Hornby, Brocklebank, Whalley	2,083
10	Nov	1	(h)	Bury	W 9-3	Kippax 2, Brocklebank 3, Whalley 2, Salmon, Hornby	2,700
11		8	(h)	Bolton W	W 2-1	Brocklebank (pen), Hornby	3,791
12		15	(a)	Bolton W	L 1-3	Gardner	2,000
13		22	(a)	Blackburn R	L 2-3	Kippax 2	1,500
14		29	(h)	Blackburn R	D 0-0		3,895
15	Dec	6	(h)	Blackpool	D 2-2	Clayton, Gardner	2,873
16		13	(a)	Blackpool	L 0-9		4,000
17		20	(a)	Oldham A	L 2-5	Kippax, Gardner	806
18		25	(h)	Oldham A	D 1-1	Waddington	5,876

FINAL LEAGUE POSITION: 19th in Football League — Northern Section (First Competition, 38 clubs competed)

19	Dec	27	(a)	Bradford C	L 1-5	Hornby	2,937
20	Jan	3	(h)	Bradford C	W 3-1	Jackson, Brocklebank (pen), Bright	2,215
21		10	(h)	Manchester C	L 1-2	Hornby	3,913
22		17	(a)	Manchester C	L 0-5		5,000
23		24	(h)	Stockport C	W 6-0	Brocklebank 2, Gardner 2, Kippax, Jackson	1,515
24		31	(a)	Stockport C	D 0-0		
25	Feb	7	(a)	Everton	L 2-3	Kippax, Gardner	
26		14	(h)	Everton	W 1-0	Gardner	6,048
27		21	(a)	Sheffield W	L 1-3	Gardner	
28		28	(h)	Sheffield W	W 3-0	Kippax, Brocklebank, Millership (og)	2,841
29	Mar	7	(a)	Blackpool	L 0-13		
30		14	(a)	Blackburn R	L 2-6	Brocklebank 2	3,534
31		21	(h)	Blackpool	L 0-6		5,091
32		28	(h)	Blackburn R	W 2-0	Jackson, Brocklebank	3,153
33	Apr	4	(h)	Liverpool	L 0-3		7,368
34		6	(a)	Liverpool	L 1-4	Gutteridge (og)	11,253
35		11	(h)	Huddersfield T	W 3-0	Waddington 2, Brocklebank	2,443
36		25	(h)	Preston NE	W 3-0	Jackson 2, Bright	2,209
37	May	2	(a)	Preston NE	L 0-2		3,000

FINAL LEAGUE POSITION: 20th in Football League — Northern Section (Second Competition, 22 clubs competed)

Matches 19-28 (10 in all) were also in the Football League War Cup, Qualifying Competition.
Matches 33-34 (2 in all) were also in the Football League War Cup, Knock-out Competition.
Matches 30 and 32 (2 in all) also counted as Lancashire Cup games.

1	2	3	4	5	6	7	8	9	10	11	
Holdcroft	Snowden	Kirkman	Gardner	Woodruff	Robinson	Coates	Brocklebank	Kippax	Hornby	Bright	1
..	..	Smith	..	..	..	..	..	..	..	..	2
..	..	Kirkman	Robinson	..	Bray	Gardner	..	..	..	Whalley	3
..	..	..	Salmon	..	Lomax	Prest	..	..	..	..	4
..	..	Mather	..	..	..	Gardner	..	..	..	..	5
..	..	Kirkman	..	..	..	..	..	..	..	..	6
Strong	..	..	..	..	..	..	..	..	..	..	7
Holdcroft	..	..	..	..	Robinson	..	..	..	..	..	8
..	..	..	..	..	..	Taylor	Gardner	Brocklebank	..	..	9
Bentley	..	..	..	..	..	Gardner	Brocklebank	Kippax	..	..	10
Holdcroft	..	..	..	..	..	..	..	..	..	..	11
..	..	..	..	..	..	..	..	..	..	..	12
..	Johnson	..	..	..	..	..	..	..	Knight	..	13
..	..	..	..	..	..	..	..	..	Hornby	..	14
..	Snowden	..	Martindale	..	..	..	..	Clayton	..	..	15
..	..	Robinson	..	..	Bray	..	..	Kippax	..	..	16
Sutcliffe	..	Kirkman	Salmon	..	..	..	..	..	Waddington	Hornby	17
Bentley	..	..	Lomax	..	Hornby	..	..	Taylor	..	Whalley	18
Bentley	Snowden	Kirkman	Martindale	Woodruff	Lawson	Gardner	Brocklebank	Taylor	Waddington	Hornby	19
Sutcliffe	..	..	Salmon	..	Harrison	..	..	H.Jackson	..	Bright	20
..	..	..	Harrison	..	Marsden	..	..	..	..	Hornby	21
..	..	..	..	..	..	..	..	Kippax	Hornby	Whalley	22
Holdcroft	Ward	..	Marsden	..	Robinson	..	..	H.Jackson	..	Kippax	23
..	..	..	..	..	..	..	..	..	..	..	24
..	..	..	..	..	Lomax	..	..	Kippax	Robinson	Bright	25
..	..	..	Robinson	..	..	P.Jackson	Gardner	..	Brocklebank	..	26
..	..	..	Marsden	..	..	Gardner	Brocklebank	Snowden	Jones	..	27
..	..	Snowden	Salmon	..	..	..	..	Kippax	Harrison	..	28
..	..	Kirkman	..	..	..	..	..	..	..	Whalley	29
Sagar	..	Snowden	Readett	Salmon	..	..	Deverall	Brocklebank	Gibson	Hornby	30
Holdcroft	Readett	..	Salmon	Woodruff	..	..	Brocklebank	H.Jackson	Waddington	Bright	31
Strong	Johnson	..	Crossland	..	Bray	..	..	..	..	Hornby	32
Holdcroft	Snowden	Richmond	Harrison	..	Robinson	..	..	Gastall	Hornby	Bright	33
..	..	..	Salmon	..	..	..	..	H.Jackson	Waddington	Hornby	34
..	Robinson	Snowden	..	..	Lomax	..	Waddington	Brocklebank	Hornby	Bright	35
..	Readett	..	Robinson	..	..	..	Brocklebank	H.Jackson	..	..	36
..	Ward	..	Readett	..	..	..	..	Bentley	..	..	37

Appearances (goals scored in brackets): G.Bentley 4, G.Bray 4, Bright 12 (2), R.Brocklebank 37 (19), J.Clayton 1 (1), F.Coates 2, Crossland 1, Deverall 1, T.Gardner 36 (10), Gastall 1, Gibson 1, Harrison 6, Holdcroft 27, R.Hornby 29 (5), H.Jackson 8 (5), P.Jackson 1, R.Johnson 3, Jones 1, F.Kippax 22 (13), Kirkman 25, G.Knight 1, Lawson 1, J.Lomax 15, Marsden 6, L.Martindale 3, H.Mather 1, Prest 1, Readett 4, Richmond 2, Robinson 20, Sagar 1, Salmon 19 (1), T.Smith 1, Snowden 30, J.Strong 2, C.Sutcliffe 4, F.Taylor 3, R.Waddington 9 (3), Ward 9, H.Whalley 17 (4), A.Woodruff 36. Own Goals 2.

1942-43

Manager: None

1	Aug	29	(a)	Blackburn R	D 3-3	O'Donnell, Bright, Brocklebank	2,000
2	Sep	5	(h)	Blackburn R	W 1-0	Taylor (og)	1,972
3		12	(h)	Oldham A	W 3-0	Gardner 2, Bright	3,126
4		19	(a)	Oldham A	W 3-1	Waddington, Bright, O'Donnell	2,000
5		26	(a)	Everton	L 1-2	Jackson	
6	Oct	3	(h)	Everton	L 1-4	Waddington	5,949
7		10	(h)	Stockport C	D 0-0		1,878
8		17	(a)	Stockport C	L 1-4	O'Donnell	
9		24	(a)	Bolton W	L 4-7	Kippax, Bright, O'Donnell, Brocklebank	2,664
10		31	(h)	Bolton W	L 1-2	Bright	2,928
11	Nov	7	(h)	Rochdale	W 5-0	Jackson 3, Waddington 2	2,018
12		14	(a)	Rochdale	L 1-2	Waddington	902
13		21	(h)	Blackpool	D 4-4	Hornby, Gardner, Waddington, Webster	5,054
14		28	(a)	Blackpool	L 1-5	Bright	
15	Dec	5	(h)	Liverpool	W 3-1	McEwan 2, Hornby	2,006
16		12	(a)	Liverpool	L 2-9	Jackson, Bright	10,000
17		19	(a)	Halifax T	D 0-0		2,500
18		25	(h)	Halifax T	D 1-1	Bright	4,865

FINAL LEAGUE POSITION: 32nd in Football League — Northern Section (First Competition, 48 clubs competed)

19	Dec	26	(a)	Blackburn R	L 1-3	Gardner	8,413
20	Jan	2	(h)	Blackburn R	D 0-0		2,640
21		9	(h)	Bury	D 0-0		2,129
22		16	(a)	Bury	L 0-3		1,908
23		23	(a)	Bolton W	L 1-4	Jackson	3,700
24		30	(h)	Bolton W	L 0-1		2,070
25	Feb	6	(h)	Southport	W 5-4	Robinson 2, Gardner (pen), Crawshaw, Manning	2,289
26		13	(a)	Southport	L 0-2		
27		20	(a)	Rochdale	L 2-4	Manning, Crawshaw	
28		27	(h)	Rochdale	D 1-1	Crawshaw	2,399
29	Mar	6	(a)	Bolton W	L 1-4	Crawshaw	2,920
30		13	(h)	Bolton W	W 4-1	Kippax 2, Brindle, Gardner	2,329
31	Apr	3	(a)	Rochdale	L 0-4		1,900
32		10	(h)	Rochdale	W 2-0	Gardner (pen), Robinson	1,347

FINAL LEAGUE POSITION: 51st in Football League — Northern Section (Second Competition, 54 clubs competed)

Matches 19-28 (10 in all) were also in the Football League War Cup. Burnley failed to qualify for the knock-out stages.

1	2	3	4	5	6	7	8	9	10	11	
Holdcroft	Snowden	Kirkman	Robinson	Woodruff	Lomax	Gardner	Brocklebank	O'Donnell	Hornby	Bright	1
..	..	..	..	..	..	..	..	..	Jackson	..	2
..	..	..	..	..	..	..	N.Dougall	Readett	Allen	..	3
..	Readett	Snowden	..	..	..	..	Waddington	O'Donnell	Hornby	..	4
..	..	..	..	..	..	..	..	Jackson	..	..	5
..	..	..	..	..	Wigglesworth	..	Brocklebank	Waddington	..	Keighley	6
..	..	..	..	..	Lomax	..	..	..	Knight	..	7
..	..	..	..	..	Bray	..	..	O'Donnell	Jackson	..	8
..	Robinson	..	Rudman	..	Webster	..	..	Kippax	O'Donnell	Bright	9
..	..	Watson	..	..	..	..	..	O'Donnell	Waddington	..	10
..	..	..	..	..	..	..	..	Jackson	..	..	11
..	Brocklebank	..	..	..	..	..	Waddington	O'Donnell	Bright	Keighley	12
Bentley	Readett	J.Taylor	..	..	..	..	..	..	Hornby	Bright	13
Holdcroft	Brocklebank	Roach	..	..	..	..	..	..	..	..	14
..	Horton	Brocklebank	..	..	..	..	McEwan	..	..	..	15
..	Brocklebank	Snowden	Marsden	..	..	..	Waddington	..	Jackson	..	16
..	..	..	Rudman	..	..	..	..	Jackson	Hornby	O'Donnell	17
..	Robinson	..	..	..	..	..	Brocklebank	..	..	Bright	18
Holdcroft	Robinson	Snowden	Rudman	Wigglesworth	Webster	Gardner	Waddington	Jackson	Hornby	O'Donnell	19
..	Snowden	Watson	..	Woodruff	..	..	Brocklebank	O'Donnell	Waddington	Kippax	20
..	..	..	..	..	..	..	Waddington	Kippax	Hornby	Bright	21
..	Robinson	Mather	..	..	..	..	Brocklebank	Snowden	..	..	22
..	Watson	..	Robinson	..	..	..	Manning	Jackson	Brocklebank	..	23
..	..	..	Rudman	..	Bray	..	..	Snowden	Robinson	..	24
..	..	Kirkman	..	..	..	..	..	Crawshaw	..	Keighley	25
..	Snowden	Watson	Wigglesworth	..	Webster	..	..	..	..	..	26
..	..	..	Robinson	..	..	..	..	..	O'Donnell	..	27
..	Robinson	..	Gardner	..	..	Shorthouse	..	..	Brocklebank	O'Donnell	28
..	Woodruff	..	Robinson	Bannister	..	Shields	..	..	Barker	..	29
..	Ward	Brocklebank	..	..	Holden	Gardner	Brindle	Kippax	Crossland	Keighley	30
..	Brocklebank	Birch	..	Woodruff	Lomax	..	Newsham	F.Taylor	Brindle	..	31
..	Riddeogh	Watson	Gardner	..	..	Smith	..	Robinson	Martindale	Carter	32

Appearances (goals scored in brackets): Allen 1, Bannister 2, Barker 1, G.Bentley 1, Birch 1, G.Bray 3, Bright 18 (8), Brindle 2 (1), R.Brocklebank 20 (2), Carter 1, Crawshaw 5 (4), Crossland 1, N.Dougall 1, T.Gardner 31 (7), Holdcroft 31, K.Holden 1, R.Hornby 12 (2), Horton 1, H.Jackson 9 (6), Keighley 9, F.Kippax 4 (3), Kirkman 4, G.Knight 1, Lomax 8, McEwan 1 (2), Manning 7 (2), Marsden 1, L.Martindale 1, Mather 3, Newsham 2, O'Donnell 17 (4), Readett 7, H.Riddeough 1, Roach 1, A.Robinson 24 (3), H.Rudman 15, Shields 1, Shorthouse 1, T.Smith 1, Snowden 19, F.Taylor 1, J.Taylor 1, R.Waddington 14 (6), Ward 1, Watson 13, Webster 19 (1), Wigglesworth 3, A.Woodruff 30. Own Goals 1.

1943-44

Manager: None

1	Aug	28	(h)	Bolton W	W 4-0	Brocklebank 2, Gardner (pen), Robinson	1,722
2	Sep	4	(a)	Bolton W	W 2-0	Kippax, Hubbick (og)	2,945
3		11	(h)	Bury	W 5-1	Snowden 2, Hornby, Hart (og), Rudman	3,599
4		18	(a)	Bury	D 1-1	Brocklebank	3,900
5		25	(h)	Everton	D 0-0		6,128
6	Oct	2	(a)	Everton	D 0-0		11,984
7		9	(a)	Oldham A	L 2-4	Hornby, Gardner	4,569
8		16	(h)	Oldham A	W 1-0	Robinson	3,649
9		23	(a)	Stockport C	D 1-1	Reid	3,000
10		30	(h)	Stockport C	D 0-0		4,116
11	Nov	6	(a)	Rochdale	L 1-3	McFarlane	3,500
12		13	(h)	Rochdale	W 2-0	Reid, Brocklebank	2,210
13		20	(a)	Blackpool	L 0-3		10,000
14		27	(h)	Blackpool	L 3-5	Sargent, Reid, Gardner	8,744
15	Dec	4	(h)	Liverpool	L 0-1		5,995
16		11	(a)	Liverpool	D 1-1	Jackson	11,368
17		18	(a)	Halifax T	D 1-1	Brocklebank	1,600
18		25	(h)	Halifax T	L 0-1		4,194

FINAL LEAGUE POSITION: 24th in Football League — Northern Section (First Competition, 50 clubs competed)

19	Dec	26	(h)	Southport	D 2-2	Gardner, Rudman	7,271
20	Jan	1	(a)	Southport	L 1-4	Brocklebank	3,000
21		8	(a)	Bolton W	L 1-2	Brocklebank	5,463
22		15	(h)	Bolton W	W 5-1	Brocklebank 3, Potts, Gardner	3,902
23		22	(h)	Rochdale	D 2-2	Sargent, Gardner	1,825
24		29	(a)	Rochdale	L 1-3	Jackson	4,762
25	Feb	5	(h)	Blackpool	W 2-1	Robinson, Brocklebank	10,282
26		12	(a)	Blackpool	W 3-1	Watson 2, Potts	
27		19	(h)	Blackburn R	W 5-1	Brocklebank 4, Watson	7,107
28		26	(a)	Blackburn R	L 0-2		5,000
29	Mar	4	(h)	Rochdale	D 3-3	Watson, Brocklebank, Gardner	6,166
30		11	(a)	Rochdale	L 1-2	Gardner	7,280
31		18	(a)	Blackburn R	L 1-2	Burns	3,000
32		25	(h)	Blackburn R	D 2-2	Gardner 2	4,769
33	Apr	1	(a)	Bury	W 4-2	Jackson 3, Gardner	1,500
34		8	(h)	Bury	W 3-1	Watson, Jackson 2	5,495
35		15	(a)	Manchester U	L 0-9		4,045
36		22	(h)	Manchester U	D 3-3	Bright 2, Gardner	2,726

FINAL LEAGUE POSITION: 37th in Football League — Northern Section (Second Competition, 56 clubs competed)

Matches 19-28 (10 in all) were also in the Football Legue War Cup, Qualifying Competition.
Matches 29-30 (2 in all) were also in the Football League War Cup, Knock-out Competition.
Matches 31-32 (2 in all) also counted as Lancashire Cup games.

1	2	3	4	5	6	7	8	9	10	11	
Strong	Smith	Snowden	Rudman	Woodruff	Robinson	Gardner	Sargent	Brocklebank	Hornby	Kippax	1
..	..	Watson	..	..	..	..	..	Kippax	Brocklebank	Hornby	2
..	Robinson	..	..	..	Webster	..	Reid	Snowden	Hornby	Kippax	3
..	Smith	..	..	..	Robinson	..	Sargent	Brocklebank	..	..	4
..	Brocklebank	Mather	Robinson	..	Watson	..	..	Snowden	..	..	5
..	Ward	Watson	Rudman	..	Webster	..	Brocklebank	..	Robinson	..	6
..	Marshall	Snowden	..	..	Hornby	..	Sargent	Smith	Brocklebank	..	7
..	..	Watson	..	..	Robinson	..	Brocklebank	Jackson	Rose	..	8
..	Taylor	Brocklebank	Robinson	..	Webster	..	Reid	Sargent	Cook	McFarlane	9
..	..	Mather	..	..	Watson	..	Dougall	Clayton	Brocklebank	Sargent	10
..	..	..	..	..	Webster	..	..	Reid	..	McFarlane	11
..	Robinson	..	Rudman	..	Bray	..	Sargent	..	..	Webster	12
..	Brocklebank	..	..	..	Williams	..	..	..	Knight	Keighley	13
..	Mather	Readay	..	..	Watson	..	Reid	Batty	Sargent	Webster	14
..	Brocklebank	Watson	..	..	Robinson	..	..	Jackson	..	..	15
..	..	..	Robinson	..	Webster	..	..	..	..	Keighley	16
..	..	..	Johnson	..	Loughran	..	Rudman	Robinson	Reid	Webster	17
..	Johnson	Robinson	Rudman	..	Mansley	..	Brocklebank	Reid	Bright	McNee	18

Strong	Johnson	Watson	Hargreaves	Woodruff	Mansley	Gardner	Rudman	Brocklebank	Hornby	Keighley	19
Slingsby	Taylor	..	Rudman	..	Holden	..	Reynolds	..	Robinson	Webster	20
Strong	..	Mather	..	..	Robinson	..	Gallon	..	Knight	..	21
Robinson	Marshall	..	Spencer	..	Bray	..	Potts	..	McGahie	Sargent	22
Strong	Robinson	Marshall	Rudman	..	Watson	..	Brocklebank	Brindle	Webster	..	23
..	Geddes	Mather	..	..	Webster	..	..	Reid	Jackson	..	24
..	..	..	Robinson	..	..	..	..	..	Watson	..	25
..	..	..	Rudman	..	..	..	Potts	Brocklebank	..	Reid	26
..	..	..	..	..	..	..	Reid	..	..	Sargent	27
..	Watson	..	..	..	..	..	Potts	..	Reid	..	28
..	Geddes	Johnson	..	..	..	..	McGahie	..	Watson	..	29
Walmsley	..	Mather	..	..	..	..	..	..	..	..	30
..	Robinson	Watson	..	..	..	..	Burns	..	Reid	Edwardson	31
Bentley	Readay	Scott	..	..	..	Smith	Gardner	..	..	Holden	32
..	..	Brocklebank	..	..	..	Gardner	Russell	Jackson	Dougall	..	33
Strong	Woodruff	..	Russell	Spencer	Bray	Rudman	Gardner	..	Watson	Webster	34
..	Sibley	Mather	Rudman	Woodruff	Kirby	Gardner	Reid	Brocklebank	Gallon	..	35
..	Horner	..	Russell	..	Webster	..	Sargent	Reid	Watson	Bright	36

Appearances (goals scored in brackets): Batty 1, G.Bentley 2, G.Bray 3, Bright 2 (2), Brindle 1, Brocklebank 33 (16), Burns 1 (1), J.Clayton 1, Cook 1, N.Dougall 3, Edwardson 1, Gallon 2, Gardner 36 (12), Geddes 6, Hargreaves 1, K.Holden 3, R.Hornby 7 (2), Horner 1, H.Jackson 6 (7), R.Johnson 4, Keighley 3, F.Kippax 8 (1), Kirby 1, G.Knight 2, J.Loughran 1 , McFarlane 2 (1), McGahie 3, McNee 1, Mansley 2, J.Marshall 4, Mather 16, H.Potts 3 (2), Readay 3, Reid 19 (3), Reynolds 1, A.Robinson 21 (3), N.Rose 1, H.Rudman 28 (2), Russell 3, Sargent 21 (2), Scott 1, Sibley 1, Slingsby 1, T.Smith 5, Snowden 5 (2), H.Spencer 2, J.Strong 30, J.Taylor 5, Walmsley 2, Ward 1, Watson 23 (5), Webster 25, Williams 1, A.Woodruff 36, Own Goals 2.

1944-45

Manager: None

1	Aug	26	(h)	Blackburn R	D 1-1	Reid	5,945
2	Sep	2	(a)	Blackburn R	W 2-0	Potts, Kinghorn	2,000
3		9	(a)	Southport	L 2-3	Gardner (pen), Potts	
4		16	(h)	Southport	W 3-1	Kinghorn 2, Brocklebank	4,275
5		23	(h)	Rochdale	D 2-2	Gardner (pen), Wyles	4,213
6		30	(a)	Rochdale	L 1-3	Jackson	
7	Oct	7	(a)	Oldham A	L 1-3	Gardner (pen)	4,232
8		14	(h)	Oldham A	W 1-0	Jackson	2,990
9		21	(h)	Bolton W	W 6-3	Brooks 3, Kinghorn 2, Burns	4,556
10		28	(a)	Bolton W	L 0-4		3,458
11	Nov	4	(a)	Halifax T	L 1-2	Mignot	2,000
12		11	(h)	Halifax T	L 1-2	Brocklebank	3,435
13		18	(h)	Accrington S	D 0-0		
14		25	(a)	Accrington S	W 5-0	Brocklebank 2, Patterson 2, Brooks	
15	Dec	2	(a)	Blackpool	W 2-0	Potts, Brooks	
16		9	(h)	Blackpool	W 5-1	Jackson 2, Gardner, Webster, Brocklebank	6,335
17		16	(a)	Preston NE	D 1-1	Gardner	3,500
18		23	(h)	Preston NE	W 5-1	Brooks 2, Brocklebank, Martindale, Kippax	8,319

FINAL LEAGUE POSITION: 20th in Football League — Northern Section (First Competition, 54 clubs competed)

19	Dec	25	(a)	Blackburn R	W 4-2	Brocklebank 2, Kippax, Gardner	9,730
20		26	(h)	Bradford	W 4-2	Brocklebank 2, Bright, Gardner (pen)	10,500
21		30	(h)	Blackburn R	W 4-1	Dryden 2, Brocklebank, Gardner	8,948
22	Jan	6	(h)	Blackpool	W 2-0	Brooks, Burns	9,643
23		13	(a)	Blackpool	L 0-4		
24		20	(a)	Accrington S	W 4-0	Jackson 2, Gardner 2	3,600
25		27	(h)	Accrington S	W 3-0	Brocklebank, Patterson, Gardner	3,236
26	Feb	3	(h)	Rochdale	W 2-0	Patterson 2	5,657
27		10	(a)	Rochdale	W 4-0	Jackson 2, Dryden 2	4,200
28		17	(a)	Preston NE	L 1-2	Gardner	
29		24	(h)	Preston NE	D 1-1	Patterson	6,813
30	Mar	3	(h)	Barnsley	W 4-0	Kinghorn, Brooks, Patterson, Brocklebank	5,660
31		10	(a)	Barnsley	L 0-2		8,903
32		17	(a)	Oldham A	W 2-1	Patterson, Martindale	4,266
33		24	(h)	Manchester U	L 2-3	Jackson, Gardner	13,947
34		29	(h)	Oldham A	W 3-1	Gardner 2, Brocklebank	5,221
35		31	(a)	Manchester U	L 0-4		25,000
36	Apr	7	(h)	Accrington S	W 1-0	Martindale	5,211
37		14	(a)	Accrington S	L 0-4		
38		21	(h)	Sheffield U	W 2-0	Brooks 2	2,879
39		28	(a)	Sheffield U	D 1-1	Smith	5,455
40	May	5	(a*)	Bradford	D 1-1	Drury	1,800
41		9	(h)	Blackburn R	W 3-1	Martindale 2, Rudman	2,308
42		12	(a)	Tranmere R	L 2-3	Martindale 2	
43		19	(h)	Tranmere R	W 5-1	Rudman 2, Drury, Martindale, Salmon	2,046
44		26	(a)	Preston NE	L 1-2	Martindale	

FINAL LEAGUE POSITION: 4th in Football League — Northern Section (Second Competition, 60 clubs competed)

*Played at Turf Moor.
Matches 19, 21-29 (10 in all) were also in the Football League War Cup Qualifying Competition.
Matches 33 and 35 (2 in all) were also in the Football League War Cup Knock-out Competition.
Matches 32, 34, 36-37 (4 in all) also counted as Lancashire Cup games.
Match 41 was also a 'VE' Game.

1	2	3	4	5	6	7	8	9	10	11	
Strong	Gallimore	Marshall	Martindale	Woodruff	Webster	Gardner	Reid	Brocklebank	Patterson	Kinghorn	1
..	..	Mather	..	..	..	..	Potts	..	..	..	2
..	Kirkman	..	..	..	..	..	..	Looms	..	..	3
..	Gallimore	..	Rudman	..	..	..	Martindale	..	Brocklebank	..	4
..	..	Webster	Martindale	..	Rudman	..	Brocklebank	Wyles	Patterson	..	5
..	..	..	Brooks	..	Edwards	..	Martindale	Jackson	Brocklebank	Holden	6
..	..	..	Martindale	..	Brooks	..	Brocklebank	Wyles	Moss	Kinghorn	7
..	McCavana	..	..	..	..	Smith	Burns	Jackson	Crossland	Holden	8
..	Gallimore	..	..	..	Rudman	Gardner	..	Brooks	Kinghorn	Kippax	9
..	..	..	Gardner	..	Martindale	Smith	Kinghorn	..	Brocklebank	..	10
..	..	Kirkman	Martindale	..	Webster	Gardner	Mignot	..	..	Kinghorn	11
..	..	..	..	..	..	Holdsworth	Gardner	..	..	Kippax	12
..	Marshall	..	..	..	Rudman	Gardner	Brocklebank	Jackson	Crossland	Kinghorn	13
..	Gallimore	..	..	..	Webster	..	..	Brooks	Patterson	Kippax	14
..	Brocklebank	Watson	..	..	..	..	Potts	..	..	Dougall	15
..	Gallimore	..	..	..	..	..	..	Jackson	Brocklebank	Kippax	16
..	..	Robinson	..	..	Holden	..	Brocklebank	Hodgeon	Patterson	Rudman	17
..	Robinson	Mather	..	..	Bray	..	..	Brooks	H.Taylor	Kippax	18
Strong	Gallimore	Mather	Webster	Woodruff	Bray	Gardner	Martindale	Brocklebank	Bright	Kippax	19
..	..	..	Robinson	..	..	..	..	..	..	..	20
..	..	Robinson	Martindale	..	Holden	..	Burns	..	Dryden	..	21
..	..	..	..	..	Webster	..	..	Brooks	Brocklebank	..	22
..	..	Kirkman	Spencer	..	..	..	Martindale	Brocklebank	Patterson	..	23
..	..	Robinson	Martindale	..	..	..	Brocklebank	Jackson	..	Dryden	24
..	..	Mather	..	..	..	..	..	Brooks	..	..	25
..	Robinson	Kirkman	..	..	..	..	..	Dryden	..	Holden	26
..	..	Mather	..	..	..	..	..	Jackson	..	Dryden	27
..	..	..	..	..	..	..	..	H.Taylor	..	Marshall	28
..	Bradford	Brooks	..	..	..	..	..	Jackson	..	Holden	29
..	..	Robinson	..	..	..	Rudman	..	Brooks	..	Kinghorn	30
..	..	..	..	..	..	Gardner	..	Bray	..	..	31
..	Gallimore	..	Webster	..	Bray	Rudman	Martindale	Brocklebank	..	Kippax	32
..	Bradford	..	Martindale	..	Webster	Gardner	Burns	Jackson	Brocklebank	..	33
Conway	..	Mather	Rudman	..	..	..	Martindale	Brocklebank	Patterson	Makin	34
Strong	Gallimore	..	Martindale	..	..	..	Brocklebank	Brooks	..	Jackson	35
Tonge	Bradford	..	Rudman	..	..	..	Martindale	Brocklebank	..	Moss	36
Strong	..	..	Martindale	..	..	..	Brocklebank	Brooks	..	Jackson	37
..	..	..	Rudman	..	Robinson	..	Martindale	..	Brocklebank	Makin	38
..	..	..	..	..	Bray	..	..	Crowther	Drury	Smith	39
..	Gallimore	..	Webster	Bradford	..	..	..	Robinson	..	Makin	40
Tonge	..	Robinson	..	Whittaker	..	..	..	Brocklebank	..	Rudman	41
Strong	Brereton	Gallimore	Salmon	Bradford	..	Henderson	..	..	..	Clarkson	42
..	Robinson	Webster	..	Whittaker	..	..	..	Brooks	..	Rudman	43
..	Bradford	..	Rudman	..	Salmon	..	..	Brocklebank	..	Bright	44

Appearances (goals scored in brackets): Bradford 12, G.Bray 10, Brereton 1, Bright 3 (1), R.Brocklebank 38 (14), Brooks 18 (11), Burns 5 (2), Clarkson 1, H.Conway 1, Crossland 2, Crowther 1, N.Dougall 1, Drury 6 (2), Dryden 5 (4), Edwards 1, F.Gallimore 25, T.Gardner 38 (15), Henderson 3, Hodgeon 1, K.Holden 6, Holdsworth 1, H.Jackson 10 (9), F.Kippax 13 (2), Kinghorn 12 (6), Kirkman 7, Looms 2, McCavana 1, Makin 3, J.Marshall 3, L.Martindale 44 (9), H.Mather 16, Mignot 1 (1), Moss 2, Patterson 21 (8), H.Potts 4 (3), Reid 1 (1), A.Robinson 17, H.Rudman 14 (3), Salmon 3 (1), Smith 3 (1), H.Spencer 1, J.Strong 41, H.Taylor 2, Tonge 2, Watson 2, Webster 36 (1), Whittaker 3, A.Woodruff 39, Wyles 2 (1).

1945-46

Manager: None

1	Aug	25	(h)	Liverpool	L 1-3	Brooks	7,481
2	Sep	1	(a)	Liverpool	W 3-2	Hold 2, Kippax (pen)	26,107
3		8	(a)	Bolton W	L 0-2		15,990
4		12	(a)	Newcastle U	W 1-0	Drury	27,100
5		15	(h)	Bolton W	D 2-2	Crowther, Drury	9,401
6		22	(h)	Bury	L 2-3	Hays, Crowther	6,255
7		29	(a)	Bury	L 0-1		8,339
8	Oct	6	(a)	Preston NE	L 0-4		9,000
9		13	(h)	Preston NE	D 0-0		8,639
10		20	(a)	Blackburn R	L 2-4	Hays 2	8,228
11		27	(h)	Blackburn R	L 1-4	Hold	7,964
12	Nov	3	(a)	Leeds U	W 2-1	Hold, Hays	11,387
13		10	(h)	Leeds U	L 2-3	Kippax, Jackson	6,925
14		17	(a)	Bradford	L 0-7		11,331
15		24	(h)	Bradford	W 2-1	Morris, Jackson	7,622
16	Dec	1	(a)	Manchester U	D 3-3	Jackson 2, Morris	17,429
17		8	(h)	Manchester U	D 2-2	Morris, Hays	8,000
18		15	(h)	Manchester C	W 1-0	Haigh	9,271
19		22	(a)	Manchester C	W 2-1	Jackson, Morris	21,000
20		25	(a)	Sunderland	D 1-1	Hornby	23,000
21		26	(h)	Sunderland	L 2-3	Chew, Jackson	22,427
22		29	(h)	Newcastle U	W 3-2	Jackson 2 (1 pen), Morris	16,877
23	Jan	1	(a)	Sheffield U	L 1-5	Jackson	
24		12	(h)	Sheffield W	D 2-2	Morris, Jackson	10,324
25		19	(a)	Sheffield W	D 1-1	Kippax	15,000
26		26	(h)	Huddersfield T	W 4-3	Morris 2, Jackson, Kippax	8,762
27	Feb	2	(h)	Middlesbrough	W 8-1	Jackson 3, Hays 2, Douglas (og), Morris, Kippax	9,906
28		16	(a)	Huddersfield T	L 2-4	Attwell, Kippax (pen)	8,851
29		23	(a)	Stoke C	D 0-0		11,159
30	Mar	9	(a)	Chesterfield	L 0-3		12,000
31		16	(h)	Chesterfield	W 3-1	Hays, Jackson, Chew	10,507
32		23	(a)	Grimsby T	D 1-1	Jackson	9,000
33		30	(h)	Grimsby T	L 1-2	Morris	14,500
34	Apr	1	(h)	Stoke	W 1-0	Morris	10,607
35		6	(a)	Barnsley	L 0-3		14,500
36		10	(a)	Middlesbrough	L 1-2	Morris	19,358
37		13	(h)	Barnsley	W 3-2	Kippax, Jackson, Pallister (og)	10,600
38		19	(h)	Blackpool	D 1-1	Kippax	18,104
39		20	(a)	Everton	L 0-2		30,635
40		27	(h)	Everton	W 1-0	Jackson	13,407
41	Apr	29	(a)	Blackpool	L 1-2	Kippax	14,000
42	May	4	(h)	Sheffield U	L 0-1		15,172

FINAL LEAGUE POSITION: 16th in Football League North

FA Cup

3	Jan	5	(a)	Stoke C	L 1-3	Morris
		7	(h)	Stoke C	W 2-1	Jackson, Kippax

1	2	3	4	5	6	7	8	9	10	11	
Strong	Roach	Innard	Wilson	Woodruff	Campbell	Gardner	Sneddon	Brooks	Drury	Kippax	1
..	Shreeve	Ancell	..	..	Rudman	..	Crowther	Hold	..	..	2
..	..	Innard	..	..	..	..	..	..	..	Chew	3
..	..	Ancell	..	..	..	..	..	..	..	Hays	4
..	Owens	Shreeve	..	..	..	..	Sneddon	Crowther	..	..	5
..	Shreeve	Innard	..	..	..	..	Burns	..	..	..	6
..	..	Mather	Rudman	..	Bray	..	..	Hold	..	Hornby	7
..	Owens	..	Wilson	..	Rudman	..	Crowther	..	..	..	8
..	Mulvaney	..	Rudman	..	Loughran	..	Meek	Hays	..	Kippax	9
..	..	..	H.Spencer	..	..	..	..	Hold	Rudman	Hays	10
Breedon	..	..	Wilson	..	Rudman	Hays	Gardner	..	Meek	Kippax	11
..	Bunker	..	McBain	..	..	Gardner	Hays	..	Chew	..	12
..	Wilson	..	..	..	Attwell	Hays	Bowden	Jackson	..	..	13
..	..	..	Rudman	..	..	..	Haigh	..	..	..	14
Hobson	Woodruff	..	..	Johnson	..	Gardner	Morris	..	Haigh	Hays	15
..	..	..	..	..	..	..	..	..	J.Knight	..	16
..	..	..	..	..	..	Chew	..	..	Haigh	..	17
Sidlow	..	..	Wilson	..	..	..	..	..	..	..	18
..	..	..	..	..	Wigglesworth	..	..	..	..	..	19
Hobson	..	..	..	..	Martindale	Hodgeon	Hays	Crowther	Chew	Hornby	20
..	..	..	..	..	Wigglesworth	Chew	Morris	Jackson	Hays	Kippax	21
Strong	..	..	Martindale	..	Attwell	..	..	..	Haigh	Hays	22
..	..	..	Wigglesworth	..	..	Hodgeon	Chew	..	..	Kippax	23
..	Shreeve	..	Wilson	Woodruff	..	Chew	Morris	..	..	..	24
..	Woodruff	..	Attwell	Johnson	Bray	..	Haigh	..	Kippax	Hays	25
..	..	..	..	..	..	..	Morris	..	Haigh	Kippax	26
..	..	Loughran	..	..	..	..	..	..	Hays	..	27
..	Loughran	Mather	..	Woodruff	..	..	..	..	..	..	28
..	Woodruff	..	..	Johnson	..	..	..	..	Haigh	..	29
..	..	..	..	..	..	..	..	..	..	Hays	30
..	..	..	Loughran	..	..	..	..	..	Hays	Kippax	31
..	..	..	..	..	..	..	..	..	Haigh	..	32
..	..	..	..	..	..	Hays	..	..	J.Knight	..	33
..	..	..	..	..	..	Milner	..	..	Burns	..	34
..	..	..	..	..	..	..	..	..	Haigh	Rudman	35
..	..	..	Rudman	..	..	F.Taylor	..	Wigglesworth	Burns	Jackson	36
Foxcroft	..	..	Loughran	..	..	Chew	..	Jackson	Haigh	Kippax	37
Strong	..	..	Soo	..	..	..	Haigh	Harrison	Jackson	..	38
..	..	..	Rudman	..	..	..	..	..	Burns	Jackson	39
..	..	..	Soo	..	..	Milner	Morris	Jackson	Haigh	Kippax	40
..	..	..	Loughran	..	..	Chew	..	..	..	..	41
..	..	..	Soo	..	..	..	Haigh	..	Potts	..	42

Foxcroft	Woodruff	Mather	Martindale	Johnson	Loughran	Hays	Morris	Jackson	Haigh	Kippax	3
Breedon	..	..	Wilson	..	..	..	..	..	..	..	

Appearances (goals scored in brackets): Ancell 2, R.Attwell 15 (1), Bowden 1, G.Bray 19, J.Breedon 4, Brooks 1 (1), Bunker 1, Burns 5, Campbell 1, J.Chew 25 (2), Crowther 7 (2), Drury 9 (2), Foxcroft 1, T.Gardner 14, G.Haigh 20 (1), R.Harrison 2, J.Hays 23 (8), Hobson 5, Hodgeon 2, O.Hold 8 (4), R.Hornby 3 (1), Innard 3, H.Jackson 29 (18), R.Johnson 26, Kippax 24 (9), J.Knight 2, J.Loughran 11, McBain 2, L.Martindale 2, H.Mather 35, W.Morris 22 (12), Meek 3, Milner 3, Mulvaney 3, Owens 2, H.Potts 1, Roach 1, H.Rudman 18, Shreeve 7, C.Sidlow 2, Sneddon 2, F.Soo 3, H.Spencer 1, J.Strong 30, F.Taylor 1, Wigglesworth 4, Wilson 15, A.Woodruff 42, Own Goals 2.
Note: Totals do not include two games played in FA Cup.

1946-47

Manager: Cliff Britton

1	Aug	31	(h)	Coventry C	D 1-1	Kippax	18,427
2	Sep	7	(a)	Birmingham C	W 2-0	Spencer, Billingham	42,309
3		9	(h)	Newport C	W 3-2	Billingham, Haigh, Chew	18,008
4		14	(h)	West Brom A	L 0-2		22,252
5		16	(a)	Barnsley	L 0-1		26,247
6		21	(a)	Newcastle U	W 2-1	Potts 2	61,255
7		28	(h)	Swansea T	W 1-0	Harrison	19,968
8		30	(h)	Barnsley	D 2-2	Bray, Harrison	24,959
9	Oct	5	(a)	Tottenham H	D 1-1	Kippax	44,351
10		12	(h)	West Ham U	W 2-1	Billingham, Kippax	22,233
11		19	(a)	Sheffield W	W 2-1	Chew, Billingham	22,083
12		26	(h)	Fulham	W 2-0	Billingham, Bray	26,905
13	Nov	2	(a)	Bury	D 2-2	Potts, Billingham	26,167
14		9	(h)	Luton T	D 1-1	Billingham	26,007
15		16	(a)	Plymouth A	D 2-2	Morris, Billingham	30,032
16		23	(h)	Leicester C	D 0-0		19,062
17		30	(a)	Chesterfield	D 0-0		16,570
18	Dec	7	(h)	Millwall	W 3-0	Billingham, Potts, Kippax	17,968
19		14	(a)	Bradford	W 1-0	Morris	10,731
20		21	(h)	Manchester C	D 0-0		31,210
21		25	(h)	Nottingham F	W 3-0	Chew 2, Kippax	21,036
22		26	(a)	Nottingham F	L 0-1		31,484
23		28	(a)	Coventry C	W 3-0	Morris 3	26,944
24	Jan	4	(h)	Birmingham C	W 1-0	Potts	36,281
25		18	(a)	West Brom A	D 1-1	Chew	43,427
26		28	(h)	Newcastle U	W 3-0	Chew, Potts 2	26,877
27	Feb	1	(a)	Swansea T	W 2-0	Harrison, Chew	18,247
28		18	(h)	Tottenham H	D 0-0		28,462
29		22	(h)	Sheffield W	W 2-0	Morris, Harrison	26,651
30	Mar	15	(a)	Luton T	W 3-1	Potts 2, Harrison	18,462
31		22	(h)	Plymouth A	W 2-1	Chew, Potts	28,287
32	Apr	4	(h)	Southampton	W 1-0	Kippax	31,713
33		5	(h)	Chesterfield	D 1-1	Potts	23,719
34		7	(a)	Southampton	W 1-0	J.Knight	20,330
35		19	(h)	Bradford	L 1-2	Potts	32,905
36	May	3	(a)	Newport C	W 3-0	Morris, Potts, Hays	14,751
37		10	(a)	Manchester C	L 0-1		69,463
38		17	(a)	Fulham	L 0-1		25,432
39		24	(a)	Leicester C	W 4-1	Billingham 2, Hays 2	21,626
40		26	(h)	Bury	D 1-1	Billingham	40,145
41		31	(a)	West Ham U	W 5-0	Potts 2, Chew, Morris, Hays	20,198
42	Jun	7	(h)	Millwall	D 1-1	Morris	15,684

FINAL LEAGUE POSITION: 2nd in Division Two (Promoted)

Appearances
Goals

FA Cup

3	Jan	11	(h)	Aston Villa	W 5-1	Morris 2, Harrison 2, Potts	38,532
4		25	(h)	Coventry C	W 2-0	Chew, Potts	39,796
5	Feb	8	(a)	Luton T	D 0-0		22,640
R		11	(h)	Luton T	W 3-0	Harrison 3	28,330
6	Mar	1	(a)	Middlesbrough	D 1-1	Morris	53,025
R		4	(h)	Middlesbrough	W 1-0*	Morris	49,244
SF		29	(n†)	Liverpool	D 0-0*		53,000
R	Apr	12	(n‡)	Liverpool	W 1-0	Harrison	72,000
F		26	(n§)	Charlton A	L 0-1*		98,215

*After extra-time. †Played at Ewood Park, Blackburn. ‡Played at Maine Road, Manchester. §Played at Wembley Stadium.

Appearances
Goals

Strong J	Woodruff A	Mather H	Spencer H	Brown A	Bray G	Chew J	Morris W	Billingham J	Potts H	Kippax FP	Haigh G	Taylor F	Rudman H	Knight G	Harrison R	Hays J	Attwell R	Marshall J	Loughran J	Hornby R	Knight J	
1	2	3	4	5	6	7	8	9	10	11												1
1	2	3	4	5	6	7	8	9	10	11												2
1	2	3	4	5	6	7		9	10	11	8											3
1	2	3	4	5	6			9	10	11	8	7										4
1	2	3		5	6		8	9		11	10		4	7								5
1	2	3		5	6			7	8		10		4		9	11						6
1	2	3		5	6			7	8		10		4		9	11						7
1	2	3		5	6	10		7	8	11			4		9							8
1	2	3		5	6	7		10	8	11			4		9							9
1	2	3		5	6	7		10	8	11			4		9							10
1	2	3		5	6	7		10	8	11			4		9							11
1	2	3		5	6	7	8	9	10	11			4									12
1	2	3		5	6	7	8	9	10	11			4									13
1	2	3		5	6	7	8	9	10	11							4					14
1		3		5	6	7	8	9	10	11							4	2				15
1		3		5	6	7	8	10		11					9		4		2			16
1	2	3		5	6	7	8		10						9	11			4			17
1	2	3		5	6	7	8	9	10	11									4			18
1	2	3		5	6	7	8	9	10							11			4			19
1	2	3		5	6	7	8	9	10	11							4					20
1	2	3		5	6	7	8	9	10	11							4					21
1	2	3		5		7			10	11	8				9		4		6			22
1	2	3		5	6	7	8	9	10							11			4			23
1	2	3		5	6	7	8	9	10	11							4					24
1	2	3		5	6	7	8		10	11					9		4					25
1	2	3		5	6	7	8		10	11					9				4			26
1	2	3		5	6	7	8		10						9				4	11		27
1	2	3		5	6	7	8		10						9	11	4					28
1	2	3		5	6	7	8		10	11					9		4					29
1	2	3		5	6	7	8		10						9	11	4					30
1	2	3		5	6	7	8		10	11					9		4					31
1	2	3		5	6	7	8		10	11					9		4					32
1	2	3		5	6			9	8	11						7	4				10	33
1	2	3		5	6			7	8						9	11			4		10	34
1	2	3		5	6		8	7	10	11					9		4					35
1	2	3		5	6	7	8		10						9	11	4					36
1	2	3		5	6	7	8		10						9	11	4					37
1	2	3		5	6	7	8		10						9	11	4					38
1	2	3		5	6	7	8	9	10							11	4					39
1	2	3		5	6	7	8	9	10							11	4					40
1	2	3		5	6	7	8	9	10							11	4					41
1	2	3		5	6	7	8		10						9	11	4					42
42	40	42	4	42	41	35	31	28	40	26	6	1	9	1	23	16	22	1	9	1	2	
			1		2	9	9	12	15	6	1				5	4					1	

1	2	3		5	6	7	8		10	11					9		4					3
1	2	3		5	6	7	8		10	11					9				4			4
1	2	3		5	6	7	8		10	11					9				4			5
1	2	3		5	6	7	8		10	11					9				4			R
1	2	3		5	6	7	8		10	11					9		4					6
1	2	3		5	6	7	8		10	11					9		4					R
1	2	3		5	6	7	8		10	11					9		4					SF
1	2	3		5	6		8	7	10	11					9		4					R
1	2	3		5	6	7	8		10	11					9		4					F
9	9	9		9	9	8	9	1	9	9					9		6		3			
						1	4		2						6							

1947-48

Manager: Cliff Britton

1	Aug	23	(a)	Portsmouth	W 1-0	Potts	33,967
2		26	(h)	Derby C	L 0-2		43,067
3		30	(h)	Bolton W	W 2-0	Morris, Potts	35,835
4	Sep	3	(a)	Derby C	D 1-1	Bray	32,565
5		6	(a)	Liverpool	D 1-1	Hays	56,074
6		8	(h)	Manchester U	D 0-0		38,517
7		13	(h)	Middlesbrough	W 3-0	Hays, Potts, Chew	34,944
8		20	(a)	Charlton A	D 1-1	Billingham	37,588
9		27	(h)	Arsenal	L 0-1		47,958
10	Oct	4	(a)	Sheffield U	D 1-1	Billingham	40,930
11		11	(h)	Blackpool	W 1-0	Potts	52,869
12		18	(a)	Blackburn R	W 2-1	Morris, Opp own-goal	41,635
13		25	(h)	Manchester C	D 1-1	Hays	41,454
14	Nov	1	(a)	Grimsby T	W 2-1	Billingham 2	17,697
15		8	(h)	Wolves	D 1-1	Potts	38,356
16		15	(a)	Everton	W 3-0	Potts, Billingham, Knight	49,442
17		22	(h)	Sunderland	W 4-0	Potts 2, Knight, Billingham	21,939
18		29	(a)	Aston Villa	D 2-2	Potts 2	56,595
19	Dec	6	(h)	Chelsea	W 1-0	Potts	30,865
20		13	(a)	Huddersfield T	W 1-0	Potts	36,375
21		20	(h)	Portsmouth	W 3-2	Billingham 3	30,131
22		25	(h)	Preston NE	W 1-0	Potts	44,645
23		26	(a)	Preston NE	L 2-3	Bray, Billingham	39,400
24	Jan	1	(a)	Manchester U	L 0-5		61,100
25		3	(a)	Bolton W	D 1-1	Harrison	43,442
26		17	(h)	Liverpool	W 3-0	Knight, Billingham 2	31,470
27		31	(a)	Middlesbrough	W 2-1	Chew, Potts	36,208
28	Feb	14	(a)	Arsenal	L 0-3		62,125
29		21	(h)	Sheffield U	D 0-0		20,667
30	Mar	6	(h)	Blackburn R	D 0-0		44,240
31		13	(a)	Manchester C	L 1-4	Opp own-goal	32,213
32		20	(h)	Grimsby T	W 4-1	Harrison, Haigh, Hornby, Opp own-goal	19,522
33		26	(h)	Stoke C	W 4-0	Chew 2, Harrison 2	28,989
34		27	(a)	Wolves	D 1-1	Morris	38,360
35		29	(a)	Stoke C	L 0-3		33,014
36	Apr	3	(h)	Everton	L 0-1		23,933
37		7	(a)	Blackpool	W 1-0	Morris	16,732
38		10	(a)	Sunderland	L 0-2		47,003
39		17	(h)	Aston Villa	W 1-0	Harrison	25,671
40		20	(h)	Charlton A	L 0-2		26,627
41		24	(a)	Chelsea	W 2-0	Billingham, Attwell	33,390
42	May	1	(h)	Huddersfield T	W 2-1	Bray, Harrison	25,443

FINAL LEAGUE POSITION: 3rd in Division One — Appearances

Goals

FA Cup

3	Jan	10	(h)	Swindon T	L 0-2		34,229

Appearances

Goals

Strong J	Woodruff A	Mather H	Attwell R	Brown A	Bray G	Chew J	Morris W	Billingham J	Potts H	Hays J	Butterfield J	Johnson R	Kippax FP	Knight J	Harrison R	Loughran J	Haigh G	Hornby R	
1	2	3	4	5	6	7	8	9	10	11									1
1	2	3	4	5	6	7	8	9	10	11									2
1	2	3	4	5	6	7	8	9	10	11									3
1·	2	3	4	5	6	7	8	9	10	11									4
1	2	3	4	5	6	7	8	9	10	11									5
1	2	3	4	5	6	7	8	9	10	11									6
1	2	3	4	5	6	7	8	9	10	11									7
1		3	4	5	6	7	8	9	10	11	2								8
1	2	3	4		6	7	8	9	10	11		5							9
1	2	3	4		6	7	8	9	10	11		5							10
1	2	3	4	5	6	7	8	9	10	11									11
1	2	3	4	5	6	7	8	9	10	11									12
1	2	3	4	5	6	7	8	9	10	11									13
1	2	3	4	5	6		8	9	10	7			11						14
1	2	3	4	5	6		8	9	10	7			11						15
1	2	3	4	5	6			9	8	7			11	10					16
1	2	3	4	5	6	7		9	8	11				10					17
1	2	3	4	5	6	7		9	8	11				10					18
1	2	3	4	5	6	7		9	8	11				10					19
1	2	3	4	5	6	7		9	8				11	10					20
1	2	3	4	5	6	7		9	8	11				10					21
1	2	3	4	5	6	7		9	8	11				10					22
1	2	3	4	5	6	7		9	8	11				10					23
1	2	3	4	5	6	7		9	8	11				10					24
1	2	3	4	5	6			7	8	11				10	9				25
1		3	4	5	6			9	10	7	2		11	8					26
1		3		5	6	7		9	10	11	2			8		4			27
1		3	4	5	6	7		9	10	11				8		2			28
1		3	4	5	6	7		9	10	11				8		2			29
1		3	4	5	6	11		9	10	7				8		2			30
1		3	4	5	6	11		9	10	7						2	8		31
1	2	3		5	6			7	8						9	4	10	11	32
1	2	3		5	6	7			8						9	4	10	11	33
1	2	3	4	5	6	7	8	9	10	11									34
1	2	3		5	6			7	8						9	4	10	11	35
1	2		4	5	6	7	8		10	11					9	3			36
1	2		4	5	6	7	8		10						9	3		11	37
1	2		4	5	6	7	8		10	11					9	3			38
1	2	3	10		6	7	8			11		5			9	4			39
1	2	3	10		6	7	8			11		5			9	4			40
1	2	3	10		6	7	8	9		11		5				4			41
1	2		4		6		8			7		5	11	10	9	3			42
42	35	38	38	36	42	34	23	35	38	37	3	6	6	16	10	15	4	4	
			1		3	4	4	13	14	3				3	6		1	1	

3 own-goals

Strong J	Woodruff A	Mather H	Attwell R	Brown A	Bray G	Chew J	Morris W	Billingham J	Potts H	Hays J	Butterfield J	Johnson R	Kippax FP	Knight J	Harrison R	Loughran J	Haigh G	Hornby R	
1	2	3	4	5	6			7	8	11				10	9				3
1	1	1	1	1	1			1	1	1				1	1				

1948-49

Manager: Cliff Britton until September, then Frank Hill

1	Aug	21	(h)	Manchester C	W 1-0	Billingham	33,621
2		25	(a)	Charlton A	L 1-3	Chew	29,397
3		28	(a)	Portsmouth	L 0-1		37,846
4		31	(h)	Charlton A	D 0-0		18,926
5	Sep	4	(h)	Newcastle U	L 0-3		32,826
6		6	(h)	Preston NE	W 1-0	Chew	35,665
7		11	(a)	Middlesbrough	L 1-4	Potts	28,903
8		15	(a)	Preston NE	W 3-0	Bray, Chew, Billingham	33,032
9		18	(h)	Birmingham C	D 2-2	Chew, Potts	34,081
10		25	(a)	Chelsea	L 0-1		53,193
11	Oct	2	(h)	Everton	W 1-0	Wilson	31,341
12		9	(a)	Arsenal	L 1-3	Chew	53,647
13		16	(h)	Huddersfield T	L 1-2	Billingham	28,976
14		23	(a)	Manchester U	D 1-1	Billingham	49,919
15		30	(h)	Sheffield U	W 2-0	Chew, Knight	26,216
16	Nov	6	(a)	Aston Villa	L 1-3	Haigh	43,323
17		13	(h)	Sunderland	W 3-1	Chew, Attwell, Hays	18,939
18		20	(a)	Wolves	L 0-3		37,096
19		27	(h)	Bolton W	W 3-0	Harrison 3	37,291
20	Dec	4	(a)	Liverpool	D 1-1	Potts	41,001
21		11	(h)	Blackpool	W 2-0	Morris, Harrison	37,969
22		18	(a)	Manchester C	D 2-2	Harrison, Attwell	26,849
23		25	(h)	Stoke C	L 1-3	Potts	39,262
24		27	(a)	Stoke C	L 1-2	Chew	39,583
25	Jan	1	(h)	Portsmouth	W 2-1	McLaren, Chew	31,045
26		15	(a)	Newcastle U	D 1-1	Morris	33,439
27		22	(h)	Middlesbrough	D 0-0		36,506
28	Feb	5	(a)	Birmingham C	D 0-0		34,003
29		19	(h)	Chelsea	W 3-0	Attwell, Harrison, Morris	28,754
30		26	(a)	Everton	L 1-2	Attwell	34,568
31	Mar	5	(h)	Arsenal	D 1-1	Potts	20,810
32		12	(a)	Huddersfield T	L 0-1		23,136
33		19	(h)	Wolves	D 0-0		31,804
34		26	(a)	Bolton W	W 1-0	Chew	26,593
35	Apr	2	(h)	Aston Villa	D 1-1	Chew	24,709
36		9	(a)	Sunderland	D 0-0		34,410
37		15	(h)	Derby C	W 3-1	Harrison, Potts, Hays	30,966
38		16	(h)	Manchester U	L 0-2		38,682
39		18	(a)	Derby C	L 0-2		26,095
40		23	(a)	Sheffield U	D 0-0		33,508
41		30	(h)	Liverpool	L 0-2		17,693
42	May	7	(a)	Blackpool	D 1-1	Potts	21,626

FINAL LEAGUE POSITION: 15th in Division One — Appearances / Goals

FA Cup

3	Jan	8	(h)	Charlton A	W 2-1*	McLaren, Clarke	37,000
4		29	(a)	Rotherham U	W 1-0	Spencer	22,000
5	Feb	12	(a)	Brentford	L 2-4	Attwell, Bray	34,000

*After extra-time — Appearances / Goals

Strong J	Woodruff A	Mather H	Attwell R	Brown A	Bray G	Chew J	Morris W	Billingham J	Knight J	Hays J	Potts H	Wilson I	Loughran J	Harrison R	Johnson R	Haigh G	Cummings T	Martindale L	McLaren A	Clarke A	Kirkham R	Spencer J	
1	2	3	4	5	6	7	8	9	10	11													1
1	2	3	4	5	6	7	8	9	10	11													2
1	2	3	4	5	6	7	8	9			10	11											3
1	2	3		5	6	7			8		10	11	4	9									4
1	2	3	4	5					8	7	10	11	6	9									5
1		3	4	5	6	7	8				10	11	2	9									6
1		3	4	5	6	7	8				10	11	2	9									7
1		3	4	5	6	7	8	9			10	11	2										8
1		3	4	5	6	7	8	9			10	11	2										9
1		3	4		6	7	8	9	10			11	2		5								10
1		3	4	5	6	7	8	9			10	11	2										11
1	2	3			6	7	8	9			10	11	4		5								12
1	2	3			6	7	8	9			10	11	4		5								13
1	5	3	4		6	7		9	8			11	2			10							14
1	5	3	4		6	7		9	8	11			2			10							15
1	5	3	4		6	7		9	8	11			2			10							16
1	5	3	4		6	7		9		11	8		2			10							17
1	5	3	4		6	7		9		11	8		2			10							18
1	5	3	4		6	7	8			11	10		2	9									19
1	5	3	4		6	7	8			11	10		2	9									20
1	5	3	4		6	7	8			11	10		2	9									21
1		3	4		6	7	8			11	10		2	9			5						22
1	5	3	4		6	7	8			11	10		2	9									23
1	5	3	4			7				11	10		2					6	8	9			24
1	5	3	4		6	7		9		11	10		2						8				25
1		3	4			7	8			11	10		2				5	6		9			26
1		3	4		6	7				11	10		2	9			5		8				27
1			4		6	7	8			11	10		2				5				3	9	28
1		3	4		6	7	8			11	10		2	9			5						29
1		3	4		6	7	8			11	10		2	9			5						30
1		3	4		6	7	8			11	10		2	9			5						31
1	2	3	4		6	7	8	9		11	10						5						32
1		3	4		6	7	8			11	10		2	9			5						33
1		3	4		6	7	8			11	10		2	9			5						34
1		3	4		6	7	8			11	10		2	9			5						35
1		3	4		6	7	8			11	10		2	9			5						36
1		3	4		6	7	8			11	10		2	9			5						37
1		3	4		6	7	8			11	10		2	9			5						38
1		3			4					7	10	11	2	9		8	5	6					39
1		3			6	7	8			11	10		2	9			5	4					40
1		3			6	7	8			11	10		2	9			5	4					41
1		3			6	7	8				10	11	2	9			5	4					42
42	19	41	35	10	39	40	31	16	8	30	36	14	38	23	3	6	18	6	3	2	1	1	
			4		1	11	3	4	1	2	7	1		7		1			1				

Strong J	Woodruff A	Mather H	Attwell R	Brown A	Bray G	Chew J	Morris W	Billingham J	Knight J	Hays J	Potts H	Wilson I	Loughran J	Harrison R	Johnson R	Haigh G	Cummings T	Martindale L	McLaren A	Clarke A	Kirkham R	Spencer J	
1	5	3	4		6	7				11	10		2						8	9			3
1		3	4		6	7				11	10		2				5			9		8	4
1			4		6	7				11	10		2				5			9	3	8	5
3	1	2	3		3	3				3	3		3				2		1	3	1	2	
			1		1														1	1		1	

1949-50

Manager: Frank Hill

1	Aug	20	(a)	Arsenal	W 1-0	Morris	47,794
2		23	(h)	Sunderland	D 2-2	Harrison, Attwell	35,599
3		27	(h)	Bolton W	W 2-1	Chew, Potts	31,581
4		31	(a)	Sunderland	L 1-2	Clarke	53,032
5	Sep	3	(a)	Birmingham C	W 1-0	Clarke	36,341
6		5	(h)	Stoke C	W 2-1	Potts 2	22,575
7		10	(h)	Derby C	L 0-1		34,600
8		12	(a)	Stoke C	D 1-1	Attwell	25,004
9		17	(a)	West Brom A	L 0-3		37,091
10		24	(h)	Manchester U	W 1-0	Spencer	41,262
11	Oct	1	(a)	Chelsea	W 1-0	Spencer	54,574
12		8	(h)	Newcastle U	L 1-2	Attwell	37,268
13		15	(a)	Fulham	L 0-1		34,313
14		22	(h)	Manchester C	D 0-0		25,063
15		29	(a)	Charlton A	D 1-1	Chew	29,195
16	Nov	5	(h)	Aston Villa	W 1-0	Spencer	24,030
17		12	(a)	Wolves	D 0-0		40,216
18		19	(h)	Portsmouth	W 2-1	Morris, Potts	28,541
19		26	(a)	Huddersfield T	W 2-1	Bray, Chew	19,154
20	Dec	3	(h)	Everton	W 5-1	Potts 3, Spencer, Hays	19,961
21		10	(a)	Middlesbrough	L 1-4	Hays	26,369
22		17	(h)	Arsenal	D 0-0		25,651
23		24	(a)	Bolton W	W 1-0	Chew	34,461
24		26	(h)	Blackpool	D 0-0		49,815
25		27	(a)	Blackpool	L 0-2		31,074
26		31	(h)	Birmingham C	D 1-1	Chew	25,473
27	Jan	14	(a)	Derby C	D 1-1	Potts	32,464
28		21	(h)	West Brom A	D 0-0		26,129
29	Feb	4	(a)	Manchester U	L 2-3	Potts, Opp own-goal	48,528
30		18	(h)	Chelsea	L 1-2	Spencer	23,446
31		25	(a)	Newcastle U	D 0-0		30,032
32	Mar	4	(h)	Fulham	D 0-0		19,858
33		11	(a)	Portsmouth	L 1-2	Spencer	26,344
34		18	(h)	Huddersfield T	W 1-0	Shannon	19,960
35		25	(a)	Aston Villa	W 1-0	Potts	29,923
36	Apr	1	(h)	Wolves	L 0-1		23,171
37		7	(h)	Liverpool	L 0-2		33,025
38		8	(a)	Manchester C	L 0-1		31,298
39		10	(a)	Liverpool	W 1-0	Clarke	43,716
40		15	(h)	Charlton A	W 1-0	Clarke	20,867
41		22	(a)	Everton	D 1-1	Clarke	35,784
42		29	(h)	Middlesbrough	W 3-2	Spencer, Clarke, Potts	12,367

FINAL LEAGUE POSITION: 10th in Division One

Appearances
Goals

FA Cup

3	Jan	7	(a)	Notts C	W 4-1	Spencer, Attwell, Potts, Wilson	43,482
4		28	(h)	Port Vale	W 2-1	Spencer, Hays	49,692
5	Feb	11	(a)	Arsenal	L 0-2		55,458

Appearances
Goals

Strong J	Loughran J	Mather H	Attwell R	Cummings T	Martindale L	Chew J	Morris W	Harrison R	Potts H	Hays J	Woodruff A	Clarke A	Wilson I	Henderson T	Spencer J	Bray G	Shannon L	Kirkham R	Hayes W	Haigh G	Hird J	Stephenson R	
1	2	3	4	5	6	7	8	9	10	11													1
1	2	3	4	5	6	7	8	9	10	11													2
1	2	3	4	5	6	7	8	9	10	11													3
1		3	4	5	6	7	8		10	11	2	9											4
1		3	4	5	6	7	8		10	11	2	9											5
1		3	4	5	6	7	8		10	11	2	9											6
1		3	4	5	6		8		10	11	2	9	7										7
1		3	4	5	6		8		10	11	2	9		7									8
1		3	4	5	6		8		10	11	2	9			7								9
1		3	4	5			7		10	11	2	9			8	6							10
1		3	4	5			7		10	11	2	9			8	6							11
1		3	4	5			7		10	11	2	9			8	6							12
1		3		5	4				10	11	2	9		7	8	6							13
1		3	4	5		7		9	10	11	2				8	6							14
1		3	4	5		7	8		10	11	2				9	6							15
1		3	4	5		7	8		10	11	2				9	6							16
1		3	4	5		7	8		10	11	2				9	6							17
1		3	4	5		7	8		10	11	2				9	6							18
1		3	4	5		7	8		10	11	2				9	6							19
1		3	4	5		7	8		10	11	2				9	6							20
1		3	4	5		7	8		10	11	2				9	6							21
1		3	4	5		7	8		10	11	2				9	6							22
1		3	4	5		7	8		10	11	2				9	6							23
1		3	4	5		7	8		10	11	2				9	6							24
1		3	4	5			8		10	11	2				9	6	7						25
1		3	4	5		7	8		10		2		11		9	6							26
1		3	4	5		7	8		10		2	9	11			6							27
1		3	4	5		7	8		10		2		11		9	6							28
1			4	5		7	8		10		2		11		9	6		3					29
1			4	5		7	8		10	11					9	6		3	2				30
1			4	5		7	8		10	11	2				9	6			3				31
1			4	5					10	11	2	9			8	6	7		3				32
1			4	5			8		10	11	2				9	6	7		3				33
1			4	5			8		10	11	2				9	6	7		3				34
1				5			8		10	11	2				9	6	7		3	4			35
1		3	4				8		10	11	5				9	6	7	2					36
1		3	4	5		11			10						9	6	7			8	2		37
1			4	5		11	8		10			9				6	7	3			2		38
1		3	4	5	10				8	11		9				6					2	7	39
1		3	4	5	10				8	11		9				6					2	7	40
1		3	4	5	10				8	11		9				6					2	7	41
1		3	4	5					8	11		9			10	6		2				7	42
42	3	34	40	41	13	25	34	4	42	36	32	17	5	2	29	33	8	5	6	2	5	4	
			3			5	2	1	11	2		6			7	1	1						

1 own-goal

Strong J	Loughran J	Mather H	Attwell R	Cummings T	Martindale L	Chew J	Morris W	Harrison R	Potts H	Hays J	Woodruff A	Clarke A	Wilson I	Henderson T	Spencer J	Bray G	Shannon L	Kirkham R	Hayes W	Haigh G	Hird J	Stephenson R	
1		3	4	5		7	8		10		2		11		9	6							3
1		3	4	5		7	8		10	11	2				9	6							4
1			4	5		7	8		10		2		11		9	6		3					5
3		2	3	3		3	3		3	1	3		2		3	3		1					
			1						1	1			1		2								

1950-51

Manager: Frank Hill

1	Aug	19	(h)	Arsenal	L 0-1		32,706
2		21	(a)	Blackpool	W 2-1	Morris 2	33,161
3		26	(a)	Sheffield W	W 1-0	Chew	40,754
4		29	(h)	Blackpool	D 0-0		38,688
5	Sep	2	(h)	Middlesbrough	W 3-1	Stephenson 2, Morris	29,779
6		4	(h)	Portsmouth	D 1-1	Kirkham	30,670
7		9	(a)	Huddersfield T	L 1-3	Stephenson	30,664
8		16	(h)	Newcastle U	D 1-1	Bray	33,283
9		23	(a)	West Brom A	L 1-2	Spencer	32,058
10		30	(h)	Stoke C	D 1-1	Lyons	23,776
11	Oct	7	(a)	Tottenham H	L 0-1		46,518
12		14	(h)	Charlton A	W 5-1	Holden 2, Hays, Morris, Stephenson	20,008
13		21	(a)	Sunderland	D 1-1	Holden	38,982
14		28	(h)	Aston Villa	W 2-0	Attwell, Holden	26,471
15	Nov	4	(a)	Manchester U	D 1-1	Holden	41,244
16		11	(h)	Wolves	W 2-0	Holden, McIlroy	36,157
17		18	(a)	Derby C	D 1-1	Morris	21,418
18		25	(h)	Liverpool	D 1-1	Chew	31,901
19	Dec	2	(a)	Fulham	L 1-4	O'Neill	25,250
20		9	(h)	Bolton W	W 2-0	Holden, McIlroy	31,124
21		16	(a)	Arsenal	W 1-0	Holden	32,374
22		23	(h)	Sheffield W	W 1-0	Morris	21,272
23		25	(a)	Everton	L 0-1		40,864
24		26	(h)	Everton	D 1-1	McIlroy	38,444
25		30	(a)	Middlesbrough	D 3-3	Chew, Morris, McIlroy	34,349
26	Jan	13	(h)	Huddersfield T	L 0-1		22,168
27		20	(a)	Newcastle U	L 1-2	Morris	40,658
28	Feb	3	(h)	West Brom A	L 0-1		19,101
29		10	(a)	Bolton W	D 1-1	Holden	35,540
30		17	(a)	Stoke C	D 0-0		20,823
31		24	(h)	Tottenham H	W 2-0	Chew 2	33,047
32	Mar	3	(a)	Charlton A	D 0-0		30,491
33		10	(h)	Sunderland	D 1-1	McIlroy	25,065
34		17	(a)	Aston Villa	L 2-3	Morris, Holden	26,347
35		23	(h)	Chelsea	W 2-1	Holden 2	22,266
36		24	(h)	Manchester U	L 1-2	Stephenson	36,656
37		26	(a)	Chelsea	W 2-0	Stephenson, Morris	23,723
38		31	(a)	Wolves	W 1-0	Lyons	20,572
39	Apr	7	(h)	Derby C	W 1-0	Lyons	21,714
40		14	(a)	Liverpool	L 0-1		24,118
41		21	(h)	Fulham	L 0-2		19,929
42	May	5	(a)	Portsmouth	L 1-2	Morris	22,510

FINAL LEAGUE POSITION: 10th in Division One

Appearances
Goals

FA Cup

3	Jan	6	(a)	Aston Villa	L 0-2	38,833

Appearances
Goals

Strong J	Woodruff A	Mather H	Martindale L	Cummings T	Bray G	Chew J	Morris W	Clarke A	Potts H	Stephenson R	Spencer J	Hays J	Kirkham R	Holden W	Samuels L	Hayes W	Rudman H	Lyons T	Attwell R	McIlroy J	O'Neill W	Aird J	Adamson J	McNulty J	
1	2	3	4	5	6	7	8	9	10	11															1
1	2	3	4	5	6	7	8	9			10	11													2
1	2	3		5	6	7	8		10		9	11	4												3
1	2	3		5	6	7	8		10		9	11	4												4
1	2	3		5	6		8			7	10	11	4	9											5
1	2	3		5	6				8	7		11	4	9	10										6
1	2	3		5	6		8		10	7		11	4	9											7
1	2	3		5	6		8		10	7		11	4	9											8
1	2			5	6		8			7	10	11	4	9		3									9
1	2			5	6				8	7	10			9		3	4	11							10
1	5	3			6	11	8		10	7				9		2	4								11
1	2	3		5	6		8		10	7		11		9					4						12
1	2	3		5	6		8			7		11		9					4	10					13
1	2	3		5	6	7	8					11		9					4	10					14
1	2	3		5	6	7	8					11		9					4	10					15
1	2	3		5	6	7	8					11		9					4	10					16
1	2	3		5	6	7	8					11		9					4	10					17
1	2	3		5	6	7	8					11		9					4	10					18
1	2	3		5	6	7						11		9					4	10	8				19
1	2	3		5	6	7	8					11		9					4	10					20
1	2	3		5	6	7	8					11		9					4	10					21
1	2	3		5	6	7	8					11		9					4	10					22
1	2	3		5	6	7	8					11		9					4	10					23
1	2	3		5	6	9	8			7		11							4	10					24
1		3		5	6	7	8				9	11				2			4	10					25
1		3		5	6	7	8					11		9		2			4	10					26
1		3		5	6	7	8					11		9		2			4	10					27
1		3		5	6	7	8					11		9					4	10		2			28
1		3		5	6	7	8					11		9						10		2	4		29
1	2	3		5	6	7	8					11		9						10			4		30
1	2	3		5	6	7	8							9				11		10			4		31
1	2	3		5	6	7	8							9				11		10			4		32
1	2	3		5	6	7	8							9				11		10			4		33
1	2	3		5	6	7	8							9				11		10			4		34
1	2	3		5	6	7	8							9				11		10			4		35
	2	3		5	6		8			7				9				11		10			4	1	36
	2	3		5	6		8			7				9				11		10			4	1	37
1	2	3		5	6		8			7				9				11		10			4		38
1	2	3		5	6		8			7				9				11		10			4		39
1	2	3		5	6					7				9				11		10			4		40
1	2	3		5	6					7				9	8			11		10			4		41
1	2	3		5	6	11	8	9		7										10			4		42
40	37	40	2	41	42	28	38	3	9	18	7	27	7	35	2	6	2	12	17	30	1	2	14	2	
					1	5	11			6	1	1	1	12				3	1	5	1				

Strong J	Woodruff A	Mather H	Martindale L	Cummings T	Bray G	Chew J	Morris W	Clarke A	Potts H	Stephenson R	Spencer J	Hays J	Kirkham R	Holden W	Samuels L	Hayes W	Rudman H	Lyons T	Attwell R	McIlroy J	O'Neill W	Aird J	Adamson J	McNulty J	
1	2	3		5	6	7	8				9	11							4	10					3
1	1	1		1	1	1	1				1	1							1	1					

1951-52

Manager: Frank Hill

1	Aug	18	(a)	Charlton A	L 0-1		21,453
2		21	(h)	Liverpool	D 0-0		25,162
3		25	(h)	Fulham	W 1-0	Holden	18,797
4		29	(a)	Liverpool	L 1-3	Morris	32,857
5	Sep	1	(a)	Middlesbrough	L 0-5		31,711
6		3	(h)	Tottenham H	D 1-1	Hapgood	27,045
7		8	(h)	West Brom A	W 6-1	Morris 4, Holden, Hapgood	23,868
8		10	(a)	Tottenham H	D 1-1	McIlroy	35,948
9		15	(a)	Newcastle U	L 1-7	Morris	51,278
10		22	(h)	Bolton W	L 1-3	Morris	37,196
11		29	(a)	Stoke C	L 1-2	Holden	28,577
12	Oct	6	(h)	Blackpool	W 2-0	Morris, Shannon	34,355
13		13	(a)	Arsenal	L 0-1		45,531
14		20	(h)	Manchester C	D 0-0		30,977
15		27	(a)	Derby C	L 0-1		21,147
16	Nov	3	(h)	Aston Villa	W 2-1	Morris 2	17,680
17		10	(a)	Sunderland	D 0-0		33,139
18		17	(h)	Wolves	D 2-2	Cummings, McIlroy	22,881
19		24	(a)	Huddersfield T	W 3-1	Holden, Shannon, Elliott	14,882
20	Dec	1	(h)	Chelsea	D 1-1	Holden	21,772
21		8	(a)	Portsmouth	D 2-2	Holden, Shannon	23,648
22		15	(h)	Charlton A	W 1-0	Holden	16,841
23		22	(a)	Fulham	W 2-1	Shannon, Adamson	20,102
24		25	(h)	Preston NE	L 0-2		36,468
25		29	(h)	Middlesbrough	W 7-1	Holden 3, Morris 3, Shannon	26,057
26	Jan	1	(a)	Preston NE	W 2-1	Chew, Morris	34,097
27		5	(a)	West Brom A	D 1-1	Morris	25,977
28		19	(h)	Newcastle U	W 2-1	Morris, Cummings	33,719
29		26	(a)	Bolton W	W 4-1	Holden 2, Morris, Elliott	38,149
30	Feb	9	(h)	Stoke C	W 4-0	Adamson, McIlroy, Elliott 2	29,714
31		16	(a)	Blackpool	L 0-1		26,079
32	Mar	1	(h)	Arsenal	L 0-1		41,040
33		12	(a)	Manchester C	W 1-0	Shannon	20,223
34		15	(h)	Derby C	L 0-1		25,129
35		22	(a)	Aston Villa	L 1-4	Shannon	31,128
36		29	(h)	Sunderland	L 0-1		11,618
37	Apr	5	(a)	Wolves	W 2-1	Shannon, McIlroy	16,737
38		11	(h)	Manchester U	D 1-1	Shannon	38,907
39		12	(h)	Huddersfield T	L 0-2		23,081
40		14	(a)	Manchester U	L 1-6	Morris	46,339
41		19	(a)	Chelsea	L 1-4	Cheesebrough	26,349
42		26	(h)	Portsmouth	W 1-0	Elliott	16,790

FINAL LEAGUE POSITION: 14th in Division One

Appearances

Goals

FA Cup

3	Jan	12	(h)	Hartlepools U	W 1-0	Shannon	38,508
4	Feb	2	(h)	Coventry C	W 2-0	Holden, Elliott	40,696
5		23	(h)	Liverpool	W 2-0	Morris, Shannon	54,031
6	Mar	8	(a)	Blackburn R	L 1-3	Chew	53,000

Appearances

Goals

Strong J	Woodruff A	Aird J	Adamson J	Cummings T	Attwell R	Stephenson R	Morris W	Holden W	McIlroy J	Shannon L	Mather H	Bray G	Hapgood A	Elliott W	Chew J	McNulty J	Clarke A	Cheesebrough A	Corr P	
1	2	3	4	5	6	7	8	9	10	11										1
1	2		4	5		7	8	9	10	11	3	6								2
1	2		4	5		7	8	9	10	11	3	6								3
1	2		4	5		7	8	9	10	11	3	6								4
1	2		4	5		7	8	9			3	6	10	11						5
1	2		4	5			8	9	10		3	6	7	11						6
1	2			5	4		8	9	10		3	6	7	11						7
1		2		5	4		8	9	10		3	6	7	11						8
1			6	5	4		8	9	10		3	2	7	11						9
1	2			5	4		8	9	10		3	6	7	11						10
1	2			5	4		8	9	10		3	6	7	11						11
1	2		4	5	6	7	8			10	3			9	11					12
1	2		4	5	6	7	8			10	3			9	11					13
1		2	4	5	6		8		9	10	3			11	7					14
1	2		4	5	6		8	9	10		3			11	7					15
1		2	4	5	6		8	9	10		3			11	7					16
1		2	4	5	6		8	9	10		3			11	7					17
1		2	4	5	6		8	9	10		3			11	7					18
1		2	4	5	6		8	9		10	3			11	7					19
1		2	4	5	6		8	9		10	3			11	7					20
1		2	4	5	6		8	9	7	10	3			11						21
1		2	4	5	6		8	9	7	10	3			11						22
1		2	4	5	6		8	9	7	10	3			11						23
1		2	4	5	6		8	9	7	10	3			11						24
1		2	4	5	6		8	9		10	3			11	7					25
1		2	4	5	6		8	9		10	3			11	7					26
1		2	4	5	6		8	9		10	3			11	7					27
1		2	4	5	6		8	9		10	3			11	7					28
1		2	4	5	6		8	9		10	3			11	7					29
1		2	4	5	6		8		10	9	3			11	7					30
		2	4	5	6		8	9		10	3			11	7	1				31
1		2	4	5	6		8	9		10	3			11	7					32
1		2	4	5	6		8	9		10	3			11	7					33
1		2	4	5	6			9	8	10	3			11	7					34
		2	4	5	6		8	9		10	3			11	7	1				35
1		2	4	5	6				8	10	3			11	7		9			36
		2	4	5	6		8		10	9	3			11	7	1				37
		2	4	5	6		8		10	9	3				7	1		11		38
		2	4	5	6		8		10	9	3				7	1		11		39
		2	4	5	6		8		10		3			11		1		7	9	40
1	2	3	4	5	6		8		10	9				11				7		41
1		2	4	5	6				8	10	3			11			9	7		42
36	13	30	38	42	37	7	39	31	28	30	40	10	7	36	24	6	2	5	1	
			2	2			18	12	4	9			2	5	1			1		

Strong J	Woodruff A	Aird J	Adamson J	Cummings T	Attwell R	Stephenson R	Morris W	Holden W	McIlroy J	Shannon L	Mather H	Bray G	Hapgood A	Elliott W	Chew J	McNulty J	Clarke A	Cheesebrough A	Corr P	
1		2	4	5	6		8	9		10	3			11	7					3
1		2	4	5	6		8	9		10	3			11	7					4
1		2	4	5	6		8	9		10	3			11	7					5
1		2	4	5	6		8	9		10	3			11	7					6
4		4	4	4	4		4	4		4	4			4	4					
							1	1		2				1	1					

1952-53

Manager: Frank Hill

1	Aug	23	(h)	Middlesbrough	L 0-1		27,386
2		26	(h)	Stoke C	W 3-2	Shannon 2, McIlroy	20,847
3		30	(a)	West Brom A	W 2-1	Chew, Elliott	31,400
4	Sep	1	(a)	Stoke C	W 3-1	McIlroy 2, Elliott	26,287
5		6	(h)	Newcastle U	W 2-1	Chew, Holden	35,068
6		8	(h)	Manchester C	W 2-1	Holden, Shannon	27,083
7		13	(a)	Cardiff C	D 0-0		45,182
8		17	(a)	Manchester C	D 0-0		25,094
9		20	(h)	Sheffield W	D 1-1	Shannon	33,049
10		27	(a)	Tottenham H	L 1-2	Holden	43,031
11	Oct	4	(h)	Derby C	L 1-2	Opp own-goal	26,248
12		11	(a)	Blackpool	L 2-4	Shannon, Elliott	35,671
13		18	(h)	Chelsea	D 1-1	Holden	27,692
14		25	(a)	Manchester U	W 3-1	McIlroy 2, Holden	38,754
15	Nov	1	(h)	Portsmouth	W 3-2	Holden, Shannon, Adamson	28,273
16		8	(a)	Bolton W	W 2-1	Holden, Opp own-goal	37,604
17		15	(h)	Aston Villa	W 1-0	Elliott	24,750
18		22	(a)	Sunderland	L 1-2	Holden	40,225
19		29	(h)	Wolves	D 0-0		30,808
20	Dec	13	(h)	Arsenal	D 1-1	Holden	32,753
21		20	(a)	Middlesbrough	D 2-2	Holden, Elliott	19,155
22		25	(h)	Liverpool	W 2-0	McIlroy, Holden	35,878
23		26	(a)	Liverpool	D 1-1	Adamson	46,589
24	Jan	3	(h)	West Brom A	W 5-0	Shannon 3, McIlroy, Elliott	35,680
25		17	(a)	Newcastle U	D 0-0		49,366
26		24	(h)	Cardiff C	D 0-0		29,491
27	Feb	7	(a)	Sheffield W	W 4-2	Holden 2, McIlroy, Shannon	41,262
28		17	(h)	Tottenham H	W 3-2	Shannon 3	13,771
29		21	(a)	Derby C	W 3-1	Chew, McIlroy, Elliott	19,646
30	Mar	3	(h)	Blackpool	L 0-1		20,874
31		7	(a)	Chelsea	W 2-0	Holden 2	39,214
32		14	(h)	Manchester U	W 2-1	Chew, Holden	45,422
33		21	(a)	Portsmouth	L 1-2	Shannon	33,413
34		28	(h)	Bolton W	L 0-1		20,392
35	Apr	3	(h)	Preston NE	D 2-2	McIlroy, Elliott	41,685
36		4	(a)	Aston Villa	L 0-2		32,404
37		6	(a)	Preston NE	L 1-2	McIlroy	39,741
38		11	(h)	Sunderland	W 5-1	Holden 4, Adamson	21,252
39		18	(a)	Wolves	L 1-5	Holden	33,474
40		22	(a)	Charlton A	D 0-0		19,303
41		25	(h)	Charlton A	W 2-0	Holden, Shannon	19,673
42	May	1	(a)	Arsenal	L 2-3	Stephenson, Elliott	51,586

FINAL LEAGUE POSITION: 6th in Division One

Appearances
Goals

FA Cup

3	Jan	10	(a)	Portsmouth	D 1-1	Stephenson	40,532
R		13	(h)	Portsmouth	W 3-1	McIlroy, Shannon, Elliott	39,385
4		31	(h)	Sunderland	W 2-0	Holden 2	53,105
5	Feb	14	(h)	Arsenal	L 0-2		51,025

Appearances
Goals

Strong J	Aird J	Mather H	Adamson J	Cummings T	Attwell R	Cheesebrough A	Morris W	Holden W	Shannon L	Elliott W	Chew J	McIlroy J	Pilkington B	Brown J	Binns E	Winton D	Thompson D	Rudman H	Stephenson R		
1	2	3	4	5	6	7	8	9	10	11											1
1	2	3	4	5	6			9	10	11	7	8									2
1	2	3	4	5	6			9	10	11	7	8									3
1	2	3	4	5	6			9	10	11	7	8									4
1	2	3	4	5	6			9	10	11	7	8									5
1	2	3	4	5	6			9	10	11	7	8									6
1	2	3	4	5	6			9	10	11	7	8									7
1	2	3	4	5	6			9	10	11	7	8									8
1	2	3	4	5	6			9	10	11	7	8									9
1	2	3	4	5	6			9	10		7	8	11								10
1	2	3	4	5	6		8	9	10		7		11								11
1	2	3	4	5	6			9	10	11	7	8									12
1	2	3	4	5				9	10	11	7	8		6							13
1	2	3	4	5	6			9	10	11	7	8									14
1	2	3	4	5	6			9	10	11	7	8									15
1	2	3	4	5	6			9	10	11	7	8									16
1		3	4	5	6			9	10	11	7	8			2						17
1		3	4	5	6			9	10	11	7	8			2						18
1		3	4	5	6			9	10	11	7	8				2					19
1	2	3	4	5			7	9	10	11	6	8									20
	2	3	4	5	6			9	10	11	7	8					1				21
	2	3	4	5	6			9	10	11	7	8					1				22
	2	3	4	5	6			9	10	11	7	8					1				23
	2	3	4	5	6			9	10	11	7	8					1				24
	2	3	4	5	6			9	10	11	7	8					1				25
	2	3	4	5				9	10	11	7	8					1	6			26
	2	3	4	5	6			9	10		7	8	11				1				27
	2	3	4	5	6			9	10	11	7	8					1				28
	2	3	4	5	6			9	10	11	7	8					1				29
	2	3	4	5	6			9	10	11	7	8					1				30
	2	3	4	5	6			9	10	11		8					1		7		31
	2	3	4	5	6			9	10	11	7	8					1				32
	2	3	4	5	6			9	10	11	7	8					1				33
	2	3	4	5	6			9	10	11	7	8					1				34
	2	3	4	5	6			9	10	11	7	8					1				35
		3	4	5	6			9	10	11	7	8			2		1				36
	2		4	5	6			9	10	11		8	7				1	3			37
	2		4	5				9	10	11		8		6		3	1		7		38
	2			5				9	10	11		8		6		3	1	4	7		39
	2		4	5				9	10	11	8			6		3	1		7		40
	2		4	5				9	10		8		11	6		3	1		7		41
	2		4	5				9	10	11		8		6		3	1		7		42
20	38	36	41	42	34	1	3	42	42	38	36	38	5	6	3	6	22	3	6		
			3					22	15	9	4	11							1		

2 own-goals

	2	3	4	5	6			9	10	11	7						1			8	3
	2	3	4	5	6			9	10	11	7	8					1				R
	2	3	4	5	6			9	10	11	7	8					1				4
	2	3	4	5	6			9	10	11	7	8					1				5
	4	4	4	4	4			4	4	4	4	3					4			1	
								2	1	1		1								1	

1953-54

Manager: Frank Hill

1	Aug	19	(h)	Wolves	W 4-1	Shannon 2, Holden, Pilkington	32,822
2		22	(a)	Charlton A	L 1-3	McIlroy	24,802
3		25	(h)	Blackpool	W 2-1	Pilkington, Opp own-goal	41,574
4		29	(h)	Sheffield W	W 4-1	Gray 2, Pilkington 2	25,813
5		31	(a)	Blackpool	L 0-2		18,113
6	Sep	5	(a)	Middlesbrough	W 3-1	Gray, Holden, Stephenson	32,597
7		7	(h)	Tottenham H	W 4-2	Gray 3, McIlroy	34,280
8		12	(h)	West Brom A	L 1-4	Stephenson	38,948
9		16	(a)	Tottenham H	W 3-2	McIlroy 2, Gray	30,472
10		19	(a)	Liverpool	L 0-4		36,643
11		26	(h)	Newcastle U	L 1-2	Holden	33,688
12	Oct	3	(a)	Manchester U	W 2-1	Gray, Stephenson	39,550
13		10	(h)	Portsmouth	W 1-0	McIlroy	28,142
14		17	(a)	Arsenal	W 5-2	Holden 3, Stephenson 2	47,353
15		24	(h)	Cardiff C	W 3-0	Gray, McIlroy, Pilkington	29,539
16		31	(a)	Manchester C	L 2-3	Adamson, Gray	32,353
17	Nov	7	(h)	Sheffield U	W 2-1	McIlroy 2	15,846
18		14	(a)	Chelsea	L 1-2	Stephenson	39,731
19		21	(h)	Aston Villa	W 3-2	Stephenson, McIlroy, Gray	26,868
20		28	(a)	Huddersfield T	L 1-3	Shannon	34,666
21	Dec	5	(h)	Sunderland	W 5-1	McIlroy, Holden, Shannon, Adamson, Gray	27,839
22		12	(a)	Wolves	W 2-1	Holden 2	35,043
23		19	(h)	Charlton A	W 2-0	McIlroy, Shannon	25,369
24		25	(h)	Preston NE	W 2-1	Shannon, Pilkington	33,398
25		26	(a)	Preston NE	L 1-2	McIlroy	32,416
26	Jan	2	(a)	Sheffield W	L 0-2		33,061
27		16	(h)	Middlesbrough	W 5-0	Gray 3, McIlroy, Holden	23,481
28		23	(a)	West Brom A	D 0-0		42,644
29	Feb	6	(h)	Liverpool	D 1-1	Pilkington	24,025
30		13	(a)	Newcastle U	L 1-3	McIlroy	29,114
31		20	(h)	Manchester U	W 2-0	Gray 2	31,402
32		27	(a)	Portsmouth	L 2-3	Adamson, McIlroy	24,155
33	Mar	6	(h)	Arsenal	W 2-1	Holden, Shannon	22,726
34		13	(a)	Cardiff C	L 0-1		33,413
35		20	(h)	Manchester C	W 3-1	Gray, McIlroy, Holden	23,061
36		27	(a)	Sheffield U	L 1-2	McIlroy	22,784
37	Apr	3	(h)	Chelsea	L 1-2	Gray	20,312
38		10	(a)	Aston Villa	L 1-5	Holden	23,043
39		16	(a)	Bolton W	D 0-0		34,394
40		17	(h)	Huddersfield T	W 2-1	Adamson, Pilkington	26,180
41		19	(h)	Bolton W	D 1-1	Holden	25,857
42		24	(a)	Sunderland	L 1-2	Adamson	28,014
	FINAL LEAGUE POSITION: 7th in Division One						Appearances
							Goals

FA Cup

3	Jan	9	(h)	Manchester U	W 5-3	Shannon 2, Holden, McIlroy, Gray	52,847
4		30	(h)	Newcastle U	D 1-1	Pilkington	52,011
R	Feb	3	(a)	Newcastle U	L 0-1		48,284
							Appearances
							Goals

Thompson D	Aird J	Winton D	Adamson J	Cummings T	Rudman H	Gray W	McIlroy J	Holden W	Shannon L	Pilkington B	Attwell R	Chew J	Stephenson R	Binns E	Mather H	Cargill D	Seith R	Milner J	McDonald C	
1	2	3	4	5	6	7	8	9	10	11										1
1	2	3	4	5	6	7	8	9	10	11										2
1	2	3	4	5		7	8	9	10	11	6									3
1	2	3	4	5		7	8	9		11	6	10								4
1	2	3	4	5		7	8	9		11	6	10								5
1	2	3	4	5		7	8	9		11	6		10							6
1	2	3	4	5		7	8	9		11	6		10							7
1	2	3	4	5		7	8	9		11	6		10							8
1			4	5		7	8	9	10		6			2	3	11				9
1			4	5		7	8	9	10		6			2	3	11				10
1	2		4	5		7	8	9	10	11	6				3					11
1	2		6	5		7		9		11		10	8		3		4			12
1	2		6			7	10	9		11			8	5	3		4			13
1	2		6			7	10	9		11			8	5	3		4			14
1	2		6			7	10	9		11			8	5	3		4			15
1	2		6			7	10	9		11			8	5	3		4			16
1	2		6			7	10	9		11			8	5	3		4			17
1	2		6			7	10	9		11			8	5	3		4			18
1	2		6	5		11	10	9	8				7		3		4			19
1	2		4	5		7	10		9	11					3		6	8		20
1	2		4	5		7	8	9	10	11					3		6			21
1	2		4	5		7	8	9	10	11	6				3					22
1	2		4	5		7	8	9	10	11	6				3					23
1	2		4	5		7	8	9	10	11	6				3					24
1	2			5		7	8	9	10	11	6				3		4			25
1	2			5		7	8	9	10	11	6				3		4			26
1	2		4	5		7	8	9	10	11	6				3					27
1	2		4	5		7		9	10	11	6		8		3					28
1	2		4	5		7	10		9	11	6		8		3					29
1	2	9	4	5		7	8		10	11	6				3					30
1	2			5		7	8	9	10	11	6				3		4			31
1	2		4	5		7	8	9	10	11	6				3					32
1	2	3	4	5		7	8	9	10	11							6			33
1	2	3	4	5		7	8	9	10	11							6			34
1	2	3	4	5		7	8	9	10	11							6			35
1	2	3	4	5		7	8	9	10	11							6			36
1	2	3	4	5		7	8	9	10	11							6			37
	2	3	4			7	8	9	10	11				5			6		1	38
	2	3	4	5		7	8	9	10	11							6		1	39
	2	3	4	5		7	8	9	10	11							6		1	40
	2	3	4	5		7	8	9	10	11							6		1	41
	2	3	4	5		7	8	9	10	11							6		1	42
37	40	19	39	35	2	42	40	39	30	39	20	3	13	9	24	2	23	1	5	
			5			19	17	14	7	8			7							

1 own-goal

1	2		4	5		7	8	9	10	11	6				3	3
1	2		4	5		7	8	9	10	11	6				3	4
1	2		4	5		7	8	9	10	11	6				3	R
3	3		3	3		3	3	3	3	3	3				3	
						1	1	1	2	1						

1954-55

Manager: Allan Brown

1	Aug	21	(h)	Cardiff C	W 1-0	Shannon	27,836
2		23	(a)	Chelsea	L 0-1		30,239
3		28	(a)	Manchester C	D 0-0		38,201
4		31	(h)	Chelsea	D 1-1	Pilkington	28,472
5	Sep	4	(h)	Everton	L 0-2		31,963
6		6	(h)	Leicester C	W 3-1	Gray, Stephenson, Holden	20,602
7		11	(a)	Newcastle U	L 1-2	Stephenson	47,346
8		13	(a)	Leicester C	D 2-2	Pilkington, Stephenson	26,413
9		18	(h)	West Brom A	L 0-2		29,727
10		25	(a)	Arsenal	L 0-4		46,190
11	Oct	2	(h)	Sheffield U	W 2-1	Gray, Holden	22,237
12		9	(a)	Charlton A	L 1-3	Stephenson	21,883
13		16	(h)	Bolton W	W 2-0	Stephenson, McIlroy	30,016
14		23	(a)	Sheffield W	D 1-1	Stephenson	28,960
15		30	(h)	Portsmouth	W 1-0	Stephenson	23,815
16	Nov	6	(a)	Wolves	L 0-5		27,524
17		13	(h)	Aston Villa	W 2-0	Holden 2	19,186
18		20	(a)	Sunderland	D 2-2	Pilkington, Holden	42,305
19		27	(h)	Tottenham H	L 1-2	McIlroy	21,973
20	Dec	4	(a)	Huddersfield T	W 1-0	Holden	17,372
21		11	(h)	Manchester U	L 2-4	Gray, Holden	24,967
22		18	(a)	Cardiff C	W 3-0	Stephenson, Holden, Opp own-goal	22,035
23		25	(h)	Preston NE	D 2-2	Gray 2	29,758
24		27	(a)	Preston NE	W 1-0	Holden	38,525
25	Jan	1	(h)	Manchester C	W 2-0	Stephenson 2	28,825
26		15	(a)	Everton	D 1-1	McIlroy	29,520
27		22	(h)	Newcastle U	L 0-1		23,467
28	Feb	5	(a)	West Brom A	D 2-2	Pilkington 2	22,749
29		12	(h)	Arsenal	W 3-0	Gray 2, Holden	24,940
30		19	(a)	Sheffield U	L 0-1		22,111
31		26	(h)	Charlton A	W 3-0	Gray, Walton, Pilkington	19,289
32	Mar	5	(a)	Manchester U	L 0-1		33,577
33		12	(h)	Sheffield W	W 2-0	Holden 2	20,082
34		19	(a)	Portsmouth	W 2-0	Holden, Pilkington	21,755
35		26	(h)	Wolves	W 1-0	Walton	23,157
36	Apr	2	(a)	Aston Villa	L 1-3	Pilkington	19,950
37		8	(h)	Blackpool	L 0-1		35,212
38		9	(h)	Huddersfield T	D 1-1	Pilkington	22,214
39		11	(a)	Blackpool	L 0-1		32,881
40		16	(a)	Tottenham H	W 3-0	Holden 2, Pilkington	23,555
41		23	(h)	Sunderland	L 0-1		19,227
42		30	(a)	Bolton W	W 1-0	Pilkington	20,671
FINAL LEAGUE POSITION: 10th in Division One							Appearances
							Goals

FA Cup

3	Jan	8	(a)	Sunderland	L 0-1		50,107
							Appearances
							Goals

McDonald C	Aird J	Mather H	Adamson J	Cummings T	Seith R	Gray W	McIlroy J	Holden W	Shannon L	Pilkington B	McKay P	Attwell R	Stephenson R	Winton D	Cargill D	Thompson D	Rudman H	Cheesebrough A	Walton J	Scott J	Smith D	Binns E	Newlands D	
1	2	3	4	5	6	7	8	9	10	11														1
1	2	3	4	5	6	7	8	9	10	11														2
1	2	3	4	5	6	7	8	9	10	11														3
1	2	3	4	5		7	8	9	6	11	10													4
1	2	3		5		7	8	9	6	11	10	4												5
1	2	3		5	4	7	10	9	6	11			8											6
1	2			5	4	7	10		6	11	9		8	3										7
1	2		4	5	6	7	10		9	11			8	3										8
1	2		4	5	6	7	10		9	11			8	3										9
1	2		4	5	6	7	8	9	10	11				3										10
1	2		4	5	6	7		9	10				8	3	11									11
1	2		4	5	6		8	9	10	11			7	3										12
1	2		4	5		7	10	9	6	11			8	3										13
1	2		4	5		7	10	9	6	11			8	3										14
1	2		4	5		7	10	9	6	11			8	3										15
1	2		4	5		7	10	9	6	11			8	3										16
			4	5		7	10	9	6	11			8	3		1	2							17
			4	5		7	10	9	6	11			8	3		1	2							18
			4	5		7	10	9	6	11			8	3		1	2							19
1				5	4	7	10	9	6	11				3			2	8						20
1				5	4	7	10	9	6	11				3			2	8						21
1			4	5		7	10	9	6				8	3			2	11						22
1				5	4	7	10	9	6				8	3			2	11						23
1			4	5		7	10	9	6				8	3			2	11						24
1			4	5		7	10	9	6				8	3			2	11						25
1			4	5		7	10		6		9		8	3			2	11						26
1			4	5		7	10	9	6	11				3			2		8					27
1			4	5		7	8	9	6	11				3			2		10					28
1			4	5		7	8	9	6	11				3			2		10					29
1			4	5		7	8	9	6	11				3			2		10					30
1			4	5		7	8	9	6	11				3			2		10					31
1			4	5		7	8	9	6					3			2		10	11				32
1			4	5		7	8	9	6	11				3			2		10					33
1			4	5		7		9	6	11			8	3			2		10					34
1			4	5		7	8	9	6	11				3			2		10					35
1			4	5		7	8	9	6	11				3			2		10					36
1			4	5		7	8	9	6	11				3			2		10					37
1			4	5		7	8	9	6	11			10	3			2							38
1	2		4	5		7	8	9	6	11			10	3										39
1			4			7	8	9	6	11				3					10		2	5		40
1			4			7	8	9	6	11			10	3							2	5		41
1			4				8	9	6	11				3					10		2	5	7	42
39	17	6	36	39	13	40	40	38	42	35	4	1	22	36	1	3	22	7	13	1	3	3	1	
						8	3	15	1	11			10						2					

1 own-goal

McDonald C	Aird J	Mather H	Adamson J	Cummings T	Seith R	Gray W	McIlroy J	Holden W	Shannon L	Pilkington B	McKay P	Attwell R	Stephenson R	Winton D	Cargill D	Thompson D	Rudman H	Cheesebrough A	Walton J	Scott J	Smith D	Binns E	Newlands D	
1			4	5		7	10	9	6				8	3			2	11						3
1			1	1		1	1	1	1				1	1			1	1						

1955-56

Manager: Allan Brown

1	Aug	20	(a)	Tottenham H	W 1-0	Pilkington	33,178
2		22	(h)	Blackpool	L 0-2		35,226
3		27	(h)	Everton	L 0-1		22,482
4		29	(a)	Blackpool	D 1-1	Pilkington	25,774
5	Sep	3	(a)	Newcastle U	L 1-3	Pilkington	41,272
6		5	(h)	Luton T	W 3-1	McKay 3	19,350
7		10	(h)	Birmingham C	W 3-2	McKay, Cheesebrough, Pilkington	22,808
8		17	(a)	West Brom A	L 0-1		23,362
9		24	(h)	Manchester U	D 0-0		26,723
10	Oct	1	(a)	Sheffield U	W 2-1	Cheesebrough, Burke	22,559
11		8	(h)	Huddersfield T	W 2-0	Gray, McKay	22,109
12		15	(a)	Cardiff C	D 2-2	McKay, Cheesebrough	24,338
13		22	(h)	Bolton W	W 2-0	McIlroy, McKay	23,839
14		29	(a)	Chelsea	D 0-0		39,069
15	Nov	5	(h)	Aston Villa	W 2-0	McKay 2	20,592
16		12	(a)	Sunderland	D 4-4	McKay 2, McIlroy, Opp own-goal	39,787
17		19	(h)	Portsmouth	W 3-0	McKay 3	20,575
18		26	(a)	Arsenal	W 1-0	Cheesebrough	37,583
19	Dec	3	(h)	Manchester C	D 2-2	Stephenson, McKay	26,217
20		10	(a)	Wolves	L 1-3	McKay	24,276
21		17	(h)	Tottenham H	W 2-0	Shannon, McKay	20,346
22		24	(a)	Everton	D 1-1	Pilkington	35,406
23		26	(h)	Preston NE	L 1-2	Stephenson	31,006
24		27	(a)	Preston NE	L 2-4	Shannon, Winton	29,524
25		31	(h)	Newcastle U	W 3-1	Pilkington 2, Gray	29,302
26	Jan	14	(a)	Birmingham C	W 2-1	Burke, McKay	27,388
27		21	(h)	West Brom A	L 1-2	Burke	23,749
28	Feb	4	(a)	Manchester U	L 0-2		27,542
29		11	(h)	Sheffield U	D 1-1	Miller	19,017
30		18	(a)	Huddersfield T	L 0-1		16,243
31		25	(h)	Cardiff C	L 0-2		18,549
32	Mar	3	(a)	Portsmouth	L 1-3	Stephenson	19,279
33		10	(h)	Chelsea	W 5-0	Pilkington 3, Cheesebrough, McKay	18,670
34		19	(a)	Aston Villa	L 0-2		15,120
35		24	(h)	Sunderland	W 4-0	Newlands, McKay, Cheesebrough, Pilkington	23,782
36		30	(a)	Charlton A	L 1-2	McKay	22,119
37		31	(a)	Bolton W	W 1-0	Burke	29,488
38	Apr	2	(h)	Charlton A	W 2-1	McKay, Burke	20,274
39		7	(h)	Arsenal	L 0-1		24,393
40		14	(a)	Manchester C	W 3-1	McIlroy 2, McKay	29,087
41		21	(h)	Wolves	L 1-2	Newlands	22,322
42		28	(a)	Luton T	W 3-2	McKay 2, Pilkington	15,999

FINAL LEAGUE POSITION: 7th in Division One

Appearances
Goals

FA Cup

3	Jan	10	(a)	Bury	W 1-0	Gray	18,346
4		28	(h)	Chelsea	D 1-1	McKay	44,857
R	Feb	1	(a)	Chelsea	D 1-1*	Pilkington	26,661
2R		6	(n†)	Chelsea	D 2-2*	McIlroy, McKay	21,921
3R		13	(n‡)	Chelsea	D 0-0*		42,757
4R		15	(n§)	Chelsea	L 0-2		27,210

*After extra-time. †Played at St Andrew's, Birmingham. ‡Played at Arsenal Stadium, Highbury, London. §Played at White Hart Lane, London.

Appearances
Goals

McDonald C	Rudman H	Winton D	Adamson J	Cummings T	Shannon L	Gray W	McIlroy J	Holden W	Walton J	Pilkngton B	Stephenson R	Cheesebrough A	McKay P	Burke R	Seith R	Smith D	Miller B	Cargill D	Newlands D	
1	2	3	4	5	6	7	8	9	10	11										1
1	2	3	4	5	6	7	8	9	10	11										2
1	2	3	4	5	6	7	9			11	8	10								3
1	2	3	4	5	6	7	9			11	8	10								4
1	2	3	4	5	6	7	9			11	8	10								5
1	2	3	4	5	6	7	8			11		10	9							6
1	2	3	4	5	6	7	8			11		10	9							7
1	2	3	4	5	6	7				11		10	9	8						8
1	2	3		5	6	7	9			11		10		8	4					9
1	2	3		5	6	7	8			11		9		10	4					10
1	2	3		5	6	7				11		10	9	8	4					11
1	2	3		5	6	7	8			11		10	9		4					12
1	2	3		5	6	7	8			11		10	9		4					13
1	2	3		5	6	7	8			11		10	9		4					14
1	2	3		5	6	7	8			11		10	9		4					15
1	2			5	6	7	8			11		10	9		4	3				16
1	2			5	6	7				11		10	9	8	4	3				17
1	2			5	6	7				11		10	9	8	4	3				18
1	2			5	6	7				11	8	10	9		4	3				19
1	2			5	6	7				11	8	10	9		4	3				20
1	2			5	6	7				11		10	9	8	4	3				21
1	2	3		5	6	7				11		10	9	8	4					22
1	2	3		5	6	7				11	8	10	9		4					23
1	2	3		5	6	7			8	11	9	10			4					24
1	2	3		5	6	7			8	11		10	9		4					25
1	2	3		5	6	7				11		10	9	8	4					26
1	2	3		5	6	7				11		10	9	8	4					27
1		3	5	2		7			10				9	8	4		6	11		28
1	2	3		5	6	7	8						9	10			4	11		29
1	2	3		5	6	7	8			11		10	9		4					30
1		3	5	2	6	7				11		10	9	8	4					31
1			5	2	6					11	7	10	9	8	4	3				32
1		3	5	2	6		8			11		10	9		4				7	33
1	2	3	5		6		8			11		10	9		4				7	34
1		3	5	2	6		8			11		10	9		4				7	35
1		3	5	2	6		8			11		10	9		4				7	36
1		3	5	2	6		8			11			9	10	4				7	37
1		3	5	2	6		8			11			9	10	4				7	38
1		3	5	2	6		8			11			9	10	4				7	39
1	2	3	5		6		8			11		10	9		4				7	40
1		3	5	2	6					11		10	9	8	4				7	41
1		3	5	2	6					11		10	9	8	4				7	42
42	31	35	21	40	41	31	24	2	5	40	8	35	34	19	33	7	2	2	10	
		1			2	2	4			12	3	6	25	5			1		2	

1 own-goal

McDonald C	Rudman H	Winton D	Adamson J	Cummings T	Shannon L	Gray W	McIlroy J	Holden W	Walton J	Pilkngton B	Stephenson R	Cheesebrough A	McKay P	Burke R	Seith R	Smith D	Miller B	Cargill D	Newlands D	
1	2	3		5	6	7				11		10	9	8	4					3
1	2	3	6	5		7	8			11		10	9		4					4
1		3	5	2		7	8			11		10	9		4		6			R
1		3	5	2		7	8			11		10	9		4		6			2R
1		3	5	2	6	7	8			11		10	9		4					3R
1	2	3		5	6	7	8			11		10	9		4					4R
6	3	6	4	6	3	6	5			6		6	6	1	6		2			
						1	1			1			2							

1956-57

Manager: Allan Brown

1	Aug	18	(h)	Chelsea	W 2-0	McIlroy, Cheesebrough	21,960
2		21	(a)	Arsenal	L 0-2		38,321
3		25	(a)	Cardiff C	D 3-3	McKay 2, McIlroy	30,769
4		28	(h)	Arsenal	W 3-1	McIlroy 2, McKay	19,049
5	Sep	1	(h)	Birmingham C	W 2-0	McKay 2	25,531
6		3	(h)	Everton	W 2-1	Smith, Pilkington	24,185
7		8	(a)	West Brom A	D 2-2	McKay 2	23,611
8		12	(a)	Everton	L 0-1		27,591
9		15	(h)	Portsmouth	D 1-1	Pilkington	22,756
10		22	(a)	Newcastle U	D 1-1	Pilkington	36,790
11		29	(h)	Sheffield W	W 4-1	McIlroy 2, McKay 2	23,559
12	Oct	6	(h)	Blackpool	D 2-2	Robson, Cheesebrough	27,694
13		13	(a)	Manchester C	W 1-0	Gray	35,981
14		20	(h)	Leeds U	D 0-0		26,440
15		27	(a)	Tottenham H	L 0-2		49,154
16	Nov	3	(h)	Luton T	D 1-1	Seith	22,891
17		10	(a)	Aston Villa	L 0-1		22,420
18		17	(h)	Wolves	W 3-0	McKay, Cheesebrough, Pilkington	25,776
19		24	(a)	Bolton W	L 0-3		26,062
20	Dec	1	(h)	Charlton A	W 2-1	McIlroy, McKay	18,348
21		8	(a)	Sunderland	L 1-2	McIlroy	29,588
22		15	(a)	Chelsea	L 0-2		18,371
23		22	(h)	Cardiff C	W 6-2	Newlands 2, McIlroy 2, Shannon, Cheesebrough	10,118
24		25	(h)	Preston NE	D 2-2	Shannon, Cheesebrough	23,737
25		26	(a)	Preston NE	L 0-1		19,265
26		29	(a)	Birmingham C	L 0-2		31,733
27	Jan	12	(h)	West Brom A	W 1-0	Cheesebrough	24,299
28		19	(a)	Portsmouth	L 0-1		22,057
29	Feb	2	(h)	Newcastle U	W 3-2	Newlands, Lawson, Pilkington	26,778
30		9	(a)	Sheffield W	D 0-0		29,583
31	Mar	9	(h)	Sunderland	W 2-0	Newlands, McIlroy	21,892
32		11	(a)	Leeds U	D 1-1	Newlands	31,956
33		16	(a)	Luton T	W 2-0	Shackleton, Cheesebrough	16,420
34		30	(a)	Wolves	W 2-1	Newlands, Cheesebrough	25,462
35	Apr	6	(h)	Bolton W	W 1-0	Shackleton	23,250
36		13	(a)	Charlton A	W 2-1	McIlroy, Shackleton	13,334
37		15	(h)	Aston Villa	W 2-1	Shackleton 2	17,381
38		19	(h)	Manchester U	L 1-3	McIlroy	37,823
39		20	(h)	Manchester C	L 0-3		16,746
40		22	(a)	Manchester U	L 0-2		41,540
41		29	(h)	Tottenham H	W 1-0	Lawson	12,048
42	May	1	(a)	Blackpool	L 0-1		13,919

FINAL LEAGUE POSITION: 7th in Division One

Appearances

Goals

FA Cup

3	Jan	5	(h)	Chesterfield	W 7-0	Lawson 4, Cheesebrough 2, Pilkington	27,608
4		26	(h)	New Brighton	W 9-0	McIlroy 3, Lawson 3, Newlands, Cheesebrough, Pilkington	41,453
5	Feb	16	(a)	Huddersfield T	W 2-1	Lawson, Cheesebrough	55,168
6	Mar	2	(h)	Aston Villa	D 1-1	Opp own-goal	49,436
R		6	(a)	Aston Villa	L 0-2		46,182

Appearances

Goals

McDonald C	Cummings T	Winton D	Seith R	Adamson J	Shannon L	Gray W	McIlroy J	McKay P	Cheesebrough A	Pilkington B	Rudman H	Newlands D	Smith D	Angus J	Robson J	Miller B	Blacklaw A	Lancaster D	Lawson I	Shackleton A	Connelly J	Wilson W	Appleby J	
1	2	3	4	5	6	7	8	9	10	11														1
1		3	4	5	6	7	8	9	10	11	2													2
1		3	4	5	6		8	9	10	11	2	7												3
1	2	3	4	5	6		8	9	10	11		7												4
1		3	4	5	6		8	9	10	11		7	2											5
1			4	5	6		8	9	10	11		7	3	2										6
1			4	5	6		8	9	10	11		7	3	2										7
1			4	5	6		8	9	10	11		7	3	2										8
1		3	4	5	6		8	9	10	11		7	2											9
1		3	4	5	6		8	9	10	11		7	2											10
1		3	4	5	6		8	9	10	11		7	2											11
1		3	4	5	6			9	10	11		7	2		8									12
1		3	4	5	6	7	8	9	10	11			2											13
1		3	4	5	6	7	8	9	10	11			2											14
1		3	4	5		7	8	9	10			11	2			6								15
1		3	4	5	6	7	8	9	10	11			2											16
1		3	4	5			8	9		11		7	2		10	6								17
1		3	4	5			8	9	10	11		7	2			6								18
1		3	4	5			8	9	10	11		7	2			6								19
1		3	4	5			8	9	10	11		7	2			6								20
1		3	4	5			8	9	10	11		7	2			6								21
1		3	4	5			8	9	10	11		7	2			6								22
		3	4	5	9		8		10	11		7		2		6	1							23
		3	4	5	9		8		10	11		7		2		6	1							24
		3	4	5	9		8		10	11		7		2		6	1							25
		3	4	5	9		8		10			7		2		6	1	11						26
		3	4	5			8		10	11		7		2		6	1		9					27
		3	4	5			8		10	11		7		2		6	1		9					28
		3	4	5			8		10	11		7		2		6	1		9					29
		3	4	5			8		10	11		7		2		6	1		9					30
1		3	4		6		8		10	11		7		2		5				9				31
1		3	4		6		8		10			7		2		5				9	11			32
1		3	4		6		8		10	11		7		2		5				9				33
1		3	4		6		8		10	11		7		2		5				9				34
1		3	4		6		8		10	11		7		2		5				9				35
1		3	4	5			8		10	11		7		2		6				9				36
1		3	4	5			8		10	11		7		2		6				9				37
1		3	4	5			8		10	11		7		2		6				9				38
1		3	4	5			8		10	11		7		2		6				9				39
1		3	4	5			8		10	11		7		2		6			9					40
1		3	4	5	6		8					7		2	10				9		11			41
1					6	7			8				3	2	10				9		11	4	5	42
34	2	38	41	36	26	7	40	22	40	37	2	36	19	23	4	25	8	1	7	9	3	1	1	
			1		2	1	13	11	8	5		6	1		1				2	5				

McDonald C	Cummings T	Winton D	Seith R	Adamson J	Shannon L	Gray W	McIlroy J	McKay P	Cheesebrough A	Pilkington B	Rudman H	Newlands D	Smith D	Angus J	Robson J	Miller B	Blacklaw A	Lancaster D	Lawson I	Shackleton A	Connelly J	Wilson W	Appleby J	
		3	4	5			8		10	11		7		2		6	1		9					3
		3	4	5			8		10	11		7		2		6	1		9					4
		3	4	5			8		10	11		7		2		6	1		9					5
		3	4	5			8		10	11		7		2		6	1		9					6
		3	4		6		8		10	11		7		2		5	1			9				R
		5	5	4	1		5		5	5		5		5		5	5		4	1				
							3		4	2		1							8					

1 own-goal

1957-58

Manager: Billy Dougall until January, then Harry Potts

1	Aug	24	(a)	Portsmouth	D 0-0		30,134
2		27	(h)	Preston NE	W 2-0	Shackleton 2	27,804
3		31	(h)	West Brom A	D 2-2	Shackleton, Cheesebrough	24,428
4	Sep	4	(a)	Preston NE	L 1-2	McIlroy	31,267
5		7	(a)	Tottenham H	L 1-3	Cheesebrough	40,108
6		9	(h)	Nottingham F	W 3-1	Shackleton 2, Pilkington	15,818
7		14	(h)	Birmingham C	W 3-1	Shackleton, Cheesebrough, Pilkington	20,522
8		18	(a)	Nottingham F	L 0-7		26,842
9		21	(a)	Chelsea	L 1-6	Cheesebrough	42,449
10		28	(h)	Newcastle U	L 0-2		18,465
11	Oct	5	(a)	Luton T	L 2-3	Pilkington 2	15,179
12		12	(h)	Sunderland	W 6-0	Shannon 2, Newlands 2, Pointer, Cheesebrough	22,868
13		19	(a)	Everton	D 1-1	Cheesebrough	45,024
14		26	(h)	Aston Villa	W 3-0	Pilkington 2, Newlands	20,860
15	Nov	2	(a)	Manchester U	L 0-1		49,689
16		9	(h)	Leicester C	W 7-3	McIlroy 3, Cheesebrough 3, Pointer	20,978
17		16	(a)	Blackpool	W 4-2	Shackleton 2, Cheesebrough, Pilkington	21,641
18		23	(h)	Leeds U	W 3-1	McIlroy, Shackleton, Pilkington	24,144
19		30	(a)	Wolves	L 1-2	McIlroy	32,888
20	Dec	7	(h)	Arsenal	W 2-1	Newlands, Cheesebrough	18,563
21		14	(a)	Bolton W	L 1-2	Newlands	20,197
22		21	(h)	Portsmouth	W 3-1	Newlands 2, Pointer	19,761
23		25	(h)	Manchester C	W 2-1	Cheesebrough, Pilkington	27,666
24		26	(a)	Manchester C	L 1-4	Pointer	47,285
25		28	(a)	West Brom A	L 1-5	Pilkington	38,183
26	Jan	11	(h)	Tottenham H	W 2-0	McIlroy 2	25,927
27		18	(a)	Birmingham C	W 3-2	White 2, Pilkington	22,281
28	Feb	1	(h)	Chelsea	W 2-1	McIlroy, Pilkington	20,599
29		15	(h)	Luton T	L 1-2	Pointer	16,869
30		22	(a)	Sunderland	W 3-2	Robson 2, Pointer	30,595
31	Mar	1	(h)	Everton	L 0-2		19,657
32		8	(a)	Aston Villa	L 0-3		25,679
33		15	(h)	Manchester U	W 3-0	McIlroy, Shackleton, Cheesebrough	37,447
34		22	(a)	Leeds U	L 0-1		24,994
35		29	(h)	Blackpool	W 2-1	McIlroy, Pilkington	20,781
36	Apr	4	(h)	Sheffield W	W 2-0	Newlands, McIlroy	18,165
37		5	(a)	Leicester C	L 3-5	McIlroy 2, Miller	26,150
38		7	(a)	Sheffield W	W 2-1	Newlands, Pointer	22,417
39		12	(h)	Wolves	D 1-1	Newlands	28,539
40		19	(a)	Arsenal	D 0-0		31,440
41		26	(h)	Bolton W	W 3-1	McIlroy 2, Seith	17,419
42		28	(a)	Newcastle U	W 3-1	Seith, Newlands, Pointer	21,610
FINAL LEAGUE POSITION: 6th in Division One							Appearances
							Goals

FA Cup

3	Jan	4	(h)	Swansea T	W 4-2	McIlroy 2, Newlands, Cheesebrough	26,193
4		25	(a)	Bristol R	D 2-2	Pointer, Connelly	35,088
R		28	(h)	Bristol R	L 2-3	McIlroy, Pointer	41,113
							Appearances
							Goals

McDonald C	Angus J	Winton D	Seith R	Adamson J	Shannon L	Newlands D	McIlroy J	Shackleton A	Cheesebrough A	Pilkington B	Smith D	Cummings T	Miller B	Wilson W	Blacklaw A	Robson J	Pointer R	White W	Connelly J	
1	2	3	4	5	6	7	8	9	10	11										1
1	2	3	4	5	6	7	8	9	10	11										2
1		3	4	5	6	7	8	9	10	11	2									3
1			4	5	6	7	8	9	10	11	3	2								4
1			4	5	6	7	8	9	10	11	3	2								5
1			4	5	6	7	8	9	10	11	3	2								6
1	2	3	4		6	7	8	9	10	11			5							7
1	2	3			6	7	8	9	10	11			5	4						8
	2	3	4	5		7	8	9	10	11			6		1					9
	2	3	4	5		7	8	9	10	11			6		1					10
	2	3	4	5		7			10	11			6		1	8	9			11
1		3	4	5	6	7			10	11	2					8	9			12
1		3	4	5	6	7	8		10	11	2						9			13
1		3	4	5	6	7	8		10	11	2						9			14
1		3	4	5	6	7	8		10	11	2						9			15
1		3	4	5	6	7	8		10	11	2						9			16
1		3	4	5	6	7	8	9	10	11	2									17
1		3	4	5	6	7	8	9	10	11	2									18
1		3	4	5	6	7	8	9	10	11	2									19
1		3	4	5	6	7	8		10	11	2					9				20
1		3	4	5	6	7	8	9	10	11	2									21
1		3	4	5	6	7	8		10	11	2						9			22
1		3	4	5	6	7	8		10	11	2						9			23
1		3	4		6	7	8		10	11	2		5				9			24
1	3	6	4			7			10	11	2		5				9	8		25
1		3	4	5	6	7	8		10	11	2						9			26
1	2	3	4	5			8			11			6				9	7	10	27
1		3	4	5	6	7	8			11	2						9		10	28
1		3	4	5	6	7	8		10	11	2						9			29
1	2	3	4	5	6	7			10	11						8	9			30
1	2	3		5	6	7			10	11			4				9		8	31
1	2	3		5	4	7			10	11			6				9	8		32
1		3		5	4	7	8	9	10	11	2		6							33
1		3		5	4	7	8	9	10	11	2		6							34
1		3		5	4	7	8	9	10	11	2		6							35
1		3		5	4	7	8	9	10	11	2		6							36
1		3		5	4	7	8	9	10	11	2		6							37
1		3			4	7	8		10	11	2	5	6				9			38
1		3		5	4	7	8		10	11	2		6				9			39
1		3	4	5		7	8		10	11	2		6				9			40
1		3	4			7	8		10	11	2	5	6				9			41
1		3	4	5	6	7	8		10	11		2					9			42
39	12	39	32	36	35	41	36	19	40	42	30	6	19	1	3	4	22	3	3	
			2		2	11	16	10	13	13			1			2	8	2		

McDonald C	Angus J	Winton D	Seith R	Adamson J	Shannon L	Newlands D	McIlroy J	Shackleton A	Cheesebrough A	Pilkington B	Smith D	Cummings T	Miller B	Wilson W	Blacklaw A	Robson J	Pointer R	White W	Connelly J	
1		3	4		6	7	8		10	11	2		5				9			3
1		3	4	5	6		8			11	2						9	7	10	4
1		3	4	5	6		8		10	11	2						9		7	R
3		3	3	2	3	1	3		2	3	3		1				3	1	2	
						1	3		1								2		1	

1958-59

Manager: Harry Potts

1	Aug	23	(h)	Manchester C	L 3-4	Pointer 2, Pilkington	31,371
2		26	(a)	Arsenal	L 0-3		41,298
3		30	(a)	Leeds U	D 1-1	Robson	22,739
4	Sep	2	(h)	Arsenal	W 3-1	Connelly, Robson, Pilkington	28,444
5		6	(h)	West Brom A	L 1-3	Shackleton	23,589
6		9	(h)	Everton	W 3-1	Shackleton 2, Pilkington	23,050
7		13	(a)	Birmingham C	L 1-2	Robson	23,926
8		17	(a)	Everton	W 2-1	McIlroy, Pilkington	50,457
9		20	(h)	Luton T	D 2-2	Seith, Newlands	23,760
10		27	(a)	Bolton W	W 2-1	Seith, Pointer	32,359
11	Oct	4	(h)	Chelsea	W 4-0	Adamson, Robson, Cheesebrough, Pilkington	22,902
12		11	(a)	Blackpool	D 1-1	Newlands	31,744
13		18	(h)	Blackburn R	D 0-0		41,961
14		25	(a)	West Ham U	L 0-1		29,387
15	Nov	1	(h)	Nottingham F	L 0-2		22,644
16		8	(a)	Manchester U	W 3-1	Pointer 2, McIlroy	48,509
17		15	(h)	Wolves	L 0-2		23,067
18		22	(a)	Portsmouth	L 2-4	Connelly 2	17,320
19		29	(h)	Aston Villa	W 3-1	Connelly, McIlroy, Pointer	14,923
20	Dec	6	(a)	Newcastle U	L 2-5	Pointer 2	42,561
21		13	(h)	Tottenham H	W 3-1	Connelly, Pointer, Robson	17,047
22		20	(a)	Manchester C	W 4-1	Connelly, Pointer 2, Robson	22,328
23		26	(a)	Leicester C	D 1-1	Pointer	32,182
24		27	(h)	Leicester C	D 3-3	Pointer 2, Connelly	24,468
25	Jan	3	(h)	Leeds U	W 3-1	McIlroy, Pointer, Harris	26,013
26		31	(h)	Birmingham C	L 0-1		22,101
27	Feb	7	(a)	Luton T	L 2-6	Miller, Connelly	15,753
28		21	(a)	Chelsea	W 3-1	Robson 3	27,564
29	Mar	7	(a)	Blackburn R	L 1-4	Pointer	27,071
30		11	(a)	West Brom A	W 4-2	Pointer 2, Connelly, McIlroy	18,164
31		14	(h)	West Ham U	W 1-0	Connelly	17,311
32		17	(h)	Blackpool	W 3-1	Pointer 2, Robson	15,881
33		21	(a)	Nottingham F	W 2-1	Connelly, Pointer	27,811
34		27	(h)	Preston NE	W 1-0	Connelly	18,322
35		28	(h)	Manchester U	W 4-2	Pointer 2, Seith, Pilkington	44,577
36		30	(a)	Preston NE	W 4-0	Pointer 2, McIlroy, Cheesebrough	17,357
37	Apr	4	(a)	Wolves	D 3-3	Cheesebrough 2, Pointer	39,810
38		8	(a)	Tottenham H	D 2-2	Cheesebrough 2	32,296
39		11	(h)	Portsmouth	W 2-1	Pointer, Pilkington	18,174
40		14	(h)	Bolton W	L 0-1		23,664
41		18	(a)	Aston Villa	D 0-0		27,097
42		25	(h)	Newcastle U	D 2-2	Cheesebrough, Pilkington	15,132
	FINAL LEAGUE POSITION: 7th in Division One						Appearances
							Goals

FA Cup

3	Jan	14	(a)	Stockport C	W 3-1	Pointer 2, Pilkington	23,147
4		28	(a)	Blackburn R	W 2-1	Robson, McIlroy	43,752
5	Feb	14	(h)	Portsmouth	W 1-0	Adamson	32,055
6		28	(a)	Aston Villa	D 0-0		53,511
R	Mar	3	(h)	Aston Villa	L 0-2		38,931
							Appearances
							Goals

McDonald C	Cummings T	Winton D	Seith R	Adamson J	Shannon L	Newlands D	McIlroy J	Pointer R	Cheesebrough A	Pilkington B	Robson J	Smith D	Connelly J	Shackleton A	Angus J	Blacklaw A	Talbut J	Miller B	Harris G	Match
1	2	3	4	5	6	7	8	9	10	11										1
1	2	3	4	5	6	7	8		10	11	9									2
1	5	3	4		6		8	9		11	10	2	7							3
1	5	3	4		6		8	9		11	10	2	7							4
1	5	3	4		6		8			11	10	2	7	9						5
1	5	3	4		6		8			11	10	2	7	9						6
1	2		4	5	6	7			10	11	8	3		9						7
1	5	3	4	6		7	10	9		11	8	2								8
1	5	3	4		6	7	10	9		11	8	2								9
1	5		4	6		7	8	9		11	10	3			2					10
	5		4	6		7		9	10	11	8	3			2	1				11
1	5		4	6		7	8	9		11	10	3			2					12
1	5		4	6		7	8	9		11	10	3			2					13
1	5		4	6			8		10	11	9	3	7		2					14
1	5		4	6			7	9	10	11	8	3			2					15
1	5	3	4	6			8	9		11	10	2	7							16
1	5	3	4	6			8	9		11	10	2	7							17
1	5		4	6			8	9		11	10	3	7		2					18
1	5		4	6			8	9		11	10	3	7		2					19
1	5		4	6			8	9		11	10	3	7		2					20
1	5		4	6			8	9		11	10	3	7		2					21
1	5		4	6			8	9		11	10	3	7		2					22
1			4	6			8	9		11	10	3	7		2		5			23
1			4	6		7	8	9			10	3	11		2		5			24
1			4	6			8	9			10	3	7		2			5	11	25
1	2		4	6			8	9		11	10	3	7					5		26
	5		4				8	9	10	11		3	7		2	1		6		27
1	2		4	6			8	9		11	10	3	7					5		28
	2		4	6			8	9		11	10	3	7			1		5		29
	2		4	6			8	9		11	10	3	7			1		5		30
1	2		4	6			8	9			10	3	7					5	11	31
	2		4	6			8	9		11	10	3	7			1		5		32
	2		4	6			8	9		11	10	3	7			1		5		33
	2		4	6			8	9		11	10	3	7			1		5		34
	5		4				8	9		11	10	3	7		2	1		6		35
	5		4				8	9	10	11		3	7		2	1		6		36
	5		4				8	9	10	11		3	7		2	1		6		37
	5		4				8	9	10	11		3	7		2	1		6		38
	5		4				8	9	10	11		3	7		2	1		6		39
	5		4	6			8	9	10	11		3	7		2	1				40
	2		4	5			8	9	10	11			7		3	1		6		41
	3		4	5			8	9	10	11			7		2	1		6		42
27	39	10	42	31	8	10	40	37	14	39	33	38	32	3	23	15	2	17	2	
			3	1		2	6	27	7	8	10		12	3				1	1	

McDonald C	Cummings T	Winton D	Seith R	Adamson J	Shannon L	Newlands D	McIlroy J	Pointer R	Cheesebrough A	Pilkington B	Robson J	Smith D	Connelly J	Shackleton A	Angus J	Blacklaw A	Talbut J	Miller B	Harris G	Round
1	5		4	6			8	9		11	10	3	7		2					3
1	2		4	6			8	9		11	10	3	7					5		4
1	5		4	6			8	9		11	10	3	7		2					5
1	5		4	6			8	9	10	11		3	7		2					6
1	2		4	6			8	9	10	11		3	7					5		R
5	5		5	5			5	5	2	5	3	5	5		3			2		
				1			1	2		1	1									

1959-60

Manager: Harry Potts

1	Aug	22	(a)	Leeds U	W 3-2	Connelly, Pointer, Pilkington	20,233
2		25	(h)	Everton	W 5-2	Connelly 2, Pointer, Robson, Pilkington	29,165
3		29	(h)	West Ham U	L 1-3	Connelly	26,756
4	Sep	2	(a)	Everton	W 2-1	Pointer 2	39,416
5		5	(a)	Chelsea	L 1-4	Connelly	36,023
6		8	(h)	Preston NE	W 2-1	Pointer, Robson	29,195
7		12	(h)	West Brom A	W 2-1	Robson, Pilkington	23,907
8		15	(a)	Preston NE	L 0-1		27,299
9		19	(a)	Newcastle U	W 3-1	Connelly 2, McIlroy	38,576
10		26	(h)	Birmingham C	W 3-1	Connelly, McIlroy, Pointer	23,848
11	Oct	3	(a)	Tottenham H	D 1-1	Miller	42,717
12		10	(h)	Blackpool	L 1-4	Robson	28,104
13		17	(a)	Blackburn R	L 2-3	Pilkington, Opp own-goal	33,316
14		24	(h)	Manchester C	W 4-3	White 2, Pointer, Pilkington	28,653
15		31	(a)	Luton T	D 1-1	Ponter	15,638
16	Nov	7	(h)	Wolves	W 4-1	Pointer 2, Connelly, Robson	27,793
17		14	(a)	Sheffield W	D 1-1	Robson	18,420
18		21	(h)	Nottingham F	W 8-0	Robson 5, Pointer 2, Pilkington	24,349
19		28	(a)	Fulham	L 0-1		29,582
20	Dec	5	(h)	Bolton W	W 4-0	McIlroy 2, Connelly, Pointer	26,510
21		12	(a)	Arsenal	W 4-2	Connelly 3, Adamson	26,056
22		19	(h)	Leeds U	L 0-1		17,398
23		26	(a)	Manchester U	W 2-1	Lawson, Robson	62,673
24		28	(h)	Manchester U	L 1-4	Robson	47,696
25	Jan	2	(a)	West Ham U	W 5-2	Connelly 2, Lawson 2, Pilkington	25,752
26		16	(h)	Chelsea	W 2-1	Robson 2	21,916
27		23	(a)	West Brom A	D 0-0		23,512
28	Feb	6	(h)	Newcastle U	W 2-1	Pointer, Robson	26,998
29		27	(a)	Bolton W	L 1-2	Connelly	28,772
30	Mar	1	(h)	Tottenham H	W 2-0	Connelly, Pointer	32,992
31		5	(h)	Blackburn R	W 1-0	Robson	32,331
32		19	(h)	Arsenal	W 3-2	Miller, Connelly, Pointer	20,327
33		30	(a)	Wolves	L 1-6	Pointer	33,953
34	Apr	2	(h)	Sheffield W	D 3-3	Miller, Connelly, McIlroy	23,123
35		9	(a)	Nottingham F	W 1-0	Pointer	24,640
36		15	(h)	Leicester C	W 1-0	Connelly	23,777
37		16	(h)	Luton T	W 3-0	McIlroy, Pointer, Robson	20,893
38		18	(a)	Leicester C	L 1-2	Meredith	24,429
39		23	(a)	Blackpool	D 1-1	Meredith	23,753
40		27	(a)	Birmingham C	W 1-0	Pilkington	37,032
41		30	(h)	Fulham	D 0-0		30,807
42	May	2	(a)	Manchester C	W 2-1	Meredith, Pilkington	65,981

FINAL LEAGUE POSITION: 1st in Division One

Appearances
Goals

FA Cup

3	Jan	9	(a)	Lincoln C	D 1-1	Pointer	21,693
R		12	(h)	Lincoln C	W 2-0	McIlroy, Pilkington	35,456
4		30	(a)	Swansea T	D 0-0		29,976
R	Feb	2	(h)	Swansea T	W 2-1	Robson 2	37,040
5		20	(a)	Bradford C	D 2-2	Connelly 2	26,244
R		23	(h)	Bradford C	W 5-0	Pointer 2, Robson 2, Connelly	52,850
6	Mar	12	(h)	Blackburn R	D 3-3	Pointer, Pilkington, Connelly	51,501
R		16	(a)	Blackburn R	L 0-2		53,892

Appearances
Goals

Blacklaw A	Angus J	Cummings T	Seith R	Miller B	Adamson J	Connelly J	McIlroy J	Pointer R	Robson J	Pilkington B	Elder A	White W	Harris G	Lawson I	Marshall W	Meredith T	Furnell J	
1	2	3	4	5	6	7	8	9	10	11								1
1	2	3	4	5	6	7	8	9	10	11								2
1	2	3	4	5	6	7	8	9	10	11								3
1	2	3	4	5	6	7	8	9	10	11								4
1	2	3	4	5	6	7	8	9	10	11								5
1	2	3	4	5	6	7	8	9	10	11								6
1	2	3	4	5	6	7	8	9	10	11								7
1	2	5		6	4	7		9	10	11	3	8						8
1	2	5		6	4	7	8	9	10	11	3							9
1	2	5		6	4	7	8	9	10	11	3							10
1	2	5		6	4	7		9	10	11	3	8						11
1	2	5		6	4	7	8	9	10	11	3							12
1	2		4	6	5		8	9		7	3	10	11					13
1	2		4	5	6	7	8	9		11	3	10						14
1	2		4	5	6	7	8	9		11	3	10						15
1	2		4	5	6	7	8	9	10	11	3							16
1	2		4	5	6	7	8	9	10	11	3							17
1	2		4	5	6	7	8	9	10	11	3							18
1	2		4	5	6	7	8	9	10	11	3							19
1	2		4	5	6	7	8	9	10	11	3							20
1	2		4	5	6	7		9	10	11	3	8						21
1	2		4	5	6	7		9	10	11	3			8				22
1	2		4	5	6	7	8	9	10	11	3							23
1	2		4	5	6	7		9	10	11	3			8				24
1	2		4	5	6	7		9	10	11	3			8				25
1	2		4	5	6	7		9	10	11	3			8				26
1	2		4	5	6	7		9	10		3		11	8				27
1	2		4	5	6	7		9	10	11	3			8				28
1	2	5		6	4	7	8	9		11	3			10				29
1	2	5		6	4	7	8	9	10	11	3							30
1	2		4	5	6	7	8	9	10	11	3							31
1	2		4	6	5	7		9	10	11	3			8				32
1		2	4	5	6	7	8	9	10	11	3							33
1	2		4	6	5	7	8	9	10	11	3							34
1	2	5		6	4		8	9	10	11					3	7		35
1	2	5		6	4	7	8	9	10	11	3							36
1	2	5		6	4		8	9	10	11	3					7		37
1	2	5		6	4		8	9	10	11	3					7		38
	2	5		6	4		8	9	10	11	3					7	1	39
1	2	5		6	4		8	9	10	11	3					7		40
1	2	5		6	4			9	10	11	3			8		7		41
1	2	5		6	4		8	9	10	11	3					7		42
41	41	23	27	42	42	34	32	42	38	41	34	6	2	8	1	7	1	
				3	1	20	6	19	18	9		2		3		3		

1 own-goal

Blacklaw A	Angus J	Cummings T	Seith R	Miller B	Adamson J	Connelly J	McIlroy J	Pointer R	Robson J	Pilkington B	Elder A	White W	Harris G	Lawson I	Marshall W	Meredith T	Furnell J	
1	2		4	5	6	7		9	10	11	3			8				3
1	2		4	5	6	7	8	9	10	11	3							R
1	2		4	5	6	7	8	9	10	11	3							4
1	2		4	5	6	7		9	10	11	3	8						R
1	2		4	5	6	7	8	9	10	11	3							5
1	2		4	5	6	7	8	9	10	11	3							R
1	2		4	5	6	7	8	9	10	11	3							6
1	2		4	5	6	7	8	9	10	11	3							R
8	8		8	8	8	8	6	8	8	8	8	1		1				
						4	1	4	4	2								

1960-61

Manager: Harry Potts

1	Aug	20	(h)	Arsenal	W 3-2	Connelly 2, Pointer	24,553
2		24	(a)	Manchester C	L 1-2	Robson	26,941
3		27	(a)	Newcastle U	W 1-0	Robson	35,485
4		30	(h)	Manchester C	L 1-3	Meredith	29,547
5	Sep	3	(h)	Cardiff C	L 1-2	Robson	19,695
6		6	(h)	Preston NE	W 5-0	Robson 3, Meredith, Pointer	19,443
7		10	(a)	West Brom A	W 2-0	Miller, Pointer	26,407
8		13	(a)	Preston NE	W 3-2	Harris 2, Pointer	25,604
9		17	(h)	Birmingham C	W 2-1	Meredith, Robson	20,749
10		24	(a)	Sheffield W	L 1-3	Robson	35,829
11	Oct	1	(h)	Fulham	W 5-0	Robson 3, Pointer 2	19,965
12		8	(a)	Blackburn R	W 4-1	Connelly 2, Robson, Adamson	26,223
13		15	(h)	Manchester U	W 5-3	Connelly 2, Joyce, McIlroy, Pointer	33,611
14		22	(a)	Chelsea	W 6-2	Robson 3, McIlroy 2, Miller	29,080
15		29	(h)	Blackpool	L 1-2	McIlroy	29,689
16	Nov	5	(a)	Aston Villa	L 0-2		35,923
17		12	(h)	Wolves	W 5-3	Pointer 2, Robson, Pilkington, McIlroy	26,813
18		19	(a)	Bolton W	W 5-3	Connelly 2, Pointer 2, Robson	23,830
19	Dec	3	(a)	Tottenham H	D 4-4	Connelly 2, Pointer, Robson	58,737
20		10	(h)	Leicester C	W 3-2	Connelly, Pointer, Robson	20,640
21		17	(a)	Arsenal	W 5-2	Pointer 3, Robson, McIlroy	37,042
22		26	(h)	Everton	L 1-3	Pointer	44,232
23		27	(a)	Everton	W 3-0	Robson 2, Connelly	74,867
24		31	(h)	Newcastle U	W 5-3	Robson 2, Harris, McIlroy, Miller	24,972
25	Jan	14	(a)	Cardiff C	L 1-2	Pointer	25,670
26		21	(h)	West Brom A	L 0-1		15,005
27	Feb	11	(h)	Sheffield W	L 3-4	Adamson, Connelly, Pointer	25,542
28		22	(a)	Fulham	W 1-0	Harris	13,139
29		25	(h)	Blackburn R	D 1-1	Miller	26,492
30	Mar	11	(h)	Chelsea	D 4-4	Lochhead 2, Harris 2	19,435
31		23	(a)	Blackpool	D 0-0		19,391
32		25	(h)	Aston Villa	D 1-1	Lawson	17,726
33		31	(h)	Nottingham F	W 4-1	Miller, Connelly, McIlroy, Pointer	18,650
34	Apr	1	(a)	Leicester C	D 2-2	Connelly, McIlroy	27,838
35		3	(a)	Nottingham F	L 1-3	Lochhead	27,965
36		8	(h)	Bolton W	W 2-0	Pointer, Fenton	22,998
37		12	(a)	Manchester U	L 0-6		24,616
38		15	(a)	Wolves	L 1-2	Harris	25,558
39		18	(h)	West Ham U	D 2-2	Connelly, Pointer	11,609
40		22	(h)	Tottenham H	W 4-2	Harris 2, Robson, McIlroy	28,991
41		27	(a)	Birmingham C	W 1-0	Adamson	15,015
42		29	(a)	West Ham U	W 2-1	Lawson, Harris	18,759

FINAL LEAGUE POSITION: 4th in Division One — Appearances

Goals

FA Cup

3	Jan	7	(h)	Bournemouth	W 1-0	Connelly	24,817
4		28	(a)	Brighton & HA	D 3-3	Miller, Pointer, Robson	28,672
R		31	(h)	Brighton & HA	W 2-0	Miller, Robson	22,726
5	Feb	18	(h)	Swansea T	W 4-0	Robson 2, Pointer, Connelly	30,977
6	Mar	4	(a)	Sheffield W	D 0-0		55,000
R		7	(h)	Sheffield W	W 2-0	McIlroy, Robson	48,894
SF		18	(n*)	Tottenham H	L 0-3		70,000

*Played at Villa Park, Birmingham. — Appearances

Goals

League Cup

2	Oct	24	(a)	Cardiff C	W 4-0	Harris 3, Connelly	8,110
3	Nov	22	(a)	Brentford	D 1-1	Lochhead	9,890
R	Dec	6	(h)	Brentford	W 2-1	Pointer, Robson	12,787
4	Jan	10	(h)	Nottingham F	W 2-1	Connelly, Robson	12,489
5	Feb	6	(a)	Southampton	W 4-2	Fenton 2, Pointer, Pilkington	26,535
SF	Apr	10	(h)	Aston Villa	D 1-1	Miller	15,908
		26	(a)	Aston Villa	D 2-2	McIlroy, Robson	23,077
R	May	2	(n†)	Aston Villa	L 1-2	Robson	7,953

†Played at Old Trafford, Manchester. — Appearances

Goals

Blacklaw A	Angus J	Elder A	Adamson J	Cummings T	Miller B	Connelly J	McIlroy J	Pointer R	Robson J	Pilkington B	Joyce W	Lawson I	Meredith T	Harris G	Lochhead A	Marshall W	Walker D	Fenton R	Furnell J	Smith D	Scott J	Talbut J	Towers I	White W	
1	2	3	4	5	6	7	8	9	10	11															1
1	2	3	4		5	7	8		10	11	6	9													2
1	2	3	4	5	6		8		10			9	7	11											3
1	2	3	4	5	6		8		10	11			7		9										4
1	2	3	4	5	6		8	9	10	11			7												5
1	2	3	4	5	6		8	9	10	11			7												6
1	2	3	4	5	6		8	9	10	11			7												7
1	2	3	4	5	6		8	9		11			7	10											8
1	2	3	4	5	6		8	9	10	11			7												9
1	2	3	4	5	6		8	9	10	11			7												10
1	2	3	5		6	7	8	9	10	11	4														11
1	2		6	5		7		9	8	11	4			10		3									12
1	2	3	5		6	7	8	9	10	11	4														13
1	2	3	5		6	7	8	9	10		4			11											14
1	2	3	5		6	7	8	9	10		4			11											15
1	2	3	5		6	7	8	9	10	11	4														16
1		3	5		6	7	8	9	10	11	4					2									17
1	2			5	6	7	8	9	10	11	4					3									18
1	2	3		5	6	7	8	9	10	11	4														19
1	2	3		5	6	7	8	9	10	11	4														20
1	2	3	5		6	7	8	9	10	11	4														21
1	2	3	5		6	7	8	9	10	11	4														22
1	2	3	5		6	7	8	9	10		4			11											23
1	2	3	5		6	7	8	9	10		4			11											24
1	2	3		5	6	7		9	10	11	4	8													25
1	2	3		5	6	7		9	10	11		8					4								26
1	2	3	5		6	7		9	10	11	4							8							27
1		3	5		6	7	8	9	10		4			11		2									28
1	2	3	5		6	7	8	9	10		4			11											29
				5								8	7	11	9	3	4	10	1	2	6				30
1	2	3	5		6	11	8	9			4		7					10							31
1	2	3		5	6	7	8		10		4	9		11											32
1	2	3	5		6	7	8	9	10		4			11											33
1	2	3	4	5	6	7	8	9	10					11											34
1	2	3	4	5		7	8		10		6			11	9										35
1	2	3		5	6	7	8	9			4			11				10							36
1	3			5		11					4		7	10	9			8		2	6				37
1	2	3		5		11		9	8		6		7	10			4								38
1	2	3		5	6	7	8	9	10		4			11											39
1	2	3		5	6	7	8	9	10		4			11											40
1	2		6								3	8		11	9		4	10				5	7		41
1	2		6	3		7		9	10		4	8		11								5			42
41	39	36	30	25	35	32	33	34	36	22	30	8	12	21	5	5	4	6	1	2	2	2	1		
			3		5	16	10	22	25	1	1	2	3	10	3			1							

Blacklaw A	Angus J	Elder A	Adamson J	Cummings T	Miller B	Connelly J	McIlroy J	Pointer R	Robson J	Pilkington B	Joyce W	Lawson I	Meredith T	Harris G	Lochhead A	Marshall W	Walker D	Fenton R	Furnell J	Smith D	Scott J	Talbut J	Towers I	White W	
1	2	3		5	6	7	8	9	10		4			11											3
1	2	3	5		6	7	8	9	10	11	4														4
1	2	3	5		6	7	8	9	10	11	4														R
1	2	3	5		6	7	8	9	10	11	4														5
1	2	3	5		6	7	8	9	10		4			11											6
1	2	3		5	6	7	8	9	10		4			11											R
1	2	3	5		6	7	8	9	10		4			11											SF
7	7	7	5	2	7	7	7	7	7	3	7			4											
					2	2	1	2	5																

Blacklaw A	Angus J	Elder A	Adamson J	Cummings T	Miller B	Connelly J	McIlroy J	Pointer R	Robson J	Pilkington B	Joyce W	Lawson I	Meredith T	Harris G	Lochhead A	Marshall W	Walker D	Fenton R	Furnell J	Smith D	Scott J	Talbut J	Towers I	White W	
1	2			5		7		9	10		4			11		3		8			6				2
													7	11	9	3	4	10	1	2	6	5		8	3
1	2	3		5	6	7	8	9	10	11	4														R
1	2	3		5	6	7		9	10	11	4	8													4
1		3	5		6	7		9	10	11	4					2		8							5
1	2	3		5	6	7	8	9			4			11				10							SF
1	2	3	4	5		7	8	9	10		6			11											
1	2		4	5	6	7		9	10		3	8		11											R
7	6	5	3	6	5	7	3	7	6	3	7	2	1	5	1	3	1	4	1	1	2	1		1	
					1	2	1	2	4	1				3	1			2							

1961-62

Manager: Harry Potts

1	Aug	19	(a)	Arsenal	D 2-2	McIlroy, Harris	42,856
2		22	(h)	Ipswich T	W 4-3	McIlroy, Harris, Pointer, Miller	24,577
3		26	(h)	Bolton W	W 3-1	Pointer 2, Robson	24,167
4		29	(a)	Ipswich T	L 2-6	McIlroy, Opp own-goal	23,835
5	Sep	2	(a)	Manchester C	W 3-1	McIlroy 2, Harris	38,171
6		5	(h)	Leicester C	W 2-0	Opp own-goals 2	22,339
7		9	(h)	West Brom A	W 3-1	Pointer 2, Connelly	22,001
8		16	(a)	Birmingham C	W 6-2	Pointer 3, McIlroy, Robson, Harris	18,764
9		20	(a)	Leicester C	W 6-2	Connelly 2, Robson 2, Pointer, Harris	25,567
10		23	(h)	Everton	W 2-1	Pointer 2	35,776
11		30	(a)	Fulham	W 5-3	Connelly 3, McIlroy, Pointer	30,665
12	Oct	14	(a)	West Ham U	L 1-2	Harris	32,238
13		21	(h)	Cardiff C	W 2-1	Harris, Robson	22,765
14		28	(a)	Tottenham H	L 2-4	Pointer 2	56,772
15	Nov	4	(h)	Aston Villa	W 3-0	Connelly, Robson, Opp own-goal	22,487
16		11	(a)	Nottingham F	L 2-3	Adamson, Miller	26,409
17		18	(h)	Wolves	D 3-3	Connelly 2, Harris	25,904
18		25	(a)	Manchester U	W 4-1	Connelly, Pointer, Robson, Harris	41,029
19	Dec	2	(h)	Sheffield U	W 4-2	Connelly, Pointer, Robson, Opp own-goal	21,526
20		9	(a)	Chelsea	W 2-1	Pointer, Harris	33,296
21		16	(h)	Arsenal	L 0-2		22,887
22		26	(h)	Sheffield W	W 4-0	Connelly 2, McIlroy, Robson	28,966
23	Jan	13	(h)	Manchester C	W 6-3	McIlroy 2, Robson 2, Harris, Opp own-goal	22,728
24		20	(a)	West Brom A	D 1-1	McIlroy	22,141
25	Feb	3	(h)	Birmingham C	W 7-1	Pointer 2, Robson, Harris, McIlroy, Connelly, Adamson	24,047
26		10	(a)	Everton	D 2-2	McIlroy, Pointer	54,369
27		20	(h)	Fulham	W 2-1	Connelly, Pointer	25,605
28		24	(a)	Blackburn R	L 1-2	Pointer	33,914
29	Mar	3	(h)	West Ham U	W 6-0	Towers 2, Robson 2, Pointer, McIlroy	24,379
30		14	(a)	Cardiff C	D 1-1	Miller	15,416
31		17	(h)	Tottenham H	D 2-2	Robson, Harris	46,810
32		24	(a)	Aston Villa	W 2-0	Connelly, Harris	36,864
33	Apr	3	(h)	Nottingham F	D 0-0		23,217
34		7	(a)	Wolves	D 1-1	Pointer	26,001
35		11	(a)	Bolton W	D 0-0		26,615
36		14	(h)	Manchester U	L 1-3	Pointer	36,240
37		17	(h)	Blackburn R	L 0-1		29,997
38		20	(h)	Blackpool	W 2-0	Cummings, Connelly	34,132
39		21	(a)	Sheffield U	L 0-2		25,003
40		23	(a)	Blackpool	D 1-1	McIlroy	31,660
41		28	(h)	Chelsea	D 1-1	Towers	29,078
42		30	(a)	Sheffield W	L 0-4		19,684

FINAL LEAGUE POSITION: 2nd in Division One

Appearances
Goals

FA Cup

3	Jan	6	(h)	Queen's Park R	W 6-1	Harris 2, Elder, Connelly, McIlroy, Opp own-goal	29,238
4		30	(h)	Leyton O	D 1-1	Harris	37,830
R	Feb	6	(a)	Leyton O	W 1-0	Miller	31,090
5		17	(h)	Everton	W 3-1	Miller, Connelly, Robson	50,514
6	Mar	10	(a)	Sheffield U	W 1-0	Pointer	54,628
SF		31	(n*)	Fulham	D 1-1	Connelly	59,989
R	Apr	9	(n†)	Fulham	W 2-1	Robson 2	31,000
F	May	5	(n‡)	Tottenham H	L 1-3	Robson	100,000

*Played at Villa Park, Birmingham. †Played at Filbert Street, Leicester. ‡Played at Wembley Stadium.

Appearances
Goals

Blacklaw A	Joyce W	Elder A	Adamson J	Cummings T	Miller B	Connelly J	McIlroy J	Pointer R	Robson J	Harris G	Angus J	Towers I	Lochhead A	Fenton R	Meredith T	Talbut J	Walker D	Simpson P	
1	2	3	4	5	6	7	8	9	10	11									1
1	2	3	4	5	6	7	8	9	10	11									2
1		3	4	5	6	7	8	9	10		2	11							3
1		3	4	5	6	7	8	9	10		2	11							4
1		3	4	5	6	7	8	9	10	11	2								5
1		3	4	5	6	7	8	9	10	11	2								6
1		3	4	5	6	7	8	9	10	11	2								7
1		3	4	5	6	7	8	9	10	11	2								8
1		3	4	5	6	7	8	9	10	11	2								9
1		3	4	5	6	7	8	9	10	11	2								10
1		3	4	5	6	7	8	9	10	11	2								11
1		3	4	5	6		8		10	11	2	7	9						12
1	3		4	5	6	7		9	10	11	2			8					13
1	4	3		5	6	7	8	9	10	11	2								14
1	4	3		5	6	7	8	9	10	11	2								15
1	2	3	4	5	6	7	8	9	10	11									16
1	2	3	4	5	6	7	8	9	10	11									17
1		3	4	5	6	7	8	9	10	11	2								18
1		3	4	5	6	7	8	9	10	11	2								19
1		3	4	5	6	7	8	9	10	11	2								20
1	4	3		5	6	7	8	9	10	11	2								21
1	4	3		5	6	7	8	9	10	11	2								22
1		3	4	5	6	7	8	9	10	11	2								23
1		3	4	5	6	7	8	9	10	11	2								24
1		3	4	5	6	7	8	9	10	11	2								25
1	6	3	4	5		7	8	9	10	11	2								26
1		3	4	5	6	7	8	9	10	11	2								27
1		3	4	5	6	7	8	9	10		2	11							28
1		3	4	5	6	7	8	9	10		2	11							29
1		3	4	5	6	7	8	9	10	11	2								30
1		3	4	5	6	7	8	9	10	11	2								31
1		3	4	5	6	7	8	9		11	2			10					32
1		3	4	5	6			9	8	11	2			10	7				33
1	4	3		5	6			9	8	11	2			10	7				34
1	4	3				7		9	8	11	2			10		5	6		35
1	6	3		5		7		9	10	11	2	8					4		36
1	6	3	4	5		7	8	9	10		2	11				5			37
1		3	4	5	6	7	8	9	10		2	11							38
1		3	4	5	6	7	8	9	10	11	2								39
1		3	4	5	6	7	8	9	10		2	11							40
1		3	4	5	6	7	8	9	10		2	11							41
1	4	3			6				10	11	2		9		7	5		8	42
42	15	41	34	39	38	38	36	40	41	34	38	10	2	5	3	3	2	1	
			2	1	3	17	15	25	15	14		3							

6 own-goals

1		3	4	5	6	7	8	9	10	11	2	3
1		3	4	5	6	7	8	9	10	11	2	4
1		3	4	5	6	7	8	9	10	11	2	R
1		3	4	5	6	7	8	9	10	11	2	5
1		3	4	5	6	7	8	9	10	11	2	6
1		3	4	5	6	7	8	9	10	11	2	SF
1	6	3	4		5	7	8	9	10	11	2	R
1		3	4	5	6	7	8	9	10	11	2	F
8	1	8	8	7	8	8	8	8	8	8	8	
		1			2	3	1	1	4	3		

1 own-goal

1962-63

Manager: Harry Potts

1	Aug	18	(h)	Everton	L 1-3	Pointer	37,100
2		22	(a)	Bolton W	D 2-2	Joyce, Connelly	28,897
3		25	(a)	West Brom A	W 2-1	Miller, Pointer	23,812
4		28	(h)	Bolton W	W 2-1	Connelly, McIlroy	27,529
5	Sep	1	(h)	Arsenal	W 2-1	Miller, Connelly	26,131
6		4	(h)	Leicester C	D 1-1	Robson	23,876
7		8	(a)	Birmingham C	L 1-5	Pointer	24,463
8		15	(h)	Leyton O	W 2-0	Lochhead, McIlroy	24,778
9		19	(a)	Leicester C	D 3-3	Pointer, Lochhead, McIlroy	26,692
10		22	(a)	Manchester U	W 5-2	Connelly 3, Lochhead, McIlroy	46,176
11		29	(h)	Blackpool	W 2-0	Connelly, Lochhead	28,351
12	Oct	6	(a)	Blackburn R	W 3-2	Lochhead 2, Harris	26,626
13		13	(h)	Sheffield U	W 5-1	Lochhead 2, Miller, Connelly, Harris	27,560
14		22	(a)	West Ham U	D 1-1	Robson	34,612
15		27	(h)	Manchester C	D 0-0		30,504
16	Nov	3	(a)	Liverpool	W 2-1	Pointer, Lochhead	43,870
17		10	(h)	Wolves	W 2-0	Lochhead, McIlroy	27,824
18		17	(a)	Aston Villa	L 1-2	Connelly	32,380
19		24	(h)	Tottenham H	W 2-1	Connelly, Pointer	44,478
20	Dec	1	(a)	Nottingham F	L 1-2	Pointer	34,171
21		8	(h)	Ipswich T	W 3-1	Miller 2, Lochhead	19,498
22		15	(a)	Everton	L 1-3	McIlroy	48,443
23		29	(h)	Sheffield W	W 4-0	Pointer 2, Miller, Harris	20,853
24	Mar	2	(a)	Sheffield U	L 0-1		26,939
25		9	(h)	West Ham U	D 1-1	Pointer	17,197
26		20	(a)	Blackpool	D 0-0		16,445
27		23	(h)	Liverpool	L 1-3	Lochhead	28,500
28		26	(a)	Manchester C	W 5-2	Harris 2, Bellamy, Lochhead, Pointer	21,985
29		30	(a)	Tottenham H	D 1-1	Lochhead	46,536
30	Apr	2	(h)	Blackburn R	W 1-0	Harris	25,746
31		6	(h)	Aston Villa	W 3-1	Pointer, Lochhead, Harris	19,605
32		12	(h)	Fulham	W 4-0	Lochhead 2, Bellamy, Pointer	22,405
33		13	(a)	Wolves	L 2-7	Pointer, Lochhead	21,562
34		15	(a)	Fulham	D 1-1	Connelly	25,869
35		20	(h)	Nottingham F	D 0-0		16,253
36		23	(a)	Sheffield W	W 1-0	Opp own-goal	24,649
37		27	(a)	Ipswich T	L 1-2	Connelly	18,645
38		30	(h)	West Brom A	W 2-1	Connelly, Lochhead	15,981
39	May	4	(h)	Manchester U	L 0-1		30,266
40		7	(a)	Leyton O	W 1-0	Towers	10,095
41		11	(a)	Arsenal	W 3-2	Elder, Irvine, Towers	23,526
42		14	(h)	Birmingham C	W 3-1	Irvine 3	14,350

FINAL LEAGUE POSITION: 3rd in Division One

Appearances

Goals

FA Cup

3	Jan	16	(a)	Tottenham H	W 3-0	Connelly, Lochhead, Harris	32,756
4		26	(h)	Liverpool	D 1-1	Connelly	49,827
R	Feb	20	(a)	Liverpool	L 1-2*	Elder	57,906

*After extra-time

Appearances

Goals

Blacklaw A	Angus J	Elder A	Joyce W	Cummings T	Miller B	Connelly J	McIlroy J	Pointer R	Robson J	Harris G	Talbut J	Walker D	Lochhead A	Adamson J	Towers I	Meredith T	Bellamy A	Buxton M	Morgan W	O'Neil B	Simpson P	Irvine W	
1	2	3	4	5	6	7	8	9	10	11													1
1	2	3	4	5	6	7	8	9	10	11													2
1	2	3	4		6	7	8	9	10	11	5												3
1	2	3	4		6	7	8	9	10	11	5												4
1	2	3	4		6	7	8	9	10	11	5												5
1	2	3	4		6	7	8	9	10	11	5												6
1	2	3	4		6	7	8	9	10	11	5												7
1	2	3			6	7	10	8		11	5	4	9										8
1	2	3			6	7	10	8		11	5	4	9										9
1	2	3			6	7	10	8		11	5	4	9										10
1	2	3			6	7	10	8		11	5	4	9										11
1	2	3			6	7	10	8		11	5		9	4									12
1	2	3			6	7	10	8		11	5		9	4									13
1	2	3			6	7		8	10	11	5			4	9								14
1	2	3			6	7	10	8		11	5		9	4									15
1	2	3			6	7	10	8		11	5		9	4									16
1	2	3			6	7	10	8		11	5		9	4									17
1	2	3			6	7	10	8		11	5		9	4									18
1	2	3			6	7	10	8		11	5		9	4									19
1	2	3			6	7	10	8		11	5		9	4									20
1	2	3			6	7	10	8		11	5		9	4									21
1	2	3			6	7	10	8		11	5		9	4									22
1	2	3			6	7	10	8		11	5		9	4									23
1	2	3			6	7		8	10	11	5		9	4									24
1	2	3			6	7		8	10	11	5		9	4									25
1	2	3			6	11		8	10		5		9	4		7							26
1	2	3			6	7		8	10	11	5	4	9										27
1	2	3			6	7		8		11	5	4	9				10						28
1	2	3			6	7		8		11	5	4	9				10						29
1	2				6	7		8		11	5	4	9				10	3					30
1	2	3			6	7		8		11	5	4	9				10						31
1	2	3			6	7		8		11	5	4	9				10						32
1	2	3			6	7		8		11	5	4	9				10						33
1	2	3			6	7		8		11	5	4	9				10						34
1	2	3			6	7		8		11	5	4	9				10						35
1	2	3			6	11			8		5	4	9				10		7				36
1	2	3			6	7			8	11	5	4	9				10						37
1	2	3			6	7			8	11	5		9							4	10		38
1	2	3			6	7			8	11	5		9							4	10		39
1	2	3			6					11	5		9	4	10	7	8						40
1	2	3			6	7				11	5			4	10		8					9	41
1	2	3			6	11				10	5			4			8		7			9	42
42	42	41	7	2	42	41	22	35	16	40	40	15	32	18	3	2	13	1	2	2	2	2	
		1	1		6	13	6	14	2	7			19		2		2					4	

1 own-goal

Blacklaw A	Angus J	Elder A	Joyce W	Cummings T	Miller B	Connelly J	McIlroy J	Pointer R	Robson J	Harris G	Talbut J	Walker D	Lochhead A	Adamson J	Towers I	Meredith T	Bellamy A	Buxton M	Morgan W	O'Neil B	Simpson P	Irvine W	
1	2	3			6	7	10		8	11	5		9	4									3
1	2	3			6	7	10		8	11	5		9	4									4
1	2	3			6	7	10	8		11	5		9	4									R
3	3	3			3	3	3	1	2	3	3		3	3									
		1				2				1			1										

1963-64

Manager: Harry Potts

1	Aug	24	(a)	Ipswich T	L	1-3	Miller	23,000
2		27	(h)	Chelsea	D	0-0		19,674
3		31	(h)	Sheffield W	W	3-1	Miller, Robson, Pointer	20,238
4	Sep	4	(a)	Chelsea	L	0-2		31,881
5		7	(a)	Everton	W	4-3	Bellamy 3, Miller	54,409
6		10	(h)	Fulham	W	4-1	Meredith, Robson, Harris, Connelly	19,349
7		14	(h)	Birmingham C	W	2-1	Bellamy, Harris	20,350
8		18	(a)	Fulham	L	1-2	Meredith	17,282
9		21	(a)	West Brom A	D	0-0		24,591
10		28	(h)	Arsenal	L	0-3		20,628
11	Oct	1	(h)	Blackburn R	W	3-0	Bellamy 2, Joyce	24,345
12		5	(a)	Leicester C	D	0-0		26,310
13		7	(a)	West Ham U	D	1-1	Harris	21,372
14		12	(h)	Blackpool	W	1-0	Harris	20,025
15		19	(a)	Blackburn R	W	2-1	Connelly 2	26,740
16		26	(h)	Sheffield U	L	1-2	Robson	21,345
17	Nov	2	(a)	Stoke C	D	4-4	Harris 2, Lochhead, Opp own-goal	36,924
18		9	(h)	Wolves	W	1-0	Connelly	19,775
19		16	(a)	Tottenham H	L	2-3	Lochhead, Harris	42,222
20		23	(h)	Aston Villa	W	2-0	Robson, Price	13,606
21		30	(a)	Liverpool	L	0-2		42,968
22	Dec	7	(h)	Nottingham F	D	1-1	Pointer	15,304
23		14	(h)	Ipswich T	W	3-1	Miller 2, Lochhead	10,558
24		21	(a)	Sheffield W	L	1-3	Miller	18,603
25		26	(h)	Manchester U	W	6-1	Lochhead 4, Morgan 2	35,766
26		28	(a)	Manchester U	L	1-5	Lochhead	48,035
27	Jan	11	(h)	Everton	L	2-3	Connelly 2	23,082
28		18	(a)	Birmingham C	D	0-0		15,917
29	Feb	1	(h)	West Brom A	W	3-2	Connelly 2, Towers	15,840
30		8	(a)	Arsenal	L	2-3	Towers, Lochhead	30,863
31		22	(a)	Blackpool	D	1-1	Morgan	12,938
32	Mar	3	(h)	West Ham U	W	3-1	Robson 2, Harris	14,428
33		7	(a)	Sheffield U	L	0-2		15,880
34		10	(h)	Leicester C	W	2-0	Morgan, Bellamy	12,664
35		21	(a)	Wolves	D	1-1	Lochhead	18,082
36		28	(h)	Stoke C	W	1-0	Elder	26,868
37		30	(a)	Bolton W	L	1-2	Irvine	14,112
38		31	(h)	Bolton W	D	1-1	Bellamy	12,554
39	Apr	4	(a)	Aston Villa	L	0-2		14,296
40		14	(h)	Liverpool	L	0-3		34,804
41		18	(a)	Nottingham F	W	3-1	Towers 2, Irvine	19,005
42		21	(h)	Tottenham H	W	7-2	O'Neil 2, Irvine 2, Harris 2, Lochhead	16,660

FINAL LEAGUE POSITION: 9th in Division One

Appearances
Goals

FA Cup

3	Jan	4	(h)	Rotherham U	D	1-1	Lochhead	24,948
R		7	(a)	Rotherham U	W	3-2	Lochhead, Connelly, Towers	23,813
4		25	(h)	Newport C	W	2-1	Morgan, Connelly	23,027
5	Feb	15	(h)	Huddersfield T	W	3-0	Pointer, Lochhead, Opp own-goal	39,326
6		29	(a)	West Ham U	L	2-3	Connelly, Pointer	36,681

Appearances
Goals

Blacklaw A	Angus J	Joyce W	Adamson J	Talbut J	Miller B	Connelly J	Lochhead A	Irvine W	Robson J	Harris G	Pointer R	Walker D	Morgan W	Meredith T	Bellamy A	O'Neil B	Price J	Buxton M	Smith F	Elder A	Towers I	Todd S	
1	2	3	4	5	6	7	8	9	10	11													1
1	2	3	4	5	6	7	8		10	11	9												2
1	2	3		5	6	11			8	10	9	4	7										3
1	2	3		5	6	11			8	10	9	4	7										4
1	2	3	4	5	6	11			9	10				7	8								5
1	2	3	4	5	6	11			9	10				7	8								6
1	2	3	4	5	6	11			9	10				7	8								7
1	2	3	4	5	6	11			9	10				7	8								8
1	2	3	4	5	6	11	9		8	10			7										9
1	2	3	4	5	6	11	9		8	10			7										10
1	2	3		5	6	11	9		10					7	8	4							11
1	2	3		5	6	11	9		8	10				7		4							12
1	2	3	4	5	6	11	9			10					8		7						13
1	2			5	6	11	9		8	10						4	7	3					14
1	2			5	6	11	9			10				7	8	4		3					15
1	2			5	6	11	9		10					7	8	4		3					16
1	2			5	6	11	8		9	10				7		4			3				17
1	2	3		5	6	11	8		9	10				7		4							18
1	2	3		5	6	11	8		9	10				7		4							19
1	2	3		5	6		9		8	10				7		4	11						20
1	2	3		5	6				8	10	9			7		4	11						21
1		3		5	6					10	9		7		8	4	11		2				22
1	3			5	6		9			10	8		7			4	11		2				23
1	2			5	6		9			10	8		7			4	11			3			24
1	2			5	6		9			10	8		7			4				3	11		25
1	2			5	6		9		10		8		7			4	11			3			26
1	2			5	6	11	9			10			7		8	4				3			27
1				5	6	11	9		10				7			4			2	3	8		28
1	2			5	6	11	9		10				7			4				3	8		29
1	2			5	6	11	9		10				7			4				3	8		30
1	2		6	5		11	9			10	8		7			4				3			31
1	2			5	6	11	9		8	10			7			4				3			32
1				5	6		9		8	10			7			4			2	3	11		33
1	2			5	6	11	9			10			7		8	4				3			34
1	2				5	11	9			10		4	7		8	6				3			35
1	2			5		11	9					4	7		10	6				3	8		36
1	2			5	6	11	9	8				4	7		10					3			37
1	2			5	6	11	9	8					7		10	4				3			38
1				5	6	11	9	8					7		10	4			2	3			39
1				5	6	11		9		10			7		8	4			2	3			40
1				5	6		8	9		10			7			4			2	3	11		41
1				5	6		8	9		10			7			4				3	11	2	42
42	35	18	10	41	40	32	33	7	25	32	10	5	25	13	17	30	8	3	8	19	8	1	
		1			6	8	11	4	6	10	2		4	2	8	2	1			1	4		

1 own-goal

Blacklaw A	Angus J	Joyce W	Adamson J	Talbut J	Miller B	Connelly J	Lochhead A	Irvine W	Robson J	Harris G	Pointer R	Walker D	Morgan W	Meredith T	Bellamy A	O'Neil B	Price J	Buxton M	Smith F	Elder A	Towers I	Todd S	
1	2			5	6	11	9			10	8		7			4				3			3
1	2			5	6	11	9			10			7			4				3	8		R
1	2			5	6	11	9			10			7			4				3	8		4
1	2		4	5		11	9			10	8		7			4				3			5
1	2			5	6	11	9			10	8		7			4				3			6
5	5		1	5	4	5	5			5	3		5			5				5	2		
						3	3				2		1								1		

1 own-goal

1964-65

Manager: Harry Potts

1	Aug	22	(h)	Blackpool	D 2-2	Lochhead, Irvine	15,773
2		25	(h)	Tottenham H	D 2-2	Irvine, Towers	21,661
3		29	(a)	Sheffield U	L 0-2		13,831
4	Sep	2	(a)	Tottenham H	L 1-4	Towers	42,326
5		5	(h)	Everton	D 1-1	O'Neil	23,703
6		8	(h)	Nottingham F	D 2-2	Bellamy, Irvine	13,420
7		12	(a)	Birmingham C	L 1-2	Morgan	16,890
8		15	(a)	Nottingham F	L 1-3	Lochhead	27,331
9		19	(h)	West Ham U	W 3-2	Pointer, Lochhead, Towers	13,541
10		23	(a)	Sheffield W	L 1-5	Lochhead	16,604
11		26	(a)	West Brom A	W 2-1	Irvine 2	15,863
12	Oct	6	(h)	Manchester U	D 0-0		31,056
13		10	(h)	Blackburn R	D 1-1	Lochhead	21,199
14		17	(a)	Arsenal	L 2-3	Angus 2	24,962
15		24	(h)	Leeds U	L 0-1		24,371
16		31	(a)	Chelsea	W 1-0	Irvine	29,040
17	Nov	7	(h)	Leicester C	W 2-1	Elder, Miller	13,780
18		14	(a)	Sunderland	L 2-3	Lochhead, Bellamy	36,102
19		21	(h)	Wolves	D 1-1	Lochhead	13,651
20		28	(a)	Aston Villa	L 0-1		18,177
21	Dec	5	(h)	Liverpool	L 1-5	Price	12,479
22		12	(a)	Blackpool	W 4-2	Lochhead 3, Irvine	11,000
23		19	(h)	Sheffield U	W 3-1	Irvine 2, Elder	10,295
24		26	(h)	Fulham	W 4-0	Irvine 3, Todd	15,602
25		28	(a)	Fulham	W 1-0	Irvine	10,162
26	Jan	2	(a)	Everton	L 1-2	Harris	42,177
27		16	(h)	Birmingham C	W 2-0	Irvine, Harris	9,971
28		23	(a)	West Ham U	L 2-3	Lochhead, Irvine	25,490
29	Feb	6	(h)	West Brom A	L 0-1		12,902
30		13	(a)	Manchester U	L 2-3	Walker, Irvine	39,135
31		24	(a)	Blackburn R	W 4-1	Irvine 2, O'Neil, Elder	15,340
32		27	(h)	Arsenal	W 2-1	O'Neil, Bellamy	12,744
33	Mar	13	(h)	Sheffield W	W 4-1	Lochhead 2, Irvine, Morgan	12,362
34		15	(a)	Leeds U	L 1-5	Morgan	38,506
35		20	(a)	Leicester C	W 2-0	Irvine, Coates	11,929
36		27	(h)	Sunderland	D 0-0		13,303
37	Apr	3	(a)	Wolves	W 2-1	Lochhead, Latcham	16,481
38		10	(h)	Aston Villa	D 2-2	Elder, Lochhead	10,105
39		17	(a)	Liverpool	D 1-1	Lochhead	30,004
40		19	(a)	Stoke C	L 0-2		19,801
41		20	(h)	Stoke C	W 1-0	Irvine	13,398
42		24	(h)	Chelsea	W 6-2	Lochhead 5, Irvine	15,213

FINAL LEAGUE POSITION: 12th in Division One

Appearances
Goals

FA Cup

3	Jan	9	(h)	Brentford	D 1-1	Irvine	15,100
R		12	(a)	Brentford	W 2-0	Irvine 2	30,448
4		30	(a)	Reading	D 1-1	Lochhead	17,872
R	Feb	2	(h)	Reading	W 1-0	Lochhead	20,591
5		20	(a)	Manchester U	L 1-2	Lochhead	54,000

Appearances
Goals

Blacklaw A	Angus J	Elder A	O'Neil B	Talbut J	Miller B	Morgan W	Lochhead A	Irvine W	Harris G	Towers I	Walker D	Smith F	Robson J	Bellamy A	Pointer R	Todd S	Price J	Buxton M	Coates R	Latcham L	Thomson H	Merrington D	
1	2	3	4	5	6	7	8	9	10	11													1
1	2		6	5	3	7	8	9	10	11	4												2
1	2		4	5	6	7		9	10			3	8				11						3
1	2		6	5	3	7	8	9	10	11	4												4
1	2		6	5	3	7	8	9	10	11	4												5
1	2	3	6	5		7		9	10	11	4			8									6
1	2	3	6	5		7	9		10	11	4			8									7
1	2	3	6	5		7	9		10	11	4			8									8
1	2	3	6		5	7	9			11	4		10		8								9
1	2	3	6		5	7	9			11	4		10		8								10
1	2	3		5	6	7	9	8		11				10		4							11
1	2	3		5	6	7	9	8		11				10		4							12
1	2	3		5	6	7	9	8		10						4	11						13
1	2			5	6	7	9	8						10		4	11	3					14
1		3		5	6	7	9	8				2		10		4	11						15
1		3		5	6	7	8	9			4	2		10			11						16
1		3		5	6	7	8	9			4	2		10			11						17
1			4	5	6	7	8					2		10	9		11	3					18
1	2	3	4	5	6	7	8	9	11					10									19
1	2	3	4	5	6	7	8		11				9	10									20
1	2	3	4	5	6	7	9		10					8			11						21
1		3	6		5		8	9	10	7		2				4	11						22
1		3	6		5			9		7		2		10		4	11		8				23
1		3	6		5		8	9	10	7		2				4	11						24
1		3	6		5		8	9	10			2		7		4	11						25
1		3	6		5		8	9	10	7		2				4	11						26
1		3	4	5	6	7	8	9	10			2		11									27
1	3		4	5	6	7	8	9	10	11		2											28
1	2	3	4	5	6	7	8		10				9	11									29
1		3	4		5			9	10	7	6	2		8						11			30
1	2	3	4	5	6		8	9		7				10						11			31
1	2		4	5	6	7	8	9						10				3		11			32
1	2	3	4	5	6	7	8	9	11					10									33
1		3	10	5	6	7	8	9			4					2			11				34
		3	4	5	6	7	8	9						10		2			11		1		35
		3	4	5	6	7	8	9	11					10		2					1		36
		3	4	5	6	7	8		10							2			9	11	1		37
		3	4	5	6	7	8	9	10							2			11		1		38
		3	4	5	6	7	8	9	10	11		2									1		39
		3	6		5	7	8	9	10	11		2				4					1		40
		3	6		5	7	8	9	10			2				4			11		1		41
		2	4		6	7	8	9	10									3	11		1	5	42
34	22	34	35	31	39	35	38	33	27	21	12	16	5	23	3	17	13	4	7	4	8	1	
	2	4	2		1	3	21	22	2	3	1			3	1	1	1		1	1			

Blacklaw A	Angus J	Elder A	O'Neil B	Talbut J	Miller B	Morgan W	Lochhead A	Irvine W	Harris G	Towers I	Walker D	Smith F	Robson J	Bellamy A	Pointer R	Todd S	Price J	Buxton M	Coates R	Latcham L	Thomson H	Merrington D	
1		3	6		5		8	9	10	7	4	2					11						3
1		3	4	5	6		8	9	10	7		2		11									R
1		3	4	5	6		8	9	10	7		2		11									4
1		3	4	5	6	7	8		10	11		2	9										R
1		3	4	5	6		8	9	10			2		7						11			5
5		5	5	4	5	1	5	4	5	4	1	5	1	3			1			1			
							3	3															

1965-66

Manager: Harry Potts

1	Aug	21	(a)	Chelsea	D 1-1	Bellamy	34,067
2		24	(h)	Blackpool	W 3-1	Lochhead, Irvine, Bellamy	15,208
3		28	(h)	Arsenal	D 2-2	Elder, Lochhead	16,741
4		30	(a)	Blackpool	W 3-1	Irvine 2, O'Neil	17,723
5	Sep	4	(a)	Everton	L 0-1		44,633
6		7	(h)	Northampton T	W 4-1	Irvine 3, Opp own-goal	14,792
7		11	(h)	Manchester U	W 3-0	Harris 2, Elder	30,137
8		15	(a)	Northampton T	W 2-1	Elder, Irvine	19,336
9		18	(a)	Newcastle U	L 2-3	Lochhead 2	35,883
10		25	(h)	West Brom A	W 2-0	O'Neil, Lochhead	20,487
11	Oct	9	(h)	Blackburn R	L 1-4	Lochhead	23,198
12		16	(a)	Leicester C	W 1-0	Morgan	17,978
13		23	(h)	Sheffield U	W 2-0	Lochhead, Harris	20,693
14		30	(a)	Leeds U	D 1-1	Irvine	41,628
15	Nov	6	(h)	West Ham U	W 3-1	Irvine 2, Lochhead	17,100
16		13	(a)	Sunderland	W 4-0	Coates 2, Harris, Irvine	38,224
17		20	(h)	Aston Villa	W 3-1	Lochhead 2, Irvine	14,281
18		27	(a)	Liverpool	L 1-2	Irvine	50,282
19	Dec	4	(h)	Tottenham H	D 1-1	Irvine	19,509
20		11	(a)	Fulham	W 5-2	Irvine 3, O'Neil, Miller	12,092
21		18	(h)	Leicester C	W 4-2	Lochhead 2, Miller, Elder	13,837
22		27	(a)	Stoke C	L 1-3	Coates	35,946
23		28	(h)	Stoke C	W 4-1	O'Neil, Bellamy, Irvine, Harris	23,214
24	Jan	1	(a)	Blackburn R	W 2-0	Irvine, Harris	28,013
25		8	(h)	Fulham	W 1-0	Angus	17,202
26		15	(a)	Sheffield U	L 1-2	Bellamy	16,072
27		29	(h)	Chelsea	L 1-2	Angus	23,825
28	Feb	5	(a)	Arsenal	D 1-1	Latcham	28,652
29		19	(h)	Everton	D 1-1	Elder	19,670
30		26	(a)	Manchester U	L 2-4	Lochhead, Irvine	50,188
31	Mar	8	(a)	Nottingham F	L 0-1		28,246
32		12	(h)	Newcastle U	W 1-0	Morgan	16,259
33		19	(a)	West Brom A	W 2-1	Elder, Harris	18,747
34		26	(h)	Nottingham F	W 4-1	Irvine 3, Lochhead	10,027
35	Apr	2	(a)	West Ham U	D 1-1	Irvine	17,665
36		9	(h)	Sunderland	W 1-0	Irvine	15,699
37		11	(h)	Sheffield W	W 2-1	Irvine 2	17,874
38		16	(a)	Aston Villa	L 1-2	Irvine	14,100
39		23	(h)	Liverpool	W 2-0	Irvine, Coates	36,530
40		30	(a)	Tottenham H	W 1-0	Lochhead	29,337
41	May	7	(h)	Leeds U	L 0-1		33,035
42		9	(a)	Sheffield W	W 2-0	Latcham, Coates	20,348

FINAL LEAGUE POSITION: 3rd in Division One

Appearances
Sub Appearances
Goals

FA Cup

3	Jan	22	(a)	Bournemouth	D 1-1	Irvine	16,082
R		25	(h)	Bournemouth	W 7-0	Lochhead 5, Irvine, Harris	21,743
4	Feb	12	(a)	Tottenham H	L 3-4	Irvine 3	50,611

Appearances
Goals

League Cup

2	Sep	22	(a)	Doncaster R	W 4-0	Lochhead 3, Towers	24,988
3	Oct	13	(h)	Southampton	W 3-2	Irvine 2, Harris	10,868
4	Nov	3	(a)	Stoke C	D 0-0		14,400
R		9	(h)	Stoke C	W 2-1	Coates, Irvine	13,666
5		17	(a)	Peterborough U	L 0-4		14,796

Appearances
Goals

Thomson H	Angus J	Elder A	O'Neil B	Talbut J	Miller B	Morgan W	Lochhead A	Irvine W	Bellamy A	Coates R	Latcham L	Towers I	Harris G	Merrington D	Blacklaw A	Buxton M	Todd S	Kinsella L	Smith D	
1	2	3	4	5	6	7	8	9	10	11										1
1	2	3	4	5	6		8	9	10	7	11									2
1	2	3	4	5	6	7	8	9*	10	11		12								3
1	2	3	4	5	6	7	8	9	12	11*			10							4
1	2	3	4	5	6	7		9	8	11			10							5
1	2	3	4	5	6	7	8	9	10				11							6
1	2	3	4	5	6	7	8	9			11		10							7
1	2	3	4	5	6	7	8	9	11				10							8
1	2	3	4	5	6	7	8	9	11				10							9
1	2	3	4	5	6	7	8	9	11				10							10
1	2	3	4	5	6	7	8	9	11				10							11
1	2	3	4	5	6	7	8	9		11			10							12
1	2	3	4		6	7	8	9		11			10	5						13
	2	3	4		6	7		9	8	11			10	5	1					14
	2	3	4		6	7	8	9		11			10	5	1					15
	2		4		6	7	8	9		11			10	5	1	3				16
	2*	3	4		5	7	8	9		11			10		1		6	12		17
		3	4		5	7		9	8	11*			10		1		6	12	2	18
	2		4		6	7	8	9		11			10	5	1	3				19
	2	3*	4		6	7	8	9		11			10	5	1		12			20
	2	3	4		6	7	8	9		11			10	5	1					21
	2	3	4		6	7	8	9		11			10	5	1					22
	2	3	4		5	7		9	8	11			10		1		6			23
	2	3	4		5	7		9	8	11			10		1		6			24
	2	3	4*		5	7	12	9	8	11			10		1		6			25
	2	3	4		5	7	8	9	11				10		1		6			26
	2	3		4	6	7	8	9		11			10	5	1					27
	2	3			5		8	9	6	11	7		10	4	1					28
1	2	3	4		5	7	8	9		11			10	6						29
1	2		4		5	7	8	9		11			10	6		3				30
	2	3	4		5		8	9		7*	11		10	6	1		12			31
	2	3	4		5	7		9		8	11		10		1		6			32
	2	3	4		5	7	8	9		11			10		1		6			33
	2	3	4		5	7	8	9		11			10		1		6			34
	2	3	4		5	7	8	9		11			10		1		6			35
		3	4		5	7	8	9		11			10		1		6		2	36
		3	4		5	7	8	9*		11			10		1		6	12	2	37
	2	3	4		5	7	8	9		11			10		1		6			38
	2	3	4		5	7	8	9		11			10		1		6			39
	2	3	4		5	7	8	9		11			10		1		6			40
	2	3	4		5	7	8	9		11			10		1		6			41
	2	3			5	7*		9	4	11	8		10		1		6	12		42
15	39	39	39	13	42	39	34	42	17	35	6		39	13	27	3	17		3	
							1		1			1					2	4		
	2	6	4		2	2	15	29	4	5	2		7							

1 own-goal

Thomson H	Angus J	Elder A	O'Neil B	Talbut J	Miller B	Morgan W	Lochhead A	Irvine W	Bellamy A	Coates R	Latcham L	Towers I	Harris G	Merrington D	Blacklaw A	Buxton M	Todd S	Kinsella L	Smith D	
	2	3	4		6	7	8	9		11			10	5	1					3
	2	3		4	6	7	8	9		11			10	5	1					R
	2	3	4	5	6	7	8	9		11			10		1					4
	3	3	2	2	3	3	3	3		3			3	2	3					
							5	5					1							

Thomson H	Angus J	Elder A	O'Neil B	Talbut J	Miller B	Morgan W	Lochhead A	Irvine W	Bellamy A	Coates R	Latcham L	Towers I	Harris G	Merrington D	Blacklaw A	Buxton M	Todd S	Kinsella L	Smith D	
1	2	3	4	5	6	7	9		10		11	8								2
1	2	3	4	5	6	7	8	9		11			10							3
	2	3	4		6	7		9	8	11			10	5	1					4
	2	3	4		6	7	8	9		11			10	5	1					R
	2		4		6	7	8	9		11			10	5	1	3				5
2	5	4	5	2	5	5	4	4	2	4	1	1	4	3	3	1				
							3	3		1		1	1							

1966-67

Manager: Harry Potts

1	Aug	20	(h)	Sheffield U	W	4-0	Harris 3, Irvine	17,380
2		23	(h)	Fulham	W	3-0	Elder, Lochhead, Irvine	18,340
3		27	(a)	West Brom A	W	2-1	O'Neil 2	21,732
4		29	(a)	Fulham	D	0-0		15,027
5	Sep	3	(h)	Leeds U	D	1-1	Harris	31,177
6		6	(a)	Everton	D	1-1	Lochhead	44,063
7		10	(a)	Newcastle U	D	1-1	Harris	25,485
8		17	(h)	Tottenham H	D	2-2	Lochhead 2	25,184
9		24	(a)	Manchester U	L	1-4	Lochhead	52,717
10	Oct	1	(h)	Blackpool	W	1-0	Irvine	16,553
11		8	(a)	Chelsea	W	3-1	Lochhead 2, Morgan	42,573
12		15	(h)	Leicester C	W	5-2	Elder, Lochhead, Irvine, Harris, Coates	20,642
13		29	(h)	Manchester C	L	2-3	Morgan, Irvine	25,596
14	Nov	5	(a)	Leicester C	L	1-5	Elder	24,394
15		9	(a)	Liverpool	L	0-2		50,124
16		12	(h)	Southampton	W	4-1	Lochhead 2, Harris 2	16,830
17		19	(a)	Sunderland	L	3-4	Irvine 2, Lochhead	32,526
18		26	(h)	Aston Villa	W	4-2	Lochhead 4	14,935
19	Dec	3	(a)	Arsenal	D	0-0		23,230
20		10	(h)	West Ham U	W	4-2	Irvine 2, Lochhead, O'Neil	19,512
21		17	(a)	Sheffield U	D	1-1	Irvine	15,751
22		26	(h)	Stoke C	L	0-2		30,097
23		27	(a)	Stoke C	L	3-4	Harris 2, Irvine	38,402
24		31	(h)	West Brom A	W	5-1	Lochhead 2, Irvine 2, Opp own-goal	18,904
25	Jan	7	(a)	Leeds U	L	1-3	Coates	37,465
26		14	(h)	Newcastle U	L	0-2		17,380
27		21	(a)	Tottenham H	L	0-2		42,187
28	Feb	4	(h)	Manchester U	D	1-1	Harris	40,265
29		11	(a)	Blackpool	W	2-0	Blant 2	16,681
30		25	(h)	Chelsea	L	1-2	Blant	20,379
31	Mar	4	(a)	Manchester C	L	0-1		32,692
32		18	(h)	Liverpool	W	1-0	Latcham	29,389
33		25	(a)	West Ham U	L	2-3	Morgan, O'Neil	24,425
34		27	(a)	Nottingham F	L	1-4	Latcham	41,586
35		28	(h)	Nottingham F	L	0-2		17,695
36	Apr	1	(h)	Sheffield W	W	2-0	Latcham, Harris	14,442
37		8	(a)	Southampton	L	0-4		23,442
38		15	(h)	Sunderland	W	1-0	Harris	13,765
39		22	(a)	Aston Villa	W	1-0	Opp own-goal	19,010
40		29	(h)	Arsenal	L	1-4	Smith	10,952
41	May	6	(a)	Sheffield W	L	0-7		21,099
42		13	(h)	Everton	D	1-1	Blant	11,634

FINAL LEAGUE POSITION: 14th in Division One

Appearances
Sub Appearances
Goals

FA Cup

3	Jan	28	(h)	Everton	D	0-0		42,482
R		31	(a)	Everton	L	1-2	Irvine	57,449

Appearances
Sub Appearances
Goals

League Cup

2	Sep	14	(a)	Shrewsbury T	D	1-1	Morgan	
R		29	(h)	Shrewsbury T	W	5-0	France, Lochhead, Talbut, Opp own-goals 2	9,049
3	Oct	5	(a)	Sheffield U	L	0-2		9,108

Appearances
Sub Appearances
Goals

Blacklaw A	Angus J	Elder A	O'Neil B	Miller B	Todd S	Morgan W	Lochhead A	Irvine W	Harris G	Coates R	Bellamy A	Kinsella L	Smith F	Latcham L	Talbut J	Murray J	France G	Merrington D	Thomson H	Blant C	Buxton M	Ternent R	Ternent S	Thomas D	
1	2	3	4	5	6	7	8	9	10	11*	12														1
1	2	3	4	5	6	7	8	9	10			11													2
1	2	3	4	5	6	7	8	9	10			11													3
1		3	4	5	6		8	9	10	7			2	11											4
1	2	3	4	5	6	7	8	9	10	11															5
1		3	4	5	6	7	8	9	10	11			2												6
1		3	4	5	6	7	8	9	10	11			2												7
1	2	3	4	5	6	7	8	9	10	11															8
1	2		4	5		7	8	9	10	11	6				3										9
1	2		4	3	12	7	8	9	10	11	6*				5										10
1	2	3	4	5		7	8		10	11	9				6										11
1	2	3	4	6		7	8	9	10	11					5										12
1	2	3	11	6		7	8	9	10		4				5										13
1	2	3	4	6		7	8		10		9				5	11									14
1	2	3	4	5	6	7	8		10	11	9*						12								15
1	2	3	4	5	6	7	8	9	10	11															16
1	2	3	4	5	6	7	8	9	10	11															17
1	2	3	4	5	6	7	8	9	10	11															18
1	2	3	4	5	6	7	8	9	10					11											19
1	2	3	4	5	6	7	8	9	10					11*			12								20
1	2	3	4	5	6	7	8	9	10					11											21
1	2	3	4	5	6	7	8	9	10					11											22
1	2		4	5	3	7	8	9	10	11								6							23
	2	3*		5	4	7	8	9	10	11				12				6	1						24
	2	3	4	5		7	8	9		11			10					6	1						25
	2	3*	4	5		7	8	9	10	11				12				6	1						26
			4	5	3	7	8		10	11			2	9				6	1						27
			4	5		7	8		10	11			3	2				6	1	9					28
			4	5		7	8		10	11			2					6	1	9	3				29
			4	6		7	8		10	11*			2	3				5	1	9	12				30
			4	5		7	8		10	11			2	3				6	1		9				31
			4	5		7	8*		10	11			2	3				6	1	9	12				32
			8	5	4	7			10	11			2	3				6	1	9					33
			8	5	4	7			10	11			2	3				6	1	9					34
	6	3	4	5			8		10	7	9		2	11					1						35
			4	5		11*	8		10	7	9		2	6		12		3	1						36
	4*			5	12	7			10	11	8			6		9		3	1			2			37
		3	4		6	7			10	11			2	8				5	1	9					38
			4	5*	12	7			10	11	6		2	8					1	9	3				39
			4			7			10	11	6		2	8				5	1	9	3				40
		3	4			7	9		10	11*	12		2	8				5	1				6		41
	5	3	12		4	7	8*		10				2	6					1	9				11	42
23	26	27	39	38	23	40	36	23	41	33	11	2	19	20	6	2		17	19	10	4	1	1	1	
			1		3						2			2		1	2				2				
		3	4			3	18	13	13	2			1	3						4					

2 own-goals

Blacklaw A	Angus J	Elder A	O'Neil B	Miller B	Todd S	Morgan W	Lochhead A	Irvine W	Harris G	Coates R	Bellamy A	Kinsella L	Smith F	Latcham L	Talbut J	Murray J	France G	Merrington D	Thomson H	Blant C	Buxton M	Ternent R	Ternent S	Thomas D	
			4	5		7	8	9	10	11			3	2				6	1						3
			4	6	12	7	8	9*	10	11			2	3				5	1						R
			2	2		2	2	2	2	2			2	2				2	2						
					1																				
								1																	

Blacklaw A	Angus J	Elder A	O'Neil B	Miller B	Todd S	Morgan W	Lochhead A	Irvine W	Harris G	Coates R	Bellamy A	Kinsella L	Smith F	Latcham L	Talbut J	Murray J	France G	Merrington D	Thomson H	Blant C	Buxton M	Ternent R	Ternent S	Thomas D	
1		3	4	5	6	7	8		10	11			2							9					2
			4	3	6	7	9			11	10		2		5		8		1						R
1	2	3	8	5	6		9		10	11*		12			4		7								3
2	1	2	3	3	3	2	3		2	3	1		2		2		2		1	1					
												1													
					1	1									1		1								

2 own-goals

1967-68

Manager: Harry Potts

1	Aug	19	(h)	Coventry C	W 2-1	Irvine, Casper	21,483
2		21	(a)	West Ham U	L 2-4	Irvine, Casper	30,414
3		26	(a)	Sheffield W	L 1-2	Casper	29,517
4		29	(h)	West Ham U	D 3-3	Bellamy, Lochhead, Harris	16,625
5	Sep	2	(h)	Tottenham H	W 5-1	Casper 2, Lochhead 2, Coates	23,337
6		9	(a)	Manchester U	D 2-2	Lochhead 2	55,809
7		16	(h)	Sunderland	W 3-0	Latcham, Morgan, Coates	19,414
8		20	(a)	Leeds U	L 1-2	Irvine	32,944
9		23	(a)	Wolves	L 2-3	Harris 2	28,151
10		30	(h)	Fulham	W 2-0	Casper, Coates	14,227
11	Oct	7	(h)	Nottingham F	D 1-1	Irvine	18,400
12		14	(a)	Stoke C	W 2-0	O'Neil, Irvine	19,538
13		24	(h)	Liverpool	D 1-1	O'Neil	29,763
14		28	(a)	Southampton	D 2-2	Irvine, Casper	22,696
15	Nov	4	(h)	Chelsea	D 1-1	Morgan	17,651
16		11	(a)	West Brom A	L 1-8	Bellamy	18,952
17		18	(h)	Newcastle U	W 2-0	Harris, Lochhead	15,447
18		25	(a)	Manchester C	L 2-4	Morgan, Casper	37,098
19	Dec	2	(h)	Arsenal	W 1-0	Harris	15,381
20		9	(a)	Sheffield U	L 0-1		14,363
21		16	(a)	Coventry C	L 1-5	Lochhead	28,560
22		23	(h)	Sheffield W	W 2-1	Lochhead, Casper	13,050
23		26	(a)	Everton	L 0-2		54,324
24		30	(h)	Everton	W 2-1	Latcham, Morgan	22,592
25	Jan	20	(a)	Sunderland	D 2-2	Casper, Coates	27,860
26	Feb	3	(h)	Wolves	D 1-1	Casper	12,643
27		10	(a)	Fulham	L 3-4	Lochhead, Casper, Opp own-goal	15,317
28		17	(h)	Manchester U	W 2-1	O'Neil, Dobson	32,165
29		24	(a)	Nottingham F	L 0-1		26,110
30	Mar	2	(h)	Manchester C	L 0-1		23,486
31		16	(a)	Liverpool	L 2-3	Coates 2	41,114
32		23	(h)	Southampton	W 2-0	O'Neil, Morgan	9,405
33		30	(a)	Tottenham H	L 0-5		26,494
34	Apr	6	(h)	West Brom A	D 0-0		11,918
35		13	(a)	Newcastle U	L 0-1		27,229
36		15	(h)	Leicester C	D 1-1	Lochhead	12,570
37		16	(a)	Leicester C	W 2-0	Dobson, Casper	20,032
38		20	(h)	Stoke C	W 4-0	Morgan 2, Lochhead, Casper	13,187
39		22	(a)	Chelsea	L 1-2	Lochhead	23,494
40		27	(a)	Arsenal	L 0-2		15,278
41	May	4	(h)	Sheffield U	L 0-2		10,244
42		11	(h)	Leeds U	W 3-0	O'Neil, Lochhead, Dobson	13,142

FINAL LEAGUE POSITION: 14th in Division One

Appearances
Sub Appearances
Goals

FA Cup

3	Jan	27	(h)	West Ham U	L 1-3	Casper	23,452

Appearances
Sub Appearances
Goals

League Cup

2	Sep	12	(h)	Cardiff C	W 2-1	Casper, Harris	11,731
3	Oct	10	(h)	Nottingham F	W 3-0	Irvine 2, Lochhead	14,421
4		31	(a)	Queen's Park R	W 2-1	Casper, Irvine	24,213
5	Nov	29	(h)	Arsenal	D 3-3	Lochhead, O'Neil, Irvine	16,032
R	Dec	5	(a)	Arsenal	L 1-2	Irvine	36,570

Appearances
Sub Appearances
Goals

Thomson H	Angus J	Latcham L	O'Neil B	Merrington D	Todd S	Morgan W	Bellamy A	Irvine W	Harris G	Casper F	Blant C	Kinsella L	Buxton M	Lochhead A	Smith F	Coates R	Ternent S	Dobson M	Waldron C	Thomas D	France G	Ternent R	Jones R	
1	2	3	4	5	6	7	8	9	10	11														1
1	2	3	4	5	6	7	8	9	10	11														2
1	2	3	4	5*		7	6	9	10	11	8	12												3
1	5	2	4			7	6	9	10	11			3	8										4
1	5	3	4			7	6		10	8				9	2	11								5
1	5	3	4			7	6		10	8				9	2	11								6
1	5	3	4			7	6		10	8				9	2	11								7
1	5	3	4	12		7	6	11*	10	8				9	2									8
1		3	4			7	6		10	8					2	11	5	9						9
1		3	4			7	6	12	10	8					2*	11	5	9						10
1	2	3	4			7	6	12	10	11				8			5	9*						11
1	2	3	4	5		7	6	8	10	11				9										12
1	2	3	4	5		7	6	9	10	11				8										13
1	2		4	5		7		9	6	11				8			10		3					14
1		3	4	5		7	10	9	6	8*						11		12	2					15
1	2	3	4			7	10	9	6					8					5	11				16
1	2	3	4			7	10	9	6	11				8					5					17
1	2	3	4	6		7	10			11	12			9					5		8*			18
1		3	4			7			6	11	9			8	2	10			5					19
1		3	4			7		9	6	10				8	2	11			5					20
1		3	4	6		7	10	9		12				8	2*				5	11				21
1		3	4	6		7	10	9		11				8					5			2		22
1		3	4	6		7*	10	9		11				8		12			5			2		23
1		3	4			7	10	9	6	12				8*		11			5			2		24
1		3		6		7	10			4	5			8		11		9				2		25
1		3			4	7	10			9	6			8		11			5			2		26
	2				4	7				9	6			8		11		10	5			3	1	27
1	2	3	10	6	4	7				9				8*		11		12	5					28
1	2*	3	10	6	4	7		8		9	12					11			5					29
1		3	10	6	4	7				9				8		11			5			2		30
1		3	4	6	10	7	8								2	11		9	5					31
1		3	4		6	7	10							8	2	11		9	5					32
1		3	4	10	6	7*				9				8	2	11		12	5					33
1		3	4		10	7	6			9				8	2	10			5					34
1		3	4		10	7	6			9				8	2	10			5					35
1	2	3	4	5	6	7	10							8		11		9						36
1	2	3			10	7	6*			9	12	5		8				4		11				37
1	2	3			4	7	10			9		6		8		11			5					38
1	2	3			6	7	10			9		5		8		11		4						39
1	2	3		6	4	7	10			9		12		8		11*			5					40
1	2	3	4	6	10	7				9				8		11			5					41
1	2	3	4	5	6	7	10			11*				8		12		9						42
41	25	40	35	21	19	42	33	17	20	36	5	3	1	34	14	25	4	11	24	3	1	7	1	
				1				2		2	3	2				2		3						
		2	5			7	2	6	5	14				13		6		3						

1 own-goal

Thomson H	Angus J	Latcham L	O'Neil B	Merrington D	Todd S	Morgan W	Bellamy A	Irvine W	Harris G	Casper F	Blant C	Kinsella L	Buxton M	Lochhead A	Smith F	Coates R	Ternent S	Dobson M	Waldron C	Thomas D	France G	Ternent R	Jones R	
1		3	4	6		7	10*	12		9				8		11			5			2		3
1		1	1	1		1	1			1				1		1			1			1		
								1																
										1														

Thomson H	Angus J	Latcham L	O'Neil B	Merrington D	Todd S	Morgan W	Bellamy A	Irvine W	Harris G	Casper F	Blant C	Kinsella L	Buxton M	Lochhead A	Smith F	Coates R	Ternent S	Dobson M	Waldron C	Thomas D	France G	Ternent R	Jones R	
1	5	3	4			7	6	12	10	8				9	2	11*								2
1	2	3	4	5		7	6	8	10	11				9										3
1	2	3	4	5		7	6	9	10	11				8*		12								4
1	2	3	4	5		7	10*	9	6	11				8		12								5
1	2*	3	4	5		7		9	6	11				8	12	10								R
5	5	5	5	4		5	4	4	5	5				5	1	2								
								1							1	2								
			1					5	1	2				2										

1968-69

Manager: Harry Potts

1	Aug	10	(a)	Nottingham F	D 2-2	Waldron, Casper	30,298
2		13	(a)	Everton	L 0-3		48,903
3		17	(h)	Newcastle U	W 1-0	Opp own-goal	13,579
4		20	(h)	Southampton	W 3-1	Casper 2, Bellamy	12,170
5		24	(a)	West Brom A	L 2-3	Lochhead, Casper	21,882
6		26	(a)	West Ham U	L 0-5		28,340
7		31	(h)	Coventry C	D 1-1	Waldron	12,939
8	Sep	7	(a)	Tottenham H	L 0-7		30,167
9		14	(h)	Manchester U	W 1-0	O'Neil	32,935
10		21	(a)	Sheffield W	L 0-1		23,270
11		28	(h)	Chelsea	W 2-1	Thomas 2	14,762
12	Oct	5	(h)	Liverpool	L 0-4		26,418
13		8	(h)	West Ham U	W 3-1	Murray, Dobson, Kindon	13,799
14		12	(a)	Stoke C	W 3-1	Coates, Blant, Murray	14,168
15		19	(h)	Leeds U	W 5-1	Casper 2, Coates, Kindon, Murray	26,434
16		26	(a)	Leicester C	W 2-0	Casper, Murray	21,307
17	Nov	2	(h)	Ipswich T	W 1-0	Blant	14,721
18		9	(a)	Queen's Park R	W 2-0	Murray, Casper	22,572
19		16	(h)	Wolves	D 1-1	Casper	20,848
20		23	(a)	Sunderland	L 0-2		19,607
21		30	(h)	Arsenal	L 0-1		16,264
22	Dec	7	(a)	Manchester C	L 0-7		31,009
23		14	(h)	Stoke C	D 1-1	Casper	10,465
24		21	(a)	Leeds U	L 1-6	Coates	31,009
25		26	(a)	Liverpool	D 1-1	Casper	52,477
26		28	(h)	Leicester C	W 2-1	Collins, Kindon	15,594
27	Jan	11	(a)	Ipswich T	L 0-2		18,858
28		18	(h)	Queen's Park R	D 2-2	Latcham, Kindon	12,674
29	Feb	1	(a)	Wolves	D 1-1	Collins	27,733
30		15	(a)	Arsenal	L 0-2		27,614
31	Mar	1	(h)	Nottingham F	W 3-1	Dobson 2, Casper	11,884
32		4	(h)	Manchester C	W 2-1	Merrington, Thomas	18,360
33		8	(a)	Newcastle U	L 0-1		32,460
34		15	(h)	West Brom A	D 2-2	Latcham, Dobson	12,218
35		22	(a)	Coventry C	L 1-4	Collins	26,584
36		29	(h)	Tottenham H	D 2-2	Probert, Coates	14,547
37	Apr	5	(a)	Chelsea	W 3-2	Collins 2, Thomas	30,266
38		7	(a)	Southampton	L 1-5	Blant	19,551
39		8	(h)	Everton	L 1-2	Coates	17,144
40		12	(h)	Sheffield W	W 2-0	Casper, Collins	9,597
41		19	(a)	Manchester U	L 0-2		52,626
42		23	(h)	Sunderland	L 1-2	Probert	10,181

FINAL LEAGUE POSITION: 14th in Division One

Appearances
Sub Appearances
Goals

FA Cup

3	Jan	4	(h)	Derby C	W 3-1	Casper 2, Blant	22,842
4		25	(a)	Liverpool	L 1-2	Latcham	53,667

Appearances
Sub Appearances
Goals

League Cup

2	Sep	4	(a)	Grimsby T	D 1-1	Lochhead	8,762
R		10	(h)	Grimsby T	W 6-0	Lochhead 2, Casper 2, Thomas, Murray	5,928
3		25	(a)	Workington	W 1-0	Blant	9,664
4	Oct	16	(h)	Leicester C	W 4-0	Thomas, Murray 2, Casper	11,486
5		30	(h)	Crystal P	W 2-0	Murray, Casper	17,879
SF	Nov	20	(h)	Swindon T	L 1-2	Coates	25,755
	Dec	4	(a)	Swindon T	W 2-1	Casper, Kindon	28,000
R		18	(n*)	Swindon T	L 2-3	Thomas, Casper	20,000

*Played at the Hawthorns, West Bromwich.

Appearances
Sub Appearances
Goals

Thomson H	Angus J	Latcham L	O'Neil B	Waldron C	Merrington D	Coates R	Lochhead A	Casper F	Bellamy A	Thomas D	Jones P	Smith F	Todd S	Dobson M	Brown W	Kindon S	Blant C	Murray J	Thomson J	Collins D	Jones R	Wrigley W	Docherty M	Kinsella L	Probert E	
1	2	3	4	5	6	7	8	9	10	11																1
1		3	4	5	6	7	8	9	10	11	2															2
1		3	4	5	6	7	8	9	10	11		2														3
1		3	4	5		7*	8	9	10	11		2	6	12												4
1		3	4	5		7	8	9	10	11*		2	6		12											5
1		3	4	5		7	8	9	6	11		2				10										6
1	2	3	4*	5	6	7	8	9	10	11							12									7
1	2	3	4	5	6	7	8	9	10	11																8
1		3	4	5	6	7	8	9	10*	11							12	2								9
1		3	4	5	6	7	8*	9		11				10			12	2								10
1		3	4	5	6*	7		9		11			10				8	12		2						11
1		3	4	5		8*	10	9		7			6				12		2	11						12
1		3		5				9		7		2	4	10		11	6	8								13
1		3		5		4		9		7		2		10		11	6	8								14
1		3		5		10		9		7		2		4		11	6	8								15
1		3		5		4		9		7		2		10		11	6	8								16
1		3		5		10		9		7*		2		4		11	6	8		12						17
1		3		5		10		9		7		2		4		11*	6	8		12						18
1		3		5		10		9		7*		2		4		11	6	8		12						19
			3					9	8	7		2		4		11	6			10	1	5				20
					3			9	8			2		10			6	11*	12	7	1	5			4	21
		3	4					9	8	7*		2		10		11	6			12	1	5				22
1		3			2			9					10	8			6		5	7			4	11		23
1		3				10		9		7		2				11	6			8		5	4			24
1		3		5	4	10		9	8	7		2				11	6									25
1		3		5		8		9	4	7		2				11	6			10						26
1		3		5	4	8		9	10	7		2					6			11						27
1		3		5	6	8		9	4	7		2				11				10						28
1		3		5		10		9	4	7		2					6		11	8						29
1		3		5		8		9	4	7*			12	2			6		11	10						30
		3		5		8		9	4	7		2		10			6			11	1					31
		3		5	4	8		9		12		2*		10			6		7	11	1					32
		3		5	4	8		9	12	7*				10			6		2	11	1					33
		3		5	4	8		9		12				10		7*	6		2	11	1					34
		3		5	4	8		9	12	7				10			6	2		11	1*					35
1	2	3		5		8		9		7				4			6			11					10	36
1	2	3	12	5		8		9		7				4*			6			11					10	37
1	2	3	4	5		8		9		7							6			11*			12		10	38
1		3	4	5		8			9							10	6	7		11			2			39
1	2	3		5		8		9		7				4*			6			11			12		10	40
1		3		5	2	8		9		7							6			11			4		10	41
1		12		5	2	8		9		7				3			6*			11			4		10	42
34	7	39	16	37	19	37	11	41	20	37	1	22	6	22		16	30	12	7	23	8	4	5	1	7	
		1	1						2	2			1	1	1		4	1	1	4			2			
		2	1	2	1	5	1	13	1	4				4		4	3	5		6					2	

1 own-goal

1		3		5	4	8		9	10	7		2					6			11						3
1		3		5		8		9	4*	7		2				12	6		11	10						4
2		2		2	1	2		2	2	2		2					2		1	2						
																1										
		1						2									1									

1	2	3	4	5	6	7	8	9	10	11																2
1	2	3	4	5	6	7	8	9	10*	11								12								R
1		3	4	5	6	7		9		11			10				8	2								3
1		3		5		10		9		7*		2	12	4		11	6	8								4
1		3		5		10		9		7		2		4		11	6	8								5
1		3	12	5*		10		9		7		2		4		11	6	8								SF
		12	4		3*			9	7	10		2		8		11	6				1	5				
1		3				8		9	10	7		2				11	6		4*			5	12			F
7	2	7	4	6	4	7	2	8	4	8		5	1	4		5	6	4	1		1	2				
		1	1										1					1					1			
						1	3	6		3						1	1	4								

1969-70

Manager: Harry Potts until February, then Jimmy Adamson

1	Aug	9	(a)	Derby C	D 0-0		29,451
2		13	(a)	Tottenham H	L 0-4		35,920
3		16	(h)	Sunderland	W 3-0	Casper 2, Kindon	13,409
4		19	(h)	Tottenham H	L 0-2		19,485
5		23	(a)	Liverpool	D 3-3	Thomas, Casper, Dobson	51,113
6		26	(h)	Leeds U	D 1-1	O'Neil	28,141
7		30	(h)	Manchester C	D 1-1	Dobson	26,342
8	Sep	6	(a)	Southampton	D 1-1	O'Neil	19,339
9		13	(h)	Arsenal	L 0-1		14,721
10		17	(a)	Chelsea	L 0-2		24,904
11		20	(a)	Wolves	D 1-1	Casper	27,556
12		27	(h)	Ipswich T	L 0-1		12,366
13	Oct	4	(a)	West Ham U	L 1-3	Kindon	26,445
14		8	(a)	Sunderland	W 1-0	Coates	20,311
15		11	(h)	Crystal P	W 4-2	Wrigley, Coates, Casper, Dobson	12,661
16		18	(h)	Sheffield W	W 4-2	Murray, Robson, Collins, Kindon	13,202
17		25	(a)	Nottingham F	D 1-1	Kindon	19,771
18	Nov	1	(h)	Newcastle U	L 0-1		16,444
19		8	(a)	Stoke C	L 1-2	Casper	18,437
20		15	(h)	Coventry C	D 0-0		11,428
21		22	(a)	Everton	L 1-2	Coates	46,380
22		29	(h)	Manchester U	D 1-1	Nulty	23,770
23	Dec	6	(a)	West Brom A	W 1-0	Kindon	18,512
24		13	(a)	Arsenal	L 2-3	Kindon, Storey (og)	21,404
25		26	(h)	Liverpool	L 1-5	O'Neil	22,954
26	Jan	6	(a)	Manchester C	D 1-1	Dobson	22,074
27		10	(h)	Wolves	L 1-3	Coates	13,193
28		17	(a)	Ipswich T	W 1-0	Casper	17,801
29		31	(h)	West Ham U	W 3-2	Coates, Thomas, Kindon	14,494
30	Feb	11	(a)	Crystal P	W 2-1	Kindon, Loughlan (og)	20,857
31		14	(h)	Derby C	D 1-1	Casper	18,470
32		21	(h)	Nottingham F	W 5-0	Kindon 3, Bellamy, Chapman (og)	11,185
33		28	(a)	Sheffield W	L 0-2		23,102
34	Mar	7	(h)	Everton	L 1-2	Kindon	21,114
35		17	(a)	Manchester U	D 3-3	Thomas 2, Kindon	38,337
36		21	(h)	West Brom A	W 2-1	Bellamy, Kindon	12,801
37		24	(h)	Southampton	D 1-1	Bellamy	11,166
38		27	(h)	Stoke C	D 1-1	Probert	16,109
39		28	(a)	Coventry C	D 1-1	Kindon	24,713
40		30	(a)	Newcastle U	W 1-0	Moncur (og)	33,264
41	Apr	4	(a)	Leeds U	L 1-2	Faulkner (og)	24,671
42		15	(h)	Chelsea	W 3-1	Kindon 2, Dobson	12,033

FINAL LEAGUE POSITION: 14th in Division One

Appearances
Sub Appearances
Goals

FA Cup

3	Jan	3	(h)	Wolves	W 3-0	O'Neil, Dobson, Casper	19,397
4		24	(a)	Chelsea	D 2-2	Dobson 2	48,282
R		27	(h)	Chelsea	L 1-3*	Coates	32,000

*After extra-time

Appearances
Sub Appearances
Goals

League Cup

2	Sep	3	(a)	Stoke C	W 2-0	Thomas, Kindon	19,294
3		24	(a)	Rotherham U	D 1-1	Dobson	10,969
R		30	(h)	Rotherham U	W 2-0	Nulty, Dobson	10,319
4	Oct	15	(h)	Manchester U	D 0-0		27,959
R		20	(a)	Manchester U	L 0-1		50,275

Appearances
Sub Appearances
Goals

Mellor P	Angus J	Latcham L	O'Neil B	Waldron C	Todd S	Thomas D	Coates R	Casper F	Docherty M	Kindon S	Probert E	Nulty G	Collins D	Bellamy A	Merrington D	Dobson M	Wilson D	Wrigley W	Murray J	Jones P	Blant C	Thomson J	Ternent R	West A	Kinsella L	Smith F	
1*	2	3	4	5	6	7	8	9	10	11	12																1
1	2	3	4	5	6	7	8	9	10	11																	2
1		3	4	5	6	7*	8	9	2	11	10	12															3
1		3	4	5	6	7	8	9	2	11			10*	12													4
1	2	3	4		6	7	8	9		11					5	10											5
1	2	3	4		6	7	8	9		11					5	10											6
1	2	3	4		6	7	8	9		11					5	10											7
1	2	3	4		6	7*	8	9		11				12	5	10											8
1	2	3	4	5	6	7*	8	9		11						10	12										9
1	2	3	4	5	6	7*	8	9		11	12					10											10
1	2	3	4	5	6	7	8	9		11						10											11
1	2	3	4	5	6	7*	8	9		11		12				10											12
1	2	3	4		6	7	8	9		11					5	10											13
1	2	3				7	8	9		11	6			4	5	10											14
1	2	3					8	9		11	6*		12	4		10		5	7								15
1		3	12	5		7*	8	9		11			10			6			4	2							16
1		3	7		6		8	9	2	11			10	4		5											17
1		3	4		6		8	9	2	11			7	10		5											18
1	3		4	5	6	7	8	9	2	11				10													19
1	3	2	4	5		12	8	9		11*	7			10							6						20
1	3*	6	4			7	8		2	11	9			10		5						12					21
1		3	4			7*	8		2	11		9		10		5	12		6								22
1		6	4			7	8		2	11		9			3	5			10								23
1		3	4			7	8		2	11		9		12	6	5			10*								24
1		3	4			10	8	12	2	11		9			6	5			7*								25
1			4				8	7		11				10	6	5	9					3				2	26
1			4			12	8	7		11*				10	6	5	9					3				2	27
1	2		4		6		8	7		11				10		5	9					3					28
1	2		4			10	8	7		11					6	5	9					3					29
1	2		4				8	7		11				10	6	5	9					3					30
1	2		4		12	10	8	7		11					6*	5	9					3					31
1	2		4		6	10	8	7		11				9		5						3					32
1	2		4		6	10	8	7		11				9		5						3					33
1	2		4		6	10	8	7		11				9		5						3					34
1	2		6		4	7		9		11				8	5	10						3					35
1	2		4		6	10	8	7		11				9		5						3					36
1	2		4		6	10	8	7		11				9		5						3					37
1						7	8		2	11	10	9				5		4					3	6			38
1			4	6	12	10	8	7	2	11	9					5						3*					39
1	2			4	6	10	8	7	3	11	9					5											40
1	2		12	4	6	10		7	3	11	9			8*		5											41
1	2			4		7		9		11	10		8			5							3		6		42
42	29	24	35	15	25	34	39	36	16	42	10	5	5	19	15	36	6	2	6	1	1	13	2	1	1	2	
			2		2	2		1			2	2	1	3			2					1					
			3			4	5	8		17	1	1	1	3		6		1	1								

5 own-goals

Mellor P	Angus J	Latcham L	O'Neil B	Waldron C	Todd S	Thomas D	Coates R	Casper F	Docherty M	Kindon S	Probert E	Nulty G	Collins D	Bellamy A	Merrington D	Dobson M	Wilson D	Wrigley W	Murray J	Jones P	Blant C	Thomson J	Ternent R	West A	Kinsella L	Smith F	
1			4				8	7		11				10	6	5	9					3				2	3
1	2		4				8	7		11				10	6	5	9					3					4
1	2	12	4				8	7		11				10	6	5	9*					3					R
3	2		3				3	3		3				3	3	3	3					3				1	
		1																									
			1				1	1								3											

Mellor P	Angus J	Latcham L	O'Neil B	Waldron C	Todd S	Thomas D	Coates R	Casper F	Docherty M	Kindon S	Probert E	Nulty G	Collins D	Bellamy A	Merrington D	Dobson M	Wilson D	Wrigley W	Murray J	Jones P	Blant C	Thomson J	Ternent R	West A	Kinsella L	Smith F	
1	2	3	4		6	7	8	9		11					5	10											2
1	2	3	4	5	6	7	8	9		11						10											3
1	2	3	4		6		7	9		11		8			5	10											R
1	2	3				7	8	9		11			10	4		5				6							4
1	2*	3	7				8	9	12	11			10	4		5				6							R
5	5	5	4	1	3	3	5	5		5		1	2	2	2	5				2							
									1																		
						1				1		1				2											

1970-71

Manager: Jimmy Adamson

1	Aug	15	(h)	Liverpool	L 1-2	Thomas	25,783
2		18	(a)	Everton	D 1-1	Thomas	44,717
3		22	(a)	Manchester C	D 0-0		36,599
4		25	(h)	Manchester U	L 0-2		29,422
5		29	(h)	Leeds U	L 0-3		26,057
6	Sep	1	(h)	Chelsea	D 0-0		14,580
7		5	(a)	Ipswich T	L 0-3		15,993
8		12	(h)	Arsenal	L 1-2	Roberts (og)	12,710
9		19	(a)	Derby C	L 0-1		26,749
10		26	(h)	Wolves	L 2-3	Waldron, Thomas (pen)	13,056
11	Oct	3	(a)	West Ham U	L 1-3	Coates	23,295
12		10	(h)	Coventry C	D 0-0		12,549
13		17	(a)	Liverpool	L 0-2		40,804
14		24	(a)	Southampton	L 0-2		19,709
15		31	(h)	Crystal P	W 2-1	Probert 2	12,870
16	Nov	7	(a)	Tottenham H	L 0-4		30,524
17		14	(h)	Huddersfield T	L 2-3	West, Kindon	18,150
18		21	(h)	Nottingham F	W 2-1	Nulty, Probert	13,013
19		28	(a)	Newcastle U	L 1-3	Probert	20,994
20	Dec	5	(h)	West Brom A	D 1-1	Kindon	12,477
21		12	(a)	Stoke C	D 0-0		13,300
22		19	(h)	Manchester C	L 0-4		19,917
23		26	(a)	Blackpool	D 1-1	Casper	28,371
24	Jan	9	(h)	Everton	D 2-2	Dobson, Casper	17,512
25		16	(a)	Manchester U	D 1-1	Dobson	38,796
26		30	(a)	Newcastle U	D 1-1	Probert	12,553
27	Feb	6	(a)	West Brom A	L 0-1		16,982
28		20	(a)	Nottingham F	L 0-1		20,873
29		23	(h)	Stoke C	D 1-1	Dobson	12,243
30		27	(a)	Crystal P	W 2-0	Dobson, Coates	20,436
31	Mar	6	(h)	Southampton	L 0-1		15,786
32		13	(a)	Huddersfield T	W 1-0	Waldron	18,793
33		20	(h)	Tottenham H	D 0-0		16,376
34		27	(h)	Ipswich T	D 2-2	Nulty, Casper	13,479
35	Apr	3	(a)	Leeds U	L 0-4		31,192
36		10	(h)	Blackpool	W 1-0	Fletcher	14,539
37		13	(h)	West Ham U	W 1-0	Nulty	15,841
38		17	(a)	Coventry C	L 0-3		18,365
39		20	(a)	Arsenal	L 0-1		47,591
40		24	(h)	Derby C	L 1-2	Casper	10,373
41		26	(a)	Chelsea	W 1-0	Kindon	14,356
42	May	1	(a)	Wolves	L 0-1		19,612

FINAL LEAGUE POSITION: 21st in Division One (Relegated)

Appearances
Sub Appearances
Goals

FA Cup

3	Jan	11	(a)	Oxford U	L 0-3		17,010

Appearances
Sub Appearances
Goals

League Cup

2	Sep	9	(a)	Aston Villa	L 0-2		28,389

Appearances
Sub Appearances
Goals

Waiters A	Angus J	Latcham L	Bellamy A	Waldron C	Thomson J	Thomas D	Coates R	Nulty G	Collins D	Kindon S	Merrington D	Probert E	Docherty M	Ternent R	Casper F	West A	Wilson D	Cliff E	Mellor P	Dobson M	James L	Welch R	Fletcher P	Wilson H	
1	2	3	4	5	6	7	8	9	10	11															1
1	2		4	5	6	7	8			11	3	9	10												2
1	2		4	5	6	7	8			11	3	9	10												3
1	2		4*	5	6	7	8		12	11	3	9	10												4
1	2		4	5	6	7	8			11	3	9	10												5
1	2			5	6	7	8			11		10	4	3	9										6
1	2		12	5	6	7	8			11		10	4	3	9*										7
1	2			5	6	7	8		10	11	3		4		9										8
1	2			5	6	7	8	11	10		3		4		9										9
1	2*			5	6	7	8	11	10		3		4		9	12									10
1	2			5		7	8	12			3	6*	4		9	11	10								11
1	2		11	5	3	7	8						4		9	6	10								12
1			11	5	3		8	2		7			4		9	6	10								13
1			4	5		7	8	6		11		9	2			10		3							14
1			4	5		7	8	6		11		9	2			10		3							15
1		12	4	5		7	8	6		11		9	2*			10		3							16
1				5		7	8	6		11		9		2	4	10		3							17
	2			5		7	8	3				9	4			10			1	6	11				18
	2			5		7		8	11		3	9	4			10			1	6					19
	2			5		7		3	10	8		9	4						1	6	11				20
	2			5		7		3	10	8*		9	4			11			1	6	12				21
	2			5		7	8	3	10			9	4			12			1	6	11*				22
1	2			5		7	8	3				9	4		11	10				6					23
1	2			5		7	8	3			12	9	4		11*	10				6					24
1	2			5		7	8			10	3	9	4		11*		12			6					25
1	2	3		5		7	8	9		11		10								6		4			26
1	2	3	4	5			8	9		11		10	12		7*					6					27
1	2	3	9	5		7	8			11		10	4							6					28
1	2	3	9	5		7	8			11		10	4							6					29
1	2	3	9	5		7	8	4		11		10								6					30
1	2	3	7	5			8	4		11		10								6			9		31
1	2	3	10	5		7	8	4		11										6			9		32
1	2	3	10	5		7*	8	4	12	11										6			9		33
1	2*	3	10	5			8	4	12	11					7					6			9		34
1		3	10				8	4		11		5	2		7					6			9		35
1	2	3	4			7*	8	6		11			12		10					5			9		36
1	2	3	10				8	6	11				4		7					5			9		37
1	2	3	10				8	6	11			12	4		7*					5			9		38
	12	3	10	2		7		6	8			11	4*						1	5			9		39
	2	3	8				7	6	11			4			10		9		1	5					40
1	2					7	8	6	10	11		4			9					5				3	41
1	2					7	8	6	11	10		4			9					5				3	42
35	35	16	24	35	12	34	38	30	14	29	10	30	29	3	21	12	4	4	7	25	3	1	9	2	
	1	1	1					1	3		1	1	2			2	1				1				
				2		3	2	3		3		5			4	1				4			1		

1 own-goal

Waiters A	Angus J	Latcham L	Bellamy A	Waldron C	Thomson J	Thomas D	Coates R	Nulty G	Collins D	Kindon S	Merrington D	Probert E	Docherty M	Ternent R	Casper F	West A	Wilson D	Cliff E	Mellor P	Dobson M	James L	Welch R	Fletcher P	Wilson H	
1	2			5		7	8	3			12	9	4			10				6	11*				3
1	1			1		1	1	1				1	1			1				1	1				
											1														

Waiters A	Angus J	Latcham L	Bellamy A	Waldron C	Thomson J	Thomas D	Coates R	Nulty G	Collins D	Kindon S	Merrington D	Probert E	Docherty M	Ternent R	Casper F	West A	Wilson D	Cliff E	Mellor P	Dobson M	James L	Welch R	Fletcher P	Wilson H	
1	2		9	5	6	7	8		12	11		10*	4	3											2
1	1		1	1	1	1	1			1		1	1	1											
									1																

1971-72

Manager: Jimmy Adamson

1	Aug	14	(a)	Cardiff C	D 2-2	Dobson, Casper	23,004
2		21	(h)	Luton T	W 2-1	Casper, Kindon	13,365
3		28	(a)	Oxford U	L 1-2	Casper	8,978
4		30	(a)	Preston NE	W 3-1	Waldron (pen), Casper, Kindon	27,284
5	Sep	4	(h)	Bristol C	D 1-1	Bellamy	13,634
6		11	(a)	Fulham	W 2-0	James 2	10,395
7		18	(h)	Queen's Park R	W 1-0	Bellamy	13,795
8		25	(a)	Charlton A	L 0-2		8,920
9		28	(h)	Orient	W 6-1	Bellamy 3, Thomas, Fletcher, James	12,433
10	Oct	2	(h)	Sunderland	L 0-1		16,496
11		9	(a)	Carlisle U	W 3-0	Casper 2, James	11,625
12		13	(a)	Norwich C	L 0-3		24,356
13		16	(h)	Cardiff C	W 3-0	Casper 2 (1 pen), Thomas	12,494
14		23	(a)	Hull C	W 2-1	Fletcher, James	15,469
15		30	(h)	Birmingham C	D 1-1	Casper (pen)	17,170
16	Nov	6	(a)	Sheffield W	L 1-2	West	23,398
17		13	(h)	Middlesbrough	W 5-2	James 2, Nulty, Bellamy, Dobson	15,720
18		20	(a)	Watford	L 1-2	Casper	11,538
19		27	(h)	Swindon T	L 1-2	Dobson	12,329
20	Dec	4	(a)	Millwall	D 1-1	West	14,747
21		11	(h)	Portsmouth	L 1-3	Waldron	11,381
22		18	(a)	Bristol C	W 2-0	Fletcher 2	12,909
23		27	(h)	Blackpool	W 2-1	Dobson, Kindon	22,015
24	Jan	1	(a)	Queen's Park R	L 1-3	Fletcher	14,614
25		8	(h)	Oxford U	D 1-1	Kindon	10,971
26		22	(a)	Orient	L 0-1		9,231
27		29	(h)	Norwich C	W 1-0	Casper (pen)	13,713
28	Feb	12	(h)	Hull C	L 0-2		11,751
29		19	(a)	Birmingham C	L 0-2		32,035
30		26	(h)	Sheffield W	W 5-3	Fletcher 2, Thomas, Casper, James	10,617
31	Mar	4	(a)	Middlesbrough	L 0-1		17,069
32		11	(h)	Carlisle U	W 3-1	Thomas, Fletcher, Collins	10,346
33		18	(a)	Luton T	L 0-1		8,490
34		25	(h)	Fulham	D 1-1	Collins	10,107
35	Apr	1	(a)	Blackpool	L 2-4	Casper 2 (1 pen)	15,931
36		3	(a)	Sunderland	L 3-4	Dobson, Casper, Probert	14,034
37		4	(h)	Charlton A	W 3-1	Casper 2, Fletcher	9,385
38		8	(h)	Watford	W 3-0	Dobson 2, Casper	8,695
39		15	(a)	Swindon T	W 1-0	Probert	11,818
40		22	(h)	Millwall	W 2-0	Dobson, Fletcher	11,271
41		25	(h)	Preston NE	W 1-0	Probert	13,067
42		29	(a)	Portsmouth	W 2-1	Dobson, Thomson	5,885

FINAL LEAGUE POSITION: 7th in Division Two

Appearances
Sub Appearances
Goals

FA Cup

3	Jan	15	(h)	Huddersfield T	L 0-1		21,563

Appearances
Sub Appearances
Goals

League Cup

2	Sep	7	(a)	Coventry C	W 1-0	Casper	15,413
3	Oct	6	(a)	Manchester U	D 1-1	James	44,600
R		18	(h)	Manchester U	L 0-1		27,511

Appearances
Sub Appearances
Goals

Waiters A	Angus J	Wilson H	Bellamy A	Waldron C	Dobson M	Thomas D	West A	Fletcher P	Casper F	Kindon S	Docherty M	Cliff E	Collins D	Mellor P	James L	Probert E	Nulty G	Parton J	Thomson J	Stevenson A	Ingham W	Rodaway W	
1	2	3	4	5	6	7	8	9	10	11													1
1	2	3	4	5	6	7	8	9	10	11													2
1			4	5	6	7	8*	9	10	11	2	3	12										3
			4	5	6	7	8	9	10	11	2	3		1									4
			4*	5	6	7	8	9	10	11	2	3	12	1									5
			4	5	6	7	8	9	10		2	3		1	11								6
			4	5	6	7	8	9	10	12	2	3		1	11*								7
			4	5	6	7	8	9*	10	12	2	3		1	11								8
			4	5	6	7	8	9	10		2	3		1	11								9
			4	5	6	7	8	9	10	12	2	3		1	11*								10
			4	5	6	7	8	9	10		2	3		1	11								11
			4*	5	6	7	8	9	10	12	2	3		1	11								12
			4	5	6	7	8	9	10		2	3		1	11								13
			4	5	6	7	8	9	10		2	3		1	11								14
			4	5	6	7	8	9	10		2	3		1	11								15
			4	5	6	7	8	9*	10		2	3		1	11	12							16
			4*	5	6	7	8	9	10	12	2			1	11		3						17
			12	5	6	7		9	10	8	2				11	4*	3	1					18
			12	5	6	7	4	9	10	11*	2				8		3	1					19
			4	5	6	7	8	9	10		2			1	11		3						20
			4	5	6	7	8	9	10		2			1	11		3						21
			4	5	6	7	8	9		10	2			1	11				3				22
			4*	5	6	7	8	9	12	10	2			1	11				3				23
			12	5	6	7*	4	9	8	10	2			1	11				3				24
				5	6	7	4	9	8	10	2			1	11				3				25
				5	6	7	4	9	8	10	2				11				3	1			26
				5	6	7	4	9	8	10	2				11				3	1			27
				5	6	7	4*	9	8	10	2				11				3	1	12		28
		3	12	5	6	7	4*	9	8		2				11	10				1			29
		3	4	5	6	7*		9	8		2		12		11	10				1			30
		3*	4	5	6			9	8	12	2		7		11	10				1			31
		3	4	5	6	7*		9	8		2		12		11	10				1			32
		3	4	5	6	7*		9	8		2		12		11	10				1			33
		3*	4	5	6			9		7	2		8		11	10				1	12		34
		3		5	6	7		9	4		2		8		11	10				1			35
		3	4	5	6			9	8		2					10			11	1	7		36
				5	6			9	8		2				11	10	3		4	1	7		37
				5	4			9	8*	12	2				11	10	3		6	1	7		38
				5	4			9	8		2				11	10	3		6	1	7		39
				5	4			9	8		2				11	10	3		6	1	7		40
					4			9	8		2				11	10	3		5	1	7	6	41
					4			9	8		2				11	10	3		5	1	7	6	42
3	2	10	27	40	42	33	28	42	39	15	40	14	3	20	36	15	11	2	14	17	7	2	
			4						1	7			5			1					2		
			6	2	9	4	2	10	18	4			2		8	3	1		1				

Waiters A	Angus J	Wilson H	Bellamy A	Waldron C	Dobson M	Thomas D	West A	Fletcher P	Casper F	Kindon S	Docherty M	Cliff E	Collins D	Mellor P	James L	Probert E	Nulty G	Parton J	Thomson J	Stevenson A	Ingham W	Rodaway W	
				5	6	7	4	9	8	10	2			1	11				3				3
				1	1	1	1	1	1	1	1			1	1				1				

Waiters A	Angus J	Wilson H	Bellamy A	Waldron C	Dobson M	Thomas D	West A	Fletcher P	Casper F	Kindon S	Docherty M	Cliff E	Collins D	Mellor P	James L	Probert E	Nulty G	Parton J	Thomson J	Stevenson A	Ingham W	Rodaway W	
			4	5	6	7	8	9	10		2	3		1	11								2
			4	5	6	7*	8	9	10	12	2	3		1	11								3
				5	6	7	8	9	10		2	3		1	11	4							R
			2	3	3	3	3	3	3		3	3		3	3	1							
										1													
									1						1								

1972-73

Manager: Jimmy Adamson

1	Aug	12	(h)	Carlisle U	D 2-2	Thomas, James	9,834
2		19	(a)	Fulham	D 1-1	James	10,285
3		26	(h)	Aston Villa	W 4-1	Dobson, Casper, Fletcher, Collins	14,941
4		29	(h)	Preston NE	W 2-0	Thomas, James	13,205
5	Sep	2	(a)	Portsmouth	W 2-0	Thomas, Fletcher	11,701
6		9	(h)	Queen's Park R	D 1-1	Casper	10,896
7		16	(a)	Hull C	D 1-1	James	8,921
8		18	(a)	Orient	D 1-1	Casper	4,924
9		23	(h)	Blackpool	W 4-3	Dobson, Waldron, Thomas, James	14,625
10		26	(h)	Middlesbrough	D 0-0		12,398
11		30	(a)	Luton T	D 2-2	James 2	12,197
12	Oct	7	(h)	Swindon T	W 2-1	Dobson, Fletcher	11,434
13		14	(a)	Sheffield W	W 1-0	James	30,394
14		21	(h)	Cardiff C	W 3-0	Fletcher 3 (1 pen)	13,442
15		28	(a)	Millwall	D 1-1	Fletcher	11,622
16	Nov	4	(a)	Middlesbrough	D 3-3	Dobson, Waldron, Fletcher	18,127
17		11	(h)	Orient •	L 1-2	Dobson	12,090
18		18	(a)	Brighton & HA	W 1-0	Dobson	17,470
19		25	(h)	Nottingham F	W 1-0	Fletcher	12,095
20	Dec	2	(a)	Sunderland	W 1-0	Fletcher	16,812
21		16	(a)	Bristol C	W 1-0	Dobson	15,334
22		23	(h)	Oxford U	D 1-1	Waldron	12,808
23		26	(a)	Blackpool	W 2-1	Casper 2	25,277
24		30	(h)	Fulham	D 2-2	Nulty, Pentecost (og)	15,512
25	Jan	6	(a)	Aston Villa	W 3-0	Newton, Nulty, Ingham	38,637
26		27	(a)	Queen's Park R	L 0-2		22,518
27	Feb	3	(h)	Huddersfield T	W 2-1	Nulty, Ingham	14,589
28		10	(h)	Hull U	W 4-1	Dobson, Nulty, Casper, Ingham	13,760
29		17	(a)	Carlisle U	D 1-1	Dobson	17,840
30		24	(h)	Bristol C	D 1-1	Dobson	13,630
31	Mar	2	(a)	Swindon T	W 1-0	Fletcher	12,730
32		10	(h)	Sheffield W	L 0-1		16,968
33		17	(a)	Cardiff C	W 1-0	Casper	11,343
34		20	(h)	Portsmouth	W 4-0	Casper 2, Nulty, Fletcher	13,610
35		24	(h)	Millwall	W 2-1	Dobson, Nulty	13,656
36		31	(a)	Nottingham F	L 0-3		12,552
37	Apr	14	(a)	Huddersfield T	W 2-0	Casper, Fletcher	13,437
38		16	(h)	Sunderland	W 2-0	Fletcher 2	22,852
39		20	(a)	Oxford U	W 2-0	Casper, Ingham	13,740
40		21	(h)	Brighton & HA	W 3-0	Dobson, Casper, James	15,968
41		24	(h)	Luton T	W 3-0	Thomson, Collins, James	17,708
42		28	(a)	Preston NE	D 1-1	Waldron	21,550

FINAL LEAGUE POSITION: 1st in Division Two (Promoted)

Appearances
Sub Appearances
Goals

FA Cup

3	Jan	13	(h)	Liverpool	D 0-0	35,730
R		16	(a)	Liverpool	L 0-3	56,124

Appearances
Sub Appearances
Goals

League Cup

2	Sep	6	(a)	Leeds U	L 0-4	20,857

Appearances
Sub Appearances
Goals

Stevenson A	Docherty M	Newton K	Dobson M	Waldron C	Thomson J	Ingham W	Casper F	Fletcher P	Thomas D	James L	West A	Collins D	Nulty G	Cliff E	Probert E	Hankin R	
1	2	3	4	5	6	7*	8	9	10	11	12						1
1	2	3	4	5	6		8	9	7	11		10					2
1	2	3	4	5	6	12	8	9	7	11*		10					3
1	2	3	4	5	6		8	9	7	11		10					4
1	2	3	4	5	6		8	9	7	11		10					5
1	2	3	4	5	6		8	9	7	11		10					6
1	2	3	4	5	6		8	9	7	11		10					7
1	2	3	4	5	6		8	9	7*	11		10	12				8
1	2	3	4	5	6		8	9	7	11		10*	12				9
1	2	3		5	6	10	8	9	7	11			4				10
1	2	3	4	5	6		8	9	7*	11		10	12				11
1	2	3	4	5	6		8	9		11		10	7				12
1	2	3	4	5	6		8	9		11		10	7				13
1	2	3	4	5	6		8	9		11		10	7				14
1	2	3	4	5	6		8	9		11		10	7				15
1	2	3	4	5	6		8	9		11		10	7				16
1	2	3	4*	5	6		8	9		11	12	10	7				17
1	2	3	4	5	6		8	9		11		10	7				18
1	2	3	4	5	6		8	9		11		10	7				19
1	2	3	4	5	6		8	9		11		10	7				20
1	2	3	4	5	6		8	9		11		10	7				21
1	2	3	4	5	6		8	9		11		10	7				22
1	2	3	4	5	6		8	9		11		10	7				23
1	2	3	4	5	6		8	9		11		10	7				24
1	2	3	4	5	6	10	8	9		11			7				25
1	2	3	4	5	6	12	8	9		11		10*	7				26
1	2	3	4	5	6	12	8	9*		11		10	7				27
1	2	3	4	5	6	9	8			11		10	7				28
1		3	4	5	6	9	8			11		10	7	2			29
1		3	4	5	6		8	9		11		10	7	2			30
1	2	3	4	5	6		8	9		11		10	7				31
1	2	3	4	5	6	12	8	9		11		10*	7				32
1	2	3	4	5	6	10	8	9		11			7				33
1	2	3*	4	5	6		8	9		11		10	7		12		34
1	2	3	4	5	6	12	8	9		11		10*	7				35
1	2	3	4	5	6	12	8	9		11		10*	7				36
1	2*	3	4	5	6	12	8	9		11		10	7				37
1		3	4	5	6	2	8	9		11		10	7				38
1		3	4	5	6	10	8	9		11			7	2			39
1		3	4	5	6	2	8	9		11		10	7				40
1		3	4	5	6	2	8*	9		11		10	7			12	41
1		3	4	5	6	2	8	9		11		10	7				42
42	35	42	41	42	42	11	42	40	11	42		37	32	3			
						7					2		3		1	1	
		1	12	4	1	4	12	15	4	10		2	6				

1 own-goal

Stevenson A	Docherty M	Newton K	Dobson M	Waldron C	Thomson J	Ingham W	Casper F	Fletcher P	Thomas D	James L	West A	Collins D	Nulty G	Cliff E	Probert E	Hankin R	
1	2	3	4	5	6	10	8	9		11			7				3
1	2	3	4	5	6	12	8	9		11		10*	7				R
2	2	2	2	2	2	1	2	2		2		1	2				
						1											

Stevenson A	Docherty M	Newton K	Dobson M	Waldron C	Thomson J	Ingham W	Casper F	Fletcher P	Thomas D	James L	West A	Collins D	Nulty G	Cliff E	Probert E	Hankin R	
1	2	3	4*	5	6		8	9	7	11		10	12				2
1	1	1	1	1	1		1	1	1	1		1					
													1				

1973-74

Manager: Jimmy Adamson

1	Aug	25	(a)	Sheffield U	W 2-0	Dobson, Collins	25,803
2		28	(h)	Chelsea	W 1-0	Casper	23,899
3	Sep	1	(h)	Coventry C	D 2-2	Dobson, Fletcher	20,683
4		5	(a)	Tottenham H	W 3-2	Collins, James, Casper (pen)	25,543
5		8	(a)	Wolves	W 2-0	Nulty, Casper	25,382
6		11	(h)	Tottenham H	D 2-2	Waldron, Nulty	25,158
7		15	(h)	Derby C	D 1-1	Hankin	24,493
8		22	(a)	Ipswich T	L 2-3	Collins, James	19,126
9		29	(h)	Manchester C	W 3-0	Fletcher 2, Dobson	24,147
10	Oct	6	(a)	West Ham U	W 1-0	Waldron	23,604
11		13	(h)	Queen's Park R	W 2-1	Nulty, Hankin	18,349
12		20	(a)	Everton	L 0-1		41,018
13		27	(h)	Manchester U	D 0-0		31,810
14	Nov	3	(a)	Southampton	D 2-2	Hankin, Fletcher	21,541
15		10	(h)	Leeds U	D 0-0		40,087
16		17	(a)	Leicester C	L 0-2		21,761
17		24	(h)	Stoke C	W 1-0	Fletcher	14,550
18	Dec	8	(h)	Norwich C	W 1-0	Ingham	13,246
19		15	(h)	Arsenal	W 2-1	Waldron, Hankin	13,169
20		22	(a)	Manchester C	L 0-2		28,114
21		26	(h)	Liverpool	W 2-1	Hankin, Fletcher	24,000
22		29	(h)	Wolves	D 1-1	Fletcher	20,196
23	Jan	1	(a)	Coventry C	D 1-1	Nulty	24,876
24		12	(a)	Derby C	L 1-5	James	24,948
25		19	(h)	Sheffield U	L 1-2	Hankin	18,878
26	Feb	2	(a)	Arsenal	D 1-1	Brady (og)	20,910
27		9	(h)	Ipswich T	L 0-1		15,497
28		23	(h)	West Ham U	D 1-1	Nulty	18,258
29		27	(a)	Queen's Park R	L 1-2	Casper	21,306
30	Mar	2	(a)	Liverpool	L 0-1		42,562
31		13	(a)	Chelsea	L 0-3		8,171
32		16	(h)	Everton	W 3-1	Waldron, Nulty, James	19,365
33		23	(a)	Leeds U	W 4-1	Fletcher 2, Nulty, Collins	39,453
34	Apr	3	(a)	Manchester U	D 3-3	James 2 (2 pens), Fletcher	33,336
35		6	(a)	Stoke C	L 0-4		19,253
36		10	(a)	Newcastle U	W 2-1	Dobson, Nulty	30,168
37		12	(h)	Birmingham C	W 2-1	Hankin 2	17,038
38		13	(h)	Leicester C	D 0-0		18,115
39		16	(a)	Birmingham C	D 2-2	Fletcher, Ingham	36,548
40		20	(a)	Norwich C	L 0-1		17,782
41		22	(h)	Southampton	W 3-0	Nulty, Fletcher, James	15,222
42		27	(h)	Newcastle U	D 1-1	Fletcher	17,145

FINAL LEAGUE POSITION: 6th in Division One

Appearances
Sub Appearances
Goals

FA Cup

3	Jan	5	(a)	Grimsby T	W 2-0	Newton, Hankin	14,152
4		26	(a)	Oldham A	W 4-1	Dobson 2, Fletcher, James	26,000
5	Feb	16	(h)	Aston Villa	W 1-0	Fletcher	29,301
6	Apr	9	(h)	Wrexham	W 1-0	Casper	35,500
SF		30	(n*)	Newcastle U	L 0-2		55,000

*Played at Hillsborough, Sheffield.

Appearances
Sub Appearances
Goals

League Cup

2	Oct	10	(a)	Cardiff C	D 2-2	James 2	8,775
R		16	(h)	Cardiff C	W 3-2	James 2, Hankin	12,397
3		30	(h)	Plymouth A	L 1-2	Hankin	11,167

Appearances
Sub Appearances
Goals

Stevenson A	Docherty M	Newton K	Dobson M	Waldron C	Thomson J	Nulty G	Casper F	Fletcher P	Collins D	James L	Noble P	Ingham W	Hankin R	Rodaway W	Flynn B	Finn M	Parton J	Brennan I	
1	2*	3	4	5	6	7	8	9	10	11	12								1
1		3	4	5	6	7	8	9	10	11	2								2
1		3	4	5	6	7	8	9*	10	11	2	12							3
1		3	4	5	6	7	8		10	11	2		9						4
1		3	4	5	6	7	8	9	10	11	2								5
1		3	4	5	6	7	8*		10	11	2	12	9						6
1		3	4	5	6	7		9	10	11	2		8						7
1		3	4	5	6	7		9	10	11	2		8						8
1		3	4	5	6	7		9	10	11	2		8						9
1		3	4	5	6	7		9	10	11	2		8						10
1		3	4	5	6	7		9	10	11*	2	12	8						11
1		3	4		5	7		9	10	11	2		8	6					12
1		3	4		5	7		9	10	11	2		8	6					13
1		3	4	5	6	7		9	10	11	2		8						14
1		3	4	5	6	7		9	10	11	2	12	8*						15
1		3	4	5	6	7		9	10	11	2	12	8*						16
1		3	4	5	6	7		9	10	11	2		8						17
1		3	4	5	6*	7		9	10	11	2	8	12						18
1		3	4	5		7		9	10	11	2	6	8						19
1		3	4	5		7		9	10	11	2	6	8						20
1		3	4	5		7		9	10	11	2	6	8						21
1		3	4	5		7		9	10	11	2	6	8						22
1		3	4	5		7		9	10	11	2	6	8						23
1		3	4	5		7		9	10	11	2	6	8						24
1		3	4	5	6	7		9	10	11	2		8						25
1		3	4	5	6	7		9	10		2	11			8				26
1		3	4	5	6	7		9	10		2	11	8						27
1		3	4	5	6	7*	12	9	10	11	2		8						28
1		3	4	5	6	7	8	9		11	2	10							29
1		3	4	5	6	7	8	9	10	11	2								30
		3	4	5	6	7	8		12	11		2	9		10*	1			31
1		3*	4	5	6	7	8		10	11	2	12	9						32
1		3	4	5	6	7	8	9	10*	11	2	12							33
		3		5	6	7		9	10	11	2	4	8				1		34
1			4	5	6	7		9	10	11	2		8					3	35
1		3	4	5		7		9		11	2	10	8	6					36
1		3	4	5		7		9	10	11	2		8	6					37
1		3	4	5		7		9	12	11*	2	10	8	6					38
1		3	4	5		7		9	10*	11	2	12	8	6					39
1			4	5	3	7		9		11	2	10	8	6					40
1			4	5	3	7		9	10	11	2		8	6					41
1		3		5		7		9	4	11	2	10	8	6					42
40	1	39	40	40	31	42	11	38	37	40	40	16	33	9	2	1	1	1	
							1		2		1	8	1						
			4	4		9	4	13	4	7		2	8						

1 own-goal

Stevenson A	Docherty M	Newton K	Dobson M	Waldron C	Thomson J	Nulty G	Casper F	Fletcher P	Collins D	James L	Noble P	Ingham W	Hankin R	Rodaway W	Flynn B	Finn M	Parton J	Brennan I	
1		3	4	5		7		9	10	11	2	6	8						3
1		3	4	5	6	7		9	10	11	2		8						4
1		3	4	5	6	7		9	10	11*	2	12	8						5
1		3	4	5	6	7	8	9	10	11		2							6
1		3	4	5	6	7	8	9	10	11	2								SF
5		5	5	5	4	5	2	5	5	5	4	2	3						
												1							
		1	2				1	2		1			1						

Stevenson A	Docherty M	Newton K	Dobson M	Waldron C	Thomson J	Nulty G	Casper F	Fletcher P	Collins D	James L	Noble P	Ingham W	Hankin R	Rodaway W	Flynn B	Finn M	Parton J	Brennan I	
1			4	5	6	7		9	10	11	2	3	8						2
1		3	4	5	6	7		9	10	11	2		8						R
1		3	4	5	6	7		9	10	11	2		8						3
3		2	3	3	3	3		3	3	3	3	1	3						
										4			2						

1974-75

Manager: Jimmy Adamson

1	Aug	17	(h)	Wolves	L 1-2	Hankin	20,187
2		21	(a)	Chelsea	D 3-3	Dobson, Hankin, Fletcher	23,745
3		24	(a)	Ipswich T	L 0-2		22,361
4		27	(h)	Chelsea	L 1-2	James (pen)	17,441
5		31	(h)	Coventry C	W 3-0	Noble, Hankin, James	14,644
6	Sep	7	(a)	Arsenal	W 1-0	Noble	23,546
7		14	(h)	Leeds U	W 2-1	Fletcher, James (pen)	25,384
8		21	(a)	Derby C	L 2-3	Todd (og), Daniel (og)	21,377
9		24	(a)	Liverpool	W 1-0	Brennan	44,639
10		28	(h)	West Ham U	L 3-5	Fletcher 2, Noble	17,644
11	Oct	5	(a)	Tottenham H	W 3-2	England (og), James, Pratt (og)	18,441
12		12	(h)	Manchester C	W 2-1	Fletcher, Clarke (og)	23,512
13		15	(h)	Ipswich T	W 1-0	Fletcher	18,011
14		19	(a)	Stoke C	L 0-2		23,561
15		26	(h)	Everton	D 1-1	Hankin	22,599
16	Nov	2	(a)	Leicester C	L 0-1		19,981
17		9	(h)	Birmingham C	D 2-2	Hankin 2	16,075
18		16	(a)	Sheffield U	D 2-2	Rodaway, Fletcher	20,784
19		23	(h)	Newcastle U	W 4-1	Noble 3, James (pen)	19,513
20		30	(a)	Luton T	W 3-2	Hankin 2, James	11,816
21	Dec	7	(h)	Queen's Park R	W 3-0	Waldron, Collins, Clement (og)	16,522
22		14	(a)	Wolves	L 2-4	James 2 (1 pen)	17,945
23		21	(h)	Middlesbrough	D 1-1	Fletcher	17,637
24		26	(a)	Leeds U	D 2-2	James 2	34,724
25		28	(h)	Carlisle U	W 2-1	Collins, James	19,729
26	Jan	11	(a)	Queen's Park R	W 1-0	Hankin	19,539
27		18	(h)	Luton T	W 1-0	Ingham	17,237
28	Feb	1	(a)	Birmingham C	D 1-1	Hankin	24,990
29		8	(h)	Leicester C	W 2-0	Newton, Hankin	16,352
30		15	(a)	Newcastle U	L 0-3		40,602
31		22	(h)	Sheffield U	W 2-1	Noble, Fletcher	18,567
32	Mar	1	(a)	Coventry C	W 3-0	Noble, Fletcher, James	17,358
33		8	(h)	Liverpool	D 1-1	Hankin	32,111
34		15	(a)	West Ham U	L 1-2	Collins	28,830
35		22	(h)	Arsenal	D 3-3	Noble, Hankin, James (pen)	17,800
36		29	(a)	Middlesbrough	L 0-2		28,922
37		31	(h)	Derby C	L 2-5	Hankin, James (pen)	24,317
38	Apr	1	(a)	Carlisle U	L 2-4	Parker, James	12,783
39		4	(a)	Everton	D 1-1	Noble	46,882
40		12	(h)	Tottenham H	W 3-2	Noble 2, James (pen)	17,865
41		19	(a)	Manchester C	L 0-2		30,723
42		26	(h)	Stoke C	D 0-0		19,322

FINAL LEAGUE POSITION: 10th in Division One

Appearances
Sub Appearances
Goals

FA Cup

3	Jan	4	(h)	Wimbledon	L 0-1		19,683

Appearances
Sub Appearances
Goals

League Cup

2	Sep	11	(a)	Hull C	W 2-1	Ingham, James	7,544
3	Oct	9	(a)	Reading	W 2-1	Newton, Noble	14,258
4	Nov	13	(a)	Manchester U	L 2-3	Noble, Hankin	46,275

Appearances
Sub Appearances
Goals

Stevenson A	Noble P	Newton K	Dobson M	Thomson J	Rodaway W	Nulty G	Hankin R	Fletcher P	Collins D	James L	Waldron C	Ingham W	Brennan I	Flynn B	Docherty M	Morris C	Bradshaw P	Parker D	Finn M	Dixey R	Scott D	
1	2	3	4	5	6	7	8	9	10	11												1
1	2	3	4		6	7	8	9	10	11	5											2
1	2	3	4		6	7	8	9	10	11	5											3
1	2	3			6		8	9	10	11	5	4	7									4
1	7	2			6		8	9	10	11	5	4	3									5
1	7	2			6		8	9	10	11	5	4	3									6
1	7	2			6		8	9	10	11	5	4	3									7
1	7	2			6		8	9	10	11*	5	4	3	12								8
1	7	2			6			9	10	11	5	4	3	8								9
1	7	2			6			9	10	11	5	4	3	8								10
1	7	2			6			9	10	11	5	4	3	8								11
1	7	2			6		8	9	10	11	5		3	4								12
1	7	2			6		8	9	10	11	5		3	4								13
1	7	2			6		8	9	10	11	5		3	4								14
1	7	2			6		8	9	10	11	5		3	4								15
1	7	2			6		8	9	10*	11	5	12	3	4								16
1	7	2			6		8	9		11	5	10	3	4								17
1	7				6		8	9	10	11	5	12	3	4*	2							18
1	7	2			6		8	9	10	11	5	4	3									19
1	7	2			6		8	9	10	11	5	4	3									20
1	7	2			6		8	9	10	11	5	4	3									21
1	7	2			6*	12	8	9	10	11	5	4	3									22
1	7	2			6		8	9	10*	11	5	4	3	12								23
1	6	2					8	9	10	11	5	4	3	7								24
1	7	2					8	9	10	11	5	4	3	6								25
1	3	2		5	6		8	9	10	11		4				7						26
1	4	3		5	6		8	9	10	11		2	7									27
1	7	2		6			8	9	10	11	5	4	3									28
1	4	2		6			8	9	10	11	5	7	3									29
1	4	2		6			8	9	10	11	5	7	3									30
1	4	2		6			8	9	10	11	5	7	3*	12								31
1	4	2		6			8	9	10	11	5	7		3								32
1	4	3		6			8	9	10	11	5	2		7								33
1	4	3		6	12		8	9	10	11	5	2		7*								34
1	4	3		6	9		8		10	11	5	2		7*			12					35
1	4	2		6			9		10*	11	5	8	3	7				12				36
1	4	2		6			9			11	5	8	3	7				10				37
	4	2					8			11	5	9	3	7				10	1	6		38
	4	3		12			8		10	11	5	9	2	7*					1	6		39
	9	2							10	11	5	4	3	7				8	1	6		40
1	9				6				10	11	5	4	3	7		12		8*			2	41
1	9				6		8		10	11	5	4	3	7							2	42
39	42	39	3	13	28	3	37	34	39	42	39	33	34	23	1	1		4	3	3	2	
				1	1	1						2		3		1	1	1				
	12	1	1		1		14	10	3	16	1	1	1					1				

6 own-goals

Stevenson A	Noble P	Newton K	Dobson M	Thomson J	Rodaway W	Nulty G	Hankin R	Fletcher P	Collins D	James L	Waldron C	Ingham W	Brennan I	Flynn B	Docherty M	Morris C	Bradshaw P	Parker D	Finn M	Dixey R	Scott D	
1	6	2		3*			8	9	10	11	5	4		7		12						3
1	1	1		1			1	1	1	1	1	1		1								
																1						

Stevenson A	Noble P	Newton K	Dobson M	Thomson J	Rodaway W	Nulty G	Hankin R	Fletcher P	Collins D	James L	Waldron C	Ingham W	Brennan I	Flynn B	Docherty M	Morris C	Bradshaw P	Parker D	Finn M	Dixey R	Scott D	
1	7	2			6		8	9	10	11	5	4	3									2
1	7	2			6		8	9	10	11	5	4*	3	12								3
1	7	2			6		8	9	10	11	5		3	4								4
3	3	3			3		3	3	3	3	3	2	3	1								
														1								
	2	1					1			1		1										

1975-76

Manager: Jimmy Adamson until January, then Joe Brown

1	Aug	16	(h)	Arsenal	D 0-0		18,831
2		19	(h)	Everton	D 1-1	Hankin	20,069
3		23	(a)	West Ham U	L 2-3	Noble, James	28,048
4		26	(a)	Ipswich T	D 0-0		23,579
5		30	(h)	Middlesbrough	W 4-1	Noble 3, Hankin	17,066
6	Sep	6	(a)	Derby C	L 0-3		24,026
7		13	(h)	Norwich C	D 4-4	Noble 4 (2 pens)	15,513
8		20	(a)	Birmingham C	L 0-4		25,830
9		23	(a)	Sheffield U	L 1-2	Noble	21,477
10		27	(h)	Leeds U	L 0-1		23,045
11	Oct	4	(a)	Coventry C	W 2-1	Hankin, James	15,432
12		11	(a)	Manchester C	D 0-0		35,003
13		18	(h)	Queen's Park R	W 1-0	Casper	20,378
14		25	(a)	Aston Villa	D 1-1	Noble	35,204
15	Nov	1	(h)	Stoke C	L 0-1		18,326
16		8	(a)	Leicester C	L 2-3	Noble (pen), James	18,344
17		15	(h)	Wolves	L 1-5	Hankin	14,530
18		22	(a)	Queen's Park R	L 0-1		17,390
19		29	(a)	Tottenham H	L 1-2	Hankin	21,222
20	Dec	6	(h)	Liverpool	D 0-0		18,524
21		13	(h)	West Ham U	W 2-0	Kennerley, Hankin	14,942
22		20	(a)	Arsenal	L 0-1		16,459
23		26	(h)	Newcastle U	L 0-1		22,736
24		27	(a)	Manchester U	L 1-2	Hankin	59,726
25	Jan	10	(a)	Norwich C	L 1-3	Newton	17,473
26		17	(h)	Derby C	L 1-2	Fletcher	21,088
27		31	(a)	Everton	W 3-2	Scott, Flynn, Noble	21,389
28	Feb	7	(h)	Ipswich T	L 0-1		17,536
29		14	(a)	Middlesbrough	D 1-1	Hankin	17,856
30		17	(h)	Leicester C	W 1-0	Newton	13,542
31		21	(a)	Wolves	L 2-3	Hankin, Fletcher	19,390
32		24	(h)	Sheffield U	W 3-1	Scott, Hankin, Flynn	14,623
33		28	(h)	Aston Villa	D 2-2	Flynn 2	17,174
34	Mar	6	(a)	Stoke C	L 1-4	Hankin	16,065
35		13	(h)	Manchester C	D 0-0		24,329
36		20	(h)	Tottenham H	L 1-2	Waldron	15,490
37		27	(a)	Liverpool	L 0-2		36,708
38	Apr	3	(a)	Leeds U	L 1-2	Hankin	25,384
39		10	(h)	Birmingham C	W 1-0	Hankin	13,679
40		17	(a)	Newcastle U	W 1-0	Noble	24,897
41		19	(h)	Manchester U	L 0-1		27,418
42		24	(h)	Coventry C	L 1-3	Parker	11,675

FINAL LEAGUE POSITION: 21st in Division One (Relegated)

Appearances
Sub Appearances
Goals

FA Cup

3	Jan	3	(a)	Blackpool	L 0-1		20,573

Appearances
Sub Appearances
Goals

League Cup

2	Sep	10	(a)	Hereford U	W 4-1	Flynn 2, Noble 2	11,360
3	Oct	7	(a)	Liverpool	D 1-1	Noble	24,607
R		14	(h)	Liverpool	W 1-0	Noble	20,022
4	Nov	11	(h)	Leicester C	W 2-0	Morgan (pen), Hankin	15,019
5	Dec	3	(h)	Middlesbrough	L 0-2		15,431

Appearances
Sub Appearances
Goals

Stevenson A	Docherty M	Newton K	Noble P	Waldron C	Thomson J	Morgan W	Hankin R	Summerbee M	Collins D	James L	Flynn B	Brennan I	Ingham W	Casper F	Fletcher P	Bradshaw P	Peyton G	Kennerley K	Loggie D	Scott D	Morris C	Rodaway W	Morley T	Pashley T	Jakub J	Parker D	
1	2	3	4*	5	6	7	8	9	10	11	12																1
1	2	3	4	5	6		8	9	10*	11	7	12															2
1	2	3	4	5	6	12	8	9	10*	11	7																3
1	2	3	4	5	6		8	9	10	11	7																4
1	2	3	4	5	6	7	8	9	10	11																	5
1	2	3	4	5	6	7	8	9	10	11																	6
1		3	4	5	6		8	9	10	11	7	2															7
1		3	4	5	6		8	9	10*	11	7	2	12														8
1	2	3	4	5	6		8	9		11	7		10														9
1	2	3		5	6	7	8	9		11	4		10														10
1	2	3	4	5	6	7	8*	9		11	10		12														11
1	2	3	4	5	6	7	8	9		11	10																12
1		3	4	5	6	7		9		11	10		2	8													13
1	2	3	4	5	6			9		11	10			8	7												14
1	2	3	4	5	6			7		11	10			8	9												15
1	2	3	4*	5	6	8	9	7		11	10		12														16
1	2	3		5	6	7	9*	8	10	11	4			12													17
1	2	3		5	6	7	9	8	10		4					11											18
1	2	3		5	6	7	9	8	10*		4				11	12											19
	2	3		5	6		9	7			10		4			11	1	8									20
	2	3		5	6		9	7			10		4			11	1	8									21
	2	3		5	6		9	7			10		4			11	1	8									22
	2	3	12	5	6		9	7			10		4*			11	1	8									23
	2	3		5	6	8	9	7	4*		10			12		11	1										24
1	2	3		5	6						8		4	11		7		9	10								25
		3	11	5	6						8		4		10	7	1	9		2							26
		3	11	5	6						8		4		10		1			2	7	9					27
		3	11	5	6			9			8		4		10		1			2			7				28
		3	11*	5	6		8	9			12				10		1			2		4	7				29
		3		5	6		8	11			10		9				1			2		4	7				30
		3		5	6		9	11			8*		12		10		1			2		4	7				31
1		3		5	6		8	11			10				9					2	7	4					32
1		3		5	6		8	11			10				9					2	7	4					33
		3		5	6		8	11			10				9		1			2	7	4*	12				34
		3			5		9	6	11		8				10		1			2		4	7				35
		3		5			9	4	11		8				10		1			2		6	7				36
		3	4	5			9	11			8				10		1			2		6	7				37
		3*	4		5		9	11			8		12		10		1			2	7	6					38
			4		5		9	11			8				10		1			2	7	6		3			39
		3	4		5		9	11			8		10				1			2	7	6					40
		3	4		5		9*	11			8		12		10		1			2	7	6					41
		3	9		5			11					4				1			2		6	7		8	10	42
22	22	41	25	36	40	12	34	39	14	17	37	2	14	4	17	8	20	6	1	17	8	15	8	1	1	1	
			1			1					2	1	6	2		1							1				
		2	13	1			13			3	4			1	2			1		2						1	

Stevenson A	Docherty M	Newton K	Noble P	Waldron C	Thomson J	Morgan W	Hankin R	Summerbee M	Collins D	James L	Flynn B	Brennan I	Ingham W	Casper F	Fletcher P	Bradshaw P	Peyton G	Kennerley K	Loggie D	Scott D	Morris C	Rodaway W	Morley T	Pashley T	Jakub J	Parker D	
	2	3		5	6	8*	9	7			10		4			11	1		12								3
	1	1		1	1	1	1	1			1		1			1	1										
																			1								

Stevenson A	Docherty M	Newton K	Noble P	Waldron C	Thomson J	Morgan W	Hankin R	Summerbee M	Collins D	James L	Flynn B	Brennan I	Ingham W	Casper F	Fletcher P	Bradshaw P	Peyton G	Kennerley K	Loggie D	Scott D	Morris C	Rodaway W	Morley T	Pashley T	Jakub J	Parker D	
1		3	4	5	6		8	9	10	11	7	2															2
1	2	3	4	5	6	7	8	9		11	10																3
1	2	3	4	5	6	7	8*	9		11	10		12														R
1	2			5	6	7	10	8	3	11	4				9												4
1	2	3	4	5	6		9	8	10*		11					7			12								5
5	4	4	4	5	5	3	5	5	3	4	5	1			1	1											
													1						1								
			4			1	1				2																

1976-77

Manager: Joe Brown

1	Aug	21	(a)	Wolves	D 0-0		19,480
2		24	(h)	Fulham	W 3-1	Noble (pen), Bradshaw, Hankin	11,506
3		28	(h)	Luton T	L 1-2	Bradshaw	12,262
4	Sep	4	(a)	Hereford U	L 0-3		9,548
5		11	(h)	Southampton	W 2-0	Noble, Hankin	9,142
6		18	(a)	Carlisle U	L 1-2	Smith	8,969
7		25	(h)	Hull C	D 0-0		10,320
8	Oct	2	(a)	Sheffield U	L 0-1		16,082
9		9	(h)	Orient	D 3-3	Cochrane, Smith, Fletcher	10,228
10		16	(h)	Charlton A	D 4-4	Noble, Cochrane, Smith, Fletcher	10,601
11		23	(a)	Nottingham F	L 2-5	Smith, Flynn	15,279
12		30	(a)	Plymouth A	W 1-0	Smith	14,704
13	Nov	6	(h)	Oldham A	W 1-0	Noble (pen)	14,305
14		9	(a)	Bolton W	L 1-2	Smith	21,737
15		20	(h)	Bristol R	D 1-1	Noble	10,371
16		27	(a)	Chelsea	L 1-2	Noble	28,595
17	Dec	4	(h)	Cardiff C	D 0-0		8,967
18		18	(h)	Millwall	L 1-3	Cochrane	8,427
19		27	(a)	Blackburn R	D 2-2	Brennan, Noble	22,189
20		28	(h)	Blackpool	D 0-0		19,682
21	Jan	3	(h)	Plymouth A	L 0-2		10,406
22		15	(a)	Fulham	D 2-2	Noble (pen), Fletcher	8,815
23		22	(h)	Wolves	D 0-0		13,638
24	Feb	5	(a)	Luton T	L 0-2		8,638
25		12	(h)	Hereford U	D 1-1	Noble	8,748
26		15	(a)	Oldham A	L 1-3	Flynn	12,438
27		19	(a)	Southampton	L 0-2		17,981
28		26	(h)	Carlisle U	W 2-0	Noble, Cochrane	10,834
29	Mar	2	(a)	Notts C	L 1-5	Smith	8,492
30		5	(a)	Hull C	L 1-4	Smith	6,636
31		12	(h)	Sheffield U	W 1-0	Smith	10,608
32		19	(a)	Orient	W 1-0	Brennan	5,610
33	Apr	2	(h)	Nottingham F	L 0-1		11,112
34		8	(h)	Blackburn R	W 3-1	Noble, Robinson, Smith	17,372
35		9	(a)	Blackpool	D 1-1	Smith	14,526
36		12	(h)	Bolton W	D 0-0		20,433
37		16	(a)	Bristol R	D 1-1	Noble	6,375
38		23	(h)	Chelsea	W 1-0	Ingham	14,977
39		26	(a)	Charlton A	L 2-5	Newton, Ingham	6,592
40		30	(a)	Cardiff C	W 1-0	Noble	11,247
41	May	7	(h)	Notts C	W 3-1	Morley 2, Fletcher	11,699
42		14	(a)	Millwall	L 0-2		6,833

FINAL LEAGUE POSITION: 16th in Division Two

Appearances
Sub Appearances
Goals

FA Cup

3	Jan	8	(h)	Lincoln C	D 2-2	Noble, Fletcher	11,583
R		12	(a)	Lincoln C	W 1-0	Fletcher	11,414
4		29	(a)	Port Vale	L 1-2	Flynn (pen)	18,068

Appearances
Sub Appearances
Goals

League Cup

2	Sep	1	(a)	Torquay U	L 0-1		7,084

Appearances
Sub Appearances
Goals

Peyton G	Scott D	Pashley T	Noble P	Thomson J	Rodaway W	Bradshaw P	Ingham W	Hankin R	Flynn B	Summerbee M	Newton K	Morley T	Jakub J	Smith M	Fletcher P	Loggie D	Stevenson A	Cochrane T	Brennan I	Robinson P	
1	2	3	4	5	6	7	8	9	10	11											1
1	2	3	4	5	6	7	8	9	10	11											2
1	2	3	4	5	6	7	8	9	10	11											3
1	2		4	5	6			9	10	11	3	7	8								4
1	2	3	4	5	6			9	10	11		7	8								5
1	2	3	4	5	6		12	9	10			7	8	11*							6
1	2	3	4	5	6				10			7	8	11*	9	12					7
1	2	3	4	5	6				10			7	8	11	9						8
	2	3	4	5	6				10			11		8	9		1	7			9
1	2	3	4	5	6				10			11		8	9			7			10
1	2	3	4	5	6				10			11		8	9			7			11
			4	5	6		7		10	11	2			8	9		1		3		12
			4	5	6		7		10	11	2			8	9		1		3		13
			4		6		7		10	11	2	9		8			1		3	5	14
			4	5	6		7*		10	11	2	12		8	9		1		3		15
			4	5	6		7		10	11	2	12		8	9*		1		3		16
			4		6				10	11	2	7		8	9		1		3	5	17
			4		6				10	11	2	9		8*	12		1	7	3	5	18
			4	5	6		11		10		2	12		8	9*		1	7	3		19
			4	5	6		11		10		2	9		8			1	7	3		20
	2		4	5	6		11		10			9		8			1	7	3		21
			4	5	6		12		10		2			11*	9		1	7	3	8	22
			4	5	6		11		10		2				9		1	7	3	8	23
			4	5	6				10		2			11	9		1	7	3	8	24
			4	5	6				10		2	11			9		1	7	3	8	25
			4	5	6				10		2	11			9		1	7	3	8	26
			4	5	6		8		10		2	11			9	7	1		3		27
			4	5	6		12		10		2	11		8	9		1	7*	3		28
	2		4	5	6				10			11		8	9		1	7	3		29
			4	5	6		10				2	11		8	9		1	7	3		30
			4		6				10		2	11		8	9		1	7	3	5	31
	12		4		6		7		10*		2	11		8	9		1		3	5	32
			4		6		7*		10		2	11		8	9		1	12	3	5	33
			4		6				10		2	11		8	9		1	7	3	5	34
		12	4		6		7		10		2	11		8	9*		1		3	5	35
			4		6		7		10		2	11		8		9	1		3	5	36
			4		6		7		10		2	11		8		9	1		3	5	37
			4		6		7		10		2	11		8	9		1		3	5	38
			4		6		7		10		2	11		8	9		1		3	5	39
			4		6		7		10		2	11			9		1	8	3	5	40
			4		6		7		10		2	11			9		1	8	3	5	41
			4		6		7		10		2	11			9		1	8	3	5	42
10	13	10	42	27	42	3	24	6	41	12	30	31	5	30	30	3	32	20	31	20	
	1	1					3					3			1	1		1			
			13			2	2	2	2		1	2		11	4			4	2	1	

Peyton G	Scott D	Pashley T	Noble P	Thomson J	Rodaway W	Bradshaw P	Ingham W	Hankin R	Flynn B	Summerbee M	Newton K	Morley T	Jakub J	Smith M	Fletcher P	Loggie D	Stevenson A	Cochrane T	Brennan I	Robinson P	
	3		4	5	6		11		10		2	12		9		1	7*		8		3
			4	5	6				10		2			9		1	7	3	8	11	R
			4	5	6		11		10		2			9		1	12	3	8*	7	4
	1		3	3	3		2		3		3			3		3	2	2	3	2	
												1					1				
			1						1					2							

Peyton G	Scott D	Pashley T	Noble P	Thomson J	Rodaway W	Bradshaw P	Ingham W	Hankin R	Flynn B	Summerbee M	Newton K	Morley T	Jakub J	Smith M	Fletcher P	Loggie D	Stevenson A	Cochrane T	Brennan I	Robinson P	
1	2		4	5	6	7*	8	9	10	11	3	12									2
1	1		1	1	1	1	1	1	1	1	1										
												1									

1977-78

Manager: Harry Potts

1	Aug	20	(h)	Bolton W	L 0-1		14,732
2		23	(a)	Sunderland	L 0-3		31,450
3		27	(a)	Stoke C	L 1-2	Burke	12,835
4	Sep	3	(h)	Crystal P	D 1-1	Nicholas (og)	10,460
5		10	(a)	Southampton	L 0-3		17,412
6		17	(h)	Brighton & HA	D 0-0		9,227
7		24	(a)	Mansfield T	L 1-4	Brennan	8,274
8	Oct	1	(h)	Millwall	L 0-2		7,242
9		4	(a)	Fulham	L 1-4	Flynn	6,895
10		8	(h)	Bristol R	W 3-1	Robinson, Cochrane, Smith	7,253
11		15	(a)	Sheffield U	L 1-2	Noble	14,151
12		22	(h)	Hull C	D 1-1	Flynn	8,592
13		29	(h)	Blackpool	L 0-1		11,243
14	Nov	5	(a)	Tottenham H	L 0-3		30,634
15		12	(h)	Notts C	W 3-1	Fletcher 2, Kindon	9,734
16		19	(a)	Cardiff C	L 1-2	Fletcher	7,069
17		26	(h)	Orient	D 0-0		8,525
18	Dec	3	(a)	Luton T	W 2-1	Hall, Kindon	6,921
19		10	(h)	Charlton A	W 1-0	Kindon	9,478
20		17	(a)	Notts C	L 0-3		7,639
21		26	(h)	Blackburn R	L 2-3	Noble (pen), Morley	27,427
22		27	(a)	Oldham A	L 0-2		15,172
23		31	(h)	Sunderland	D 0-0		12,726
24	Jan	2	(a)	Bolton W	W 2-1	Brennan 2	28,232
25		14	(h)	Stoke C	W 1-0	Kindon	11,101
26		21	(a)	Crystal P	D 1-1	Noble	15,367
27	Feb	4	(h)	Southampton	D 3-3	Kindon 2, Cochrane	10,592
28		11	(a)	Brighton & HA	L 1-2	Scott	22,694
29		25	(a)	Millwall	D 1-1	Noble (pen)	7,166
30	Mar	4	(a)	Bristol R	D 2-2	Kindon 2	7,520
31		11	(h)	Sheffield U	W 4-1	Cochrane 2, Noble (pen), Ingham	11,801
32		14	(h)	Mansfield T	W 2-0	Fletcher, Kindon	9,893
33		18	(a)	Hull C	W 3-1	Ingham, Fletcher, Noble (pen)	5,936
34		25	(h)	Oldham A	W 4-1	Cochrane 2, Kindon, Brennan	13,529
35		27	(a)	Blackburn R	W 1-0	Cochrane	24,379
36		28	(a)	Blackpool	D 1-1	Smith	13,393
37	Apr	1	(h)	Tottenham H	W 2-1	Noble, Ingham	16,916
38		15	(h)	Cardiff C	W 4-2	Kindon 2, Ingham, Fletcher	11,610
39		18	(a)	Orient	L 0-3		5,795
40		22	(a)	Charlton A	L 2-3	Cochrane, Smith	6,511
41		25	(h)	Fulham	W 2-0	Noble, Fletcher	9,465
42		29	(h)	Luton T	W 2-1	Smith, P.Futcher (og)	11,648

FINAL LEAGUE POSITION: 11th in Division Two

Appearances
Sub Appearances
Goals

FA Cup

3	Jan	7	(h)	Everton	W 1-0	Fletcher	10,984
4		31	(a)	Chelsea	L 2-6	Fletcher, Kindon	32,168

Appearances
Sub Appearances
Goals

League Cup

1	Aug	13	(h)	Chester	W 2-0	Cochrane 2	4,792
		17	(a)	Chester	L 0-1		4,097
2		30	(h)	Norwich C	W 3-1	Ingham, Noble, Morley	6,492
3	Sep	25	(h)	Ipswich T	L 1-2	Fletcher	9,581

Appearances
Sub Appearances
Goals

Stevenson A	Newton K	Brennan I	Burke M	Robinson P	Rodaway W	Morley T	Ingham W	Loggie D	Flynn B	Cochrane T	Smith M	Scott D	Noble P	Pashley T	Higgins R	Fletcher P	Thomson J	Overson R	Hall B	Kindon S	
1	2	3	4	5	6	7	8	9*	10	11	12										1
1	2	3	4	5	6	11	8		10	7	9										2
1		3	12	5	6	8	7		10	11	9*	2	4								3
1		3	4	5	6	11	8		10	7		2	9								4
1		3		5	6	11	8		10	7	9	2	4								5
1		3		9	6	11	8*		10	7	12		4	2	5						6
1		3		9	6	11*	12		10	7			4	2	5	8					7
1	2	3		5	6*		8	9	11	7	10		4	12							8
1	2	3		5			8		10	7	11		4		6	9					9
1	2	3		5		11			10	7	8		4			9	6				10
1	2	3		5		12	11		10	7*	8		4			9	6				11
1	2	3				11	7		10		8		4			9	6	5			12
1			10	12	5	11				7	8*	2	4	3		9	6				13
1	11		10		5					7	8	2	4	3		9	6				14
1	2	3			6	11				7			4			9	5		8	10	15
1	2	5			4	11				12			6	8*		9	3		7	10	16
1	2	3			6	11				7			4			9	5		8	10	17
1	2	3			6	11	7						4			9	5		8	10	18
1	2	3			6	11				7			4			9	5		8	10	19
1	2	3			6	11	7			12			4			9*	5		8	10	20
1	2	3			6	11	7*			12			4			9	5		8	10	21
1		3	7*		6	11				12		2	4			9	5		8	10	22
1		3			6	11				7	12	2	4			9	5		8*	10	23
1		3		10	6	11	7			8		2	4			9	5				24
1		3			6	11	8			7		2	4			9	5			10	25
1	11	3			6		8			7		2	4			9	5			10	26
1	6	3				11	8			7		2	4			9	5			10	27
1	6	3				11	8			7		2	4			9	5			10	28
1		3			6	11	8			7	9	2	4				5			10	29
1		3			6	11	8			7		2	4			9	5			10	30
1		3			6	11	8			7		2	4			9	5			10	31
1		3			6	11	8			7		2	4			9	5			10	32
1		3			6		8			7	11	2	4			9	5			10	33
1		3			6	12	8			7	11	2	4			9	5			10*	34
1		3			6		8			7	11	2	4			9	5			10	35
1		3			6		8			7	11	2	4			9	5			10	36
1		3			6		8			7	11	2	4			9	5			10	37
1		3		5	6		8			7	11	2	4			9				10	38
1		3		5	6*		8			7	11	2	4			9			12	10	39
1		3		5			8			7	11	2	4			9	6			10	40
1		3		6			8			7	11	2	4			9	5			10	41
1		3		6			8			7	11	2	4			9	5			10	42
42	18	40	6	17	33	27	32	2	12	36	21	26	40	5	3	34	31	1	9	27	
			1	1		2	1			4	3			1					1		
		4	1	1		1	4		2	8	4	1	8			7			1	12	

2 own-goals

Stevenson A	Newton K	Brennan I	Burke M	Robinson P	Rodaway W	Morley T	Ingham W	Loggie D	Flynn B	Cochrane T	Smith M	Scott D	Noble P	Pashley T	Higgins R	Fletcher P	Thomson J	Overson R	Hall B	Kindon S	
1		3			6	11	8			7	12	2	4			9*	5			10	3
1	11*	3			6	12	8			7		2	4			9	5			10	4
2	1	2			2	1	2			2		2	2			2	2			2	
						1					1										
																2				1	

Stevenson A	Newton K	Brennan I	Burke M	Robinson P	Rodaway W	Morley T	Ingham W	Loggie D	Flynn B	Cochrane T	Smith M	Scott D	Noble P	Pashley T	Higgins R	Fletcher P	Thomson J	Overson R	Hall B	Kindon S	
1	2	3		5	6		7		10	11	8		4			9					1
1	2	3	12	5	6*		7		10	11	8		4			9					
1		3	4	5	6	11	8		10	7		2	9								2
1	2	3			5	11			10	7	8		4			9	6				3
4	3	4	1	3	4	2	3		4	4	3	1	4			3	1				
			1																		
						1	1			2			1			1					

1978-79

Manager: Harry Potts

1	Aug	19	(h)	Leicester C	D 2-2	Noble (pen), Fletcher	12,048
2		22	(a)	Charlton A	D 1-1	Cochrane	8,580
3		26	(a)	Fulham	D 0-0		6,135
4	Sep	2	(h)	Notts C	W 2-1	Brennan, Noble (pen)	9,787
5		9	(h)	West Ham U	W 3-2	Brennan, Thomson, Fletcher	12,392
6		16	(a)	Sheffield U	L 0-4		15,355
7		23	(h)	Sunderland	L 1-2	Morley	13,368
8		30	(a)	Millwall	W 2-0	Noble, Fletcher	5,389
9	Oct	7	(h)	Oldham A	W 1-0	Smith	11,835
10		14	(a)	Stoke C	L 1-3	Ingham	18,434
11		21	(h)	Brighton & HA	W 3-0	Ingham 2, Brennan	10,321
12		28	(a)	Preston NE	D 2-2	Noble (pen), Kindon	14,975
13	Nov	4	(h)	Crystal P	W 2-1	Brennan, Fletcher	11,129
14		11	(a)	Leicester C	L 1-2	Ingham	12,842
15		18	(h)	Fulham	W 5-3	Kindon, James, Noble 3 (2 pens)	10,566
16		21	(a)	Notts C	D 1-1	Ingham	8,520
17		25	(a)	Cambridge U	D 2-2	Ingham, Fletcher	6,502
18	Dec	9	(a)	Orient	L 1-2	Fletcher	4,754
19		16	(h)	Bristol R	W 2-0	Ingham 2	9,257
20		23	(a)	Newcastle U	L 1-3	Noble	23,639
21		26	(h)	Blackburn R	W 2-1	Noble, Fletcher	23,133
22		30	(h)	Cardiff C	D 0-0		9,821
23	Feb	3	(a)	Sunderland	L 1-3	James	23,030
24		24	(h)	Stoke C	L 0-3		13,890
25	Mar	3	(a)	Brighton & HA	L 1-2	Ingham	19,379
26		6	(h)	Sheffield U	D 1-1	Fletcher	8,208
27		10	(h)	Preston NE	D 1-1	Noble	15,270
28		13	(h)	Luton T	W 2-1	Noble 2 (1 pen)	7,691
29		21	(a)	Wrexham	W 1-0	Fletcher	8,840
30		24	(h)	Charlton A	W 2-1	Scott, James	8,560
31		31	(h)	Cambridge U	D 1-1	Robinson	8,234
32	Apr	7	(a)	Luton T	L 1-4	Noble (pen)	6,466
33		10	(h)	Newcastle U	W 1-0	Hall	7,771
34		14	(a)	Blackburn R	W 2-1	Hall, Morley	14,761
35		16	(h)	Wrexham	D 0-0		9,401
36		21	(a)	Bristol R	L 0-2		5,947
37		24	(a)	West Ham U	L 1-3	Noble	24,139
38		28	(h)	Orient	L 0-1		7,195
39	May	5	(a)	Cardiff C	D 1-1	Kindon	10,254
40		8	(h)	Millwall	L 0-1		5,837
41		11	(a)	Crystal P	L 0-2		51,482
42		14	(a)	Oldham A	L 0-2		6,791

FINAL LEAGUE POSITION: 13th in Division Two

Appearances
Sub Appearances
Goals

FA Cup

3	Jan	9	(a)	Birmingham C	W 2-0	Morley, James	15,535
4	Feb	21	(h)	Sunderland	D 1-1	Thomson	20,852
R		26	(a)	Sunderland	W 3-0	Ingham, Fletcher, Kindon	37,507
5		28	(a)	Liverpool	L 0-3		47,161

Appearances
Sub Appearances
Goals

League Cup

2	Aug	29	(h)	Bradford C	D 1-1	Cochrane	9,185
R	Sep	5	(a)	Bradford C	W 3-2	Noble, Cochrane, Ingham	9,192
3	Oct	3	(h)	Brighton & HA	L 1-3	Brennan	9,076

Appearances
Sub Appearances
Goals

Stevenson A	Scott D	Brennan I	Noble P	Thomson J	Rodaway W	Cochrane T	Ingham W	Fletcher P	Kindon S	Smith M	Hall B	James L	Morley A	Robinson P	Arins A	Jakub J	Young K	Robertson S	
1	2	3	4	5	6	7	8	9	10	11									1
1	2	3	4	5	6	7	8	9	10	11									2
1	2	3	4	5	6	7	8	9	10*	11	12								3
1	2	3	4	5	6	7	8	9	10	11									4
1	2	3	4	5	6	7		9	10	11	8								5
1	2	3	4	5	6	7		9	10		8	11							6
1	2		4	5	6		3		10	9	8	11	7						7
1	2	3	4	5	6		8	9	10	7		11							8
1	2	3	4	5	6		8	9	10	7		11							9
1	2	3	4	5	6		8	9	10	7		11							10
1	2	3	4	5	6		8	9	10		7	11							11
1	2	3	4	5	6		8	9	10		7	11							12
1	2	3		5	6		8	9	10		7	11		4					13
1	2	3	4	5	6		8	9	10		7	11							14
1		3	4	5	6		8	9	10*		7	11		12	2				15
1		3	4	5	6		8	9	10		7	11			2				16
1		3	4	5	6		8	9	10		7*	11		12	2				17
1		3	4	5	6		8	9	10*		7	11		12	2				18
1		3	4	5	6		8	9	10		7	11			2				19
1	2	3	4	5	6		8	9	10		7	11*		12					20
1	2	3	4	5	6		8	9	10		7	11*	12						21
1	2*	3	4	5	6		8	9	10		7	11	12						22
1	2	3	4	5	6		9		10		8	11	7						23
1	2	3	4	5	6		8	9	10			11		7					24
1	2	3	4	5	6		8	9	10		7	11							25
1	2	3	4	5	6		8	9*	10			11	12			7			26
1	2	3	4	5	6		8*	9	10			11	12			7			27
1	2	3	4	5	6			9	10		12	11		8*		7			28
1	2	3	4	5	6		8	9	10			11				7			29
1	2	3	4	5	6		8	9				11	10			7			30
1	2	3	4	5			8	9	10*			11	12	6		7			31
1	2	3	4	5			8	9	12			11	10	6		7*			32
1	2		4	5	6		8	9*	10		7	11	12			3			33
1			4	5	6		8	9	10*		7	11	12		2	3			34
1			4	5	6			9			7	11	10		2	3	8*	12	35
1	2	3	4	5	6		8	9*			7	11	10	12					36
1	2	3	4	5	6		8				12	11	10	9		7*			37
1	2	3	4		6				9		8	11	10	5		7			38
1	2	3	4	5	6		8		9		7	11	10						39
1	2	3	4	5	6		8	12	9		7*	11	10						40
1	2	3	4	5	6		8		9		7	11	10						41
1	2	3	4	5			8		9			11	10	6		7			42
42	35	38	41	41	39	6	37	34	37	9	25	37	12	8	7	13	1		
								1	1		3		7	5				1	
	1	4	14	1		1	9	9	3	1	2	3	2	1					

Stevenson A	Scott D	Brennan I	Noble P	Thomson J	Rodaway W	Cochrane T	Ingham W	Fletcher P	Kindon S	Smith M	Hall B	James L	Morley A	Robinson P	Arins A	Jakub J	Young K	Robertson S	
1	2	3	4	5	6		8		10		7	11	9						3
1	2	3	4	5	6		8	12	10		7	11	9*						4
1	2	3	4	5	6		8	9	10			11		7					R
1	2	3	4	5	6		7	9	10		8	11							5
4	4	4	4	4	4		4	2	4		3	4	2	1					
								1											
				1			1	1	1			1	1						

Stevenson A	Scott D	Brennan I	Noble P	Thomson J	Rodaway W	Cochrane T	Ingham W	Fletcher P	Kindon S	Smith M	Hall B	James L	Morley A	Robinson P	Arins A	Jakub J	Young K	Robertson S	
1	2	3	4	5	6	7	8	9		11			10						2
1	2	3	4	5	6	7	8	9	10	11									R
1	2	3	4	5	6	7	8	9	10			11							3
3	3	3	3	3	3	3	3	3	2	2		1	1						
		1	1			2	1												

1979-80

Manager: Harry Potts until October, then Brian Miller

1	Aug	18	(a)	Orient	D 2-2	Kindon, James	6,151
2		21	(h)	Charlton A	D 1-1	Kindon	6,924
3		25	(h)	Notts C	L 0-1		7,005
4	Sep	1	(a)	Swansea C	L 1-2	Noble	16,670
5		8	(h)	Oldham A	D 1-1	Kindon	6,974
6		15	(a)	Fulham	L 1-3	Noble (pen)	6,633
7		22	(h)	Sunderland	D 1-1	Dobson	8,872
8		29	(a)	West Ham U	L 1-2	Scott	18,327
9	Oct	6	(h)	Chelsea	L 0-1		8,458
10		9	(a)	Charlton A	D 3-3	Noble, Dobson, James	5,279
11		13	(h)	Cardiff C	L 0-2		6,450
12		20	(a)	Preston NE	L 2-3	James, Dobson	12,323
13		27	(a)	Queen's Park R	L 0-7		11,261
14	Nov	3	(h)	Orient	L 1-2	Arins	6,777
15		10	(a)	Leicester C	D 1-1	James	17,191
16		17	(h)	Luton T	D 0-0		7,119
17		24	(h)	Cambridge U	W 5-3	Burke, James, Dobson, Tate, Biley (og)	6,873
18	Dec	1	(a)	Bristol R	D 0-0		5,373
19		8	(h)	Watford	W 1-0	Burke	8,608
20		15	(a)	Birmingham C	L 0-2		13,997
21		21	(h)	Wrexham	W 1-0	Burke	7,042
22		26	(h)	Newcastle U	W 3-2	Dobson (pen), Hamilton, Smith	16,634
23		29	(a)	Notts C	W 3-2	Cavener 2, Hamilton	7,596
24	Jan	1	(a)	Shrewsbury T	L 0-2		10,504
25		12	(h)	Swansea C	D 0-0		8,853
26	Feb	2	(h)	Fulham	W 2-1	Burke, James	6,977
27		9	(a)	Sunderland	L 0-5		21,855
28		19	(h)	West Ham U	L 0-1		9,030
29		23	(a)	Cardiff C	L 1-2	Hamilton	6,342
30	Mar	1	(h)	Preston NE	D 1-1	Dixon	11,046
31		4	(a)	Oldham A	L 1-2	Arins	9,519
32		8	(h)	Queen's Park R	L 0-3		7,579
33		15	(a)	Chelsea	L 1-2	Busby	16,519
34		22	(h)	Leicester C	L 1-2	Scott	7,173
35		29	(a)	Luton T	D 1-1	Hamilton	8,507
36	Apr	4	(a)	Wrexham	L 0-1		6,605
37		5	(h)	Shrewsbury T	D 0-0		6,333
38		7	(a)	Newcastle U	D 1-1	Hamilton	18,863
39		12	(h)	Bristol R	D 1-1	Hamilton	5,353
40		19	(a)	Cambridge U	L 1-3	Hamilton	4,727
41		26	(h)	Birmingham C	D 0-0		10,388
42	May	3	(a)	Watford	L 0-4		11,931

FINAL LEAGUE POSITION: 21st in Division Two (Relegated)

Appearances
Sub Appearance
Goals

FA Cup

3	Jan	5	(h)	Stoke C	W 1-0	Dobson	13,478
4		26	(a)	Bury	L 0-1		17,722

Appearances
Sub Appearance
Goals

League Cup

2	Aug	26	(h)	Wolves	D 1-1	Dobson	6,163
	Sep	4	(a)	Wolves	L 0-2		17,411

Appearances
Sub Appearances
Goals

Stevenson A	Scott D	Brennan I	Noble P	Thomson J	Rodaway W	Ingham W	Dobson M	Fletcher P	Kindon S	James L	Jakub J	Arins A	Robinson P	Hall B	Young K	Tate J	O'Rourke W	Overson V	Cavener P	Overson R	Dixon P	Burke M	Hamilton W	Smith M	Busby M	Robertson S	McAdam S	Laws B	
1	2	3	4	5	6	7	8	9	10	11																			1
1	2	3	4	5	6	7	8	9	10	11																			2
1	2	3	4	5	6	7	8		10	11	9																		3
1	2	3	4*	5	6	7	8			11	9	10	12																4
1	2	3*		5	6	7	8	10	12	11	9	4																	5
1	2		4	5	6	7	8	9	10	11	3																		6
1	2			5	6		8	9	10	11	3			4	7														7
1	2	12		5	6		8	9	10	11	3			4	7*														8
1	2		4*	5	6	12	8	9		11	3			7	10														9
1	2		4	5	6		8			11	3			7	10	9													10
1	2		4	5	6		8		12	11	3			7	10	9*													11
1	2	3	4	5	6		8	9	11	7					10														12
	2	3	4	5	6		8	9	11	7					10		1												13
			4	5*			8	9	11	10		2			3		1	6	7	12									14
1		3			12		8	9		7		2			10	11		5		4	6*								15
1		3					8	9		7		2			10	11		5		4*	6	12							16
1		3					8	9*		7		2			10	11		5	12		6	4							17
1		3					8			7		2			10			5			6	4	9	11					18
1	12	3					8			7		2			10			5			6*	4	9	11					19
1		3			6		8			7		2			10			5		11		4	9						20
1		3			6		8			7		2			10			5				4	9	11					21
1		3			6		8			7*		2			10			5	12			4	9	11					22
1	2	3			6		8								10			5	7			4	9	11					23
1	2	3			6		8								10			5	7			4	9	11					24
1	2				6		8			7					10*			5	12		3	4	9	11					25
1	2				6		8			7	3							5	10			4	9	11					26
1	2				6		8			7	3							5	10			4	9	11					27
1		3					8			7		2			10			5	12		6	4*	9	11					28
1		3			5					7		2	8		10						6	4	9	11					29
1		3					8			7		2			10*			5	12		6		9	11	4				30
1		3								7	10	2	8					5	12		6		9	11	4*				31
1		3								7	10	2						5	8	4	6		9	11					32
1		3								7	10	2						5	8		6		9	11	4				33
1	4	3								7	11	2	8					5			6		9		10				34
1	4	3								7	10	2						5			6		9	11		8			35
1	4	3								7	10	2						5			6		9	11		8			36
1	2	3		5	6					7	10				12							4	9	11*		8			37
1	2			5	6					7	10											4	9	11		8	3		38
1	2			5	6					7	10				12							4*	9	11		8	3		39
1	4			5	6					7	10	2											9	11		8	3		40
1	4			5	6					7	10	2											9	11		8	3		41
1	4			5*	6	11					10				12				7				9			8	3	2	42
40	27	27	11	20	28	7	29	13	9	39	23	22	3	5	22	5	2	22	8	4	15	16	25	22	4	8	5	1	
	1	1			1	1			2				1		3				6	1		1							
	2		3				5		3	6		2				1			2		1	4	7	1	1				

1 own-goal

Stevenson A	Scott D	Brennan I	Noble P	Thomson J	Rodaway W	Ingham W	Dobson M	Fletcher P	Kindon S	James L	Jakub J	Arins A	Robinson P	Hall B	Young K	Tate J	O'Rourke W	Overson V	Cavener P	Overson R	Dixon P	Burke M	Hamilton W	Smith M	Busby M	Robertson S	McAdam S	Laws B	
1	2				6		8								10			5	7		3	4	9	11					3
1	2	3			6		8			7					10*			5	12			4	9	11					4
2	2	1			2		2			1					2			2	1		1	2	2	2					
																			1										
							1																						

Stevenson A	Scott D	Brennan I	Noble P	Thomson J	Rodaway W	Ingham W	Dobson M	Fletcher P	Kindon S	James L	Jakub J	Arins A	Robinson P	Hall B	Young K	Tate J	O'Rourke W	Overson V	Cavener P	Overson R	Dixon P	Burke M	Hamilton W	Smith M	Busby M	Robertson S	McAdam S	Laws B	
1	2	3	4	5	6	7	8		10	11	9																		2
1	2	3		5	6	7	8	10	12	11	9*	4																	
2	2	2	1	2	2	2	2	1	1	2	2	1																	
									1																				
							1																						

1980-81

Manager: Brian Miller

1	Aug	16	(h)	Newport C	D 1-1	Cassidy	6,733
2		20	(a)	Walsall	L 1-3	Taylor	4,714
3		23	(h)	Chesterfield	W 1-0	Dobson (pen)	5,880
4		30	(a)	Charlton A	L 0-2		5,445
5	Sep	6	(h)	Colchester U	W 1-0	Hamilton	4,436
6		13	(a)	Exeter C	D 0-0		4,534
7		16	(h)	Hull C	W 2-0	Young, Taylor	4,933
8		20	(a)	Chester	D 0-0		3,660
9		27	(h)	Millwall	W 5-0	Taylor 3 (1 pen), Hamilton, Dobson	5,620
10		30	(a)	Hull C	D 0-0		5,497
11	Oct	4	(a)	Fulham	W 2-0	Laws, Potts	4,673
12		7	(h)	Sheffield U	W 3-2	Taylor 2, Hamilton	7,308
13		11	(h)	Rotherham U	D 1-1	Dobson	9,352
14		18	(a)	Portsmouth	L 2-4	Scott 2	13,449
15		21	(a)	Huddersfield T	D 0-0		15,741
16		25	(h)	Brentford	W 2-0	Dobson (pen), Cavener	7,324
17	Nov	1	(a)	Swindon T	W 3-0	Scott 2, Carter (og)	6,436
18		4	(a)	Sheffield U	D 0-0		14,585
19		8	(h)	Reading	L 1-2	Hamilton	6,925
20		11	(h)	Walsall	D 0-0		5,573
21		15	(a)	Newport C	W 2-1	Hamilton, Taylor	5,370
22		29	(h)	Gillingham	W 3-2	Scott, Taylor, Weatherly (og)	5,797
23	Dec	2	(h)	Barnsley	L 0-1		9,109
24		6	(a)	Oxford U	W 2-0	Scott, Young	3,513
25		20	(h)	Plymouth A	W 2-1	Taylor 2	5,695
26		26	(a)	Carlisle U	L 2-3	Scott, Taylor	7,136
27		27	(h)	Blackpool	W 4-1	Laws, Holt, Potts, Taylor	10,782
28	Jan	3	(a)	Brentford	D 0-0		6,379
29		27	(h)	Portsmouth	L 1-3	Hamilton	6,689
30		31	(a)	Chesterfield	L 0-3		7,637
31	Feb	7	(h)	Exeter C	W 1-0	Dobson (pen)	5,496
32		14	(a)	Colchester U	L 1-2	Hamilton	3,082
33		17	(h)	Charlton A	L 0-1		5,786
34		21	(a)	Millwall	D 2-2	Hamilton, Taylor	4,691
35		28	(h)	Chester	W 1-0	Young	4,997
36	Mar	7	(h)	Fulham	W 3-0	Dobson 2 (1 pen), Hamilton	5,472
37		28	(a)	Barnsley	L 2-3	Phelan, Scott	13,689
38		31	(a)	Rotherham U	L 0-1		9,762
39	Apr	4	(h)	Swindon T	D 0-0		4,736
40		7	(a)	Gillingham	D 0-0		4,412
41		11	(a)	Reading	W 3-1	Taylor 2, Phelan	3,977
42		14	(h)	Huddersfield T	W 4-2	Overson, Scott, Potts, Brown (og)	11,075
43		18	(a)	Blackpool	D 0-0		7,198
44		21	(h)	Carlisle U	L 0-3		5,126
45		25	(a)	Plymouth A	L 1-2	Cavener	4,331
46	May	2	(h)	Oxford U	D 1-1	Potts	3,947

FINAL LEAGUE POSITION: 8th in Division Three

Appearances
Sub Appearances
Goals

FA Cup

1	Nov	22	(h)	Scarborough	W 1-0	Hamilton	7,789
2	Dec	13	(h)	Port Vale	D 1-1	Potts	7,497
R		16	(a)	Port Vale	L 0-2		7,684

Appearances
Sub Appearances
Goals

League Cup

1	Aug	9	(a)	Wrexham	W 3-1	Thomson, Cassidy, Davis (og)	5,126
		12	(h)	Wrexham	W 2-1	Scott, Dobson (pen)	4,448
2		26	(h)	West Ham U	L 0-2		6,673
	Sep	2	(a)	West Ham U	L 0-4		15,216

Appearances
Sub Appearances
Goals

Stevenson A	Wood I	Holt D	Scott D	Thomson J	Rodaway W	Cassidy T	Dobson M	Hamilton W	Taylor S	Cavener P	Young K	Laws B	Overson V	Robertson S	Potts E	Anderson C	Wharton A	O'Rourke W	Phelan M	Steven T	Wardrobe M	
1	2	3	4	5	6	7	8	9	10	11												1
1	2	3	4	5	6	7	8	9	10	11												2
1	2	3	4	5	6		8	9	10	11	7											3
1		3	4			7	6	9	10	11	8	2	5									4
1		3				7	6	9	10	11	8	2	5	4								5
1		3	4			7	6	9	10	11	8	2	5									6
1	12	3	4			7	6	9*	10	11	8	2	5									7
1		3	4			7	6	9	10	11		2	5		8							8
1		3	4			7	6	9	10	11		2	5		8							9
1		3	4			7	6	9	10	11		2	5		8							10
1		3	4*			7	6	9	10	11		2	5		8	12						11
1		3	4			7	6	9	10	11		2	5		8							12
1	12	3*	4			7	6	9	10	11		2	5		8							13
1	3		4			7	6	9	10	11		2	5		8							14
1	3		4			7	6	9	10	11		2	5		8							15
1	3		4			7	6	9	10	11		2	5		8							16
1		3	4			7	6	9	10	11		2	5		8							17
1		3	4			7	6	9	10	11		2	5		8							18
1		3	4			7	6	9	10	11		2	5		8							19
1		3				7	6	9	10	11	4	2	5		8							20
1		3	4			7	6	9	10	11		2	5		8							21
1			4				6	9	10	11	7	2	5		8		3					22
1			4				6	9	10	11	7	2	5		8		3					23
1			4				6	9	10	11	7	2	5		8		3					24
1		3	4			7	6	9	10	11		2	5		8							25
1		3	4			7	6	9	10	11		2	5		8							26
1		3	4*			7	6	9	10	11	12	2	5		8							27
		3				7	6	9	10	11	4	2	5		8			1				28
	4	3			5		6	9	10	11	7	2			8			1				29
1	4	3			5		6	9	10*		7	2			8	11			12			30
1	4	3					6	9		11	7	2		10	8				5			31
1		3					6	9	12	11	7	8	5	10*			2		4			32
1		3					6	9	10	11	7	4		8			2		5			33
1		3					6	9	10	11	7	2	4	8					5			34
1		3					6	9	10	11	7	2	4	8					5			35
1		3	10				6	9		11*	7	2	4	8	12				5			36
1		3	10				6	9		12	7		5	8	11		2		4*			37
1		3					6	9	10		7	2	5	8	11				4			38
1		3					6	9	10	12	7	2	5	8	11*				4			39
1		3					6	9	10	4	7	2	5	8	11							40
1	12	3*					6	9	10		7	2	5	8	11				4			41
1	2		10*				6	9			7	3	5	8	11				4	12		42
1	2		10				6	9			7	3	5	8	11				4			43
1	2					10	6	9			7*	3	5	8	11				4		12	44
1	2					10	6	9		12	7	3	5	8	11				4*			45
1	3*					4	6	9		12	7	2	5	8	11				10			46
44	14	35	29	3	5	27	46	46	37	36	28	42	39	17	34	1	6	2	15			
	3								1	4	1				1	1			1	1	1	
		1	9			1	7	9	16	2	3	2	1		4				2			

3 own-goals

Stevenson A	Wood I	Holt D	Scott D	Thomson J	Rodaway W	Cassidy T	Dobson M	Hamilton W	Taylor S	Cavener P	Young K	Laws B	Overson V	Robertson S	Potts E	Anderson C	Wharton A	O'Rourke W	Phelan M	Steven T	Wardrobe M	
1		3	4				6	9	10	11	7	2	5		8*		12					1
1		3	4				6	9		11	7	2	5		8						10	2
1		3	4			7	6	9	10*	11	12	2	5		8							R
3		3	3			1	3	3	2	3	2	3	3		3						1	
											1						1					
								1							1							

Stevenson A	Wood I	Holt D	Scott D	Thomson J	Rodaway W	Cassidy T	Dobson M	Hamilton W	Taylor S	Cavener P	Young K	Laws B	Overson V	Robertson S	Potts E	Anderson C	Wharton A	O'Rourke W	Phelan M	Steven T	Wardrobe M	
1	2	3	4	5	6	7	8	9	10	11												1
1		3	4	5	6		8	9	10	11	7	2										
1	2		4	5	6	7*	8	9	10	11	12	3										2
1	12	3	4*			7	6	9	10	11	8	2	5									
4	2	3	4	3	3	3	4	4	4	4	2	3	1									
	1										1											
			1	1		1	1															

1 own-goal

1981-82

Manager: Brian Miller

1	Aug	29	(a)	Gillingham	L	1-3	Taylor	4,663
2	Sep	5	(h)	Plymouth A	W	1-0	Dobson (pen)	3,476
3		12	(a)	Bristol R	L	1-2	Kite (og)	5,083
4		19	(h)	Huddersfield T	D	0-0		6,524
5		22	(h)	Doncaster R	L	0-1		3,799
6		26	(a)	Millwall	L	3-4	Laws, Overson, Potts	4,796
7		29	(a)	Carlisle U	L	0-1		3,983
8	Oct	3	(h)	Swindon T	L	0-2		3,377
9		10	(a)	Portsmouth	W	2-1	Wharton, Young	9,891
10		17	(h)	Exeter C	D	3-3	Overson, Taylor, Laws (pen)	3,982
11		20	(a)	Preston NE	D	1-1	Wharton	7,521
12		24	(h)	Fulham	D	2-2	Hamilton, Taylor	4,124
13		31	(a)	Brentford	D	0-0		6,929
14	Nov	3	(h)	Chester	W	1-0	Cassidy	3,484
15		7	(h)	Wimbledon	D	2-2	Overson, Hamilton	4,242
16		14	(a)	Reading	D	1-1	Steven	4,337
17		28	(a)	Bristol C	W	3-2	McGee 2 (1 pen), Young	5,255
18	Dec	5	(h)	Oxford U	W	2-1	Cassidy, Hamilton	4,380
19	Jan	9	(h)	Plymouth A	D	1-1	Young	5,065
20		16	(h)	Newport C	W	2-1	Overson, Taylor	4,730
21		30	(a)	Huddersfield T	W	2-1	Taylor 2	10,269
22	Feb	2	(h)	Gillingham	W	1-0	Wharton	5,848
23		6	(h)	Bristol R	W	4-0	Scott, Hamilton, Taylor, Mabbutt (og)	5,784
24		9	(a)	Doncaster R	W	1-0	Wharton	5,638
25		13	(a)	Swindon T	W	2-1	Cassidy, Taylor	5,296
26		20	(h)	Millwall	D	1-1	Hamilton	7,081
27		27	(h)	Portsmouth	W	3-0	Phelan, Scott, Taylor	7,013
28	Mar	2	(a)	Walsall	D	1-1	Hamilton	4,196
29		6	(a)	Exeter C	L	1-2	Allen	3,136
30		13	(a)	Fulham	D	1-1	Young	7,214
31		17	(a)	Chester	W	1-0	Laws (pen)	3,509
32		20	(h)	Brentford	D	0-0		7,906
33		27	(a)	Wimbledon	D	0-0		2,641
34		31	(a)	Lincoln C	D	1-1	Steven	6,188
35	Apr	3	(h)	Reading	W	3-0	Hamilton 2, Young	6,661
36		10	(h)	Lincoln C	W	1-0	Hamilton	10,911
37		12	(a)	Chesterfield	W	2-1	Laws, Dobson	7,732
38		17	(a)	Oxford U	D	0-0		10,407
39		20	(h)	Southend U	L	3-5	Steven, McGee, Otulakowski (og)	8,171
40		24	(h)	Bristol C	W	2-0	Laws, Dobson	7,063
41	May	1	(a)	Newport C	D	0-0		4,094
42		4	(h)	Carlisle U	W	1-0	McGee	9,760
43		8	(h)	Walsall	W	2-1	McGee, Young	8,537
44		11	(h)	Preston NE	W	2-0	Hamilton 2	13,911
45		14	(a)	Southend U	W	4-1	McGee 2, Laws, Wharton	5,123
46		18	(h)	Chesterfield	D	1-1	Young	18,711

FINAL LEAGUE POSITION: 1st in Division Three (Promoted)

Appearances
Sub Appearances
Goals

FA Cup

1	Nov	21	(h)	Runcorn	D	0-0		6,112
R		24	(a)	Runcorn	W	2-1	McGee 2	5,500
2	Jan	2	(a)	Bury	D	1-1	Taylor	9,200
R		4	(h)	Bury	W	2-1	Steven, Hamilton	9,108
3		18	(h)	Altrincham	W	6-1	Hamilton 3, Taylor 2, Steven	10,174
4		23	(a)	Shrewsbury T	L	0-1		7,679

Appearances
Sub Appearances
Goals

League Cup

1	Sep	1	(a)	Tranmere R	L	2-4	Hamilton, Potts	2,034
		15	(h)	Tranmere R	D	3-3	Holt 2, Cassidy	2,363

Appearances
Sub Appearances
Goals

Stevenson A	Laws B	Holt D	Scott D	Phelan M	Dobson M	Cavener P	Taylor S	Hamilton W	Cassidy T	Potts E	Young K	Overson V	Steven T	Robertson S	Dixon P	Wharton A	Anderson C	McGee P	Allen M	Flynn B	
1	2	3	4*	5	6	7	8	9	10	11	12										1
1	2	3			6	7	8	9	10	11	4	5									2
1	2	3	4		6	7*	8	9		11		5	10	12							3
1	2	3	4		6	7		9	10			5	8	11							4
1	2	3	4		6		12	9	10*	7		5	8	11							5
1	2	3	4		6		10	9*		7		5	8	11	12						6
1	2		4	9	6		10			7		5	8	11		3					7
1	2		4	9	6		10			7	12	5	8	11*		3					8
1	2		4*	7	6		10	9		12	11	5	8			3					9
1	2		4	7	6		10	9			11	5	8			3					10
1	2		9	3	4		11	10			7	5	6			8					11
1	2		4	7	6		10	9			11	5	8			3					12
1	2		4*	7	6		10	9			11	5	8			3	12				13
1	2			7	6		10	9	4	12	11*	5	8			3					14
1	2			6				9	4	7	11	5	8			3		10			15
1	2			6				9	4	7	11	5	8			3		10			16
1	2			6	7			9	4	12	11	5	8*			3		10			17
1	2			6	7			9	4		11	5	8			3		10			18
1	2				6		10	9	8		11	5	7		4	3					19
1	2				6		10	9	7		11	5	8		4	3					20
1	2	6	12		7		10	9	4		11	5	8*			3					21
1	2	6	8		7		10	9	4		11	5				3					22
1	2	6	8		7		10	9	4		11	5				3					23
1	2	6	8	12	7		10	9	4		11	5*				3					24
1	2	6	8	5*	7	12	10	9	4	11						3					25
1	2	6	8	5	7		10	9	4		11					3					26
1	2	6	8	5	7		10*	9	4	12	11					3					27
1	2	6	8	5	7			9	4	10	11					3*			12		28
1	2	6	8*	5	7			9	4	10	11	3							12		29
1	2	3	4	6	7			9			11	5	8							10	30
1	2	3	4	6	7			9		12	11	5	8							10*	31
1	2	3	4	6	7			9			11	5	8					10			32
1	2		4	6*	7			9		12	11	5	8				3	10			33
1	2				7			9		4	11	5	8		6	3		10			34
1	2	6			7	4		9			11	5*	8			3	12	10			35
1	2	6	4		7	12		9			11		8		5	3*		10			36
1	2	6			7	4		9			11		8		5		3	10			37
1	2	6	4		7			9			11		8		5	3		10			38
1	2	6	4		7	12		9			11		8		5	3*		10			39
1	2	6			7			9	4		11	5	8			3		10			40
1		6	2		7			9	4	11		5	8			3		10			41
1	2	6			7			9	4		11	5	8			3		10			42
1		6	2*		7			9	4	12	11	5	8			3		10			43
1	2	6			7			9	4		11	5	8			3		10			44
1	2	6			7			9	4		11	5	8			3		10			45
1	2	6			7			9	4		11		8		5	3		10			46
46	44	30	29	22	44	6	21	44	27	14	37	36	36	5	8	34	2	19		2	
			1	1		3	1			7	2			1	1		2		2		
	6		2	1	3		9	11	3	1	7	4	3			5		7	1		

3 own-goals

Stevenson A	Laws B	Holt D	Scott D	Phelan M	Dobson M	Cavener P	Taylor S	Hamilton W	Cassidy T	Potts E	Young K	Overson V	Steven T	Robertson S	Dixon P	Wharton A	Anderson C	McGee P	Allen M	Flynn B	
1	2			6				9	4	7	11	5	8			3		10			1
1	2			6	7			9	4		11	5	8			3		10			R
1	2				7		10	9	4		11	5	8		6	3					2
1	2				7		10	9	4		11	5	8		6	3					R
1	2				7		10	9	4		11	5	8		6	3					3
1	2				7		10	9	4	12	11	5	8		6*	3					4
6	6			2	5		4	6	6	1	6	6	6		4	6		2			
										1											
							3	4					2					2			

Stevenson A	Laws B	Holt D	Scott D	Phelan M	Dobson M	Cavener P	Taylor S	Hamilton W	Cassidy T	Potts E	Young K	Overson V	Steven T	Robertson S	Dixon P	Wharton A	Anderson C	McGee P	Allen M	Flynn B	
1	2	3		5	6	7	8	9	10	11	4										2
1	2	3*	4		6	12		9	10	7		5	8	11							
2	2	2	1	1	2	1	1	2	2	2	1	1	1	1							
						1															
		2						1	1	1											

1982-83

Manager: Brian Miller until January, then Frank Casper

1	Aug	28	(h)	Bolton W	D 0-0		10,562
2	Sep	4	(a)	Middlesbrough	W 4-1	Laws, Dobson, Hamilton, Young	8,036
3		7	(h)	Carlisle U	W 4-1	Hamilton 3 (1 pen), McGee	7,703
4		11	(h)	Rotherham U	L 1-2	Steven	9,169
5		18	(a)	Barnsley	L 0-3		11,938
6		25	(h)	Shrewsbury T	L 1-2	Wharton	6,480
7	Oct	2	(a)	Queen's Park R	L 2-3	Steven 2	9,165
8		9	(h)	Crystal P	W 2-1	Hamilton, Taylor	6,480
9		16	(a)	Charlton A	L 1-2	Phelan	5,940
10		20	(a)	Leeds U	L 1-3	Muir	13,827
11		23	(a)	Fulham	L 1-3	Laws (pen)	9,040
12		30	(h)	Oldham A	L 1-2	Hamilton	7,265
13	Nov	6	(a)	Newcastle U	L 0-3		20,961
14		13	(h)	Cambridge U	W 2-1	Taylor 2	6,039
15		20	(a)	Sheffield W	D 1-1	Steven	16,329
16		27	(h)	Derby C	D 1-1	McGee	7,513
17	Dec	4	(a)	Chelsea	L 1-2	Laws	8,184
18		11	(h)	Leicester C	L 2-4	Steven, Taylor	6,503
19		18	(a)	Grimsby T	L 2-3	Laws (pen), Moore (og)	5,448
20		27	(h)	Blackburn R	L 0-1		20,439
21		28	(a)	Wolves	L 0-2		21,961
22	Jan	1	(h)	Sheffield W	W 4-1	Taylor 3, Hamilton	9,548
23		3	(h)	Middlesbrough	D 1-1	Scott	9,205
24		15	(a)	Bolton W	L 0-3		8,894
25		22	(h)	Barnsley	W 3-1	Steven, Hamilton, Taylor (pen)	10,358
26	Feb	5	(a)	Rotherham U	D 1-1	Taylor	6,079
27		26	(h)	Charlton A	W 7-1	Hamilton 3, Taylor 3, Steven	7,040
28	Mar	5	(h)	Fulham	W 1-0	Flynn	8,774
29		19	(h)	Newcastle U	W 1-0	Donovan	14,069
30		26	(a)	Cambridge U	L 0-2		3,549
31	Apr	2	(h)	Wolves	L 0-1		9,643
32		4	(a)	Blackburn R	L 1-2	Scott	13,434
33		9	(h)	Leeds U	L 1-2	Steven	12,205
34		12	(a)	Oldham A	L 0-3		6,126
35		16	(a)	Carlisle U	D 1-1	Phelan	5,081
36		23	(h)	Chelsea	W 3-0	Hamilton 2, Donovan (pen)	7,452
37		30	(a)	Derby C	L 0-2		14,674
38	May	3	(a)	Shrewsbury T	W 2-1	Phelan, Donovan	3,573
39		7	(h)	Grimsby T	D 1-1	Donovan (pen)	7,136
40		10	(h)	Queen's Park R	W 2-1	Donovan 2	7,215
41		14	(a)	Leicester C	D 0-0		29,453
42		17	(a)	Crystal P	L 0-1		22,743

FINAL LEAGUE POSITION: 21st in Division Two (Relegated)

Appearances
Sub Appearances
Goals

FA Cup

3	Jan	8	(a)	Carlisle U	D 2-2	Taylor, Wharton	6,998
R		11	(h)	Carlisle U	W 3-1	Flynn, Steven, Laws (pen)	9,439
4		29	(h)	Swindon T	W 3-1	Hamilton 2, Steven	9,786
5	Feb	19	(a)	Crystal P	D 0-0		14,949
R		28	(h)	Crystal P	W 1-0	Taylor (pen)	16,240
6	Mar	12	(h)	Sheffield W	D 1-1	Cassidy	23,134
R		15	(a)	Sheffield W	L 0-5		41,731

Appearances
Sub Appearances
Goals

League Cup

1	Aug	31	(a)	Bury	W 5-3	Phelan, McGee, Scott, Wharton, Steven	3,111
	Sep	14	(h)	Bury	W 3-1	Hamilton, Laws (pen), Cruikshank (og)	3,714
2	Oct	5	(h)	Middlesbrough	W 3-2	Phelan, Hamilton, Young	3,909
		26	(a)	Middlesbrough	D 1-1	Laws	10,328
3	Nov	9	(a)	Coventry C	W 2-1	McGee 2	7,437
4		30	(h)	Birmingham C	W 3-2	McGee, Taylor, Brazier (og)	10,726
5	Jan	19	(a)	Tottenham H	W 4-1	Roberts 2 (2 ogs), Hamilton 2	30,771
SF	Feb	8	(a)	Liverpool	L 0-3		33,520
		15	(h)	Liverpool	W 1-0	Scott	22,228

Appearances
Sub Appearances
Goals

Stevenson A	Laws B	Ray P	Scott D	Phelan M	Holt D	Dobson M	Steven T	Hamilton W	McGee P	Young K	Wharton A	Taylor S	Cassidy T	Cavener P	Muir I	Donachie W	Flynn B	O'Rourke W	Walsh M	Miller D	Donovan T	Overson V	Dixon L	
1	2	3	4	5	6	7	8	9	10	11														1
1	2		4	5	6	7	8	9	10	11	3													2
1	2		4	5	6	7	8	9	10	11	3													3
1	2		4*	5	6	7	8	9	10	11	3	12												4
1	2		4	5	6	7	8	9	10*		3	12	11											5
1	2		4	5	6	7	8	9	10		3	12	11*											6
1	2		4	5	6	7	8	9		11	3	10												7
1	2		4	5	6	7		9		11	3	10		8										8
1	2		4	5	6	7*		9		11	3	10		8	12									9
1	2		4	5	6	7		9		11	3			8	10									10
1	2		4*	5	6	7	12	9		11	3	10		8										11
1	2		10	5	6	7*	8	9	4	11	3			12										12
1	2		6	4	5	7	8	9	10	11	3													13
1	2		6	5		7	8		10	11		9	4			3								14
1	2		12	5		7	8	9	11			10	4			3*	6							15
1	2			5		7	8	9	11		3	10	4				6							16
1	2		12	5*		7	8	9	11		3	10	4				6							17
1	2			5	3	7	8	9	11			10	4				6							18
1	2			5	3	7	8	9	11			10	4				6							19
	2			5	3	7	8	9				10	4				6	1	11					20
	2		11	5	3	7	8	9				10	4				6	1						21
	2		11*	5		7	8	9				10				3	6	1	4	12				22
	2		11	5	7		8	9				10				3	6	1	4					23
	2		7	5	4		8	9		11	12	10*				3	6	1						24
1			2	4		5	8*	9		11	12	10		7		3	6							25
1	2		7	4		5	8	9		11*		10	12			3	6							26
1	2		7	4		5	8	9		11		10				3	6							27
1	2			4		5	8	9		11		10	7			3	6*				12			28
1	2		7	4		5	8	9		11						3	6				10			29
1	2		7	4		5	8			11		9				3	6				10			30
1	2		7	4		5	8			11*		9				3	6				10	12		31
1	2		7	4		5	8	9		11		10				3	6							32
1	2		7	4		5	8	9		11*			12			3	6				10			33
1	2		7*	4		5	8	9				12				3	6				10	11		34
1	2			4		5	8	9			11		7			3	6				10			35
1	2		11	4		5	8	9					7			3	6				10			36
1	2		11	4		5	8	9					7			3	6				10			37
	2		11	4		5	8	9					7*			3	6	1			10	12		38
	2		11	4		5	8	9					7*			3	6	1			10	12		39
			11	4			8	9	12	7*						3	6	1			10	5	2	40
			11	4		5	8	9		7						3	6	1			10		2	41
			11	4		5*	8	9			7					3	6	1			10	12	2	42
32	38	1	34	42	19	39	38	39	14	24	16	22	16	5	1	23	28	10	3		13	2	3	
			2				1		1		2	4	2	1	1					1	1	4		
	4		2	2		1	8	13	2	1	1	12			1		1				6			

1 own-goal

Stevenson A	Laws B	Ray P	Scott D	Phelan M	Holt D	Dobson M	Steven T	Hamilton W	McGee P	Young K	Wharton A	Taylor S	Cassidy T	Cavener P	Muir I	Donachie W	Flynn B	O'Rourke W	Walsh M	Miller D	Donovan T	Overson V	Dixon L	
	2		7	4	5		8	9		11	12	10				3	6*	1						3
	2		7*	5	4		8	9		11	12	10				3	6	1						R
1			2	4		5	8	9		11		10	12	7*		3	6							4
1	2		7	4		5	8	9		11		10				3	6							5
1	2		7	4		5	8	9		11		10				3	6							R
1	2			4		5	8	9		11*		10	7			3	6				12			6
1	2		7	4		5*	8	9		11		10				3	6				12			R
5	6		6	7	2	5	7	7		7		7	1	1		7	7	2						
											2		1								2			
	1						2	2			1	2	1				1							

Stevenson A	Laws B	Ray P	Scott D	Phelan M	Holt D	Dobson M	Steven T	Hamilton W	McGee P	Young K	Wharton A	Taylor S	Cassidy T	Cavener P	Muir I	Donachie W	Flynn B	O'Rourke W	Walsh M	Miller D	Donovan T	Overson V	Dixon L	
1	2		4*	5	6	7	8	9	10	11	3	12												1
1	2		4	5	6	7	8	9	10*		3	12	11											
1	2		4	5	6	7	8*	9		11	3	10	12											2
1	2			5	6	7	8	9	4	11	3			10										
1	2		6	4	5	7	8		10	11		9	3											3
1	2			5		7	8	9	11		3	10	4				6							4
1	2		7	5		4	8	9		11		10				3	6							5
1	2		7	4		5	8	9		11		10				3	6							SF
1	2		7	4		5	8	9		11		10*	12			3	6							
9	9		7	9	5	9	9	8	5	7	5	6	3	1		3	4							
												2	2											
	2		2	2			1	4	4	1	1	1												

4 own-goals

1983-84

Manager: John Bond

1	Aug	27	(a)	Hull C	L 1-4	Reeves	8,394
2	Sep	3	(h)	Bournemouth	W 5-1	Hamilton 3, Dobson, Reeves	5,525
3		6	(h)	Newport C	W 2-0	Reeves, Hamilton	6,755
4		10	(a)	Oxford U	D 2-2	Flynn, Hamilton	5,824
5		24	(a)	Brentford	D 0-0		8,042
6		27	(a)	Bolton W	D 0-0		9,709
7	Oct	1	(h)	Plymouth A	W 2-1	Scott, Hamilton	6,845
8		9	(a)	Millwall	L 0-2		6,707
9		15	(h)	Gillingham	L 2-3	Hamilton, Dobson	5,590
10		18	(h)	Southend U	W 3-0	Reeves, Hamilton, Miller	5,307
11		22	(a)	Lincoln C	L 1-3	Hamilton	3,793
12		29	(h)	Wigan A	W 3-0	Flynn, Hutchison, Reeves	7,458
13	Nov	2	(a)	Exeter C	D 1-1	Flynn	3,714
14		5	(h)	Preston NE	W 2-1	Reeves, Hamilton	8,095
15		8	(h)	Sheffield U	W 2-1	Donachie, Dobson	9,574
16		12	(a)	Bristol R	L 1-2	Reeves	7,021
17		26	(h)	Port Vale	W 7-0	Reeves 3, Donachie, Flynn, Hutchison, Hamilton	6,385
18	Dec	3	(a)	Rotherham U	D 1-1	Flynn	5,544
19		17	(a)	Wimbledon	W 4-1	Scott 2, Reeves, Hamilton	2,883
20		26	(h)	Bradford C	L 1-2	Jackson (og)	12,327
21		27	(a)	Walsall	D 1-1	Hamilton	8,131
22		31	(h)	Scunthorpe U	W 5-0	Flynn, Hutchison, Reeves, Dobson, Tueart	7,668
23	Jan	2	(a)	Orient	W 2-1	Flynn, Hamilton	4,457
24		21	(a)	Sheffield U	D 0-0		13,892
25	Feb	4	(a)	Plymouth A	D 1-1	Tueart	5,104
26		11	(h)	Brentford	D 2-2	Tueart, Hamilton	7,027
27		14	(h)	Exeter C	W 4-0	Phelan, Flynn, Tueart, Biggins	5,968
28		18	(a)	Wigan A	L 0-1		7,509
29		25	(h)	Lincoln C	W 4-0	Biggins 3, Flynn	6,652
30	Mar	2	(a)	Southend U	D 2-2	Hamilton, Hutchison	2,864
31		6	(a)	Preston NE	L 2-4	Donachie, Tueart	8,813
32		10	(h)	Bristol R	D 0-0		6,306
33		17	(h)	Millwall	W 1-0	Biggins	5,088
34		24	(a)	Gillingham	W 1-0	Biggins	4,319
35		27	(h)	Oxford U	D 1-1	Daley	8,058
36		31	(h)	Bolton W	D 2-2	Miller, Hamilton	8,350
37	Apr	7	(a)	Newport C	L 0-1		2,306
38		9	(a)	Bournemouth	L 0-1		4,113
39		14	(h)	Rotherham U	D 2-2	Scott, Biggins	4,676
40		21	(a)	Bradford C	L 1-2	Biggins	5,578
41		23	(h)	Walsall	L 0-2		3,948
42		28	(a)	Port Vale	W 3-2	Daley 3	3,061
43	May	5	(h)	Orient	L 2-3	Phelan, Hamilton	3,301
44		7	(a)	Scunthorpe U	L 0-4		2,720
45		12	(h)	Wimbledon	L 0-2		3,382
46		15	(h)	Hull C	L 0-2		8,051

FINAL LEAGUE POSITION: 12th in Division Three

Appearances
Sub Appearances
Goals

FA Cup

1	Nov	19	(a*)	Hyde U	W 2-0	Reeves, Waldron	7,723
2	Dec	10	(a)	Chesterfield	D 2-2	Dobson, Reeves	5,788
R		19	(h)	Chesterfield	W 3-2	Hamilton 2, Reeves	8,286
3	Jan	7	(h)	Oxford U	D 0-0		11,672
R		11	(a)	Oxford U	L 1-2	Hamilton	10,497

*Drawn away but played at Turf Moor, Burnley.

Appearances
Sub Appearances
Goals

League Cup

1	Aug	30	(a)	Crewe A	L 0-1		3,043
	Sep	13	(h)	Crewe A	L 3-4	Flynn 2, Wharton	5,659

Appearances
Sub Appearances
Goals

Hansbury R	Dixon L	Donachie W	Phelan M	Gallagher J	Flynn B	Scott D	Reeves K	Hamilton W	Young K	Hutchison T	Wharton A	Overson V	Dobson M	Gow G	Donovan T	Miller D	Waldron M	Daley S	Tueart D	Kennedy S	Biggins W	Baker S	Glendon K	Malley P	
1	2	3	4	5	6	7	8	9	10	11															1
1			4		6	2	8	9		11	3*	5	7	10	12										2
1		2	4		6		8	9		11	3	5	7	10											3
1		2	4		6	12	8	9		11	3*	5	7	10											4
1			4		6	2		9	11*	7	3	5	8	10		12									5
1			4		6	2		9		11	3	5	7	8			10								6
1			4		6	2	12	9		11	3	5	7	8			10*								7
1			4		6	2	8	9		7	3		11	10			5								8
1		3	4		6	12	8	9		7		5*	11	10			2								9
1		3	4		6		8	9		7		5	11			10	2								10
1		3	4		6	2	8	9		7		5	11	12		10*									11
1		3	4		6	2	8	9		7		5	11			10									12
1		3	4		6	2	8	9		7		5				10	11								13
1		3	4		6	2	8	9		7		5	11				10								14
1		3	4		6	2	8	9		11		5	10				7								15
1		3	4		6	2	8	9		7		5	11*				10	12							16
1		3	4		6	2	8	9		7		5	11*				10	12							17
1		3	4		6	2	8	9		7		5					11	10							18
1		3	4			2	8	9		7		5	11				6	10							19
1		3	4		6	2	8	9		7		5					11	10							20
1		3	4		6	2	8	9		7		5	11					10							21
1		3*	4		6	2	8	9		7		5	11				10		12						22
1			3		6		8	9		7		4	5				2	10	11						23
1		3			6	2		9		7		5	11					8	10	4					24
1		3	4		6	2		9		11		5	8					10	7						25
1		3	4		6	2		9		11		5	8						7		10				26
1		3	4		6	2		9		11		5	8						7		10				27
1		3	4		6*	2		9		11		5	8				7	12			10				28
1		3	4		6	8		9		11			5					7			10	2			29
1		3	4		6*	8		9		11			5			12		7			10	2			30
1		3	4			8		9		11			5					6	7		10	2			31
1		3	4		6	8		9		11			5					7			10	2			32
1		3	4		6	8*		9		11		5				7			12		10	2			33
1		3	4		6*			9		11		5				8		7	12		10	2			34
1		3	4		6			9		11		5				8*		7	12		10	2			35
1		3	4		6			9		11		5				8		7*	12		10	2			36
1		3	4		6*	8		9		11		5							12		10	2	7		37
1		3				8		9		11		5				6			7	4	10	2			38
1		3	4		6	8		9		11		5						7		2	10				39
1		3*	4		6	2		9		11		5				8			12	7	10				40
1		3	4		6*	8		9		11						5			7	2	10			12	41
1			4		6	8		9		11						5		7		2	10		3		42
1			4		6	2		9		11		5				8		7		10			3		43
1			4		6	2		9		11		5				8		7			10		3		44
1		3	4		6	2		9		11		5				8		7			10				45
1		3	4		6	2		9		11		5						7			10			8	46
46	1	37	44	1	43	38	20	46	2	46	7	38	28	8		15	16	20	8	7	20	10	4	1	
						2	1							1	1	2		3	7					1	
		3	2		9	4	12	18		4			4			2		4	5		8				

1 own-goal

Hansbury R	Dixon L	Donachie W	Phelan M	Gallagher J	Flynn B	Scott D	Reeves K	Hamilton W	Young K	Hutchison T	Wharton A	Overson V	Dobson M	Gow G	Donovan T	Miller D	Waldron M	Daley S	Tueart D	Kennedy S	Biggins W	Baker S	Glendon K	Malley P	
1		3	4		6	2	8	9		7		5	11				10								1
1		3	4		6	2	8	9		7		5	11					10							2
1		3	4		6	2	8	9		7		5					11	10							R
1		3	4*		6	2	8	9		7		5	11					12	10						3
1		3			6	2	8*	9		7		5	11				4	12	10						R
5		5	4		5	5	5	5		5		5	4				3	2	2						
																		2							
							3	3					1				1								

Hansbury R	Dixon L	Donachie W	Phelan M	Gallagher J	Flynn B	Scott D	Reeves K	Hamilton W	Young K	Hutchison T	Wharton A	Overson V	Dobson M	Gow G	Donovan T	Miller D	Waldron M	Daley S	Tueart D	Kennedy S	Biggins W	Baker S	Glendon K	Malley P	
1	2*		4		6	7	8	9		11	3	5	10		12										1
1		2	4	5	6	7	8*	9		11	3			10						12					
2	1	1	2	1	2	2	2	2		2	2	1	1	1											
															1					1					
					2						1														

1984-85

Manager: John Benson

1	Aug	25	(h)	Plymouth A	D 1-1	Taylor	4,644
2		31	(a)	Doncaster R	L 0-2		3,368
3	Sep	8	(h)	Bristol R	D 0-0		4,573
4		15	(a)	Derby C	D 2-2	Hird, Biggins	11,755
5		18	(a)	Orient	W 2-0	Taylor, Foster (og)	2,359
6		22	(h)	Hull C	D 1-1	Biggins	5,526
7		29	(a)	Rotherham U	L 2-3	Biggins 2	4,646
8	Oct	2	(h)	Newport C	W 2-0	Grewcock, Flynn	3,666
9		6	(a)	Bournemouth	D 1-1	Hird	3,180
10		13	(h)	Lincoln C	L 1-2	Hird (pen)	4,315
11		20	(a)	Reading	L 1-5	Biggins	4,024
12		23	(h)	Brentford	W 3-1	Hird (pen), Biggins, Roberts (og)	2,916
13		27	(h)	Bolton W	W 3-2	Hird, Grewcock, Miller	6,501
14	Nov	3	(a)	Preston NE	D 3-3	Biggins 2, Whatmore	4,995
15		6	(h)	Gillingham	L 0-1		3,595
16		10	(a)	Cambridge U	W 3-2	Hird, Grewcock, Biggins	2,505
17		24	(h)	Bradford C	L 1-2	Biggins	7,060
18	Dec	1	(a)	Millwall	L 1-2	Hird	5,376
19		15	(h)	Swansea C	D 1-1	Lawrence	3,798
20		22	(h)	Walsall	L 1-2	Hird	3,350
21		26	(a)	York C	L 0-4		6,397
22		29	(a)	Bristol C	L 0-4		8,282
23	Jan	1	(h)	Wigan A	L 1-2	Biggins	5,235
24	Feb	2	(h)	Rotherham U	W 7-0	Hird 3 (1 pen), Biggins 2, Devine, Lawrence	3,907
25		9	(a)	Hull C	L 0-2		6,478
26		16	(h)	Orient	D 1-1	Hird	3,744
27		23	(h)	Preston NE	W 2-0	Scott, Biggins	4,768
28	Mar	2	(a)	Bolton W	W 3-1	Hampton, Grewcock, Devine	6,468
29		5	(a)	Brentford	L 1-2	Hird	3,267
30		9	(h)	Reading	L 0-2		3,955
31		12	(h)	Doncaster R	L 0-1		3,020
32		16	(a)	Lincoln C	L 1-3	Hird	2,137
33		23	(h)	Bournemouth	D 1-1	Biggins	2,784
34		26	(a)	Plymouth A	D 2-2	Hird, Biggins	3,165
35		29	(a)	Gillingham	D 1-1	Biggins	5,935
36	Apr	2	(a)	Newport C	L 1-2	Grewcock	1,689
37		6	(h)	York C	D 1-1	Phelan	3,844
38		8	(a)	Wigan A	L 0-2		3,517
39		13	(h)	Cambridge U	W 2-0	Taylor 2	2,843
40		16	(a)	Bristol R	L 0-4		4,866
41		20	(a)	Bradford C	L 2-3	Biggins, Grewcock	8,156
42		23	(h)	Derby C	L 0-1		3,873
43		27	(h)	Millwall	D 1-1	Overson	3,586
44	May	4	(a)	Swansea C	W 1-0	Taylor	5,221
45		6	(h)	Bristol C	L 0-1		4,570
46		11	(a)	Walsall	W 3-2	Taylor 2, Hird	3,396

FINAL LEAGUE POSITION: 21st in Division Three (Relegated)

Appearances
Sub Appearances
Goals

FA Cup

1	Nov	17	(a)	Penrith	W 9-0	Hird 3 (1 pen), Taylor 3, Powell 2, Grewcock	1,813
2	Dec	8	(h)	Halifax T	W 3-1	Hird, Devine, Biggins	5,543
3	Jan	5	(a)	Wimbledon	L 1-3	Devine	3,381

Appearances
Sub Appearances
Goals

League Cup

1	Aug	23	(h)	Crewe A	L 1-2	Grewcock	3,043
	Sep	4	(a)	Crewe A	W 3-0	Overson, Hird, Grewcock	3,067
2		26	(a)	Manchester U	L 0-4		28,383
	Oct	9	(h)	Manchester U	L 0-3		12,690

Appearances
Sub Appearances
Goals

Hansbury R	Scott D	Hampton P	Phelan M	Overson V	Hird K	Grewcock N	Powell B	Taylor A	Biggins W	Hutchison T	Flynn B	Miller D	Kennedy S	Whatmore N	Malley P	Gallagher J	Devine P	Palmer G	Lawrence L	Neenan J	Rhodes M	Chilton A	
1	2	3	4	5	6	7	8	9	10	11													1
1	2	3	4	5	6	7	8*	9	10	11	12												2
1	2	3	4	5	6	7		9	10	11		8											3
1	2	3	4	5	6	7	12	9	10	11		8*											4
1	2	3	4	5	6	7	8	9	10	11													5
1	2	3	4	5	6	7	8	9*	10	11	12												6
1	2*	3	4	5	6	7	8	12	10	11	9												7
1		3	4	5	6	7			10	11	8		2	9									8
1		3	4	5	6	7			10	11	8	12	2*	9									9
1		3	4	5	6	7		12	10	11	8	2		9*									10
1		3*	4	5	6	7	12		10	11	8	2		9									11
1		3	4	5	6	7			10	11	12	8*		9	2								12
1		3	4	5	6	7			10	11		8		9	2								13
1		3		5	6	7			10	11*	12	8		9	2	4							14
1		3		5	6	7		12	10	11		8		9	2	4*							15
1		3		5	6	7	4	9*	10	11		8	2				12						16
1		3	4	5	6	7	8		10	11								2	9				17
1		3	4		6	7	8		10	11			5					2	9				18
1		3	4	5	6	7	8		10	11								2	9				19
1		3	4	5	6	7			10	11		8						2	9				20
1		3	4	5	6	7			10	11		8						2	9				21
1		3	4		6	7			10	11			5		8		12	2	9*				22
1		3*	4		6	7			10	11			5		8	12	9	2					23
		3*	4	5	6	7			10	11			8				9	2	12	1			24
	12	3	4	5	6	7			10	11			8*				9	2		1			25
	8	3	4	5	6	7			10	11							9	2		1			26
	8	3	4		6	7			10	11						5	9	2		1			27
	8	3	4	5	6	7			10	11							9	2		1			28
	8	3	4	5	6	7			10	11							9	2		1			29
	8	3	4	5	6	7			10	11							9	2		1			30
	8	3	4	5	6	7			10	11							9*	2	12	1			31
	8	3	4	5	6	7			10	11						9		2*	12	1			32
1	8	3	4	5	6	7			10	11							9	2					33
1	8	3	4	5	6	7*			10	11							9	2	12				34
1	8	3	4	5	6	7			10	11							9	2					35
1	8	3	4	5	6	7			10	11							9	2					36
1	8	3	4	5	6	7		9	10	11								2					37
1	8	3*	4	5	6	12		9	10	11								2			7		38
1	8		4	5		7		9	10	11					2						6	3	39
1	8*	12	4	5		7		9	10	11		2			3						6		40
1	2	3	4	5	6	12		8*	10	11							9				7		41
1	2	3*	4	5	6	7		9	10	11							12				8		42
1	2	3	4	5	6	7			10	11					12		9*				8		43
1	2	3	4	5	6	7		9	10	11											8		44
1	2	3	4	5	6	7*		9	10	11		12									8		45
1		3	4	5	6	7		9	10*	11							12	2			8		46
37	27	44	43	42	44	44	9	16	46	46	5	12	8	8	8	4	15	23	6	9	9	1	
	1	1				2	2	3			4	2			1	1	4		4				
	1	1	1	1	16	6		7	18		1	1		1			2		2				

2 own-goals

Hansbury R	Scott D	Hampton P	Phelan M	Overson V	Hird K	Grewcock N	Powell B	Taylor A	Biggins W	Hutchison T	Flynn B	Miller D	Kennedy S	Whatmore N	Malley P	Gallagher J	Devine P	Palmer G	Lawrence L	Neenan J	Rhodes M	Chilton A	
1		3	4	5*	6	7	8	9	10	11		2	12										1
1		3	4	5	6	7	8		10	11							9	2					2
1		3	4	8	6	7			10	11			5				9	2					3
3		3	3	3	3	3	2	1	3	3		1	1				2	2					
													1										
					4	1	2	3	1								2						

Hansbury R	Scott D	Hampton P	Phelan M	Overson V	Hird K	Grewcock N	Powell B	Taylor A	Biggins W	Hutchison T	Flynn B	Miller D	Kennedy S	Whatmore N	Malley P	Gallagher J	Devine P	Palmer G	Lawrence L	Neenan J	Rhodes M	Chilton A	
1	2	3	4	5	6	7	8	9	10	11													1
1	2	3	4	5	6	7		9	10	11		8											
1	2	3	4	5	6	7	8	9*	10	11	12												2
1		3	4	5	6	7			10	11	8	2		9									
4	3	4	4	4	4	4	2	3	4	4	1	2		1									
											1												
				1	1	2																	

1985-86

Manager: Martin Buchan until 10 October 1985, then Tommy Cavanagh.

1	Aug	17	(h)	Northampton T	W 3-2	Biggins 2, Hird	4,279
2		23	(h)	Stockport C	L 0-1		3,909
3		26	(h)	Port Vale	L 1-2	Taylor	3,995
4		31	(a)	Aldershot	W 2-0	Taylor 2	1,744
5	Sep	7	(h)	Hartlepool U	W 2-0	Heggarty, Biggins	3,175
6		14	(a)	Hereford U	D 2-2	Hird (pen), Malley	3,411
7		17	(a)	Preston NE	L 0-1		5,585
8		21	(h)	Rochdale	W 1-0	Biggins	4,241
9		28	(a)	Peterborough U	D 0-0		3,700
10	Oct	1	(h)	Colchester U	L 0-2		3,424
11		5	(a)	Chester C	L 0-4		2,974
12		12	(h)	Swindon T	L 0-2		3,022
13		19	(a)	Crewe A	L 1-3	Taylor	1,998
14		22	(h)	Torquay U	W 3-0	Taylor 2, Hird (pen)	2,295
15		26	(a)	Halifax T	D 2-2	Parker, Grewcock	2,334
16	Nov	2	(h)	Southend U	L 1-3	Robinson	2,673
17		5	(h)	Mansfield T	W 2-1	Hird, Taylor	2,020
18		9	(a)	Cambridge U	W 4-0	Hird, Devine, Taylor, Parker	1,917
19		23	(h)	Exeter C	W 3-1	Hird 2 (2 pens), McNichol (og)	2,893
20		30	(a)	Scunthorpe U	D 1-1	Hoskin	2,001
21	Dec	14	(h)	Orient	W 1-0	Taylor	3,007
22		20	(a)	Stockport C	D 1-1	Heesom	3,472
23		26	(a)	Tranmere R	L 1-2	Taylor	3,188
24	Jan	1	(h)	Wrexham	W 5-2	Parker 2, Deakin, Grewcock, Taylor	4,106
25		3	(a)	Southend U	W 3-2	Taylor 2, Deakin	2,619
26		18	(a)	Northampton T	L 0-2		3,095
27		25	(h)	Hereford U	W 3-2	Taylor 2, Lawrence	3,936
28	Feb	1	(a)	Hartlepool U	L 1-3	Lawrence	3,359
29		4	(a)	Torquay U	L 0-2		1,335
30		24	(a)	Port Vale	D 1-1	Lawrence	3,030
31	Mar	1	(h)	Peterborough U	D 1-1	Paris (og)	2,676
32		8	(h)	Chester C	W 1-0	Lawrence	3,742
33		11	(h)	Aldershot	L 1-2	Grewcock	2,675
34		15	(a)	Swindon T	L 1-3	Lawrence	7,311
35		18	(a)	Rochdale	L 0-1		2,406
36		22	(h)	Halifax T	L 1-3	Hampton	3,326
37		29	(a)	Wrexham	W 1-0	Hoskin	2,057
38		31	(h)	Tranmere R	W 3-1	Grewcock 2, Malley	3,132
39	Apr	5	(a)	Mansfield T	D 0-0		3,678
40		12	(h)	Cambridge U	D 1-1	Grewcock	2,796
41		15	(h)	Crewe A	L 0-1		1,988
42		19	(a)	Exeter C	W 2-0	Taylor, Parker	2,019
43		22	(h)	Preston NE	D 1-1	Deakin	3,835
44		26	(h)	Scunthorpe U	L 1-2	Grewcock	2,542
45	May	3	(a)	Orient	L 0-3		1,955
46		6	(a)	Colchester U	D 2-2	Devine, Lawrence	2,726

FINAL LEAGUE POSITION: 14th in Division Four

Appearances
Sub Appearances
Goals

FA Cup

1	Nov	16	(a)	Nuneaton B	W 3-2	Devine 2, Malley	4,500
2	Dec	7	(a)	Rotherham U	L 1-4	Parker	4,264

Appearances
Sub Appearances
Goals

League Cup

1	Aug	20	(h)	Bury	W 2-1	Taylor, Biggins	3,303
	Sep	3	(a)	Bury	L 3-5	Taylor 2, Hird	3,762

Appearances
Sub Appearances
Goals

Neenan J	Palmer G	Hampton P	Heggarty J	Overson V	Deakin R	Hird K	Malley P	Taylor A	Biggins W	Grewcock N	Chippendale B	Devine P	Peacock D	Rhodes M	Robinson A	Parker D	Heesom D	Hoskin A	Harrington P	Edwards N	Lawrence L	Kilner A	Haddock P	Holden R	
1	2	3	4	5	6	7	8	9	10	11															1
1	2	3	6	5	11	4	8	9	10	7															2
1	2	3	6	5	11	4	8	9	10	7*	12														3
1	2	3	6	5	11	4	8	9*	10	7		12													4
1	2	3	6	5	11	4	8	9	10*		7	12													5
1	2	3	6	5	11	4	8	9	10		7														6
1	2	3	6	5	11	4	8	9*	10		7	12													7
1	2	3	6	5	11	4	8		10	7*	12	9													8
	2	3	6		5		8	9*	10	7	4	12	1	11											9
	2	3	6		5		8	12	10	7	4*	9	1	11											10
	2	3	6		5	4	8	9	10		7*	12	1	11											11
		3	5		6	4*	2	9	10			11	1	12	7	8									12
		2	6		5	4	10*	9		12		11	1		7	8	3								13
		2	5		6	4	8	9				11	1		7	10	3								14
		2	5		6	4*	8	9		12		11	1		7	10	3								15
			5*		6	2	8	9		4		11	1		7	10	3	12							16
		2	5		6	4*	8	9		7		11				10	3	12	1						17
			5		6	2	8	9		7		4				10	3	11*	1	12					18
1			5		6	2	8	9*		7		4				10	3	11			12				19
1			5		6	2	8	9		7		4				10	3	11							20
1		12		5	6	2	8	9		7		4				10	3	11*							21
1		11		5	6	2	8	9		7		4				10	3								22
1		11*	4	5	6	2	8	9		7						10	3				12				23
1			4	5	6	2	8	9		7		11*				10	3					12			24
1			4	5	6	2		9		7		8				10	3					11			25
1		4		5	6	2		9		7		8				10*	3				12	11			26
1		11		5	6	2	4	9		7		8					3				10				27
1		11		5	6	2	4	9		7		8					3*				10	12			28
1		11		5	6	2	4	9*		7		8					3				10	12			29
1		11		5	6	2	4	9		7		8					3				10				30
1		11		5	6	2	4	9		7		8					3				10				31
1		11	12	5	6	2	4	9		7		8*					3				10				32
1		11	12	5	6	2	4	9		7		8*					3				10				33
1		3	6	5	8	2	4	9		7								11			10				34
1		3	6	5	8	2	4*	9				7					12	11			10				35
1		3	6	5	8	2	4	9*		7		12						11			10				36
1		3			6	2	4	9		7		8						11			10		5		37
1		3			6	2*	4	9		7		8					12	11			10		5		38
1		2	4		6			9		7		8					3	11			10		5		39
1		2	12		6		4	9		7		8					3*	11			10		5		40
1		3	2	6	8		4	9				7*				10		11			12		5		41
1		3	2	6	8		4	9		7						10		11					5		42
1		3	2	6	8		4	9		7						10		11					5		43
1		3	6	5*	8	2	4	9		7						10		11			12				44
1		3	5		6	2	4	9		7		8						11*			10			12	45
1		3	5		6	2	4	9		7		8						11			10				46
36	11	39	33	28	46	39	43	44	12	36	6	31	8	3	5	19	23	17	2		16	2	7		
		1	3					1		2	2	6		1			2	2		1	5	3		1	
		1	1		3	7	2	16	4	7		2			1	5	1	2			6				

2 own-goals

Neenan J	Palmer G	Hampton P	Heggarty J	Overson V	Deakin R	Hird K	Malley P	Taylor A	Biggins W	Grewcock N	Chippendale B	Devine P	Peacock D	Rhodes M	Robinson A	Parker D	Heesom D	Hoskin A	Harrington P	Edwards N	Lawrence L	Kilner A	Haddock P	Holden R	
1			5		6	2	8	9		7		4				10	3	11							1
1	2		5		6	4	8	9		7						10	3	11							2
2	1		2		2	2	2	2		2		1				2	2	2							
							1					2				1									

Neenan J	Palmer G	Hampton P	Heggarty J	Overson V	Deakin R	Hird K	Malley P	Taylor A	Biggins W	Grewcock N	Chippendale B	Devine P	Peacock D	Rhodes M	Robinson A	Parker D	Heesom D	Hoskin A	Harrington P	Edwards N	Lawrence L	Kilner A	Haddock P	Holden R	
1	2	3	6	5	11	4	8	9	10	7															1
1	2	3	6	5	11	4	8	9	10*	7		12													
2	2	2	2	2	2	2	2	2	2	2															
												1													
						1		3	1																

1986-87

Manager: Brian Miller

1	Aug	23	(a)	Torquay U	D 1-1	Parker	2,144
2		30	(h)	Scunthorpe U	W 1-0	James (pen)	3,008
3	Sep	6	(a)	Hereford U	L 0-2		2,796
4		13	(h)	Hartlepool U	D 1-1	Entwistle	2,465
5		16	(h)	Swansea C	D 1-1	Entwistle	2,775
6		20	(a)	Wolves	W 1-0	Grewcock	5,786
7		27	(h)	Halifax T	W 3-0	Parker 2, Hoskin	3,296
8		30	(a)	Tranmere R	L 1-2	Britton	2,017
9	Oct	4	(h)	Preston NE	L 1-4	James (pen)	5,974
10		11	(a)	Aldershot	L 0-2		2,061
11		18	(h)	Stockport C	W 2-0	Regis, Matthewson (og)	2,410
12		22	(a)	Northampton T	L 2-4	James, Hoskin	5,718
13		25	(a)	Exeter C	L 0-3		3,198
14	Nov	1	(h)	Peterborough U	D 0-0		2,229
15		4	(h)	Colchester U	W 2-1	Grewcock, Hoskin	1,696
16		8	(a)	Cambridge U	L 1-3	James (pen)	2,572
17		22	(h)	Lincoln C	W 3-1	Rodaway, Murphy, James	2,177
18		28	(a)	Southend U	L 1-2	Gallagher	3,309
19	Dec	13	(a)	Orient	L 0-2		2,413
20		19	(h)	Cardiff C	L 1-3	Hoskin	1,717
21		26	(a)	Wrexham	D 2-2	Parker, Murphy	4,568
22		27	(h)	Crewe A	W 4-0	Malley, Murphy, James, Hoskin	2,560
23	Jan	1	(h)	Rochdale	L 0-3		4,217
24		3	(a)	Lincoln C	L 1-2	Murphy	2,343
25		24	(h)	Hereford U	L 0-6		1,961
26		31	(a)	Hartlepool U	D 2-2	Malley, Grewcock	1,506
27	Feb	6	(a)	Swansea C	D 2-2	Murphy, Hoskin	6,015
28		14	(h)	Wolves	L 2-5	Grewcock, James	2,947
29		21	(a)	Halifax T	D 2-2	Grewcock, James	1,735
30		28	(h)	Tranmere R	D 2-2	Rodaway, Grewcock	2,394
31	Mar	4	(a)	Peterborough U	D 1-1	Grewcock	4,304
32		7	(h)	Exeter C	D 0-0		1,792
33		13	(a)	Stockport C	W 1-0	Hoskin	2,500
34		17	(h)	Northampton T	W 2-1	Gallagher, Hoskin	2,691
35		21	(h)	Aldershot	L 0-1		2,690
36		28	(a)	Preston NE	L 1-2	Parker	10,716
37	Apr	4	(h)	Cambridge U	L 0-2		1,874
38		10	(a)	Colchester U	L 0-1		2,635
39		14	(h)	Torquay U	D 2-2	Britton, James (pen)	2,718
40		18	(a)	Rochdale	W 2-0	Gallagher, Devaney	5,739
41		20	(h)	Wrexham	D 0-0		4,090
42		25	(a)	Cardiff C	L 0-1		2,003
43		28	(a)	Scunthorpe U	L 1-2	Malley	1,770
44	May	2	(h)	Southend U	W 2-1	Grewcock, James	3,991
45		4	(a)	Crewe A	L 0-1		4,175
46		9	(h)	Orient	W 2-1	Grewcock, Britton	15,696

FINAL LEAGUE POSITION: 22nd in Division Four

Appearances
Sub Appearances
Goals

FA Cup

1	Nov	15	(a)	Telford	L 0-3		4,145

Appearances
Sub Appearances
Goals

League Cup

1	Aug	26	(a)	Rochdale	D 1-1	James	1,937
	Sep	2	(h)	Rochdale	L 1-3	James (pen)	2,605

Appearances
Sub Appearances
Goals

Neenan J	Malley P	Hampton P	Rodaway W	Gallagher J	Deakin R	Britton I	Parker D	Entwistle W	James L	Hoskin A	Grewcock N	Kennedy S	Regis R	Leebrook P	Heesom D	Harris J	Murphy P	Woodworth A	Caughey M	Devaney P	Hardy J	
1	2	3	4	5	6	7	8	9	10	11												1
1	2	3	4	5	6	7	8		10	11	9											2
1	2	3	4	5	6	7*	8	12	10	11	9											3
1	2*	3	4	5	6	8	9	12	10	11	7											4
1		3	2	5	6	4	8	9	10	11	7											5
1		3	2	5	6	4	8	9	10	11	7											6
1		3	2	5	6	4	8	9	10	11	7											7
1		3	2	5	6	4	8	9	10	11	7											8
1		3	2	5	6	4	8	9	10	11	7											9
1	2	3	4	5	6	8	9		10	11	7											10
1	2*	3	4	5	6	7			10	11	9	8	12									11
1		3	2	5	6	8	9		10	11	7	4										12
1		3	4	5	6	7	8		10	11	9	2										13
1	2	3	4	5	6	7			10	11	9		8									14
1	2	3	4	5	6	7			10	11	9		8									15
1	2	3	4	5	6	7			10	11	9		8									16
1			4	5	6				10	11	9			2	3	7	8					17
1			4	5	6				10	11	7			2	3	8	9					18
1			4	5	6				10	11	9			2	3	7	8					19
1			4	5	6	7			10	11				2	3	8	9					20
1			4	5	6	7	8		10	11				2	3		9					21
1	5		4		6	7	8		10	11				2	3		9					22
1	5		4		6	7	8		10	11				2	3		9					23
1	5		4		6		8		10	11	7			2	3		9					24
	5		4		6	12	8		10	11	7			2	3		9*	1				25
1	5		4		6		8		10	11	7			2	3		9					26
1	5			4	6	12	8		10*	11	7			2	3		9					27
1	5			4	6		8		10	11	7			2	3		9					28
1			5	4	6	8			10	11	7			2	3				9			29
1	11	3	4	5	6	8			10		7			2					9			30
1	11	3	4	5	6	8			10		7			2					9			31
1	11	3	4	5	6	8			10		7			2			12		9*			32
1	8	3	4	5	6	11				10	7			2					9			33
1	11	3	4	5	6	8				10	7			2					9			34
1	8	3*	4	5	6	10				11				2					9	7	12	35
1	8	3	4*	5	6	10	7			11				2			12		9			36
1	8	3	4	5	6	7	9*		10	11				2			12					37
1	8	3	4	5	6	10	9		11	12	7			2								38
1	8	3	4	5	6	7	9*		10	11				2						12		39
1	8	3	4	5	6	10			9	11				2						7		40
1	8	3	4	5	6	9*			10	11	12			2						7		41
1	8	3	4	5	6	9*			10	12	11			2						7		42
1	8	3	4	5	6				9	11	7			2						10		43
1	8	3	4	5	6	11			10		7			2						9		44
1	8	3	4	5	6	11			9		7			2						10		45
1	8	3	4	5	6	11			9		7			2						10		46
45	33	33	44	41	46	37	24	6	42	38	35	3	3	30	13	4	12	1	8	8		
						2		2		2	1		1				3			1	1	
	3		2	3		3	5	2	10	8	9		1				5			1		

1 own-goal

Neenan J	Malley P	Hampton P	Rodaway W	Gallagher J	Deakin R	Britton I	Parker D	Entwistle W	James L	Hoskin A	Grewcock N	Kennedy S	Regis R	Leebrook P	Heesom D	Harris J	Murphy P	Woodworth A	Caughey M	Devaney P	Hardy J	
1	2	3†	4	5	6	7*	9		10	11	8		12		14							1
1	1	1	1	1	1	1	1		1	1	1											
													1		1							

Neenan J	Malley P	Hampton P	Rodaway W	Gallagher J	Deakin R	Britton I	Parker D	Entwistle W	James L	Hoskin A	Grewcock N	Kennedy S	Regis R	Leebrook P	Heesom D	Harris J	Murphy P	Woodworth A	Caughey M	Devaney P	Hardy J	
1	2	3	4	5	6	7	8	9	10	11												1
1	2	3	4	5	6	7*	8	12	10	11	9											
2	2	2	2	2	2	2	2	1	2	2	1											
								1														
									2													

1987-88

Manager: Brian Miller

1	Aug	15	(h)	Colchester U	L 0-3		5,419
2		22	(a)	Newport C	W 1-0	Oghani	2,016
3		29	(h)	Carlisle U	W 4-3	Taylor, Oghani, Zelem, Deakin	5,781
4	Sep	1	(a)	Leyton O	L 1-4	Farrell	3,560
5		5	(h)	Swansea C	W 1-0	Oghani	4,787
6		11	(a)	Tranmere R	W 1-0	Comstive	4,209
7		15	(h)	Wrexham	W 1-0	Farrell	5,650
8		19	(h)	Cambridge U	L 0-2		5,789
9		26	(a)	Rochdale	L 1-2	Oghani	4,655
10		29	(h)	Crewe A	D 0-0		5,408
11	Oct	3	(a)	Scarborough	L 0-1		4,782
12		10	(h)	Hartlepool U	W 1-0	Comstive	5,216
13		17	(a)	Exeter C	W 2-1	Oghani 2 (1 pen)	2,780
14		20	(h)	Scunthorpe U	D 1-1	Taylor	6,353
15		24	(a)	Torquay U	W 3-1	Britton, Comstive, Taylor	2,836
16		31	(h)	Stockport C	D 1-1	Davis	6,642
17	Nov	3	(a)	Halifax T	L 1-2	Taylor	3,419
18		7	(a)	Wolves	L 0-3		10,002
19		21	(h)	Bolton W	W 2-1	Reeves, Britton	7,544
20		28	(a)	Peterborough U	L 0-5		3,394
21	Dec	12	(h)	Hereford U	D 0-0		4,217
22		19	(a)	Cardiff C	L 1-2	Davis	3,401
23		26	(h)	Rochdale	W 4-0	Britton, Farrell, Oghani, Comstive	7,013
24		28	(a)	Darlington	L 2-4	Reeves 2	3,325
25	Jan	1	(a)	Carlisle U	W 4-3	Deakin, Davis, Oghani, Wright (og)	4,260
26		2	(h)	Tranmere R	D 1-1	Comstive	7,401
27		9	(h)	Newport C	W 2-0	Comstive, Reeves	5,256
28		16	(a)	Cambridge U	L 0-2		2,146
29	Feb	2	(a)	Wrexham	W 3-1	Oghani, Hoskin, Bowden (og)	1,821
30		6	(a)	Swansea C	D 0-0		3,498
31		13	(h)	Darlington	W 2-1	Reeves 2	6,440
32		19	(a)	Colchester U	W 1-0	Reeves	2,520
33		27	(h)	Scarborough	L 0-1		7,645
34	Mar	1	(a)	Crewe A	W 1-0	Gage (og)	3,720
35		5	(h)	Exeter C	W 3-0	Davis, Reeves, Taylor	6,052
36		12	(a)	Hartlepool U	L 1-2	Oghani	2,893
37		18	(a)	Stockport C	L 0-2		4,423
38		22	(h)	Leyton O	W 2-0	Oghani 2	5,842
39	Apr	2	(h)	Wolves	L 0-3		10,386
40		4	(a)	Bolton W	L 1-2	Oghani	9,921
41		8	(h)	Halifax T	W 3-1	Comstive, Taylor, Davis	5,833
42		23	(a)	Scunthorpe U	D 1-1	Britton	5,347
43		30	(h)	Peterborough U	L 1-2	Comstive (pen)	6,315
44	May	2	(a)	Hereford U	L 1-2	Deakin	2,304
45		4	(h)	Torquay U	W 1-0	McGrory	5,075
46		7	(h)	Cardiff C	L 1-2	Oghani	8,421

FINAL LEAGUE POSITION: 10th in Division Four

Appearances
Sub Appearances
Goals

FA Cup

1	Nov	14	(h)	Bolton W	L 0-1		10,788

Appearances
Sub Appearances
Goals

League Cup

1	Aug	18	(a)	Wrexham	L 0-1		2,301
		25	(h)	Wrexham	W 3-0	Farrell, Comstive, Oghani (pen)	3,788
2	Sep	22	(h)	Norwich C	D 1-1	Oghani	7,912
	Oct	7	(a)	Norwich C	L 0-1		6,168

Appearances
Sub Appearances
Goals

Pearce C	Leebrook P	McGrory S	Daniel P	Zelem P	Deakin R	Grewcock N	Farrell A	Oghani G	Comstive P	Britton I	Hoskin A	Gardner S	Taylor S	James L	Malley P	Davis S	Reeves D	Devaney P	
1	2	3*	4	5	6	7	8	9	10	11†	14	12							1
1	2		4	5	3	7	8	9	10			6	11						2
1	2		4	5	3	7	8	9	10			6	11						3
1	2		4	5	3	7	8	9	10*		12	6	11						4
1	2		4	5	3	8	7	9	10			6	11						5
1	2		4		3	8	7	9	10			6	11	5					6
1	2		4		3	8	7	9	10			6	11	5					7
1	2		4		3	8	7	9	10			6	11	5					8
1	2*				3	8	7	9	10		12	6	11	5	4				9
1	2*		14		3†	8	7	9	10		12	6	11	5	4				10
1	2					8	7	9	10		12	6	11	3	4*	5			11
1	2	3				8	7	9	10			6	11	4		5			12
1		3	2			8	7	9	10			6	11	4		5			13
1		3	2			8	7	9	10			6	11	4		5			14
1		3*	2			8	7		10	9		6	11	4	12	5			15
1			2	14		8	7†	9	10	12		6	11	4	3*	5			16
1			2			8	7	9	10			6	11	4	3	5			17
1			2		3	8	7*	9	10	12		6	11	4		5			18
1				5	3	8	2		10	7		6	11			4	9		19
1				5*	3	8	2		10	7	12	6	11			4	9		20
1			2		3	8	7	9*	10	14		6	12	4†		5	11		21
1	2				3		7	9	10	4	11	6				5	8		22
1	2				3	8	7*	9	10	4	12	6	14			5	11†		23
1	2				3	8	7	9*	10	4		6	12			5	11		24
1	2				3	8	7	9	10	4		6				5	11		25
1	2			6	3	8	7	9†	10	4*	12		14			5	11		26
1	2*			6	3	8	7		10	4	12		9			5	11		27
1					3	8	2		10	4	7	6	9			5	11		28
1		10	2		3		7	9		4	11	6	8			5			29
1			2		3		7	9*	10	4	11	6				5	8	12	30
1			2		3	12	7		10	4	11*	6	9			5	8		31
1			2*		3	12	7		10	4	11	6	9			5	8		32
1		3	2			12	7*	14	10	4	11	6	9†	5			8		33
1		3	2			12	7		10	4	11*	6	9	5			8		34
1			2		3	11	7		10	4		6	9			5	8		35
1	2	3			10		7	8		4	11		9	6		5			36
1		2			3		7	8*	10	4	11	6	9			5		12	37
1	2				3		7	8	10	4	11	6	9			5			38
1	2*				3		7	8	10	4	11	6	9			5		12	39
1	2				3		7	8	10	4		6	9	11		5			40
1		2			3		7	8	10	4	11	6	9			5			41
1		3	2		6			8	10	4	11		9		7	5			42
1		2			3		7*	8†	10	4	11	6	9		12	5		14	43
1		3	2		6		7	8	10	11		4	9			5			44
1		11	2		3		7	8	10	4		6	9			5			45
1		11	2		3		7	8	10	4		6	9	5					46
46	22	16	26	9	37	28	45	36	44	29	15	41	38	19	6	33	16		
			1	1		4		1		3	9	1	4		2			4	
		1		1	3		3	14	8	4	1		6			5	8		

3 own-goals

Pearce C	Leebrook P	McGrory S	Daniel P	Zelem P	Deakin R	Grewcock N	Farrell A	Oghani G	Comstive P	Britton I	Hoskin A	Gardner S	Taylor S	James L	Malley P	Davis S	Reeves D	Devaney P	
1			2*	5	3	8	7	9†	10	12	14	6	11	4					1
1			1	1	1	1	1	1	1			1	1	1					
										1	1								

Pearce C	Leebrook P	McGrory S	Daniel P	Zelem P	Deakin R	Grewcock N	Farrell A	Oghani G	Comstive P	Britton I	Hoskin A	Gardner S	Taylor S	James L	Malley P	Davis S	Reeves D	Devaney P	
1	2	3	4	5	6	7	8	9*	10	11	12								1
1	2		4	5	3	7	8	9	10			6	11						
1	2				3	8	7	9	10			6	11	5	4				2
1	2	3				8	7	9	10			6	11	4		5			
4	4	2	2	2	3	4	4	4	4	1		3	3	2	1	1			
											1								
							1	2	1										

1988-89

Manager: Brian Miller until 13 January, then Frank Casper

1	Aug	27	(h)	Rochdale	W 2-1	Farrell, Comstive	7,511
2	Sep	3	(a)	Halifax T	W 2-1	Comstive, O'Connell	4,071
3		10	(h)	York C	W 6-0	Atkinson, Comstive 2 (1 pen), O'Connell, Britton, Oghani	7,258
4		16	(a)	Stockport C	D 0-0		6,676
5		20	(a)	Torquay U	L 0-2		3,021
6		24	(h)	Colchester U	W 2-0	O'Connell, Rowell	7,177
7	Oct	1	(a)	Darlington	D 1-1	O'Connell	3,409
8		4	(h)	Rotherham U	W 1-0	Oghani	9,290
9		8	(h)	Exeter C	W 3-0	O'Connell, Oghani, Zelem	7,894
10		15	(a)	Peterborough U	L 0-3		5,023
11		22	(h)	Leyton O	D 2-2	O'Connell, Comstive (pen)	8,503
12		25	(a)	Carlisle U	D 0-0		4,543
13		29	(h)	Cambridge U	W 2-0	Oghani, O'Connell	8,669
14	Nov	5	(a)	Scunthorpe U	L 1-2	O'Connell	6,358
15		8	(h)	Lincoln C	L 1-4	Comstive (pen)	8,445
16		12	(a)	Scarborough	L 0-1		5,258
17		26	(a)	Doncaster R	L 0-1		2,724
18	Dec	3	(h)	Hartlepool U	D 0-0		6,289
19		17	(a)	Hereford U	D 0-0		2,442
20		26	(h)	Wrexham	L 1-3	O'Connell	9,174
21		31	(h)	Grimsby T	W 1-0	Oghani	7,367
22	Jan	2	(a)	Tranmere R	L 1-2	Britton	7,974
23		14	(h)	Halifax T	W 2-1	Oghani 2	8,298
24		21	(a)	Rochdale	L 1-2	Farrell	5,812
25		28	(h)	Stockport C	W 1-0	Britton	6,942
26	Feb	4	(h)	Torquay U	W 1-0	O'Connell	6,626
27		10	(a)	Colchester U	D 2-2	White 2 (1 pen)	3,831
28		18	(a)	Exeter C	L 0-3		3,672
29		25	(h)	Peterborough U	D 1-1	Measham	6,853
30	Mar	4	(a)	Leyton O	L 0-3		3,944
31		11	(h)	Scunthorpe U	L 0-1		6,813
32		14	(a)	Cambridge U	L 1-2	White	2,555
33		18	(a)	York C	D 0-0		3,164
34		21	(h)	Carlisle U	D 0-0		5,283
35		25	(h)	Tranmere R	D 2-2	Comstive 2	6,839
36		27	(a)	Wrexham	L 2-4	Grewcock, McGrory	3,956
37	Apr	1	(h)	Hereford U	D 3-3	Monington, James 2 (2 pens)	5,534
38		4	(h)	Crewe A	W 1-0	Hardy	5,677
39		8	(a)	Grimsby T	L 0-1		4,856
40		15	(h)	Darlington	L 0-1		5,577
41		22	(a)	Rotherham U	L 1-3	Farrell	5,726
42		29	(h)	Doncaster R	W 3-0	O'Connell 2, Comstive	4,211
43	May	1	(a)	Lincoln C	W 3-2	White 2, O'Connell	3,594
44		6	(a)	Hartlepool U	D 2-2	Farrell, James (pen)	2,038
45		9	(a)	Crewe A	L 0-4		3,597
46		13	(h)	Scarborough	L 0-1		6,206

FINAL LEAGUE POSITION: 16th in Division Four

Appearances
Sub Appearances
Goals

FA Cup

1	Nov	19	(h)	Chester C	L 0-2		8,474

Appearances
Sub Appearances
Goals

League Cup

1	Aug	30	(a)	Rochdale	D 3-3	Oghani, O'Connell, Comstive (pen)	3,669
	Sep	6	(h)	Rochdale	W 2-1	O'Connell 2	6,674
2		27	(a)	Luton T	D 1-1	Comstive (pen)	6,282
	Oct	11	(h)	Luton T	L 0-1		14,036

Appearances
Sub Appearances
Goals

Pearce C	Daniel P	Deakin R	Farrell A	Davis S	Gardner S	Britton I	Oghani G	Rowell G	Comstive P	James L	O'Connell B	Atkinson P	Taylor S	Zelem P	White W	McGrory S	Hoskin A	Morley A	Measham I	Miller D	Jones D	Hardy J	Monington M	Grewcock N	Williams D	Hooper S	
1	2	3	4	5	6	7	8	9*	10	11	12																1
1	2	3	4	5	6	7	8		10		9	11															2
1	2	3	4	5	6	7	8		10		9	11															3
1	2	3	4	5	6	7	8		10		9	11															4
1	2	3	4	5	6	7	8		10		9	11															5
1	2	3*	4	5	6	7	8	12	10		9	11															6
1	2		3	5	6	7	8	4	10		9	11*	12														7
1	2		3		6	7	8	4	10		9	11		5													8
1	2		3		6	7	8	4	10		9	11		5													9
1	2		3		6	7	8	4	10		9	11		5													10
1	2		4	6	3	11*	8	12	10		9			5	7												11
1	2		4	6			8	11*	10		9			5	7	3	12										12
1	2		4		6		8		10		9			5	7	3		11									13
1	2		4		6		8		10		9			5	7	3		11									14
1			4	6	2*		8	12	10		9			5	7	3		11									15
1			4	5	6		8		10		9				7	3		11	2								16
1			3	5	6	4	8*	12	10		9	11†			14			7	2								17
1			3	5	6	4	8*	14	10		9	11†	12		7				2								18
1			3	5	6	4	8		10		9	11			7				2								19
1			3	5	6	4	8		10		9	11*			7		12		2								20
1			3	5	6	4	8		10		9				7	12	11		2*								21
1			2	5	6	4	8		10		9		12		7	3	11*										22
1			3	5	6	4	8		10*	11	9			12	7				2								23
1			3	5	6	4	8		10	11*	9				7	12			2								24
1			3	5	6	4	8		10	11	9				7				2								25
1			3	5	6	4	8		10	11*	9				7†	14	12		2								26
1		11	3*	5	6	4	8	12	10		9				7				2								27
1		11	12	5		4	8	14	10†		9				7	3*			2	6							28
1		11		5	3	4	8	10*		12	9				7				2	6							29
1			3	5	10	4	8†	12		11					7*				2	6	9	14					30
1			7	5	6	4	8			11		14			12				2	10*	9†	3					31
1				5	6	4	8†	14	10*	12	9				7				2			3	11				32
1				5	6	4	8		10		9				7*				2			3	11	12			33
1					6	4	8*	12	10		9				7				2			3	5	11			34
1					6	4	8		10		9				7				2			3	5	11			35
1					6	4†		8	10	12	9				7*	14			2			3	5	11			36
1					6*	4	8		10†	11	9				12	14			2			3	5	7			37
1				5	6	4	8			11	9					10			2			3		7			38
				5	6	4				11	9				12	10			2		8*	3		7	1		39
				5	6	4				11*	9				12	10			2		8†	3	14	7	1		40
			4	5	6	12				11	9				8	10†			2			3		7*	1	14	41
		11	4	5	6				12		9				8	10*			2			3		7	1		42
		11	4	5	6				10		9				8				2			3		7	1		43
		11	4	5	6				10	9					8				2			3		7	1		44
		11	4†	5	6				10*	12	9				8	14			2			3		7	1		45
1		11	4	5	6	10*				7†	9				8	14			2			3	12				46
39	14	14	35	37	44	36	37	8	37	14	42	13		8	30	12	2	5	30	4	4	16	6	12	7		
			1			1		10	1	4	1	1	3	1	5	7	3					1	2	1		1	
			4			3	7	1	9	3	13	1		1	5	1			1			1	1	1			

Pearce C	Daniel P	Deakin R	Farrell A	Davis S	Gardner S	Britton I	Oghani G	Rowell G	Comstive P	James L	O'Connell B	Atkinson P	Taylor S	Zelem P	White W	McGrory S	Hoskin A	Morley A	Measham I	Miller D	Jones D	Hardy J	Monington M	Grewcock N	Williams D	Hooper S	
1			4*	5	6	12	8		10		9	11			7	3			2								1
1			1	1	1		1		1		1	1			1	1			1								
						1																					

Pearce C	Daniel P	Deakin R	Farrell A	Davis S	Gardner S	Britton I	Oghani G	Rowell G	Comstive P	James L	O'Connell B	Atkinson P	Taylor S	Zelem P	White W	McGrory S	Hoskin A	Morley A	Measham I	Miller D	Jones D	Hardy J	Monington M	Grewcock N	Williams D	Hooper S	
1	2	3	4	5	6	7	8		10	11	9																1
1	2	3	4	5	6	7	8		10		9	11															
1	2		3	5	6	7	8	4	10		9	11															2
1	2		3		6	7	8	4	10		9	11		5													
4	4	2	4	3	4	4	4	2	4	1	4	3		1													
							1		2		3																

1989-90

Manager: Frank Casper

1	Aug	19	(a)	Rochdale	L 1-2	White (pen)	5,420
2		26	(h)	Stockport C	D 0-0		6,537
3	Sep	2	(a)	Chesterfield	W 1-0	Mumby	4,061
4		9	(h)	Exeter C	W 1-0	White (pen)	5,431
5		16	(a)	Gillingham	D 0-0		3,853
6		23	(h)	Hereford U	W 3-1	O'Connell 2, Mumby	5,828
7		26	(h)	York C	D 1-1	Mumby	7,205
8		30	(a)	Torquay U	W 1-0	Grewcock	2,214
9	Oct	7	(a)	Maidstone U	W 2-1	O'Connell, Deary	3,769
10		14	(h)	Hartlepool U	D 0-0		7,450
11		17	(h)	Peterborough U	L 1-2	Grewcock	7,189
12		21	(a)	Doncaster R	W 3-2	Davis, Jakub, White (pen)	2,900
13		28	(h)	Aldershot	D 0-0		6,451
14		31	(a)	Southend U	L 2-3	O'Connell, Farrell	3,765
15	Nov	4	(h)	Colchester U	D 0-0		6,145
16		11	(a)	Scunthorpe U	L 0-3		4,745
17		25	(a)	Lincoln C	L 0-1		4,079
18	Dec	2	(h)	Grimsby T	D 1-1	Jakub	5,647
19		26	(h)	Carlisle U	W 2-1	Futcher, Jakub	12,277
20		30	(h)	Halifax T	W 1-0	Futcher	9,109
21	Jan	1	(a)	Cambridge U	W 1-0	Bent	3,738
22		9	(h)	Scarborough	W 3-0	Bent 2, Futcher	7,330
23		13	(a)	Stockport C	L 1-3	White	5,210
24		20	(h)	Rochdale	L 0-1		8,174
25	Feb	10	(h)	Gillingham	L 1-2	Walker (og)	7,274
26		17	(a)	Grimsby T	L 2-4	Francis 2	5,973
27		24	(h)	Lincoln C	D 0-0		5,897
28	Mar	3	(a)	Scarborough	L 2-4	Futcher 2	2,961
29		6	(h)	Torquay U	W 1-0	Farrell	4,533
30		10	(a)	York C	W 3-1	White 2 (1 pen), Deary	3,216
31		13	(a)	Wrexham	L 0-1		4,346
32		17	(h)	Maidstone U	D 1-1	Galley (og)	5,050
33		20	(a)	Hartlepool U	L 0-3		3,187
34		24	(a)	Peterborough U	L 1-4	Futcher (pen)	3,841
35		28	(a)	Hereford U	W 1-0	Francis	2,391
36		31	(h)	Doncaster R	L 0-1		5,066
37	Apr	3	(h)	Chesterfield	D 0-0		3,959
38		6	(a)	Aldershot	D 1-1	Jakub	2,325
39		10	(h)	Southend U	D 0-0		3,967
40		14	(h)	Cambridge U	L 1-3	Futcher	3,975
41		16	(a)	Carlisle U	D 1-1	Saddington (og)	6,738
42		21	(h)	Wrexham	L 2-3	Jakub, Mumby	4,513
43		24	(a)	Halifax T	D 0-0		2,556
44		28	(h)	Scunthorpe U	L 0-1		4,098
45	May	1	(a)	Exeter C	L 1-2	Francis	7,544
46		5	(a)	Colchester U	W 2-1	White (pen), Taylor (og)	2,788

FINAL LEAGUE POSITION: 16th in Division Four

Appearances
Sub Appearances
Goals

FA Cup

1	Nov	18	(h)	Stockport C	D 1-1	White (pen)	8,030
R		22	(a)	Stockport C	W 2-1	O'Connell, Futcher	6,257
2	Dec	9	(a)	Scunthorpe U	D 2-2	Deary, Mumby	5,698
R		12	(h)	Scunthorpe U	D 1-1*	Eli	7,682
2R		18	(h)	Scunthorpe U	W 5-0	Eli 2, Futcher 2, Hardy	7,429
3	Jan	6	(a)	Blackpool	L 0-1		7,790

*After extra-time

Appearances
Sub Appearances
Goals

League Cup

1	Aug	22	(a)	Blackpool	D 2-2	White, Mumby	4,540
		29	(h)	Blackpool	L 0-1		6,085

Appearances
Sub Appearances
Goals

Pearce C	Measham I	Deakin R	Eli R	Monington M	Harris M	White W	Mumby P	O'Connell B	Jakub J	Farrell A	Hancock A	Deary J	Grewcock N	Davis S	Hardy J	McGrory S	Atkinson P	Futcher R	Davis S	Bent J	McKay P	Francis J	Gardner S	Smith N	Rowell G	Buckley N	Williams D	Howarth N	
1	2	3	4*	5	6	7	8†	9	10	11	14	12																	1
1	2	3*	4	5	6	7	8†	9	10	11	14	12																	2
1	2	3		5	6	7	8		10		9	4	11																3
1	2	3		5	6	7	8		10		9	4	11																4
1	2	3		5		7	8	12	10		9*	4		6	11														5
1	2	3		5		7	8	11	10		9	4		6															6
1	2	3	12	5		7	8	11	10		9*	4		6															7
1	2	3		5		7	8	11	10		9*	4	12	6															8
1	2	3	14	5		7	8*	11	10		9†	4	12	6															9
1	2	3	5			7	8	11	10		9*	4	12	6															10
1	2	3		5		7	8*	9	10		12	4	11	6															11
1	2	3	12	5		7	8†	9	10			4	11*	6		14													12
1	2	3		5		7	8*	9	10	11†	12	4		6	14														13
1	2		14	5*		7	8	9	10	11	12	4		6	3†														14
1	2		5			7*	8	9	10	11	12	4		6	3														15
1	2		5			7	8*	9	10	11	12			6	3		4												16
1	2					7	12	9	10	4	6*				3	5	11†	8	14										17
1	2					7	8		10	4				5	3*	12		9	6	11									18
1	2		8			7			10	5		4		6	3		11*	9	12										19
1	2		8†			7			10	5		4		6	3*			9	11	14	12								20
1	2					7*			10	5		4		6	3†	14		9	11	8	12								21
1	2*		12			7			10	5		4		6	3			9	11	8									22
1			2			7*			10	5	12	4		6	3†		14	9	11	8									23
1			2			7			10	5		4		6		3*	12	9	11	8									24
1			2			7			10	5				6	3*			9	4	8	12	11							25
1		3	2			7			10	5				6			8*	9		12	4†	11	14						26
1		3	2						10	5		8						9		7	4	11	6						27
1		3	8*			12		7	10	5		4						9			2	11	6						28
1		3				12		7	10	5		4				8*		9			2	11	6						29
1		3				9		7	10	5		4				8					2*	11	6	12					30
1		3				9	14	7	10	5		4				8†					2*	11	6	12					31
1		3	8*			9		7	10	5		4						14			2†	11	6	12					32
1		3	2			9		7	10*	5		4						8				11	6		12				33
1	2	3	8						10	5		4		7				9				11				6			34
	2	3	8			7			10	5		4		6				9				11					1		35
	2	3				7†	12		10	5		4		6	11*			9						14		8	1		36
	2	3*	8			7			10	5		4		6	12			9								11	1		37
	2		11			7			10	5		4		6	3			9								8	1		38
	2	6	11			7			10	5		4			3*			9				12				8	1		39
	2	12	8			7*			10	5†		4			3			9				11	6	14			1		40
1	2	6	8				14		10	5		4			3*	12		9†				11		7					41
1	2	3	8				12		10	5		4		6	14	11†						9		7*					42
1	2	3	8				7*		10	5		4		6	11						12	9							43
1	2	3					8		10	5		4		6	11*		14				7†	9		12					44
1	2	3				12	8		10	5		4		6	11							9		7*					45
	2	3				7			10	5		4		6		12	11*					9		8†			1	14	46
39	35	32	24	13	4	37	20	20	46	36	9	39	4	31	20	6	5	22	7	7	8	18	8	4		5	7		
		1	5			3	5	1			8	2	3		3	5	3	1	2	2	4	1	1	6	1			1	
						7	4	4	5	2		2	2	1				7		3		4							

4 own-goals

Pearce C	Measham I	Deakin R	Eli R	Monington M	Harris M	White W	Mumby P	O'Connell B	Jakub J	Farrell A	Hancock A	Deary J	Grewcock N	Davis S	Hardy J	McGrory S	Atkinson P	Futcher R	Davis S	Bent J	McKay P	
1	2		5*			7		9	10	4	12			6	3		11	8				1
1	2					7	12	9	10	4	6*				3	5	11	8				R
1	2					7	3		10	4		8		6		5	11	9				2
1	2		12			7	8*		10	5		4		6	14	3	11†	9				R
1	2		8†			7			10	5		4		6	12	3*	11	9			14	2R
1	2		8			7			10	5	12	4		6	3			9			11*	3
6	6		3			6	2	2	6	6	1	4		5	3	4	5	6			1	
			1				1				2				2						1	
			3			1	1	1				1			1			3				

Pearce C	Measham I	Deakin R	Eli R	Monington M	Harris M	White W	Mumby P	O'Connell B	Jakub J	Farrell A	Hancock A	Deary J	Grewcock N	
1	2	3	4	5*	6	7	8	9	10	11		12		1
1		3*	2	5	6	7	8†	9	10	4*	14	11	12	
2	1	2	2	2	2	2	2	2	2	2		1		
											1	1	1	
						1	1							

1990-91

Manager: Frank Casper

1	Aug	25	(h)	Lincoln C	D 2-2	Deary, Jakub	6,106
2	Sep	1	(a)	Darlington	L 1-3	Futcher	3,671
3		8	(h)	Scarborough	W 2-1	Futcher, Grewcock	4,723
4		14	(a)	Stockport C	D 2-2	Futcher 2 (1 pen)	3,523
5		18	(a)	Blackpool	W 2-1	Deary, Mumby	4,737
6		22	(h)	Aldershot	W 3-0	Jakub, Francis (pen), Mumby	5,517
7		28	(a)	Carlisle U	D 1-1	Edwards (og)	5,205
8	Oct	2	(h)	Northampton T	W 3-0	Francis 2, Eli	6,271
9		6	(h)	York C	D 0-0		6,808
10		13	(a)	Hereford U	L 0-3		3,688
11		20	(a)	Peterborough U	L 2-3	Futcher 2	5,102
12		23	(h)	Maidstone U	W 2-1	Davis, Futcher	5,567
13		27	(h)	Rochdale	W 1-0	White	7,971
14	Nov	3	(a)	Wrexham	W 4-2	Jakub, Francis, Mumby 2	3,997
15		10	(a)	Walsall	L 0-1		5,710
16		24	(h)	Halifax T	W 2-1	Francis, Mumby	6,620
17	Dec	1	(h)	Cardiff C	W 2-0	Deary, Francis	6,348
18		15	(a)	Gillingham	L 2-3	Futcher (pen), Deary	3,679
19		22	(h)	Hartlepool U	W 4-0	Davis, Francis 2, Deary	8,514
20		29	(a)	Torquay U	L 0-2		4,210
21	Jan	1	(h)	Scunthorpe U	D 1-1	Francis	8,557
22		12	(h)	Darlington	W 3-1	Futcher, Francis, Davis	8,491
23		19	(a)	Lincoln C	L 0-1		4,167
24		26	(h)	Stockport C	W 3-2	Futcher, Eli, Deary	8,946
25	Feb	16	(a)	Halifax T	W 2-1	Francis 2 (1 pen)	4,755
26		23	(h)	Walsall	W 2-0	Eli, Grewcock	7,883
27		26	(a)	Doncaster R	L 1-2	Deary	3,080
28	Mar	1	(a)	Cardiff C	L 0-3		3,591
29		5	(a)	Chesterfield	L 1-2	White	4,022
30		9	(h)	Gillingham	D 2-2	Futcher (pen), Davis	6,459
31		12	(a)	Northampton T	D 0-0		3,710
32		16	(h)	Carlisle U	W 2-1	Farrell 2	6,635
33		19	(h)	Hereford U	W 2-1	Futcher, Eli	5,716
34		23	(a)	York C	L 0-2		4,407
35		26	(a)	Scarborough	W 1-0	Francis	2,373
36		30	(h)	Chesterfield	L 0-1		8,373
37	Apr	1	(a)	Hartlepool U	D 0-0		4,967
38		6	(h)	Torquay U	D 1-1	Futcher (pen)	6,661
39		13	(a)	Scunthorpe U	W 3-1	Futcher, Eli, Davis	4,449
40		16	(a)	Aldershot	W 2-1	Eli 2	2,473
41		20	(h)	Peterborough U	W 4-1	Eli 2, Futcher 2 (1 pen)	10,018
42		23	(h)	Blackpool	W 2-0	Eli, Futcher (pen)	18,395
43		27	(a)	Maidstone U	L 0-1		3,130
44		30	(h)	Doncaster R	W 1-0	Futcher	10,410
45	May	4	(a)	Rochdale	D 0-0		7,344
46		11	(h)	Wrexham	W 2-0	Francis 2	10,161

FINAL LEAGUE POSITION: 6th in Division Four

Appearances
Sub Appearances
Goals

Play-offs

	May	19	(a)	Torquay U	L 0-2		5,600
		22	(h)	Torquay U	W 1-0	Evans (og)	13,620

Appearances
Sub Appearances
Goals

FA Cup

1	Nov	17	(a)	Stafford R	W 3-1	White, Collymore (og), Mumby	4,117
2	Dec	12	(h)	Stoke C	W 2-0	Francis, White	12,949
3	Jan	6	(h)	Manchester C	L 0-1		20,331

Appearances
Sub Appearances
Goals

League Cup

1	Aug	27	(a)	Stockport C	W 2-0	Hamilton, Futcher	2,786
	Sep	4	(h)	Stockport C	L 0-1		3,912
2		26	(a)	Nottingham F	L 1-4	Mumby	17,897
	Oct	10	(h)	Nottingham F	L 0-1		11,399

Appearances
Sub Appearances
Goals

Pearce C	France P	Bray I	Deary J	Farrell A	Davis S	Mumby P	Futcher R	Francis J	Jakub J	Grewcock N	Hamilton D	White W	Deakin R	Measham I	Pender J	Eli R	Williams D	Smith N	Sonner D	Lancashire G	
1	2†	3	4	5	6	7*	8	9	10	11	14	12									1
1		3*	4	5	6	14	9	8	10		2	7†	11	12							2
1			4	5	6	7	8	9	10*	12	11		3	2							3
1			4	14	6	7†	8*	9	10	12	11		3	2	5						4
1			4	12	6	8		9	10		11	7*	3	2	5						5
1			4		6	8		9	10		11	7*	3	2	5	12					6
1			4	11	6	8		9	10			7	3	2	5						7
1			4	11	6	8		9	10			7	3	2	5*	12					8
1			4	5	6	8*	14	9	10	12		7	3	2		11†					9
1			4	11*	6	8	14	9	10	12		7†	3	2	5						10
1			4	11	6		8	9	10			7*	3	2	5	12					11
1			4		6	12	8	9	10	11*		7	3	2	5						12
1			4		6	12	8*	9	10	11		7	3	2	5						13
1			4		6	8		9	10	11		7	3	2	5						14
1			4		6	9		8	10	11*		7	3	2	5	12					15
1			4	12	6	8		9	10	11		7	3	2	5*						16
1			4	14	6	8	12	9	10	11		7*	3	2	5†						17
1			4	5	6		8	9	10	11		7	3	2							18
1			4	12	6	14	8	9	10	11†		7	3	2	5*						19
			4		6		8	9	10	11		7*	3	2	5	12	1				20
1			4	12	6		8	9	10	11		7*	3	2	5						21
1				4	6		8	9	10			7	3	2	5	12		11*			22
1				4	6		8	9	10	11			3	2	5	12		7*			23
1			4	7	6		8		10	11			3	2	5	9					24
			4	7	6			9	10	11			3	2	5	8	1				25
			4	5	6			8	10	11		7	3	2		9	1				26
1	12		4	7	6			8	10	11†		14	3	2	5*	9					27
1			4	7†	6		12	8	10	11		14	3	2	5	9*					28
1			4		6		8	9	10	12	11*	7	3	2	5						29
1			4		6		8*	9	10	11		7	3	2	5	12					30
1			4		6		8	9	10		11	7	3	2	5						31
1			4	12	6		8	9	10	11*		7†	3	2	5	14					32
1			4	7	6		8	9	10				3	2	5	11					33
1			4	7	6	12		9	10			8*	3	2	5	11					34
1			4	7	6		8	9	10			11	3	2	5						35
1			4	7	6	11*	8	9	10				3	2	5	12					36
1			4	7	6	11*	8	9	10	12			3	2	5						37
1		14	4	7	6		8	9	10	11*			3†	2	5	12					38
1		3	4	7	6		8	9*	10					2	5	11			12		39
1		3	4	7	6		8	9	10					2	5	11					40
1		3	4	7	6		8†	9	10	14	12			2	5*	11					41
1		3	4	7	6		8	9	10					2	5	11					42
1		3*	4	7	6		8	9	10	12				2	5	11					43
1		3	4	7	6		8	9	10					2	5	11					44
1		3	4*	7	6		8	9†	10	14	12			2	5	11					45
1		3		7	6			9	10	8	4*			2	5				11	12	46
43	1	10	43	30	46	15	30	45	46	21	8	26	37	44	40	15	3	2	1		
	1	1		7		5	4			9	3	3		1		11			1	1	
			7	2	5	5	18	15	3	2		2				10					
																					1 own-goal
1		3		7	6			9	10		4		8	2	5	11*			12		
1		3	4	7	6		8	9	10					2	5*	11			12		
2		2	1	2	2		1	2	2		1		1	2	2	2					
																			2		
																					1 own-goal
1			4		6	8*	12	9	10	11		7	3	2	5						1
1			4*	12	6	14	8†	9	10	11		7	3	2	5*						2
1			4	14	6		8	9	10	11†	12	7*	3	2	5						3
3			3		3	1	2	3	3	3		3	3	3	3						
				2		1	1				1										
						1		1				2									
																					1 own-goal
1		3	4	5	6		9	8	10		2	7	11								1
1		3	4	5	6		9	8	10		2	7	11								
1			4	12	6	8†		9	10		11*	7	3	2	5	14					2
1			4	5		7		9	10	11*		8	3	2	6	12					
4		2	4	3	3	2	2	4	4	1	3	4	4	2	2						
				1												2					
						1	1				1										

FA Cup 1885 to 1888

1885-86

1	Oct	17	(a)	Darwen Old W	L 0-11	
						Appearances
						Goals

1886-87

1	Oct	23	(a)	Astley Bridge	D 3-3	Place Snr, 2 Unknown
R		30	(h)	Astley Bridge	D 2-2	2 Unknown
						Appearances
						Goals

1887-88

1	Oct	15	(h)	Darwen Old W	W 4-0	Friel, McFettridge, 2 Unknown
2	Nov	5	(a)	Accrington	L 2-3	2 Unknown
						Appearances
						Goals

McConnell J	Whitaker	Birnie	McFettridge W	Smith H	McCrae R	Place W Snr	Friel D	Sugg F	Howarth	Jackson	Fulton	Bury W	Lang A	Abrams J	Waugh D	Elston	Gallocher P	Keenan J	
																			1

It proved impossible to find the team for the 1885 FA Cup tie against Darwen Old Wanderers. Burnley had to field the Reserves, because the first team were all professionals, and the local newspapers decided to largely ignore the game.

McConnell J	Whitaker	Birnie	McFettridge W	Smith H	McCrae R	Place W Snr	Friel D	Sugg F	Howarth	Jackson	Fulton	Bury W	Lang A	Abrams J	Waugh D	Elston	Gallocher P	Keenan J	
1	2	3	5	6	7	8	9	10	11									4	1
1	2	3	11	6	7	8	9			5	10							4	R
2	2	2	2	2	2	2	2	1	1	1	1							2	
						1													

4 scorers unknown

McConnell J	Whitaker	Birnie	McFettridge W	Smith H	McCrae R	Place W Snr	Friel D	Sugg F	Howarth	Jackson	Fulton	Bury W	Lang A	Abrams J	Waugh D	Elston	Gallocher P	Keenan J	
1			6		8		7	5				2	3	4	9	10	11		1
1					8		9	5				2	3	4	10	11	7	6	2
2			1		2		2	2				2	2	2	2	2	2	1	
			1				1												

4 scorers unknown

Burnley in Other Competitions

ASSOCIATE MEMBERS CUP

1983-84
Round 1
Feb 21 v Bolton Wanderers (h) 2-1
Donachie, Biggins
Hansbury; Dobson, Donachie, Phelan, Overson, Flynn, Miller, Daley, Scott, Biggins, Hutchison.
Att: 3,355
Round 2
Mar 13 v Darlington (h) 2-1
Baker, Biggins
Hansbury; Baker, Donachie, Phelan, Overson, Flynn (Tueart), Daley(Miller), Scott, Hamilton, Biggins, Hutchison.
Att: 1,978
Round 3
Mar 20 v Doncaster Rovers (a) 3-1 a.e.t.
Biggins, Daley, Flynn
Hansbury; Baker, Donachie, Phelan, Overson, Flynn, Daley, Miller(Tueart), Hamilton, Biggins, Hutchison.
Att: 3,504
Northern Semi-final
Apr 17 v Tranmere Rovers (a) 0-2 a.e.t.
Hansbury; Kennedy, Donachie, Phelan, Overson, Flynn, Daley, Scott, Hamilton, Biggins, Hutchison.
Att: 3,928

FREIGHT/ROVER TROPHY

1984-85
Round 1 (1st leg)
Jan 29 v Stockport County (h) 5-1
Biggins 2, Phelan, Hutchison, Devine
Neenan; Palmer, Hampton, Phelan(Malley), Overson, Hird, Grewcock, Kennedy, Devine, Biggins, Hutchison(Lawrence).
Att: 1,432
Round 1 (2nd leg)
Feb 4 v Stockport County (a) 1-0 (agg 6-1)
Hird
Neenan; Palmer, Malley, Phelan, Overson, Hird, Grewcock, Gallagher, Devine(Lawrence), Biggins, Hutchison.
Att: 1,568
Round 2
Mar 19 v Tranmere Rovers (a) 2-2 a.e.t.
Burnley lost 4-5 on penalties.
Devine, Phelan
Hansbury; Palmer, Hampton, Phelan, Overson, Hird, Grewcock, Gallagher, Devine, Biggins, Hutchison.
Att: 1,325
Round 3
Apr 10 v Mansfield Town (a) 1-1 a.e.t.
Burnley lost 3-5 on penalties.
Taylor
Hansbury; Palmer, Malley, Phelan, Overson, Hird (Devine), Rhodes, Scott, Taylor, Grewcock, Hutchison.
Att: 2,540

1985-86
Preliminary Group
Jan 21 v Chesterfield (a) 2-1
Taylor, Lawrence
Neenan; Hird, Heesom, Malley, Overson, Deakin, Grewcock, Devine, Taylor, Lawrence, Hampton.
Att: 1,053
Mar 13 v Darlington (h) 1-1
Taylor
Neenan; Hird, Hampton, Malley, Overson, Heggarty, Grewcock(Devine), Deakin, Taylor, Lawrence, Hoskin.
Att: 1,138

1986-87
Preliminary Group
Dec 9 v Blackpool (a) 3-2
Murphy 2, Hoskin
Neenan; Leebrook, Heesom, Rodaway, Gallagher, Deakin, Grewcock, Harris, Murphy, James(Malley), Hoskin.
Att: 1,448
Dec 16 v Bolton Wanderers (h) 0-2
Neenan; Leebrook, Heesom, Rodaway, Southern, Deakin, Britton, Harris, Murphy, Malley, Hoskin.
Att: 1,465
Round 1
Jan 27 v Bolton Wanderers (a) 1-2
Parker
Neenan; Leebrook, Heesom, Rodaway, Malley, Deakin, Grewcock, Parker, Murphy, James, Hoskin.
Att: 3,698

SHERPA VAN TROPHY

1987-88
Preliminary Group
Oct 27 v Tranmere Rovers (a) 2-1
Oghani, Grewcock
Pearce; Daniel, Malley, James, Zelem, Gardner, Farrell, Grewcock, Oghani, Comstive, Taylor (Britton).
Att: 1,801
Nov 24 v Rochdale (h) 3-2
Grewcock, Farrell, Reeves
Pearce; Farrell, Deakin, Davis, Zelem, Gardner, Britton, Grewcock(Hoskin), Reeves, Comstive, Taylor (Devaney).
Att: 2,677
Round 1
Jan 19 v Chester City (h) 1-0
Oghani
Pearce; Farrell, Deakin, Britton, Davis, Gardner, Hoskin, Grewcock, Oghani, Comstive, Taylor.
Att: 3,436
Round 2
Feb 9 v Bury (a) 1-0
Comstive (pen)
Pearce; Daniel, Deakin, Britton, Davis, Gardner, Farrell, Reeves, Taylor, Comstive, Hoskin.
Att: 4,672
Round 3
Northern Semi-final
Mar 8 v Halifax Town (h) 0-0 a.e.t.
Burnley won 5-3 on penalties.
Pearce; Daniel, Deakin, Britton, Davis, Gardner (McGrory), Farrell, Oghani, Taylor, Comstive, Grewcock(Hoskin).
Att: 10,222
Northern Final (1st leg)
Apr 12 v Preston North End (h) 0-0
Pearce; McGrory, Deakin, Britton, Davis, Gardner, Farrell, Oghani, Taylor, Comstive, Hoskin.
Att: 15,680
Northern Final (2nd leg)
Apr 19 v Preston North End (a) 3-1 a.e.t. (agg 3-1)
Oghani, Hoskin, Comstive
Pearce; McGrory, Deakin, Britton, Davis, Gardner, Farrell(Malley), Oghani, Taylor, Comstive, Hoskin.
Att: 17,592
Final
May 29 v Wolverhampton Wanderers (Wembley) 0-2
Pearce; Daniel, Deakin, Britton, Davis, Gardner, Farrell, Oghani, Taylor, Comstive, McGrory(James).
Att: 80,841

1988-89
Preliminary Group
Nov 22 v York City (a) 2-0
Comstive (pen), O'Connell
Pearce; Measham, Farrell, Britton, Davis, Gardner, Morley, Oghani, O'Connell, Comstive, Atkinson.
Att: 1,648
Nov 29 v Hartlepool United (h) 3-0
White, Davis, O'Connell
Pearce; Measham, Farrell, Britton, Davis, Gardner, White, Oghani, O'Connell, Comstive, Atkinson.
Att: 3,478
Round 1
Jan 17 v Crewe Alexandra (h) 1-1 a.e.t.
Burnley lost 4-2 on penalties.
Macowat (og)
Pearce; Measham, Farrell, Britton, Davis, Gardner, White(Taylor), Oghani, O'Connell, Comstive, James (Zelem).
Att: 6,392

LEYLAND DAF TROPHY

1989-90
Preliminary Group
Nov 7 v Preston North End (a) 0-3
Pearce; Measham, Hardy(McGrory), Deary, Eli, Davis, White, Mumby, O'Connell, Jakub, Farrell.
Att: 5,241
Nov 28 v Stockport County (h) 0-2
Pearce; Measham, Hardy, Farrell, S.Davis, Hancock (Mumby), White, Futcher, O'Connell, Jakub, McGrory(Smith).
Att: 3,352

1990-91
Preliminary Group
Nov 6 v Crewe Alexandra (h) 2-1
White, Francis
Pearce; Measham, Deakin, Deary, Pender, Davis, White, Francis, Mumby, Jakub, Grewcock.
Att: 3,481
Jan 8 v Stockport County (a) 1-1
Farrell
Williams; Measham, Deakin, Deary, Pender, Davis, White, Futcher, Francis, Jakub, Farrell.
Att: 1,707
Round 1
Jan 22 v Stockport County (h) 3-2 a.e.t.
Eli, Jakub, White
Pearce; Measham, Deakin, Deary, Pender, Davis, Farrell, Futcher(White), Eli, Jakub, Grewcock.
Att: 3,378
Round 2
Jan 29 v Bradford City (a) 1-0
Futcher
Pearce; Measham, Deakin, Deary, Pender, Davis, Farrell, Futcher(Francis), Eli, Jakub, Grewcock.
Att: 5,432
Round 3
Feb 19 v Preston North End (a) 1-6
Bray
Williams; Measham, Deakin, Deary, Pender, Davis, Farrell, Francis, Eli(Bray), Jakub, Grewcock(White).
Att: 12,016

LANCASHIRE MANX CUP

1982-83
Group Matches
Aug 14 v Oldham Athletic (h) 1-1
Hamilton
Stevenson; Laws, Wharton, Cassidy, Phelan, Holt, Dobson, Steven, Hamilton, Taylor, Young.
Att: 4,459
Aug 17 v Rochdale (a) 0-0
Stevenson; Laws, Ray, Scott, Phelan, Holt, Dobson, Steven, Hamilton(Allen), Taylor, Wharton.
Att: 2,191
Aug 21 v Bury (h) 0-0
Stevenson; Laws, Wharton(Miller), Scott, Phelan, Holt, Dobson(Harrison), Steven, Hamilton, Taylor, Young.
Att: 2,588

1983-84
Group Matches
Aug 13 v Preston North End (a) 2-1
Reeves, Wharton
Hansbury; Dixon, Donachie, Phelan, Gallagher, Laws, Scott, Reeves, Dobson, Donovan, Wharton.
Att: 3,513
Aug 16 v Blackburn Rovers (h) 1-1
Scott
Hansbury; Laws, Donachie, Phelan, Gallagher, Wharton, Hutchison, Reeves, Scott, Dobson, Donovan.
Att: 6,488
Aug 20 v Blackpool (h) 0-0
Hansbury; Dixon, Donachie, Phelan, Gallagher, Flynn, Scott, Reeves, Hamilton, Gow, Hutchison.
Att: 3,989

1984-85
Group Matches
Aug 11 v Blackpool (h) 1-0
Hird
Hansbury; Scott, Hampton, Phelan, Overson, Flynn, Malley, Powell, Devine(Butler), Biggins, Hird.
Att: 2,035
Aug 14 v Rochdale (a) 0-1
Turner; Scott, Hampton, Phelan, Overson, Flynn, Miller, Powell, Devine, Biggins, Hird.
Att: 1,344
Aug 18 v Wigan Athletic (h) 1-2
Scott
Turner; Scott, Hampton, Phelan, Overson, Flynn, Malley, Powell, Devine, Biggins, Hird.
Att: 1,659

1985-86
Group Matches
Aug 3 v Bury (h) 1-3
Taylor
Neenan; Malley, Hampton, Heggarty, Overson, Deakin, Grewcock(Rawstron), Devine(Rhodes), Biggins, Taylor, Chippendale.
Att: 1,970
Aug 6 v Rochdale (a) 7-0
Biggins 3, Grewcock 2, Hampton, Chippendale
Neenan; Palmer, Hampton, Heggarty, Overson, Deakin, Grewcock, Malley, Taylor, Biggins, Chippendale.
Att: 1,099
Aug 10 v Bolton Wanderers (h) 4-0
Biggins 3, Grewcock
Neenan; Palmer, Hampton, Heggarty, Overson, Deakin, Grewcock, Malley, Taylor, Biggins, Chippendale(Hird).
Att: 2,720
Final
Aug 13 v Blackburn Rovers (a) 0-1
Neenan; Palmer, Hampton, Heggarty, Overson, Deakin, Grewcock, Malley, Taylor, Biggins, Hird.
Att: 6,017

1986-87
Group Matches
Aug 9 v Wigan Athletic (a) 1-1
Hoskin
Neenan; Malley, Hampton, Rodaway, Heggarty, Deakin, Grewcock, Britton, Regis, James, Hoskin.
Att: 1,899
Aug 12 v Bolton Wanderers (h) 2-3
Heggarty, Hoskin
Neenan; Malley, Hampton, Rodaway, Heggarty, Deakin, Grewcock, Britton, Regis, James, Hoskin.
Att: 2,149
Aug 16 v Preston North End (h) 0-0
Neenan; Malley, Hampton, Rodaway, Heggarty (Gallagher), Deakin, Grewcock, Britton, Entwistle, James, Hoskin.
Att: 1,586

1987-88
Group Matches
Aug 1 v Blackpool (h) 0-2
Pearce; Leebrook, McGrory, Daniel, James, Deakin (Monington), Grewcock, Farrell, Oghani, Comstive, Hoskin.
Att: 2,508
Aug 4 v Blackburn Rovers (h) 2-1
Comstive, Britton
Pearce; Leebrook, McGrory, Daniel, Gardner, Deakin, Grewcock, Farrell(Malley), Oghani, Comstive, Britton.
Att: 5,358
Aug 7 v Bolton Wanderers (a) 1-1
Oghani
Pearce; Malley, McGrory, Daniel, Gardner, Deakin, Grewcock, Farrell, Oghani, Comstive, Britton(Hoskin).
Att: 2,501

1988-89
Group Matches
Aug 6 v Preston North End (h) 0-1
Pearce; Daniel, Deakin, Farrell, Davis, Gardner, Rowell, Oghani(Taylor), O'Connell, Comstive, Britton (Hoskin).
Att: 5,456
Aug 9 v Blackburn Rovers (h) 1-3
Comstive (pen)
Williams; Daniel(Britton), Deakin, Farrell, Davis, Gardner, Rowell, Oghani, O'Connell, Comstive, Atkinson.
Att: 7,506
Aug 13 v Blackpool (a) 1-2
Oghani
Williams; Farrell, Deakin, Britton, Zelem, Gardner (McGrory), Rowell, Oghani, O'Connell, Comstive, Atkinson.
Att: 3,042

1989-90
Group Matches
Aug 5 v Bolton Wanderers (h) 2-2
Farrell, Mumby
Pearce; Measham, McGrory, Deakin, Monington, Eli(Mumby), Grewcock, Hancock(White), O'Connell, Farrell, Jakub.
Att: 4,547
Aug 8 v Blackburn Rovers (h) 0-2
Pearce; Measham(Comstive), Jakub, Deakin, Monington, Harris, Grewcock, Mumby, O'Connell, Farrell, White(Rowell).
Att: 9,007
Aug 12 v Wigan Athletic (h) 0-2
Pearce; Farrell, Deakin, Deary, Monington, Harris, White, Mumby, O'Connell, Hancock(Grewcock), Jakub.
Att: 3,277

1990-91
Group Matches
Aug 11 v Blackpool (h) 2-2
Francis, Futcher
Pearce; France, Bray(Deakin), Deary, Farrell, Smyth, Mumby(Hamilton), Futcher, Francis, Jakub, White.
Att: 3,060
Aug 14 v Wigan Athletic (h) 3-1
Francis, Farrell, Futcher
Williams; Measham, Deakin, Deary, Farrell(Smyth), Davis, Hamilton, Futcher, Francis, Jakub, Grewcock.
Att: 2,380
Aug 18 v Bolton Wanderers (a) 0-3
Pearce; Measham, Bray, Deary, Smyth, Davis, Mumby (Hamilton), Futcher, Francis, Jakub, White.
Att: 2,649

WATNEY CUP

1972-73
Round 1
Jul 29 v Lincoln City (a) 1-0
James
Stevenson; Docherty, Newton, Dobson, Waldron, Thomson, Ingham, Casper, Fletcher, Probert(West), James.
Att: 7,428
Round 2
Aug 2 v Bristol Rovers (h) 0-2
Stevenson; Docherty, Newton, Dobson, Waldron, Thomson, Ingham(Bradshaw), Casper, Fletcher, Probert(West), James.
Att: 10,589

TEXACO CUP

1970-71
Round 1 (1st leg)
Sep 15 v Heart of Midlothian (h) 3-1
Docherty, Merrington, Kindon
Waiters; Merrington, Angus, Docherty, Waldron, Thomson, Thomas, Coates, Casper, Collins, Kindon (Bellamy).
Att: 10,106
Round 1 (2nd leg)
Sep 30 v Heart of Midlothian (a) 1-4 (agg 4-5)
Casper
Waiters; Latcham, Merrington, Docherty, Waldron, West, Thomas, Coates, Casper, Bellamy, Collins.
Att: 16,500

1973-74
Round 1 (1st leg)
Sep 18 v East Fife (h) 7-0
Fletcher 3, Nulty 2, James, Noble
Stevenson, Noble, Newton, Ingham, Waldron, Thomson, Nulty, Hankin, Fletcher, Collins(Pashley), James.
Att: 10,374
Round 1 (2nd leg)
Oct 3 v East Fife (a) 3-2 (agg 10-2)
Fletcher, Noble, Hankin
Stevenson; Noble, Newton, Dobson, Waldron, Thomson, Nulty, Hankin, Fletcher, Ingham, James.
Att: 2,000
Round 2 (1st leg)
Oct 24 v Heart of Midlothian (a) 3-0
Dobson, Noble, James
Stevenson; Noble, Newton, Dobson, Thomson, Rodaway, Nulty, Hankin, Fletcher, Ingham, James.
Att: 22,000
Round 2 (2nd leg)
Nov 6 v Heart of Midlothian (h) 5-0 (agg 8-0)
Hankin 2, Fletcher, Collins, Nulty
Stevenson; Ingham, Newton, Dobson, Waldron, Rodaway, Nulty, Hankin, Fletcher, Collins, James.
Att: 9,063
Round 3 (1st leg)
Nov 27 v Norwich City (h) 2-0
James, Noble
Stevenson; Noble, Newton, Dobson, Waldron, Thomson, Nulty, Ingham, Fletcher, Collins, James.
Att: 4,858
Round 3 (2nd leg)
Dec 12 v Norwich City (a) 3-2 (agg 5-2)
Hankin, Waldron, Noble
Stevenson; Noble, Newton, Dobson, Waldron, Ingham, Nulty, Hankin, Fletcher, Collins, James.
Att: 11,797
Final
Apr 24 v Newcastle United (a) 1-2 a.e.t.
Fletcher
Stevenson; Noble, Newton, Dobson(Collins), Waldron, Rodaway, Nulty, Hankin, Fletcher, Ingham, James.
Att: 34,540

ANGLO-SCOTTISH CUP

1976-77
Preliminary Group
Aug 7 v Blackburn Rovers (a) 1-1
Flynn
Peyton; Scott, Newton, Noble, Thomson, Rodaway, Morris, Hankin, Ingham, Flynn(Loggie), Summerbee.
Att: 11,012
Aug 11 v Blackpool (a) 1-2
Noble
Stevenson; Scott, Newton, Noble, Thomson, Rodaway, Morris, Fletcher, Hankin, Flynn, Summerbee.
Att: 9,386
Aug 14 v Bolton Wanderers (h) 1-0
Ingham
Peyton; Scott, Newton, Noble, Thomson, Rodaway, Morris, Ingham, Hankin, Flynn, Summerbee.
Att: 9,028

1977-78
Preliminary Group
Aug 2 v Blackburn Rovers (h) 2-1
Ingham, Smith
Stevenson; Newton, Brennan, Noble, Robinson, Rodaway, Ingham, Smith, Fletcher, Flynn, Cochrane.
Att: 8,119
Aug 6 v Bolton Wanderers (a) 0-1
Stevenson; Newton, Brennan, Noble, Robinson, Rodaway, Ingham, Smith, Loggie, Flynn, Cochrane.
Att: 8,250
Aug 9 v Blackpool (h) 0-4
Stevenson; Newton, Brennan, Noble(Pashley), Robinson, Rodaway, Ingham, Smith, Loggie, Flynn, Cochrane.
Att: 5,515

1978-79
Preliminary Group
Aug 5 v Preston North End (h) 3-2
Ingham, Kindon, Fletcher
Stevenson; Scott, Brennan, Noble, Thomson, Rodaway, Cochrane, Ingham, Fletcher, Kindon, Smith.
Att: 7,456
Aug 8 v Blackpool (h) 3-1
Ingham, Cochrane, Smith
Stevenson; Scott, Brennan, Noble, Thomson, Rodaway, Cochrane, Ingham, Fletcher, Kindon, Smith.
Att: 4,750
Aug 12 v Blackburn Rovers (a) 1-1
Smith
Stevenson; Scott, Brennan, Noble, Thomson, Rodaway, Morley, Ingham, Fletcher, Kindon, Smith.
Att: 9,791
Quarter-final (1st leg)
Sep 12 v Celtic (h) 1-0
Kindon
Stevenson; Scott, Brennan, Noble, Thomson, Rodaway, Cochrane, Hall, Fletcher, Kindon, James.
Att: 30,000
Quarter-final (2nd leg)
Sep 27 v Celtic (a) 2-1 (agg 3-1)
Brennan, Kindon
Stevenson; Scott, Brennan, Noble, Thomson, Rodaway, Smith, Ingham, Fletcher, Kindon, James.
Att: 28,000
Semi-final (1st leg)
Oct 31 v Mansfield Town (a) 2-1
Kindon, James
Stevenson; Scott, Brennan, Noble, Thomson, Rodaway, Hall, Ingham, Fletcher, Kindon, James.
Att: 5,517
Semi-final (2nd leg)
Nov 7 v Mansfield Town (h) 0-1 a.e.t. (agg 2-2)
Burnley won 8-7 on penalties.
Stevenson; Scott, Brennan, Noble, Thomson, Rodaway, Hall, Ingham, Fletcher, Kindon, James.
Att: 6,871
Final (1st leg)
Dec 5 v Oldham Athletic (a) 4-1
Kindon 2, Thomson, Noble
Stevenson; Arins, Brennan, Noble, Thomson, Rodaway, Hall, Ingham, Fletcher, Kindon, James.
Att: 10,456
Final (2nd leg)
Dec 12 v Oldham Athletic (h) 0-1 (agg 4-2)
Stevenson; Arins, Brennan, Noble, Thomson, Rodaway, Hall, Ingham, Fletcher, Kindon, James.
Att: 10,865

1979-80
Preliminary Group
Aug 4 v Blackburn Rovers (a) 2-2
Kindon, Metcalfe (og)
Stevenson; Scott, Jakub, Noble, Thomson, Rodaway, Ingham, Dobson, Fletcher, Kindon, James.
Att: 7,749
Aug 7 v Blackpool (a) 2-3
Noble, Ingham
Stevenson; Scott, Brennan, Noble, Robinson, Rodaway, Ingham, Dobson, Fletcher, Kindon, James.
Att: 5,003
Aug 11 v Preston North End (h) 1-2
Brennan
Stevenson; Scott, Brennan, Noble, Thomson, Rodaway, Ingham, Dobson, Fletcher, Kindon, James.
Att: 6,171

1980-81
Preliminary Group
July 29 v Bury (a) 1-2
Dobson
Stevenson; Wood, Holt, Dobson, Dixon, Rodaway, Cavener, Cassidy, Hamilton, Taylor, Ingham(Young).
Att: 3,887
Aug 2 v Oldham Athletic (h) 3-1
Scott, Taylor, Cavener
Stevenson; Wood, Holt, Scott, Overson, Thomson, Cassidy, Dobson, Hamilton, Taylor, Cavener.
Att: 4,083
Aug 5 v Shrewsbury Town (h) 1-1
Cassidy
Stevenson; Wood, Holt, Scott, Overson, Dixon, Cassidy(Young), Dobson, Hamilton, Taylor, Cavener.
Att: 3,354

FOOTBALL LEAGUE GROUP CUP

1981-82
Group Matches
Aug 15 v Carlisle United (h) 4-2
Taylor 2, Hamilton 2
Stevenson; Laws, Holt, Scott, Overson, Dobson, Cavener, Taylor, Hamilton, Cassidy, Potts.
Att: 2,305
Aug 18 v Preston North End (a) 1-0
Hamilton
Stevenson; Laws, Holt, Scott, Phelan, Dobson, Cavener, Taylor, Hamilton, Cassidy, Potts.
Att: 5,269
Aug 22 v Blackpool (a) 0-0
Stevenson; Laws, Holt, Scott, Phelan, Dobson, Cavener, Taylor, Hamilton, Cassidy(Overson), Young.
Att: 3,464
Quarter-final
Dec 8 v Watford (h) 2-1
Scott, Holt
Stevenson; Dixon, Holt, Scott, Overson, Phelan, Cavener, Potts, Taylor, Anderson, Young.
Att: 2,658
Semi-final
Feb 16 v Wimbledon (a) 0-5
O'Rourke; Miller, Ray, Holt, Dixon, Anderson, Scott, Cavener, Wright(Allen), Potts, Young.
Att: 1,267

Note: The Football League Group Cup replaced the Anglo-Scottish Cup which was discontinued when the Scottish clubs withdrew after the 1980-81 competition. Originally started in 1970-71 under the sponsorship of Texaco, the tournament first embraced teams from Northern Ireland as well as England and Scotland. It became the Anglo-Scottish Cup in 1975-76.

Burnley in the FA Charity Shield

The Clarets have participated in this annual curtain-raiser on three occasions, and have had mixed success.

16 May 1921 v Tottenham Hotspur (a) 0-2
Dawson; Smelt, Taylor, Bassnett, Boyle, Watson, Nesbitt, Kelly, Anderson, Cross, Mosscrop.
Att: 20,000

13 Aug 1960 v Wolverhampton Wanderers (h) 2-2
Connelly, Miller
Blacklaw; Angus, Elder, Adamson, Cummings, Miller, Connelly, McIlroy, Pointer, Robson, Pilkington.
Att: 20,000
(Trophy shared, each club retaining it for six months)

18 August 1973 v Manchester City (a) 1-0
Waldron
Stevenson; Docherty, Newton, Dobson, Waldron, Thomson, Nulty, Casper, Fletcher, Collins, James.
Att: 23,988

Burnley in Europe

EUROPEAN CUP
1960-61

Round 2 (1st leg)
Nov 16 v Reims (h) 2-0
McIlroy, Robson
Blacklaw; Angus, Elder, Joyce, Adamson, Miller, Connelly, McIlroy, Pointer, Robson, Pilkington.
Att: 36,742
Round 2 (2nd leg)
Nov 30 v Reims (a) 2-3 (agg 4-3)
Connelly, Robson
Blacklaw; Angus, Elder, Joyce, Adamson, Miller, Connelly, McIlroy, Pointer, Robson, Pilkington.
Att: 45,000

Round 3 (1st leg)
Jan 18 v SV Hamburg (h) 3-1
Pilkington 2, Robson
Blacklaw; Angus, Elder, Joyce, Adamson, Miller, Connelly, McIlroy, Pointer, Robson, Pilkington.
Att: 47,000
Round 3 (2nd leg)
Mar 15 v SV Hamburg (a) 1-4 (agg 4-5)
Harris
Blacklaw; Angus, Elder, Joyce, Adamson, Miller, Connelly, McIlroy, Pointer, Robson, Harris.
Att: 71,000

EUROPEAN FAIRS CUP
1966-67

Round 1 (1st leg)
Sep 20 v VfB Stuttgart (a) 1-1
Irvine
Blacklaw; Angus, Elder, O'Neil, Miller, Bellamy, Morgan, Lochhead, Irvine, Harris, Coates.
Att: 74,000
Round 1 (2nd leg)
Sep 27 v VfB Stuttgart (h) 2-0 (agg 3-1)
Lochhead, Coates
Blacklaw; Angus, Miller, Bellamy, Talbut, Todd, Morgan, Lochhead, Irvine, Harris, Coates.
Att: 23,716
Round 2 (1st leg)
Oct 19 v Lausanne-Sports (a) 3-1
Coates, Harris, Lochhead
Blacklaw; Angus, Elder, O'Neil, Talbut, Miller, Morgan, Lochhead, Bellamy, Harris, Coates.
Att: 4,000
Round 2 (2nd leg)
Oct 25 v Lausanne-Sports (h) 5-0 (agg 8-1)
Lochhead 3, O'Neil, Irvine
Blacklaw; Angus, Elder, Bellamy, Talbut, Miller, Morgan, Lochhead, Irvine, Harris, O'Neil.
Att: 18,573

Round 3 (1st leg)
Jan 18 v Napoli (h) 3-0
Lochhead, Latcham, Coates
Thomson; Angus, Smith, O'Neil, Miller, Todd, Morgan, Lochhead, Coates, Harris, Latcham.
Att: 24,519
Round 3 (2nd leg)
Feb 8 v Napoli (a) 0-0 (agg 3-0)
Thomson; Smith, Todd, O'Neil, Miller, Merrington, Morgan, Lochhead, Coates, Harris, Latcham.
Att: 60,000
Round 4 (1st leg)
Apr 4 v Eintracht Frankfurt (a) 1-1
Miller
Thomson; Smith, Angus, O'Neil, Miller, Merrington, Morgan, Bellamy, Coates, Harris, Latcham.
Att: 25,000
Round 4 (2nd leg)
Apr 18 v Eintracht Frankfurt (h) 1-2 (agg 2-3)
Miller
Thomson; Smith, Elder, O'Neil, Miller, Merrington, Morgan, Bellamy, Coates, Harris, Latcham.
Att: 25,161

Burnley Internationals

*Many players won additional caps with other clubs but the totals given here are solely for appearances made while Burnley players. Before 1924 there was only one 'Ireland' team. In that year the Republic of Ireland began separate matches and that position is reflected here. The date given for each match is the actual year in which it was played. *Denotes World Cup final stages.*

ENGLAND

John Angus (1) 1961 v Austria.
William Bannister (1) 1901 v Wales.
Tommy Boyle (1) 1913 v Ireland.
Jack Bruton (3) 1928 v France, Belgium; 1929 v Scotland.
Ralph Coates (2) 1970 v Northern Ireland; 1971 v Greece (sub).
John Connelly (10-4 goals) 1959 v Wales, Sweden (1 goal), Northern Ireland; 1960 v Scotland; 1961 v Wales, Portugal (1 goal); 1962 v Austria, Switzerland (1 goal), Wales (1 goal); 1963 v France.
James Crabtree (3) 1894 v Ireland; 1895 v Ireland, Scotland.
Jerry Dawson (2) 1921 v Ireland; 1922 v Scotland
Martin Dobson (4) 1974 v Portugal, East Germany, Bulgaria, Yugoslavia.
Billy Elliott (5-3 goals) 1952 v Italy, Austria, Northern Ireland (1 goal), Wales, Belgium (2 goals).
Bert Freeman (3-2 goals) 1912 v Ireland (1 goal), Wales (1 goal), Scotland.
Gordon Harris (1) 1966 v Poland.
Jack Hillman (1) 1899 v Ireland.
Jack Hill (8) 1925 v Wales; 1926 v Scotland, Northern Ireland; 1927 v Scotland, Belgium, France, Ireland, Wales.
Bob Kelly (11-6 goals) 1920 v Scotland (2 goals), Ireland (1 goal); 1921 v Wales, Scotland; 1922 v Wales (1 goal), Scotland; 1923 v Scotland (1 goal), Ireland; 1924 v Northern Ireland (1 goal); 1925 v Wales, Scotland.
Colin McDonald (8) 1958 v Soviet Union, Soviet Union*, Brazil*, Austria*, Soviet Union*, Northern Ireland, Soviet Union, Wales.
Brian Miller (1) 1961 v Austria.
Eddie Mosscrop (2) 1914 v Wales, Scotland.
Louis Page (7-1 goal) 1927 v Wales, Scotland, Belgium (1 goal), Luxembourg, France, Ireland, Wales.
Brian Pilkington (1) 1954 v Northern Ireland.
Ray Pointer (3-2 goals) 1961 v Luxembourg (1 goal), Wales, Portugal (1 goal).
George Waterfield (1) 1927 v Wales.
Willie Watson (3) 1913 v Scotland; 1914 v Ireland; 1919 v Ireland.
Jack Yates (1-3 goals) 1889 v Ireland (3 goals).

SCOTLAND

Jock Aird (4) 1954 v Norway, Norway, Austria, Uruguay.

Adam Blacklaw (3) 1963 v Norway, Spain; 1965 v Italy.
Willie Morgan (1) 1967 v Northern Ireland.

WALES

Stan Bowsher (1) 1929 v Northern Ireland.
Brian Flynn (33-3 goals) 1974 v Luxembourg (sub); 1975 v Hungary (sub), Scotland (1 goal), England, Northern Ireland, Austria, Luxembourg (sub); 1976 v England, Yugoslavia, England, Northern Ireland, Yugoslavia, Scotland; 1977 v Czechoslovakia, Scotland, England, Northern Ireland, Kuwait, Kuwait, Scotland; 1982 v Yugoslavia (1 goal); 1983 v England, Bulgaria, Scotland, Northern Ireland, Brazil (1 goal), Norway, Romania, Bulgaria, Yugoslavia; 1984 v Scotland, Norway, Israel.
Leighton James (22-3 goals) 1971 v Czechoslovakia, Romania; 1972 v Scotland (sub), England; 1973 v England, Poland (1 goal), Scotland, England, Northern Ireland, Poland; 1974 v England, Scotland, Northern Ireland, Austria, Hungary, Luxembourg; 1975 v Hungary, Luxembourg (2 goals), Scotland, England, Northern Ireland; 1978 v Turkey.
Billy Morris (5) 1947 v Northern Ireland; 1948 v England; 1951 v Scotland, Rest of UK; 1952 v Northern Ireland.

NORTHERN IRELAND

Tommy Cassidy (4) 1980 v Sweden, Portugal; 1981 v Israel, Honduras* (sub).
Terry Cochrane (4) 1978 v Scotland (sub), England (sub), Wales (sub), Republic of Ireland (sub).
Alex Elder (34-1 goal) 1960 v Wales, England, West Germany, Scotland; 1961 v Wales, Greece, West Germany, Scotland, Greece, England; 1962 v Poland, England, Scotland, Poland; 1963 v Wales, Spain; 1964 v Wales, Uruguay, England, Switzerland, Switzerland, Scotland; 1965 v Holland, Wales, Holland, Albania, Scotland, England, Albania; 1966 v Wales, Mexico (1 goal), England, Scotland; 1967 v Wales.
William Emerson (5) 1922 v Wales, England; 1923 v Scotland, Wales, England.
Hugh Flack (1) 1929 v Scotland.
Billy Hamilton (34-5 goals) 1980 v Scotland (1 goal), England, Wales, Australia, Australia, Sweden, Portugal; 1981 v Scotland (1 goal), Portugal, Scotland, Sweden, Scotland, Israel; 1982 v England, Wales, Yugoslavia*, Honduras*, Spain*, Austria* (2 goals), France*, Austria, West Germany, Albania; 1983 v Albania, Scotland, England, Wales, Austria (1 goal), Turkey, West Germany, Scotland; 1984 v England, Wales, Finland.
Willie Irvine (17-6 goals) 1963 v Wales, Spain (1 goal); 1964 v Switzerland, Scotland (1 goal); 1965 v Holland, Wales, Holland, Albania, Scotland (1 goal), England (1 goal), Albania (1 goal); 1966 v Wales (1 goal), Mexico, England, Scotland; 1967 v England; 1968 v Wales.
Jimmy McIlroy (51-10 goals) 1951 v Scotland, England; 1952 v Wales, England, Scotland; 1953 v Wales, Scotland, England; 1954 v Wales, England, Scotland; 1955 v Wales, Scotland, England; 1956 v Wales, England (1 goal), Scotland; 1957 v Portugal, Wales, Italy, Portugal (1 goal), Scotland, England (1 goal), Italy; 1968 v Italy (1 goal), Wales, Czechoslovakia*, Argentina*, West Germany*, Czechoslovakia*, France*, England, Spain (1 goal), Scotland (1 goal); 1959 v Wales (1 goal), Scotland, England; 1960 v Wales, England, West Germany; 1961 v Wales, Greece (1 goal), West Germany (1 goal), Scotland, Greece, England (1 goal); 1962 v Holland, Poland, England, Scotland, Poland.

Andy McCluggage (11-1 goal) 1927 v Scotland, Wales, England; 1928 v Wales, Scotland, England; 1929 v Wales (1 goal), Scotland; 1930 v Wales, England; 1931 v Wales.
Tom Morrison (4) 1899 v Wales; 1900 v Wales; 1902 v Scotland, England.
Sammy Todd (8) 1966 v Mexico (sub), England; 1968 v Wales; 1969 v England, Scotland, Wales, Soviet Union; 1970 v Scotland.
Tom Willighan (2) 1932 v Wales; 1933 v Scotland.

UNDER-23 INTERNATIONALS

ENGLAND

John Angus (7) 1959 v West Germany; 1960 v East Germany, Poland, Israel, Italy; 1961 v Wales; 1962 v Scotland.
Albert Cheesebrough (1) 1956 v France.
Ralph Coates (8) 1967 v Wales, Greece, Bulgaria, Turkey; 1968 v Holland; 1969 v Belgium, Portugal, Holland.
John Connelly (1) 1960 v Italy.
Martin Dobson (1) 1970 v Bulgaria.
Paul Fletcher (4) 1973 v Denmark (sub); 1974 v Wales, Yugoslavia, France (1 goal).
Ray Hankin (3) 1974 v Czechoslovakia, (sub), Scotland; 1975 v Wales.
Gordon Harris (2) 1961 v Israel; 1963 v Yugoslavia.
Brian Miller (3) 1960 v East Germany, Poland, Israel.
Brian O'Neil (1) 1966 v Turkey.
Ray Pointer (5) 1959 v Italy, Hungary; 1960 v East Germany, Poland, Israel.
Jimmy Robson (1) 1959 v West Germany.
Alan Stevenson (11) 1972 v Wales; 1973 v Holland, Scotland, Czechoslavakia, Holland, Denmark; 1974 v Scotland, Turkey, France, Czechoslovakia, Portugal.
John Talbut (7) 1964 v Wales, Hungary, Israel, Turkey; 1965 v West Germany, Scotland, France.
David Thomas (8) 1970 v Bulgaria, Scotland, West Germany, Sweden, Wales; 1971 v Switzerland, Scotland; 1972 v East Germany.
Alan West (1) 1972 v Wales.

SCOTLAND

Adam Blacklaw (2) 1959 v Wales; 1960 v England.
Andy Lochhead (1) 1962 v Wales.
Willie Morgan (1) 1968 v England.

WALES

Brian Flynn (2) 1975 v England, Scotland.
Leighton James (7) 1972 v England, Scotland; 1973 v England, Scotland; 1974 v England; 1975 v England, Scotland.
Jeff Parton (3) 1972 v England, Scotland; 1974 v England.

NORTHERN IRELAND

Alex Elder (1) 1964 v Wales.
Willie Irvine (3) 1963 v Wales; 1964 v Wales; 1965 v Wales.
Sammy Todd (4) 1965 v Wales; 1967 v Wales; 1968 v Wales; 1969 v Italy.

ENGLAND YOUTH CAPS

John Angus 1957-1958 (2)
Paul Bradshaw 1971-1972 (2)
Mick Docherty 1969 (1)
Ray Hankin 1973 (1)
Peter Jones 1968 (1)
Andy Kilner 1984 (1)
Steve Kindon 1968-1969 (2)
Ian Lawson 1958 (1)
Mike Phelan 1981 (1)
Eric Probert 1970 (1)
Trevor Steven 1982 (1)
David Thomas 1968-1969 (2)
Harry Wilson 1971 (1)

FOOTBALL LEAGUE REPRESENTATIVES

Jimmy Adamson 1960-61 v Irish League.
John Angus 1960-61 v Irish League.
Reg Attwell 1948-49 v Scottish League.
Billy Bannister 1900-01 v Scottish League.
Tommy Boyle 1911-12 v Scottish League; 1912-13 v Scottish League; 1913-14 v Scottish League.
Allan Brown 1947-48 v Irish League.
Jack Bruton 1928-29 v Irish League.
Frank Casper 1968-69 v Scottish League.
Ralph Coates 1968-69 v Scottish League; 1969-70 v Scottish League; 1970-71 v Scottish League, Irish League.
John Connelly 1959-60 v Irish League, League of Ireland; 1960-61 v Scottish League; 1961-62 v League of Ireland, Irish League, Italian League; 1962-63 v Italian League.
James Crabtree 1893-94 v Scottish League, Irish League; 1894-95 v Scottish League.
Benny Cross 1922-23 v Irish League; 1926-27 v Scottish League.
Tommy Cummings 1950-51 v Irish League.
Jerry Dawson 1909-10 v Scottish League; 1910-11 v Scottish League; 1921-22 v Scottish League, Irish League.
Martin Dobson 1973-74 v Scottish League.
Billy Elliott 1952-53 v Irish League, League of Ireland, Scottish League.
Bert Freeman 1911-12 v Scottish League; 1912-13 v Irish League; 1913-14 v Irish League.
Gordon Harris 1961-62 v Irish League; 1965-66 v League of Ireland.
Jack Hill 1923-24 v Scottish League; 1924-25 v Scottish League; 1925-26 v Scottish League.
Jack Hillman 1898-99 v Scottish League; 1899-1900 v Irish League.
Teddy Hodgson 1913-14 v Scottish League.
Bob Kelly 1919-20 v Scottish League; 1920-21 v Scottish League; 1921-22 v Scottish League; 1923-24 v Scottish League, Irish League; 1924-25 v Scottish League, Irish League.
Peter Kippax 1946-47 v Scottish League, Irish League.
Colin McDonald 1957-58 v Scottish League; 1958-59 v Irish League, League of Ireland.
Jimmy McIlroy 1960-61 v Irish League, Italian League.
Brian Miller 1961-62 v Irish League, Scottish League.
Hugh Moffat 1909-10 v Southern League.
Eddie Mosscrop 1913-14 v Scottish League.
Brian O'Neil 1965-66 v League of Ireland.
Louis Page 1929-30 v Irish League.
Brian Pilkington 1958-59 v Scottish League.

Ray Pointer 1961-62 v League of Ireland, Italian League.
Alec Robinson 1934-35 v Irish League; 1935-36 v Irish League.
Wilf Toman 1898-99 v Scottish League.
Willie Watson 1913-14 v Irish League; 1914-15 v Irish League, Southern League; 1919-20 v Irish League; 1921-22 v Irish League.
Arthur Woodruff 1946-47 v League of Ireland; 1947-48 v Irish League.

'B' INTERNATIONALS

ENGLAND

Jimmy Adamson 1953 v Scotland 'B'.
Tommy Cummings 1953 v Scotland 'B'; 1956 v Scotland 'B', Switzerland 'B'.
Bill Holden 1953 v Scotland 'B'.
Brian Pilkington 1954 v Scotland 'B'; 1957 v Scotland 'B'.
Les Shannon 1952 v France 'B'; 1954 v West Germany 'B'; 1956 v Scotland 'B'.

NORTHERN IRELAND

Alex Elder 1960 v France 'B'.
Billy Marshall 1958 v Romania 'B'; 1960 v France 'B'.
Billy Wilson 1958 v Romania 'B'.

SCOTLAND

Jock Aird 1953 v England 'B'; 1954 v England 'B'.
Doug Winton 1957 v England 'B'.

OTHER INTERNATIONAL GAMES

Jimmy McIlroy 1956 Great Britain v Rest of Europe.
Billy Morris 1946 Wales v Italy (Unofficial International).
Peter O'Dowd 1931 England v Canada (Unofficial Tour).
Willie Watson 1919 England v Wales (Victory International).

AMATEUR INTERNATIONALS

Arthur Bell 1907 England v Holland; 1908 England v Wales, Holland.
Peter Kippax 1948 (Olympic Games); Great Britain v Holland, France, Yugoslavia.

Burnley's Leading Appearances

Football League		FA Cup		League Cup		Other		Total	
J.Dawson	522	J.Adamson	52	A.Stevenson	36	A.Stevenson	36	J.Dawson	569
J.McIlroy	439	J.McIlroy	50	M.Dobson	34	R.Deakin	35/1	A.Stevenson	543
J.Angus	438/1	B.Miller	50	J.Angus	25	D.Scott	32	J.Angus	520/1
A.Stevenson	438	J.Dawson	46	D.Scott	24	A.Farrell	30	J.McIlroy	497
T.Cummings	434	J.Angus	45	C.Waldron	23	N.Grewcock	29/2	M.Dobson	495/4
J.Adamson	426	A.Blacklaw	44	R.Coates	22/2	W.Rodaway	28	J.Adamson	486
M.Dobson	406/4	A.Elder	39	F.Casper	22	L.James	27/1	T.Cummings	479
F.Barron	400	J.Connelly	38	L.James	22	C.Pearce	27	B.Miller	455
B.Miller	379	T.Cummings	38	B.O'Neil	21/1	W.Ingham	26	F.Barron	423
G.Waterfield	371	R.Pointer	35	J.Thomson	21	M.Dobson	24	L.James	397/6
W.Watson	346	B.Pilkington	33	P.Noble	19	P.Fletcher	24	G.Waterfield	394
L.James	331/5	A.Stevenson	33	B.Flynn	18/2	P.Noble	24	A.Blacklaw	383
J.Taylor	323	W.Watson	33	L.Latcham	18/1	J.Thomson	23	W.Watson	380
A.Blacklaw	318	M.Dobson	31	P.Fletcher	18	S.Davis	22	J.Thomson	360/3
G.Beel	316	G.Harris	30	W.Rodaway	18	V.Overson	21/1	D.Scott	356/8
C.Waldron	308	H.Mather	28	A.Bellamy	16	M.Phelan	20	C.Waldron	356
H.Mather	301	D.Taylor	28	W.Hamilton	16	I.Britton	18/2	J.Taylor	352
B.Pilkington	300	R.Seith	27	G.Harris	16	S.Taylor	18/2	P.Fletcher	349/3
J.Thomson	294/3	R.Attwell	25	M.Phelan	16	P.Malley	17/4	B.Pilkington	340
P.Fletcher	291/2	T.Boyle	25	D.Thomas	16	P.Comstive	17/1	G.Beel	337

Burnley's Leading Goalscorers

Football League		FA Cup		League Cup		Other		Total	
G.Beel	178	J.Connelly	15	F.Casper	9	W.Biggins	11	G.Beel	187
R.Pointer	118	J.Robson	14	A.Lochhead	9	S.Kindon	8	R.Pointer	133
J.McIlroy	116	J.McIlroy	13	W.Irvine	8	P.Noble	8	J.McIlroy	131
L.Page	111	R.Pointer	13	L.James	8	P.Fletcher	7	A.Lochhead	128
B.Freeman	103	B.Freeman	12	P.Noble	8	A.Lochhead	6	B.Freeman	115
A.Lochhead	101	A.Lochhead	12	W.Hamilton	5	P.Comstive	5	L.Page	115
R.Kelly	88	W.Hamilton	10	G.Harris	5	N.Grewcock	5	J.Connelly	105
J.Connelly	86	G.Beel	9	T.Cochrane	4	W.Ingham	5	J.Robson	100
W.Bowes	79	E.Hodgson	9	M.Dobson	4	L.James	5	W.Irvine	97
J.Robson	79	W.Irvine	9	B.Flynn	4	G.Oghani	5	R.Kelly	97
W.Irvine	78	R.Kelly	9	R.Hankin	4	A.Farrell	4	F.Casper	89
W.Holden	75	J.Anderson	8	P.McGee	4	W.Hamilton	4	P.Fletcher	86
F.Casper	74	I.Lawson	8	J.Murray	4	R.Hankin	4	W.Bowes	84
P.Fletcher	71	T.Boyle	7	J.Robson	4	A.Hoskin	4	G.Harris	81
R.Smith	71	M.Dobson	7	O.Thomas	4	D.Scott	4	L.James	81
G.Harris	69	P.Fletcher	7	P.Comstive	3	A.Taylor	4	P.Noble	80
B.Pilkington	67	E.Hancock	7	W.Ingham	3	W.Toman	4	W.Holden	79
L.James	66	B.Pilkington	7	B.O'Connell	3			W.Hamilton	77
J.Anderson	64	R.Harrison	6	G.Oghani	3			B.Pilkington	77
M.Dobson	63	W.Morris	6	D.Scott	3			R.Smith	76
P.Noble	63	A.Ogden	6	A.Taylor	3				

Leading Goalscorers Season-by-Season

(League only)

Season				
1888-89	A.Brady 7	P.Gallocher 6	W.McKay 6	
1889-90	R.Haresnape 5	C.Lambie 5		
1890-91	C.Lambie 16	A.McLardie 14		
1891-92	T.Nicol 17	A.McLardie 10		
1892-93	W.Bowes 8	R.Buchanan 8		
1893-94	P.Turnbull 15	A.Brady 6	W.Bowes 6	
1894-95	T.Nicol 11	W.Bowes 8		
1895-96	H.Robertson 10	T.Nicol 8		
1896-97	W.Bowes 11	T.Chambers 5	D.Black 5	H.Robertson 5
1897-98	J.Ross 23	W.Toman 15		
1898-99	W.Toman 11	W.Bowes 10		
1899-1900	E.Chadwick 10	W.Bowes 6		
1900-01	W.Bowes 9	W.Jenkinson 9		
1901-02	C.Hogan 10	M.Brunton 8		
1902-03	C.Hogan 7	F.Barron 3	J.Crawford 3	E.Lee 3
1903-04	D.McFarlane 8	H.Williams 8		
1904-05	D.McFarlane 14	R.Smith 8		
1905-06	D.McFarlane 10	A.Davidson 7	R.Smith 7	
1906-07	R.Smith 17	F.Whittaker 13		
1907-08	R.Smith 24	A.Smith 10		
1908-09	R.Smith 13	J.Morley 7		
1909-10	B.Green 18	W.Lomas 11		
1910-11	B.Green 11	W.Lomas 10		
1911-12	B.Freeman 32	R.Lindley 15		
1912-13	B.Freeman 31	E.Hodgson 15		
1913-14	B.Freeman 16	E.Hodgson 12		
1914-15	E.Hodgson 19	B.Freeman 12		
1919-20	B.Freeman 12	R.Kelly 9		
1920-21	J.Anderson 25	R.Kelly 20		
1921-22	J.Anderson 20	R.Kelly 16		
1922-23	R.Kelly 17	B.Cross 12		
1923-24	G.Beel 19	R.Kelly 8		
1924-25	T.Roberts 15	G.Beel 10		
1925-26	L.Page 26	G.Beel 14		
1926-27	G.Beel 24	L.Page 13		
1927-28	G.Beel 35	L.Page 22		
1928-29	G.Beel 30	L.Page 17		
1929-30	L.Page 15	J.Mantle 14		
1930-31	G.Beel 25	L.Page 13		
1931-32	G.Beel 11	J.Kelly 9		
1932-33	T.Jones 16	C.Smith 14		
1933-34	C.Smith 17	E.Hancock 10		
1934-35	G.Brown 21	C.Smith 8		
1935-36	C.Smith 10	E.Hancock 7	S.Kilcar 7	

1936-37	C.Fletcher 12	T.Lawton 11	
1937-38	R.Brocklebank 14	W.Miller 13	
1938-39	J.Clayton 10	R.Brocklebank...8	
1946-47	H.Potts...........15	J.Billingham.....12	
1947-48	H.Potts...........14	J.Billingham.....13	
1948-49	J.Chew 11	R.Harrison........7	H.Potts 7
1949-50	H.Potts...........11	J.Spencer..........7	
1950-51	W.Holden 12	W.Morris 11	
1951-52	W.Morris 18	W.Holden 12	
1952-53	W.Holden 22	L.Shannon 15	
1953-54	W.Gray...........19	W.Holden 14	
1954-55	W.Holden 15	B.Pilkington.....11	
1955-56	P.McKay 25	B.Pilkington.....12	
1956-57	J.McIlroy........13	P.McKay 11	
1957-58	J.McIlroy........16	A.Cheesebrough13	B.Pilkington.....13
1958-59	R.Pointer 27	J.Connelly.......12	
1959-60	J.Connelly.......20	R.Pointer 19	
1960-61	J.Robson 25	R.Pointer 22	
1961-62	R.Pointer 25	J.Connelly.......17	
1962-63	A.Lochhead.....19	R.Pointer 14	
1963-64	A.Lochhead.....11	G.Harris 10	
1964-65	W.Irvine 22	A.Lochhead.....21	
1965-66	W.Irvine 29	A.Lochhead.....15	
1966-67	A.Lochhead.....18	G.Harris 13	W.Irvine 13
1967-68	F.Casper 14	A.Lochhead.....13	
1968-69	F.Casper 13	D.Collins..........6	
1969-70	S.Kindon 17	F.Casper...........8	
1970-71	E.Probert..........5	F.Casper...........4	M.Dobson 4
1971-72	F.Casper 18	P.Fletcher........10	
1972-73	P.Fletcher........15	F.Casper 12	M.Dobson.......12
1973-74	P.Fletcher........13	R.Hankin 8	
1974-75	L.James 16	R.Hankin 14	
1975-76	R.Hankin 13	P.Noble 13	
1976-77	P.Noble 13	M.Smith 11	
1977-78	S.Kindon 12	T.Cochrane 8	P.Noble............8
1978-79	P.Noble 14	P.Fletcher 9	W.Ingham.........9
1979-80	W.Hamilton 7	L.James............6	
1980-81	S.Taylor..........16	W.Hamilton 9	D.Scott 9
1981-82	W.Hamilton.....11	S.Taylor 9	
1982-83	W.Hamilton.....13	S.Taylor..........12	
1983-84	W.Hamilton.....18	K.Reeves.........12	
1984-85	W.Biggins........18	K.Hird............16	
1985-86	A.Taylor 16	N.Grewcock 7	K.Hird 7
1986-87	L.James 10	N.Grewcock 9	
1987-88	G.Oghani 14	P.Comstive 8	D.Reeves 8
1988-89	B.O'Connell.....13	P.Comstive 9	
1989-90	R.Futcher 7	W.White...........7	
1990-91	R.Futcher........18	J.Francis 15	

Burnley's Hat-Trick Heroes

Only one player, Louis Page, has scored a double hat-trick in a senior match for Burnley. Other players have scored five or four goals in a game and there are a host of hat-trick heroes. Below is a chronological list of all those who have netted three or more goals in a senior game for the Clarets. In that list, the player is named with a figure in brackets stating how many goals he scored. After that is the date, the venue and opponents, the final result and the competition. After that, the list is redefined to show the strikers in order of success (ie sixes, fives, fours and hat-tricks).

Claude Lambie (3) 1 March 1890, at home to Bolton Wanderers (7-0)..........Football League
Claude Lambie (3) 8 November 1890, away to Aston Villa (4-4).................Football League
Claude Lambie (4) 15 November 1890, at home to Derby County (6-1) ....Football League
Claude Lambie (3) 24 January 1891, away to Derby County (4-2) ....Football League
Tom Nicol (3) 7 March 1891, at home to Preston North End (6-2) ....Football League
Tom Nicol (3) 9 January 1892, at home to Darwen (9-0)..........................Football League
Alex McLardie (3) 9 January 1892, at home to Darwen (9-0)....................Football League
James Hill (3) 1 January 1896 to Bury (4-3)..Division One
Tom Nicol (3) 13 April 1896, at home to Blackburn Rovers (6-0)...................Division One
Jimmy Ross (5) 28 March 1898, at home to Loughborough Town (9-0) ....Division Two
Wilf Toman (3) 21 April 1898, away to Blackburn Rovers (3-1).......................Test Match
Jimmy Ross (4) 3 December 1898, at home to Sheffield Wednesday (5-0)..........Division One
Edgar Chadwick (3) 29 December 1899, at home to Glossop (3-1)..................Division One
Matthew Brunton (3) 28 December 1901, at home to Doncaster Rovers (7-0) ....Division Two
Dave Walders (3) 31 October 1903, away to Keswick (8-0) ....FA Cup
Billy Jackson (4) 31 October 1903, away to Keswick (8-0)................................FA Cup
Dick Smith (3) 25 February 1905, at home to Port Vale (5-0).......................Division Two
Dick Smith (3) 15 February 1908, at home to Barnsley (4-1)........................Division Two
Dick Smith (3) 22 February 1908, away to Chesterfield (4-2) ....Division Two
Dick Smith (4) 3 October 1908, at home at Gainsborough Trinity (5-2)............Division Two
Arthur Ogden (3) 16 January 1909, away to Bristol Rovers (4-1) ....FA Cup
Dick Smith (3) 10 February 1909, at home to Crystal Palace (9-0) ....FA Cup
Walter Abbott (3) 13 November 1909, at home to Wolves (4-2) ....Division Two
Ben Green (3) 25 December 1909, at home to Blackpool (5-1) ....Division Two
Bert Freeman (3) 28 October 1911, away to Fulham (4-3)..........................Division Two
Bert Freeman (3) 30 December 1911, at home to Glossop (4-0).....................Division Two
Dick Lindley (3) 20 January 1912, at home to Hull City (5-1)......................Division Two
Bert Freeman (3) 2 March 1912, at home to Fulham (5-1) ....Division Two
Bert Freeman (4) 14 December 1912, at home to Leicester Fosse (5-1)............Division Two
Dick Lindley (3) 4 January 1913, at home to Clapton Orient (5-0) ....Division Two
Teddy Hodgson (3) 27 September 1913, at home to Chelsea (6-1)...................Division One
Teddy Hodgson (3) 31 January 1914, at home to Derby County (3-2)....................FA Cup
Bert Freeman (3) 11 April 1914, at home to Derby County (5-1)....................Division One
Joe Lindsay (3) 13 January 1920, at home to Thorneycrofts (5-0) ....FA Cup
Joe Anderson (3) 17 April 1920, at home to Everton (5-0) ....Division One
Bob Kelly (4) 27 November 1920, at home to Oldham Athletic (7-1) ....Division One
Joe Anderson (4) 25 December 1920, at home to Sheffield United (6-0)...........Division One
Joe Anderson (4) 8 January 1921, away to Leicester City (7-3)............................FA Cup
Joe Anderson (5) 5 February 1921, at home to Aston Villa (7-1)....................Division One
Bob Kelly (3) 24 December 1921, at home to Middlesbrough (3-1) ....Division One
George Richardson (3) 8 April 1922, at home to West Bromwich Alb (4-2) ....Division One
Benny Cross (3) 4 November 1922, at home to Nottingham Forest (8-2) ....Division One
George Beel (3) 17 November 1923, at home to West Ham United (5-1)............Division One
Tom Roberts (3) 29 November 1924, at home to Bury (4-0) ....Division One
Tom Roberts (3) 5 September 1925, at home to Leicester City (4-0) ....Division One
Louis Page (3) 26 December 1925, at home to Leeds United (6-3) ....Division One
Louis Page (6) 10 April 1926, away to Birmingham (7-1) ....Division One
George Beel (3) 1 September 1926, away to Newcastle United (5-1).................Division One

George Beel (3) 11 September 1926, at home to Bolton Wanderers (4-3) .... Division One
George Beel (3) 20 November 1926, at home to Tottenham Hotspur (5-0) .... Division One
George Beel (3) 1 October 1927, at home to Derby County (4-2) .... Division One
George Beel (3) 21 January 1928, at home to Sheffield United (5-3) .... Division One
George Beel (3) 29 August 1928, away to Newcastle United (7-2) .... Division One
George Beel (3) 24 November 1928, away to Birmingham (6-3) .... Division One
George Beel (3) 1 December 1928, at home to Portsmouth (4-1) .... Division One
George Beel (3) 23 February 1929, at home to Leeds United (5-0) .... Division One
Louis Page (3) 12 April 1930, at home to Liverpool (4-1) .... Division One
Joe Mantle (3) 26 April 1930, at home to Derby County (6-2) .... Division One
George Beel (3) 3 February 1931, at home to Wolves (4-2) .... Division Two
Tom Jones (4) 29 October 1932, away to West Ham United (4-4) .... Division Two
Cecil Smith (3) 11 March 1933, at home to West Ham United (4-0) .... Division Two
Harry O'Grady (3) 9 December 1933, at home to Lincoln City (3-1) .... Division Two
George Brown (3) 3 November 1934, away to Hull City (3-1) .... Division Two
Cecil Smith (3) 18 January 1936, at home to Barnsley (3-0) .... Division Two
Tommy Lawton (3) 10 October 1936, at home to Tottenham Hotspur (3-1) .... Division Two
Jimmy Stein (3) 20 November 1937, at home to Southampton (4-0) .... Division Two
James Clayton (3) 26 November 1938, at home to Tranmere Rovers (3-1) .... Division Two
Billy Morris (3) 28 December 1946, away to Coventry City (3-0) .... Division Two
Ray Harrison (3) 11 February 1947, at home to Luton Town (3-0) .... FA Cup
John Billingham (3) 20 December 1947, at home to Portsmouth (3-2) .... Division One
Ray Harrison (3) 27 November 1948, at home to Bolton Wanderers (3-0) .... Division One
Harry Potts (3) 3 December 1949, at home to Everton (5-1) .... Division One
Billy Morris (4) 8 September 1951, at home to West Bromwich Alb (6-1) .... Division One
Billy Holden (3) 29 December 1951, at home to Middlesbrough (7-1) .... Division One
Billy Morris (3) 29 December 1951, at home to Middlesbrough (7-1) .... Division One
Les Shannon (3) 3 January 1953, at home to West Bromwich Alb (5-0) .... Division One
Les Shannon (3) 12 February 1953, at home to Tottenham Hotspur (3-2) .... Division One
Billy Holden (4) 11 April 1953, at home to Sunderland (5-1) .... Division One
Billy Gray (3) 7 September 1953, at home to Tottenham Hotspur (4-2) .... Division One
Billy Holden (3) 17 October 1953, away to Arsenal (5-2) .... Division One
Billy Gray (3) 16 January 1954, at home to Middlesbrough (5-0) .... Division One
Peter McKay (3) 5 September 1955, at home to Luton Town (3-1) .... Division One
Peter McKay (3) 19 November 1955, at home to Portsmouth (3-0) .... Division One
Brian Pilkington (3) 10 March 1956, at home to Chelsea (5-0) .... Division One
Ian Lawson (4) 5 January 1957, at home to Chesterfield (7-0) .... FA Cup
Ian Lawson (3) 26 January 1957, at home to New Brighton (9-0) .... FA Cup
Jimmy McIlroy (3) 26 January 1957, at home to New Brighton (9-0) .... FA Cup
Jimmy McIlroy (3) 9 November 1957, at home to Leicester City (7-3) .... Division One
Albert Cheesebrough (3) 9 November 1957, at home to Leicester City (7-3) .... Division One
Jimmy Robson (3) 21 January 1959, away to Chelsea (3-1) .... Division One
Jimmy Robson (5) 21 November 1959, at home to Nottingham Forest (8-0) .... Division One
John Connelly (3) 12 December 1959, away to Arsenal (4-2) .... Division One
Jimmy Robson (3) 6 September 1960, at home to Preston North End (4-2) .... Division One
Jimmy Robson (3) 1 October 1960, at home to Fulham (5-0) .... Division One
Jimmy Robson (3) 22 October 1960, away to Chelsea (6-2) .... Division One
Gordon Harris (3) 24 October 1960, away to Cardiff City (4-0) .... League Cup
Ray Pointer (3) 17 December 1960, away to Arsenal (5-2) .... Division One
Ray Pointer (3) 16 September 1961, away to Birmingham City (6-2) .... Division One
John Connelly (3) 30 September 1961, away to Fulham (5-3) .... Division One
John Connelly (3) 22 September 1962, away to Manchester United (5-2) .... Division One
Willie Irvine (3) 14 May 1963, home to Birmingham City (3-1) .... Division One
Arthur Bellamy (3) 7 September 1963, away to Everton (4-3) .... Division One
Andy Lochhead (4) 26 December 1963, home to Manchester United (6-1) .... Division One
Andy Lochhead (3) 12 December 1964, away to Blackpool (4-2) .... Division One
Willie Irvine (3) 26 December 1964, at home to Fulham (4-0) .... Division One
Andy Lochhead (5) 24 April 1965, at home to Chelsea (6-2) .... Division One
Willie Irvine (3) 7 September 1965, at home to Northampton Town (4-1) .... Division One

Andy Lochhead (3) 22 September 1965, away to Doncaster Rovers (4-0)............League Cup
Willie Irvine (3) 11 December 1965, away to Fulham (5-2)..........................Division One
Andy Lochhead (5) 25 January 1966, at home to Bournemouth & BA (7-0).............FA Cup
Willie Irvine (3) 12 February 1966, away to Tottenham Hotspur (3-4) ....FA Cup
Willie Irvine (3) 26 March 1966, at home to Nottingham Forest (4-1) ....Division One
Gordon Harris (3) 20 August 1966, at home to Sheffield United (4-0) ....Division One
Andy Lochhead (3) 25 October 1966, at home to Lausanne Sports (5-0) ....European Fairs Cup
Andy Lochhead (4) 26 November 1966, at home to Aston Villa (4-2)...............Division One
Steve Kindon (3) 21 February 1970, at home to Nottingham Forest (5-0) ....Division One
Arthur Bellamy (3) 28 September 1971, at home to Orient (6-1) ....Division Two
Paul Fletcher (3) 21 October 1972, at home to Cardiff City (3-0) ....Division Two
Paul Fletcher (3) 18 September 1973, at home to East Fife (7-0) ....Texaco Cup
Peter Noble (3) 23 November 1974, at home to Newcastle United (4-1) ....Division One
Peter Noble (3) 30 August 1975, at home to Middlesbrough (4-1)...................Division One
Peter Noble (4) 13 September 1975, at home to Norwich City (4-4).................Division One
Peter Noble (3) 18 November 1978, at home to Fulham (5-3) ....Division Two
Steve Taylor (3) 27 September 1980, at home to Millwall (5-0).....................Division Three
Billy Hamilton (3) 18 January 1982, at home to Altrincham Town (6-1) ....FA Cup
Billy Hamilton (3) 7 September 1982, at home to Carlisle United (4-1) ....Division Two
Steve Taylor (3) 1 January 1983, at home to Sheffield Wednesday (4-1) ....Division Two
Billy Hamilton (3) 26 February 1983, at home to Charlton Athletic (7-1)..........Division Two
Steve Taylor (3) 26 February 1983, at home to Charlton Athletic (7-1) ....Division Two
Billy Hamilton (3) 3 September 1983, at home to AFC Bournemouth (5-1)......Division Three
Kevin Reeves (3) 26 November 1983, at home to Port Vale (7-0)..................Division Three
Wayne Biggins (3) 25 February 1984, at home to Lincoln City (4-0) ....Division Three
Steve Daley (3) 28 April 1984, away to Port Vale (3-2).............................Division Three
Kevin Hird (3) 17 November 1984, away to Penrith (9-0)..................................FA Cup
Alan Taylor (3) 17 November 1984, away to Penrith (9-0).................................FA Cup
Kevin Hird (3) 2 February 1985, at home to Rotherham United (7-0) ....Division Three
Wayne Biggins (3) 6 August 1985, away to Rochdale (7-0)........................Lancashire Cup
Wayne Biggins (3) 10 August 1985, at home to Bolton Wanderers (4-0).........Lancashire Cup

SIX

Louis Page

FIVE

Andy Lochhead (2)
Joe Anderson, Jimmy Robson, Jimmy Ross

FOUR

Joe Anderson (2) and Andy Lochhead (2)
Bert Freeman, Billy Holden, Bob Kelly, Billy Jackson, Tom Jones, Claude Lambie, Ian Lawson, Billy Morris, Peter Noble, Jimmy Ross, Dick Smith.

THREE

George Beel (11)
Willie Irvine (6)
Bert Freeman (4), Billy Hamilton (4), Jimmy Robson (4), Dick Smith (4)
Wayne Biggins (3), John Connelly (3), Claude Lambie (3), Andy Lochhead (3), Tom Nicol (3), Peter Noble (3), Steve Taylor (3).
Arthur Bellamy (2), Paul Fletcher (2), Billy Gray (2), Gordon Harris (2), Ray Harrison (2), Kevin Hird (2), Teddy Hodgson (2), Billy Holden (2), Dick Lindley (2), Jimmy McIlroy (2), Peter McKay (2), Billy Morris (2), Louis Page (2), Ray Pointer (2), Tom Roberts (2), Les Shannon (2), Cecil Smith (2).
Walter Abbott, Joe Anderson, John Billingham, George Brown, Matthew Brunton, Edgar Chadwick, Albert Cheesebrough, James Clayton, Benny Cross, Steve Daley, Ben Green, James Hill, Bob Kelly, Ian Lawson, Tommy Lawton, Joe Lindsay, Steve Kindon, Alex McLardie, Joe Mantle, Arthur Ogden, Harry O'Grady, Brian Pilkington, Harry Potts, Kevin Reeves, George Richardson, Jimmy Stein, Alan Taylor, Wilf Toman, Dave Walders.

BURNLEY CAREER RECORDS

This list contains every player who has appeared for Burnley in any League, FA Cup or League Cup match. The statistics listed under 'Other' are totals of appearances and goals made by a player in either the European Cup, Fairs Cup, FA Charity Shield, Texaco Cup, Anglo-Scottish Cup, Watney Cup, Associate Members Cup, Lancashire Manx Cup, Group Cup, Test Matches and Play-offs. The abbreviations 'cs' signifies close season, (p/m) player-manager and (Man) manager. Matches played at the start of the 1939-40 season are not included.

Player	Born	From	To	League App	League Gls	FA Cup App	FA Cup Gls	FL Cup App	FL Cup Gls	Other App	Other Gls	Total App	Total Gls
Abbott *Walter*	Birmingham 7 Dec 1877	Everton cs 1908	Birmingham cs 1910	57	15	8	3	0	0	0	0	65	18
Abrams *J*		*c.*1887	1889	13	1	3	0	0	0	0	0	16	1
Adams *Edward F*	Anfield 30 Nov 1906	Southport Feb 1936	Retired Wartime	111	0	7	0	0	0	0	0	118	0
Adamson *James*	Ashington 4 Apr 1929	Ashington Jan 1947	Coach 1964	426	17	52	1	3	0	5	0	486	18
Aird *Jock*	Glencraig 18 Feb 1926	Jeanfield Sw Aug 1948	Dundee cs 1955	132	0	11	0	0	0	0	0	143	0
Alderman *Albert E*	Alvaston 30 Oct 1907	Derby Aug 1934	cs 1935	19	2	0	0	0	0	0	0	19	2
Allen *Mark S*	Newcastle 18 Dec 1963	Apprentice Dec 1981	Released cs 1982	0/2	1	0	0	0	0	0/2	0	0/4	1
Almond *James*		Nelson Nov 1896	Swindon Feb 1897	1	0	0	0	0	0	0	0	1	0
Anderson *Colin R*	Newcastle 26 Apr 1962	Apprentice Apr 1980	Torquay cs 1982	3/3	0	0	0	0	0	2	0	5/3	0
Anderson *Joseph*	Bishopton 1895	Clydebank Mar 1920	Clydebank Oct 1923	121	64	4	8	0	0	1	0	126	72
Angus *John*	Amble 2 Sep 1938	Juniors Sep 1955	Retired 1972	438/1	4	45	0	25	0	12	0	520/1	4
Appleby *James*	Shotton 15 Jun 1934	Wingate Feb 1953	Blackburn Feb 1958	1	0	0	0	0	0	0	0	1	0
Arins *Anthony F*	Chesterfield 26 Oct 1958	Apprentice Jul 1976	Leeds May 1980	29	2	0	0	1	0	2	0	32	2
Armitage *John H*	Chapeltown 21 Aug 1897	Mexborough May 1924	Oldham May 1926	44	1	0	0	0	0	0	0	44	1
Arnott *James*		Fair City C Oct 1897	1899	12	0	0	0	0	0	0	0	12	0
Ashbridge *Kenneth*	Burnley 12 Nov 1916	Local Jnrs Oct 1935	Halifax Sep 1938	1	0	0	0	0	0	0	0	1	0
Ashcroft *Gordon*	Lea 1902	Coppull Cen Nov 1925	Lancaster Nov 1929	1	0	0	0	0	0	0	0	1	0
Ashworth *John*		1889	1890	2	2	0	0	0	0	0	0	2	2
Aspden *Thomas E*		Kettering cs 1903	Brighton cs 1904	29	4	2	0	0	0	0	0	31	4
Astin *James*	Hapton 16 Aug 1900	Army Sep 1921	Bury Oct 1923	13	0	0	0	0	0	0	0	13	0
Atkinson *George*		cs 1904	1905	14	0	0	0	0	0	0	0	14	0
Atkinson *Paul G*	Pudsey 14 Aug 1961	Oldham Jul 1988	Released cs 1990	18/4	1	6	0	3	0	4	0	31/4	1
Attwell *Reg*	Oakengates 23 Mar 1920	West Ham Oct 1946	Bradford C Oct 1954	244	9	25	2	0	0	0	0	269	11
Baker *Steven*	Newcastle 16 Jun 1962	Southampton Feb 1984	On loan until Apr 1984	10	0	0	0	0	0	2	1	12	1
Bamford *Thomas F*	Horwich	Darwen cs 1909	Rochdale Sep 1920	137	0	20	0	0	0	0	0	157	0
Bannister *William*	Burnley 1879	Earley cs 1899	Bolton Nov 1901	55	4	3	1	0	0	0	0	58	5
		Leicester Sep 1910	Leicester Imp 1912										
Barron *Fred*	Stockton	Stockton St M cs 1898	Retired cs 1911	400	13	23	1	0	0	0	0	423	14
Bassnett *Alfred*	St Helens 10 Apr 1893	Eccles Jun 1919	Lincoln Nov 1926	147	5	9	0	0	0	1	0	157	5
Bates *Charles*	West Bromwich	cs 1910	1912	15	5	0	0	0	0	0	0	15	5
Beard *Arthur H*		cs 1904	1904	1	0	0	0	0	0	0	0	1	0
Beddows *Jonathan H*		Man Utd cs 1907	1909	16	7	0	0	0	0	0	0	16	7
Beel *George W*	Bracebridge H 26 Feb 1900	Chesterfield Apr 1923	Lincoln Feb 1932	316	178	21	9	0	0	0	0	337	187
Bell *Arthur*	Burnley Nov 1882	Burnley Belv Mar 1902	Retired 1909	101	29	3	1	0	0	0	0	104	30
Bellamy *Arthur*	Blackhill 5 Apr 1942	Juniors Jun 1959	Chesterfield Jul 1972	204/13	29	9	0	16	0	7/1	0	236/14	29
Bellamy *James*	Barking Oct 1881	Motherwell Oct 1912	Fulham Jul 1914	21	3	1	0	0	0	0	0	22	3
Bellis *George A*	India 8 Jun 1904	Wolves Dec 1932	Bournemouth Jun 1935	86	0	5	0	0	0	0	0	91	0
Bennie *Peter*	Larkhall 10 Jun 1898	Albion Rov Jun 1923	Bradford C Sep 1924	36	7	7	0	0	0	0	0	43	7
Bennion *S Raymond*	Wrexham 1 Sep 1896	Man Utd Nov 1932	Coach cs 1934	31	0	4	0	0	0	0	0	35	0
Bent *Junior*	Huddersfield 1 Mar 1970	Huddersfield Nov 1989	On loan until Feb 1990	7/2	3	0	0	0	0	0	0	7/2	3
Beveridge *David*		Albion R cs 1896	Grimsby May 1899	20	0	4	1	0	0	4	0	28	1
Biggins *Wayne*	Sheffield 20 Nov 1961	Matlock Feb 1984	Norwich Oct 1985	78	30	3	1	6	1	14	11	101	43
Billingham *John*	Daventry 3 Dec 1914	Bristol C May 1938	Carlisle Sep 1949	93	36	3	0	0	0	0	0	96	36
Binns *Eric*	Halifax 13 Aug 1924	Goole Mar 1949	Blackburn May 1955	15	0	0	0	0	0	0	0	15	0
Birchall *Joseph*		Jan 1902	Preston Feb 1903	12	1	0	0	0	0	0	0	12	1
Birchenough *Frank*	Crewe	West Ham Aug 1920	1921	2	0	0	0	0	0	0	0	2	0
Birnie		*c.*1886	1887	0	0	2	0	0	0	0	0	2	0
Black *David*	29 Mar 1896	Wolves Dec 1896	Tottenham cs 1897	12	5	1	0	0	0	0	0	13	5
Blacklaw *Adam*	Aberdeen 2 Sep 1937	Juniors Oct 1954	Blackburn Jul 1967	318	0	44	0	12	0	9	0	383	0
Blant *Colin*	Rawtenstall 7 Oct 1946	Rossendale Aug 1964	Portsmouth Apr 1970	46/7	7	2	1	7	1	0	0	55/7	9
Blinkhorn *Fred*	Bolton 2 Aug 1901	Horwich RMI May 1925	Retired cs 1928	15	0	0	0	0	0	0	0	15	0
Boden *Roland*		cs 1909	cs 1910	5	0	0	0	0	0	0	0	5	0
Bolton *William*		Apr 1915	1916	1	0	0	0	0	0	0	0	1	0
Booth *Jerry*		Burnley Belv cs 1903	1903	1	0	0	0	0	0	0	0	1	0
Bowes *William*	Armadale 1870	Broxburn Feb 1891	Released cs 1901	269	79	18	4	0	0	8	1	295	84
Bowsher *Stanley J*	Newport 3 Oct 1899	Newport Jan 1929	Rochdale Mar 1933	82	2	3	0	0	0	0	0	85	2

Player	Born	From	To	League App	League Gls	FA Cup App	FA Cup Gls	FL Cup App	FL Cup Gls	Other App	Other Gls	Total App	Total Gls
Boyd *Henry*	Lanchester 1866	Sunderland Alb cs 1892	West Brom Oct 1892	4	1	0	0	0	0	0	0	4	1
Boyle *Thomas W*	Hoyland 29 Jan 1888	Barnsley Sep 1911	Wrexham Apr 1923	210	36	25	7	0	0	1	0	236	43
Bradshaw *Ernest*	Padiham	cs 1911	cs 1914	8	0	0	0	0	0	0	0	8	0
Bradshaw *Paul*	Sheffield 2 Oct 1953	Apprentice Oct 1970	Sheff Wed Sep 1976	11/2	2	1	0	2	0	0/1	0	14/3	2
Bradshaw *William*		Burton U cs 1907	1907	11	1	0	0	0	0	0	0	11	1
Brady *Alexander*	Cathcart	Partick Th cs 1888	Sunderland Feb 1889	20	7	0	0	0	0	0	0	20	7
Brady *Arthur*		Feb 1893	1894	24	8	0	0	0	0	0	0	24	8
Brady *W*		1888	Newcastle WE 1889	9	2	2	2	0	0	0	0	11	4
Brae *James*		cs 1896	Released Nov 1896	6	0	0	0	0	0	0	0	6	0
Bray *George*	Oswaldtwistle 11 Nov 1918	Gt Harwood Oct 1937	Coaching Staff 1953	241	8	18	1	0	0	0	0	259	9
Bray *Ian M*	Neath 6 Dec 1962	Huddersfield cs 1990		10/1	0	0	0	2	0	4/1	1	16/2	1
Breedon *Jack*		Man Utd Oct 1945	1945	0	0	1	0	0	0	0	0	1	0
Brennan *Ian*	Easington 25 Mar 1953	Apprentice Oct 1970	Bolton Dec 1980	173/2	11	9	0	13	1	14	2	209/2	14
Brewis *Robert*		Lincoln cs 1908	cs 1909	2	0	0	0	0	0	0	0	2	0
Brierley *Herbert J*		Mar 1899	cs 1899	2	0	0	0	0	0	0	0	2	0
Britton *Ian*	Dundee 19 May 1954	Blackpool Aug 1986	Released cs 1989	102/6	10	1/2	0	7	0	18/2	1	128/10	11
Brocklebank *Robert E*	Barnet 23 May 1908	Aston Villa Mar 1936	Ch'field Sep 1945(Man)	121	33	7	5	0	0	0	0	128	38
Brodie *John C*	Kilmarnock	Kilmarnock Nov 1890	Kilmarnock Mar 1891	2	0	0	0	0	0	0	0	2	0
Brophy *Thomas*	St Helens 8 Jan 1897	St Helens Sep 1920	St Helens May 1922	3	0	0	0	0	0	0	0	3	0
Brown *Allan W*	Corbridge 26 Aug 1914	Huddersfield Feb 1946	Notts Co Oct 1948	88	0	10	0	0	0	0	0	98	0
Brown *David C*		cs 1896	1896	4	0	0	0	0	0	0	0	4	0
Brown *George*	Mickley 22 Jun 1903	Aston Villa Oct 1934	Leeds Sep 1935	35	24	6	3	0	0	0	0	41	27
Brown *Harry*		Mar 1902	cs 1902	7	0	0	0	0	0	0	0	7	0
Brown *James*	Motherwell 1907	East Fife May 1927	Man Utd Jun 1935	228	5	13	0	0	0	0	0	241	5
Brown *Joe*	Cramlington 26 Apr 1929	Middlesbro Aug 1952	Bournemouth Jun 1954	6	0	0	0	0	0	0	0	6	0
Brown *Jonathan*	Clayton le Moors	Gt Harwood Dec 1913	Wartime Fatality	1	0	0	0	0	0	0	0	1	0
Brown *Robert N*	Cambuslang Aug 1870	Bolton Mar 1897	on loan until cs 1897	4	1	0	0	0	0	4	0	8	1
Brown *William*	Falkirk 5 Feb 1950	Juniors Feb 1967	Carlisle Jul 1969	0/1	0	0	0	0	0	0	0	0/1	0
Brunton *Matthew*	Burnley 20 Apr 1878	Accrington cs 1901	Accrington cs 1902	30	8	2	0	0	0	0	0	32	8
Bruton *John*	Westhoughton 21 Nov 1903	Horwich RMI Mar 1925	Blackburn Dec 1929	167	42	9	2	0	0	0	0	176	44
Buchanan *Robert*	Johnstone 1868	Sunderland Alb cs 1892	W Arsenal Sep 1894	40	12	2	0	0	0	0	0	42	12
Buckley *Neil*	Hull 25 Sep 1968	Hull Mar 1990	On loan until Apr 1990	5	0	0	0	0	0	0	0	5	0
Burke *Marshall*	Glasgow 26 Mar 1959	Apprentice Mar 1977	Leeds May 1980	22/2	5	2	0	1/1	0	0	0	25/3	5
Burke *Robert G*	Ballymena 5 Nov 1934	Albertville Sep 1955	Chester Jun 1958	19	5	1	0	0	0	0	0	20	5
Burley *George M*	West Ham 23 Dec 1900	Chester Oct 1926	Colwyn Bay Jul 1929	4	0	0	0	0	0	0	0	4	0
Bury *William H*	Darwen 1865	Padiham 1886	Brierfield 1891	43	0	6	1	0	0	0	0	49	1
Busby *Martin G*	Slough 24 Mar 1953	Queen's PR Feb 1980	On loan until Mar 1980	4	1	0	0	0	0	0	0	4	1
Butler *John*		Trialist Aug 1984		0	0	0	0	0	0	0/1	0	0/1	0
Butterfield *Jack*	Barnsley 30 Aug 1922	Tamworth Feb 1946	Club Scout Nov 1949	3	0	0	0	0	0	0	0	3	0
Buxton *Michael*	Corbridge 29 May 1943	Juniors Jun 1960	Halifax Jun 1968	16/2	0	0	0	1	0	0	0	17/2	0
Caldow *G*		cs 1889	Released Nov 1889	6	0	0	0	0	0	0	0	6	0
Campbell *J*		Darwen cs 1889	1890	14	3	1	0	0	0	0	0	15	3
Campbell *T Fred*	Burnley	Oct 1905	Queen's Park Nov 1907	9	0	1	0	0	0	0	0	10	0
Cargill *David A*	Arbroath 21 Jul 1936	Juniors Jul 1953	Sheff Wed Sep 1956	5	0	0	0	0	0	0	0	5	0
Carr *Z*		Preston Hornets 1890	1890	1	0	0	0	0	0	0	0	1	0
Carson *James*		Crystal P May 1936	Alloa Aug 1937	6	0	0	0	0	0	0	0	6	0
Casper *Frank*	Barnsley 9 Dec 1944	Rotherham Jun 1967	Coach 1976	230/7	74	11	5	22	9	5	1	268/7	89
Cassidy *Tommy*	Belfast 18 Nov 1950	Newcastle Jul 1980	Released cs 1983	70/2	4	8/1	1	8/2	2	7	1	93/5	8
Caughey *Mark*	Belfast 27 Aug 1960	Hibernian Feb 1987	On loan until Mar 1987	8	0	0	0	0	0	0	0	8	0
Cavener *Philip*	Tynemouth 2 Jun 1961	Apprentice May 1979	Gillingham cs 1983	55/14	4	5/1	0	6/1	0	8	1	74/16	5
Cawthorne *Rupert*		Clitheroe C May 1906	1909	24	0	0	0	0	0	0	0	24	0
Chadburn *JH*		Nov 1908	1910	9	4	0	0	0	0	0	0	9	4
Chadwick *W Edgar*	Blackburn 1870	Everton May 1899	Southampton Aug 1900	31	10	1	0	0	0	0	0	32	10
Chambers *Robert*	Newcastle 11 Dec 1899	Lincoln Mar 1922	Rotherham Jun 1923	4	0	0	0	0	0	0	0	4	0
Chambers *Thomas*		Sep 1892	Hearts 1893	26	9	2	0	0	0	0	0	28	9
		Hearts cs 1896	St Bernards 1897										
Chambers *William T*	Wednesbury 10 Aug 1906	Darlaston May 1929	Darlaston 1931	2	0	0	0	0	0	0	0	2	0
Charlton *Tom*	Middlesbrough	Mar 1913	Blackpool Nov 1913	7	3	0	0	0	0	0	0	7	3
Chedgzoy *Sydney*	Liverpool 17 Feb 1912	Everton May 1933	Millwall May 1934	5	1	0	0	0	0	0	0	5	1
Cheesebrough *Albert*	Burnley 17 Jan 1935	Juniors Jan 1952	Leicester Jun 1959	142	35	16	5	0	0	0	0	158	40
Chester *Thomas H*	Glasgow	Bury Mar 1937	Notts Co Jun 1939	51	1	3	0	0	0	0	0	54	1
Chew *Jackie*	Blackburn 13 May 1920	Blackburn cs 1945	Bradford C Jun 1954	225	39	23	2	0	0	0	0	248	41
Chilton *Anthony*	Maryport 7 Sep 1965	Feb 1985	Released cs 1985	1	0	0	0	0	0	0	0	1	0
Chippendale *Brian A*	Bradford 29 Oct 1964	York Aug 1985	Preston Oct 1985	6/2	0	0	0	0	0	3	1	9/2	1
Clacher *John*	Kirkcaldy 1912	Altrincham May 1934	Darlington May 1937	30	1	0	0	0	0	0	0	30	1
Clarke *Alfred*	Hollinwood 23 Aug 1926	Crewe Dec 1948	Oldham Aug 1952	24	6	3	1	0	0	0	0	27	7
Clarke *George*		Mar 1909	1909	3	0	0	0	0	0	0	0	3	0
Clarkson *William*	Padiham 1891	Nelson cs 1914	Rotherham Aug 1920	2	0	0	0	0	0	0	0	2	0
Clayton *James GT*	Sunderland 1910	Aston Villa Oct 1938	Retired Wartime	16	10	0	0	0	0	0	0	16	10

Player	Born	From	To	League App	League Gls	FA Cup App	FA Cup Gls	FL Cup App	FL Cup Gls	Other App	Other Gls	Total App	Total Gls
Cliff *Eddie*	Liverpool 30 Sep 1951	Apprentice Oct 1968	Notts Co Sep 1973	21	0	0	0	3	0	0	0	24	0
Coates *Ralph*	Hetton le Hole 26 Apr 1946	Apprentice Jun 1963	Tottenham May 1971	214/2	26	12	1	22/2	2	9	3	257/4	32
Cochrane *Terry*	Killyleagh 23 Jan 1953	Coleraine Oct 1976	Middlesbro' Oct 1978	62/5	13	4/1	0	7	4	6	1	79/6	18
Collins *Douglas*	Newton 28 Aug 1945	Grimsby Sep 1968	Plymouth May 1976	172/15	18	9	0	12/1	0	7/1	1	200/17	19
Collins *Henry*	Wynlaton 1876	Hebburn Arg cs 1900	Queen's PR cs 1901	30	0	3	0	0	0	0	0	33	0
Comrie *Malcolm*	Denny	Man City May 1934	Crystal P Jun 1935	8	0	0	0	0	0	0	0	8	0
Comstive *Paul T*	Southport 25 Nov 1961	Wrexham Aug 1987	Bolton Sep 1989	81/1	17	2	0	8	3	17/1	5	108/2	25
Connelly *John*	St Helens 18 Jul 1938	St Helens Nov 1956	Man Utd Apr 1964	215	86	38	15	7	2	5	2	265	105
Conway *Herman*	Gainsborough 11 Oct 1908	Gainsboro' Tr Feb 1930	West Ham Jun 1934	81	0	6	0	0	0	0	0	87	0
Conway *Thomas*	Belfast	Willowfield May 1928	Northampton Jul 1932	3	0	1	0	0	0	0	0	4	0
Corr *Pat M*	Derry 31 Mar 1927	Coleraine Oct 1951	Released cs 1952	1	0	0	0	0	0	0	0	1	0
Cox *W*		Hibernian Nov 1888	Everton Jan 1890	26	0	2	0	0	0	0	0	28	0
Coyle *B*		1889	1890	2	0	0	0	0	0	0	0	2	0
Crabtree *James W*	Burnley 23 Dec 1871	Local Jnrs 1888	Rossendale Apr 1890	72	9	5	0	0	0	0	0	77	9
		Heywood cs 1892	Aston Villa cs 1895										
Cragg *Richard*	Burnley 1893	Army May 1919	Stockport Sep 1920	15	5	2	1	0	0	0	0	17	6
Crawford *James*	Stirling	Kings Park cs 1902	1903	45	4	3	1	0	0	0	0	48	5
Cretney *Jonathan*	Workington 1879	Newcastle cs 1905	Gainsboro' Tr 1911	167	7	10	2	0	0	0	0	177	9
Crompton *Wilfred*	Blackburn 1 Apr 1908	Blackburn May 1932	Gillingham Jun 1934	31	8	4	0	0	0	0	0	35	8
Cross *Benjamin*	Birkenhead 20 Aug 1898	Runcorn Apr 1920	Retired 1929	237	57	17	4	0	0	1	0	255	61
Crossley *Thomas H*		1891	1891	1	0	0	0	0	0	0	0	1	0
Cummings *Tom S*	Castledown 12 Sep 1928	Stanley U Oct 1947	Mansfield Mar 1963	434	3	38	0	6	0	1	0	479	3
Cunliffe *Arthur*	Blackrod 5 Feb 1909	Middlesbro Apr 1937	Hull Jun 1938	9	0	0	0	0	0	0	0	9	0
Daley *Steven*	Barnsley 15 Apr 1953	Seattle Nov 1983	Released cs 1984	20/3	4	2/2	0	0	0	4	1	26/5	5
Daniel *Peter W*	Hull 12 Dec 1955	Lincoln cs 1987	Retired 1988	40/1	0	1	0	6	0	9	0	56/1	0
Davidson *Andrew*		Clyde cs 1905	Croydon Com cs 1907	47	10	1	0	0	0	0	0	48	10
Davidson *James*	Edinburgh 1873	Celtic cs 1895	Lincoln Mar 1897	65	7	2	0	0	0	0	0	67	7
		Apr 1900	cs 1902										
Davis *Stephen*	Hexham 30 Oct 1968	Southampton Nov 1989	On loan until Feb 1990	7/2	0	0	0	0	0	1	0	8/2	0
Davis *Steve P*	Birmingham 26 Jul 1965	Crewe Oct 1987		147	11	9	0	7	0	22	1	185	12
Dawson *Arthur*		Nelson cs 1908	1908	1	0	0	0	0	0	0	0	1	0
Dawson *Jeremiah*	Cliviger 18 Mar 1888	Cliviger Feb 1907	Retired cs 1929	522	0	46	0	0	0	1	0	569	0
Dawson *Jonathan*		cs 1906	1907	1	0	0	0	0	0	0	0	1	0
Deakin *Raymond J*	Liverpool 19 Jun 1959	Bolton Aug 1985	Released May 1991	212/1	6	7	0	15	0	35/1	0	269/2	6
Deary *John S*	Ormskirk 18 Oct 1962	Blackpool Jul 1989		82/2	9	7	1	5/1	0	11	0	105/3	10
Devaney *Philip*	Huyton 12 Feb 1969	Apprentice Jul 1985	Released cs 1988	8/5	1	0	0	0	0	0/1	0	8/6	1
Devine *Joseph*	Motherwell 8 Aug 1905	Bathgate May 1925	Newcastle Jan 1930	114	27	7	2	0	0	0	0	121	29
Devine *Peter*	Blackburn 25 May 1960	Nov 1984	Retired cs 1986	36/10	4	3	4	0/1	0	8/2	2	47/13	10
Dickinson *H James*	Padiham	Sep 1901	Padiham Jan 1902	2	0	0	0	0	0	0	0	2	0
Dixey *Richard*	Leicester 2 Sep 1956	Enderby Dec 1974	Released cs 1976	3	0	0	0	0	0	0	0	3	0
Dixon *Arthur*	Barrowford 5 Oct 1879	Local Jnrs cs 1900	Tottenham May 1907	175	7	8	0	0	0	0	0	183	7
Dixon *Ernest*	Pudsey 10 Jul 1901	Halifax Mar 1924	Halifax Dec 1924	3	0	0	0	0	0	0	0	3	0
Dixon *Lee M*	Manchester 17 Mar 1964	Juniors Jul 1982	Chester Feb 1984	4	0	0	0	1	0	2	0	7	0
Dixon *Paul K*	Londonderry 22 Feb 1960	Apprentice Jun 1978	Released May 1983	23/1	1	5	0	0	0	4	0	32/1	1
Dobinson *Harold*	Darlington 2 Mar 1898	Durham C Jan 1922	Queen's PR Jun 1923	2	0	0	0	0	0	0	0	2	0
Dobson *Martin*	Rishton 14 Feb 1948	Bolton Aug 1967	Everton Aug 1974	406/4	63	31	7	34	4	24	2	495/4	76
		Everton Aug 1979	Bury (p/m) March 1984										
Docherty *Michael*	Preston 29 Oct 1950	Apprentice Apr 1967	Man City Apr 1976	149/4	0	5	0	9/2	0	5	1	168/6	1
Dodd *Robert*	Blackburn	cs 1910	1911	5	0	0	0	0	0	0	0	5	0
Dollins *JW*		cs 1908	cs 1910	8	0	0	0	0	0	0	0	8	0
Donachie *Willie*	Glasgow 5 Oct 1951	Portland Nov 1982	Oldham cs 1984	60	3	12	0	4	0	7	1	83	4
Donaghey *Bernard*		cs 1907	1908	5	2	0	0	0	0	0	0	5	2
Donovan *Terry*	Liverpool 27 Feb 1958	Aston Villa Feb 1983	Rotherham Sep 1983	13/2	6	0/2	0	0/1	0	2	0	15/5	6
Dougall *Peter*	Denny 1909	Denny Pace Nov 1926	Clyde Feb 1929	6	2	0	0	0	0	0	0	6	2
Dougall *William*	Denny	Falkirk Feb 1926	Coach 1929	60	1	3	0	0	0	0	0	63	1
Dougan *Patrick*		Feb 1910	1910	1	0	0	0	0	0	0	0	1	0
Douglas *George H*	Stepney 18 Aug 1893	Leicester Feb 1921	Oldham May 1922	5	0	0	0	0	0	0	0	5	0
Douglas *Thomas A*	Ayr 11 Sep 1910	Blackpool Sep 1933	Witton A cs 1936	63	13	2	0	0	0	0	0	65	13
Down *William*	Ryhope 22 Jan 1898	Doncaster Sep 1927	Torquay Nov 1930	80	0	2	0	0	0	0	0	82	0
Downes *Percy*	Notts 12 Sep 1904	Stockport May 1934	Oldham May 1936	61	6	8	0	0	0	0	0	69	6
Drabble *Frank*		Dec 1911	1912	2	0	0	0	0	0	0	0	2	0
Drinnan *James M*	Harthill 28 May 1906	Luton Jun 1930	1931	6	2	0	0	0	0	0	0	6	2
Driver *Fred*		cs 1900	Trawden cs 1903	17	2	0	0	0	0	0	0	17	2
Drummond *Robert G*	Dalmeny 1898	Bathgate May 1924	Pembroke Dock cs 1925	3	0	0	0	0	0	0	0	3	0
Dryden *John*	Broomhill 1911	Sheff Utd May 1938	Peterborough cs 1939	4	2	0	0	0	0	0	0	4	2
Duckworth *Harry*		Oct 1900	cs 1903	9	2	0	0	0	0	0	0	9	2
Duckworth *Robert W*	Bury 1872	*c.*1886	Rossendale Apr 1890	5	1	0	0	0	0	0	0	5	1
Duerden *J*		*c.*1888	Rossendale cs 1891	3	0	0	0	0	0	0	0	3	0
Dunn *Thomas*		Wolves Dec 1896	1897	7	0	0	0	0	0	0	0	7	0

Player	Born	From	To	League App	League Gls	FA Cup App	FA Cup Gls	FL Cup App	FL Cup Gls	Other App	Other Gls	Total App	Total Gls
Earle *Edwin*	Newbiggin 17 Jun 1905	Nelson Dec 1926	Boston Jul 1928	3	1	0	0	0	0	0	0	3	1
Edmondson *William*		Local Jnrs Jan 1903	1903	2	0	0	0	0	0	0	0	2	0
Edwards *Neil*	Liverpool 2 Jul 1967	Liverpool cs 1985	Released cs 1986	0/1	0	0	0	0	0	0	0	0/1	0
Edwards *Reginald T*	Coseley 1912	Brierley Hill cs 1931	Walsall Sep 1933	18	5	0	0	0	0	0	0	18	5
Egan *T William*	Chirk 1872	Ardwick Mar 1894	Ashton NE May 1895	10	1	0	0	0	0	0	0	10	1
Elder *Alex*	Glentoran 25 Apr 1941	Glentoran Jan 1959	Stoke Aug 1967	271	15	39	2	11	0	9	0	330	17
Eli *Roger*	Bradford 11 Sep 1965	Bury cs 1989		39/16	10	3/1	3	2/2	0	7	1	51/19	14
Elliott *William H*	Bradford 20 Mar 1925	Bradford Sep 1951	Sunderland Jun 1953	74	14	8	2	0	0	0	0	82	16
Elston		*c.*1887	1888	0	0	2	0	0	0	0	0	2	0
Emerson *William*	Enniskillen 1891	Glentoran Mar 1922	Glentoran Sep 1924	44	0	1	0	0	0	0	0	45	0
Entwistle *Wayne P*	Bury 6 Aug 1958	Bolton Aug 1986	On loan until Oct 1986	6/2	2	0	0	1/1	0	1	0	8/3	2
Espie *John*	Hamilton 1868	Burnbank Sw Dec 1891	Man City Feb 1896	93	9	2	0	0	0	0	0	95	9
Evans *James H*	Rhyl 29 Dec 1894	Southend Apr 1923	Swansea Jul 1925	20	0	0	0	0	0	0	0	20	0
Fairburn *James*		Darlington cs 1899	Released Mar 1900	1	0	0	0	0	0	0	0	1	0
Fairhurst *Richard*	St Helens 5 Sep 1911	Skelmersdale Nov 1931	Hartlepools Aug 1934	23	3	0	0	0	0	0	0	23	3
Farrell *Andrew J*	Colchester 7 Oct 1965	Colchester Aug 1987		146/8	11	8/2	0	13/1	1	30	4	197/11	16
Fenton *Ron*	South Shields 2 Sep 1940	Juniors Sep 1957	West Brom Nov 1962	11	1	0	0	4	2	0	0	15	3
Fergus *Alexander*	Kirkintilloch	Bathgate May 1924	Coventry Mar 1927	38	0	3	0	0	0	0	0	41	0
Ferguson *William*		Celtic Mar 1897	Man City Nov 1899	33	7	2	1	0	0	2	1	37	9
Finn *Michael G*	Liverpool 1 May 1954	Apprentice Dec 1971	Released cs 1976	4	0	0	0	0	0	0	0	4	0
Fisher *John*	Hodthorpe 4 Aug 1897	Chesterfield Mar 1922	Chesterfield Apr 1923	32	3	1	0	0	0	0	0	33	3
Fisher *Peter*	Glasgow	Watford Jan 1937	1939	23	2	0	0	0	0	0	0	23	2
Fitton *Frederick*	Bury	Adlington May 1928	Oldham Jun 1930	15	2	0	0	0	0	0	0	15	2
Flack *Hugh*	Belfast 1903	Crusaders May 1927	Swansea May 1929	3	0	0	0	0	0	0	0	3	0
Fletcher *Charles A*	Homerton 28 Oct 1905	Brentford Feb 1936	Plymouth Nov 1937	62	21	3	1	0	0	0	0	65	22
Fletcher *Paul J*	Bolton 13 Jan 1951	Bolton Mar 1971	Blackpool Feb 1980	291/2	71	16/1	7	18	1	24	7	349/3	86
Flynn *Brian*	Port Talbot 12 Oct 1955	Apprentice Oct 1972	Leeds Nov 1977	193/9	19	17	2	18/2	4	14	2	242/11	27
		Leeds Mar 1982	On loan										
		Leeds Nov 1982	Cardiff Nov 1984										
Forrest *Alexander*	Hamilton 2 Apr 1908	Bo'ness Mar 1927	Chesterfield Jun 1933	108	4	8	0	0	0	0	0	116	4
Foxcroft		1945	1946	0	0	1	0	0	0	0	0	1	0
France *Garry L*	Stalybridge 5 May 1946	Stalybridge Apr 1966	Bury Jul 1968	1/2	0	0	0	2	1	0	0	3/2	1
France *Paul*	Huddersfield 10 Sep 1968	Bristol C cs 1990		1/1	0	0	0	0	0	1	0	2/1	0
Francis *John*	Dewsbury 21 Nov 1963	Sheff Utd Jan 1990		63/1	19	3	1	4	0	8/1	3	78/2	23
Freeman *Albert*	Preston 21 Oct 1899	Leyland Mar 1923	Swansea May 1929	78	19	4	0	0	0	0	0	82	19
Freeman *Bertram C*	Handsworth Oct 1885	Everton Apr 1911	Wigan B cs 1921	166	103	23	12	0	0	0	0	189	115
Friel *Daniel*		Accrington Oct 1883	Released Nov 1889	27	1	6	1	0	0	0	0	33	2
Fulton		*c.*1886	1887	0	0	1	0	0	0	0	0	1	0
Furnell *James*	Clitheroe 23 Nov 1937	Juniors Nov 1954	Liverpool Feb 1962	2	0	0	0	1	0	0	0	3	0
Futcher *Ron*	Chester 25 Sep 1956	Port Vale Nov 1989	Released July 1991	52/5	25	8/1	3	2	1	8	3	70/6	32
Galbraith *Hugh*		Midds Iron Nov 1891	Luton Nov 1892	5	2	0	0	0	0	0	0	5	2
Gallacher *William*	Dalmuir	Renton Jan 1920	Released Mar 1920	4	0	0	0	0	0	0	0	4	0
Gallagher *Joe*	Liverpool 11 Jan 1955	West Ham Aug 1983	Released cs 1987	46/1	3	1	0	3	0	6/1	0	56/2	3
Gallocher *Pat*	Scotland 1864	Padiham 1884	Accrington cs 1889	20	6	4	2	0	0	0	0	24	8
Gardner *Steve*	Middlesbrough 3 Jul 1968	Man Utd Aug 1987	Released cs 1990	93/2	0	2	0	7	0	16	0	118/2	0
Gardner *Tom*	Huyton 28 May 1910	Aston Villa Apr 1938	Wrexham Dec 1945	39	3	1	0	0	0	0	0	40	3
Gastall *John WH*	Blackburn 1913	Bacup May 1936	Accrington May 1938	21	7	0	0	0	0	0	0	21	7
Gee *Harold*	Haydock 25 Dec 1895	Newton Com cs 1921	New Brighton Jul 1923	5	0	0	0	0	0	0	0	5	0
Gillatt *Ernest*	Wensley	Clapton O Sep 1923	Barnsley Feb 1925	1	0	0	0	0	0	0	0	1	0
Glendon *Kevin W*	Manchester 21 Jun 1961	Hyde Dec 1983	Released cs 1984	4	0	0	0	0	0	0	0	4	0
Goodison *Percy*	Burnley	Livingstone cs 1911	Accrington 1912	1	0	0	0	0	0	0	0	1	0
Goodwin *Fred*		Nov 1906	1906	1	0	0	0	0	0	0	0	1	0
Gow *Gerry*	Glasgow 29 May 1952	Rotherham Aug 1983	Released cs 1984	8/1	0	0	0	1	0	1	0	10/1	0
Graham *William*		cs 1891	Lincoln Dec 1892	24	3	2	0	0	0	0	0	26	3
Graham *William*	Hetton le Hole 3 Oct 1914	Blyth S Sep 1932	Bury May 1935	5	2	0	0	0	0	0	0	5	2
Gray *William P*	Durham 24 May 1927	Chelsea Aug 1953	Nottm For Jun 1957	120	30	10	2	0	0	0	0	130	32
Green *Benjamin H*	Penistone 23 Feb 1883	Birmingham Sep 1909	Preston cs 1911	71	29	6	4	0	0	0	0	77	33
Green *William*	Gravesend 1882	Brentford cs 1903	Bradford Dec 1908	147	0	6	0	0	0	0	0	153	0
Greenhalgh *John S*	Bolton 1898	Leyland Oct 1921	Barrow cs 1923	7	0	0	0	0	0	0	0	7	0
Greenwood *Jonathan W*	Todmorden	Local Jnrs cs 1905	Nelson cs 1906	11	0	0	0	0	0	0	0	11	0
Greenwood *Thomas*		Local Jnrs cs 1899	1899	1	0	0	0	0	0	0	0	1	0
Grewcock *Neil*	Leicester 26 Apr 1962	Shepshed C cs 1984	Released May 1991	180/22	27	10	1	12/1	2	29/1	5	231/24	35
Grice *Reuben*	Ruddington	cs 1914	Retired wartime	2	0	0	0	0	0	0	0	2	0
Gunton *Samuel*	Norwich	Gainsboro' Tr Feb 1913	1913	1	0	0	0	0	0	0	0	1	0
Haddock *Peter M*	Newcastle 9 Dec 1961	Newcastle Mar 1986	On loan until Apr 1986	7	0	0	0	0	0	0	0	7	0
Haddow *Andrew*	Glasgow	Morton May 1927	Clyde Feb 1929	1	0	0	0	0	0	0	0	1	0
Haddow *David*	Dalserf 12 Jun 1869	Motherwell Dec 1895	New Brighton T Aug 1898	38	0	5	0	0	0	4	0	47	0
Haigh *Gordon*	Barnsley 18 Aug 1921	Ransons 1945	Bournemouth Apr 1950	18	3	2	0	0	0	0	0	20	3
Hall *Brian W*	Glasgow 22 Jan 1946	Plymouth Nov 1977	Released cs 1980	39/4	3	3	0	0	0	5	0	47/4	3

Player	Born	From	To	League App	League Gls	FA Cup App	FA Cup Gls	FL Cup App	FL Cup Gls	Other App	Other Gls	Total App	Total Gls
Hall *John*		Hetton Jnrs Aug 1930	1932	38	4	3	0	0	0	0	0	41	4
Halley *George*	Cronberry 29 Oct 1887	Bradford Mar 1913	Southend Nov 1922	137	4	16	1	0	0	0	0	153	5
Hamilton *David*	South Shields 7 Nov 1960	Chester Aug 1990		8/3	0	0/1	0	3	1	2/2	0	13/6	1
Hamilton *William R*	Belfast 9 May 1957	Queen's PR Nov 1979	Oxford Aug 1984	200	58	23	10	16	5	13	4	252	77
Hampson *Thomas*	Burg 20 May 1898	West Ham Dec 1925	West Stanley 1926	6	0	0	0	0	0	0	0	6	0
Hampson *Walker*	Radcliffe 24 Jul 1889	Colne Feb 1914	South Shields Sep 1919	4	0	0	0	0	0	0	0	4	0
Hampton *Peter*	Oldham 12 Sep 1954	Stoke Jul 1984	Rochdale cs 1987	116/2	2	4	0	8	0	14	1	142/2	3
Hancock *Anthony E*	Manchester 31 Jan 1967	Stockport cs 1989	Preston Jan 1990	9/8	0	1/2	0	0/1	0	3	0	13/11	0
Hancock *Edward*	Rotherham 29 Mar 1907	Liverpool Feb 1933	Luton Nov 1936	112	23	11	7	0	0	0	0	123	30
Hankin *Raymond*	Wallsend 2 Feb 1956	Apprentice Feb 1973	Leeds Sep 1976	110/2	37	5	1	12	4	9	4	136/2	46
Hannigan *Richard*		W Arsenal Dec 1899	1900	8	3	0	0	0	0	0	0	8	3
Hansbury *Roger*	Barnsley 26 Jan 1955	Hong Kong Aug 1983	Cambridge cs 1985	83	0	8	0	6	0	10	0	107	0
Hapgood *E Anthony*	Kettering 13 Jun 1930	Juniors Mar 1948	Watford Jul 1953	7	2	0	0	0	0	0	0	7	2
Haresnape *Robert*	Blackburn 1866	Blackburn cs 1889	Irwell Springs Nov 1891	27	7	1	0	0	0	0	0	28	7
Hardy *Jason*	Manchester 14 Dec 1969	Trainee 1986		36/5	1	3/2	1	0	0	2	0	41/7	1
Hargreaves		*c.*1888	1889	0	0	1	0	0	0	0	0	1	0
Hargreaves *A*		Oct 1894	Released cs 1895	3	0	0	0	0	0	0	0	3	0
Hargreaves *A*		Nov 1905	cs 1906	1	0	0	0	0	0	0	0	1	0
Hargreaves *Ellis*		1892	1897	1	0	0	0	0	0	0	0	1	0
Hargreaves *Harold*	Higham 3 Feb 1899	Tottenham Mar 1926	Rotherham cs 1928	26	6	0	0	0	0	0	0	26	6
Harker *William*	Brierfield 1911	Nelson cs 1931	Torquay Jun 1933	24	7	2	1	0	0	0	0	26	8
Harrington *Philip*	Bangor 20 Nov 1963	Blackpool Nov 1985	On loan	2	0	0	0	0	0	0	0	2	0
Harris *Gordon*	Worksop 2 Jun 1940	Firbeck Col Jan 1958	Sunderland Jan 1968	258	69	30	5	16	5	9	2	313	81
Harris *Jason*	Bacup 26 Dec 1969	Apprentice Jul 1986	Released cs 1989	4	0	0	0	0	0	2	0	6	0
Harris *Joshua*	Glasgow 5 Nov 1891	Ashfield Sep 1910	Bristol City cs 1912	57	5	5	0	0	0	0	0	62	5
Harris *Mark*	Reading 15 Jul 1963	Crystal P Aug 1989	On loan until Sep 1989	4	0	0	0	2	0	2	0	8	0
Harrison *Raymond W*	Boston 21 Jun 1921	Boston Apr 1946	Doncaster Jan 1950	60	19	10	6	0	0	0	0	70	25
Harrison *Wayne M*	Whitehaven 16 Oct 1957	Blackpool Aug 1982	Released 1982	0	0	0	0	0	0	0/1	0	0/1	0
Hartley *Abraham*	Dumbarton 8 Feb 1872	W Arsenal Dec 1899	cs 1900	13	5	0	0	0	0	0	0	13	5
Hartley *James*		Sunderland Nov 1896	Lincoln Mar 1897	1	0	0	0	0	0	0	0	1	0
Hastie *Henry*	Padiham	Jul 1919	1920	7	0	0	0	0	0	0	0	7	0
Hayes *William E*	Cork 7 Nov 1915	Huddersfield Feb 1950	Released cs 1951	12	0	0	0	0	0	0	0	12	0
Hays *C Jack*	Ashington 12 Dec 1918	Bradford 1939	Bury Sep 1951	146	12	8	1	0	0	0	0	154	13
Heap *Clifford*	Burnley 14 Feb 1906	Local Jnrs Aug 1925	Thames Jul 1930	5	0	0	0	0	0	0	0	5	0
Heesom *Darren*	Warrington 8 May 1968	Apprentice Jul 1984	Released cs 1987	36/2	1	2/1	0	0	0	4	0	42	1
Heggarty *James*	Larne 4 Aug 1965	Brighton Aug 1985	Released Oct 1986	33/3	1	2	0	2	0	8	1	45/3	2
Henderson *Robert*		Bee Hole cs 1904	Clitheroe 1905	10	0	0	0	0	0	0	0	10	0
Henderson *Robert*		Sep 1929	New Brighton Aug 1931	3	0	0	0	0	0	0	0	3	0
Henderson *Tom*	Burnley 1 Oct 1927	Juniors 1945	Released cs 1949	2	0	0	0	0	0	0	0	2	0
Heslop *Archibald*	Co Durham	Annfield Pl Dec 1927	Luton May 1930	24	4	1	0	0	0	0	0	25	4
Hetherington *Thomas B*	Walker 1912	Walker Cel Dec 1933	Jarrow 1938	67	0	0	0	0	0	0	0	67	0
Heyes *L*		Darwen cs 1889	Hyde Feb 1890	11	2	1	0	0	0	0	0	12	2
Heys *Stephen*	Accrington	Colne cs 1906	1907	1	0	0	0	0	0	0	0	1	0
Hibbert *Jack*	Darwen	*c.*1888	1888	1	0	0	0	0	0	0	0	1	0
Higgins *Robert*	Bolsover 23 Dec 1958	Apprentice Jul 1976	Released cs 1980	3	0	0	0	0	0	0	0	3	0
Hill *James*	Paisley	St Mirren Dec 1889	Stoke Jan 1897	151	36	11	5	0	0	0	0	162	41
Hill *John H*	Hetton le Hole 2 Mar 1897	Plymouth cs 1923	Newcastle Oct 1928	184	13	14	0	0	0	0	0	198	13
Hillam *Charles E*	Burnley	Clitheroe May 1932	Man Utd May 1933	19	0	2	0	0	0	0	0	21	0
Hillman *Jack*	Tavistock 30 Jun 1870	Local Jnrs cs 1891	Everton Feb 1895	175	0	9	0	0	0	4	0	188	0
		Dundee Mar 1898	Man City Jan 1902										
Hindmarsh *John S*	Ashington	Sheff Wed cs 1935	Notts Co May 1937	39	1	2	0	0	0	0	0	41	1
Hird *Kevin*	Colne 11 Feb 1955	Leeds Jul 1984	Released cs 1986	83	23	5	4	6	2	10/1	2	104/1	31
Hodgson *Edward*	Chorley 1886	Chorley Sep 1911	Deceased Aug 1919	120	53	17	9	0	0	0	0	137	62
Hogan *Cornelius*		Watford Nov 1901	Released cs 1903	43	17	3	2	0	0	0	0	46	19
Hogan *James*	Nelson 16 Oct 1882	Rochdale Sep 1903	Fulham Oct 1905	50	12	2	0	0	0	0	0	52	12
Holden *Rick*	Skipton 9 Sep 1964	1985	Halifax cs 1986	0/1	0	0	0	0	0	0	0	0/1	0
Holden *TH*		Sep 1906	cs 1907	1	0	0	0	0	0	0	0	1	0
Holden *William*	Bolton 1 Apr 1928	Everton Nov 1949	Sunderland Dec 1955	187	75	12	4	0	0	0	0	199	79
Holt *David*	Padiham 26 Feb 1952	Oldham Jul 1980	Retired cs 1983	84	1	5	0	10	2	11	1	110	4
Hooper *Stewart*	St Annes on Sea 16 Jun 1970	Trainee 1987	Released cs 1989	0/1	0	0	0	0	0	0	0	0/1	0
Hornby *Ronald*	Rochdale 13 Apr 1914	Stalybridge May 1934	Retired cs 1949	123	16	12	3	0	0	0	0	135	19
Hoskin *Ashley*	Accrington 27 Mar 1968	Apprentice Jul 1984	Released cs 1989	72/16	11	3/1	0	2/1	0	12/4	4	89/22	15
Howarth		*c.*1886	1887	0	0	1	0	0	0	0	0	1	0
Howarth *Neil*	Farnworth 15 Nov 1971	Trainee July 1988		0/1	0	0	0	0	0	0	0	0/1	0
Howarth *William*		Dec 1899	cs 1903	14	0	0	0	0	0	0	0	14	0
Howarth *William*	Bury	Feb 1908	cs 1909	9	0	1	0	0	0	0	0	10	0
Hubbick *Henry*	Jarrow 12 Nov 1914	Spennymoor Mar 1935	Bolton Feb 1937	58	1	5	0	0	0	0	0	63	1
Hughes *Alexander*	Hetton le Hole	Hetton Jnrs cs 1931	Accrington Aug 1933	3	0	0	0	0	0	0	0	3	0
Hughes *Leonard*	Edmonton 1899	Leyton O Jan 1925	Accrington Sep 1926	28	1	2	0	0	0	0	0	30	1

Player	Born	From	To	League App	League Gls	FA Cup App	FA Cup Gls	FL Cup App	FL Cup Gls	Other App	Other Gls	Total App	Total Gls
Hunt *Patrick*	Glasgow	Hamilton Nov 1928	Belfast Cel Dec 1930	8	0	3	0	0	0	0	0	11	0
Husband *William*	Kilmarnock	St Mirren May 1912	Hamilton cs 1914	39	7	6	0	0	0	0	0	45	7
Hutchinson *Alexander*	Musselburgh	Bo'ness Oct 1929	Blackpool Oct 1930	5	2	0	0	0	0	0	0	5	2
Hutchison *Tommy*	Cardenden 22 Sep 1947	Hong Kong Aug 1983	Swansea cs 1985	92	4	8	0	6	0	10	1	116	5
Hutchinson *William*		cs 1904	1904	1	0	0	0	0	0	0	0	1	0
Ingham *William C*	Stakeford 22 Oct 1952	Apprentice Nov 1969	Bradford City Aug 1980	181/30	22	13/2	1	12/1	3	26	5	232/33	31
Irvine *Willie*	Carrickfergus 18 Jun 1943	Juniors Jun 1960	Preston Mar 1968	124/2	78	9/1	9	8/1	8	3	2	144/4	97
Jackson		c 1886	1887	0	0	1	0	0	0	0	0	1	0
Jackson *Harry*	Blackburn 30 Dec 1918	Darwen 1940	Man City Jun 1946	0	0	2	1	0	0	0	0	2	1
Jackson *Thomas*	Sunderland 1896	Sunderland WE Feb 1920	Dundee Jan 1921	1	0	0	0	0	0	0	0	1	0
Jackson *William*		Barrow cs 1903	1904	22	6	2	4	0	0	0	0	24	10
Jakub *Yanek*	Falkirk 7 Dec 1956	Apprentice Dec 1973	Bury Oct 1980	134	8	9	0	8	0	18	1	169	9
		Chester cs 1989											
James *Leighton*	Llwchwyr 16 Feb 1953	Apprentice Feb 1970	Derby Oct 1975	331/5	66	17	2	22	8	27/1	5	397/6	81
		Queen's PR Sep 1978	Swansea May 1980										
		Newport Aug 1986	Coach cs 1988										
Jeavons *William H*	Woodhouse Mill 9 Feb 1912	Chesterfield cs 1932	Accrington Jun 1933	1	0	0	0	0	0	0	0	1	0
Jeffrey *William*	Dalderby 1868	Gainsboro' Tr Aug 1891	W Arsenal Mar 1892	7	0	0	0	0	0	0	0	7	0
Jenkins *Evan T*	Ynyshir 1906	Lincoln May 1930	Lincoln cs 1932	66	16	4	1	0	0	0	0	70	17
Jenkinson *William*	Burnley	Local Jnrs Jan 1897	West Ham cs 1901	50	12	4	2	0	0	0	0	54	14
		West Ham cs 1903	cs 1904										
Jennings *Samuel*		Jan 1932	cs 1932	6	2	0	0	0	0	0	0	6	2
Johnson *David*		Barrow Dec 1906	cs 1907	4	0	0	0	0	0	0	0	4	0
Johnson *E*		Glentoran Feb 1894	Glentoran Apr 1895	9	0	1	0	0	0	0	0	10	0
Johnson *Robert E*	Fencehouses 25 Oct 1911	Bishop Auck Sep 1934	Nelson (p/m) cs 1949	81	0	7	0	0	0	0	0	88	0
Jones *Clifford*	Rotherham	Gainsboro' Tr Feb 1913	Accrington Dec 1922	82	0	3	0	0	0	0	0	85	0
Jones *David*	Harrow 3 Jul 1964	Leyton O Mar 1989	Released cs 1989	4	0	0	0	0	0	0	0	4	0
Jones *Peter A*	Ellesmere Pt 25 Nov 1949	Apprentice May 1967	Swansea Jul 1971	2	0	0	0	2	0	0	0	4	0
Jones *Rodney E*	Ashton 23 Sep 1945	Rotherham Mar 1967	Rochdale Jun 1971	9	0	0	0	1	0	0	0	10	0
Jones *Thomas W*	Shrewsbury	Oakengates Nov 1930	Blackpool Sep 1933	94	24	5	0	0	0	0	0	99	24
Joyce *Walter*	Oldham 10 Sep 1937	Juniors Oct 1954	Blackburn Feb 1964	70	3	8	0	7	0	4	0	89	3
Kavanagh		*c.*1887	1888	1	0	0	0	0	0	0	0	1	0
Kay *Robert*		*c.*1887	1888	5	0	2	0	0	0	0	0	7	0
Kaye *Archibald*	Glasgow 1869	Glasgow Th Jan 1890	Left cs 1891	28	0	0	0	0	0	0	0	28	0
Keenan *John*	Clitheroe 1864	Clitheroe Aug 1884	Retired cs 1893	68	0	10	0	0	0	0	0	78	0
Kelly *John*	Hetton le Hole 2 Mar 1913	Hetton Jnrs Oct 1930	Newcastle Apr 1933	30	12	0	0	0	0	0	0	30	12
Kelly *Robert*	Ashton-in-M 16 Nov 1894	St Helens Nov 1913	Sunderland Dec 1925	277	88	21	9	0	0	1	0	299	97
Kennedy *Steven*	Audenshaw 22 Jul 1965	Apprentice Jul 1983	Released 1987	18	0	1/1	0	0/1	0	2	0	21/2	0
Kennerley *Kevin R*	Chester 26 Apr 1954	Arsenal May 1972	Port Vale May 1976	6	1	0	0	0	0	0	0	6	1
Kenyon *Joseph*		Failsworth May 1906	cs 1907	29	0	1	0	0	0	0	0	30	0
Kilcar *Stephen P*	Bo'ness	Chester May 1935	Bournemouth Sep 1936	24	7	2	0	0	0	0	0	26	7
Kilner *Andrew*	Bolton 11 Oct 1966	Apprentice cs 1983	Released cs 1986	2/3	0	0	0	0	0	0	0	2/3	0
Kindon *Steven M*	Warrington 17 Dec 1950	Apprentice Dec 1967	Wolves Jul 1972	175/10	46	10/1	2	14/2	2	13	8	212/13	58
		Wolves Nov 1977	Huddersfield Dec 1979										
King *George*	Dunblane	Sunderland Alb cs 1892	Millwall cs 1894	33	2	2	0	0	0	0	0	35	2
Kinsella *Leonard*	Alexandria 14 May 1946	Apprentice May 1963	Carlisle Sep 1970	7/6	0	0	0	0/1	0	0	0	7/7	0
Kippax *F Peter*	Burnley 17 Jul 1922	Juniors 1940	Liverpool cs 1948	32	6	11	1	0	0	0	0	43	7
Kirkham *Reginald*	Ormskirk 8 May 1919	Wolves Mar 1947	Retired cs 1951	13	1	2	0	0	0	0	0	15	1
Knight *George R*	Bolton 12 May 1921	Holdens T cs 1938	Retired 1949	9	2	0	0	0	0	0	0	9	2
Knight *Jack*	Bolton 12 Sep 1922	Juniors 1938	Preston Dec 1948	26	5	1	0	0	0	0	0	31	5
Knox *William*		Bathgate cs 1927	Luton May 1930	23	0	0	0	0	0	0	0	23	0
Lambie *Claude*	Glasgow 1868	Glasgow Th Jan 1890	Clyde Mar 1891	29	21	2	1	0	0	0	0	31	22
		Highland Lt Inf	On leave Dec 1892										
Lambie *William A*		Hamilton Oct 1901	Released Oct 1901	1	0	0	0	0	0	0	0	1	0
Lancashire *Graham*	Blackpool 19 Oct 1972	Trainee July 1989		0/1	0	0	0	0	0	0	0	0/1	0
Lancaster *Desmond*	Burnley 16 Jul 1937	Juniors Aug 1954	Darlington Mar 1958	1	0	0	0	0	0	0	0	1	0
Lancaster *Wilfred*	Backbarrow	Dick Kerr's Dec 1924	cs 1925	4	0	0	0	0	0	0	0	4	0
Lane *John W*	Birmingham 29 May 1898	Cradley Hth Dec 1920	Chesterfield Jul 1923	5	0	0	0	0	0	0	0	5	0
Lang *Alexander*	Bridge of Weir 1864	Padiham 1885	Released cs 1895	123	2	11	1	0	0	0	0	134	3
Latcham *Leslie*	Stanley 22 Dec 1942	Juniors Jan 1961	Plymouth Jul 1971	149/4	10	6/1	1	18/1	0	5	1	178/6	12
Lawrence *Leslie O*	Wolverh'ton 18 May 1957	Rochdale Nov 1984	Peterborough Jul 1986	22/9	8	0	0	0	0	2/2	1	24/11	9
Laws *Brian*	Wallsend 14 Oct 1961	Apprentice Oct 1979	Huddersfield Aug 1983	125	12	15	1	14	2	8	0	162	15
Lawson *Ian*	Onslow 24 Mar 1939	Juniors Mar 1956	Leeds Mar 1962	23	7	5	8	2	0	0	0	30	15
Lawton *Jack*		Manchester NE Apr 1934	cs 1936	3	0	0	0	0	0	0	0	3	0
Lawton *Thomas*	Bolton 6 Oct 1919	Rossendale U May 1935	Everton Jan 1937	25	16	0	0	0	0	0	0	25	16
Leake *Alexander*	Small Heath 11 Jul 1871	Aston Villa Dec 1907	Wednesbury cs 1910	81	2	9	0	0	0	0	0	90	2
Lee *Edward*		cs 1902	cs 1903	26	3	1	0	0	0	0	0	27	3
Leebrook *Peter*	Saltburn 18 Sep 1968	Apprentice Jul 1985	Released cs 1988	52	0	0	0	4	0	5	0	61	0
Lester *Edmund*		Fleetwood Mar 1898	cs 1899	1	0	0	0	0	0	0	0	1	0

Player	Born	From	To	League App	League Gls	FA Cup App	FA Cup Gls	FL Cup App	FL Cup Gls	Other App	Other Gls	Total App	Total Gls
Liggins *John G*	Altrincham 26 Mar 1906	Leicester Nov 1935	cs 1936	4	1	0	0	0	0	0	0	4	1
Lindley *Richard*	Bolton	Oswaldtwistle Mar 1908	Bradford C May 1920	137	42	15	4	0	0	0	0	152	46
Lindsay *James*	Stockton 1879	Newcastle Jul 1900	Bury Apr 1901	30	0	3	0	0	0	0	0	33	0
Lindsay *James J*	Glasgow	Glentoran cs 1914	Larne cs 1923	74	18	6	3	0	0	0	0	80	21
Lindsay *Neil*	1875	Thornliebank Apr 1895	Clitheroe Oct 1895	2	0	0	0	0	0	0	0	2	0
Livingstone *Archibald*	Bothwell 9 Nov 1877	Third Lanark Mar 1893	Nelson cs 1900	169	2	8	0	0	0	4	0	181	2
Lochhead *Andrew*	Millgie 9 Mar 1941	Renfrew J Dec 1958	Leicester Oct 1968	225/1	101	19	12	15	9	6	6	265/1	128
Lockhart *George*	Barrhill 1877	Bolton Mar 1900	Released cs 1903	93	0	5	0	0	0	0	0	98	0
Loggie *David M*	Newbiggin 31 May 1957	Apprentice Jun 1974	York Jun 1978	6/1	0	0/1	0	0/1	0	2/1	0	8/4	0
Lomas *William*		Heywood U Sep 1909	Bury Feb 1911	36	21	1	0	0	0	0	0	37	21
Longair *William*	Dundee	Sunderland Nov 1896	Dundee cs 1897	12	0	1	0	0	0	0	0	13	0
Loughran *Joseph*	Consett 12 Aug 1915	Luton 1940	Southend Sep 1949	65	0	8	0	0	0	0	0	73	0
Lovett *Jonathan*		Local Jnrs Jan 1906	1906	1	0	0	0	0	0	0	0	1	0
Lowe *Robert H*		Congleton Jan 1904	1904	3	0	0	0	0	0	0	0	3	0
Lowe *Luke*		Dec 1911	1912	1	0	0	0	0	0	0	0	1	0
Lumsden *Frank*		Queen's PR May 1937	1937	1	0	0	0	0	0	0	0	1	0
Lyons *Terry*	Bradford 14 Apr 1929	Juniors Oct 1949	Bradford Sep 1951	12	3	0	0	0	0	0	0	12	3
McAdam *Steven*	Portadown 2 Apr 1960	Portadown May 1978	Oldham Aug 1980	5	0	0	0	0	0	0	0	5	0
McCallum *Charles*		Dec 1910	cs 1911	4	0	0	0	0	0	0	0	4	0
McColl *William*	Drymen 1865	Morton Dec 1889	cs 1890	9	2	1	0	0	0	0	0	10	2
McConnell *James*		Padiham *c.*1886	1890	1	0	5	0	0	0	0	0	6	0
McCluggage *Andrew*	Larne 1 Sep 1900	Bradford May 1925	Dundalk Sep 1931	204	22	9	2	0	0	0	0	213	24
McCrae *Robert*		Vale of Leven *c.*1886	Released cs 1889	2	0	5	0	0	0	0	0	7	0
McDonald *Colin A*	Tottington 15 Oct 1930	Hawkshaw Oct 1948	Retired 1959	186	0	15	0	0	0	0	0	201	0
McEleny *Charles*		Celtic Nov 1895	New Brighton T cs 1896	15	1	3	0	0	0	0	0	18	1
MacFarlane *Dugald*	Barrow 24 Aug 1880	Barrow cs 1903	Tottenham Jul 1908	121	35	4	0	0	0	0	0	125	35
McFettridge *William*	Govan 1862	Padiham 1886	Retired Nov 1892	85	2	10	1	0	0	0	0	95	3
McGee *Paul G*	Sligo 19 Jun 1954	Preston Nov 1981	On loan until Dec 1981	33/1	9	2	2	5	4	0	0	40/1	15
		Preston Mar 1982	Released cs 1983										
McGrory *Robert*	Bishopton 17 Oct 1895	Dumbarton Aug 1920	Stoke Apr 1921	3	0	0	0	0	0	0	0	3	0
McGrory *Shaun*	Coventry 29 Feb 1968	Coventry cs 1987	Released cs 1990	34/12	2	5	0	2	0	8/3	0	49/15	2
McIlroy *James*	Lambeg 25 Oct 1931	Glentoran Mar 1950	Stoke Mar 1963	439	116	50	13	3	1	5	1	497	131
McInnes *Angus*		St Bernards Mar 1898	1899	38	4	2	0	0	0	0	0	40	4
		cs 1902	Padiham Oct 1903										
McKay *Paul*	Banbury 28 Jan 1971	Trainee July 1987		8/4	0	1/1	0	0	0	0	0	9/5	0
McKay *Peter W*	Newburgh 23 Feb 1925	Dundee U May 1954	St Mirren May 1957	60	36	6	2	0	0	0	0	66	38
McKay *William*		c 1888	Newcastle WE cs 1889	14	6	0	0	0	0	0	0	14	6
McKnight *John*		Darwen cs 1894	Released Apr 1895	22	6	0	0	0	0	0	0	22	6
McLardie *Alexander*	Paisley 1868	St Mirren Mar 1890	Pais Abercorn cs 1892	43	24	4	2	0	0	0	0	47	26
McLaren *Andrew*	Larkhall 24 Jan 1922	Preston Dec 1948	Sheff Utd Mar 1949	3	1	1	1	0	0	0	0	4	2
McLaren *William*	Glasgow	Cowdenbeath Dec 1910	Huddersfield Dec 1913	63	0	10	0	0	0	0	0	73	0
McLean *James T*	Scotland 1881	Bradford C Nov 1908	cs 1910	41	0	8	0	0	0	0	0	49	0
McLintock *Thomas*	Maybole	Kilmarnock cs 1893	Kilmarnock Dec 1903	233	14	13	0	0	0	8	0	254	14
McLoughlin *William*		Feb 1909	1910	6	0	0	0	0	0	0	0	6	0
McMahon *Ross*		*c.*1888	1889	2	0	2	0	0	0	0	0	4	0
McMillan *William*		cs 1898	Released Mar 1900	3	0	0	0	0	0	0	0	3	0
McNab		1906	1906	1	0	0	0	0	0	0	0	1	0
McNab *William*	Glasgow 1870	Sep 1892	W Arsenal Dec 1893	14	5	2	1	0	0	0	0	16	6
McNulty *Joseph*	Dundalk 17 Jul 1923	Ards May 1949	Sheff Utd Jun 1952	8	0	0	0	0	0	0	0	8	0
McVean *Malcolm*		Liverpool Mar 1897	Dundee cs 1897	4	0	0	0	0	0	4	0	8	0
Malley *Philip*	Felling 1 Nov 1965	Hartlepool Feb 1984	Released cs 1988	91/4	5	3	1	5	0	17/4	0	116/8	6
Manns *Thomas*	Rotherham	Eastwood WMC cs 1931	Man Utd May 1933	10	0	0	0	0	0	0	0	10	0
Mantle *Joseph*	Hetton le Hole 9 May 1908	Hetton Jnrs Mar 1926	Plymouth Mar 1931	50	22	2	0	0	0	0	0	52	22
Marr *Robert*		1890	Released cs 1891	9	4	0	0	0	0	0	0	9	4
Marshall *John G*	Bolton 25 May 1917	Juniors Nov 1936	Bury (coach) 1949	26	0	1	0	0	0	0	0	27	0
Marshall *Thomas*		Bolton Oct 1904	1906	23	4	2	2	0	0	0	0	25	6
Marshall *William*	Belfast 11 Jul 1936	Distillery Oct 1953	Oldham Aug 1962	6	0	0	0	3	0	0	0	9	0
Martindale *Leonard*	Bolton 30 Jun 1920	Juniors cs 1937	Accrington Dec 1951	69	2	4	0	0	0	0	0	73	2
Mather *Harold*	Bolton 24 Jan 1921	Juniors 1939	Released 1955	301	0	28	0	0	0	0	0	329	0
Matthew *James*	Dundee	Lincoln cs 1891	Accrington 1893	26	1	2	0	0	0	0	0	28	1
Mays *Albert W*	Ynyshir 1902	Notts Co May 1930	Walsall Jan 1931	2	0	0	0	0	0	0	0	2	0
Mayson *Thomas*	Whitehaven 8 Dec 1886	Walker Dec 1907	Grimsby Oct 1911	67	14	4	3	0	0	0	0	71	17
Measham *Ian*	Barnsley 14 Dec 1964	Cambridge Nov 1988		109/1	1	10	0	3	0	16	0	138/1	1
Mee *George W*	Bulwell 12 Apr 1900	Derby Sep 1932	Mansfield cs 1933	18	3	3	2	0	0	0	0	21	5
Meechan *John S*	Falkirk	St Mirren Jun 1933	Released Sep 1933	2	0	0	0	0	0	0	0	2	0
Mellor *Peter J*	Prestbury 20 Nov 1947	Witton A Apr 1969	Fulham Feb 1972	69	0	4	0	8	0	0	0	81	0
Meredith *Trevor G*	Kidderminster 25 Dec 1936	Kidderminster Nov 1957	Shrewsbury Apr 1964	37	8	0	0	1	0	0	0	38	8
Merrick *Charles*	Pendleton	Walsden cs 1929	Swindon Jun 1933	12	0	0	0	0	0	0	0	12	0
Merrington *David R*	Newcastle 26 Apr 1945	Apprentice Feb 1962	Bristol C Jul 1971	96/2	1	9/1	0	13	0	5	1	123/3	2

Player	Born	From	To	League App	League Gls	FA Cup App	FA Cup Gls	FL Cup App	FL Cup Gls	Other App	Other Gls	Total App	Total Gls
Midgeley *T*		*c.*1888	1888	1	0	0	0	0	0	0	0	1	0
Miller *Brian G*	Hapton 19 Jan 1937	Juniors Feb 1954	Coach 1967	379	29	50	4	13	1	13	3	455	37
Miller *David*	Burnley 8 Jan 1964	Apprentice Jan 1982	Tranmere cs 1985	31/5	3	1	0	2	0	4/2	0	38/7	3
		Preston Feb 1989	On loan until Mar 1989										
Miller *John*	Maryhill 1878	Birtley Nov 1899	1900	18	2	1	0	0	0	0	0	19	2
Miller *Thomas H*	Hamilton	Oakengates Apr 1932	Released Feb 1934	5	1	0	0	0	0	0	0	5	1
Miller *William*	Bainsford	Everton Oct 1936	Tranmere Nov 1938	74	18	3	1	0	0	0	0	77	19
Milligan *George*	Glasgow	Nov 1911	Clyde cs 1914	2	0	0	0	0	0	0	0	2	0
Milner *James E*	Newcastle 3 Feb 1933	Blyth Sp Dec 1952	Darlington Dec 1957	1	0	0	0	0	0	0	0	1	0
Minion *Fred*		cs 1907	cs 1909	2	0	0	0	0	0	0	0	2	0
Moffat *Hugh*	Congleton Jan 1885	Congleton T Jan 1904	Oldham Dec 1910	201	13	13	0	0	0	0	0	214	13
Mole *George*	Stockton 1879	Newcastle cs 1900	1901	9	2	3	1	0	0	0	0	12	3
Monington *Mark D*	Bilsthorpe 21 Oct 1970	Trainee July 1987		19/2	1	0	0	2	0	3/1	0	24/3	1
Mooney *Joseph*		Apr 1906	cs 1906	1	0	0	0	0	0	0	0	1	0
Moorwood *Leonard*	Wednesbury 1888	West Brom Oct 1920	cs 1924	18	0	0	0	0	0	0	0	18	0
Morgan *William*	Burnley 16 Dec 1896	Local Jnrs Mar 1920	Retired cs 1924	28	0	6	0	0	0	0	0	34	0
Morgan *William*	Glasgow 2 Oct 1944	Juniors Oct 1961	Man Utd Aug 1968	195/1	19	13	1	15	2	8	0	231/1	22
		Man Utd Jun 1975	Bolton Mar 1976										
Morley *Anthony W*	Ormskirk 26 Aug 1954	Preston Feb 1976	Aston Villa Jun 1979	83/13	5	3/2	1	3/1	1	2	0	91/16	7
		West Brom Oct 1988	On loan until Nov 1988										
Morley *Jonathan B*	Carlisle	Sunderland cs 1908	Preston Dec 1912	96	15	12	2	0	0	0	0	108	17
Morris *Colin*	Blyth 22 Aug 1953	Apprentice Sep 1971	Southend Jan 1977	9/1	0	0/1	0	0	0	3	0	12/2	0
Morris *William*	Colwyn Bay 30 Jul 1918	Llandudno Jan 1939	Retired 1952	211	47	19	6	0	0	0	0	230	53
Morrison *Thomas*	Ireland 1874	Glentoran Feb 1894	Glentoran Sep 1895	179	26	11	2	0	0	5	0	195	28
		Glentoran Feb 1897	Man Utd Dec 1902										
		Man Utd 1905	Glentoran 1907										
Mosscrop *Edwin*	Southport 16 Jun 1892	Southport C cs 1912	Retired Nov 1922	176	19	21	1	0	0	1	0	198	20
Mountford *Harry W*	Hanley	Everton Apr 1911	Third Lanark Nov 1913	28	10	1	0	0	0	0	0	29	10
Mudie		*c.*1888	1889	1	0	0	0	0	0	0	0	1	0
Muir *Ian*	Coventry 5 May 1963	Queen's PR Oct 1982	On loan	1/1	1	0	0	0	0	0	0	1/1	1
Mullineaux *James E*	Blackburn 1872	Lincoln Mar 1892	Burton W Sep 1894	26	0	3	0	0	0	0	0	29	0
Mumby *Peter*	Bradford 22 Jun 1969	Leeds cs 1989		35/10	9	3/2	2	4	2	6/2	1	48/14	14
Munn *Stuart*		cs 1894	Released Feb 1895	2	0	0	0	0	0	0	0	2	0
Murphy *Bernard*		Duntocher cs 1905	1905	6	2	0	0	0	0	0	0	6	2
Murphy *Philip*	Liverpool 21 Nov 1960	Witton A Nov 1986	Released cs 1987	12/3	5	0	0	0	0	3	2	15/3	7
Murray *John*	Newcastle 2 Mar 1948	Juniors Mar 1965	Blackpool Mar 1970	20/2	6	0	0	4/1	4	0	0	24/3	10
Murray *T*		Dundee Harp Oct 1889	Released Feb 1890	7	1	0	0	0	0	0	0	7	1
Mustard *John*	Durham	Preston Mar 1933	Southend Dec 1933	15	4	0	0	0	0	0	0	15	4
Napier *Walter*		cs 1895	Released Nov 1895	1	0	0	0	0	0	0	0	1	0
Nash *Joseph*	Uxbridge	Uxbridge cs 1889	Nelson cs 1891	5	0	2	0	0	0	0	0	7	0
Neenan *Joe P*	Manchester 17 Mar 1959	Scunthorpe Feb 1985	On loan until Mar 1985	90	0	3	0	4	0	14	0	111	0
		Scunthorpe Jul 1985	Peterborough cs 1987										
Nesbitt *William*	Todmorden	Hebden Br Sep 1911	Bristol City Oct 1923	172	19	19	1	0	0	1	0	192	20
Nevin *George W*	Lintz 16 Dec 1907	Man Utd May 1935	Lincoln cs 1937	26	0	0	0	0	0	0	0	26	0
Newlands *Douglas*	Edinburgh 29 Oct 1931	Aberdeen Mar 1955	Stoke Jul 1959	98	21	6	2	0	0	0	0	104	23
Newton *Frank*		Jan 1911	cs 1911	6	2	3	0	0	0	0	0	9	2
Newton *Keith R*	Manchester 23 Jun 1941	Everton Jun 1972	Retired 1978	209	5	13	1	14	1	16	0	252	7
Nicol *Alfred*		Stockton cs 1898	cs 1899	2	0	0	0	0	0	0	0	2	0
Nicol *Thomas*	Linlithgow 1870	Mossend SW Feb 1891	Blackburn Dec 1896	140	42	9	2	0	0	0	0	149	44
Nisbet *Gavin*		Preston Sep 1935	1935	2	0	0	0	0	0	0	0	2	0
Noble *Peter*	Newcastle 19 Aug 1944	Swindon Jun 1973	Blackpool Jan 1980	241/2	63	14	1	19	8	24	8	298/2	80
Norris *Patrick*	Broughton	Salford cs 1919	Stockport cs 1920	2	0	0	0	0	0	0	0	2	0
Nulty *Geoffrey*	Prescot 13 Feb 1949	Stoke Jul 1968	Newcastle Dec 1974	123/7	20	8	0	4/1	1	8/1	3	143/9	24
Nunnick *William*	Colne 1877	Trawden For cs 1898	Nelson 1898	1	0	0	0	0	0	0	0	1	0
O'Beirne *Joseph*	Manchester	Stalybridge cs 1923	Nelson Jun 1924	5	0	0	0	0	0	0	0	5	0
O'Connell *Brendan*	Waterloo 12 Nov 1966	Exeter cs 1988	Barnsley Mar 1990	62/2	17	3	1	6	3	11	2	82/2	23
O'Dowd *J Peter*	Halifax 26 Feb 1908	Blackburn Mar 1930	Chelsea Nov 1931	65	8	2	0	0	0	0	0	67	8
Ogden *Arthur*	Burnley	Local Jnrs cs 1906	Released cs 1910	45	12	7	6	0	0	0	0	52	18
Oghani *George W*	Manchester 2 Sep 1960	Bolton Jun 1987	Released Apr 1989	73/1	21	2	0	8	3	15	5	98/1	29
O'Grady *Harry*	Tunstall 16 Mar 1907	Leeds May 1933	Bury May 1934	13	8	2	0	0	0	0	0	15	8
Oliver *John*	Gateshead	Stoke May 1935	cs 1937	3	0	0	0	0	0	0	0	3	0
O'Neil *Brian*	Bedlington 4 Jan 1944	Juniors Jan 1961	Southampton May 1971	231/4	22	18	1	21/1	1	7	1	277/5	25
O'Neill *William A*	Cork 29 Dec 1919	Chelmsford Jun 1949	Walsall Jan 1951	1	1	0	0	0	0	0	0	1	1
O'Rourke *Peter*		New Brighton cs 1897	Lincoln May 1899	18	1	0	0	0	0	0	0	18	1
O'Rourke *William J*	Nottingham 2 Apr 1960	Apprentice Feb 1978	Released cs 1983	14	0	2	0	0	0	1	0	17	0
Oswald *John*		Notts Co cs 1890	Released Jan 1891	15	1	1	1	0	0	0	0	16	2
Overson *Richard J*	Kettering 3 Jun 1959	Apprentice Jun 1977	Hereford May 1980	5/1	0	0	0	0	0	0	0	5/1	0
Overson *Vincent D*	Kettering 15 May 1962	Apprentice Nov 1979	Birmingham Jun 1986	207/4	6	19	0	9	1	21/1	0	256/5	7
Page *Louis A*	Kirkdale 27 Mar 1899	Northampton May 1925	Man Utd Mar 1932	248	111	11	4	0	0	0	0	259	115

Player	Born	From	To	League App	League Gls	FA Cup App	FA Cup Gls	FL Cup App	FL Cup Gls	Other App	Other Gls	Total App	Total Gls
Page *Samuel*	Blackheath	Halesowen Nov 1921	St Johnstone Nov 1925	12	0	1	0	0	0	0	0	13	0
Pake *Ralph R*	Tynemouth 1913	Newcastle cs 1936	cs 1937	5	1	0	0	0	0	0	0	5	1
Palmer *Geoffrey*	Cannock 11 Jul 1954	Wolves Nov 1984	Wolves Dec 1985	34	0	3	0	2	0	7	0	46	0
Parker *Derrick H*	Wallsend 7 Feb 1957	Apprentice Feb 1974	Southend Feb 1977	48/1	12	3	1	2	0	1	1	54/1	14
Parker *Jonathan*	Barrow	Barrow St Mat cs 1905	Bradford Nov 1908	32	1	0	0	0	0	0	0	32	1
Parker *Samuel*	Hurlford	Newton Heath Oct 1894	Southport C Feb 1895	5	0	0	0	0	0	0	0	5	0
		Oldham Oct 1985	Released cs 1987										
Parkin *George*	Hunslet 20 Aug 1903	Halifax Mar 1924	Chester Sep 1929	125	2	3	0	0	0	0	0	128	2
Parkinson *William*		Feb 1901	cs 1901	2	0	0	0	0	0	0	0	2	0
Parton *Jeffrey J*	Swansea 24 Feb 1953	Apprentice Mar 1970	Northampton Jul 1975	3	0	0	0	0	0	0	0	3	0
Pashley *Terry*	Chesterfield 11 Oct 1956	Apprentice Oct 1973	Blackpool Aug 1978	16/2	0	0	0	0	0	0/2	0	16/4	0
Paterson *Thomas*	Quarter 1874	Motherwell Nov 1895	1896	7	3	0	0	0	0	0	0	7	3
Patterson *T*		1890	Released Jan 1891	2	0	0	0	0	0	0	0	2	0
Peacock *Dennis M*	Lincoln 19 Apr 1953	Doncaster Sep 1985	On loan until Nov 1985	8	0	0	0	0	0	0	0	8	0
Pearce *Christopher L*	Newport 7 Aug 1961	Wrexham Jul 1987		167	0	11	0	14	0	27	0	219	0
Pearson *John C*	Dudley 14 Mar 1896	Cradley Hth Feb 1921	Brentford Aug 1923	1	0	0	0	0	0	0	0	1	0
Pender *John P*	Luton 19 Nov 1963	Bristol C Sep 1990		40	0	3	0	2	0	7	0	52	0
Peyton *Gerry*	Birmingham 20 May 1956	Atherstone May 1975	Fulham Dec 1976	30	0	1	0	1	0	2	0	34	0
Phelan *Michael C*	Nelson 24 Sep 1962	Apprentice Jul 1980	Norwich Jul 1985	166/2	9	16	0	16	2	20	2	218/2	13
Picken *Jonathan*	Hurlford	Man Utd cs 1911	Bristol City Oct 1913	18	10	1	0	0	0	0	0	19	10
Pickering *William*	Glasgow	cs 1912	Wartime fatality 1917	13	6	1	0	0	0	0	0	14	6
Pilkington *Brian*	Leyland 12 Feb 1933	Leyland M Apr 1951	Bolton Mar 1961	300	67	33	7	3	1	4	2	340	77
Pinkerton *Henry*	Glasgow	Port Vale May 1936	Falkirk 1938	3	0	0	0	0	0	0	0	3	0
Pinnell *A*		cs 1898	1899	5	0	1	0	0	0	0	0	6	0
Place *Walter (Snr)*	Burnley 1870	Local Jnrs 1886	Left 1886	136	7	9	2	0	0	4	0	149	9
		Bacup 1890	Released cs 1900										
Place *Walter (Jnr)*	Burnley	Local Jnrs 1893	W Arsenal May 1900	152	30	9	4	0	0	6	0	167	34
Pointer *Raymond*	Cramlington 10 Oct 1936	Dudley W Aug 1957	Bury Aug 1965	223	118	35	13	7	2	5	0	270	133
Poland *F*		*c.*1888	1888	9	5	0	0	0	0	0	0	9	5
Pollard *Walter*	Burnley 26 Sep 1906	Local Jnrs Sep 1924	West Ham Jun 1929	20	4	0	0	0	0	0	0	20	4
Porterfield *Alfred*	1869	Kings Park Apr 1895	cs 1895	2	0	0	0	0	0	0	0	2	0
Potts *Eric*	Liverpool 16 Mar 1950	Preston Sep 1980	Bury cs 1982	48/8	5	4/1	1	2	1	4	0	58/9	7
Potts *Harry*	Hetton le Hole 22 Oct 1920	Juniors Nov 1937	Everton Oct 1950	165	47	16	3	0	0	0	0	181	50
Powell *Barry I*	Kenilworth 29 Jan 1954	Hong Kong Aug 1984	Swansea Feb 1985	9/2	0	2	2	2	0	3	0	16/2	2
Prest *Thomas W*	Darwen	Darwen Jan 1930	Brighton Jun 1935	80	16	2	1	0	0	0	0	82	17
Price *John*	Easington 25 Oct 1943	Horden CW Nov 1960	Stockport May 1965	21	2	1	0	0	0	0	0	22	2
Probert *Eric W*	South Kirkby 17 Feb 1952	Apprentice Feb 1969	Notts Co Jul 1973	62/5	11	1	0	2	0	2	0	67/5	11
Provan *John*		cs 1895	1896	4	0	0	0	0	0	0	0	4	0
Rawstron *Mark*	Littleborough 21 Jan 1967	Apprentice cs 1984	Released cs 1986	0	0	0	0	0	0	0/1	0	0/1	0
Ray *Philip*	Wallsend 21 Nov 1964	Apprentice Nov 1982	Released cs 1985	1	0	0	0	0	0	2	0	3	0
Raynor *Frank*	Goldthorpe	Mexborough Mar 1935	Notts Co Jun 1939	79	7	4	0	0	0	0	0	83	7
Readett *Harold*	Darwen	Hurst cs 1934	1934	3	0	0	0	0	0	0	0	3	0
Reeves *David*	Birkenhead 19 Nov 1967	Sheff Wed Nov 1987	On loan until Jan 1988	16	8	0	0	0	0	2	1	18	9
		Sheff Wed Feb 1988	On loan until Mar 1988										
Reeves *Kevin P*	Burley 20 Oct 1957	Man City Jul 1983	Coach 1984	20/1	12	5	3	2	0	3	1	30/1	16
Regis *Robert*	Huddersfield 24 Apr 1967	Huddersfield Feb 1986	Released Mar 1987	3/1	1	0/1	0	0	0	2	0	5/2	1
Reid *Andrew*	Aberdeen	Bo'ness Mar 1927	Bradford Jul 1928	3	0	0	0	0	0	0	0	3	0
Reid *Robert*	Newtongrange	Cowdenbeath cs 1910	Huddersfield Oct 1914	84	0	5	0	0	0	0	0	89	0
Reynolds *Jeremiah*		Celtic cs 1895	1899	107	0	9	0	0	0	8	0	124	0
Reynolds *Walter*	Sheffield 24 Nov 1906	Leeds cs 1932	Newport cs 1933	19	3	1	0	0	0	0	0	20	3
Rhodes *Mark N*	Sheffield 26 Aug 1957	Rotherham Mar 1985	On loan until May 1985	12/1	0	0	0	0	0	1/1	0	13/2	0
		Rotherham Aug 1985	Released Nov 1985										
Richards *Percy*	Manchester 15 May 1905	New Mills Feb 1926	Plymouth Jan 1928	9	8	0	0	0	0	0	0	9	8
Richardson *Arthur*		Oct 1936	Chesterfield cs 1938	11	2	4	1	0	0	0	0	15	3
Richardson *George*	Horden	Horden Ath Jan 1921	Derby May 1923	9	5	0	0	0	0	0	0	9	5
Richmond *Gilbert*	Bolton 2 Apr 1909	Clitheroe May 1932	1939	176	1	17	1	0	0	0	0	193	2
Ridsdale *George*		cs 1901	cs 1902	3	0	0	0	0	0	0	0	3	0
Ridsdale *J*		*c.*1888	1888	1	0	0	0	0	0	0	0	1	0
Riley *James E*		Jan 1906	cs 1907	3	0	0	0	0	0	0	0	3	0
Riley *Richard*	Padiham	Colne cs 1912	Third Lanark Oct 1913	3	2	0	0	0	0	0	0	3	2
Roberts *Lawrence*		Renton Feb 1920	Hamilton Feb 1920	1	0	0	0	0	0	0	0	1	0
Roberts *William T*	Handsworth 29 Nov 1898	Preston Oct 1924	Preston cs 1926	49	28	1	1	0	0	0	0	50	29
Robertson *Hugh*	Scotland	Millwall cs 1895	Lincoln cs 1897	40	15	3	2	0	0	3	0	46	17
Robertson *Peter*		Polton Vale cs 1895	1895	1	0	0	0	0	0	0	0	1	0
Robertson *Stuart*	Glasgow 29 Sep 1959	Apprentice Jul 1977	Exeter Mar 1982	30/2	0	0	0	1	0	0	0	31/2	0
Robinson *Alexander*	Leigh	Bury Oct 1933	Retired wartime	204	8	17	1	0	0	0	0	221	9
Robinson *Andrew C*	Oldham 10 Mar 1966	Man Utd Oct 1985	On loan until Nov 1985	5	1	0	0	0	0	0	0	5	1
Robinson *James W*	Ruyton	cs 1923	Nelson cs 1925	4	0	0	0	0	0	0	0	4	0
Robinson *Peter*	Ashington 4 Sep 1957	Apprentice cs 1974	Sp Rotterdam cs 1980	48/7	3	4	0	3	0	4	0	59/7	3

Player	Born	From	To	League App	League Gls	FA Cup App	FA Cup Gls	FL Cup App	FL Cup Gls	Other App	Other Gls	Total App	Total Gls
Robson *James*	Pelton 23 Jan 1939	Juniors Jan 1956	Blackpool Mar 1965	202	79	29	14	6	4	5	3	242	100
Robson *William P*	Newcastle 14 Jan 1908	Stoke Oct 1937	1938	10	2	2	1	0	0	0	0	12	3
Rodaway *William*	Liverpool 26 Sep 1954	Apprentice Sep 1971	Peterborough Jul 1981	245/2	3	12	0	18	0	28	0	303/2	3
		Tranmere Aug 1986	Released cs 1987										
Ross *Andrew*		Barrow cs 1904	cs 1905	24	2	2	0	0	0	0	0	26	2
Ross *Henry*	Brechin 1881	Brechin Harp Feb 1899	Fulham cs 1904	106	2	5	0	0	0	0	0	111	2
Ross *James D*	Edinburgh 28 Mar 1866	Liverpool Mar 1897	Man City Feb 1899	51	29	5	2	0	0	7	1	63	32
Rowell *Gary*	Seaham 6 Jun 1957	Carlisle cs 1988	Released cs 1990	8/11	1	0	0	2	0	3/1	0	13/12	1
Rudman *Harold*	Whitworth 4 Nov 1924	Juniors 1942	Rochdale Jul 1957	71	0	4	0	0	0	0	0	75	0
Ryan *William*		Sep 1892	Padiham Nov 1894	1	0	0	0	0	0	0	0	1	0
Samuels *Leslie*	Oldham 8 Dec 1928	Juniors Dec 1949	Exeter Jul 1953	2	0	0	0	0	0	0	0	2	0
Savage *James*		cs 1899	cs 1902	36	11	5	0	0	0	0	0	41	11
Sawers *Alexander*		Clyde Sep 1892	1893	2	0	1	0	0	0	0	0	3	0
Sawley *Alfred*		cs 1900	Trawden cs 1903	13	1	0	0	0	0	0	0	13	1
Schofield *John*	Waterfoot 1913	Bacup cs 1931	Accrington May 1935	9	0	0	0	0	0	0	0	9	0
Scott *Derek E*	Gateshead 8 Feb 1958	Apprentice Feb 1975	Bolton Jul 1985	277/8	24	23	0	24	3	32	4	356/8	31
Scott *James*	Hetton le Hole 7 Sep 1934	Juniors Sep 1951	Oldham Jun 1961	3	0	0	0	2	0	0	0	5	0
Scott *Robert A*	Liverpool 29 Oct 1913	Liverpool May 1933	Wolves Feb 1936	57	0	8	0	0	0	0	0	65	0
Seeburg *Max P*	Leipzig 19 Sep 1884	Leyton O cs 1910	Reading cs 1912	17	0	1	0	0	0	0	0	18	0
Seith *Robert*	Coatbridge 9 Mar 1932	Juniors Mar 1949	Dundee cs 1960	211	6	27	0	0	0	0	0	238	6
Sellars *William*	Sheffield 7 Oct 1907	Southport Jul 1933	Bradford cs 1934	19	0	1	0	0	0	0	0	20	0
Sewell *W Ronald*	Wingate 19 Jul 1890	Gainsboro Tr Feb 1913	Blackburn Feb 1920	23	0	4	0	0	0	0	0	27	0
Shackleton *Alan*	Padiham 3 Feb 1934	Juniors May 1954	Leeds Oct 1958	31	18	1	0	0	0	0	0	32	18
Shannon *Leslie*	Liverpool 12 Mar 1926	Liverpool Nov 1949	Released cs 1959	262	39	19	5	0	0	0	0	281	44
Short *William*		cs 1907	cs 1908	3	0	0	0	0	0	0	0	3	0
Simpson *Peter W*	Sunderland 21 Sep 1940	Juniors Nov 1957	Bury Aug 1963	3	0	0	0	0	0	0	0	3	0
Sims *Stephen*	Bedminster 11 Dec 1895	Bristol Rov Jul 1922	Weymouth cs 1924	11	0	0	0	0	0	0	0	11	0
Smelt *Leonard*	Rotherham 10 Dec 1885	Gainsborough Mar 1919	Barrow cs 1926	229	0	18	0	0	0	1	0	248	0
Smethams *Charles*		Sep 1907	Blackburn cs 1910	60	4	9	2	0	0	0	0	69	6
Smith *Albert*	Burnley	Local Jnrs Oct 1905	Bradford Nov 1908	105	21	2	0	0	0	0	0	107	21
Smith *David B*	Dundee 22 Sep 1933	Juniors Sep 1950	Brighton Jul 1961	99	1	8	0	1	0	0	0	108	1
Smith *Ernest*	Shirebrook 1912	Sutton Jnc Nov 1931	1932	7	1	0	0	0	0	0	0	7	1
Smith *F Cecil*	Marchwiel 30 Oct 1904	Stalybridge cs 1932	Cardiff May 1936	106	49	13	5	0	0	0	0	119	54
Smith *Frederick G*	W.Sleekburn 25 Dec 1942	Juniors Dec 1959	Portsmouth May 1970	84	1	10	0	8/1	0	4	0	106/1	1
Smith *H*		*c.*1886	1887	0	0	2	0	0	0	0	0	2	0
Smith *Joseph*		Keswick cs 1904	cs 1905	15	1	1	1	0	0	0	0	16	2
Smith *Malcolm*	Stockton 21 Sep 1953	Blackpool Sep 1976	York Aug 1980	82/3	17	4/1	0	5	0	7	3	98/4	20
Smith *Nigel*	Leeds 21 Dec 1969	Leeds cs 1989	Released May 1991	6/6	0	0	0	0	0	0/1	0	6/7	0
Smith *Philip*		cs 1910	1910	7	0	0	0	0	0	0	0	7	0
Smith *Richard*	Workington	Sep 1904	Released cs 1910	174	71	11	5	0	0	0	0	185	76
Smith *Wilfred*		Blackpool Oct 1933	Crystal P Jul 1935	29	0	2	0	0	0	0	0	31	0
Smith *William S*	Haggate	1885	cs 1895	7	0	0	0	0	0	0	0	7	0
Smith *William S*	South Shields 22 Oct 1903	Crystal P May 1936	1938	53	0	3	0	0	0	0	0	56	0
Smyth *John*	Dundalk 28 Apr 1970	Liverpool cs 1990	Released May 1991	0	0	0	0	0	0	2/1	0	2/1	0
Snowden *Thomas H*		South Shields Oct 1911	1912	14	0	1	0	0	0	0	0	15	0
Sommerville *George*	Glasgow	Hamilton cs 1926	Bristol C cs 1932	118	0	6	0	0	0	0	0	124	0
Sonner *Daniel J*	Wigan 9 Jan 1972	Wigan cs 1990		1/1	0	0	0	0	0	0/2	0	1/3	0
Southern *Michael*		cs 1986	Released 1987	0	0	0	0	0	0	1	0	1	0
Spargo *Stephen*	Burnley 29 Dec 1903	Local Jnrs Nov 1924	Nelson Aug 1929	3	0	1	0	0	0	0	0	4	0
Spencer *Harold*	Burnley 30 Apr 1919	Juniors cs 1939	Wrexham Jul 1950	4	1	0	0	0	0	0	0	4	1
Spencer *Jack S*	Bacup 24 Aug 1920	Jun 1948	Accrington Jun 1951	37	8	6	3	0	0	0	0	43	11
Spiers *Daniel*	Ayrshire 1868	Morton Dec 1889	1891	27	1	0	0	0	0	0	0	27	1
Splitt *Thomas*	Lochgelly	Cowdenbeath Dec 1909	Halifax cs 1913	47	0	1	0	0	0	0	0	48	0
Stage *William*	Edinburgh 22 Mar 1893	Bury Jun 1928	Southampton cs 1930	25	1	3	0	0	0	0	0	28	1
Steel *John*	Denny	Hamilton Nov 1925	1930	145	5	7	0	0	0	0	0	152	5
Stein *James*	Coatbridge 7 Nov 1907	Everton Oct 1936	New Brighton Jun 1938	42	8	5	2	0	0	0	0	47	10
Stephenson *Roy A*	Crook 27 May 1932	Juniors Jun 1949	Rotherham Sep 1956	78	27	2	1	0	0	0	0	80	28
Steven *Trevor M*	Berwick 21 Sep 1963	Apprentice Sep 1981	Everton Jul 1983	74/2	11	13	4	10	1	3	0	100/2	16
Stevenson *Alan*	Staveley 6 Nov 1950	Chesterfield Jan 1972	Rotherham Aug 1983	438	0	33	0	36	0	36	0	543	0
Stewart *Alexander*	Greenock 1869	Morton Dec 1889	Everton Dec 1892	66	8	0	0	0	0	0	0	66	8
		Northampton Aug 1901	Leicester Aug 1902										
Stirling *James*		Polton Vale Apr 1895	Released Oct 1895	2	0	0	0	0	0	0	0	2	0
Storer *Harry*	West Derby 2 Feb 1898	Derby Feb 1929	Coventry May 1931(Man)	52	5	2	0	0	0	0	0	54	5
Storey *Cuthbert W*		Burnley Belv Jan 1903	1903	4	1	0	0	0	0	0	0	4	1
Storey *Thomas*	Foulridge 1914	Nelson Oct 1935	Accrington Sep 1938	35	7	1	0	0	0	0	0	36	7
Strong *James G*	Morpeth 7 Jun 1916	Walsall 1946	Retired 1953	264	0	21	0	0	0	0	0	285	0
Sugden *Thomas*		Dec 1901	1902	7	0	0	0	0	0	0	0	7	0
Sugg *Frank*		*c.*1884	1888	0	0	3	0	0	0	0	0	3	0
Summerbee *Michael G*	Cheltenham 15 Dec 1942	Man City Jun 1975	Blackpool Dec 1976	51	0	1	0	6	0	3	0	61	0

Player	Born	From	To	League App	League Gls	FA Cup App	FA Cup Gls	FL Cup App	FL Cup Gls	Other App	Other Gls	Total App	Total Gls
Sutherland *James*	Inverness 1881	Invern Cal Dec 1899	1901	11	1	0	0	0	0	0	0	11	1
Sutherland *Malcolm*		Darwen cs 1894	Released Nov 1894	1	0	0	0	0	0	0	0	1	0
Swain *Joseph*		Feb 1904	1904	1	0	0	0	0	0	0	0	1	0
Swainston *Henry*		cs 1899	Released Mar 1900	2	0	0	0	0	0	0	0	2	0
Swift *Henry*	Accrington	Accrington Apr 1910	Third Lanark cs 1913	64	2	4	0	0	0	0	0	68	2
Syme *Robert*	S.Queensferry	Man City cs 1934	Released Feb 1935	9	0	0	0	0	0	0	0	9	0
Tait *W*		*c.*1888	1888	5	4	0	0	0	0	0	0	5	4
Talbut *John*	Oxford 20 Oct 1940	Juniors Oct 1957	West Brom Dec 1966	138	0	14	0	5	1	3	0	160	1
Tate *Jeffrey*	Blyth 11 May 1959	Juniors Aug 1978	Released cs 1981	5	1	0	0	0	0	0	0	5	1
Tatham *William*	Burnley	Local Jnrs Feb 1895	Nelson Sep 1901	51	0	2	0	0	0	0	0	53	0
Tattersall *William*		Heywood 1895	Nelson Mar 1897	5	0	0	0	0	0	0	0	5	0
Taylor *Alan D*	Hinckley 14 Nov 1953	Hull cs 1984	Bury May 1986	60/4	23	3	3	5	3	7	4	75/4	33
Taylor *Archibald*		Cambuslang May 1937	1939	3	1	0	0	0	0	0	0	3	1
Taylor *David*	Bannockburn	Bradford C Dec 1911	St Johnstone May 1924 (Man)	221	5	28	0	0	0	1	0	250	5
Taylor *Fred*	Burnley 24 Feb 1920	Cambuslang May 1936	New Brighton Jul 1948	49	7	1	0	0	0	0	0	50	7
Taylor *Joseph*	Burnley	Local Jnrs Nov 1893	Retired cs 1907	323	12	21	2	0	0	8	0	352	14
Taylor *Stephen*	Royton 18 Oct 1955	Mansfield Jul 1980 Preston Aug 1987	Wigan Aug 1983 Rochdale Mar 1989	118/13	43	14	5	14/2	1	18/2	3	164/17	52
Taylor *William*	Southwell 1886	Notts Co Apr 1919	Oldham Nov 1920	17	2	2	0	0	0	0	0	19	2
Ternent *Raymond*	Blyth 9 Sep 1948	Apprentice Sep 1965	Southend Jun 1971	13	0	1	0	1	0	0	0	15	0
Ternent *Stanley*	Gateshead 16 Jun 1946	Apprentice Jun 1963	Carlisle May 1968	5	0	0	0	0	0	0	0	5	0
Thomas *David*	Kirkby 5 Oct 1950	Apprentice Oct 1967	Queen's PR Oct 1972	153/4	19	4	0	16	4	2	0	175/4	23
Thompson *Desmond*	Southampton 4 Dec 1928	York Nov 1952	Sheff Utd May 1955	62	0	7	0	0	0	0	0	69	0
Thompson *George*	Ashington	Apr 1914	Rotherham Jun 1921	5	0	0	0	0	0	0	0	5	0
Thomson *Harry W*	Edinburgh 25 Aug 1940	Bo'ness Aug 1959	Blackpool Jul 1969	117	0	5	0	15	0	4	0	141	0
Thomson *James*	Glasgow 1 Oct 1946	Chelsea Sep 1968	Released cs 1981	294/3	3	22	1	21	1	23	1	360/3	6
Thorpe *Levy*	Seaham H 18 Nov 1889	Blackpool Oct 1913	Blackburn Feb 1920	72	3	7	2	0	0	0	0	79	5
Tillotson *Stephen*	Brierfield	cs 1909	cs 1911	9	0	0	0	0	0	0	0	9	0
Todd *Samuel*	Belfast 22 Sep 1945	Glentoran Sep 1962	Sheff Wed May 1970	108/8	1	0/1	0	7/1	1	3	0	118/10	2
Toll *Jack P*	Bradford 7 Feb 1914	Bridlington Nov 1935	1937	20	9	3	3	0	0	0	0	23	12
Toman *Wilfrid*	Bishop Auckland 1873	Victoria U Dec 1896	Everton Apr 1899	63	30	6	1	0	0	5	4	74	35
Tonner *James*	Glasgow	Bo'ness Oct 1924	Hamilton Oct 1926	37	2	0	0	0	0	0	0	37	2
Towers *Ian J*	Blackhill 11 Oct 1940	Juniors Oct 1957	Oldham Jan 1966	43/1	12	6	1	1	1	0	0	50/1	14
Towler *Edwin*		Nov 1902	1904	23	0	1	0	0	0	0	0	24	0
Trainer *Stephen*	Coatbridge	cs 1906	cs 1907	3	0	0	0	0	0	0	0	3	0
Tranter *Richard A*	Bolton	Padiham Jan 1914	Retired wartime	5	0	0	0	0	0	0	0	5	0
Tresadern *John*	Leytonstone 26 Sep 1890	West Ham Oct 1924	Northampton May 1925 (p/m)	22	0	1	0	0	0	0	0	23	0
Tueart *Dennis*	Newcastle 27 Nov 1949	Stoke Dec 1983	Retired cs 1984	8/7	5	2	0	0	0	0/2	0	10/9	5
Turnbull *Peter*		Glasgow Th Mar 1893	Bolton Mar 1895	46	21	2	0	0	0	0	0	48	21
Turner *John G*	Peterlee 23 Dec 1954	Weymouth cs 1984	Peterborough Oct 1984	0	0	0	0	0	0	2	0	2	0
Twiss *James*	Haydock 1897	Skelmersdale Dec 1919	cs 1920	4	1	0	0	0	0	0	0	4	1
Twist *Richard*		Dec 1931	1932	10	0	1	0	0	0	0	0	11	0
Valentine *F*		cs 1907	cs 1910	18	3	0	0	0	0	0	0	18	3
Wadsworth *Samuel J*	Darwen 13 Sep 1896	Huddersfield Sep 1929	Lytham 1931	7	0	0	0	0	0	0	0	7	0
Waiters *Anthony*	Southport 1 Feb 1937	Liverpool Jul 1970	Released 1971	38	0	1	0	1	0	2	0	42	0
Walders *David*	Barrow 1884	Barrow Jul 1903	Oldham May 1906	93	3	4	3	0	0	0	0	97	6
Walders *Jonathan*	Barrow	Barrow cs 1904	Oldham cs 1906	48	2	1	0	0	0	0	0	49	2
Waldron *Colin*	Bristol 22 Jun 1948	Chelsea Oct 1967	Man Utd Jun 1976	308	16	14	0	23	0	11	2	356	18
Waldron *Malcolm*	Emsworth 6 Sep 1956	Southampton Sep 1983	Portsmouth Mar 1984	16	0	3	1	0	0	0	0	19	1
Walker *David*	Colne 15 Oct 1941	Juniors May 1959	Southampton May 1965	38	1	1	0	1	0	0	0	40	1
Walker *John*		cs 1890	Clyde cs 1892	40	0	2	0	0	0	0	0	42	0
Wallace *James*	Milton of Campsie	Clyde Jan 1929	Chester cs 1930	39	8	0	0	0	0	0	0	39	8
Wallace *Thomas H*	Jarrow 1911	Sunderland May 1933	1936	61	1	6	0	0	0	0	0	67	1
Waller *William*	Bolton	Nelson cs 1922	Scunthorpe Aug 1923	1	0	0	0	0	0	0	0	1	0
Walsh *Michael T*	Manchester 20 Jun 1956	Everton Dec 1982	On loan until Jan 1983	3	0	0	0	0	0	0	0	3	0
Walton *John A*	Horwich 21 Mar 1928	Bury Feb 1954	Coventry Oct 1956	18	2	0	0	0	0	0	0	18	2
Warburton *Arthur*	Bury 30 Oct 1903	Man Utd Nov 1933	Nelson cs 1934	25	4	2	0	0	0	0	0	27	4
Warburton *T*		Nov 1895	1896	1	0	0	0	0	0	0	0	1	0
Wardrobe *Michael*	Newcastle 24 Mar 1962	Apprentice Mar 1980	Stockport Aug 1981	0/1	0	1	0	0	0	0	0	1/1	0
Waterfield *George S*	Swinton 2 Jun 1901	Mexborough Oct 1923	Crystal Pal Jun 1935	371	5	23	0	0	0	0	0	394	5
Watkins *William*		cs 1898	cs 1902	44	7	0	0	0	0	0	0	44	7
Watson *D*		cs 1893	1894	2	0	0	0	0	0	0	0	2	0
Watson *William*	Birkdale 11 Sep 1890	Southport C Mar 1909	Accrington cs 1925	346	18	33	2	0	0	1	0	380	20
Waugh *David*		*c.*1885	1888	0	0	2	0	0	0	0	0	2	0
Weale *Thomas J*	Merthyr 1911	Crewe Feb 1934	cs 1935	15	2	0	0	0	0	0	0	15	2
Weaver *Robert S*		Altrincham Dec 1930	cs 1932	6	0	0	0	0	0	0	0	6	0
Weaver *Walter*	Birkenhead 9 Nov 1898	S.Liverpool Aug 1919	Everton Dec 1924	106	15	10	3	0	0	0	0	116	18

Player	Born	From	To	League App	League Gls	FA Cup App	FA Cup Gls	FL Cup App	FL Cup Gls	Other App	Other Gls	Total App	Total Gls
Weightman *David*		Dec 1909	cs 1912	4	0	0	0	0	0	0	0	4	0
Welch *Ronald*	Chesterfield 26 Sep 1952	Apprentice Oct 1969	Brighton Dec 1973	1	0	0	0	0	0	0	0	1	0
Welsh *Fred*		Bacup cs 1902	1902	1	0	0	0	0	0	0	0	1	0
West *Alan*	Hyde 18 Dec 1951	Apprentice Dec 1968	Luton Oct 1973	41/4	3	2	0	3	0	1/2	0	47/6	3
Weston *John M*	Halesowen	Halesowen cs 1926	Northampton Jul 1928	2	1	0	0	0	0	0	0	2	1
Wharton *Andrew*	Bacup 21 Dec 1961	Apprentice Dec 1979	Chester Feb 1984	63/2	6	6/3	1	7	2	5	1	81/5	10
Whatmore *Neil*	Ellesmere Port 17 May 1955	Oxford Aug 1984	Mansfield Nov 1984	8	1	0	0	1	0	0	0	9	1
Wheelhouse *Ben*	Rothwell 23 Sep 1902	Halifax Mar 1924	cs 1925	13	0	0	0	0	0	0	0	13	0
Whitaker		*c.*1886	1887	0	0	2	0	0	0	0	0	2	0
White *E Thomas*	Uxbridge	Uxbridge cs 1889	Club secretary 1890	21	0	1	0	0	0	0	0	22	0
White *E Winston*	Leicester 26 Oct 1958	Colchester Oct 1988	West Brom Mar 1991	93/11	14	10	3	6	1	10/3	3	119/14	21
White *William H*	Liverpool 13 Oct 1936	Juniors Jan 1954	Wrexham Mar 1961	9	4	2	0	1	0	0	0	12	4
Whiteley *Charles*	Burnley	Local Jnrs cs 1905	cs 1907	3	0	0	0	0	0	0	0	3	0
Whittaker *Edgar*		Burnley Belv Nov 1902	1902	1	0	0	0	0	0	0	0	1	0
Whittaker *Fred*	Nelson	Local Jnrs Mar 1905	Bradford C Nov 1908	60	21	1	1	0	0	0	0	61	22
Whittam *Arthur*		Local Jnrs Oct 1903	1904	4	1	0	0	0	0	0	0	4	1
Whitty *Ernest*		Dec 1931	Released Feb 1932	2	0	0	0	0	0	0	0	2	0
Wilcox *Herbert*		cs 1907	cs 1909	3	0	0	0	0	0	0	0	3	0
Wilde *James*	Sheffield	Rotherham Jan 1915	Reading cs 1920	1	0	0	0	0	0	0	0	1	0
Williams *David*	Liverpool 18 Sep 1968	Oldham Mar 1988		17	0	0	0	0	0	5	0	22	0
Williams *Henry*	Bolton	Bolton cs 1903	Man Utd cs 1904	32	8	2	0	0	0	0	0	34	8
Williams *John*	Pendleton	Rossendale May 1924	cs 1925	4	2	1	0	0	0	0	0	5	2
Willighan *Thomas*	Belfast	Willowfield Mar 1928	Retired May 1934	59	0	2	0	0	0	0	0	61	0
Wilson		1945	1946	0	0	1	0	0	0	0	0	1	0
Wilson *Ian G*	Fife 11 Feb 1923	Preston Jun 1948	Leicester Mar 1950	19	1	2	1	0	0	0	0	21	2
Wilson *David EJ*	Wolverhampton 4 Oct 1944	Walsall Sep 1969	Chesterfield Jun 1971	10/3	0	3	0	0	0	0	0	13/3	0
Wilson *Harry*	Hetton le Hole 29 Nov 1953	Apprentice Dec 1970	Brighton Dec 1973	12	0	0	0	0	0	0	0	12	0
Wilson *William JR*	Portadown 23 Sep 1936	Portadown Sep 1955	Released cs 1958	2	0	0	0	0	0	0	0	2	0
Winton *Douglas*	Perth 6 Oct 1929	Jeanfield Sep 1947	Aston Villa Jan 1959	183	1	15	0	0	0	0	0	198	1
Wolstenholme *Tom*		Bolton cs 1907	Bradford cs 1908	38	0	1	0	0	0	0	0	39	0
Wood *Alfred*	Workington	Blackpool cs 1905	Workington cs 1906	5	1	1	0	0	0	0	0	6	1
Wood *Ian T*	Radcliffe 15 Jan 1948	Oldham May 1980	Released cs 1981	14/3	0	0	0	2/1	0	3	0	19/4	0
Wood *William H*	Mereclough 5 Apr 1910	Local Jnrs Apr 1930	Blackburn Mar 1933	32	0	0	0	0	0	0	0	32	0
Wood *William*	Blackburn	Blackburn Mar 1933	Released cs 1934	7	0	0	0	0	0	0	0	7	0
Woodruff *Arthur*	Barnsley 12 Apr 1913	Bradford C cs 1936	Workington Jul 1952	271	0	21	0	0	0	0	0	292	0
Woods *James*		*c.*1888	1889	1	0	0	0	0	0	0	0	1	0
Woods *Jonathan*	Workington	Jan 1911	1912	2	0	0	0	0	0	0	0	2	0
Woodward *Harry*		Oct 1908	1910	3	0	0	0	0	0	0	0	3	0
Woodworth *Anthony*	Manchester 5 Mar 1968	Apprentice Jul 1984	Released cs 1987	1	0	0	0	0	0	0	0	1	0
Woolfall *Thomas*	Darwen	Darwen cs 1899	cs 1900	33	0	1	0	0	0	0	0	34	0
Wright *Robert*		cs 1907	1907	2	0	0	0	0	0	0	0	2	0
Wright *William H*	Corbridge 4 Nov 1962	Juniors Jan 1981	Released cs 1983	0	0	0	0	0	0	1	0	1	0
Wrigley *Wilfred*	Clitheroe 4 Oct 1949	Juniors Jul 1968	Retired cs 1970	6	1	0	0	2	0	0	0	8	1
Wynne *Fred*		cs 1902	1902	10	0	0	0	0	0	0	0	10	0
Yates *John*	Blackburn 1861	Accrington cs 1888	cs 1894	29	7	2	0	0	0	0	0	31	7
Young *Kevin*	Sunderland 12 Aug 1961	Apprentice May 1977	Bury cs 1984	114/6	11	17/1	0	10/1	1	5/2	0	146/10	12
Zelem *Peter R*	Manchester 13 Feb 1962	Preston cs 1987	Released cs 1989	17/2	2	1	0	3	0	3/1	0	24/3	2
			Own Goals	-	97	-	6	-	7	-	3	-	113
			Scrimmages	-	33	-	1	-	0	-	0	-	34
			Unknown	-	0	-	8	-	0	-	0	-	8

SUBSCRIBERS

Presentation Copies
1 Burnley Football Club
2 The Football League • 3 The Football Association

4 F J Teasdale
5 Frank Casper
6 Edward Lee
7 Ray Simpson
8 J A Harris
9 Stephen Joseph Berry
10 Donald Speak
11 Rod Fuller
12 Peter Wharton
13 Matthew Red Kay
14 Keith Turner
15 David Ellis
16 John E Ashworth
17 Jim Stark
18 K Cocker
19 Vincent Heywood
20 James Anderson
21 Paul Cookson
22 P J Birtwistle
23 Darren Mawson
24 Keiron Anthony Farnworth
25 Andrew Thomas Hall
26 Kenneth F Webb
27 Steve Whipp
28 David Carrington
29 Ian Carrington
30 A R Fergus
31 Stephen Campbell
32 Mr Jeremy Aldous
33 Peter Marsden
34 Ian W Gregory
35 Keith Crabtree
36 Ernest Woods
37 Edward McKane
38 Gerald James Summers
39 Simon Naylor
40 Paul Brennan
41 Paul Egar
42 Alan Magnall
43 John D Magnall
44 Clive Spencer
45 Philip Klobcar
46 John Rogerson
47 Raymond John Lord
48 Nicholas Gordon Rae
49 Brian Mark Cook
50 Adrian Colin Pate
51 Michael Riley
52 B Boardwell (South Africa)
53 K Longrigg
54 Alan Aggett
55 Scott Mitchell
56 Border Bookshop, Todmorden
57 Richard Lund
58 Ben Laycock
59 Brian Pilkington JP
60 Dennis Dransfield
61 Michael Berry
62 M J Greenwood
63 Stephen Harrison
64 Martin Richard Smith
65 Matthew Gilmartin
66 Steven Kelly
67 Paul Clark
68 Nathan J Holden
69 Niel Brierley
70 Don Anslow
71 Michael John Thompson
72 Peter John Wilson
73 Keith Burrows
74 Michael McGinn
75 Eddie Shapland
76 Andrew D J Tomlinson
77 Dave Mack
78 Lee Lawrence
79 Barry Heard
80 Ian Gray
81 Michael Cook
82 Matt Barnes
83 James Grieg Avinou Snr
84 James Riley
85 Martin Townshend
86 Jack G Davies
87 Mr O L Clegg
88 A S Graham
89 James Grieg Avinou Jnr
90 Mr & Mrs John Melia
91 Mr Raymond Lorimer
92 Robert A Bancroft
93 Craig Hartley
94 Jack Heaton
95 Leslie Hurrell
96 Nick Hirst
97 A Wilkinson
98 Peter F Townsend
99 Malcolm Fielder
100 Jennifer Thornton
101 Steven Grimes
102 Steve Hawkes
103 Darren Blackhurst
104 J Goddard
105 Graham Shutt
106 Andrew Cowell
107 Mr S Hartley
108 John M Edgar
109 Philip Wilcock
110 Philip Wilcock
111 Ron Hughes
112 Michael G Parker
113 Graham Fox
114 John D Connolly
115 Allen Bolton
116 Errick Peterson
117 Terry Wilson
118 Iain Beattie
119 Andrew Dickinson
120 Greig A Bridge
121 Douglas E Cockcroft
122 Allen Hollingworth
123 David Hothersall
124 Michael Guilfoyle
125 Richard Guilfoyle
126 Nigel Sullivan
127 Alban Holden
128 David Ormerod
129 Mrs E Watson

130 Lynn Jones
131 Alex & Jayn Pearson
132 Michael West
133 B H Standish
134 Brian Spridgens
135 Brian H Hobbs
136 Raymond Shaw
137 John Motson
138 Philip Healey
139 Ian J Brookes
140 David Spencer
141 Steven Gough
142 Andrew Parker
143 C P Wheeler
144 Steven C M Trippier
145 Paul Haworth
146 Anthony Anderson
147 Neil Kay
148 Steven Shaw
149 Andrew Powell
150 Alastair Binns
151 Phillip Redfearn
152 Michael Redfearn
153 Graham Seabrook
154 Peter Raines
155 Robert J Whipp
156 Stephen C Whipp
157 John Philip Ramsden
158 Adrian Thomas
159 Mr John Fielding
160 Mr Steven Fielding
161 Robert Turk
162 Miss Debra Tomlinson
163 Daniel Stepinac
164 Andy Cox (Leyland)
165 Derek Smith
166 David J Taylor
167 C J Rawson
168 Colin E Wood
169 Colin D Wood
170 Graham J Wood
171 C G & R E Fryers
172 J V Merritt
173 S J Rogers
174 David Sullivan
175 K P Wood
176 Mike Young
177 Harry Kay
178 David Coulson
179 Duncan Watt
180 Frank Stoddart
181 Lloydy, Sutton
182 G Foster
183 Paul Southward
184 A Pitman
185 Trevor Slack
186 Derek W Jenkins
187 Derek W Jenkins
188 Shaun David Smith
189 Philip Brecknell
190 Olav Gjesteland
191 Kelvin Spencer
192 Mr G N Boocock
193 Keith Edwards
194 Paul Heaton
195 'Sizzle'
196 Revd David Wiseman
197 Don Haworth
198 Roy K Shoesmith
199 David Earnshaw
200 D T Bryant
201 Mark Southwell
202 Ian Willott
203 Mike Holgate
204 Mark Davidson
205 E C Simmons
206 Lars-Olof Wendler
207 John Treleven
208 John Clancy
209 David Keats
210 P J Cooke
211 Janine McHale
212 Jane Davis
213 J Atherton & D Yates
214 David S Roe
215 Stephen F Roe
216 Alan Newby
217 Ste Garrard
218 Mr B White
219 Anthony Jones
220 Paul A Kilburn
221 Damian P Kilburn
222 Chris Kilburn
223 Michael Kilburn
224 David N Kilburn
225 Andrew Wood
226 Ashley Eastwood
227 Mary Barker
228 Mary Barker
229 W D Phillips
230 David Downs
231 Michael Holtom
232 Barry Marlow
233 Roger Pill
234 Neil Sanderson
235 Peter Denison
236 Gordon Cooper
237 Henry Metcalfe
238 John Rawnsley
239 Mr E R Maudsley
240 Martin Hill
241 Steve Denwood
242 P I & R D Pomeroy
243 R M Minton
244 Ian Tasker
245 Petrer Alldred
246 Dominic Rayner
247 Roy Holtom
248 Peter Jackson
249 Richard Price
250 R J Preston
251 Simon Lacey
252 L Bone
253 Tony Williams
254 Jonny Stokkeland
255 Ewan Pidgeon
256 Geoffrey Richard Billington
257 Bryan North
258 Mark Butterworth
259 Stephen Foster
260 Chris Redman
261 Neil Robert Pilling
262 Barry Pollard
263 D N A Racing
264 Michael Briggs
265 Ian Rowbottom
266 John Hewitson
267 Stephen Berry
268 Sharon Lister
269 L R Newby
270 Edward Wilkinson
271 A M Wilson
272 Shaun Anthony Kay
273 Terry Hephrun
274 Tom England
275 Kevin Shaun Wareing
276 Mr Nigel Swinbank
277 Mark Child
278 Alan Kerr
279 David J Marshall
280 Dale Barton
281 E W Green

282 David C Green
283 Paul Banner
284 A B Smith
285 Bob Watson
286 David Watson
287 Richard Watson
288 C R Flintoff
289 Paul Sayer
290 Gary Chadwick
291 Shaun R Taylor
292 Dr Graham Tennant
293 P H Whitehead
294 Alan Wheatley
295 Moira & Frederick Furness
296 Douglas Lamming
297 J M Moore
298 William Briggs
299 Paul Drury
300 John Riley
301 Ian & Carol Barnes
302 A N Davis
303 Dave Hillam
304 John Harrison
305 R Digby Collinson
306 M D Wilkinson
307 M McIntyre
308 Andrew M Leach
309 David Opacic
310 Eddie Lee
311 K Andrews
312 Mr John C Stead
313 Gary Wynne
314 John Lathan
315 Sam Ashworth
316 Iain Macintyre
317 Mr K Foster
318 Mr J S Hargreaves
319 Mr R Wilkinson
320 Leighton James Butterworth
321 John Whittingham
322 Dave Ashworth
323 A & J A Waterman
324 Dave Harrison
325 Mr Kieran Doran
326 B Magee
327 Howard F Bracewell
328 Garry N Veevers
329 Carl Wilkinson
330 Steve Kershaw
331 Harold Barton
332 Alan Parry
333 Tony Parry
334 Timothy Parry
335 Terry Mundy
336 Sports Marketing
337 J Ringrose
338 Fred Beale
339 Fred Lee
340 C J Morton
341 David J Godfrey
342 Gordon Small
343 Jeremy D F Smith
344 David Chew
345 Keith Bullough
346 Michael Fenton
347 Michael John Pownall
348 Adam Braddock
349 Henry Lumley
350 Horace Pickles
351 John Pickles
352 Steven Pickles
353 Peter Davis
354 Andrew Roberts
355 Chris Doyle
356 R A Scoffield
357 Steve Barnes
358 Glen Isherwood
359 Martyn Brassington
360 Anders Johansson
361 Mick Garman
362 Peter McNabb
363 Peter McNabb
364 Mr Nigel Taylor
365 Paul Hindle
366 George Rushworth Capstick
367 Mark Francis Dugdale
368 Garth I Dykes
369 Richard D N Wells
370 Donald Noble
371 Douglas Bidgood
372 Liam Kelly
373 T R Thornton
374 David Scott
375 Karen Ogden
376 Glen Aspinall
377 William Grier
378 Ian Middleton
379 Göran Schönhult
380 Roberto J Gamble
381 Phillip Hart
382 Michael Blakeway
383 Michael E Benyon
384 Robert Thomas
385 Nik Ingham
386 Ralph R Brodie
387 David Acreman
388 Terry Frost
389 Malc Hartley
390 Stephen Golby
391 Stephen Lee
392 Robert Simon McNabb
393 Paul Cattle
394 Stephen B Smith
395 David Newton
396 Ray Marsden
397 Maurice Curtin
398 Graeme D Harley
399 Eric Ronald Hargreaves
400 M R Duxbury
401 Colin Roberts
402 Geoffrey Wright
403 Trond Isaksen
404 David Turner
405 A Beresford
406 D J Stevenson
407 J C Stevenson
408 Paul Cannon
409 J Musgrove
410 M P Waters
411 David Walker
412 Bill Willmer
413 Colin Jose
414 Alan Hardy
415 Peter Sanderson
416 Ian Rigg
417 Andrew John Ritchings
418 Lewis Bramley
419 Edward V Phillips
420 Adrian Whitehead
421 Graham Veevers
422 David J Caddy
423 Kevin Webb
424 Paul D Berry
425 Paul Wells
426 Mrs Carol Booth
427 Carl J Taylor
428 W H Halshaw
429 B H Hargreaves
430 Albert & Alice Howorth
431 L A Zammit

432 Robert Wilson
433 Harold Boothman
434 Andrew Gee
435 Harold Gee
436 Ken McMaster
437 Michael Pendlebury
438 Eric Turner
439 Martyn Helm
440 J S Pyke
441 Filippo Rossi
442 Christer Svensson
443 Geir Juva
444 Andrew Anderson
445 Leroy Anderson
446 Sheila Rogers
447 D J Nelson
448 R S Hickey
449 Russ Nevison
450 Ian Phillip Kemp
451 Nicholas Brown
452 S J Jackson
453 David Redhead
454 Kevin Hitchon
455 David Sutcliffe
456 Peter Pickup
457 David Gregg
458 Graham Wilkinson
459 Paul Turner
460 Peter Harrand
461 Rampton Hospital Library
462 Michael Brett
463 Jonathan Ward
464 Mr David Chapman
465 Lewis Anthony Haworth
466 David C Verran
467 Roy Sproule
468 Brian King
469 Guy Lövgreen
470 Mr Leslie John Butcher
471 Norman Haworth
472 David Edmondson
473 Stephen Jolly
474 A G Cooks
475 Shaun Borman
476 J Gardiner
477 D M Timberlake
478 Ronald Dixon
479 Peter L Hodson
480 Christopher Bond
481 S G & J Patrick
482 J M Maunders
483 H W Lewthwaite
484 Martin Pratt
485 Phil Hall
486 Jeff Lawson
487 R Staniforth
488 G Daggett
489 David Alexander
490 Mr W Lamont
491 Stephen Baldwin
492 Malcolm Wood
493 Andrew Tomlinson
494 John Barraclough
495 Igor Wowk
496 Ken Armstrong
497 Barrie Gallagher (Oldham)
498 Andy Perry
499 Andrew Burns
500 Stanley Woodhead
501 Gary W Cummins
502 David Wilson
503 J D M Whitaker
504 Mark 'Mouse' Fielding
505 N J Magnall
506 C J Wilby
507 J M Hartley
508 Mr D Pollard
509 Mr D Pollard
510 Mr Andrew Lord
511 Nigel D Higgins
512 Mr H Sumner
513 Phil Haworth
514 Rob Thorpe
515 M J Bracken
516 Frank Grande
517 Keith B Ducher
518 T D Culshaw
519 P Marks
520 Paul H Bannister
521 Geoffrey Hall
522 Jim Walker
523 John Bloodworth
524 Anthony Connor
525 Peter Heywood
526 Julian Ambrose
527 P M Ambrose
528 N N Brunton
529 Andrew Smith
530 Ian Petrie
531 Maurice Golesworthy
532 Paul Franks
533 Martin Davies
534 Mr K McHale
535 Gavin Barker
536 Ian Barker
537 Catherine Nicholls
538 Alan J Frankland
539 Garry D Watson
540 R Norcliffe
541 Keith Andrew Blackwell
542 Stephen Allen
543 Victor Allen
544 Ian Walmsley
545 Jack Foy
546 Martin Miller
547 Casper
548 Derek Wheatcroft
549 Mike Purkiss
550 Robert Baines
551 Michael Hothersall
552 Simon Pettit
553 Ian Schofield
554 Michael McColgan
555 Ken Hanson
556 Mark Horsfall
557 David Jesson
558 Paul Johnson
559 Neil Matthew
560 Steven Dunkley
561 Peter Griffiths
562 Angus W Rodger
563 Eric N Hayton
564 John van den Elsen
565 Derek Hyde
566 Ingemar Stromberg
567 A Young
568 Souris Lamplighters FC PEI
569 Colin Cameron
570 David Lumb
571 Martin Simons
572 Hartmut Vilmar
573 M Swart
574 S P Tomlin
575 Mario Sirianni
576 G D Painter
577 Stephen Laski
578 Christopher Minchin
579 QCM Olsthoorn
580 Kimmo Kukkola
581 Harry Thompson

582 Harald Lohr
583 Anders Johansson
584 Kåre M Torgrimsen
585 Andrew Tweddle
586 A H Atkins
587 R G Woolman
588 Richard Lane
589 Ake Axelsson
590 David Helliwell
591 John Knibbs
592 A P J M Otten
593 Trevor Chapman
594 Graham Chapman
595 Robert Nutter
596 Mr Paul Moore
597 D Aisthorpe
598 Christopher E C Hooker (Canada)
599 John S Whyte
600 Terence S Denslow
601 David Broom
602 Ian Duffy
.603 Peter Ruston
604 Coats
605 Michael Edroff
606 M R Pearce
607 John Gray
608 Paul Vibert
609 Brian Tabner
610 Derry Good
611 Steve Drake
612 Andrew C Heap
613 Nicholas Heap (New Zealand)
614 C W Hopkins
615 Michael Joyce
616 Paul Jerome
617 Ivan Ponting
618 Colin Cavanagh
619 Kevin Goss
620 Andrew & Gareth Davies
621 David Pring
622 John Phillips
623 Kevin Green
624 Peter Green
625 S Mackrell
626 David J Moorhouse
627 E Kautonen
628 Diamant Yozef
629 Mike Jackman
630 Gerald Hill
631 Dave Smith
632 Stanley A Robinson
633 Roger Wash
634 Christopher J Plant
635 Ken Spencer
636 Gilbert Monnereau
637 Juergen Hohmann
638 Ian Griffiths
639 Alan Hindley
640 David Crawford
641 Michael McConkey
642 Gerald Fitzpatrick
643 Shaun Smith
644 David Clarke
645 Tim Buckel
646 Scott David Wylie
647 Terry Butterworth
648 Peter Greenwood
649 Theodoros Mantzouranis
650 Norman Green
651 P Baxter
652 Derek Baisbrown
653 David Pease
654 Dave Green
655 Audrey Harper
656 Steve Cartman
657 Paul Brown
658 W J & M G Beckwith
659 James H Stevenson
660 Chris Allen
661 Graham Smith
662 Richard Smith
663 Les Dearden
664 Michael Fort
665 Anthony Fort
666 Peter Jackson
667 Surapot Saengchote
668 Eric Heesom
669 F Parkinson
670 Thomas K Goldie
671 John S Ratcliffe
672 S Robinson
673 T W Stevenson
674 Ian D Chase
675 Brian Charles Hollingworth
676 Marcia Dixon
677 Stephen Rapson
678 Duncan Pierce
679 Andrew Anderson
680 Steven F Thomas
681 Richard Stocken
682 David J Simmons
683 Wesley Lloyd Tattersall
684 David S Allen
685 Ian Harraden
686 Christopher Ellis
687 Jonathan & Fiona Tillotson
688 A J Thomas
689 I M Thomas
690 Brian McKenna
691 Jonathan & James McKenna
692 Martin Langrish
693 Graham R Haworth
694 D Burnley
695 Mrs R M Simpson
696 Alan Crilly
697 Alan Crilly
698 R H Bubb
699 Andrew M Wade
700 Ian Short
701 Matthew Short
702 Andrew Short
703 Tony Scott
704 R W Marsden
705 Kevin Hodkinson
706 Roger Hudson
707 K Day
708 K Day
709 S J Wilkinson
710 Sandra Hetherington
711 Glenys, Helen & Philip Simpson
712 John & Anne Lee
713 Eddie Simpson
714 Philip & Becky Lee
715 Steven & Leigh Hetherington
716 Les Simpson
717 Wallace Chadwick
718 Alan Rycroft
719 Mike Davage